COLD NEW WORLD

WILLIAM FINNEGAN

COLD

Growing Up

NEW

in a Harder Country

WORLD

 Random House · New York

Portions of this work appeared, in different form, in *The New Yorker.*

Grateful acknowledgment is made to Alfred A. Knopf, Inc., for permission to reprint three lines from "An Ordinary Evening in New Haven" from *Collected Poems* by Wallace Stevens. Copyright © 1950 by Wallace Stevens. Copyright renewed 1978 by Holly Stevens. Reprinted by permission of Alfred A. Knopf, Inc.

Library of Congress Cataloging-in-Publication Data

Finnegan, William.
    Cold new world: growing up in a harder country / William Finnegan.
        p.   cm.
    Includes index.
    ISBN 0-679-44870-5
    1. Teenagers—United States—Social conditions.   2. Subculture—
United States.   3. Poverty—United States.   4. United States—
Social conditions—1980–   I. Title.
HV1431.F56   1998
305.235′098—dc21   97-45927

Random House website address: www.randomhouse.com
Printed in the United States of America on acid-free paper
2 3 4 5 6 7 8 9
First Edition

For my parents, Bill and Pat,
and for Caroline

MIRANDA

How beauteous mankind is! O brave new world,
That has such people in't!

PROSPERO

'Tis new to thee.

—Shakespeare, *The Tempest,* Act V, Scene 1

CONTENTS

"It's all about working-class." This was the earnest and curious refrain I heard from the Antelope Valley Sharps—a group of young antiracist skinheads in an outer suburb of Los Angeles—each time I asked why they were skins. By the time I got to the Antelope Valley, in late 1995, I had spent the better part of six years knocking around the United States, immersed in the stories you are about to read. The experience had left me something of a specialist in the unexpected. My previous work as a reporter had been mostly in other countries, which may be why I started out with a set of relatively neat, received ideas about what I would find in this country under headings like race, class, poverty, and the drug trade. My tidy ideas were upended, in any case, at every turn. American real life is rowdier, more disturbing, more charming than anything dreamt of in your or my philosophy.

This country was (and is) in a strange, even an unprecedented, condition. While the national economy has been growing, the economic prospects of most Americans have been dimming. For young people and males and those without advanced degrees—for, that is, the large majority of working Americans—real hourly wages have fallen significantly over the past twenty-four years. Even during the time since I began this book, a period marked economically by low inflation, one of the great bull markets in Wall Street history, and an unemployment rate that has reached, as I write, its lowest level in twenty-four years, the median household income has fallen and the national poverty rate has risen. What the triumphalism of most American business writing ignores is a frightening growth in the number of low-wage jobs. This growth has left 30 percent of the country's workers earning too little to lift a family out of poverty. A new American class structure is being born—one that is harsher, in many ways, than the one it is replacing. Some people are thriving in it, of course. This book is about some families who are not. More particularly, it's about their children who are teenagers and young adults, about their lives and times, how they speak and act as they try to find their way in this cold new world.

I spent time with families in four communities: New Haven, Connecticut; San Augustine County, Texas; the Yakima Valley, in Washington State; and the Antelope Valley, in northern Los Angeles County. A rough logic drove this se-quence. New Haven is a poor Northern city, ravaged by deindustrialization and middle-class flight, with a large black ghetto that can stand for the many stricken inner cities that have come, collectively, to represent "poverty" in our national imagination and political debate—despite the fact that most poverty in America is, as many researchers have pointed out, neither Northern nor urban nor black. Terry Jackson's family has been in New Haven since his great-grandparents moved there after the Second World War. The family's ex-perience with downward mobility has been unequivocal: each generation has been poorer than the one before it.

San Augustine County is in the rural Deep South (never mind that it's in Texas). It is, figuratively speaking, the home place where most African Ameri-cans, even those who have lived for many years in cities like New Haven, have or locate their roots. Although social change tends to occur more slowly and subtly in poor rural communities, I found San Augustine racked by distinctly contemporary struggles. Crack addiction, AIDS, and the federal government's war on drugs had each dealt heavy blows to Lanee Mitchell's family before we met. To a poor black family in the South, new troubles inevitably appear in a context of traditional oppression. And yet the shutdown of emigration to the cities as a hopeful option for ambitious young people seemed to have given things a newly apocalyptic cast.

The Yakima Valley is a rich farming region whose economy depends entirely on cheap Mexican labor. Getting there from the South was less of a stretch than it might seem. Black people in San Augustine complain about job competition from Mexicans—in the local pea and watermelon fields and timber mills as well as in the cities, such as Houston and Los Angeles, where union jobs that they or their relatives once held are increasingly filled by undocumented immigrants working nonunion. Rafael and Rosa Guerrero, a couple from the Mexican state of Zacatecas who have "settled out" in the Yakima Valley (and who happen to be militants in the local farmworkers' union), came to this country in search of *una vida mejor* for themselves and their children. My story is about what they— and, especially, what their oldest son, Juan—found instead.

Finally, I went to Los Angeles. Jacqueline Jones, a historian of American poverty, has written about how the "postmodern poverty" of the late twenti-eth century is creating "a multitude of 'underclasses,' " many of them white. I went to L.A. to see how vulnerable white people were dealing with recent up-heavals in the Southern California economy. Some of the kids I met there de-clared, as I say, that their lives were "all about working-class." Karl Marx might have said that they were, more precisely, about being forced down into the lumpen proletariat—into what is popularly known nowadays as the underclass. Mindy Turner and her friends, while clearly desperate to avoid that fate, often seemed to be doing everything in their power to bring it on: bagging school, getting pregnant as teenagers, abusing dangerous drugs, forming violent gangs, doing time in jail. Even when one of them killed another one—this happened in the midst of my reporting—it seemed to give almost nobody pause. At times the downward momentum in their suburban world felt all-consuming.

My reporting method was unscientific. In the communities that interested me, I tried to find hard-pressed people whom I liked enough to spend months with. They also had to be willing, of course, to let me hang around. Because I'm particularly interested in how people understand their own situations, I tried to let them show me, when possible, where their story was and what it might mean. Some of the most eloquent commentary I found came, therefore, not from interviews or as straightforward analysis, but in jokes, asides, quarrels, incidents, display. I can't think of a more nuanced expression, for instance, of the "double truth," as Benjamin DeMott calls it, "that within our borders an opportunity society and a caste society coexist" than Terry Jackson's decision to "go Yale" in the New Haven black community's spring-cleaning parade, which passes through the Yale University campus. Terry was a fifteen-year-old school dropout and street cocaine dealer at the time, and he used his drug earnings to outfit himself for the parade in Yale sweatpants, a blue Yale sweatshirt, and a Yale baseball cap. The costume was a hit with the crowd. "It was *dope*," Terry said afterward. Indelibly, I thought.

I did not go looking for "types." Some readers of an earlier version of Terry Jackson's story, which appeared in *The New Yorker,* complained that by writing about him I was reinforcing a stereotype: the young black inner-city drug dealer. I think the point is valid, although the further complaint, made by a few antidrug crusaders, that I should not be writing *sympathetically* about such a person, is, I think, not. I *am* sympathetic to Terry, and to the many other kids in his situation. The fact is that the illegal drug trade offers more economic opportunity to more young men than anything else going in the inner city. Depicting this reality may indeed play into the powerful (and politically destructive) association, in the public mind, of poor blacks with crime. I make a sharp distinction, however (one that the law does not always make), between violent criminals and people merely involved in the drug trade. Terry's story is both common and, I think, commonly misunderstood.

I generally failed to keep my journalistic distance. The sheer amount of time we spent together tended to erode the lines between me and my subjects. Often, their ideas about me became elements of my story about them. People usually took me at first for a "news reporter," a notion that invariably wilted as the months passed and nothing I wrote appeared in print. I was sometimes suspected, even accused to my face, of being a cop. At other times my bluff was called more shrewdly. Laverne Clark, Lanee Mitchell's mother and the materfamilias of the all-black village in San Augustine County where I landed up, liked to probe my racial views, hoping to find out "what it is about you and black people, Bill." She seemed to have me down, at least initially, as what Zora Neale Hurston used to call, during the Harlem Renaissance, a Negrotarian—a *de haut en bas* patron of black aspiration. Although Laverne's view of me seemed to soften with time, we often argued—about local history, the causes of poverty, Clarence Thomas and Anita Hill. I found our debates, some of them conducted in the school bus Laverne drives for a living, both rewarding and upsetting. They were also remarkable for how unhampered she seemed by the fact that she had never finished the ninth grade.

There is, just as fashionable cultural theory has it, no privileged place to stand. I never found such a place while writing this book, anyway. The moral authority of the social order that once might have allowed me to pass unambivalent judgments on the lives of poor Americans—an authority packed tight, at the best of times, with unexamined assumptions about power and virtue—has, in my view, simply grown too weak to support such exertions. A white middle-class reporter inspecting the souls of poor African Americans is, given our history, an especially dubious proposition. So I've tried to keep one eye on my limitations as observer and analyst, and to reflect, where possible, the densely freighted power relations between me and some of my subjects.

There is still, however, privilege itself, vast rangelands of it. Particularly because my main subjects here are kids, I felt compelled, on a couple of occasions, to intervene, most unjournalistically, in their lives, calling on my relatively grand resources to try to prevent one disaster or another. In both cases these interventions came after the publication of earlier, magazine versions of the stories in question, when I felt less constrained by the canons of the guild. These episodes now figure in the more comprehensive accounts here.

I've changed the names of a number of people in Terry Jackson's story, some for legal reasons that will be self-evident, some for reasons of privacy. All of these stories contain, for that matter, highly sensitive material. But it was only in the New Haven section that the arguments for changing names outweighed the claims of maximum veracity.

I was born in the 1950s, and grew up in a country very different from the America described in this book. Disparities of class and race account for some of that difference, but the rest is generational—the fallout from, above all, economic stagnation and decline. The peculiar, morale-sapping toxicity of that fallout is hardly news, but it really struck me, in an oddly personal way, one night in the Antelope Valley while talking to a white kid named Jaxon Stines (he was Mindy Turner's boyfriend at the time). Jaxon was eighteen, intelligent, with a shaved head and a big silver ring through his nose. He and I had been raised, I discovered, in some of the same Los Angeles suburbs. I had been back to the area only rarely since finishing high school in 1970—hanging out in the Antelope Valley was thus a sort of homecoming for me—and I thought I understood why Jaxon said he loathed it. (Bright kids from the 'burbs almost always abhor the 'burbs.) But when I asked him about other places he had visited, he said sourly, "I've hitchhiked all up and down California and every place is just as boring as this is." I was stunned—if only because I still remembered how, when I left home at seventeen, I did so with a sense of possibility that was radically unlimited. My politics were utopian, my hopes jejunely unclouded. I found no place boring—or, if I did, I kept moving. I knew Jaxon's remark was partly just trendy nihilism (he played in a punk band called Wallpaper) but it was also piercingly sad. Some fierce *constriction* has taken place, especially among young Americans, over the past twenty-five years.

Nostalgia, I hasten to add, is on the list of banned substances for this book. Although some of the people I write about are preoccupied, even obsessed, with their memories or fantasies of better times, I've tried to resist the temptation to gild the past myself, particularly when it comes to my own generation's experience. The sense of extreme freedom I enjoyed when I was Jaxon's age was anomalous—an unearned blessing anchored in the belief that, when my friends and I got around to becoming working adults, our options would be ample. Many of the parents in these stories are my age, and, if this is a singularly difficult time to be a teenager, it is clearly not a much better time to be the parent of one. Still, I hold the fecklessness and self-absorption of my generation substantially responsible for the darkening, fearsome world that younger Americans face today. As Christopher Lasch, the late social critic, wrote, "If young people feel no connection to anything, their dislocation is a measure of our failure, not theirs."

This generational failure is not merely cultural—a hapless abdication of parental roles and family obligations by adults who themselves never quite grew up. It's also material. And it is the work not just of baby boomers but also of *their* parents. Between 1970 and 1995, thanks to progressive public policy, poverty among Americans over the age of sixty-five was reduced by more than 50 percent. During the same period, poverty among American children rose by 37 percent. The success of the assault on poverty among the elderly is to be applauded, obviously, and yet there is no doubt about who, generationally speaking, has paid for it. Our national child-poverty rate is by far the highest among the world's advanced economies. The 1996 welfare "reform" bill was signed into law by President Clinton despite predictions from his own Department of Health and Human Services that a million more American children would be pushed into poverty as a result. Meanwhile, Social Security benefits are politically sacred. It is clearly no coincidence that the 1996 budget of the Children's Defense Fund, the leading national lobby for children's interests, was $15 million while the equivalent lobby for the elderly, the American Association of Retired Persons, in the same year spent $449 million.

The official and political neglect of children, particularly poor children, includes a brutal squeeze on public school funding in much of the country (most spectacular in California), as taxpayers increasingly shirk their traditional obligations to the young. Kids know that their schools very often, as they would put it, suck, that a high school diploma is increasingly worthless, that their prospects when they leave school, even if they manage to earn a college degree, are darker, on the whole, than their parents' were—and this awareness is, I believe, a prime reason why the horizons of possibility seem to be constricting for so many young Americans.

Just as damaging, however, as the shortage of technical competence being produced by an increasingly inequitable educational system is the shortage of historical understanding it creates. Everywhere I traveled for this book, history was being debated, contested, and re-narrated in one way or another by ordinary people, old and young, poor and otherwise. I found the kids in the Antelope Valley, for instance, arguing about slavery and Adolf Hitler and Charles Manson. Their source materials were notably scant. A local community-college teacher told me, "There are no books at home, no ideas, no sense of history. The kids reach out to these historical figures, but it's through TV, through comic books, through word-of-mouth." Though often characterized as indifferent to history and ideas, Americans—including many who are indifferently *educated*—actually have a great unsatisfied hunger for narratives that may help explain the deep, diffuse crisis that they and their communities seem to be in. Laverne Clark, for her part, had a solid grasp of the importance of history. In her community the broadcast of the TV miniseries *Roots* had been controversial. Laverne's mother could not bear to watch it, and her sister didn't think it should have been shown because of the passions it stirred up. Laverne disagreed. "I'm glad they went and showed it, even if it did upset a lot of people, upset the white children to see how their people done treated our people. It started some fights, I know, but people got to know what happened here, how we got to this."

The problem of race, which is a main theme of *Cold New World*, boils over into explicit, militant racism only in its final section. My treatment of the subject there may be, as such, slightly misleading. That is, I think it is important to know that a kid like Jaxon Stines, who lived in a middle-class gated community, can nowadays describe himself without embarrassment as "a racist," while his mother, a liberal Democrat with an anthropology degree, throws up her hands in helplessness and horror. And I find the struggles of Mindy Turner to survive the violent tides of white supremacism and neo-Nazism swirling around her at school and among her peers a startling, compelling story. But I don't think that the dilemma of the millions of poor and working-class Latinos and African Americans who are being locked out of the great American middle class by falling wages and shrinking educational opportunity will be eased in any conceivable measure if Mindy's personal struggle is ultimately won by the good angels whispering to her that some black people are nice. Color caste lines are not a product of individual moral failures. And their current hardening is not the work of racist fringe movements.

There is, rather, a far broader backlash going on. Put simply, it's a society-wide shift of priorities and resources away from the movement toward racial equality (abetted by an upward transfer of wealth that is reducing equality generally). Resegregation has become the norm in American schools and housing. In 1997 the Harvard Project on School Desegregation reported the largest shift back toward segregation since the 1954 Supreme Court decision, *Brown* v. *Board of Education,* and it predicted worse ahead. The extraordinary growth of the African American middle class over the past generation has leveled off. I don't write much about that growth here—though it does provide a context for some of the violent racism among downwardly mobile whites in places like the Antelope Valley, and it does provide much of the cover for white politicians contending that "enough has been done" to dismantle the American racial caste system. I've written instead about a few black people among the millions who are losing ground, people whose lives are being determined largely by their inherited place in that system.

Formal political action is not the only way that racial domination gets dismantled; there is in fact great pressure from below on the assorted, less-than-scientifc ethnic categories that prop up American color caste. "Mixed marriages" in every combination are on the increase, which contributes to a cultural and demographic paradox: on the one hand, growing income inequality and racial polarization in an increasingly rigid, neo-Victorian economic dispensation; on the other, a social universe in which traditional categories are becoming ever more fluid. Young people grasp this paradox— and the "racial" nettles that surround it—far more readily than their elders. And their responses often break the mold—e.g., the antiracist skinheads mentioned above.

Another fraught, essential topic here is drugs—essential because illegal drugs are a salient feature of nearly every young American's world; because the drug trade is the heart of the nation's underground economy, which flourishes alongside poverty; and because drugs have become political code, in various contexts, for race. While the devastation caused by drug abuse and by the violence of the drug trade, especially in our inner cities, is obviously real, the public perception that drugs are predominantly a black problem is mistaken. Selective news coverage and selective drug-law enforcement both contribute to this distortion. James A. Morone of the University of Chicago recently ticked off some of the relevant figures: "African Americans constitute 12 percent of the population and an estimated 13 percent of American drug users. They account for 35 percent of the arrests for drug possession, 55 percent of all convictions for drug possession, and . . . 74 percent of all prison sentences." While I am concerned that my tales of the drug trade in urban and rural black communities will do nothing to offset prevailing misconceptions, I trust that my reporting on the rampant methamphetamine problem among suburban whites will help to balance the picture.

Given the ethnic and geographic range of these stories, and the tribalistic passions of youth, this book is inevitably, in part, a survey of American subcultures. But the cultural "balkanization" regularly decried by conservatives in recent years—a presumed splintering of the national identity usually attributed to heightened ethnic self-awareness and the growth of multiculturalism in education—is being met, it seems to me, by countervailing forces that are at least as strong. The entertainment and advertising industries are the most obvious of these centripetal, homogenizing cultural forces; Afrocentrism is but a frail reed in their gale.

The tension between mass culture and its local alternatives ripples through each of the stories here. In Laverne Clark's youth, black Texans celebrated, with community barbecues and parades, a holiday known as "June Teenth," which commemorated the date—June 19, 1865—when the slaves were freed in Texas. June Teenth had become neglected and Laverne fretted that black kids in San Augustine knew (and cared) more about Disney World than they did about East Texas. Her husband, Cecil, a Baptist preacher and pulpwood logger, would pore over his Bible in their crowded house in the evenings, looking for passages that would speak to the hard lives of his congregation, while all around him his children and grandchildren zoned out on the cheesy ironies of David Letterman and *Seinfeld.*

The mismatch between experience and its mass media simulacra is a live issue for most Americans, whose bodies and bank statements rarely resemble those of the rich and famous whose "lifestyles" have become so inescapable. But it has special ferocity among the disaffected—poor people, young people, new immigrants, members of low-caste minorities—among those, in other words, who lack the skills, not to mention the money, to participate in the high-consumption, high-debt culture being touted all around them. People in these marginalized groups necessarily develop an embattled, ambivalent relationship to the center, to its institutions and its denizens. Among the comfortable (and the comfortably monocultural), this ambivalence—this apparent reluctance to seize every opportunity for law-abiding self-advancement—tends to be looked upon with bafflement. (I've felt my share of this bafflement.

"What do you mean you *forgot* your Job Corps interview?") Thus, well-meaning people often talk about the need to convert poor kids to "mainstream values," or "mainstream culture."

I am convinced, however, that nearly all Americans already belong to basically the same culture. There is certainly no distinct "culture of poverty." There are, rather, innumerable adaptations to slight or shrinking opportunities. Some of these adaptations are antisocial or self-destructive. Many are simply survival strategies whose rationales are not always obvious to middle-class outsiders. There is also, as has often been observed, a high degree of social isolation among the very poor. But even this isolation does not preclude a constant barrage of mass culture into the daily life of nearly every American, much of it delivered by commercial television.

The central ideology of "mainstream culture," the belief system that most of us share, is liberal consumerism—a secular, individualist creed that essentially adds more shopping hours to the old exaltation of life, liberty, and the pursuit of happiness. Our children are being raised in this tepid faith with what amounts to fanatic zeal: the average American child, by the time he or she leaves high school, has been subjected to more than 380,000 TV commercials. The role of advertising in our daily lives has grown so immense that it has become difficult to remember what it was like before the subliminal flood of "brand synergies" came to fill every corner of public space. Billions of dollars and fantastic amounts of energy are, after all, devoted annually to the creation ex nihilo of new desires—anxieties that, by design, only more consumption can console. Some American communities are less completely converted to these "mainstream values" than others. In San Augustine County, which does not have a shopping mall—the demographics of income and population density don't even meet the minimums required by Wal-Mart, K mart, Kentucky Fried Chicken, or McDonald's in order to license a franchisee—I found many remnants of an older, less homogenized country, and perhaps a limited exception to my argument that all Americans belong to the same culture.

Liberal consumerism's main competitor today, both in the United States and abroad, is fundamentalism in its myriad forms. As it happens, each of the four young people I write about here was confronting, I found, at least one backward-looking culture of absolute belief. Terry, in New Haven, worked for a while for the Nation of Islam—not a fundamentalist group, religiously speaking, but one whose black nationalism vehemently expresses the classic separatist (and conservative) response to cultural and economic domination, and whose essentialism on the subject of race is starkly premodern. Terry also had an uncle who was a fundamentalist Christian. Terry spent a lot of time thinking about each of these faiths and resisting their conversion efforts. Lanee Mitchell, in San Augustine, was in her early twenties when we met and often wished aloud that she had her parents' (and her grandparents') passionate

faith in a Southern Baptist God—anything to deliver her from what she regarded as a fallen modern world. Juan Guerrero, in the Yakima Valley, was far
too much the MTV ironist for the folk-romanticism of Latino gang life—
except, he said, when he was in jail, where suddenly it was important to be
Mexican and he turned into an ethnic nationalist. And Mindy Turner, in the
Antelope Valley, was not only flirting with white supremacism but, at seventeen, had already had flings with Mormonism and even Judaism in her search
for some sustaining circle in the spiritual vacuum of a bedroom community in
economic free-fall.

Poverty is relative. The worst poverty in the United States is mild compared
with the absolute scarcity that haunts large parts of the globe. But the experience of poverty is also relative, and it has everything to do with one's
surroundings, one's neighbors, and one's ideas about the world. For a fundamentalist, poverty is unpleasant, but it may make sense. For a liberal consumer, poverty is agony, unameliorated by the promise of heavenly reward.
And this sort of pain is only intensified by the hoary presence of consumerism's mythic twin, the American Dream: the idea that anyone can
achieve success and prosperity in this country through his or her own efforts.
The sociologist Jennifer Hochschild found in a recent study that this belief is
not only still widely held among the poorest Americans but is even more popular among, say, poor African Americans than among their middle-class
counterparts. Certainly the four young people who fill the main roles in this
book all subscribe, in sometimes heartbreaking ways, to the American Dream.
They're down for it, as they might say. The key difference, finally, between a
poor American teenager's relation to "mainstream culture" and a comfortably
middle-class teenager's relation to it is the difference between their access to its
rewards.

From their situations, however dire, kids also *make* culture: music, language
(slang), dance, fashion, politics, and the profusion of quasi-tribal arrangements generically known as gangs. (The youth-gang phenomenon is so widespread—there is scarcely an American town of any size now without a gang
problem—that gangs figure in three of the four stories here.) I haven't tried to
produce a comprehensive inventory of any aspect of the youth subcultures described in these pages. They are simply too lush and swiftly changing. They are
also enmeshed in a constant, impenetrable exchange with the youth-culture
industry, a multibillion-dollar, transnational trade that both leads and follows
youth taste. Most of the kids I got to know for this book seemed perfectly aware
that they are a prized market, and seemed also to feel ambivalent about being
so relentlessly targeted by adults intent on selling them entertainments and
accessories. Some were experts at cross-cutting and satirizing the nonstop
sales pitch that is the white noise of their lives—although, because I'm less flu-

ent in the language of pop music and ads, especially TV commercials, I know I missed a lot.

There's more to downward mobility than decreased purchasing power. No dollar figure can be placed on the loss to individual members when a community declines, or a family breaks up, or a closely knit village must be left behind. The savage tension between postindustrial capitalism's imperatives and the claims of family and community, whether celebrated by free-marketers as creative or denounced by social democrats as destructive, hangs as a frame around all the stories I tell here. But it's the people inside that frame, trying to build lives for themselves in this premillennial America, who really interest me. The kids, especially—those lavish producers of the consistently unexpected. They made this long, strange prodigal's trek feel more like a voyage of discovery than work.

BOOK ONE

Work Boy

We keep coming back and coming back
To the real: to the hotel instead of the hymns
That fall upon it out of the wind.

—Wallace Stevens,
    "An Ordinary Evening in New Haven"

Beulah Morgan had lived in Newhallville, a working-class neighborhood of New Haven, Connecticut, since 1953. She moved there with her parents from Ansonia, a mill town a few miles west, because, she said, "black people couldn't buy a house in a good neighborhood in Ansonia." By Beulah's parents' lights, Newhallville was a very good neighborhood. Its leafy streets and well-built three-family houses had been home to a stable population of factory workers and their families for more than a century. The neighborhood got its name from George T. Newhall, whose Carriage Emporium was, in 1855, the largest manufacturer of carriages in the world. After the Civil War put Newhall, whose main trade was in the South, out of business, the Winchester Repeating Arms Company became New Haven's—and Newhallville's—largest employer. After the Winchester plant was sold to Olin Industries, a Midwestern ammunition and brass company, in 1931, Olin became the neighborhood's mainstay. Newhall Street, where Beulah's parents bought their house, dead-ended at the Olin plant. In 1953, there was every reason to believe that Beulah's family's social mobility would be, in the American way, upward.

New Haven has had an African American community since the seventeenth century, but until the Second World War, its members usually found themselves blocked from the better industrial jobs—compelled to accept instead lower-wage employment as, typically, waiters or porters at Yale University. For many years, they were also blocked from living outside a ghetto, near Yale, known as Dixwell. Factory work, like housing in Newhallville, went first to Irish immigrants, later to Germans and Eastern Europeans, and then to Italians. When the era of immigration from Europe ended, however, many of the jobs generated by the wartime industrial boom of the 1940s went to blacks. New Haven's black community grew from 5,000 in 1930 to 10,000 in 1950, then to 23,000 in 1960. Most of the new arrivals were from the South—most came, in fact, from one particular area of North Carolina—and in the 1950s and 1960s many black families settled in Newhallville. The Olin plant was going strong; in 1954, it employed 6,500 people. Although none of the men in Beulah Morgan's family worked at Olin, they all worked in factories. Her first husband worked at Scoville Manufacturing, in Waterbury. Her second husband, Carl Morgan, whom she married in 1954, worked at Simkins Industries, in New Haven. Beulah herself was a doctor's receptionist on Dixwell Avenue for twenty-two years. In 1990, when we met, she was working as a receptionist for a dentist in Newhallville. Her husband was still, after forty-five years, at Simkins Industries.

Like every old industrial city in America, New Haven fell into a steep economic decline starting in the 1950s and 1960s. Factories began to cut back and then to close. Unemployment mushroomed. By 1981, when the Olin plant was sold to a local consortium, it employed barely a thousand people. The city's middle class, which had been trickling off to the suburbs since at least the First World War, started leaving in earnest. And while the overall population of the city shrank, from 150,000 in 1960 to 119,000 in 1994, its black population continued to grow. By 1980, there were 40,000 black people in New Haven; by 1990, there were more than 47,000. An influx of Latinos, mostly from Puerto Rico—and mostly, like the swelling population of blacks, unskilled and ill educated—also began in the 1960s. Poverty came to engulf large parts of the city. The 1980 federal census found New Haven to be the seventh-poorest city in America. The 1990 census found neighborhoods where the poverty rate ran as high as 40 and 50 percent.

The arc of New Haven's decline was mirrored by an arc within Beulah Morgan's family. Her parents sold the house on Newhall Street in 1975 and, for their retirement, bought a house in Hamden, just outside New Haven. Their standard of living remained much the same. And Beulah and Carl, when we met, still owned a modest house in Newhallville. But none of Beulah's five children—the youngest was born in 1961; they all still lived in New Haven—owned a house of any kind. Indeed, four of them were unemployed and could not afford even to rent. Two had moved back in with Beulah and Carl. The other two had each lived on and off with their parents since becoming adults, and both were living, at the time we met, in apartments paid for entirely by public assistance. Beulah's six grandchildren, meanwhile, had all lived with her at various times. She had effective custody of one, and her mother had legal custody of three. In other words, none of Beulah's children had been able to form and maintain a two-parent family for their children. And each generation's social and economic prospects were looking worse, not better, than those of their parents.

This alarming eversion of the normal American expectation of generational progress was the grim backdrop, as I see it now, for the months I spent with one of Beulah's grandsons. Terry Jackson, as I shall call him, was sixteen when we met. His mother—let's call her Anjelica—was thirty-three, never married, with two sons by different fathers. Let's call Terry's younger brother Buddy.

Terry and I are eating spaghetti at the kitchen table in his mother's apartment on Wallace Street. It's mid-December. Anjelica, a glass of wine in her hand, is standing in a doorway watching us eat. The telephone rings. Terry stops eating and watches his mother. Something about the way she mumbles tells him that the caller is his grandmother. He goes back to his supper. Terry's girlfriend, Lakeeda, has been calling every few minutes. Terry and Lakeeda, who is eighteen, have been estranged lately. Anjelica has been trying to broker a reconciliation. Lakeeda has just invited Terry over to her house. Hence his rush to eat.

Talking to her mother seems to turn Anjelica into a teenager. She pouts, murmurs, and pouts some more. Anjelica is a slight, fine-featured woman with short straight hair and clear chestnut-colored skin. She is dressed tonight in sweatpants and a T-shirt advertising the Connecticut state lottery with the slogan YOU CAN'T WIN IF YOU DON'T PLAY. Buddy, who is six, is playing Nintendo on the television in the living room. Somebody has cut Buddy's hair in a stubbly fade that makes him look like a tiny Mike Tyson. He's a stocky child, wearing flannel pajamas. I think Buddy should come and have some spaghetti. Buddy doesn't agree. I realize I've never seen Buddy eat anything that isn't sweet.

Beulah is in the hospital for surgery. Anjelica is trying to explain why she and Terry have started visiting her in shifts. Somebody, it seems, is trying to break into their apartment. Twice she has come home and found the doorjamb scratched and smashed. Leaving the apartment empty even for an hour is now out of the question. Anjelica thinks she knows who the would-be burglar is. She and her sons moved in here four months ago. They had no problems—*nothing*—for a month and a half. Then a Puerto Rican woman moved in upstairs. The woman's boyfriend is the suspect. He drinks and he beats her up. Whoever it is trying to break in, Anjelica has a plan to catch him. She will have her own boyfriend come over late at night, park on the next block, and slip in the back door. In the morning, she and her sons will leave the house. Her boyfriend will stay inside, making no noise. When somebody tries to break in—*boom*. Her boyfriend is big and strong and, Anjelica says, crazy. He works as a painter, off and on, at Yale.

Anjelica says good-bye to her mother and moves to the living-room doorway. She stands there studying Terry. A huge, soft smile slowly lights her face. "I remember first love," she says. Her voice is husky. She shakes her head. "I was *crazy*. I was sixteen, too. When I got upset, I went and got a gun and I was going to *kill* him, then kill myself."

Terry, devouring the last of his spaghetti, does not look up from his plate.

His mother still wears a dreamy smile as she says, "After all the time we was going together, he met somebody else and a month later he married her."

Anjelica turns to watch Buddy, who is twisting frantically in front of the TV, pushing buttons on a remote control unit to make Mario, an animated character in plumber's overalls, jump over lethal creatures and bounce into stars that make him temporarily invulnerable. "Use your bullets!" Anjelica shouts.

Terry, dropping his fork and rising from the table, pauses to watch Buddy play. Terry is the household Nintendo champion. "I'm a *crazy* Nintendo freak," he says. But Lakeeda is waiting. He dodges into a bedroom to dress.

Anjelica and I join Buddy while Terry agonizes over what to wear. He keeps reappearing in different shirts and sweaters. Anjelica and I tell him, without looking away from the TV, that the white turtleneck and the boots look great. Yes, he has used enough cologne. Terry starts singing, in a wild falsetto, "The girls, the girls, they love me."

Terry, who is tall and lithe, stands in the doorway. Wearing a manic grin and a high-low cut that rises in a solid cylinder at least four inches above his head, he looks electrified: fifty thousand volts of high spirits surging through his frame. He hunches his shoulders, splays his arms, and starts an explosive little hip-hop dance. The apartment seems suddenly too small to hold him. I offer to drive him to Lakeeda's.

In the car, with the Gothic ramparts of Yale's Payne Whitney Gymnasium rolling by on our right, Terry says, "My mother *love* Lakeeda." Terry is wearing a Chicago Bears parka over his turtleneck, and a tall blue ski cap. "And Lakeeda's mother love me. And Lakeeda's little son, Tyrone, he love me *dearly*. I love him, too. And me and Lakeeda, we love each other. So, I guess, when push come to shove, me and her just gotta be together."

Terry is gazing raptly up at a red stoplight. He is a strikingly good-looking boy, long-eyelashed and fine-jawed. The most striking thing about him, though, is an eerie purity of self-expression. He can say "I love him" with utter naturalness. And when he tells me stories, which he does a lot, he always tells them the same way—eagerly, easily, with no discernible embarrassment or pride—regardless of whether the story he is telling reflects well or shamefully on him. His indifference to manipulating me sometimes seems too good to be real, and yet I've noticed few inconsistencies in his accounts of his adventures. I can't imagine what he thinks of me, this white dude from New York with a notebook and a million questions. I give him rides and buy him meals, and he says he enjoys our chats.

"Welcome to the Terrordome," Terry murmurs. This is a rap lyric, and hearing it reminds me suddenly of something Lisa Sullivan, a black Yale graduate student and community activist, told me. "The older folks just don't understand that being a teenager these days is *brutal*," Sullivan said. "It's much worse than it was to be a teenager in the forties, when people were afraid of the Klan, of being called 'nigger,' of having somebody spit on them. These kids know that the whole society hates who they are. And they can't *help* who they are. Why do you think their favorite band calls itself Public Enemy Number One?"

"Welcome to the Terrordome" is the latest release by Public Enemy, which is indeed Terry's favorite band. We are now passing a Kentucky Fried Chicken that is a notorious teen hangout. Terry cranes to see who is inside. "'Round about midnight, that's when it's *showtime* there," he says. "All the crazy cars, all the crazy girls, all the crazy clothes. I bet some of my homeboys will be there tonight. I won't be, though. I'll be with Lakeeda!"

I drop Terry on the west side of town—on a dark, quiet street lined with large white houses—and start back toward his mother's. On Edgewood Avenue, black teenage boys in bulky parkas and tall ski caps stand on every corner, despite the cold, selling drugs. At the western edge of the Yale campus, the drug dealers abruptly disappear. On the radio, a woman chants, rap-style, "I wanna see a bank account with lots of zeroes after the first five numbers, I wanna see *Hamiltons.*" Downtown New Haven looks deserted. The road passes under an immense concrete parking garage. Wallace Street lies east of the city, in a ramshackle, unfocused neighborhood, one of the many areas of New Haven marooned by postwar highway construction. It is miles from Newhallville, Anjelica's real home. Anjelica studies me through a window before she lets me in. We sit at the kitchen table drinking an ice-cold rosé wine called Canei.

"I was sixteen when Terry was born," Anjelica says. "It was my freshman year. His father was a couple years older. After he graduated, he joined the service. Terry's real name is Peter, same as his father. He has his last name, too. But I call him Terry because me and his father never got along. He never took responsibility for his son. On the day after Terry was born, though, I met this other guy, who worked at the hospital. Me and him fell in love. We was high school sweethearts. Then he went to the Air Force. He stayed away ten years. He just came back a few years ago."

Anjelica smiles to herself. Then she frowns. "He never should've come back," she says. "He's smart. He's had some damn good jobs. He was a manager of Wendy's. But he blew it. Now he just sits around his house smoking cocaine. I heard he broke into someplace and was out on the street, selling stuff. Uh-uh. He blew it."

The phone rings. Anjelica picks it up, grunts a few times, and hangs up without saying good-bye.

"Let's see," she says. "I graduated from Hillhouse High in 1975. Then I went to secretarial school. But I was mainly into drugs. In high school, we just smoked reefer and took acid and black beauties—some kind of speed pill. But then I got into snorting coke, and freebasing. My big sister, Charlayne, was really into it. She was into P-dope—that's like heroin. And my other sister, Darla, she'd take anything you gave her. She *still* will. And my little brother, Button, he got to be a dealer. He was into freebasing. He used to bug out."

Anjelica laughs. "One night, Button took a glass basing pipe and just broke it in his hand," she says. "He was *crazy*. We was all lookouts for Button. I was a bag lady, too. I held the drugs. I never had to buy no drugs because I got paid in drugs. I used to make runs to New York sometimes. I was the pickup girl. Reefer, cocaine. I only tried P-dope once, on my twenty-fifth birthday. I didn't like it. And I never injected *nothing*."

Anjelica pours us both some more Canei. "But Terry got kind of tired of me. He said he didn't want me no more. He went to live with my mother. That's when I landed on the street. I was twenty, twenty-one years old. I ended up living a lot of different places. Had a house on Brewster Street. Stayed at the Pond Lily Motel. I always kept a room for Terry, but he just liked living with my mother more than he liked living with me. He stayed with his father's parents, too, over on Bassett Street. They were good to him. When I was twenty-eight or twenty-nine, I got down to ninety-six pounds. I was freebasing. I was dehydrated. My mother, she was hysterical. She put me on a special diet, with lots of water and fruit juices and meat. I kept getting high, though, even when I was staying with her. I went into the hospital for a month, but when I come out I got right back into it. I just couldn't get away from it. Living with my mother and my brother, it was like living in a hell house. They're always picking fights. They're crazy about money. You come in with any money, they want it. Soon as I put Buddy down to sleep, I was gone, into the street."

Buddy comes into the kitchen. He starts clamoring for Jell-O. Anjelica ignores him. "Buddy's father came up here from North Carolina. He's a car mechanic, had him a good job, but he got too involved with the street life, so he had to go back. I went down later, in 1986, with Buddy and Terry both. Mount Olive, North Carolina. It's real quiet. Terry settled down good there. He stayed about a year. I just came back. This is my first Christmas back up here."

Buddy is now crashing around under the kitchen table, running a plastic tractor over our feet. The tractor is a Christmas present from his father that came today in the mail. The remains of its foam packing are scattered across the kitchen floor. "I was going to get him one of these," Anjelica says, nodding toward the tractor. "But I put it back on the shelf and got him a bigger one. More money. Forty-nine dollars. He's going to freak when he opens that box. That truck is *bad*. Buddy!" Anjelica seizes the tractor. She stuffs it back in its torn box. "Put this under the tree," she tells Buddy. A Christmas tree stands near the television, a bright heap of presents beneath it.

Anjelica starts making sandwiches. They are for Beulah, she says, who may or may not be out of the hospital for Christmas. "One thing about my mother, she never tried to get custody of Terry," Anjelica says. "He's still mine. I have to thank her for that. The state never tried to take him, neither. My caseworker, Mr. Johnson, he's a good guy."

Anjelica puts the sandwiches in the refrigerator and returns to the kitchen table. "You know, I haven't got high since we moved here," she says. "If you don't go out there on the street, you don't got problems. My problem is, I just don't like being alone for too long. That's why I'm going to school now—try to keep busy. I'm taking a two-year course at South Central Community College—word processing. When it's over, and I got a certificate, I'll get a job. I can type seventy words a minute."

The phone rings. Anjelica answers it, listens, grins. "Good," she says, and hangs up. "Sounds like Terry and Lakeeda's getting along good."

Anjelica goes to the sink and starts washing dishes. "My older brother, Kenny," she says over her shoulder, "he got into drugs a little bit, but not like the rest of us. He never let it take over his life. He's thirty-five. Works for the lottery. He's divorced. No kids. *Smart.*" She guffaws. "He used to help with Terry. But he was too rough with him, always jumping on him. Button tried to be a father to Terry, too. But he couldn't make Terry follow him, neither. Nowadays, the only thing Button does is try to get everybody to go to church with him. No wonder Terry's confused. He was living in a house full of nuts!"

Buddy runs in from the living room, shouting, "Five sixty-five! Five sixty-five!" It's a winning lottery number. He heard it on TV.

Anjelica stares at Buddy. She looks like she wants to spit. "*This keeps happening,*" she says heatedly. "I been playing five sixty, a dollar a box, all week. We're going to win something, I swear we are. My grandmother, she gave us all the stuff for this house—the beds, sheets, towels, blankets, everything. So I been playing her house number, five sixty, a dollar straight, a dollar a box, all week."

Buddy runs back into the living room.

Anjelica dries her hands. "I'm going to send him down to his father in North Carolina next summer. And I'm going to San Diego to see my grandfather. Flying in an airplane. I never been in an airplane before. I sure hope it don't get hijacked. California's supposed to be beautiful. One thing I know, anywhere is better than here."

Peter Jackson, Terry's father, had spent six years in the Air Force. He was a youthful, intense, good-looking man, sharp of speech, dress, and carriage. Although he paid Anjelica twenty-five dollars a month toward Terry's support, he had very little to do with her. Peter married soon after returning to New Haven. His wife had a good job with a cable-television company. They had two young sons and lived in a racially mixed neighborhood. Peter did some substitute teaching after getting out of the service. (He went to community college while in the Air Force.) Then, in 1984 his father, who was a high school custodian—Peter's mother worked at the public library—helped him get a job as a custodian at a New Haven junior high school, where he eventually became the night-crew leader.

Peter didn't have much to do with Terry, either. He worried that as a small child Terry was "exposed to lots of the wrong kind of excitement—cussing, fighting, drinking, drugs." He also worried that Anjelica's family "gives him no positive input about myself." Finally, he worried that Beulah and Anjelica indulged his son. According to Peter, Terry had not been happy living with his paternal grandparents because they were disciplinarians. Beulah, he said, had always let Terry "follow the grotesque fashions of the day." Peter had tried to offer a corrective to this policy. When Terry was a student at the junior high where Peter worked, for instance, all fashion-conscious boys were wearing their shoelaces untied. Peter, seeing that his son was *à la mode,* one day hauled him out of class and into a rest room where he tucked in his shirt and tied his shoelaces—"nice and neat, the way the athletes wear them when they play basketball"—before sending him back to class. Terry was humiliated. Beulah was furious. She phoned Peter and berated him for his insensitivity. Peter was unrepentant. Beulah's permissiveness, he believed, was one of the reasons Terry "doesn't show me or my parents the respect he should." But now, when it came to Terry's upbringing, Peter said, "I choose, on the advice of my parents, to remain pretty much neutral."

Indulgence is actually not Beulah Morgan's most apparent trait. She is an ample, bespectacled, vinegary woman, the owner of a piercing glance and a biting tongue. When I ask her about Terry's childhood, she immediately starts apportioning blame. "Terry's father used to come and take him downtown, saying he was going to buy him all kinds of things. But then he would just buy himself something. He used to bring Terry back with nothing." Anjelica, according to Beulah, was even worse. "She couldn't take care of him. She was too busy running the street."

We are talking in Beulah's living room. It's a jumbled, comfortable place, poorly ventilated and loosely arranged around a television set, which is playing loudly. Beulah's son Button, her eldest daughter, Charlayne, Charlayne's three children, the eight-year-old son of Beulah's youngest daughter, Darla, and assorted other children come and go, sometimes pausing to watch TV, or to glance shyly at me, while Beulah sits beside me on the couch, crocheting an afghan—the third one since her surgery last month, she says—and watching TV and monitoring the outerwear of each child who heads out the front door. I wonder in passing where Beulah's husband, Carl, is; he never seems to be here when I come by. Terry, who does not get along with his grandfather, has told me I should be thankful for that.

Peter's parents were actually pretty good to Terry, Beulah says, and their strictness was not a problem. "It didn't work out because Anjelica wouldn't give them any of the state money she was collecting on Terry," Beulah says.

"That's all it was. But Peter's mother used to complain about the money *in front of Terry*. That used to make him cry." Anjelica never gave *her* any of the money she collected for Terry, either, Beulah says, in all the years he lived with her. If anyone indulged Terry, she says, it was his mother. "When he was nine or ten, he realized that if I told him he couldn't do something he could always just run over to her and *she* would say okay. Now she's messing up Buddy the same way. She won't hit him. All he eats is candy, which is why he's so hyper. Not to mention what it does to his teeth." Anjelica's problem, Beulah says, is not lack of intelligence. "She's smart. She just thinks everything is funny. That's why she lets her kids do whatever they want. Now Terry's getting the same attitude. Nothing matters. Everything's funny." Beulah and the noise on TV both pause, and for a moment the only sound is the light clacking of her crochet hooks. "I've been a foster mother," she goes on. "I've taken in a lot of kids. And it's always the same. When the real mother gets visiting rights, they start messing up."

If it was true that nothing mattered to Terry, that he simply thought everything was funny, then he did a good job of concealing the fact from me. And yet it was true that he was more serene, less accusatory, than the adults in his life when he talked about his own upbringing; he seemed to regard himself as more than the product of his family's failings. One dereliction of duty that all his guardians agreed occurred—but that each ascribed to someone else—had to do with Terry's eyesight. He had poor vision but had rarely worn glasses. His reading ability, which was normal in early primary school, later fell far behind that of his classmates, at least partly because of his poor sight. Terry said merely that he stopped wearing his glasses because they gave him headaches. He also became, he said, something of a class clown. His antics eventually gained him a series of interviews with school psychiatrists. The interviews got more interesting as Terry got older. "When I was little, I used to hold my problems in," he said. "Now, I'm just, like, *out* with 'em. Holding things in just make you madder. If a shrink talk to me now, I really act the fool, I play *crazy*."

Terry did not fool around, though, when it came to after-school work. He started selling newspapers on downtown street corners at the age of eleven. At twelve, he got his first real job—with forged employment papers, saying he was sixteeen—as a busboy at the Ponderosa Restaurant, on Dixwell Avenue in Hamden. According to a family friend who used to see him there, Terry showed aptitude for the "restaurant business." He was fast and diligent and the customers liked him. He was worried, though, the family friend said, when she saw him at work that she might reveal his true age. Terry cleared about forty dollars a week and spent his pay on clothes, music, fast food, and video binges with his friends.

But the importance of his income could not be measured simply by its disposition. To judge from the stories told by his family, Terry's entire life had been spent within earshot of violent arguments over money. He had been the object of many of these arguments—the cost of keeping him, the squandering of the state money received on his account, the failure of his father to buy him gifts—and he had been hurt and frightened by them, but utterly powerless to act. Now, finally, he was making money himself. Beulah and Anjelica approved of his working and let him keep his wages. Terry eventually left the Ponderosa for Kevin's Seafood, another Dixwell Avenue restaurant, where his main occupation was folding boxes. He also worked at Jimmies, a seafood restaurant in Hamden.

Terry's memories of his restaurant days were fond ones. One evening, at least, he and I were at a café in New Haven when he started fingering a pile of not-yet-folded pizza boxes. "I love these things," he said dreamily. "I got really good at folding boxes at Kevin's Seafood. The better you fold 'em, the more you can do." At Kevin's, Terry was earning about fifty dollars a week. Then a friend of a friend offered him work that paid a thousand dollars a week.

The illegal drug business enjoyed a spectacular boom in the late 1980s in New Haven. The city's heroin trade had been large but stable since the 1960s and the demand for marijuana, although it peaked in the early 1970s, remained strong. The boom drug was cocaine. Demand soared, both in the city itself—which had an estimated 5,000 hardcore cocaine and heroin addicts (many of whom used both drugs) and many more occasional users—and in the surrounding suburbs. The number of suburban users was hard to measure but some 400,000 people live in the New Haven hinterland, and most of the users there tend to do their drug shopping in the city, so the cocaine boom gave New Haven a marked economic boost. Again, it was difficult to measure the dollar volume, but it was easy to see that many people were making great money—not only drug dealers but car dealers, owners of jewelry and sportswear stores, lawyers, bankers, and bail bondsmen.

Perhaps because of its rapid growth, the drug trade in New Haven remained loosely organized. Numerous small gangs, each affiliated to some degree with a neighborhood-based federation known as a posse, operated more or less independently. The posses had names like the Ninjas, the Wild Wild West, the Underworld, and the Jungle, and they underwent constant mutations. They formed alliances with and declared war on one another; factions within a posse might also fight. Although there were Latino posses, girl gangs, and a small number of grown men involved, most posse members were black teenage boys. The drug industry's demand for labor was fierce and the pay it offered was unprecedented, but the huge risks incurred by those in its retail sector, especially at the street level, ensured that only the most desperate—those with the fewest other prospects—accepted such employment. That meant poor blacks, particularly young males, who typically possessed the further qualifications of fleetness, physical strength, and profound illusions about their own immortality. The average age of New Haven's drug dealers had been falling steadily during the boom. The city's public defender for juveniles could recall seeing only one drug case in the eight or nine years prior to early 1987. By mid-1990, he had more than fifty drug cases pending and most of his clients were under sixteen. One of his clients was a ten-year-old boy charged with selling marijuana at a New Haven school.

Terry and his friends saw—and smoked—some marijuana in junior high. "But drugs wasn't the thing then still," he said. "Drugs was like a sneak tip still. Then it just started coming out. We started hearing about cocaine, cocaine, cocaine. People started getting nice clothes. Girls started wanting all kinds of crazy things—gold, leather, fur. They'd be sayin', 'It's all about the dividend.' I was working, but I couldn't find a job that would give me enough money. And there was always another guy who was up, you know what I'm sayin'? He'd have his nice outfit, and he'd be sayin', 'Yo, man, you should get down, you should get down.'"

The decision to get down—to start dealing drugs—is not, of course, simply economic. It is also social, flowing in some (usually large) degree out of a background of family and friends, often opening up whole new vistas of friendship, and meanwhile shutting down others. In Terry's case, the fact that his mother, his uncle, and his two aunts had all been involved in drugs made the drug world a relatively familiar place. His failures in school no doubt also helped dispose him to try his luck in another area. (Among his peers, the ramifications of the decision to get down were, at least in their details, opaque to me. The terms of our relationship precluded my meeting his male friends—strange white men were violently suspect in their world, where they represented not just authority in general but the New Haven police in particular.)

As for the suggestion that girls drive boys into dealing, by their demands for expensive gifts—this was a popular suggestion among the boys involved—I heard inner-city teenage girls reverse the equation with persuasive scorn. "Drugs changed guys," a sixteen-year-old mother from a New Haven housing project told me. "They used to be pissants. They never knew about styles. Then they started getting all this money, these cars, thinking they hot. 'You be my girl, I get you some boots, some crazy earrings, a shearling coat'—that's what they say." But I also heard girls reluctantly confirm a sort of feminist nightmare. "Most these girls out here ain't goin' anyplace, and they know it," an eighteen-year-old girl in New Haven told me. "But they like cars, and going shopping, just like anybody else. They might not like it that a guy could get killed anytime, or go to jail, but most of them will still go out with a dealer. They're *impressed* when a guy says, 'I'll shoot that nigger if he mess with you.' They say, 'Hey, he really likes me, he'll *shoot* that guy.' Girls want to be well known, just like anybody else, and if they're not well known themselves, they want to be with a guy who is well known. Drug dealers *are* well known. They always got the latest styles. So if a guy asks her out for a date, a girl will say, 'What kind of car you got?' And he better say, 'BMW,' or 'Mercedes,' or 'Volvo.'

Because if he say, 'I don't got a car. Maybe we can take a taxi, or my parents can drive us,' she gonna say, 'What? This other brother, he takes me shopping in New York, and you want to go for a *walk?*' A guy who's poor, he don't have no chance of gettin' a girlfriend here. That's why a lot of them become drug dealers, and get down with the posses."

Despite the fact that Terry was living in Beulah's house in Newhallville, where the Newhallville Dogs (usually known simply as the Ville) reigned, he got down first with the Island Brothers, a large posse whose home turf was in east New Haven. The Island, as it was called, was allied with the Ville, and Terry figured that it would be safer, from a friends-of-his-grandmother point of view, to sell drugs in a neighborhood where he was not known. Terry liked the Island boys he had met—they seemed to work hard and to think highly of him. So he joined one of the crews then active in Quinnipiac Terrace, an exceptionally bleak public housing project on the Quinnipiac River. (The first time I saw what is commonly called Q Terrace, my companion, a black youth counselor from Brooklyn, muttered, "I grew up around poverty, but this place, this is *slave quarters.*")

Though Terry was only fifteen and inexperienced, he was made a "work boy." He was stationed in a second-floor hallway, where his task was to sell small capsules of cocaine, at ten dollars apiece, to customers directed to him by "piss boys" stationed out on the streets. Because he handled money he was paid better than the piss boys, who are hired less for their intelligence or probity than for their willingness to use force—piss boys normally carry guns—against competitors and would-be thieves. For a twelve-hour shift—noon to midnight—six days a week, Terry was paid a thousand dollars in cash. Sunday was his day off.

The work was scary. You had to watch out for rip-offs—customers who might try to grab the drugs and run—and for boys from a rival posse, and watch out, too, for undercover police officers posing as customers. The customers at Q Terrace were black, white, and Latino; most were in their twenties or thirties. Q Terrace, being near the junction of Interstate Highways 91 and 95, not only served New Haven's resident drug users but was a "stop 'n' cop" for buyers from the suburbs and outlying towns. Terry and his coworkers called their customers "baseheads" and thoroughly despised them. The young dealers did not use cocaine themselves—Terry had still not tried it when we met—and, according to him, they would not sell it to other teenagers. "It make people comatose," he said. "Everybody know that."

On a good day, Terry handled three or four hundred sales. His crew kept its supplies in a guarded apartment near the hallway where, as he said, he "worked the work, pumpin' it off." They mostly sold powder in the ten-dollar capsules—users could either snort it; dissolve it in water and inject it; or cook it into crack or freebase and smoke it—but sometimes they sold crack directly, in twenty-five-dollar rocks in little yellow bags. Terry was not involved in the supply line that brought the drugs to Q Terrace, but he heard that it ran through New York City.

It was a heady time. The crushing financial pressure that had haunted most of Terry's life was decisively eased. He was no longer dependent on his family. "Quick fast in a hurry, I was makin' crazy dollars," he said. "I was livin' large. I started buyin' all kinds of things—new clothes, and gold, stuff for my mother, stuff for my grandmother, stuff for the girls. Yeah, I started gettin' all *kinds* of girls—crazy girls, material girls. You know, there's a lot of girls out there that *just* want to go with a drug dealer."

Although Q Terrace is miles from Newhallville, black New Haven can be a small town, and Anjelica soon heard that Terry had started dealing. "I used to buy a lot of coke out at Quinnipiac myself," she said. "So when I heard Terry was there I went and got my gun and went out there. I couldn't find him that time. But then I started noticing him coming in about one A.M., and I knew they closed their shop at twelve midnight out there, and he had a lot of money on him suddenly now, so I knew. Then I *really* knew when I heard the girls talking in the Laundromat about a new boy working out at Quinnipiac. They said he was wearing a blue leather bomber jacket and a blue leather cap, and I knew that wasn't nobody but my son.

"I was scared to death. Kids were getting shot all over the place." She recalled telling Terry, "This ain't gonna work."

But Terry just recalled his mother's saying, "I can't tell you what to do. You gotta do what you gotta do. I just wish you the best of luck."

Things began to get hot at Q Terrace. "The big boys," as Terry calls the police, bought drugs with marked bills and arrested several dealers. They ran a sting operation, posing as dealers, and caught a number of would-be buyers. Terry decided to take a break. One week after he stopped working at Q Terrace, the young man who had recruited him was arrested.

"It was close," Terry said. "So I got me another job in a restaurant, and for a while I just chilled."

When the *New Haven Register* surveyed public opinion on the city's worst problems in 1980, "drugs" did not make the top ten. A similar poll in 1989 found drug abuse ranked third. Drug-related crime came in first. Meanwhile, the New Haven chief of police estimated that 80 percent of all crime in the city was drug-related. In 1988, there were 19,425 serious crimes reported in New Haven. Residents and nonresidents alike considered large parts of the city unsafe. At the entrances to many buildings at Yale were racks of crime advisories from the university police, including maps of the Yale area showing the locations of all assaults and robberies in the previous three weeks, and flyers about how to protect your car or bicycle, secure your office, engrave your valuables, report suspicious persons, and take precautions to avoid being mugged or raped. A nurse at a New Haven hospital, a white woman who lives in a nearby suburb (most of New Haven's workers now live outside the city and whites account for less than half of the city's residents), told me that she had not set foot downtown for many years, and that she even told her adult children never to shop there. "If you have to drive through, keep your doors locked and windows rolled up, even in summer," she said. "And always look in the backseat of your car before you get in it." On the day before we spoke, her suspicions about downtown New Haven had been dramatically confirmed by a multiple shooting on the steps of the state courthouse, which faces the New Haven Green. Only three people were injured, none of them seriously, but it seemed likely that many in the midday Christmas-shopping crowd who had to dive for cover might also be persuaded to stick to suburban malls thereafter. There were more than 320 shootings in New Haven in 1989, and 34 murders—more murders per capita than in Chicago, Los Angeles, or New York City.

The belief that nearly all this mayhem was "drug-related" was not universal—critics of the police claimed the term was a catchall for every crime the police couldn't solve—but there was no argument about the explosive growth of the drug problem. In 1988, the New Haven police made 2,700 drug-related arrests—nearly five times the number they had made in 1984. The city's superintendent of schools estimated, when I interviewed him, that one third of New Haven's kindergartners had cocaine-addicted mothers. The weapons being confiscated from dealers showed clearly their increasing wealth and seriousness: .38s and .45s had been replaced by AK-47 assault rifles and 9-millimeter semiautomatic pistols. Major dealers in New Haven used walkie-talkies and police scanner radios and wore bulletproof vests. They fortified their homes against police attacks, installing barred windows and thick oak doors that could stand up to a battering ram.

The main impact of the drug boom had been, without question, on the black community. Twenty-nine of the thirty-four murder victims in 1989 were black. Many black neighborhoods had drug dealers standing on virtually every corner, day and night. Gunfire was so common that residents were careful not to sit in windows that faced the street. After bond for two of the suspects in the courthouse shootings was set at half a million dollars apiece (the suspects were members of the Kensington Street International, or KSI, posse; the victims were members of the Ville and the Island), many black New Haveners noted how shootings in *their* neighborhoods never provoked such a serious judicial response. Was it that certain neighborhoods had simply been ceded by the authorities as free-fire zones?

When I first started going to New Haven, I was taken on a tour of the city's neighborhoods by two black residents. Their conversation reminded me of others I've heard—in countries suffering from chronic guerrilla war.

"Who was that waved hello to you?"

"He was the guy that was with that girl who got shot in the eye."

"The fourteen-year-old?"

"That's right."

"How's she doing?"

"She gettin' better."

"Who did the shooting?"

"The Ville got blamed for it, because some of their boys was following that guy around, because he's KSI, so it's another beef now. But the Ville say they didn't do it."

"That don't make no difference."

Virtually every black person in New Haven knew someone who had been shot. One of my guides, a college student home on vacation, told me about a friend of hers, a twenty-two-year-old man, who had just been shot to death on the street by a sixteen-year-old dealer. On Newhall Street, not far from his grandmother's house, Terry Jackson heard shots one afternoon, ran out, and found a seventeen-year-old friend lying on the sidewalk. "It was my boy Gary," he told me, with even more than his usual dissociation. "He wasn't moving, but he was still alive. If I had a car, I would've throwed him in it and drove him to the hospital. The ambulance came and took him, but he died anyway. He was shot right here." Terry indicated a spot just below his left eye and he kept his finger there, drilling abstractedly into his cheek, for a full minute.

An inordinate number of the people getting shot in New Haven were teenagers—a fact clearly connected to the number of teenagers selling drugs. This connection could be overdrawn, however. It was the booming underground economy—primarily cocaine money—that financed the proliferation of guns, but once guns are in circulation they take on a life of their own. Among teenage boys, especially, they become status items. They get endlessly traded around. They signify power, safety, glamour, excitement, manhood. And they end up settling petty disputes that previously were settled with fists. In several visits to New Haven public high schools, I heard little talk about drug abuse (the drug of choice among students remained, overwhelmingly, alcohol; cocaine abuse had, if anything, declined in recent years) but a great deal of talk about who was "packing," and who might have a "death wish," issued by some enemy, hanging over his head. In such an atmosphere, as a school counselor put it to me, "every young man is mainly concerned with survival, with being the biggest beast on his block, which means being down with the baddest posse."

I caught a glimpse of this type of natural selection at work one December afternoon at Wilbur Cross High in New Haven. I was sitting in a second-floor classroom talking to a social studies teacher. School was just letting out. A series of sharp pops erupted outside and we looked out and saw two cars parked at odd angles in the street. The boys inside the cars—at least three of them turned out to be Wilbur Cross students—were firing pistols at each other. Students were running, diving behind hedges and snowbanks. One of the cars started backing up very fast, then roared off up a side street. The other car squealed away in another direction. The scene had a heavy, panic-edged quality as people began to pick themselves up and look around to see who, if anyone, had been hit. Nobody seemed to be hurt. But then the car that had left by the side street—a large, muddy, dark blue Buick—came barreling back out and slid to a halt in front of the school. People began to run again as the Buick lurched around, bumped over the curb, and then sped off in the direction the other car had taken. That was the end of the excitement. A white motorist who had been forced to a stop by the shoot-out sat banging on his steering wheel and shouting. The principal of Wilbur Cross High later reported that the motorist was yelling, "Drugs are *killing* this city!"

But the shoot-out was not about drugs. It seemed that a girl at Wilbur Cross had made fun of a disabled boy, calling him a cripple. He "illed" her in return. She telephoned her boyfriend, who was a member of the Ghetto, a small posse based in a housing project in east New Haven. He came to the school with some of his friends. The handicapped boy was a member of the Island Brothers, who were, along with the Ville, one of the dominant posses at Wilbur Cross, so this promised to be a serious confrontation. Many students knew it was coming. One even walked into a classroom, pointed to a girl whose boyfriend was down with the Island, and announced, "Your baby's father goin' be killed." I heard this from a self-possessed twelfth-grade girl who went on to explain, "This school's affiliated with the Island. The Ghetto, only their little piss boys go here. Also, the Island is *cute*. You know, the Ghetto, they're ugly, they're from the projects, they stink. So they want to show everybody they're on top." The Ghetto had put on a great performance on the street after school, she said. "They was *profilin'*." She imitated them: boys walking around with arms akimbo, a little like gunfighters ready to quick-draw, but with exaggerated side-to-side steps that suggested extremely fat men waddling. I had seen the walk before; it was both frightening and very funny. The Island, she said, had matched this display and things had quickly escalated to gunfire.

The social studies teacher with whom I watched the shoot-out had her own theory. She thought that it might be the beginning of a race war. She said that a white boy at the school (Wilbur Cross was less than one third white; Hillhouse High, New Haven's other comprehensive public high school, was 94 percent black) had been threatened recently by one of the posses. This was a first, she said, and very ominous, particularly since a white man had been murdered in the projects the same week. (The white man in question—he was twenty years old and well known locally as a champion swimmer—had been, according to witnesses, trying to steal drugs. He had gone to Rockview Circle—possibly the most dangerous housing project in town—to score, and had there been accused of having fled, a few days earlier, without paying for the drugs he took. The dealer's "beatmaster," whose job it was to make sure such things didn't happen, shot the accused thief in the head as he and a companion drove their pickup truck out of Rockview Circle.)

While the social studies teacher was telling me her theory—this was immediately after the shoot-out—three boys ran into her classroom. It seemed that they all lived in the projects where the Ghetto was based, and they were afraid they might be the Island's next targets. We shut the door and made them sit on the floor while we watched the corridor and the street. We tried to find out more from the boys. Each wore a ski cap. All denied being involved with the posses. Other than that, we learned nothing. The boys were obviously not pleased to find themselves being interrogated by a couple of white adults. The word "niggers" occurred in every sentence fragment they muttered. Afterward, I tried to imagine what the world felt like to those boys, and what I would do if I were in their place—if I felt myself in mortal danger, with no help coming from adults—and had to go home to the projects that night. And I knew: I would get down with a posse; I would get myself a gun.

Terry lopes out of the dark before I've even come to a stop in front of Lakeeda's house. As he gets in the car, his face looks clouded and bunched up in the snapshot of dome light, and as we pull away he shoots glances up and down the street. I ask what's happening; he mutters something unintelligible. Later, he tells me, "Me and Lakeeda and Tyrone was out this afternoon, just takin' a walk, and these three niggers from KSI come rollin' up on us. They had guns. They even had a pit bull. I had a beef with 'em one time, but it was iced, it was over. But they seen me, and they just decided to start it up again. I was ready to fight, and they seen I was ready, and they got scared. I walked away, but I never turned my back on 'em—I ain't takin' no bullet off them. I know what time it is. We got away okay, but I was scared, and I was mad. I'm *still* mad."

Terry broods as we drive through east New Haven. He points out a poorly lit housing project. "That's a Terrordome in there," he says. A few minutes later, he points down a cross street and says, "This is the hottest block in America. Niggers running all *over* in there." In the middle of a factory district, a nightclub looms surreally: MONTEGO BAY, says the neon script beneath painted palm trees. Terry twists in his seat to inspect the cars parked outside the club. "I gotta get me a fake I.D.," he says. "People be sayin' this is the best club in town."

The rental car we're driving has a telephone. Terry keeps picking it up and pretending to make calls. "That's right, we're coming up Church Street now," he says. "We'll be there in five minutes, so don't leave, and don't let the girls leave, neither. Roger, okay, over and out." Terry is mugging with the phone—

profiling—for the people in the cars around us. To me, he says, "Who should I call?"

"Eddie Murphy."

"Okay," he says, and pretends to dial. "Yo, Eddie, it's me, Terry. I'm with Mr. Bill. We're just out cruising, nothing too much, what are you doing? Yeah? Well, have fun. Later."

"What's he doing?"

"Nothing. Watching TV with his girlfriend."

Eddie Murphy is one of Terry's heroes. Terry's favorite movies are all Murphy vehicles—*Harlem Nights, Beverly Hills Cop, Raw*. Terry doesn't seem to know anything, when I ask, about Murphy's life offscreen, but he finds his work "funny, funny, *funny*."

"What would you have done if those KSI guys had attacked you?"

"Just go crazy."

Going crazy was Terry's all-purpose self-defense technique. He was not especially muscular, but he rarely had trouble with bigger boys, he said, because of his reputation for going wild when cornered. One of his nicknames, a play on the rap star Tone Loc's name, was Loco Tone—LOCO was even embroidered on his ski cap. Anjelica confirmed her son's reputation for fearless, windmill-style fighting. She also confirmed that Terry met her brother Button's efforts to discipline him with a fierce display of lunacy. Terry told me, "I broke bottles, windows, everything I could reach when he tried that old-fashioned stuff on me. Pulled knives. Finally, he gave up, and now we get along fine."

I ask Terry what the beef with the boys from KSI was about. He shrugs. "They say I dissed 'em," he says. "I don't even remember. It's just posse stuff."

Posse stuff. Although KSI and the Ville were warring, gang life in New Haven was not the organized, paramilitary affair that it is in some cities (and many movies). I'd seen members of the Ville sporting haircuts with a bushy V in back, and I'd heard that they could sometimes be identified by two nicks cut in their eyebrows—KSI members wore three nicks—but the local posses didn't wear "colors" or scrawl territorial warnings on neighborhood walls as more full-blown gangs do, and they didn't have formal structures. Though Terry was down with the Ville, he had never been to a Ville meeting, because there had never been one, and he could not name the posse's leader, because there wasn't one. Posses provided members a measure of protection on the streets, and a structure for selling drugs (though not all members were involved in the trade), and perhaps an opportunity, within the recondite confines of the local youth culture, to become "well known," but that seemed to be about it.

To become well known in the wider world, a posse member usually had to make an appearance in the *New Haven Register* or, better yet, on local television. On the day of the courthouse shootings, Terry and I watched the afternoon news on Anjelica's TV. Terry recognized one of the victims, who was shown being loaded into an ambulance. "That's my boy! That's my boy!" Terry shouted. "Those are Villains that got shot!" He seemed thrilled. It had been a big news day for him. Less than twenty-four hours earlier, a seventeen-year-old cousin of his had been arrested, along with two other boys, for shooting up a house on Springside Avenue. The cousin was being held on $85,000 bond. Terry read the *Register*'s story about the incident raptly. "They gonna be *staying* in jail," he said. "All them niggers in there, bet they havin' a ball. Hey, Mom! You do ten percent of your time now, right?"

Studiously Anjelica said, "Yes, that's right."

Terry went back to the *Register.* " 'Leader of Crack Ring Guilty,' " he read out. "Huh. That was that kingpin." As he pored over the paper, I recalled hearing a New Haven public defender say, "In the newspaper, what they used to call the police blotter page, that's my clients' Social Register." Animated by all the flash and celebrity of the hour, Terry turned to me and declared, "The name of your book should be *Blood, Money, or Jail*."

Anjelica agreed.

On the evening after the close call with KSI, Terry and I cruise the peaceful, lamplit streets of the Whitney-Orange neighborhood, an area dense with Yale graduate students, and then, crossing Whitney Avenue, find ourselves among the great Gilded Age mansions on Prospect Street. The mansions, many of them built by factory owners (and many of them now owned by Yale), look directly down on Newhallville, where the factory workers once lived. Terry studies the vast houses set back in their vast yards but says nothing.

We stop at an ice cream parlor near Yale. While we lick cones and watch the students come and go outside, Terry says, "My friend got him a kitchen job in one of these colleges. He says Yale don't work you too hard and he gets some real good food out of there."

A minute later, apropos of nothing that I can see, Terry says, "I never took acid, but I heard it make you alert. Like when you get in a fight or something? You're *alert*. I never seen it, but I'd *like* to see somebody fighting on acid."

I propose that we take a walk around Yale. Terry says that outsiders are not allowed on the campus. The college compounds are locked, I reply, but the walkways and libraries and the Old Campus are not. Dubiously, Terry accompanies me on a stroll around the Law School and Sterling Memorial Library, where a security guard studies us closely but says nothing. I point out to Terry the snickering schoolboys carved in the library's nave, try to explain the significance of posters at the Law School hailing an award of tenure to a popular black professor, and show him how to use the library's computer catalogue. Terry, who says he has never touched a computer keyboard before, is fascinated by the silence and seriousness of the students all around us.

On another evening, as if in response to this little tour, Terry takes me to see

Harlem Nights. In the film, Eddie Murphy, who also wrote and directed, plays the adopted son of a nightclub owner in the 1930s. They are the leaders of an all-black band of rich, stylish gangsters who drive beautiful cars, wear beautiful clothes, and sleep with beautiful women. When a rival gang, led by fat white racists and in league with the police (also fat white racists), tries to take over their operations, Murphy and company annihilate them. I find *Harlem Nights* an utterly awful film but I don't say so to Terry. He says he loves it more every time he sees it.

THREE

On a cold November night, the Reverend Kevin Houston led a small group of marchers across Dixwell Avenue into the Elm Haven public housing project. Each marcher carried a lighted candle in a small glass jar wrapped in red, green, and black ribbon. Houston had called the march "to pray for the spirits of all the young brothers" who had died on the streets of New Haven since the beginning of the year. The idea was to visit each place—the alley or street corner or empty lot—where someone had been killed: thirty sites in all. The Elm Haven buildings are long, low barracks of dirty, crumbling brick. Startled by the sight of a silent line of people carrying candles, residents shouted from the shadows, "What's up?" Houston called back, "It's a vigil for the young brothers that have died!"

Under a weak street light in a windy alley—the spot where William Knox had been shot twice in the head, in April—the marchers stopped, formed a circle, joined hands, and sang the James Weldon Johnson hymn, "Lift Every Voice." While the other marchers cupped the flames of their candles against the wind, Mustafa Abdul-Salaam, a community activist, poured springwater on the ground in symbolic purification of the site. Someone else sprinkled charcoal and salt and then a stream of colored water. Next, Houston dripped candle wax on the spot, explaining that these substances represented the flesh, the blood, and the spirit of William Knox. The group then chanted "A Prayer for Liberation," a long rap-style poem written for the occasion by Houston, that began with the lines "Almighty Supreme One: Remove these chains from our brains so that the community's soul will be free to stroll down the road towards true perfection," and ended, "Supreme One: Free your children!!!"

After a minute of silent prayer, the march resumed. A young woman who had been watching the ceremony in the alley ran after the group, demanding to know what this was about. Hearing the answer, she said, "I can deal with that," and joined the march. Back out on Dixwell Avenue where the ceremony, complete with hymn and poem, was repeated in memory of Eugene Deis, who had died in February, two teenage boys in ski caps joined in, along with a pair of students from Yale Divinity School. Except for those two teenagers (who hung back slightly and did not carry candles), none of the dozen or so marchers who headed up Dixwell Avenue—past the funeral homes and liquor stores, the barber shops and churches and soul food restaurants—were in the age group directly involved in the violence. Most of the marchers, in fact, were community activists. Houston had showered the neighborhood with flyers inviting young people to join the march, but none had come, perhaps because of the cold.

As the procession headed south of Dixwell, the young woman from Elm Haven dropped out, and a haggard-looking man took her place. Although the march was supposed to be silent, the newcomer managed to let me know, between ceremonies, that he was a heroin addict with AIDS. By the time we got back to Dixwell Avenue, we were all stupid with cold. Many spots marked on Houston's map were still unvisited, but we decided to go to only one more that night. We sang and prayed and performed our libations on a street corner in Newhallville for Javan Green, who had died just three weeks before, and then, at Houston's insistence, we all gave each other big, backslapping "spirit hugs." After that, we headed back to the Elks Club on lower Dixwell, where we had left our cars, and where the man with AIDS hit me up for five dollars.

I asked Houston if he was disappointed by the turnout. He said he was, but he vowed to go on with the march the next night, and the next, even if he had to walk alone, until he had visited every murder site and prayed for each victim's soul. Rev Kev, as he was known, had a visionary streak. The first time we talked, he had regaled me with a lecture on ancient African religions, Memphite theology, the Nubian Empire, and with his own plans to start not a church but what he called a "spiritual consciousness house." Rev Kev was a big, quick man, thirty years old, with long hair braided in cornrows and a fondness for homemade clerical garb; on the candlelight march, he wore a black robe with a scarlet ankh (an Egyptian symbol of life) sewn on the front. Rev Kev came from Far Rockaway in New York City, where he grew up in poverty. He was a college graduate, a Yale Divinity School dropout, a senior adviser to the NAACP Youth Council in New Haven, and the youth director for the Elks Club on Dixwell, where his job description could just as well have read "Get black youth interested in anything that won't get them killed or arrested."

To that end, Houston and his fellow activists filled the calendar with dances, meetings, marches, and classes for young people. Rev Kev also wrote lyrics for local rap groups, preaching black unity and pride and denouncing drugs and violence. The previous August, he and other young black activists had held a "peace summit" for New Haven's warring posses. Twenty-one posse members came, including boys who had shot one another, and an agreement was reached to "chill out with the violence." A "peace council" was formed, with regular meetings and a rotating chair, to settle differences. Within a few months, the peace council seemed to be defunct, and yet Rev Kev and the other activists were still in touch with the posses, still trying to get them to chill. Some of the younger members of the NAACP Youth Council were, at the same time, posse members. "We have this one little guy, thirteen years old," Rev Kev told me. "You can just see him, every day, trying to decide which is more glamorous, the Youth Council or the Foote Street posse. The Foote Street boys offer him five hundred dollars a week to be a lookout. All we can offer is knowledge. They win hands down most every time!"

Houston and his friends gained the trust of the posses by making it clear that they did not talk to the police and did not blame the teenagers themselves for their situation. They saw the government's "war on drugs" as primarily a war on black youth, and, like many, many other black Americans, described the drug onslaught and its associated violence as "genocide." Rev Kev used the term "dominant culture" to describe the perpetrators of this genocide; most folks simply said "white people." The true object of the war on drugs, they said, was to confine the violence to the ghetto. Soaring arrest rates were part of a conspiracy to "warehouse black youth." Through the Youth Council and other groups, Rev Kev and his friends tried to organize inner-city teenagers politically, campaigning for better schools, parks, jobs, and training. Rev Kev himself went further, evangelizing against "materialism" while celebrating "knowledge." He carried this message—along with his enthusiasm for African religion and history—everywhere he went. To the summer basketball team he coached, he shouted "Babylon!" and "Timbuktu!" Those were the names of plays. "Insurrection!" was one of the team's defensive setups.

The young black activists in New Haven were all cultural nationalists, intent on replacing Eurocentric models with Afrocentric ones. Thus, around Christmastime, Rev Kev filled the Elks Club's main hall with a celebration of Kwanzaa, an "African-based" holiday. (It was actually invented in 1966 by Maulana Ron Karenga, born Ronald McKinley Everett, a professor at the University of California, Los Angeles, as a black nationalist substitute for Christmas.) Local merchants set up booths, musical and dance groups performed, and, in the evening, a Kwanzaa ceremony was enacted. One evening, Roger Vann, a trim, soft-voiced young activist in a gray leather cap, gave a running explanation of the ceremony. Kwanzaa, he said, is a Swahili word meaning "the first fruits of the harvest." The holiday lasts seven days (this was the first) and each day is dedicated to one of the seven principles of Kwanzaa: unity, self-determination, collective work and responsibility, cooperative economics, purpose, creativity, faith. On each of the seven days, a candle is lit, and gifts are exchanged. While Vann talked, seven small children came onto the stage and each lit a candle. Kwanzaa is a family holiday, Vann explained, dedicated to the veneration of elders and ancestors. "For your Kwanzaa setting, put out one ear of corn for each child you have," he told parents. "If you educate your children correctly in the seven principles, they won't turn on you when they become teenagers, the way they do today."

Preventing teenage boys from turning on their parents was Vann's day job. He worked across the street from the Elks Club at the Dixwell Community House, known as the Q House, where he ran a "rites of passage" program called Simba (Swahili for lion). The Q House was founded in 1924 to give black children—who in those days were forbidden to use the YMCA—a place to play, and now offered classes and workshops as well as sports. The Simba program was based on African initiation rituals. It was started in 1988, when a group of twelve-year-old boys began coming each afternoon to the Q House, where Vann helped them with their homework, taught them African and African American history, and, because he was working, he said, against a terrific current of peer pressure on the boys *not* to be good students, tried to offer them another model for black manhood. Not one of the boys in the program that year had a father living at home. (84 percent of families living in poverty in Newhallville were, according to the 1990 census, headed by women. Indeed, nearly 70 percent of *all* family households with children in Newhallville were headed by women.) Vann, who was twenty-four and a graduate of Brown, took the group to shows and museums in New York City as well as in New Haven. When I asked him how the Simba program differed from traditional organizations like the Boy Scouts, he said that it emphasized not only African culture but sex education, and that it also tried to shape the boys' attitudes toward women—confronting the contempt they learned from peers, from pop music, and, often, from their families, and trying to replace it with respect. At the end of the year, the boys in the program were ritually welcomed to manhood—but Vann, heedful of the constant perils of inner-city adolescence, was also expanding Simba so that boys could participate until they finished high school.

At the Kwanzaa celebration, Vann was joined on the stage first by Rev. Houston, who made all members of the audience hold hands, close their eyes, and listen to his poetry, and then by Muata Langley, another young activist, who wore a blue dashiki and matching bandanna and spoke of the importance of remembering one's ancestors. Langley publicly thanked his own late grandfather and great-grandfather for their contributions to his family, and then invited the audience to praise their ancestors.

"My great-great-grandmother—Matilda Crump Pierce!" a woman shouted.

"My grandfather—Wilbur H. Knight, Jr.!" another woman called.

Langley repeated each name, affirming the contribution of each to the community, and Roger Vann said that people should rely on their forebears whenever the stress of modern life got to be too much. "Call on Malcolm, or Martin, or your grandpa," he urged. On the wall behind the stage, alongside a huge American flag and a banner proclaiming this to be the POCAHONTAS TEMPLE, NO. 55 OF THE IBPOEW, hung three framed photographs of elderly black men wearing white fezzes. These, I assumed, were leading local Elks from bygone days: ancestors. (The initials stand for the Improved Benevolent Protective Order of Elks of the World, and the "Improved" is significant because membership in the BPOE, the original Elks organization, was, until 1973, restricted to white American males, leading to the founding, in 1898, of an Elks for black men, which endures.)

Meanwhile, most of the living elders of the community were downstairs, in the basement of the Elks Club, at the bar. The Elks basement was, as bars went, a great one. In fact, when people in Dixwell and Newhallville spoke of the Elks, they usually meant the bar, which was spacious and well appointed, had a dance floor, and accommodated an unending stream of parties, dances, and benefits. (Beulah Morgan attended her share of these.) And even on a cold weekday afternoon, with the dance floor in darkness, I could find fifteen or twenty Elks, all men in their fifties or sixties or seventies, bellied up to the bar, which is long and dim and warm. Some of the drinkers would be wearing phone-company overalls; others were clearly retired. An old man with a gravel laugh would be telling a story about how he once outwitted the police in Orange, Connecticut—and everybody listening could recall how dangerous it was, back in the forties and fifties, for a black man even to drive through Orange—while two old friends down the bar argued Baptist Church politics. Every time someone came in, pulling off his hat and coat and rubbing his cold hands together, a small welcoming wave of jokes and greetings would break in his direction. The Rev Kev might come in—an apparition from another era, with his braids and bright robes—working the bar like a politician, slapping backs and naming names. Rev Kev and the bar regulars had had their differences—in the summer, when the bar basically moved out into the Elks Club parking lot, he had told the members that their public drinking sent the wrong message to the community's youth, who were forever being harangued about drugs and alcohol—and yet the regulars' relations with the youth director were generally good. The Elks' bar was a haven, a throwback, where the self-consciousness of Afrocentrism was unknown, the hip-hop beat of angry youth was rarely, if ever, heard, and reminiscence ruled.

Nostalgia was rampant in black New Haven. Everyone over forty remembered when the housing projects were well maintained, with managers living on the premises, and with tiny lawns and flower gardens in front of the ground-floor units; the maintenance office in Elm Haven even kept a lawnmower for tenants to use. Down at the Elks, middle-aged men recalled with astonishment the innocent sorts of mischief they once pursued: robbing a neighbor's cherry tree; getting a wino to buy a half pint of brandy for a whole group of boys to share. There was marijuana around, but it was associated with visiting bandleaders, "hopheads." And heroin began to appear in the late fifties. But even the junkies in New Haven were nostalgic. They recalled a camaraderie, a time when dealers were just supporting their own habits, when there was little violence, and drugs were advanced to users who could not pay. The cocaine boom of the 1980s, the rise of violent posses, and the devolution of street dealing onto younger and younger boys had made the addict's world a far colder, more frightening place. "Scoring these days is like going to a convenience store," an ex-addict told me. "A *dangerous* convenience store." These new, young dealers were heartless, the addicts said. Hearing that, I remembered a New Haven high school counselor saying, "Bottom line: These kids hate adults." Apparently, there were few adults the young drug dealers hated more than their own customers.

In reality, New Haven's ghetto was always a tough place, full of deprivation and suffering. Even so, it was not nostalgic bunk that the factory jobs had disappeared, or that the streets were once vastly safer, or that there was once a great deal more in the way of organized after-school activity for teenagers. Recreation centers had closed; sports leagues had folded. The collapse of the city's tax base after the flight of the middle class was usually blamed for the loss of city services and facilities, but it was also widely agreed that there were fewer adults prepared to work with children—to coach teams or teach classes or referee games—than there once were. "Reason is, everybody who works nowadays works *two* jobs," a white-haired Dixwell Elk told me.

And yet much of black New Haven, old and young, had been galvanized in 1989 by a mayoral campaign. In the Democratic primary (Democrats in the city outnumber Republicans ten to one, so their primary is the main event), an Italian American–dominated party machine put up an Italian American candidate against John Daniels, a five-term state senator seeking to become New Haven's first African American mayor. Although Daniels was a moderate's moderate—and on racial matters a staunch integrationist—the city's young black activists, Rev Kev and Roger Vann and their friends, decided to work for him. They expanded a previous voter registration project, adding three thousand names, most of them African Americans under the age of twenty-five, to the city's rolls. They also spearheaded a fierce effort to get out the vote, and, when Daniels won, were generally believed to have made a crucial difference. Though Daniels received support from white and Latino voters, his election was plainly the latest chapter of a centuries-long story in New Haven politics—in urban American politics generally—in which successive immigrant groups have replaced their ethnic predecessors in City Hall. Certainly Daniels could be expected to devote special attention to the problems of the city's black youth.

Daniels could also be expected to be held up as an example to every black child in New Haven. He grew up in the Elm Haven projects himself. He was a school sports star, was New Haven's "Boy of the Year" for 1954, and attended Villanova University on an athletic scholarship. He even still found time to referee high school football games.

And yet John Daniels's election did not herald the social and economic rise of his people the way the election of Irish and Italian mayors in New Haven had. Blacks have always faced far more daunting obstacles than have European immigrants to America, but now the structure of economic opportunity itself had changed, abruptly and profoundly. Middle-class blacks might be only marginally more vulnerable to these changes than middle-class whites, but poor blacks were being economically slaughtered. Between 1975 and 1992, the average income of the poorest 20 percent of black families in America declined by 32 percent. In such circumstances, even a John Daniels might be able to understand the attractions of the underground economy. In the February after his election, anyway, Daniels's younger brother, Robert, was arrested for selling two hundred dollars' worth of cocaine to an undercover police officer.

"I never vote," Anjelica says, making it sound almost as if her nonregistration were a matter of principle. At the same time, she is pleased that John Daniels has been elected mayor. "Maybe he can *do* something." Anjelica has never heard of Kwanzaa, or the Simba program, and all she knows about Timbuktu is that it's a long way away.

Anjelica knows telephones, though, and simple computer programming— and I was glad for that when, one January morning, I called Terry to confirm plans for a meeting at their apartment and he told me they were no longer staying on Wallace Street. They had been forced to flee, he said, after his mother called the police on the Puerto Rican people upstairs. The nightly blows and screams from the Puerto Ricans' apartment had reached homicidal levels, Terry said, and when the police finally hauled away the boyfriend of the woman who lived there, he and Anjelica got a nasty scare. Despite being bloody, handcuffed, shirtless, and barefoot in the snow, the Puerto Rican fought his captors valiantly, meanwhile swearing mortal vengeance on everyone in earshot. As the one who had called the police, Anjelica immediately saw the unwisdom of being at home if and when he was released, so she and her sons were staying with friends in West Haven. How had my call found them? "Total Phone," Terry said. Anjelica subscribed, he explained, to a deluxe package of phone services, and she knew how to program the family phone so that calls could be forwarded wherever she happened to be.

It is some weeks later now, and Anjelica and her sons are back on Wallace Street; the upstairs batterer is reportedly still in jail. I have stopped in to see Terry, who is not home. Although the television and radio are both playing, and Anjelica has invited me inside, I suspect I have woken her from an afternoon nap, so I haven't taken a seat. Instead, I'm leaning awkwardly against the refrigerator, asking interview-like questions about voting and the Q House, while Anjelica sits at the table in a baby blue bathrobe, smoking a cigarette and looking sallow and weary. Buddy's at school, she says dully.

The phone rings. It's Beulah. I gather from the ensuing conversation that Anjelica's data entry skills are in demand at the dentist's office where Beulah works. While Beulah was in the hospital, the dentist's computer lost a batch of files. Now Beulah is back on the job, and Anjelica has been asked to come in and work, off the books, retyping the lost files. This conversation appears to be doing wonders for Anjelica's mood. "I can probably come in tomorrow," she says, sounding officious and overbooked but looking pleased and proud. Anjelica has a vivid, mischievous, missing-bicuspid smile that she flashes in my direction as she talks to her mother. All Anjelica ever needed, I think suddenly, was to be needed, to have her skills valued. It's not true, of course. She has needed—and not gotten—much more than that. And when she has been needed—by Terry, for instance—she has usually, according even to herself, been too busy getting high to perform. But this is the kind of lunging, broad-brush thought that often strikes me in Anjelica's company. Anything to explain, in a sound bite, her perpetual quandary.

After she gets off the phone, we talk briefly about Terry's slang. Anjelica says she doesn't understand half the things that come out of his mouth. I say our parents probably felt the same way about us, and she agrees, with a short laugh. "But every generation gets worse," she says.

I ask what she means.

"That older generation, they cared better," she says. "They had hearts. They communicated better than we do. That's why these older couples stay together." Anjelica studies her cigarette for a long minute. "It's the drug world," she says, finally. "It took over the whole world. There's nothing left. This is the end."

We segue, somehow, into birth control. I ask Anjelica what she's told Terry on the subject.

"I give him condoms, and I tell him to use 'em," she says. "And he does use 'em, on all the girls except Lakeeda. He just won't use 'em on her, I don't know why."

Recalling how delighted Anjelica has seemed about Terry and Lakeeda's romance, and how much she, according to Terry, likes Lakeeda, I wonder aloud how she would feel if Lakeeda were to get pregnant.

"Uh-uh," Anjelica says. "Uh-*uh*. I'm too young to be a grandmother."

Anjelica still looks sleepy. I ask her to tell Terry I came by, and leave. But the image of her as a grandmother—or, rather, of her insisting that she's too young to be any such thing—stays with me. A few days later, Terry and I are driving in Newhallville. It's a warm, snowmelt morning. Terry points out two people walking on the roadside up ahead. His mother and his Aunt Darla, he says. I would have taken them both for teenagers. Darla is a head taller than Anjelica, who has to skip and trot to keep up. Both wear baggy denim jackets and sunglasses. Anjelica also wears huge gold earrings, and a baseball cap with an extra-long bill, which makes her look like a street urchin from another era—the seventies, perhaps, or the twenties. She does not look, in any case, old enough to be a mother, let alone a grandmother. Terry rolls down his window and shouts at his mother and aunt, "What you two doing out here this time of day?" He points at them, they point at him, everybody laughs, and we all keep moving.

"They do look like they should be in school," I say. Terry does not disagree.

When I ask Terry about birth control, he seems less embarrassed about it than I am. He confirms that he and Lakeeda do not use condoms. "I love her too much," he says. In fact, he says, she may be pregnant already. "You see how I'm always sleeping all the time? That's because when she gets pregnant you get her symptoms. So if you see me getting all kinds of strange craving—well, that's it, then we know for sure."

How does Terry feel about the possibility that Lakeeda is pregnant?

"I'm too young to be a father," he says.

But he seems less opposed than ambivalent. The responsibilities of parenthood are no doubt daunting, but the allure of a child to call his own, and of a permanent connection to Lakeeda and Tyrone, may, if I know Terry, often be more real. Also, I have to remind myself, Terry has always lived in a world of largely fatherless families; as a result, his notion of a father's role in a child's life—of a father's responsibilities—is presumably quite different from, say, mine. His notions, for that matter, about manhood generally have inevitably been shaped by his long experience of families in which men are transient players and women are the solid, central figures—and he has missed the benefit of intervention by a Roger Vann.

Lakeeda turned out not to be pregnant, though, and when she and I talked she made it clear that she was not leaving such things to chance. "I already have one baby," she said. "I know what's involved."

Lakeeda was two years older than Terry, but she seemed older than that. She had a deliberate, Southern manner, with a very high, very soft voice. Though she wore a lot of gold, the effect it created on her was less teenage trashy than African aristocratic: when her dark, full, beautifully molded face was framed by gold it became more grave and imposing still. Solidly built and not tall, Lakeeda presented a sharp physical contrast to the lithe reed Terry. She also presented a scholastic contrast. Despite Tyrone, she graduated with her original high school class, having kept up her studies through a program for teen mothers. During her senior year she won a college scholarship in a statewide art competition.

Lakeeda and Terry had been an item for nearly a year before she discovered the true difference in their ages; Terry had, with a little help from Anjelica, managed to add a couple of years to his. This was not a trifling concern for Lakeeda. It seemed to explain a great many things—why, for instance, Terry sometimes seemed to her like a little brother. At the same time, Terry was more like a father to Tyrone than Tyrone's real father was, and his devotion to the boy made up for a lot.

Terry found absolutely everything about Tyrone charming. "He do the grownedest things," Terry told me. "Like I gave him a baseball and we was playin' with it last night, and he said, 'You gave me this baseball. How come you playin', too?' He's a little *man*. Sometimes he make me wanna cry." Terry's absorption with Tyrone was so intense that I sometimes thought it bordered on identification.

In the Wallace Street apartment one afternoon, Terry tells me about how, when he was small, he used to love to pull the blankets over his head and just lie in bed all day, not asleep but safe inside a little blanket world. "That was my favorite thing," he says, with a relish suggesting that it might still be pretty high on his list. "One of these days," he goes on, "I'm gonna unplug the phone, and lock the door, and shut the drapes, and just lie in bed in here all day, just sleep and sleep, and not let nobody bother me."

I note down this fantasy with the same kind of embarrassment I feel asking questions about birth control. None of it is my business; all of it is of interest. I sometimes wonder if Terry and his family offer me stories and insights simply in the hope that I will see a pattern that will satisfy me and thus complete my project. Of course, the anomalies and contradictions of character always outstrip neat definition. While I am scrawling "circle of love" and "replacement family" alongside notes from a conversation with Terry about Lakeeda and Tyrone, he telephones Lakeeda. She is asleep, her mother says. Terry hangs up the phone and jumps to his feet. He needs to go downtown immediately, he announces. The coast is clear for him to "see a couple of my sneak tips," he says.

I give him a ride downtown. His destination is the Chapel Square Mall, off the New Haven Green. We get stuck in traffic two blocks east of the Green, and Terry jumps out to walk, thanking me with a quick double-clutch handshake. Traffic starts to move, slowly, and I find myself keeping pace with Terry, who does not see me as he moves along the sidewalk toward the mall. He is in a good mood, and he cuts through the crowd on the sidewalk with a vivid, rising step. I notice other pedestrians shying from him, and suddenly I see him through the eyes of an elderly white woman with a shopping bag who grimaces and braces herself as Terry sweeps past her. He does not look in her direction—his eyes are fixed on the mall ahead—but he is a young black male, strong and fast, in a parka and sneakers and a ski cap that says LOCO, and that's all the woman needs to see to feel a cold wave of fear. That's all, I realize, that most of us need to see.

The Chapel Square Mall has been the hangout of choice for New Haven's teenagers since it was built, in the 1960s. Covering two large blocks in the heart of the city, it was built as the centerpiece of a vast urban renewal project that filled ninety-six acres of downtown New Haven and included a nineteen-story hotel, a fourteen-story office building, and a colossal parking garage—the garage designed by Paul Rudolph, the chair of the Yale School of Architecture. At the time of the mall's construction—in the brief era of federal support for urban renewal—New Haven was a leader among American cities, winning so much support that, while John Lindsay's New York was being called Fun City, New Haven was known as Fund City. Richard Lee, New Haven's mayor from 1954 to 1970, was a pioneering advocate of urban renewal, and the city's cause was not hurt in Washington by Lee's friendship with President John F. Kennedy. "Our goal is a slumless city—the first in the nation," Lee declared, and he even set a deadline for achieving that goal: 1969.

And yet, for all its achievements (Project Head Start, the single most successful program in the War on Poverty, was inspired in New Haven) and national renown (in 1964, Willard Wirtz, the Secretary of Labor, pronounced New Haven to be already "the greatest success story in the history of the world"), New Haven's urban renewal effort produced few happy results. Like slum-clearance projects across the country, it displaced far more poor people—in New Haven, one fifth of the population was uprooted between 1956 and 1974—than it ever provided with new housing. The social and economic forces that were increasing segregation and concentrating poverty in American central cities in the 1970s and 1980s were too powerful to be countered by the increasingly modest programs offered against them. The Chapel Square Mall, Richard Lee's pride and joy, never had a chance of spearheading an urban retail renaissance. When we spoke, Lee bitterly described the present-day mall as "a junk shop."

That was harsh. It was true that Lee was unable to persuade Saks Fifth Avenue, Lord & Taylor, or Brooks Brothers to open branches in New Haven, leaving it to a slightly forlorn Macy's to anchor the south end of the mall. But the mall itself had had two facelifts since its construction—"each time adding another layer of mauve," a longtime patron told me—and it could certainly hold its head up among American shopping malls. The artificial waterfall was nicely lighted, the air was stunningly sweet, anthemic jazz emanated from every floor tile, and the two levels of shops each enjoyed near-complete tenancy. At the north end, overlooking the New Haven Green, was a complex of fast food stands known as Picnic on the Green, with patio furniture, retro neon signs, and stands named 1 Potato 2, Everything Yogurt, and Wannacookie.

The teenagers who thronged the mall each afternoon collected around the fast food stands, which tended to be staffed by their friends, but they also constantly promenaded up and down the mall. The owners of many mall businesses considered the youth hordes a problem—believing, among other things, that they scared off adult customers. So the superintendent of New Haven's schools had been trying to persuade the city's transportation department to alter its bus routes—the current routes ensured that hundreds of teenagers had to change buses downtown on their way home from school—in such a way that students would be delivered directly to their neighborhoods. The superintendent told me that the mall's businesses were so enthusiastic about this idea that in exchange for his efforts they might even be willing to contribute money to the development of after-school programs at the schools.

The teenagers probably did scare off customers. The courthouse steps where the Christmas shoot-out occurred were visible from Wannacookie. And the posses were active around the mall—Terry told me that he had to avoid it at certain hours, when KSI was likely to be there and his allies in the Ville were not. But the posse wars had never surfaced inside the mall, and for an adult visitor, even at the height of the afternoon adolescent swarm, it actually held zero physical menace. White teenagers in heavy-metal drag promenaded alongside black teenagers in hip-hop drag with no evidence of tension.

There *was* real menace in the mall. It just happened to be impalpable—and its objects were the teenagers themselves. The mall was a total environment—a totalitarian environment, one could even say. Everything was packaged and stamped, fragrant and bright, alluring and on offer—except that if you loitered or lingered or seemed to be doing anything other than shopping, the security guards descended on you. As a hangout for teenagers, there could scarcely be a worse choice than shopping malls; they are a universe in which consumption is the only value. In New Haven, shearling coats and yellow leather shirts hung spotlit in the display windows, their hefty prices forming major markers of power and worth in the captive world of adolescents circulating in the mall. And for pure purchasing power, of course, no one could compete with the drug dealers.

There were merchants in New Haven who discouraged the custom of drug dealers. Body and Sole, a sporting goods store on Chapel Street, half a block west of the mall, had a large sign in its window: IF YOU DEAL DRUGS, WE DON'T WANT YOUR BUSINESS! SPEND YOUR MONEY SOMEWHERE ELSE! Wally Grigo, the owner of Body and Sole, said, "You can't tell someone, 'You're a drug dealer, I won't sell you shoes.' But you can hope to insult them, so they won't come in, and you can send a message to other kids—that not all of the merchants in town are bending over to service the dealers, that the hypocrisy stops here. Drug dealers are *not* legitimate business people. They're killing their own communities, and I'm not going to profit from them." Grigo, who was wiry, ebullient, white, and thirty-odd, said that the worst reactions to the sign had come from his suppliers. "One guy, who is very high up in a major company, told me, 'Look, you're an inner-city store. You gotta hook up the drug dealers, really cater to them. You gotta shake four or five hundred dollars out of them every time they come in the store.'" A representative of another company told Grigo, "Drug dealers are half our business." The owners of other sporting goods stores, he said, joked about the situation. "They say, 'Oh, this good customer is now in jail' or 'This good customer is dead.'" But when the sign maker saw the message he wanted for his window, Grigo said, he did the work for free. It seemed that the sign maker had been getting a lot of business himself from dealers who wanted custom lettering for their cars and, when the cars got shot up in gunfights, wanted the lettering done again, and he was feeling guilty about doing it for them.

On Whalley Avenue, which divided the Ville's territory from that of KSI, I noticed an automobile dealer displaying a new silver Porsche Speedster. Price: $92,000. I asked a young salesman who might be expected to buy such a car and he laughed. "We get these very young guys coming in here with these huge wads of cash and their grandmothers to sign the papers," he said. Typically, such a customer would buy a new Mercedes or Audi, he said, paying between twenty thousand and seventy thousand dollars, with 50 percent down in cash.

A few blocks away, also on Whalley, I dropped into a waterbed shop called Rubber Match. In the back of the shop, which was crammed with merchandise, loud with acid rock, and stinking of incense, stood the proprietor. He was an overweight, middle-aged, bearded white man, and he was busy telling a female customer all about a cruise he had recently taken to Mexico and Aruba, and then about a trip to Atlantic City he was planning. The shelves around him overflowed with off-color novelties, including camouflage-patterned condoms, and with the tools of the drug dealer's trade: water pipes, crack pipes, triple-balance-beam scales, jars of lactose and mannitol (for adulterating cocaine), and glassine envelopes of all sizes, complete with color codings. While I browsed, a tall black teenager wearing a baseball cap rushed in. He bought a large jar of lactose, paying from a fat wad of cash, then ran out, hopped into a new, root-beer–colored Ford Explorer minivan, and roared off, his stereo booming that month's hit tune, "Gangsta Gangsta," by the Los Angeles rap group N.W.A, or Niggaz Wit' Attitude.

"**I** was chillin'," Terry said. "But then my homeboy come in March, and he shoot me up to get down with him."

Terry's homeboy, in this case, was Frank Black. Frank was several years older than Terry and had always, according to Anjelica, taken an avuncular interest in her son. Frank had graduated from Hillhouse High and was living with his girlfriend and her infant son on Foote Street, in the Elm Haven projects. He was down with the Ville and was doing fairly well in the drug business, but he needed more street-level dealers. Boys under sixteen were preferred, because when they were arrested they were usually not charged as adults. Terry was fifteen and bright. Frank offered him what amounted to a profit-sharing partnership. "He told me if he ever got to the top he would take me with him," Terry said. "He was going to get a 190, I was going to get a 190. A yellow 190 Mercedes-Benz."

Frank's sales outlet was an empty lot in Newhallville known as the Mudhole. It was perilously close to Beulah's house, but had such an evil reputation in the neighborhood that Terry hoped he could evade detection simply by staying back in the weeds and trees, where respectable folk like his grandmother and her friends never ventured. The Mudhole was laid out brilliantly for drug dealing. Straddling a disused rail line running north from the old Winchester plant, it could be reached from either of two busy streets and was also a popular pedestrian shortcut. To the immediate south were housing projects. To the east was Shelton Avenue, where an old liquor store, an even older bar called Sonny & Viv's, and a grimy little windowless gambling club called the Shelton Avenue Social Club (but usually known as Pepper's, or simply as the Mudhole) drew a crowd of grimy, drunken hangers-on who helped to disguise the goings-on in the Mudhole itself. The customers were virtually all local, which meant that many of them knew Terry—his own Aunt Darla, who lived behind Sonny & Viv's, was a regular—but they were used to buying from neighborhood children, and used to concealing the fact.

The volume of business in the Mudhole was, as it had been in Quinnipiac Terrace, phenomenal, and Terry's pay was even better. He no longer received a weekly salary but got a cut of the day's take—a cut that could come to as much as five hundred dollars. Frank ran his crew differently, too; there were no piss boys, as in Q Terrace, and little hierarchy. Terry was Frank's lieutenant, but he did not give orders to the other sellers or the lookouts. "We didn't even call them workers," Terry said. "We just say, 'They's down with us.' It was more like a big family. Everybody watch each other's back. If I see the police first, I yell 'Raise up!' That mean 'Get away from your bundle!'" The Mudhole was open for business from nine A.M. to nine P.M., and in the evenings Frank often brought around a bottle of brandy, which the boys drank with Coca-Cola. After a good day, Frank might bring Courvoisier, which the boys liked to drink straight from the bottle. Squalid as the Mudhole was, with its deep rubble of old tires, couches, baby carriages, and car parts, it really resembled nothing so much as a great children's haunt—and Terry had in fact, been playing along the tracks there since he was small. Selling drugs was like playing hide-and-seek, but more exciting, and much better paid.

Frank's main traffic was in cocaine, which he brought in from New York City himself. When he first took Terry with him to New York—they rode the train to 125th Street in Harlem—Terry was scared. "I almost dookied myself," he said. "But Frank just kept telling me, 'Act like you live here.' And he knew where to go, so things was okay." They made regular trips to New York, buying four or five ounces of cocaine each trip, paying five or six hundred dollars an ounce, then returning to New Haven, where they mixed the cocaine with lactose, packed it into small glassine bags, and sold it in the Mudhole for profits that ranged from 150 to 200 percent. Learning the trade was easy, Terry said. "Whatever Frank did, I just did it the exact same way." The work itself could be hard, requiring long hours and constant vigilance; you never knew when the police might appear in the Mudhole or in New York or on the train. Terry's favorite job was counting the take. "I got to flip the money," he said. "Fold it all up. Each crease, that's one hundred dollars. Get it all flipped, take my part, put it in my pocket, a nice fat bundle, go down to the mall, and *play the girls.*"

Playing the girls meant buying them clothes and jewelry—gold bracelets, necklaces, and earrings were especially appreciated; the massive, staple-shaped "Jumbo" and "Colombo" door-knocker earrings could cost as much as four hundred dollars in the Chinese jewelry stores downtown—but it also meant "getting all geared down," as Terry put it, himself. He bought silk shirts, leather shirts, Gucci sneakers, a Rolex watch. He became a regular customer at the tonier mall shops, got gold caps to sheathe his teeth—"sparked my whole *mouth* out"—and took to wearing finely tailored Italian trousers. He bought clothes and jewelry for his male friends, too, and gave many gifts to his mother and Buddy, including a huge stuffed bear for Anjelica on Mother's Day.

Beulah was not so easy to please. When Terry gave her an expensive porcelain poodle on Mother's Day, "she just acted like it was nothin'," he said. Then she refused to let him pay for her car to be repaired, even though it was giving her trouble. It seemed that a friend of Beulah's had seen Terry in the Mudhole after all, and had told his grandmother about it. "Then I was getting ready one night to go to Nick & Neil's," Terry said. "That's a teen club in Orange. I go there with my posse on Saturdays. So I was taking a bath, and she saw my clothes there. I had bought myself a *nice* little outfit—I bought my boy one, too—and she wanted to know where I got the money for it. I said my mother gave me the money, and she didn't say nothin'. But then I got dressed, and I said, 'Grandma, how do I look?' And she said, 'Like a drug dealer.' After that, she told me to get on out of her house."

Terry moved into the Elm Haven projects with Frank and his girlfriend and her son. "I was on my own," he said. "Nobody telling me what to do, nobody telling me when to come home." Although Frank and Terry had to come and go carefully—Frank's girlfriend's rent was paid by public assistance, and only she and her child were legal tenants—life on Foote Street was, in Terry's view, basically one long party. Even in this paradise, though, this world without adults, where sex, liquor, and money flowed freely, Terry and Frank and the crew worked hard, sometimes staying up all night to cut and bag cocaine. "Pour in some cut, stir it up, flip it, flip it, throw in some more rocks, stir it up," Terry said, showing the same pleasure in the production process that he showed when he talked about folding pizza boxes. "Take a dime-size amount— do it all by eye—bag it, staple it, shake it down. It take a couple hours to cut and bag an ounce. And if somebody fall asleep when you're baggin' you get to slap 'em. The sleep game, we call it. Slap!" Terry laughed. "Then, never mind if we work all night, only sleep one hour, we get up and go straight out to the block in the morning. Go make that money!"

As in other retail businesses, packaging and reputation were critical. Frank's crew was known as White Bag, and the quality of its product was well established. Other crews tried to distinguish their product by putting stars on the bags they sold. This, according to Frank, was unwise. The courts regarded stars on bags as evidence of the involvement of "organized crime," he said, and the sentences given to dealers arrested with star-marked bags were harsh. The question of arrest loomed larger in Terry's mind after he turned sixteen, in May, but business in the Mudhole thrived all spring and into the summer without any notable interruption by the police. There were close calls. Once, a police cruiser, complete with German shepherd, arrived without warning, and Terry had to flee across the backyards of Newhallville with the dog in pursuit. He cut his mouth in a fall while vaulting a fence and he lost his Rolex, but he managed to get away, and that same evening he was back in the Mudhole, defiantly making crazy dollars.

Frank's crew sold marijuana—they called it "sess," or "Larry," and they made excellent profits from it just as long as they did not smoke too much themselves—but their best-selling item remained cocaine, which they marketed in powdered form. Crack, the smokable form of the drug, had not caught on widely in New Haven, seemingly because of rumors spread by local dealers that street crack might contain a lethal dose of rat poison. These rumors had been part of a fierce campaign to resist the incursion of Jamaican crack dealers from New York City into the New Haven market. The resistance also involved violence, including the murders of local dealers suspected of working with the Jamaicans, and the campaign seemed to have been successful. Jamaican crack dealers dominated the cocaine trade in other Connecticut cities, such as Bridgeport, but remained a minor force in New Haven. "The Jamaicans are crazy," Terry said. "We just *crazier*." Most of the crack addicts in New Haven (who included Terry's Aunt Darla) continued to buy powder and make the crack themselves.

In Frank's crew, contempt for the customers was, if anything, even more virulent than it had been among the dealers in Q Terrace. This was not a stop 'n' cop but a neighborhood concession, where everybody knew everybody else, and the desperation and degradation of the addicts were always on display. Again, all the baseheads were adults, and none of the young dealers used cocaine. Terry considered trying it once. "But Frank stopped me," Terry said. "He whipped my ass and he said, 'We *see* what this stuff do to people.' He was right. I thank him for it."

Anjelica was apparently never a customer of Terry's. She quarreled with Beulah after her mother made Terry leave her house, though. She and Buddy had also been staying with Beulah but now they moved out. Anjelica's caseworker found them a room at the Sleeping Giant Motel, a roadhouse six miles north of New Haven, while they waited for an apartment in town. A taxi ride to Sleeping Giant cost twenty-five dollars each way, but Terry still managed to visit them regularly, and he continued to shower both Buddy and his mother with gifts. He was not yet the family breadwinner—some of his fellow dealers, including some even younger than him, paid their mothers' rents and bought them cars—but Beulah disapproved of Anjelica's taking anything at all from her son. Anjelica worried about Terry's safety, especially after a rash of drive-by shootings and subsequent series of police sweeps on street dealers, but she accepted his gifts, including tuition money for a summer camp program for Buddy. (Anjelica found other uses for this money, however, and Buddy never got to camp.)

Terry's father heard rumors that his son was dealing and he expressed his disapproval to Terry. If he needed money, Peter said, he should simply ask for it. "Ask *him* for money?" Terry said, his voice sharp with disbelief. "I never did and I never will. But, you know, I had *so much money* on me that day. If he had patted me down, he would have found it. And I would have said, 'Yeah, that's right, I'm out there. *I'm way, way out there.*'" In truth, Peter was disinclined to carry the matter any farther. As he explained to me later, "There could be problems if I intervened in that sort of thing and I've reached an age where I don't need problems." Among the problems he didn't need, he said, "there's violence, there's death." But the aspect of the drug world that seemed to bother Peter the most was its denizens' indifference to the resale value of luxury cars. "It just turns me off," he said, "seeing all these Mercedeses, Volvos, BMWs, Saab 9000s, with tinted windows, telephones, bubble windows. With all that customizing, those cars *are not going to sell.* The real society doesn't want any part of those cars."

Though the drive-by shootings and the posse wars were, for the most part, taking place elsewhere in New Haven, Frank's crew kept a pistol at the Mudhole for emergencies. Sometimes, particularly when he had been drinking, Frank liked to fire off a few rounds at the end of the evening. His notion was that the gunfire would bring the police, which it normally did, and that the police officers snooping around the Mudhole would scare off any other dealers who might be thinking of setting up shop after his crew quit for the night. Frank's gunplay was apparently unappreciated by nearby residents—especially when he fired a shotgun, as he sometimes did—but his crew's franchise at the Mudhole was uncontested. Quarrels with other drug dealers did, however, occasionally break out. One night, a member of Frank's crew was attacked in the Mudhole by another dealer, with a baseball bat. "He had messed up some of this nigger's money," Terry said. "But I didn't care about that. He was trying to hurt one of my boys. So I took the gun and I unloaded a whole clip at him. Six shots. I didn't hit him, but he *ran.*"

News of this clash flew through Newhallville and soon reached Anjelica by telephone out at Sleeping Giant. What she heard was that somebody had come after the Mudhole crew with a baseball bat and that Terry had been firing a gun. She panicked. The last bus to New Haven had just passed Sleeping Giant. Anjelica ran down the road after it. And she kept on running, never quite catching the bus, mile after mile, all the way to the center of Hamden. Again, the bus pulled away without her. At that point she gave up and started trudging back to Sleeping Giant. But the story of Anjelica's frantic maternal rescue marathon made a big impression on Terry when he heard it. I heard him repeat the story more than once, and he told it with almost as much pride and wonderment as Anjelica did.

The Freddie Fixer Parade used to be confined to black New Haven. Nowadays it finishes up downtown after passing an official reviewing stand on the New Haven Green. Still, the parade remains what it has always been: a celebration of the city's African American community. Dreamed up by Dr. Fred Smith, a longtime Dixwell physician, as an occasion for involving children in neighbor-hood spring cleaning, the parade draws marching bands and marching units from the Elks, the Masons, the Boy Scouts, the Firebirds, the Silver Shields, the fire department, and other civic-minded organizations, both local and out-of-town. It's a showcase for finery, and virtually everybody in Dixwell and New-hallville takes the opportunity to display theirs. By the late eighties, nobody was putting on a better show than the communities' nouveaux riches—the le-gions of young drug dealers. During the time when Terry was making crazy money in the Mudhole, he could have marched in silk or Gucci or leather—or, for that matter, ridden, as some dealers did, on a sparkling new motorcycle—but he chose instead to make a subtler statement. He went Yale. He wore Yale sweatpants, a blue Yale sweatshirt, and a Yale baseball cap, all bought at the Yale Co-op. It was a clever choice (the parade actually passes through Yale) and the outfit was well received. "It was *dope*," Terry said. "People *liked* it."

Yale dominates New Haven and has done so for more than two hundred years. Since the mid-nineteenth century, when the town's founding Puritan elite was displaced from the leadership of city government by the self-made businessmen of the industrial era, Yale's grip on direct local political power has been relatively weak, and relations between the university and the city have often been strained. Still, Yale's influence remains pervasive. The univer-sity is the city's largest private landowner (much of its property is untaxed), and its largest employer. Warren Kimbro, a New Haven native and a former member of the Black Panther Party, distills his long experience in city politics this way: "If Yale wants the parade to go down Church Street, we ain't *takin'* it down Chapel Street." As for Yale's influence on black New Haven, Kimbro says, "We all grew up in the shadow of Yale. Everybody secretly wanted to be a Yalie. In the fifties, we all wore the white bucks, the gray flannel pants, the cord jackets, the tweed jackets, the button-down shirts, the argyle socks, the college-stripe ties. We bought our clothes at J. Press, on York Street, when we could afford it. Later on, of course, we started waking up. 'Hey, you niggers never gonna be Yalies,' we said."

Very few black New Haveners do attend Yale. Those who go to college tend to go to the University of Connecticut, to local schools such as the University of New Haven and Southern Connecticut State University, or to traditionally black colleges in the South. Dr. John Dow, a recent superintendent of New Haven's schools, was a booster of the Southern colleges, and his administra-tion regularly helped high school seniors make reconnaissance trips to At-lanta and other centers of black education. In the days of cocaine posse warfare, the wisdom of sending inner-city teenagers as far as possible from their homes had never been more compelling, and the South has in fact been serving this R & R purpose for New Haven families for at least a generation.

Terry's year in North Carolina stood, clearly, as an island of calm and steady school attendance in an ocean of truancy and disorder.

But the cognitive dissonance between tranquil campus and ghetto streets can make the transition difficult even for the academically prepared. A former member of the Underworld, suddenly recast as a college student in Georgia, told me that even brief trips home to New Haven could be schizophrenic. "I gotta step back out of the college life, out of being collegiate," he said. "Like last summer, the Jungle tried to bum-rush my crib"—attack his house. "It was crucial. My brother had beat up one of their guys, so they were coming with baseball bats. That's when you gotta pump yourself up. You can't show fear. I soup myself up, I stop being rational. I'm like Jekyll and Hyde—it's the only way. This particular beef stayed just sticks—it wasn't a gun affair. I snuffed one of their guys head-up"—beat him in a fist fight—"and they left. But then some of our guys started basing"—smoking cocaine—"so they were perceived as weak. So the Jungle came back, this time with a police battering ram. And we went out, and they were defeated again. But I was really upset. Now it was like I might have to start carrying a gun to NAACP meetings. Another time, the Jungle aired out"—shot up—"my crib. Then I *knew* I had to carry a gun." This young man, who once spent ten months in juvenile detention after a precocious career as a thief (his favorite target was the Macy's in the Chapel Square Mall; his favorite method was to start a fire near the elevators and, during the ensuing hubbub, clean out the men's department), never had much success as a drug dealer. "I was always hustling backwards," he said—consuming his profits when there were any. The choice between the streets and "going legit" came down to a decision one morning, he said, "whether to get nice with my homeboys—we had some good sess—or to go work in Jesse's campaign"—Jesse Jackson's 1988 campaign for the Democratic presidential nomination—"like I said I would." He had always been a capable student when he chose to work, but his ability to weigh more than the most immediate considerations when he made a decision hinged, he said, on a single conviction: "I'm a leader. That knowledge helps me do the right thing."

Another child of New Haven's streets who became a student at one of the elite black colleges in Atlanta talked about the pain of breaking with her old friends. "They say, 'You're being funny. You think you're too good for us now.'" She was never a drug dealer herself but two of her brothers (she is one of twelve children) and several of her high school boyfriends were. "You just can't get away from it here," she said. "Older people don't understand. In their generation, it was, 'Should I go out with this person? Should I give him a kiss?' Now it's, 'Should I go out with this drug dealer?' Saying, 'Don't talk to this guy because he's a drug dealer,' is like saying, 'Don't have any involvement with any guys.'" Her own decision to study hard and to go away to college caused rifts with nearly all her friends, though the only recriminations came from girlfriends. The boys, she said, were strangely understanding. "This one guy, he was a dealer, and we were really close, and he just said, 'You gotta leave people like me alone.' Even though he wanted me, wanted a pretty girl to sport around and show off, he just gave me a hug and left." She wiped away a sudden rush of tears. "Now I just keep telling him to get out of New Haven, to join the service—*anything*. He got shot by KSI—he's down with the Ville—on our graduation night. But he's still here, and he's still out there."

These two students got help and inspiration from the NAACP Youth Council, where they both worked in the election campaigns of Jesse Jackson and John Daniels. Political and community volunteer work is an essential part of most successful ghetto-escape plans. It is where inner-city kids can meet educated activists, who can provide both advice and institutional contacts; it's also a way to widen their understanding of their problems. Terry once attended a meeting of the Youth Council—by judicial order. He was still living with Beulah, and he and his Uncle Button had been quarreling over Button's attempts to discipline him. One of their fights grew violent, Beulah called the police, and the family-court judge ordered Terry to attend a Youth Council meeting. Terry found the meeting "corny." He did not see any future for himself in such a setting—"I'm a leader" is not *his* mantra—and he did not attend another. To Terry, the Youth Council was much like school—just another scene in which he found no inspiration and saw no chance for success.

Dr. James Comer, a professor of child psychiatry at Yale, says that children begin to understand in about the third grade whether they are part of the American mainstream or part of another, more marginal country—and sometimes they sense the distinction years earlier. If they see that they are on the margins, Dr. Comer says, their academic performance usually suffers immediately: "They sense already that they are not getting—not from their family, their school, their neighborhood—the skills, the socialization they need to participate in the mainstream economy." By early adolescence, according to Dr. Comer, most kids in this situation simply stop trying to bond with school and teachers. Black Americans, in particular, have been trapped by a disastrous historical lag in their access to education, says Dr. Comer, who is himself black. On the average, he estimates, three generations of continuous access are necessary if a family is to gain the type of education that will allow its members to function successfully in the postindustrial economy. But few black families had achieved that continuity before deindustrialization began to shatter the hopes of working-class people. "Large and pervasive as the drug problem is, it's still only a symptom," Dr. Comer says. "It's like the headache one gets with a cerebral hemorrhage. It's not the headache that's going to kill you;

it's the hemorrhage." And the hemorrhage in this case, he says, is the profound and ongoing failure to educate poor Americans.

The drug world, of course, provides an alternative sphere of opportunity for the marginalized. Some teenagers see dealing drugs as merely an after-school job. Most realize, certainly, that it is not a viable career over the long run. But to those who have already sensed that their own chances of entering the mainstream economy are effectively nil—and whose interest in "credentialing," in avoiding a police record and building a work and school record that will increase their chances of economic success, is also near zero—the reasons not to deal drugs must seem weak indeed. The appeal of dealing is not, moreover, always simply financial. For users, the drug itself may be a prime attraction. The idea of selling blissful oblivion, in an environment notably short of bliss, also has its charms. Finally, there is the importance of being "well known," and of its psychological concomitant, self-respect. In an age that celebrates entrepreneurial ardor above all, when the idea of the dignity of labor has come to seem quaint at best, washing dishes or flipping burgers for a risible wage becomes an act of either blind faith or sheer desperation.

In school, the marginalized child's perception that the die is already cast has its objective correlative in the practice of "tracking," in which students with greater academic skills—normally gained only by children with adequate social support systems—are prepared, more or less exclusively, for college entrance. Tim Shriver, the supervisor of an ambitious "social development" program (inspired in large measure by Dr. Comer's ideas) in New Haven's schools, said that, as a rule, only children with extraordinary parents can do well in inner-city schools. "Those who get only average parenting," he said, "just don't make it."

The social development program in New Haven's schools sought to balance extensive instruction in basic problem solving—teaching students self-control, especially stress management—with instruction in social skills. Superintendent Dow spoke of the need for "institutional parenting," and emphasized basic skills—how to shake hands, look people in the eye, say please and thank you—while the Yale psychologists who designed the program preferred to put the emphasis on "social critical-thinking skills," encouraging the use of such devices as a Feelings Dictionary, which can help children identify "problem feelings" such as anger, loneliness, and fear. Everyone agreed, though, on the need to develop a greater common language between teachers, who in New Haven's schools tend to be white, and students, who tend to be black or Latino, and on the need to make more connections between schoolwork and students' lives. If a class is taking a trip to an art museum, for example, a well-designed preparatory lesson for inner-city students would include not just Van Gogh, but what sort of clothes to wear on the day, what to expect en route, how to behave in a museum, how to cope with boredom, and, finally, perhaps, how to cope with the feelings you may have when you get home and your mother doesn't want to hear about Van Gogh.

I attended a social development class for eleventh graders at Wilbur Cross High. The lesson consisted of a role-playing skit and a discussion. The teacher, a young white woman, played an "African American teenage girl in the Chapel Square Mall." A white female student played a "nervous white male security guard." As the security guard began to harass the teenager, both characters' tempers flared, and the teacher playing the teenager cried, "Freeze!" Then the class discussed the problem—feelings, goals, solutions. A heavily built white boy in a hockey shirt thought the girl should simply obey the guard. "Go talk to your friends outside," he said. "Go talk on the Green." Perhaps because the temperature outside was near zero, this solution struck some of the other students as preposterous. A black girl with a Jamaican accent kept exclaiming "Go talk on the Green!" and then dissolving in giggles. And yet the discussion struck me as remarkably clear and unrancorous. When the teacher asked, "How would I feel if I just left?" a black boy with a dramatic high-low said, "You might feel like you got *beat*. And then you might go home and take it out on other people." I found myself thinking about how these were, by rights, Terry's classmates. He was enrolled in school. He just never went.

After class, I asked the teacher whether there had been any drug dealers in the class. She said that there had been two at the beginning of the semester but both had dropped out. I later attended another social development class, and when I asked its teacher about a boy who slept soundly through the entire session, she explained that he was a drug dealer in the Franklin Street projects and had probably been up all night working. He also had emotional problems, she said, because he had accidentally shot a friend to death.

One sunny summer afternoon, the New Haven police sent four plainclothes officers in an unmarked car to the Mudhole after receiving a telephone complaint about a black male there wearing a red shirt and brandishing a handgun. As the policemen approached on West Hazel Street, they saw six or seven black male teenagers gathered in the vacant lot ahead. None of them was wearing a red shirt. One of the boys began walking away, however, when the officers arrived. As he walked, according to the police, he threw a brown paper bag to the ground. He was ordered to halt. The paper bag was retrieved and found to contain fifteen small pink bags of a plantlike material, which field tests showed to be marijuana. The boy was searched, and a quantity of cash—twenty-seven dollars, according to the police—was confiscated. He was arrested and charged with intent to sell marijuana within a thousand feet of a school (Martin Luther King Elementary was two blocks away across Dixwell Avenue)—a felony.

"I shoulda dipped," Terry said. "I coulda got away. I don't know why I stopped, I just did. I panicked. The big boys said I only had twenty-seven dollars on me. I had at least two hundred. They just took it. Then they was going to take me out back of Wilbur Cross and beat me up. That's what they usually do. Call it the Beat Down Posse. But there was too many people around, too many witnesses, so they had to take me downtown. I was in there for eight hours before my mother got me out. I was hungry, but all they give you in jail is a baloney sandwich. That's the worst part of jail, if you ask me. Baloney—*that's not me.*"

After his release, Terry went straight back to work in the Mudhole. "I had taken a downfall," he said. "I had to get back on *top*. Plus I needed money for a lawyer. I had witnesses who saw the big boys didn't find no drugs on me. They found the work in some weeds way over *there*. But it was real, real hot in the Mudhole after that, and I couldn't afford to get popped again."

Reluctantly, Terry stopped selling drugs. He moved from Frank's girlfriend's place to the Sleeping Giant Motel. At his trial, he was represented not by a private lawyer specializing in drug cases—he couldn't afford such counsel—but by a New Haven public defender. The prosecutor asked for a sentence of three years, suspended after ninety days, with three years' probation. If Terry had been charged with intent to sell cocaine, his lawyer said, the prosecutor might have gotten his wish. As it was, Terry's lawyer persuaded the court to reduce the charge to possession of marijuana, a misdemeanor, in exchange for a guilty plea. Terry received a suspended sentence of one year, with two years' probation.

The suspended sentence was a big relief. In the weeks after his arrest, Terry had become so worried about the possibility of a jail term that he had started going to church—to the Catholic church where Beulah had taken him when he was small—and praying for forgiveness. He had also written a letter to the judge who would hear his case. The letter, printed in pencil on lined paper, was thick with spelling and other mistakes and looked more like the work of a third grader than a high school student. But it included a promise that Terry would "start fresh" in school in September, the news that he and Anjelica and Buddy were on the verge of getting an apartment of their own, and a declaration that, "I am really trying to get my head on write." The letter also listed every place where Terry had applied for a job since his arrest, including Kentucky Fried Chicken, Burger King, Yale University, Yale–New Haven Hospital, the Hospital of Saint Raphael, Pathmark, two New Haven country clubs, and three local restaurants. He was about to start two new jobs, Terry wrote, one at a discount department store in Hamden, the other at the Ponderosa Restaurant on Dixwell Avenue.

In the meantime, though he did not mention it to the judge, Terry was cooking at Shabazz, a lunch counter on Shelton Avenue, in Newhallville. Shabazz was owned and operated by a Black Muslim named Scott X and it doubled as a storefront office for the Nation of Islam. Posters of Louis Farrakhan and Martin Luther King, Jr., hung in the front windows; inside was the well-known photograph of Malcolm X holding an automatic rifle and peering warily out a window, over the caption BY ANY MEANS NECESSARY. The Nation of Islam's newspaper, *The Final Call*, was on sale, along with books like *The Fall of America*, by the late Black Muslim leader, Elijah Muhammad. Among the videotapes for rent were thirty-seven speeches by Farrakhan, one of which was usually playing on a television in the shop's front window. The food sold at Shabazz was simple, but even the menu on the wall evangelized. After "Box of Fish" and "Fish Sandwich," it said "Stop Calling Each Other Niggers."

"Scott's got some *good* messages," Terry said.

I was interested in those messages, but I had a hard time discovering just what they were. Terry's version of Scott's views was murky—"Tell you the truth, I don't really catch on to that stuff," he said—and it was Scott's policy not to talk to white reporters. "Why should I help you make money?" he asked me. "What good would it do *our* community?"

Scott X was in his late twenties, trim, severe, light-skinned, with Marine Corps posture and a Marine Corps haircut. He said, when I asked, that he was indifferent to politics, but in fact he worked closely with Kevin Houston, Roger Vann, and the other young black activists in New Haven, and the previous year's peace agreement among the posses, though it ultimately failed to stop the violence, might not have come about at all, according to participants, without the esteem in which the posses held Scott. It seemed that the posses liked the mixture of street toughness and religious right living he projected: Scott X not only read the Koran and preached a scorching sermon against the powers that be, but he also cruised around town in a late-model white Isuzu Trooper with a telephone. Scott counseled the neighborhood's youth, particularly the boys, and when a boy was in trouble he might even give him work at Shabazz. That's what he did with Terry, and the job helped Terry break away from selling drugs.

"Who do you think is bringing all these drugs into our community?" Scott asked me. "Who do you think is bringing in all these guns? *We* don't own no gun factories. *We* don't own no jet airplanes. So who is it?"

I knew the preferred answers to these questions, but I said, "I don't know. Who?"

This conversation took place on the sidewalk in front of Shabazz, with a small crowd listening and Louis Farrakhan orating with pointed finger on the television in the window. Scott, losing patience, pointed at my chest. "You got a good heart?" he asked.

I snapped back, "Who's to say?"

The conversation ended right there. Over the weeks that followed, I often stopped by Shabazz, however, and finally Scott invited me to a public meeting at a nearby elementary school where Conrad Muhammad, the Nation of Islam's Minister of Youth, was scheduled to speak. On the appointed evening I showed up, but Muhammad did not, and Scott, wearing the old-fashioned black suit and red bow tie that constitute the Nation of Islam's curious uniform, had to do the miserable honors of turning people away, which he did with gruff aplomb.

A few nights later, he agreed to try to explain his no-interview policy to me again. "It's simple," he said. "Your people have kept my people in chains for four hundred years. We don't owe you *anything.* You say you're interested in the troubles of the black community. We say you are *responsible* for those troubles. You say you can't stop the drugs from coming in. We don't believe that. You can throw a satellite up to Neptune, but you can't control the borders of your own country? We are about helping the black community, and I can't see how anything you write is going to help us."

I found myself offering the most basic arguments for the existence of journalism, but he brushed my points aside. If I was really interested in his views, he said, I could read *The Final Call.* Everything he had to tell me was in there. I had to wonder if Scott actually meant to endorse, say, Elijah Muhammad's claim, reprinted in the issue of the paper he had on sale, that a fleet of fifteen hundred bombing planes, parked for now inside a giant, wheel-shaped Mother of Planes, was preparing to destroy "the white man's evil world." I didn't ask, though. Things were complicated enough.

They are far less complicated, of course, for fundamentalists, and the Nation of Islam seems to owe much of its popularity to the fierce and rigid answers it supplies to the bottomless conundrums and bottomless pain of being black and poor in America. I found it hard to gauge the Nation's real strength in New Haven. Its forces had never been mobilized locally for high-profile campaigns, such as that of the Dopebusters, who, with some help from the news media, had recently chased the drug dealers out of two housing projects in the District of Columbia. And there was no New Haven contingent of the Fruit of Islam, the cohort of grim young men who give the Nation's public events such a Fascistic look. But I often saw teenagers outside Shabazz, half-watching the Farrakhan videos, and I often heard Scott X and the Nation credited with "knowledge." (On the subject of Jews, Terry could recall only one saying of Scott's: "Jews are for jewelry." This is actually an infamous Public Enemy trope. When I asked after his own views, Terry shrugged. "Jews? They're people. That's all I can say. They like to keep their money, I heard.") For people whose lives are chaotic or desperate, the structure and pride that Nation membership can provide clearly have a powerful appeal; the Nation has been strong among convicts for decades. Indeed, it seemed to be only the movement's asceticism, particularly its dietary laws and prohibition on alcohol, that kept many young New Haveners from joining. Terry said he knew *he* could never be a good Muslim, because "I love pigs' feet too much." Young women might be put off as well by the retrograde treatment of females. There were other, more traditional Muslim congregations in black New Haven, which also offered the rare joy of shedding one's "slave name." And Mustafa Abdul-Salaam, the community activist, who was a disciple of Elijah Muhammad's son, Warith Deen Muhammad, told me that there was *nothing* more personally liberating than that.

In the end, Scott X was more forthcoming with work than he was with payment, and after a couple of months Terry left Shabazz for a job as a dishwasher in a convalescent home.

. . .

Terry's Uncle Button was also a fundamentalist. He went to the Bible Gospel Center in Newhallville at least five days a week, and he spent most of his non-church time at home—he was unemployed and, at thirty-one, still lived with his mother—praying and reading the Bible. "The Catholic Church was very boring compared to where I'm at now," Button told me. He smiled knowingly. "Bible Gospel got more *oomph.*" Button is slight and well spoken, with big, feline eyes and a wary, ironic manner. In appearance he strongly resembles his sister Anjelica. "I got saved in 1983," he said. "Before that, I was just into drinking and drugs and that whole life. In 1979, I got shot by a guy who was trying to take my money—he didn't get it, either. Then a friend who had been saved took me to church with him. It took six or seven months before I finally quit drinking. But, I can tell you, this works better than any drug program."

I remembered hearing Anjelica, who had been through her share of drug treatment programs, and who had always been close to her younger brother, talk about the time Button took her to his church. "I always told him, 'If I go in the church, the ceiling gonna fall on me,'" she said. "But I did go with him once. And the preacher said, 'There's somebody in here screaming for help, going the wrong way, but don't know how to change. I'm going to walk down the aisle and when my feet stop, that's going to be the person.' And he started coming, and I turned to Button and I said, 'Don't start.' But when the preacher got to us he stopped, and he started turning toward me. I just jumped up and ran. I ran out onto Winchester Avenue, and there were all the drug dealers and everybody hanging out, and I just kept running. I got home, and my father said, 'Girl, what's wrong with you?' I couldn't sleep all night, and I'll never go near that church again."

It was easy to picture Anjelica spooked—she often seemed to be in permanent flight from her own hobgoblins and guilts—but it was hard to picture her finding salvation down the same path that Button had taken. She lacked all trace of his asceticism, his irony, his evident need for a rock-solid structure of meaning around him. Poor people have, of course, always employed religion, including fundamentalist sects, to help make their lot more bearable, but Button's belief had an existential quality, an intensity, that did not call to mind the traditional comforts offered to those on the bottom of the pile by their pastors. Terry once told me, "My uncle used to sit out on the porch and smoke sess and read the Bible. Now tell me *that* ain't wack." Terry was describing a phase of Button's conversion, and it didn't sound the least bit wack to me. Button's own tales of his hell-raising youth were another matter; they were difficult to reconcile with the gentle, balding, lemurlike man I met. I could definitely see him, though, bugging out and deliberately breaking a glass basing pipe in his hand.

Button and I are in Beulah's living room. His big sister Charlayne, hearing

Button speak of the extra oomph offered at his church, joins our conversation, saying, "It's true. They got it all at Bible Gospel. Singing, shouting, speaking in tongues—you name it, they do it." Charlayne laughs. Button grins, and does not seem offended. Charlayne, at forty, has leading-lady bone structure and a worldly manner, even in a grubby bathrobe. She does not look like a career drug addict who has lost custody of her three children. But that is what she is, and she, too, is unemployed and living here with Beulah.

"Charlayne just can't handle all the excitement at my church," Button says. "But my mother, she comes."

Beulah, who is crocheting and watching TV, briskly confirms this statement. I say, "I hear Anjelica can't handle it, either."

Button and Charlayne, presumably recalling Anjelica's headlong flight from church, guffaw. Beulah does not smile. "Anjelica," she says. "Anjelica can't handle a whole bunch of things. That's because she used so many drugs. She still does use them, and she agreed to Terry getting into drugs by taking the money he gave her. She even took money for summer camp tuition for Buddy and spent it on herself. Terry was very upset about that."

Charlayne and Button are staring at the TV, having tuned out as their mother talks.

Anjelica is painting her kitchen. Her boyfriend has come over to help. He is the painter who sometimes works at Yale, and who was the key element in her plan to catch the suspected burglar from upstairs, who is blessedly still in jail. Anjelica's boyfriend's name is Robert. He is big, as advertised, but he doesn't seem the least bit crazy. Rangy and deep-voiced, somewhere in his forties, he is singing along with a Joe Tex tape when I arrive. Three walls are already painted and the kitchen looks much, much better. It was grimy off-white; now it's white. Buddy is wielding a long-handled roller, painting the remaining wall—he is manic, barefoot, paint-spattered. Anjelica looks to be in a great mood—her data entry gig at her mother's office is still going strong. She and Robert are sitting on paint cans, drinking Canei and Scotch. I take a glass of Scotch.

Anjelica and Robert are discussing local family fortunes—who left what house or car or grocery to whom, and who tried to get it away from them, and who was cut out of whose will. This is a favorite topic of Anjelica's and she can expand on it with or without Robert, whose knowledge of black New Haven's secret social and economic history seems nearly as thorough as hers, but who is also easily seduced by the chorus of "Try a Little Tenderness." Buddy, meanwhile, has run out of paint and is frantically running his roller up and down the wall, leaving only a faint streak of white. "More paint! More paint!" he cries. Robert and Anjelica ignore him even as he tries to get them up off the cans he needs to open. Anjelica is exulting over the case of the rich old lady who failed to leave a *dime* to her daughter, who never recovered from the shock.

Anjelica's other favorite subject is intoxication, particularly its wilder varieties (how crazy somebody got on what drug) and her own adventures: the time she was tricked into smoking PCP, or the time when, extremely stoned, she ran from the police through the old New Haven cemetery at midnight. Tonight, these stories provide a sort of Dionysian chorus to the recitations on ancestry. Even when Anjelica's drug tales are cautionary and grim, her rascally, missing-bicuspid smile breaks out; the idea of getting high simply fills her with a delight she can't hide. This, it occurs to me, is another way in which Anjelica is still a teenager at heart. (The adolescent fascination with getting high, and with exotic new drugs, seems to me inextinguishable. The exciting new drug in New Haven at that time, causing a great stir among teenagers, was "ice"—smokable methamphetamine. After hearing that I lived in New York City, many kids brought it up. "It got double the chemicals," a Puerto Rican teenager told me brusquely. Then he looked at me sidelong. "That right?" A young white cocaine addict from West Haven said dreamily, "I imagine it kind of dusty and blue." Even Terry, who seemed not to have inherited his mother's obsession with inebriation, had his curiosity. For instance, he really wanted, as noted, to see somebody on LSD box.)

Tonight, Terry is, I assume, at Lakeeda's.

No, says Anjelica, he's with Frank.

I'm alarmed to hear it.

"Frank's a nice kid," Anjelica assures me. "He took good care of Terry when Terry was out there. He took a *lot* better care of him than some other dealers would have."

I'm not reassured. Terry has time on his hands these days, and no money in his pocket. He lost the job washing dishes in a convalescent home, and he did not "start fresh" in school in the fall, as he told the judge he would. He went to school only intermittently, failed to make any stronger connection there than he had in preceding years, and, having been told by a school official that he had already missed too many classes to pass this year, has stopped going altogether. Anjelica says now, "If he goes to school, I'll buy him clothes. If he don't go, he ain't gettin' nothin'." Together with Frank's reappearance, this sounds to me like a formula for Terry's return to dealing. In principle, that is none of my business, but keeping my reporter's distance, not interfering with my subject's life, has been difficult from the start with Terry, and this prospect raises the stakes sharply. My role is already ambiguous as far as Terry's family is concerned. When I met his Aunt Darla, she glared at me for a full minute— through what appeared to be a brutal hangover—before recognition broke in her face and she said, "Oh, *you're* the guy trying to get Terry back on the right track."

I ask Anjelica what sort of future she imagines for Terry.

"The best thing would be the Air Force," she says. "But first he has to get a diploma. You can't do nothin' without that piece of paper." Maybe Terry can get a high-school-equivalency diploma in an adult education course, she says, and *then* join the Air Force. "Terry's problem is, he's lazy," she goes on. "Buddy loves to work. He always got to be doing something. But Terry, he's not like that."

Anjelica is right about Buddy, at least, who is now swinging his paint roller wildly in an effort to dislodge her and Robert from the paint cans. "More paint! More paint!" Buddy has been pleading for more paint for an hour now. I've tried to suggest to Anjelica and Robert that he really could use some more paint, but I, too, am ignored. The scene has become painful to watch. I gulp Scotch and hum along with Joe Tex and get up and wander around the apartment. On top of the television, which is playing unwatched, are two studio portraits of Buddy, looking toothlessly cute and unnaturally calm, and a copy of Anjelica's high school diploma, in a cardboard frame.

Hearing Anjelica disparage Terry's interest in work reminds me of something Beulah said. "Terry's just not motivated to go to school, or get a job, or do anything," she said. "It's dangerous. Doing nothing becomes a habit. It's partly his mother's fault and partly his probation officer's." Someone, I realize, is always telling me what someone else's problem is. Beulah says Anjelica's problem is a failure to take life seriously; Anjelica says Terry's problem is laziness. Beulah and Anjelica both sense that I want an explanation: what is wrong. *Something* is wrong—why else would I be coming around? And yet, at some level, we all know that there is in fact no explanation, no insight that can possibly sum up a life or character. It may be my job to tease out such a thing, but the truth is that a life—Terry's, Anjelica's, Beulah's, even black New Haven's—is not an illness in need of a diagnosis.

At the same time, events have obviously conspired to cripple—socially, economically, educationally—a vast number of black poor and working-class families. If I had to choose a root cause for all this distress, I might single out structural unemployment—the cruelest edge of the American economy's deindustrialization and increasing reliance on untrained, insecure labor, and a close cousin to the pervasive undereducation in public schools in poor and working-class neighborhoods. But Beulah and Anjelica speak a more personal language, and in their terms *my* problem may be just my deep reluctance to diagnose.

Above all, I realize, I'm reluctant to sit in judgment on Anjelica's maternal performance. The state can do that. (And so far it has judged Charlayne's performance more harshly.) Anjelica has not come stomping uninvited into *my* life and, on the basis of a few conversations with my family, presumed to judge my performance as a son or a spouse or a citizen.

Of course, my reluctance to diagnose or to sit in moral judgment on Anjelica does not change the real power relations between us.

I end my tour of the apartment. Buddy still hasn't got his paint. Robert re-
fills my glass. Anjelica, waving her glass, says, "Frank's problem is, he drinks
too much. And now Terry is drinking, too. I told him he's gotta stop. He can't
handle it. The boy goes crazy."

"**I** was lost in the sand," Terry says. "I didn't know what I was doin', even before we got to Nick & Neil's. I got in a fight with this nigger from Bridgeport. They shut the club early. So we went to the Milford Arcade and some dude there started *shootin'* at us. He was one of the Bridgeport guys, I guess. He had a pistol. We just ran, my posse and me. I don't even know where. I'm *still* lost in the sand. You can look in my face and tell."

Terry's face doesn't actually look much the worse for wear, though he is speaking unusually slowly. It's Saturday morning. We are in the New Haven station, setting off on a long-planned excursion to New York City. I ask Terry what he was drinking last night.

"Yukon Jack." Pause. "Vodka." Pause. "Rum."

Nick & Neil's doesn't serve liquor—the club doesn't even let anyone over twenty-one inside—so all this was apparently parking-lot tippling. Nick & Neil's has, if nothing else, an abundance of parking lot. A flimsy-looking white one-story building lashed together with strings of pink and turquoise neon, the club sits out on an endless suburban shopping strip, some ten miles west of New Haven, surrounded by Sound Playgrounds and Showcase Furniture Showrooms and drive-in banks, and vast expanses of parking. The club, on a weekend night, has hundreds of black teenagers, most of them from the ghettos of New Haven, Bridgeport, Stamford, or Norwalk, being served and chaperoned and occasionally manhandled by a staff of uneasy, muscle-bound young white men in bow ties. The hip-hop scratches and blasts, and the dance floor thrashes. I ask Terry what the fight was about.

"I don't even remember," he says. "I just remember I got this guy down and I was stomping his head." Terry demonstrates, lifting his feet exaggeratedly, as if he had on lead boots, and bringing each foot down with great force on the station platform. It is a strange, stylized dance, reminiscent of the waddling, fat-man walk that posse members use to "profile." "I was *stompin'* that nigger's head," Terry says. Then, perhaps noticing that I seem horrified, he adds, "I don't know why. Something in me just wanted to do it."

Terry's opponent, it turns out, managed to get up and escape, with unspecified damage, but the story leaves me bemused—not for the first time—by Terry's capacity for violence. His habit of "going crazy" notwithstanding, he normally seems to me far less inclined to actual violence than, say, the average high school football player. So when he first told me about the time he "unloaded a clip"—fired six shots—at someone in the Mudhole I assumed that he meant only to scare off the attacker. No, he assured me. "I wanted to catch me a body." It's a salutary reminder that success in the drug business virtually requires violence—to hold territory, prevent rip-offs, enforce agreements, and so on. Since leaving the business, Terry says, he has realized that violence is wrong. "Before, I used to be like, 'Word, word,' when somebody said, 'Yo, I wanna take somebody out.' But now I'm like, 'No way.'" And yet there are still those situations in which, as he says, something in him just wants to do it. (Late that same night, on upper Broadway in Manhattan, I see such a situation suddenly develop. We are standing outside a Korean grocery discussing whether to pick up something for breakfast. An older Korean man emerges from the store with a large knife in his hand. When he sees Terry, he stops, and gives Terry a long, amazingly frank look, right in the face. Then the old man glances at me and turns away to start cutting the stems off a shipment of tulips. My heart is slamming. Terry, I notice, is grinning strangely. We move on quickly, and as we walk up the street Terry says, "Did you see that dude? I thought he was going to stick me with that knife. That's why I was smiling. I was going to grab his arm like *this*, and twist him around like *this*, and then start choking him. I would have stomped the *dooky* out of him.")

As we board the train for New York, Terry points to a street that runs past the New Haven police station. "Me and Frank used to go that way when we came back from New York," he says. "We walk right past the po-lice station. We have four, five ounces. He carry the coke but I be carrying crazy paraphernalia. Big old package of lactose for cut. We was ready to run, but we never got stopped."

"How is Frank?"

Terry smirks. "He fine. No job. No money."

As the train leaves New Haven, I notice Terry playing with a belt-mounted telephone beeper. "This don't work," he assures me. "I just carry it around to play the front with the girls. If they think you're a dealer, they got more time for you."

I mention that I've heard of boys' wearing automatic garage door openers for the same purpose, and Terry laughs.

"Other dealers see you with one of these, they think you're dealing, too," he says. "Then they don't try to shoot you up. They leave you alone. That's another reason I got this. But if the big boys find a beeper on you, that's organized crime. That's why I make sure I got one that don't work."

Terry pulls his ski cap down over his eyes, curls up in his seat, and sleeps all the way to 125th Street. There, as we descend the stairs from the station platform, he points to a police car in the shadows. "Check it out," he says. "He's waitin' for somebody who looks like me, see if he can catch him with a bundle." Terry grins and yawns.

"I been in this part of New York lots of times," he says. We're riding west in a cab on 125th Street. "Me and Frank used to buy the work right by here. But I was usually drunk, so it's hard to remember. I bought me a jacket in there once." Terry points to a discount clothing store called Dr. Jays.

Terry's knowledge of New York City does turn out to be limited. A walk in Central Park is a revelation: he has never seen the park before, or heard of it. A ride on the subway, same thing. His eyes dart eagerly, studying the train, the stations, and our fellow passengers, and he repeatedly checks with me to make sure he is behaving correctly, saying, "I never really been down here before in this whatchacallit."

"Subway."

"Yeah. This is like an *experiment* for me."

But the comforts of the familiar are never far away. We come and go from my apartment, and each time we stop there we find a telephone message from Anjelica. She and Terry spend hours discussing nothing in particular on the phone. Among my records and tapes Terry quickly finds the few rap recordings, and then raps along with Public Enemy and MC Lyte. And at the end of a long day of sight-seeing and moviegoing he drags a television into my study, where a bed has been set up for him, explaining that he can't get to sleep without out a TV going.

In the morning, I find him asleep in front of the TV. All the lights in the study are blazing. Terry has the sheets pulled over his head. The shouts and sirens of some ancient police show wash over him.

A vast part of what Terry knows and believes about the world he learned from television, and on critical topics such as violence and drugs his electronic education has been a toxic soup of mixed moral messages. Since infancy, his brain has been filled, willy-nilly, with flashy, violent fantasies. Lately, alongside a torrent of antidrug propaganda—itself a powerful lure for any self-respecting teenager, on the durable theory that anything adults bother to prohibit must be fun—an equal but opposite torrent of images has been flowing, mingling the drug world indelibly with visions of glamour and wealth. Rap music moves to the channel-zapping rhythms of TV, and Terry's heroes, Public Enemy, appear onstage wearing combat fatigues and surrounded by bodyguards with machine guns. If Terry is impervious to fundamentalism (Christian, Islamic, or black nationalist), it is because his own religion, his ideology—consumer individualism, imbibed since childhood from commercial television—is itself profoundly rooted. Of course, consumerism and lifelong poverty make a painful combination. So any source of fast money—such as dealing drugs— that might offer some relief gets seen, naturally, in the slanting light of economic man's moral relativism. It is a question of belief systems.

Wrong, said Virginia Henry. A genial grandmother of twelve, Ms. Henry lived in the Quinnipiac Terrace housing project, and helped run a group called Tenants Against Drugs, Dammit! "Talking about poverty is a copout," Ms. Henry told me one afternoon in her apartment. "I'm sorry, but these kids know right from wrong. I was brought up poor. I guess I'll always be poor. But I brought up my kids to know right from wrong. That's all you gotta do. These kids *know* drugs are wrong. *And I better not see you on the corner.*"

Ms. Henry and her comrades—TADD had chapters in housing projects all over New Haven—did not confront dealers or their customers. "We just observe," she told me. "We're mothers taking our kids to the park, or looking out our windows while we're cooking. We make notes on who's where, what they're wearing, where they're hiding their drugs, and we give that information to the police." Ms. Henry indicated the street outside her window. "There's been drug dealing going on out here all day. I've called the police twice already. They came, so there's not too much going on right now, because it's hot."

Ms. Henry's tidy, homey apartment seemed an unlikely conning tower, but there it was.

"I moved to Q Terrace fifteen years ago," she said. "It was a lot different then. There were trees, and grass, kids out playing. Buildings were kept up. People met out at the clothesline. But then everything changed. People stopped caring. Drugs really hit about four or five years ago. By about two years ago, it was so bad you'd get off the bus, coming home from work, and you could hardly get to your own front door because of the dealers. That's when I knew it was time to get involved."

I wondered if her work was dangerous.

"They never come after me personally," she said. "I guess they say things to my brother about me, but that's all. Over in Eastern Circle"—another housing project in east New Haven—"they been making threats, and the TADD people over there had to let up. But the rest of us have kept on going. Things got better for a while, but lately it's been bad again. We've had a lot of shootings. Just last week, three kids from Q Terrace got shot, and while the mother of one was bringing him back from the hospital *she* got shot. There's a war going on here. It's KSI against the Island Brothers. You probably heard about the posses."

I said I had.

"They got so many *guns,*" Ms. Henry said, shaking her head. "Three weeks ago, I heard some shots and I jumped up, and I saw a boy out here in back just falling down. I know I'm supposed to jump *down*, but that's just not my nature."

Ms. Henry had surprisingly few complaints about the New Haven police, or about the public housing authority's failure to maintain her building. "The maintenance men stopped coming," she said. "But I can see why they won't go in the cellar to fix the boiler—it's just too dangerous. They're not policemen. They're not trained."

I asked about the drug trade itself.

"Most of the buyers we see out here are white," she said. "They come in cars. Some women who live here are also involved. They let the dealers hide in their apartments. There's been a lot of drug-related evictions here—that's why you see so many empty apartments. I almost got evicted myself after my son was arrested. But most of the dealers you see in Q Terrace don't actually live around here."

I decided against mentioning that I knew a former Q Terrace dealer. I asked Ms. Henry about her son's arrest.

"He's twenty-five," she said. "He's been in prison now eight months. He was a strong young man, active in sports. Then, suddenly, he was into drugs. He has two children, with different women. *My* theory is that his girlfriend was into drugs, and she told him that sex would be better if he took drugs. But I don't know. He thinks I turned him in, but I didn't. He got arrested in a sting, selling drugs to an undercover officer. His sentence is seven years."

We sat in silence, sipping our coffee, as the winter daylight faded. A heavy-set young man emerged from a bedroom to raid the refrigerator. "That's one of the two I still got at home," Ms. Henry said. "He's unemployed. One of my other sons is a roofer. But I'm more afraid of him walking these streets than I am of him up on that roof. *That's* why I'm always jumping up to see what's going on out there—because of all the other mothers."

Silence overtook us again. Ms. Henry, who worked as a custodian at Yale, mentioned that she had expected me to be a Yalie. I didn't ask what that meant. Finally, she said, "I work. I try to make an honest living. It ain't no sin to be poor."

I wondered how many impoverished young people would agree with her. From the bedroom where her unemployed son sat we could hear a television playing.

"Check it out," Terry says. "Italian." He drops a pair of pleated wool trousers in my lap, where a pale blue silk shirt and a pair of beige silk trousers are already piled. I asked to see, and now Terry is showing me, some of the things he bought while he was livin' large. "Look at that lining."

Earlier today, in a social service agency's office where Terry, as a condition of his probation, must report each week, I noticed a stack of well-thumbed

GQ magazines; Terry's quondam wardrobe might have been plucked from the pages of *GQ*. He pulls out a pair of green suede loafers. "Bally," he says. "Hundred eighty dollars." A pair of leather sneakers: "Gucci. Hundred fifty dollars." A black leather shirt: "Had me a whole bunch of these. Two hundred fifty each."

Gold chains?

"Nah," Terry says. "They didn't *excite* me. I had a big gold ring, though, with dollar signs on it. That thing was huge. Cost me two hundred ten dollars, plus tax. I was gonna get diamonds put in it, and rubies. But I could never wear it, because of my grandma, so I sold it to another dealer. Now this stuff is all I got left. Everything else I sold or gave away or lost."

Even when he was making thousands a week, Terry says, he never opened a bank account. "The life I was living," he explains, "I coulda got killed today." And he never tried to buy a car. "I wanted one, and I coulda paid, but I was afraid," he says. "You get a car, a sixteen-year-old guy with no job, that make you *hot*."

Terry and I are at the kitchen table. Anjelica, who has been playing Nintendo in the living room, appears in the doorway. "I wish he'd got a car," she says. "I woulda *found* some way to cover for a car."

Anjelica is wearing her lottery T-shirt—YOU CAN'T WIN IF YOU DON'T PLAY. It occurs to me that Terry's brief run of affluence may have been the closest Anjelica has ever come to tasting the sweet wine of success herself. She disliked the fact that he was in danger—and the spoils he grabbed were a sad imitation, certainly, of the trappings of real membership in the monied classes—but the mere heft of his cash roll must have been, in a world fundamentally defined by the lack of money, somewhat unhinging for her. Anjelica has tasted a hundred brands of failure, as have most of her friends and family, and in such a psychological universe any facsimile of success, even a child's drug income, must have immense weight—enough to warp whole family systems.

As for Terry, his vision of "getting to the top" still seems to revolve around a yellow Mercedes-Benz 190. I've asked him many times about his role models, about who he wants to be when he grows up. When his answer is not Eddie Murphy (playing a gangster) or a rap star (with a gangster style), it is an older New Haven dealer who "made it to the top." This dealer is now in prison, and when Terry proudly shows me the two houses he allegedly still owns in New-hallville, they turn out to be crumbling, unpainted dives. The fact is that the drug trade in New Haven is too poorly organized for anyone in it to rise very far. Entrepreneurs may make a killing, but there is no local organization large enough to allow a bright young dealer to move into middle management—where the risks of injury, death, or arrest might become manageable, and where there might be some future.

This may or may not be why Terry advises against a career in the drug trade.

"I used to tell kids not to get involved, even when I was involved myself," he says. "I always wanted to do a drug commercial. I'll be the dealer, and here's a wannabe, you know what I mean? I'd do it *up*. Give me two minutes, I'd make people realize that it ain't no joke when you get in a gang."

There is also the moral aspect. When I ask Terry about the overall impact of drugs on New Haven, he says, "Bad, bad, bad."

And yet he dearly misses dealing drugs, and is increasingly candid about the fact with me. "Sometimes I want to get back out there so bad I can taste it in my mouth," he says. He takes the pile of silk and leather finery from my lap, carries it into the bedroom, and throws it listlessly into a closet. "But I don't want to go to jail. I wish I was still fifteen! If you're fifteen and the big boys catch you, nothing really happens. If I was fifteen, I'd still be out there actin' the fool, like everybody else."

Out There: Anjelica, who has returned to her Nintendo, talks about it constantly, as if it were a destination on a map. If she doesn't keep busy, if she gets too bored or lonely, she'll go Out There again, she knows she will. It's dangerous Out There, and hard—you're often broke, and may have no place to live— but it's exciting, and the worries of ordinary life recede. To me, these two states of being are not always distinct, but to those who move between them they are. Darla, for example, is Out There now, even though her family often sees her; Charlayne and Anjelica, meanwhile, are safely ensconced in domestic routine, keeping regular hours and maintaining stable addresses. Terry, too, is within the fold, though without the parental duties that help keep his mother and his aunt off the street. But Terry has been Out There, and he clearly remembers with mixed feelings the thrills, terror, and family dramatics of it all.

Terry's frank nostalgia for dealing unnerves me. I mention his mother's notion that he should join the Air Force. Terry says he thinks he would miss Lakeeda and Tyrone too much. If he were to go, he would try to learn computers, because that's where the money is, but he doubts it will ever happen. What he would really like to do, he says, is act. He once took an acting class and he loved it. Somehow, I'm not surprised to hear this—Terry's weird purity of expression often makes him seem like an actor waiting for a character—but neither am I especially heartened. Why not? Here is a good—perhaps even an inspired—idea with which to try to fill the terrible void of Terry's future: acting. Why am I lukewarm? Because, I realize, I have little faith in his ability to stick to a difficult craft like acting. With failure as the dominant object lesson in his world, Terry has learned, or so I imagine, never to extend himself, never to try too hard. If you don't care too much, don't want anything too much, failing to get it won't hurt too much. I can too easily imagine Terry letting thespian matters slide. I guiltily try to hide my doubts from him, but he surely senses them, and he drops the subject.

It's time for me to go. Hearing that I'm bound for the offices of the *New Haven Register,* where I plan to browse in the paper's files, Terry asks a favor: Could I get him a copy of the story from last summer about his arrest? The *Register* often publishes the names of people charged with narcotics offenses. The idea is to increase the shame of arrest. The idea seems not to have worked in Terry's case. Then again, why should it? What has brought me to him, if not his criminal adventures? Kids who go to school, who stay out of trouble—do they have reporters coming from New York every week, writing down everything they say and do and wear?

Warren Kimbro, the former Black Panther, runs a halfway house for ex-convicts in New Haven. Kimbro knows from experience the difficulty of reentering society after prison. He served four and a half years for murder—then went to Harvard, where he earned a master's degree in education. From his office on Congress Avenue, in a rundown neighborhood known as the Hill, Kimbro points to the street outside, where drug dealers stand on every corner, and says, "I can't find any of these guys out here a job that pays them as much as they make dealing drugs. A lot of them are ex-clients, that's how I know."

Kimbro is tweedy, jovial, and not given to dramatic remarks. He talks easily about local black political history and about the bureaucratic details of his work. But his tone softens and darkens as he says, "Drugs are like a new form of slavery. Maybe it's true that cigarettes and liquor kill more people than drugs, but cigarettes and liquor do not destroy a culture, a people, a way of *life*, the way cocaine has."

Roger Vann, who majored in African American studies at Brown, agrees. "African Americans have been through a lot of bad stuff," he says. "But this drug thing is the worst. We really may be down for the count this time."

Sitting in my car outside Kimbro's office, watching the dealers on Congress Avenue work in the weak winter midday sun, I catch a glimpse of the horror that inspires such statements. Rusting, shuttered storefronts and broken-windowed warehouses form the backdrop for a scene of monumental desolation. Business is slow, and the white suburbanites, whom ghetto residents and the police both like to blame for financing the cocaine boom, are nowhere to be seen. (I know that such customers exist, because I am constantly signaled and approached by dealers when I drive through black New Haven.) Young women with toothpick legs in filthy jeans, wearing headscarves and bomber jackets; spectral men in filthy sweaters, shivering; small boys in down coats and ski caps, presumably "running" for someone else—these customers come and go, following dealers into alleys and doorways and sideyards to make their purchases. I can see eight or nine dealers posted along three or four blocks. They range from battered, ageless addicts to burly teenagers; all are black and male. Even from a distance, the shaky, furtive figures of the older dealers emanate defeat. But the teenage dealers radiate something else—some deadly mixture of industry and ice-cold rage. Selling death, risking jail, injury, and death themselves, they are agents and, at the same time, victims of a man-made plague—and their rage, and all the talk of "genocide," suddenly seem entirely reasonable.

Of course, this scene—it's like an Edward Hopper painting reworked by Anselm Kiefer—is repeated, with few variations, every day in the ghettos of every city in America. And the plague metaphor is only deepened by the AIDS virus, which has cut a terrifying swath through the heart of New Haven. By early 1997, 1,557 city residents had developed full-blown AIDS, and more than 800 of them had died. Nearly two thirds of the city's AIDS victims were black, and over two thirds were under the age of forty. New Haven was one of only fifteen cities in the United States where AIDS was the leading cause of death among both men and women between the ages of twenty-five and forty-four. Drug abuse—sharing dirty needles—was by far the most common source of infection, accounting for more than three times as many cases as homosexual contact between men. While everyone in the black community knew someone—if not many people—who had died of AIDS, the disease retained an intense stigma that silenced discussion in most quarters, both public and private. Young mothers were dying without their children ever being told why; infected children themselves were dying without knowing the name of their illness.

Mayor John Daniels told me that, while the quality of daily life in black New Haven was certainly worse in the 1990s than when he was young, "opportunities are greater now." We spoke just a few days after his inauguration, and his confidence in the options available to black youth may have been, understandably, at a high-water mark. But Daniels's manner, his language—deliberate, modest, lawyerly—seemed to derive from another country, another America, a place with only the faintest relation to the barbaric, twilight world inhabited by inner-city children today. Truly, the distance between the childhood world of Daniels and his contemporaries—such as Warren Kimbro, with whom he once coached football—and "the dominant culture," as Kevin Houston called middle-class America, seems negligible when compared with the huge gulf that separates the ghetto from middle-class life today.

That gulf is perfectly apparent, of course, to those growing up on its far edge. At a drug rehabilitation center in western Connecticut, I talked with a sixteen-year-old boy from the projects of South Norwalk. He was a former cocaine dealer and mugger—he used to take the train to New Haven, he said, and stick up people there just to prove that he could do it on someone else's turf—and he had been convicted of ordering a shooting. He told me he was determined to stay for at least a year in the rehab center, where daily life was heavily regimented and the operating philosophy was behavior modification. "I got all that street in me," he explained. "I got to get it *all out*. I got to *talk* different." In the meantime, dialect aside, the boy spoke with a terrible, introspective gravity that suggested he already knew exactly how deep in him ran the roots he was proposing to tear up.

Few black teenagers have much historical perspective on their predicament. Even their parents are, in many cases, too young to remember the civil rights movement. In New Haven, only the middle-aged and elderly remember the Black Panthers, or the 1970 murder trial of Bobby Seale, when thousands demonstrated on the New Haven Green, or the nights of rioting that began on Congress Avenue in 1967. What all black kids do know, in their bones, is that racial inequality has always been the American rule, and that, for as long as they *can* remember, life for the poor has been getting harder: prices have gone up, but wages and welfare payments have not; the streets and the housing projects have gotten wildly more dangerous; and drugs and the drug trade have come to permeate everything. Many know, too, that life in middle-class neighborhoods is profoundly different from life in their own. Connecticut contains some of the nation's worst ghettos—Hartford, the state capital, is actually poorer than even basket cases like Newark and East Los Angeles—and yet it still manages to have the highest per capita income of any state. This is a contrast worthy of the bad old days in South Africa. I once taught in a black high school under apartheid in South Africa, and I rarely, if ever, saw there scenes any more desolate than Congress Avenue or Quinnipiac Terrace or the Elm Haven projects in Dixwell.

Newhallville is different. On a sunny winter morning, with its long rows of Victorian houses decked with sparkling snow, it is an unlikely-looking ghetto. The Mudhole and the two or three worst blocks of Winchester and Newhall avenues are unusual in Newhallville for their overt seediness and violence. And yet in the cramped apartments inside many of the large houses, poverty and drugs are pervasive, and the streets are dominated by the posses and their feuds. Older people are terrorized. A middle-aged resident told me, "When I was a kid, an adult saw us on the street, he'd say, 'What you kids doin'? You ain't got nothin' to do?' Nowadays, I walk down the street, I see a bunch of kids standing around, I'd be a *fool* to say something to them. They got *guns* under those coats." The owner of a Newhallville dry cleaner's told the *Register* that his business was in trouble because 60 percent of the clothes being dropped off now were never picked up; the drug dealers, he said, simply had too much ready cash to bother.

These are all small parts of what Warren Kimbro means when he says the drug trade is destroying a way of life. And though the police have rarely been popular in black communities, the situation has given rise to a near-unanimous sentiment in favor of more police action. Even the ex–Black Panther talks as if he would like to see martial law declared. A New Haven drug treatment administrator told me, "The middle class wants to see martial law after a hurricane. Well, there is the equivalent of a hurricane hitting some of these neighborhoods now."

The New Haven police shut down the Mudhole for a while with an operation they called Citizens and Police Against Criminal Transgression. CAPACT, which was introduced in 1988 to combat drug dealing, involved parking a manned police van twenty-four hours a day in a high-crime neighborhood and using it as a base for sweeps. In Newhallville, the CAPACT van was parked directly across Shelton Avenue from the Mudhole, making it impossible for Frank Black's crew to work there. When I stopped by the Mudhole one Saturday morning, the CAPACT van was there. A liquor store at the edge of the lot was doing a steady business. An elderly black man leaving the store, already quite drunk, spotted me and said, "You come up here this morning? You must be struggling for Jesus!" He gave a big laugh. He seemed to think I was a cop.

After I got to talking to a group of men gathered in front of the Shelton Avenue Social Club, and told them I was a reporter, they were all eager to tell me about how they had run off the young drug dealers. "*We're* the Mudhole gang!" bellowed Milton Click, a man in his sixties. "And I'm the mayor of the Mudhole!" Everybody in the group was over thirty, drunk, and ready to impugn the courage of the absent young dealers. The social club was also doing a steady business—dapper elderly men came and went past a sign that said MEMBERS ONLY. I had assumed that my companions on the sidewalk would not be welcome inside the club, but then Milton Click excused himself and went in. The main activity inside was gambling, somebody said—cards and numbers.

I headed across the street to talk to the policeman in the CAPACT van. I found him absorbed in a comic book. He seemed startled when I tapped on his window. CAPACT, according to police spokespeople, represented "community-based," as opposed to merely reactive, police work. The young officer I found at the Mudhole said he thought that the van and its related operations were "well accepted by the community," and that the neighborhood was far safer than it had been. "We still get shootings—we had one last night," he said. "But not every forty-five minutes, like it was before." Drug dealing was still going on two blocks away, he said, and would undoubtedly return to the Mudhole after CAPACT left, but nobody believed that CAPACT was the answer to the drug problem anyway. (CAPACT was, in fact, discontinued soon thereafter.)

The commander of CAPACT operations told me, in his downtown office, "We're just trying to give the public some one-on-one with the police." Over several months, however, during which I passed CAPACT vans in Newhallville and Dixwell dozens of times, I never saw a policeman talking to a resident. Once, I approached a CAPACT van parked outside the Elm Haven projects, intending to ask directions. I found I had interrupted a card game—all four players had had their backs to the street—and I was angrily interrogated for my trouble. Although Dixwell and Newhallville are completely black neighborhoods, every policeman I ever saw at a CAPACT post was white.

The New Haven Police Department was often accused by black activists of having its back turned, figuratively, to the African American community, a state of affairs symbolized by the downtown station, a mud-colored fortress that sits off by itself near the train station. (Its long, slitlike, black-glass windows make it look like a particularly sinister, high-tech riot helmet.) The department's Narcotics Enforcement Unit was, however, actually based for a time in Newhallville—inside a building of the old Winchester Repeating Arms plant. Much of the plant had been turned into an office complex called Science Park, designed to lure high-technology firms to New Haven. Science Park had itself been a source of community resentment; the complex had a number of high-tech tenants, but only 10 percent of the roughly one thousand jobs it provided had gone to Newhallville residents. The Narcotics Enforcement Unit had its headquarters inside the complex—far from the streets—mainly for security reasons. Most narcotics officers are plainclothes; many work undercover. It obviously wouldn't do to have these officers going in and out of the downtown station for anyone to see. The guarded gates at Science Park presented a less informative picture to their enemies.

Captain Rafael Garcia, who was then the head of the narcotics unit, was a big, plainspoken man. He believed that a major cause of the drug problem was "a lack of effective deterrents"—the fact that there was so little room in Connecticut's jails that most of the thousands of people convicted of drug offenses each year received light or suspended sentences. Captain Garcia had no faith in drug treatment—"We see the same druggies out here year after year." He didn't have much faith in interdiction, either. When I met him, he and his men had recently seized five pounds of cocaine, worth an estimated $100,000, in a raid on Orange Street, near Yale, but Captain Garcia was still pessimistic about the chances of reducing the drug problem in New Haven. "This is a billion-dollar industry," he said simply. The only good news on the local crime front, he said, was that muggings were down. As I prepared to leave his office, however, Captain Garcia asked where my car was parked. I said I was on foot, and he wanted to know my next destination. I mentioned an address on Shelton Avenue, and he and a fellow officer roared their disapproval. I would be lucky to get there, they said—a white man on foot in Newhallville. They offered me a ride. I declined—I was on my way to see Scott X, all of whose suspicions about me would be confirmed if I showed up in the car of a well-known policeman. I had to wonder, though, what Captain Garcia and his colleague would have said if muggings had been *up*.

Shortly before Christmas, I joined Captain Garcia and his men on a raid in the Franklin Street projects. Before we left the narcotics unit's warehouselike headquarters, he and a lieutenant briefed the raiding party, which consisted of a dozen men. The evening's targets, they said, were George Chapman, twenty-three, and his girlfriend, Virginia Ford, forty. The lieutenant, a powerfully built young man with a dark mustache, drew a plan of the apartment to be searched in red felt pen on a white marker board. The latest news from the department's informer was that Chapman had received a shipment of a half-pound of cocaine two hours earlier. "He should be bagging it at the kitchen table when we arrive," the lieutenant said. "The kitchen will be on our left as we come in. George is about five-eight. Virginia's kind of heavyset now. George might have a gun. He has been known to sell shotguns." Ford's children, we were told, might be in the apartment—a nine-year-old girl and a ten-year-old boy.

"You make a buy there?" one of the raiders asked.

"Yeah," said the lieutenant.

"What kind of bag?"

"Red with black lines."

Bulletproof vests were strapped on, weapons checked. One officer was carrying a shotgun; two others held a heavy gray battering ram. Except for the weapons (everyone but me had a handgun), we looked and sounded, I thought, like a parks-league softball team—lots of baseball caps, blue jeans, running shoes, low-key banter. One of the two black officers in the party was carrying a video camera. Our departure was delayed briefly by a round of Final Jeopardy on a desktop TV; everybody except the cameraman guessed the North American river that generates the most hydroelectricity wrong (it's the Columbia). Then we set off, heading out in a caravan of half a dozen unmarked cars. I rode with Captain Garcia, who brought up the rear in a souped-up Trans Am. As we snaked through New Haven, I had to hold my bulletproof vest away from my throat to keep from choking.

Upon arriving at the Franklin Street projects, the raiders all parked and jumped from the cars and ran headlong toward a dark brick building. Two officers peeled away to watch the front windows of Virginia Ford's second-floor apartment, two more ran to make sure that no guns, drugs, or suspects came out the back windows, and the rest of the squad charged up a stinking, pitch-black flight of stairs. The men with the battering ram went first; Captain Garcia and I were at the back of the column. The battering ram made a terrifying noise as it smashed into the apartment door, echoing fearfully in the dark, narrow hallway. Three smashes and the door was down. The police poured into the apartment, shouting, their guns drawn. By the time I got inside, most of them were in one of the bedrooms, loudly subduing someone. A shocked-looking black woman was sitting on a couch in the living room clutching two crying children. A television was playing. Next to the couch was a fully deco-rated Christmas tree, with colored lights glowing and presents stacked be-neath. Apparently, the children and their mother—and perhaps the person now being handcuffed in the bedroom—had been watching TV when the door next to the set was smashed down. Now the police cameraman stood in the shattered doorway filming.

A knot of officers emerged from the bedroom with a slight young black man in handcuffs. The man looked frightened, yet not intimidated. He was saying, "I'm not George Chapman, I'm George *Brown*." The officers sat him on the couch. The woman, who quietly identified herself as Virginia Ford, rose from the couch and, with an arm around each of her children, turned them and stood facing into the Christmas tree. She apparently did not want their faces on police videotape. The childrens' thin backs shook with sobs.

Meanwhile, the police were turning the apartment inside out. In a kitchen cupboard decorated with a bumper sticker advising CAUTION: JESUS CHRIST CAN WATCH YOUR LIFE they found dozens of small red bags of white powder. The bags had black lines on them, and the powder field-tested positive for cocaine. In the same cupboard they found a bag full of grimy cash—three or four hundred dollars in fives, tens, and twenties. The cash and the cocaine were placed in an aluminum evidence suitcase, along with a jar of lactose and various pieces of identification. "*Somebody* around here is named George Chapman," an officer muttered, showing me a driver's license in that name.

Virginia Ford asked to see a search warrant, which she studied by the light of the Christmas tree. George asked to see it, too, and it was held up for his in-spection. When an officer waved a bag of white powder in front of the camera and said he had found it in George's pocket, George turned to the camera and said that it had not been in his pocket.

Although one or two officers invited me to notice what a dirty, unkempt place we were in, I found it hard to remember what the apartment had looked like before ten minutes of searching had rendered it a wreck. One policeman pointed to a box standing on end in the kitchen. The picture on its side showed a toy Chevy Corvette the size of a small refrigerator. "You know how much one of these costs?" he asked me. "I know, because I just tried to buy one for *my* kid for Christmas. A hundred and twenty-nine dollars, that's how much. I couldn't afford one!"

Captain Garcia said, "Virginia, you got anybody can take care of your kids? Neighbor? Otherwise, we're gonna have to get CYS"—Connecticut's Depart-ment of Children and Youth Services—"to take 'em. Because you're goin' downtown, too."

"I don't want nobody takin' my kids," Ford said.

Garcia pointed out that they would need some clothes in any case, and I took the children back to their rooms to pack. The little girl, Shaneesha, stuffed a bag full of pink jeans, pink socks, and pink sneakers, and pulled on a pink jacket. I noticed a hamster on her dresser. It was chewing frantically on the bars of its cage. Shaneesha said her hamster's name was Pepsi. I suggested it should be fed before we left, and she ran to the kitchen for fresh lettuce. Her brother, Maurice, packed a Nintendo game and a pair of pajamas. He was a tall, thin boy with a beautiful face. Large tears rolled down his cheeks. I thought about telling him I was not a policeman, but decided against it. As far as Maurice was concerned, I was a policeman. He said nothing to me—not a word. On the walls of his room were posters of Magic Johnson and Babe Ruth.

Back out in the living room, George was snarling, "I'll do all my time before I help youse." He meant he would not answer any police questions. He grinned defiantly, then noticed the black officer with the video camera and stopped smiling. "You the worst of 'em," he sneered.

A neighbor had arrived to take charge of Maurice and Shaneesha. Virginia and George were led outside. A cat had already fled through the broken door, but there was a puppy in a box in the kitchen who was clearly not ready to survive outdoors. The officer who had marveled at the toy Corvette put out water for the puppy. I turned off the television. Then the last of us left the apartment, and Captain Garcia began nailing the door back in place. That was necessary, he explained to me, to prevent looting.

I hoped the apartment would be reopened before the puppy and the hamster starved.

Back at headquarters, Captain Garcia started erasing the diagram of Virginia Ford's apartment with Windex. "Bye, George," he said. "This wasn't his first time, won't be his last. Tonight was the hundred and thirty-fourth search warrant, or maybe the hundred and thirty-fifth, we served this year."

That night's raid was part of a series of raids that the police department was calling Operation Scrooge. Although this holiday-season blitzkrieg had already resulted in the arrests of seventy-one street-level dealers, the New Haven chief of police told the *Register* the following week that he himself had no illusions. Operation Scrooge would have little lasting impact, he said, on the city's drug problem.

"St. Raphael's dissed me," Terry says. "They said I wasn't whatchacallit."

"Qualified?"

"Yeah."

The dishwashing job at the hospital had sounded like a sure thing.

"But I ain't worried," Terry says. "There's another job washing dishes, in an old people's home in Hamden, making six-fifty an hour. If I get it, then I be stackin', and when I see the niggers on the street, and they want me to be sellin' again, I can tell them I *am* sellin', that's where my money come from, and they leave me alone."

We are setting off by car from the house on Wallace Street. It's a bright, unseasonably warm day in late January. I ask Terry about some marks on his neck and cheeks—they look like bruises or old burns.

"Hickeys," he says. "Lakeeda don't trust me no more, so she put these on me. She goin' crazy."

We pass the Franklin Street projects, where the midday drug trade appears heavy. "State checks come yesterday," Terry says.

I ask if he knows George Chapman.

He says he doesn't know anybody in this part of town. "The Ville, that's me," he says, without enthusiasm. "And the Island."

Terry seems sulky and preoccupied. "Lakeeda got a lawsuit on Monday," he says. "She fell down in a bus or something. So she went and bought me three outfits, plus a ring, and some K-Swiss sneakers, red ones, just like I wanted. But I didn't call her for three days, so she took it all back."

We pass beneath Interstate 91, then head downtown.

"If I get shot downtown, I'll sue," Terry suddenly announces. "I'll sue the city. Those guys who got shot at the courthouse, they're suing. If I get shot in the mall, I'll sue the mall. I'll sue them for my safety."

We pass a big, well-dressed black woman walking with a child. Terry waves. "I know her," he says. "I tried to get with her."

"She's too old for you!"

"She just look old," Terry says. He drums on his knees. "All I need is a Macy's charge card." He sighs, then says, "Where you get this car?"

It's a rental. Normally, Terry makes an immediate critical appraisal of whatever car I show up in. His distractedness today has delayed his assessment. Now he turns and studies the backseat. "I got *arrested* in this car," he declares. "The big boys rent cars for undercover, and I was in this same one. Same colors, same smell—everything." Somehow, the memory doesn't sound altogether awful. "I was handcuffed, like sitting on my hands," he says. "People could look at me, and I couldn't do nothing." It still doesn't sound all bad. Terry's tone is dreamy, as if his arrest might have been a rendezvous with his own fate, rather than a nasty event in a world of free will.

I ask what he will do with the clipping from the *Register* about his arrest.

"Nothin'," he says.

How did it feel, seeing it again?

"That was the worst day in my life," he says emphatically. "My name in the paper, my family all seein' it." After a minute, he adds, "That's the bad thing about havin' a big family. You can't do what you want."

We go by Body and Sole, the sporting goods store with the sign in the window saying IF YOU DEAL DRUGS, WE DON'T WANT YOUR BUSINESS! Terry says he would never shop in there. "That's insulting the customer, isn't it?"

We stop for lunch at a large, fern-filled restaurant near Yale. Terry orders Buffalo chicken wings, his favorite dish, but then pronounces the wings he is served inferior to those at Jimmies, where he used to work as a busboy, and where we often eat. These smell funny, he says. I notice him, between bites, giving a quick raised-fist salute to someone behind me. I look back and see no likely recipient of this greeting; the restaurant is full of Yale students and their parents. I ask who's here. "My boy," Terry says. He nods toward the kitchen. Framed by a pass-through, a black dishwasher toils above a sink. He looks to be in his late twenties—not exactly a "boy"—but he probably is, it strikes me, a peer of Terry's in the sense that he and Terry compete in the same labor market, working nonunion, high-turnover restaurant jobs for the same sort of pay. (In the restaurants where we eat, Terry routinely asks for job applications.)

Terry spots in my bag a paperback copy of *The Autobiography of Malcolm X.* He asks to see it, and for the next several minutes he is completely absorbed in a chapter called "Hustler." This is his favorite part of the book, he says. At one point, he bursts out laughing. I ask what's funny. Terry looks embarrassed. "He says here this other guy was a 'beefy-faced Irishman.'"

After Terry finishes reading, I ask where he has seen *The Autobiography* before.

"In Scott's shop," he says. "But I only read this page"—he points to the first page of "Hustler"—"not the whole thing." He points to the facing page. The rest of the book, which culminates in Malcolm X's political awakening and conversion to Islam ("Hustler" is about his early days as a petty thief and gangster in Harlem), Terry hasn't read yet. "When I was little, I *loved* to read," he says. "But now I just do it if I don't got nothin' else to do."

After lunch, we head for the convalescent home in Hamden where Terry hopes to find a job. En route, while we're stopped at a light in Newhallville, Terry suddenly makes a strange noise in his throat. I follow his gaze, which is baleful, across the intersection, and there see three black teenage boys climbing out of a black, late-model Mercedes-Benz with smoked windows.

"That's the Read Street boys. Little crew works over by the Mudhole. That guy who was driving, he's fifteen years old and he got another car, a Jaguar, back home in his garage. Other two both got cars, too. That coulda been *me*."

The Read Street boys, who radiate youthful confidence and criminal menace at sixty yards, vanish into a house. I drive us out of Newhallville, into the shopping mall wilderness of Hamden.

"I'd like to be a cop," Terry murmurs. "It sounds like braggin', but I think I'd be good, because I know what time it is. I wouldn't be crooked. At least, I don't think I would be. I'd just clean up the town. They'd have to kill me to stop me, because they couldn't pay me off."

Would he arrest his friends?

"Anybody who's out there."

Frank?

Terry gives a short laugh. "Frank's in jail now," he says. "That's what his girlfriend say. His probation officer violated him."

I'm half relieved, on Terry's account, to hear it. But when I mention that, in any case, the police are still camped out at the Mudhole, Terry says, "Things get going in the Mudhole again, I know I'll want to be back in it."

The route to the convalescent home is long and complicated, but Terry directs me easily through sprawling hillside suburbs. As we start up a walkway to the home's front entrance, Terry turns to me and asks, "How's my hair? Is it all peazy?"

I don't know what "peazy" means (or how to spell it). I tell Terry his hair looks fine. But once we're inside the building, which is hushed and clean and pastel, Terry does look incongruous, with his cheap bomber jacket and high-low haircut—and black skin. For the first time in the months we've spent together, I see Terry caught in the alien light beam of racial self-consciousness. He has always fended off my questions on the subject—yes, of course he has white friends; no, he doesn't mean anything special by the word "nigger"; nor does he mean anything in particular when he claims, as he occasionally does, to have "good hair"—and he may, in fact, *not* be feeling especially strange here in this convalescent-home corridor, where the white woman behind the counter certainly seems unfazed by his halting request for a job application form. But I see his whole identity under siege: his language, appearance, manners, culture—his humanity itself—viewed skeptically by every doctor, nurse, secretary, or shuffling white-haired resident who passes. And Terry, I think, can hardly be unaware of the deep estrangement that exists between him and white Americans, of the profound "twoness," as W.E.B. Du Bois called it, of being a black American.

We sit together on a couch, laboring over the application form. As offhandedly as I can manage, I ask, "You sure you want to work here?"

"In the kitchen," Terry says, and he gives me a wry look that says that, although there may be no black people in sight, there must be some working in the kitchen. Under POSITION SOUGHT he writes, with some spelling help, "dietary." He claims to be eighteen years old; he makes up a Social Security number. For an employer reference, he ignores my suggestion that he list Scott X and writes in the name of a friend's mother, who, he says, owns a hardware store in Dixwell. "She'll cover for me," Terry whispers. "She's like my aunt." I find myself wondering if his decision not to list Scott X has anything to do with a Star of David I can see hanging on the corridor wall.

On the way back to New Haven, I ask Terry how he plans to travel to work if he gets the job at the convalescent home.

"Bus, and by foot," he says.

How long will that take?

"Two hours, probably. It's a long walk."

Although it's common knowledge in the inner city that even the unskilled jobs have moved to the suburbs, this commute sounds to me prohibitive. I doubted before that Terry would get this job; now I doubt he'll keep it if he does get it.

As if reading my thoughts, he says, "I *gotta* get this job. It's only two weeks to Valentine's Day."

Valentine's Day?

"I gotta get flowers for my mother, for my grandmother, and for Lakeeda," Terry says. "And maybe for a couple of my sneak tips. And candy. Maybe some jewelry. All that cost crazy dollars. Where am I gonna get that kind of money if I don't got a job?" He pauses, then says, "If I don't got a job, you *know* where I'm gonna get it."

Terry was hired as a dishwasher at the convalescent home in Hamden. His first paycheck was late, though, because of his phony Social Security number, and on Valentine's Day he had nothing to give his mother, his grandmother, or Lakeeda. The commute did prove grueling, particularly after Terry was moved to a split shift, which meant two round trips, or nearly eight hours' travel, a day. He soon quit.

Lakeeda did receive flowers and candy on Valentine's Day—from an eighteen-year-old drug dealer. The flowers, she later estimated, were worth about a hundred dollars, and the box of chocolates, she told me, weighed three and a half pounds. A few days later, for her nineteenth birthday, the same young man gave her an expensive gold ring. Lakeeda said she refused it.

On the night of her birthday, a quarrel with her grandmother drove Lakeeda out of her mother's apartment. She and Tyrone moved in with Terry, Anjelica, and Buddy on Wallace Street. She and Anjelica shared the baby-sitting, and both went to school. Terry resumed job-hunting. Nothing more was heard from Lakeeda's suitor. At the end of February, however, his sister, who was a friend of Lakeeda's, invited her to their family's house. Terry assented to the visit, and even walked Lakeeda and Tyrone halfway there. But then he proceeded to the Mudhole where he found Frank Black, who had been released from jail. Frank had a bottle of brandy. He and Terry got drunk.

When Terry returned to Wallace Street late that night, he was jealous and belligerent. He woke Lakeeda and accused her of planning to leave him. His shouting woke Tyrone. Terry demanded to know if Tyrone still loved him or if he now loved Lakeeda's friend's brother, the drug dealer, instead. His shouting woke Anjelica. When she emerged from her bedroom, she found Terry on the telephone. He was talking to a friend, and he was swearing freely. Anjelica ordered Terry not to swear on her telephone. Terry said, "Fuck your phone," and he yanked the cord from the wall. Anjelica plugged the phone back in and called the police.

When the police arrived, Terry fled out the back door. He hid under a car in the alley. After the police had passed his hiding place, he crept back to the house. Anjelica would not let him in. He pounded on the door and cried, "Don't do this to me." The police returned and arrested him, charging him with domestic violence. Terry spent the night in jail.

I arrived at the house on Wallace Street the next day around noon. Lakeeda and Tyrone were asleep. Anjelica was at the courthouse, where Terry was being arraigned. Lakeeda wanted to go with me to the courthouse, but she was afraid to leave the apartment before the mail arrived. Anjelica's state check would come today, Lakeeda explained, and the Puerto Rican people upstairs would steal it if she weren't there to collect it. The woman's boyfriend had finally gotten out of jail, and he had already broken into Anjelica's apartment once, stealing a radio.

I drove to the courthouse. Anjelica, it turned out, had just dropped the charges, and Terry had just been released, on the condition that he immediately move from his mother's apartment to a halfway house for young male offenders. The three of us returned to Wallace Street to collect Terry's things. He and Lakeeda greeted each other with a long, wordless embrace. Although Terry was sleepy and hungry and rushed, he found the time and energy to tell his mother and Lakeeda about how, when he had arrived at the jail the night before, he had entertained the guards and the other inmates, several of whom he knew. "I was *cuttin'*, and they was *laughin'*." One of the guards on duty was "a cousin," Terry said, who had let him make a number of phone calls, including one to his father. His father had declined to come downtown and bail him out.

The phone rang. It was Terry's paternal grandmother. Terry talked to her—or, rather, he listened and every now and then said quietly, "Now, don't say that, Grandma. Please don't say that." Apparently, she had heard from her son about Terry's night in jail. By the time Terry got off the phone, he was in tears. He disappeared into the bathroom. Anjelica, Lakeeda, and I waited awkwardly, saying nothing. It seemed as if, between Terry and his mother and Lakeeda, the events of the night before were forgotten already. Even the telephone looked undamaged.

Terry emerged from the bathroom and started throwing clothes in a bag. He kept glancing, though, at Tyrone, who lay asleep on his bed. Finally, Terry muttered to Lakeeda, "I can't leave this house without saying good-bye to this nigger. Wake him up." Lakeeda shook Tyrone, who opened his eyes and, when he saw Terry, sleepily raised his arms. Terry threw himself on the bed, put his arms around Tyrone, and lay there silently for several minutes, with Tyrone's fat little arms around his neck. At last, he rose, and we headed out to my car—I had agreed to drive him to the halfway house. By then, Terry, Anjelica, and Lakeeda were all crying.

Terry stayed two weeks at the halfway house, ostensibly job-hunting but often going home to see Lakeeda. Shortly after he moved back to the apartment on Wallace Street, however, Lakeeda and Anjelica quarreled over baby-sitting duties, and Lakeeda and Tyrone moved back to Lakeeda's mother's house. A few days later, Anjelica threw Terry out, flinging his clothes into the street. The reasons for his eviction were never made clear to me, though everyone I asked emphasized the fact that Anjelica had started freebasing cocaine again. The apartment on Wallace Street certainly became a wilder place. Whenever I called or visited, there seemed to be a party going on. I grew worried about Buddy. So did Beulah. Lakeeda's mother told me that she was thinking about "calling the state on" Anjelica—urging the child welfare people to remove Buddy from her care.

By this time, Lakeeda and Tyrone had moved into "emergency housing"—a first step toward receiving their own place from the state. Emergency housing consisted, in this case, of a bare one-bedroom apartment in a tough neighborhood—the Hill, near Congress Avenue. Terry began staying there, too, even though his presence endangered Lakeeda's housing benefits. He had to come and go carefully, and if there was a knock at the door he hid in the bedroom. It was archetypal welfare family life—Lakeeda was "married to the state," as activists say, while Terry, because of his poverty, became a skulking shadow. The state, in this view, is a jealous mate, determined to marginalize all rivals. Certainly, all metaphors aside, welfare eligibility rules have had a devastating impact on poor black families over several generations, and Terry seemed to be slipping all too easily into the role of the marginalized male. Lakeeda's mother now took care of Tyrone while Lakeeda went to school. Terry began spending his days in the Mudhole. He wasn't dealing drugs, Lakeeda said—mostly because the police were still camped out there. "But he *shouldn't* deal drugs," she told me. "Some people can do it without getting caught. Other people just get caught. Terry is one of those people who will always get caught. So he shouldn't even try it."

Terry, too, insisted he was "just hanging out." Frank was around. When they could scrounge a bottle, they drank it together. It sounded like they were forming a youth wing to Milton Click's bedraggled "Mudhole Gang." Of course, the street dealers of the modern cocaine boom and the "streetcorner men" who have haunted black urban neighborhoods for more than a century exist in a continuum. Both have abandoned the world of conventional achievement. Both have ready to hand the consolations of street life, where failure in the greater world tends to be forgiven and forgotten. Many of today's young hustlers are surely tomorrow's drunkards and addicts.

In April, Lakeeda threw Terry out. Beulah offered to take him in, but not on terms he could accept. Terry was now homeless—Out There again. The circle of love that he had hoped to draw around himself was broken. In a moment of clear-minded pique, he informed Anjelica's welfare caseworker that he was no longer living with his mother—causing a reduction in her benefits. In dire need of money, Terry went to see the leader of a drug crew on Winchester Avenue who had often tried to recruit him. He took a small consignment of cocaine—two hundred dollars' worth, already bagged—and went to a quiet spot on the railroad tracks behind the Mudhole. He managed to pump off all the coke that evening, netting four hundred dollars, but on the way back to pay his supplier he was accosted by three young men who took not just the cash but his jacket, shoes, and trousers. Half naked, Terry made his way to his Aunt Darla's room. Humiliated, he did not try to get in touch with the Winchester Avenue crew to explain what had happened to their money. They could be expected to assume the worst—that he had stolen it—and to come looking for him. Terry was now on the run.

I watched all this from a distance, talking by telephone with Beulah, Lakeeda, Lakeeda's mother, Anjelica, and, when I could reach him, Terry. I thought I had completed my street reporting about Terry's life, and I was trying to stay out of New Haven. As Terry's situation got more desperate, however, I felt drawn back in. He was sixteen years old, his life was careering out of control—he *didn't* know what time it was—and the adults around him all seemed to be throwing up their hands. Now his life was in danger. He clearly had to get out of New Haven. I suggested he come stay with me as a temporary measure. He said he might.

A counselor at the Q House had suggested that Terry go into the Job Corps. There was a residential center in Massachusetts, she said, where he could learn a trade while earning a high-school-equivalency diploma. When I first heard the idea, I thought it sounded unpromising. Terry would undoubtedly be homesick. The baleful aspects of the inner-city streets would certainly extend to a Job Corps center, perhaps in an even more concentrated form than in New Haven. Moreover, "learning a trade" sounded Victorian, like an abandonment of all hope of higher education. Now, however, I thought the idea had merit. At least, it would get him out of New Haven. And Terry professed himself interested. He would like to learn masonry, he said.

I tried to expedite his application. Progress was infuriatingly slow. The recruiter who took the application, which had to include a guardian's signature (Beulah filled in for Anjelica, who could not be found) and a report from Terry's probation officer, held on to it for weeks. It seemed he was a "subcontractor," who was awaiting payment for an earlier batch of applications before he turned in the next ones. Then the probation officer's report was deemed inadequate. Then the mere fact that Terry was *on* probation was given as a reason to deny his application. The public defender who had represented Terry offered to try to get his probation terminated. She needed authorization from Terry, though, and he could not seem to get to her office during business hours to sign the papers. He had by now moved back into the apartment on Wallace Street, and Anjelica would presumably be able to start collecting money for him from the state again. But he was rarely there, and Anjelica never seemed to know where he was. In the Mudhole, she guessed. She was worried sick he was going to get shot.

The Job Corps prospect abruptly receded one night in late April, when Terry was arrested and charged with conspiracy to distribute cocaine. He was picked up not in the Mudhole but on the Hill, along with fourteen other young black males, during a police raid on two houses on Arch Street. Police spokespeople called the suspects the Arch Street Gang. The raid was the lead story in the *Register* the next day; a brief wire-service story even appeared in *The New York Times*. The police said they found quantities of cocaine and cash, a twelve-gauge shotgun, a loaded .44-caliber Magnum handgun, beepers, and apparent records of drug transactions. Terry, along with several other suspects, was on the porch of one of the houses when the police arrived. He had no drugs, cash, weapons, or other incriminating evidence on him, but two of the arresting officers recognized him from the Mudhole, and he was accused of acting as a lookout for the Arch Street Gang. Terry said he had merely been visiting a girl who lived across the street, had noticed a friend of his among the boys on the porch, and had gone over to chat only minutes before the raid occurred.

Terry's bond was set at $25,000. Because Anjelica was in New York City for the weekend, it fell to Beulah to bail him out. Terry assumed that his grandmother would be too ashamed to come to the jail, but she surprised him, and he was released that night on a promise to appear, with Beulah's house offered as collateral. Terry's freedom while awaiting trial was precarious, though. He could "be violated," as the saying goes, at any time by his probation officer, because of his new arrest, and compelled to start serving the one-year term of his suspended sentence. He made several court appearances in May. His lawyer did not show up for any of them—the public defender's office had been swamped by the fifteen simultaneous arrests and needed more time to sort out the cases—and continuances were granted. But Anjelica never showed up in court, either, and on the third occasion the prosecutor asked that Terry be locked up as a minor without parental supervision. Terry's pleas that his mother was at school persuaded the judge not to jail him then and there, but prison seemed to be closing in on him from all sides. Conspiracy to distribute cocaine is a felony, and the prosecutor was offering Terry a seven-year sentence, suspended after three and a half years, in exchange for a guilty plea.

"I ain't *guilty*," Terry told me. "So I don't want to say I am." In many ways, though, Terry seemed to be preparing himself for jail. Just as he had done after his domestic violence arrest, he bragged about the figure he had cut in jail. "I was all matchin' when I went downtown," he said. "Green shoes, green hat, green-and-white sweatsuit." It was as if the swagger imperative of the jailhouse were already overcoming his natural modesty.

And the outfit Terry wore one morning in late May when I turned up on Wallace Street did nothing to belie this impression. It included not only the green shoes (the Bally suedes from the high old days in the Mudhole, now heavily worn) and the green hat (a bright, high-crowned, short-billed affair in a style once popular among Rastafarians—when worn sideways, as Terry wore it, the hat spoke of a scary, low-rent decadence) and a matching kelly green turtleneck, but also two gold tooth caps and a large imitation-gold chain. I had never seen Terry dressed anything like this before. He didn't even *like* gold chains. It was as if he had resolved to fulfill some grotesque expectation of him, perhaps hoping to disarm the amorphous authority/predator he could feel bearing down on him. One of the tooth caps even had a dollar sign carved into it.

Over lunch at Jimmies, Terry informed me that he had a new girlfriend. She was in her twenties, he said, and had a three-year-old son. "She nice, and she got a *blazin'* job. She at the post office, but she ain't workin' now, because she broke her kneecap. She got a lawsuit, too." Still, Terry had not forgotten Tyrone. "If I go to jail, Tyrone gonna *miss* me," he said. Then he changed the subject.

In order to eat, Terry had to remove his tooth caps. He showed them to me in an outstretched hand, watching me closely. They were disgusting little objects, and it occurred to me that Terry might have gotten himself all decked out today as a way of testing me, the coat-and-tie white man who professed to be his friend. All I really cared about now, though, was keeping him out of jail. After lunch, we went to see his probation officer. Later, we went to see his lawyer. I noticed that Terry took out the tooth caps and tucked the fake-gold chain inside his shirt before each meeting. Both his lawyer and his probation officer were serious young white women with little patience for inner-city display. And when the lawyer told Terry that, if he wanted to convince a judge he was not a drug dealer he had better find a job immediately, Terry took her point. After we left the courthouse, he had me drop him near a McDonald's where he thought he might find work.

NINE

While Terry's case on the conspiracy charges meandered toward trial, an article I had written about him and his family appeared in *The New Yorker.* This released me, as I saw it, from some of my journalistic obligation not to meddle in his affairs—an obligation I had never entirely honored anyway.

His court case wasn't looking good. He had been assigned a new lawyer, who told me that she thought he should take the seven-year sentence the prosecutor was offering. She could insure that he would be sent to a terrific youth facility, she said, in a little town not too far from New Haven, and that he would be released within three years. I asked her how Terry felt about this deal. She said that, because her office was in Bridgeport, she and he hadn't met—or spoken—yet. When I asked her for directions to the youth facility, so that Terry and I could check it out, it emerged that she had never been there and wasn't sure exactly where it was. When I said I believed Terry's claim that he was not involved with the Arch Street Gang, she politely questioned my credulity. The prosecution's evidence was strong, she said. She acknowledged that Terry had had no drugs, money, or weapons on him when he was arrested, but, she said, she had seen him on a police videotape.

I asked her to describe the videotape.

She did. It was clearly a videotape of Terry's arrest.

I pointed out that nobody was disputing that he had been arrested. The question was whether Terry appeared on a *surveillance* videotape. In any case, I said, how could she have recognized him on the police videotape if she had never met him?

A few weeks later, I went with Terry to the New Haven courthouse for a hearing on his case. We hung around in the hallways for half the morning while his lawyer bustled back and forth, attending to a hundred different things. Finally, she stopped and told Terry that he had been granted a continuance for four more weeks and could leave. I hurried after her to find out more details, and was told that the continuance was to give the court the time to get a "psychological profile" of Terry. She hadn't mentioned any "psychological profile" to him, and no arrangements for such a thing actually looked like they were going to be made.

That was when I took it upon myself to find Terry another lawyer. An experienced criminal defense attorney in New Haven agreed to take his case pro bono. Soon, Terry was offered an extraordinary deal by the prosecutor: pass a drug test, and the charges would be dismissed. The deal seemed extraordinary partly because there had never been any suggestion that Terry *used* drugs, and partly because it was so generous. Terry took the test, passed it, and the charges were dropped.

When I thanked the pro bono attorney, exclaiming over his brilliance, he insisted it was no big thing. The case was just a little weak, and a little old, and he had a little credibility around the courthouse, that was all. Terry's previous lawyer had done the right thing, he said, by getting a series of continuances, letting time pass, and he had just come in and finished it off. He hadn't looked any harder at the evidence than his predecessor had, or got to know Terry any better than she had.

That, I thought, might all be so. But the court-appointed lawyer had been ready to plead him out, consigning him to three years of incarceration for a crime he probably hadn't committed. This, moreover, was standard treatment for kids like Terry—kids who had the bad luck to be born poor and black. Anybody who wondered why most black Americans were still skeptical about the justice system could have learned something here.

Terry was, of course, relieved. And yet he didn't seem terribly interested in the details of his case. It was a process over which he clearly felt he had no influence. Deals were made, up above his head somewhere, settling his fate. These were deals between adults—white adults, mainly—and he just found out afterward what was in store for him. My advocacy, such as it was, didn't change his relationship to the process.

But I was flush now with interventionist fervor. I took Terry to get a pair of glasses, and lectured him about not losing them. I tried to get him registered in school, ran into a bureaucratic wall, and then, over the course of a couple of weeks, with the help of his new girlfriend, Yvette, bulled through it. We finally got him into Hillhouse High. Again, I got the impression that without a noisy white adult on his side, Terry would have been out of luck.

It was still early fall, so Terry looked set for the school year. He was now living with Yvette—a wry, fast-talking, no-nonsense young woman—and her son and her mother in Fair Haven, in a household that seemed eminently calm and stable. It seemed like a good time for me to withdraw.

A couple of months later, I checked back in—and learned that things had gone sour. Yvette said she rarely saw Terry. He had quit school, she said, after a few weeks. She had enrolled him in night school, but he had also quit that. "His mother's back using that stuff, real strong," Yvette said. "And Terry, he want to stay *out* in the street. Won't even come home to change his clothes and take a bath. Like he gonna miss something. Only thing he gonna miss is a bullet, or seein' his name in the paper. Ten o'clock, he wake up, ten-ten he out the door—runnin' to the Mudhole or wherever." Yvette was disgusted. She was also pregnant. She had no advice about how I might contact Terry. She hadn't seen him in a week. I decided not to ask her if he still had his glasses.

I tried to keep in touch. Terry spent the spring dealing cocaine and marijuana with Frank out of an old house across from the Mudhole. He bought a couple of cars. The first one, an old Pontiac, he wrecked. The second one, an old Chevy station wagon, Frank totaled when he got drunk and rammed it into a church on Shelton Avenue. Somehow the two of them managed to stay out of jail.

Yvette and Terry's daughter, Latifah, was born in July. Terry seemed thrilled to be a father. He stopped dealing, and tried to get a job through his grandfather at Simkins Industries, but ended up boxing bagels for $6.30 an hour at a bakery near the Franklin Street projects.

I went to New Haven to meet Latifah. Yvette and Terry, who seemed to be back on terms, showed her off proudly. She looked like Beulah, I thought. Terry had a flashy new haircut—shaved on the sides, boxed on top, with a lightning bolt on one side and two thin parallel strips of hair running all the way around his chin. I was surprised that he had enough beard to grow such a thing. "I'm eighteen now, Mr. Bill," he said.

I stopped in to see Anjelica, who seemed unusually full of energy. She went to the store and came back with a big bag of pork chops, which she began busily breading and frying. I'd heard that Yvette and Anjelica were feuding, but Anjelica denied being jealous of Yvette's relationship with Terry—"I don't gotta be jealous of some fuckin' kid." Yvette had told me that Terry couldn't even let his mother know where he was working, for fear that if she got mad at him she might call his boss and say something crazy and get him fired. But Anjelica seemed to know quite well where Terry was working. He sometimes had her call his boss with a story, she said, when he didn't want to go to work. And she didn't mind being a grandmother so much after all, she said. Latifah was *cute.*

Terry, on an impulse, came back to New York with me. On the train, a golfer tossed his clubs into the overhead luggage rack, then had to scramble to keep the clubs from sliding out of their bag onto a woman seated below. Terry watched, wide-eyed, and said, "That lady almost had herself a good suit—a *law* suit."

New York that night seemed to get on his nerves. "I don't like it," he announced. "Too much walking. Too many freaky things be happening. Even the M & Ms ain't never fresh here. They old. I like 'em *fresh.*" He professed himself shocked not to be able to find the *New Haven Register* on a newsstand. We retreated to my apartment, where Terry whipped up some homemade onion dip and we watched *New Jack City* on video. He had seen *New Jack City* more times than he could count. What he liked about it, he said, was that there were no good guys in it. In the film Wesley Snipes plays a successful drug dealer who becomes power-mad and paranoid. The moral, according to Terry: "This is what happens to you when you get too much like Scarface." I went to bed. Terry watched the video again. In the morning, when I got up, he was sleeping with his face two feet from the TV screen, while *New Jack City* played for the fourth time.

He was interested again in Job Corps, Terry told me. He was no longer on probation, and he was now convinced that, to get out of the drug trade for good and to finish high school, he needed to leave New Haven. I was happy to hear it, and happy to help with another round of applications. Again, though, it seemed absurdly difficult to get the paperwork in order. The recruiter managed to lose Terry's birth certificate, and then seemed to do everything in slow motion. I started to wonder if he was waiting for a bribe. I made calls, wrote letters, and issued unpersuasive threats to expose the incompetence of the Job Corps bureaucracy with an article about Terry's experience. The system's wheels ground along at their own oblivious pace. Finally, late in the year, Terry was accepted by a Job Corps center in Grafton, Massachusetts.

He claimed to be elated. A week before he was scheduled to leave New Haven, however, Yvette reported that Terry was on the verge of blowing it; he was Out There again, raising hell with Frank. "He just wanna be back in the street while he can, say good-bye to all them niggers," she said angrily. "Frank and them, they tell him, 'You ain't goin' *nowhere.*' And if something happen this week, they gonna be right. Frank and them *hate* to see Terry try to make something of himself. If they don't see him around the Mudhole, they always be asking me, 'Where Terry at? He think he too good for us now?'" Yvette thought Anjelica, too, might try to sabotage Terry's departure. "Just before it's time for him to go, she'll throw him in the street or something, make him miss the bus."

Terry got to Grafton in one piece, and then seemed to settle quickly into the routine there, earning, he told me in a phone call, two "certificates" almost immediately. He'd chosen building and apartment maintenance as his first course of study, he said, with masonry to follow. The other boys were all from different towns, he said, so there were no posses at the center. "Everybody's kind of on their owns." I thought it sounded lonely—particularly after I heard that all of Terry's clothes had been stolen during his first week. "I mean *every-*

thing," Yvette said. "Even underclothes. All of it new, and every little thing with his name on it, like they told us to do." Worst of all, somehow, was Terry's suspicion that the thief was not another student at the center but a teacher.

The siren call of the New Haven streets rose, meanwhile, to a new pitch. A few weeks after he got to Grafton, Terry told me, he called Frank to see how he was doing, and Frank promptly offered him two thousand dollars "to shoot a guy he's beefing with." Frank reasoned that since Terry wasn't living in New Haven anymore it would be easy for him to shoot somebody there and get away with it. Terry didn't sound tempted. He did sound broke, though—Anjelica was apparently not sending him his share of their welfare benefits. I offered to put together a care package. Terry asked for candy (*fresh* M & Ms, if New York had any), packets of Kool-Aid, and rap magazines. I should wait till after New Year's to send it, though, he said, because the center shut down for the holidays. He had a job lined up in a New Haven restaurant for the two weeks he would be home.

But Terry never made it back to Grafton. He and Yvette had a fight on New Year's Eve, he stormed off, and then, according to an administrator at the Grafton center, he "AWOLed out of the program" by not returning on time. He could apply for readmission in six months, the administrator said, with zero enthusiasm. Yvette, as was her wont, blamed Anjelica. "Terry had nobody to support him," she said. "His mother was always saying she would give him things, but she never did. '*Yvette's* your mother now,' she told him. So, when he couldn't come to me, he had no support at all."

I happened to get this news while giving a lecture at a prep school near New Haven—a speech that was largely about Terry. I went looking for him afterward. Both Anjelica and Yvette figured he was probably in the Mudhole with Frank. But I couldn't find him anywhere. Most likely, I decided, he didn't want me to find him now.

It was a year before Terry and I spoke again. By then he was back living with Anjelica and Buddy, who had moved to West Haven, a small shore town next to New Haven. Terry said he had been too ashamed after messing up Job Corps to talk to me or anybody else about it. Now, however, he was ready to reminisce candidly. "Job Corps was more like jail," he said. "A place for bad kids. It was *fun.* Sneaking in drinks. There was a lot of liquor. The food was here and there—you know." He laughed, and said, "It was *nasty.*" Then he added, "It was like college, really. Just like they said it would be."

In fact, while 40 percent of Job Corps participants drop out (or get kicked out) of the program in their first three months, it is, along with its Great Society cousin, Head Start, one of the more successful federal antipoverty efforts.

The local street drug trade was in the doldrums, Terry said, after a series of major busts. "People are scared now, so they're just getting, like, *jobs.* It's real,

real dead around here." The Mudhole, he said, was history. "They're turning it into a *farm* or something." He wasn't working himself, but he was collecting food stamps and something he called "city welfare." He was also hoping to make some money from a fall he had taken on an icy sidewalk in front of an apartment complex. "I hurt my back, so I'm trying to catch a little lawsuit," he said. His plan, if he managed to collect enough money, was to open a restaurant. "There's a lot of room at the Chapel Square Mall," he said. "People from the courthouse go there to eat lunch. There's a lot of restaurants in there, but no *fish* restaurants. You know, like seafood. So that's what I wanna buy. This economy's so bad you can't make no money workin' for somebody else. You gotta own your own."

His other ambition, Terry said, was to go to acting school. "I'm writing memos to myself," he said. This was something he had learned to do at Job Corps, I gathered. It was meant to fix goals and priorities. I said I would look into acting schools in New York that gave scholarships—and hoped my voice didn't betray my skepticism.

In any event, the next time I heard from Terry, he was back in jail. It seemed he had started selling drugs in West Haven, and had gotten caught. He'd pleaded guilty to possession of cocaine with intent to sell, and had been sentenced to two years in state prison. "I know that you may not be happy that I am in here and all, but I am making this a learning experiment," he wrote to me in a letter. "I have learned my lesson this time for sure."

I went to the prison, a sprawling, low-security place in Cheshire, Connecticut. Terry looked different—older, less energetic, shiftier, more ordinary. His chin-strap beard was no longer pencil thin but full and scraggly and vaguely rabbinical. We talked about the classes he was taking in jail (he had been provided with a pair of glasses) and the high-school-equivalency diploma he hoped to earn. I told him about a trade school in Rhode Island that offered a four-year program in culinary arts and full scholarships for needy inner-city students. He would need his equivalency diploma to apply, though. Terry seemed interested—not least because he was again convinced that he needed to stay out of New Haven to stay out of trouble. If he left jail without a plan, he said, he would end up going back to his mother's place—where all roads seemed to lead down. (Even Anjelica's new place in West Haven had become, according to Yvette, "a hellhole. More drugs coming in and out of there than anywhere.")

Terry showed me a book he was reading: *I Wanna Be the Kind of Father My Mother Was.* It was written by a Black Muslim from New York, he said, and was highly regarded among the inmates, many of whom were Muslims. Terry liked the book, but still didn't think he'd become a Muslim—"I'll just stay my Christian self." His tastes and loyalties seemed unchanged generally. When I asked what I could send him, he said, "Black gangster books."

Terry was worried about his grandparents' house. It seemed that Carl had finally retired from Simkins Industries, and Beulah was also talking of retiring,
and their income would no longer be enough to pay the mortgage and taxes.
Indeed, they were already behind on their payments, and the bank was already muttering about repossession. Terry passionately wanted to save the
day. He reckoned that, if he just got out of jail before it was too late, "I could get
me two jobs and some roommates and lift up the house myself." He had it all
figured out—how much he had to earn each week, how much rent the roommates would pay. He also planned to start helping Yvette with money for Latifah. Such heavy financial pressure would almost certainly force him back into
dealing, I thought. I didn't say so, though. Terry's earnestness was too poi-
gnant. And his release was, in any case, still a long way away.

I later talked to his teacher, who was cautiously optimistic about his chances
of earning an equivalency diploma. He was trying hard, she said, and unlike
many of his fellow inmates he could read. He even volunteered to read out
loud in class. His worst subject was science, but he needed to improve in every
subject to pass the diploma exam. She thought he should start taking a special
pre-exam class. "The problem is, it starts at eight-thirty A.M.," she said. "And
he doesn't know if he can get up that early. Jane Whitney really does us in
here. She has a late night talk show on TV—one to two A.M—and they *all* stay
up and watch it, so they're all too tired to get up for school."

The risks of Jane Whitney addiction notwithstanding, I found myself har-
boring a heretical thought: that Terry was, for now, better off in jail. Being
locked up seemed to give him what he could never find on the outside: the
calm, sober space and daily structure that allowed him to study. If he could
just get his diploma, and we could just get him into the trade school in Rhode
Island, his path into adult life might finally begin to open up.

I was dismayed, then, to hear, a couple of months later, that because of
prison overcrowding Terry had been granted early release. He could be
reached, I was told, through his mother—who had just given birth to her first
daughter, LaToya.

That was in 1994. New Haven had by then changed in some significant ways
since the first months I spent there with Terry. The regional economy had con-
tracted severely. Southern Connecticut, which is often described as the most
Pentagon-dependent area in the United States, had been especially battered by
post–Cold War cutbacks in military spending. The state had lost an estimated
200,000 jobs, most of them defense-related, in just four years, and when the
rest of the country began to recover from recession in 1992, Connecticut
lagged far behind. The real estate market throughout the Northeast also collapsed in the early 1990s, with property values in Connecticut leading the
plunge. The state's cities, already poor and weak, were hit hardest. In New

Haven, the Macy's that had anchored the Chapel Square Mall closed for good in 1993. The city's population continued to plummet—between 1990 and 1995, it fell by more than 10,000 people.

Mayor John Daniels, worn down by the struggle to halt the city's decline, chose not to run for a third two-year term in 1993. His successor, following the zigzag ethnic-political pattern being set in other cities (including New York), was an Italian American, John DeStefano. The son of a local cop, De-Stefano was a young, energetic technocrat from the old Democratic machine. He quickly (and quixotically) attacked one of the sources of New Haven's debilitating weakness in relation to its suburbs by campaigning for state property-tax reform—Connecticut's tax structure blatantly disadvantages its cities—and he won over many working-class families with an innovative home-ownership program. He improved city services, and began an ambitious school rebuilding effort. More dramatically, he undertook a new kind of urban redevelopment: not the displacement, razing, and massive building of yore, but a "downsizing" that accepted the inevitable shrinking of the city and sought to make the best of it, bulldozing abandoned buildings and replacing them with small parks and playgrounds. Other old cities, like Baltimore and Philadelphia, were also adopting this approach.

Relations between the police and the community had improved noticeably under an iconoclastic new police chief, Nicholas Pastore, who abandoned his predecessor's SWAT team approach to the drug trade, and disbanded the notorious Beat Down Posse. Rank-and-file cops were restive, even rebellious—and many veteran hard-liners, including Captain Garcia, took retirement rather than work under the new regime—but Pastore became widely popular in black New Haven as he hired more black officers, put many more cops on the street, established innovative youth counseling programs, and listened closely to the concerns of residents in high-crime neighborhoods. The city's crime rate, particularly its murder rate, dropped sharply. The streets were still dangerous (and so were the schools—at Wilbur Cross High, scene of the school-front shoot-out I happened to see, a student was shot on campus in 1994) and the drug trade still bustled, but several of the big drug posses were, as Terry said, broken up or driven underground by a series of successful joint (city/state/federal) investigations. The Ville took a big hit in 1992, the Jungle took one in 1993, and by 1994 most of the leadership of KSI was in jail.

Of course, all the busts of local black gangs may have only cleared space for other dealers. In September 1995, a big joint-agency drug raid in Fair Haven took in more than thirty Latino suspects, some of whom, the police said, were working directly for the Cali cocaine cartel—the first known Colombian connection in New Haven. And even these headline-grabbing busts and the general drop in crime failed to endear Chief Pastore to his troops, or to many white people in and around New Haven—who tended to see him as a minority-loving liberal. And when Pastore was forced to resign, in early 1997, because of a scandal over a child he had fathered with a black prostitute, it was not clear what sort of policing New Haven could anticipate.

Some of the young black community activists I'd met had prospered: Roger Vann was now president of the Greater New Haven NAACP and a popular radio talk show host; Lisa Sullivan had gone to Washington, D.C., to work for the Children's Defense Fund; and Scott X, after forming a political base with a militant youth group he called Elm City Nation, had gone to work for the Board of Education and had become, if not part of the city's political estab- lishment, certainly a figure to be reckoned with—sitting, for instance, on the board of the New Haven Coliseum. Kevin Houston, the Rev Kev, who had con- cerned himself with remembering the young who had fallen, had died prema- turely, of heart failure, in 1991.

The young black New Haveners to whom the activists ministered were, while shooting each other at a somewhat reduced rate, still facing a larger world no less cold, no less segregated. Inner-city youth style had made an odd adaptation, though, forsaking extravagant, born-to-lose, gold chain display for a restrained, preppy look: rugby shirts and North Face windbreakers. At the prep schools where I sometimes lectured about the inner city, meanwhile, many kids were dressed in what had been ghetto style: extra-baggy pants, ski caps, NFL warmup jackets. Some of the prep school boys—little gangstas of entitlement—could even talk the hip-hop talk.

A more substantial penetration of the suburbs by the ghetto was also taking place. A new interpretation of federal law had made all federal housing subsi- dies portable, and a lot of poor people were taking the opportunity to escape dangerous cities like New Haven. That was how Anjelica and Buddy—along with many other poor blacks and Latinos—had made their way to West Haven. The imploded real estate market in Connecticut had left an oversupply of housing everywhere, which meant cheap rents. Of course, suburbs and small towns were rarely pleased to see welfare families moving into their midst, and many were erecting barriers against such immigration, including, in West Haven, starkly inferior maintenance and services in the parts of town that were now suddenly black and brown.

The best hope for many deteriorating American cities is, in fact, radical ex- pansion—incorporating, somehow, their entire metropolitan area into a sin- gle administrative unit, with shared tax burdens and revenues. There is some resistance within entrenched city-government elites (some of them black) to this obvious route to renewal, but the deep resistance is in the suburbs, where residents naturally prefer to use the city's resources without paying its taxes, and to shoulder as little as possible of the burden of urban poverty. In Con- necticut, as elsewhere, how to bind the cities economically and politically to their wealthier neighbors remains the fundamental problem for those truly interested in halting the cities' long decline.

Anjelica, bucking the demographic trend, was determined, the last time we talked, to move back to New Haven. This was in late 1996. West Haven had become intolerable. Rowdy neighbors were tearing up her apartment building; drugs were epidemic. So she had her eye on a nice place on Dixwell Avenue, back in the old neighborhood. She was working, she said, on an assembly line in Milford, the next town west, for six dollars an hour, but after Christmas—after she had paid for all the Christmas presents she was buying—she planned to look for word-processing work. She had just finished learning Lotus and WordPerfect 6.1 at a secretarial school, and she figured she should be able to make ten or even twelve dollars an hour. Her baby, LaToya, was fine, she said, and on weekends she often took her granddaughter, Latifah, off Yvette's hands. It sounded like Anjelica and Yvette were getting along for a change. In fact, Anjelica sounded impressively sober and stable. Buddy, she said, when I asked, was no longer living with her. He had gone down south to live with his father in Mount Olive, North Carolina, where he was doing well in school. "But he's gettin' homesick," she said, chuckling with satisfaction. "I can tell. He'll be back."

Anjelica's family was rumbling along. Beulah hadn't retired, after all—she was still working as a receptionist for the dentist on Dixwell Avenue. Beulah's father, however, had died, and she and Carl had moved up to Hamden to live with her mother, leaving Button to look after the house in Newhallville, which remained on the verge of repossession. Button got a job as an orderly at Yale–New Haven Hospital. Darla continued to struggle with drug addiction—but found the time to bear two more children. Then, in late 1996, the Newhallville house burned down. No one was injured in the fire, and the insurance settlement that Carl and Beulah received presumably made this ending—for it was the end of an era, the end of the family's postwar working-class dream of steady work and home-ownership—slightly less bitter.

Terry hung around in New Haven for a couple of years after he got out of prison. He dealt some drugs. He worked for a while at a convalescent home, in "dietary." He took up with a woman named Juliet. "She my heart," he told me. "She got a piece of paper, a CNA—that's certified nursing aide—and a real good job. We livin' together, and she makin' me be more mature. She don't want none of that drug scenery."

If anyone, I thought, was ever going to make a difference for the better in Terry's life, it was going to be a woman. Certainly it would not be me. I remained interested in his fate, and ready to help him in the ways I could, but my days of vain (in both senses of the word) intervention were over.

Whenever we talked, Terry had a new ambition: trade school, modeling, working on a cruise ship. For trade school, though, he needed a diploma. And to get into modeling he needed a portfolio, which he could not afford. To apply for a cruise ship job, all he needed, he said, were a résumé and a cover letter. He knew what a résumé was, but wasn't so sure about a cover letter—"That's where you talk about how you feel about yourself, I think." The cruise ship company was in Miami. It never happened.

Terry finally "got a lawsuit," after a fall at the convalescent home. He settled out of court for ten thousand dollars, of which he ultimately received less than two thousand.

He and Yvette remained on friendly terms, though he rarely had money to contribute to the support of their daughter.

He lost touch with Lakeeda and Tyrone, but heard that she had another baby, a girl.

Terry remained convinced that, to get ahead, he had to leave New Haven. If I told him I had recently been in, say, England, his first question was always the same: "Yeah, well, how's the economy down there?" He'd heard that "in California there's *lots* of opportunities. You can just walk in the door out there. Hollywood, everything."

When Terry finally made his move, however, he went not to sunny California but to, of all places, Detroit. "It's not as bad as everybody thinks," he said. This was two months after he got there, near the end of 1996. Juliet had just joined him. Terry had called to wish me a merry Christmas. "We don't live in the worst neighborhood," he said. "Or the best. Rent's nice and low. We're in the city, just pay city prices. In the suburbs, you pay top money." He already had a job, he said, cooking in a convalescent home in the suburbs, making nine dollars an hour. He got a ride to work from neighbors. He also had distant cousins in Detroit—I guessed that was where the idea to move there had come from. "I'm getting myself together before it's too late," he said simply. Then he had to run. It was Sunday morning, and time for church.

What a dazzling idea—lighting out for the territory in postindustrial America and landing at ground zero of the white-flight urban apocalypse, the biggest Rust Belt fiasco of them all: Detroit, city of opportunity. Terry's reports remained bravely upbeat. In the spring of 1997, he called to say that he had become the manager of two kitchens at the convalescent home. The work was hard, but it was good preparation, he figured, for the day when he got a restaurant of his own.

BOOK TWO

A Tight Fight with a Short Stick

Leviathan split the stand-together
Leviathan fix the rise-ups good

—Suzanne Gardinier,
"Leviathan"

ONE

In the piney-woods country known as Deep East Texas, two black men from San Augustine County went to a cattle auction. Roger Hale and Willie Earl Dade each wore a huge white cowboy hat. In the version of the story I heard, told by the Reverend Cecil Clark at his home in San Augustine in 1992, Hale's hat was about four feet tall and roughly six feet across at the brim—a lid for a piney-woods Paul Bunyan. Though neither Hale nor Dade had any money, Hale decided to purchase some stock. His bidding technique was, according to Rev. Clark, exquisitely subtle. He would lay an index finger alongside his nose and, when he wanted to bid on an animal, would lift the finger ever so slightly. Rev. Clark demonstrated the technique, his expression unnaturally blank, again and again. Each time he did it, his wife, Laverne, and I would howl and pound the couch, helpless with laughter. Although it was only Clark's impression of Hale's imitation of a white rancher's puffed-up sangfroid, we finally had to beg him to stop.

"Okay. So Roger, who was wearing a lot of jewelry he got from someplace, bought himself a whole eighteen-wheeler full of fine cattle," Clark went on. "He just signed for 'em. 'Roger Hale,' 'Roger Hale.' Gave his address. Payment on delivery. And the truck showed up next day down there at his sorry little place in Brushy, full of cattle. But all Roger could afford to *pay* for was one little cow so weak it had to lean on the side of the truck not to fall over. Had to send the rest all back."

Laverne imitated the undernourished, listing cow. "Had to lean on the fence in Roger's yard, too," she said. "Sorriest little cow you ever saw." She shook her head, sighing with spent laughter and wiping her eyes. "Oh, Roger," she said. "Bless his heart."

By the time the Clarks told me this story, Hale was in federal prison in Louisiana. Because he and Laverne were cousins, the Clarks received a lot of collect calls from him. "Sometimes, when Roger calls, he just curses," Laverne said. "Right up to the top. And I tell him, 'I know you're angry, but I don't got to be paying this phone bill to listen to this. You should be praying, not cursing.'"

I actually couldn't imagine anyone cursing at Laverne. She wasn't stuffy, but she was a religious woman, forty-six years old, and sober in her ways. As the mother of eight, grandmother of eleven, and a school bus driver by trade, she also knew a few things about keeping misbehavers in line. In fact, the Clarks had, as of that evening, eleven kids and grandkids living with them in their tiny brick house on Farm-to-Market Road 1277. Earlier, I had had four squirming children in my lap tunelessly screeching hymns while I leafed through Laverne's sheet music—she plays piano in her church's choir—but now it was late, and gently raining, and the house was unusually quiet.

The case that had put Roger Hale in prison was known as Operation White Tornado. It had been a combined effort by federal, state, and local law enforcement to shut down a cocaine-trafficking network based in San Augustine County. Some two hundred agents had descended on San Augustine on June 2, 1989, and arrested dozens of residents, including Hale. At a press conference the next day, the U.S. Attorney for the Eastern District of Texas announced that the local drug trade had been "what you would expect to find in a large metropolitan area." He said that seventy-five pounds of cocaine—with a street value of more than $3 million—had been moving through San Augustine each week.

This was startling news, if only because San Augustine is, even by East Texas standards, poor, isolated, and sparsely populated. The county, which is half the size of Rhode Island, has only eight thousand inhabitants, nearly 30 percent of whom live below the federal poverty line (the poverty rate for blacks is nearly 50 percent). Though it is on no interstate highway, and is at least eighty miles from a town of any size, San Augustine, according to the authorities, had become a major regional distribution center for cocaine. I wanted to know how that had happened—and how such a small, close-knit community had absorbed the impact of an Operation White Tornado.

Cecil Clark called it Operation Black Tornado, for of fifty-four people ultimately convicted on various charges, fifty were black. (San Augustine County is 28 percent black.) There were few black families in the county that had not lost members in the raid. One of Laverne's older brothers had been arrested and spent a year in state prison; two of the Clarks' nephews were serving ten years each at a federal pen outside Fort Worth. The meaning and the value of the great drug bust were bitterly contested, politically divisive questions in San Augustine, and the facts of the case were already richly encrusted with rumor and myth. As a loupe for examining the community's inner life and self-understanding, White Tornado was, I found, uncommonly powerful.

Roger Hale was actually a minor figure in the San Augustine drug trade, according to the police. In part, I went to see him simply because he was related to a lot of people I had gotten to know. His wife, for instance, a soft-voiced young woman known as Fanny, waitressed at the Hill Top Barbecue, a family-run joint where I often ate lunch. After I told Fanny I was going to visit her husband, she sent the same message Laverne Clark did: "Just tell Roger we love him."

We met in an empty prison visiting room. Hale came on like a tough guy. In a harsh, level voice, he told extravagant stories of wheeling and dealing in guns and jewelry—but not drugs—and made extravagant threats against people in San Augustine who he felt had sold him down the river. His standard pronouncement on his enemies was: "He's no earthly good, and he knows I know it." He himself had never really done anything wrong—"just devilment," he said—but he had become unpopular as a result of his work as a repo man (work that had required him to carry a sawed-off shotgun) and his involvement in what he called "politics." Hale's social philosophy might also have hurt his popularity, I thought. "People who had less than me, I never messed with 'em because I couldn't make nothing off 'em," he said. "I never had much time for black people. I mostly associated with up-to-date white people."

Hale believed that he was in prison solely because of his association with Nathan Tindall, a not especially up-to-date white person who had been the sheriff of San Augustine County for the better part of forty years. Hale had worked in various capacities for Mr. Nathan, as he called him, his entire adult life. Indeed, people in San Augustine still described Hale, who was in his forties, as "Nathan's hey-boy," a nasty little tag that Hale may have had in mind when he informed me vehemently, "I'm my own man. I ain't no boy."

Nathan Tindall was, by all accounts, the chief target of Operation White Tornado. He had left the sheriff's office just a few months before the raid, after losing an election, and federal indictments had fallen all around him. Roger Hale went to prison on drug charges, and so did Hale's two grown sons. Willie Earl Dade, Tindall's last chief deputy, was convicted of conspiracy to distribute cocaine. Dave Husband, a local liquor wholesaler and a longtime friend and political ally of Tindall's, was one of the white defendants in the case. Roger Hale said, "Me and the white boy, we got the hard time just because we wouldn't give them the sheriff." By "the white boy," he meant Husband, and in Husband's case Hale was certainly right. Although Husband had cooperated by pleading guilty to drug, gun, and tax charges—and no drugs had been found on his property, and he had no prior felony convictions, and none of the crimes he was charged with involved any violence—he had, after refusing to incriminate Tindall, been sentenced to life imprisonment without parole. This extraordinary sentence was one of the many things that interested me about Operation White Tornado. I also wondered, naturally, how it was that Tindall had escaped indictment.

A mystery of a different kind was Laverne Clark's affection for her con man cousin Roger. The two resembled each other physically. Both were very dark, with narrow eyes and powerful, strongly planed features. Otherwise, they were about as different as they could possibly be. In the months I spent in and around San Augustine, I never heard a story about Hale that put him in anything but a dubious light—boasting, stealing, bullying, lying. During the hours I spent with him, he radiated anger and malice and precious little else. He didn't smile once, and he seemed to live in a moral universe with only one inhabitant: himself. Laverne, meanwhile, whose vast family called her Sister, was the steady, hymn-singing, comfort-dispensing center of more people's lives than I could count.

Laverne's stories about Hale were much like everyone else's. "He could come in here, convince you he had two or three thousand dollars in his pocket when he didn't have ten cents," she told me. "He was always like that—mean, and wantin' to be a big shot." And yet Laverne, it was clear, genuinely liked Hale. "Roger got the brains," she told me. "He just don't have the . . . background."

Hale's orneriness, in other words, arose from the bitter gap between his ambitions and his lot. Even from the depths of his crushing prison sentence, he kept returning, during my interview with him, to the prospects and requirements of various business enterprises—trucking companies, gaming rooms—which he discussed with great energy. Because of his . . . background, he had spent much of his life hauling pulpwood. (Pulpwooding is a dangerous, low-overhead form of logging, and it is what most black men in East Texas do for a living.) But Hale's heart was clearly not in the woods but in the office, the bank, the auto dealership. When I asked about the drug raid's community impact, he fairly snarled, "Operation White Tornado just put every black man with any business talent in San Augustine in prison."

Why did we find the story of Hale at the cattle auction so funny? It was something about his peculiar fury, his lifelong poverty, his stiff-necked hustler's dignity. The six-foot cowboy hat helped, as did the super-subtle bidding technique. In my own case, it also had to do with the fact that, by the time I heard Cecil Clark tell the story, I had spent much of a long, rainy winter hanging around San Augustine. The harsh facts of local black life provided the only backdrop against which Hale's "devilment" could possibly be seen. I found myself asking Laverne, "Did Roger ever laugh at himself?"

"Of course he did," she said. She pursed her dark lips thoughtfully over gold-capped teeth. "That's the whole point."

It was the whole point, perhaps, of her affection—that Hale's self-awareness, and their ability to laugh together, made his swaggering tolerable, even charming. But it was also the point, I realized, of my stint in San Augustine, at least as Laverne understood it: that I should begin to see how people there amused themselves, consoled each other, and kept alive their self-respect.

Cecil, though a popular and talented Baptist preacher, with two congrega-tions and plenty of funeral work, still had to haul pulpwood. Indeed, he had been in the woods that day, and had come home too tired to change his clothes—his jeans were caked with dried red mud. Lanky, sad-faced, fifty-two years old, he had a cross tattooed on his left forearm.

Toward the end of the evening, Lanee Mitchell, Cecil and Laverne's eldest daughter, trudged in from work. She was twenty-three, light-skinned, long-legged, slim like her father. Lanee was working as what she called a "chicken plucker" in a Tyson chicken-processing plant in the next county north. Her commute, which she made by car pool with other local women, was a forty-mile round trip, and the job's long hours meant that Lanee didn't see much of her six-year-old son, Johnathan. Tonight, he had gone to bed hours ago. "But you know there ain't no good jobs round here," Lanee said, collapsing onto the couch beside me. I stared without comment at the plastic showercap she was wearing—it was required equipment at the Tyson plant—and Lanee tore it off, guffawing.

I did know—everybody knew—that there weren't many good jobs in East Texas, particularly for young blacks. People looking for more opportunity had been streaming out of the region for a hundred years. In fact, San Augustine County has fewer people living in it today than it did in 1900. But the cities that absorbed the great exodus north and west while they grew and prospered no longer need cheap labor from the South. Their factories have, as in New Haven, mostly closed their gates. And so Lanee and her siblings and cousins and friends—her cohort, as demographers say—now largely stay home, get-ting by as best they can. And this was what interested me most about San Au-gustine: how people got by there. Lanee, who loves to talk, had been one of my faithful tutors on this subject, serenely ignoring all the queer looks and mut-tering we got as we rambled around the county, ignoring even the vehement testimony of one of her own sisters that I was in reality a "narc" who had par-ticipated in the big drug raid.

Tonight, however, Lanee was, as she said, "tahrd, tahrd, tahrd." So I put my notebook away, and she and her folks and I just sank back into the velveteen couch and watched TV. One thing I remember from that evening's viewing was a commercial. It showed a street crack deal going down in Lufkin, a town in the next county west: a young dealer on foot selling a bundle through the window of a pickup truck, with a voiceover offering one thousand dollars for tips leading to the arrest and conviction of a crack dealer. "Now there's a way to make some legal money," Cecil said dryly.

East Texas resembles the Deep South far more than it does the open prairies of the rest of Texas. Dense pine and hardwood forests shroud rolling terrain; lakes and bayous are fed by fifty inches of rain a year. White farmers and their black slaves first settled the area while migrating west at the beginning of the nineteenth century. In San Augustine their cotton plantations thrived in the "redlands" that run in a wide, fertile band across the county. The town of San Augustine, laid out in 1833, nowadays bills itself as "The Oldest Anglo Town in Texas." Several leaders of the Texas Republic came from San Augustine; Sam Houston himself lived there in the 1830s. When members of some of the older white families talk about their ancestors signing the Declaration of Independence, they mean, I learned, the *Texas* Declaration of Independence.

Present-day San Augustine teems with ghosts, particularly in the woods, where innumerable small family graveyards lie overgrown, and ancient farmhouses and abandoned schools rot and collapse beside red mud roads. Traces of a pre-Anglo Texas survive in the names of a few rural families, such as the Y Barbos (who pronounce their name Why Barbo), but it's the slavery era that left the deepest print on the place. Startling numbers of people, black and white, share the same few family names: Polk, Cartwright, Edwards, Davis, Garrett, Holman, Jones, Price, Sexton, Sowell, Sublette. These biracial clans were created when former slaves took the names of their owners after Emancipation, and some residents still hear those atavistic echoes, still see those relationships spread across the modern county like some deep map of the local soul. "Her people belonged to my people," an old white man in the western part of the county once told me. He was speaking of Laverne Clark's mother, Ruby Kelly, née Davis.

The Clark family's roots run as deep in the region as anyone's. On Laverne's side, her mother's father, Clark Davis, was born into slavery in the Brushy community. Her father's grandfather, John Randle, was born into slavery in East Liberty, a few miles north of San Augustine. Laverne's parents, Hulon and Ruby Kelly, were of the Depression generation that left their farms and sharecroppers' shacks for the cities in vast numbers. Ruby went to Houston and, during the Second World War, she and Hulon, then newly married, lived in Orange, Texas, a port city where Hulon worked in a shipyard. While family obligations drew Hulon and Ruby back to San Augustine, many of their brothers and sisters settled permanently in places like Houston and Oakland, California. Ruby, a short, wiry woman with a long, sweet face, still has to pause to control her feelings, sixty years later, when she talks about the sacrifices her parents made to help her go to high school, and her disappointment at being called home before she could go to college to become a teacher or a nurse in Houston.

On Cecil's side, there were legendary great-great-grandparents who "swam the Red River to escape slavery" in Louisiana, an Indian great-grandmother, and an ex-slave named Claiborne Greer whose descendants filled a rural community of black landowners called Greertown, where Cecil was raised, in the northern part of the county. One of Cecil's grandfathers was a white barber—

Cecil's grandmother had worked in the barber's household as a young woman—and Cecil's father, Archie Clark, "could have passed for white," according to Cecil. Instead, Archie was raised and spent his life in Greertown, marrying a black Greer, farming, and driving trucks. There are black Clarks throughout the county's early records, most of them related to Cecil. I found one ancestor in the family graveyard, near a settlement that used to be known as Clarktown, who was born, according to her headstone, in 1821. I even found a second cousin of Cecil's, a formidable church elder named T. G. Clark, who claimed that a mutual ancestor, an ex-slave known as Old Tom Clark, had been fathered by a white man (Tom Clark is in fact listed in the county's 1870 census as a "mulatto") whose family later produced one of modern San Augustine's leading citizens, a banker named Edward Clark.

White San Augustine, like much of the white South, never recovered from the Civil War. Sharecropping, which lasted nearly a century, perpetuated the old master-servant relations, and Jim Crow laws and the Ku Klux Klan helped maintain social and economic distinctions between black and white small farmers. The great tide of American industrial prosperity bypassed everyone, though. Like the rest of the "black belt" of the rural South, San Augustine after the Civil War settled into a general poverty, endured by all but a small elite. Cotton farming declined, then vanished with the invention of harvest machinery that required flat terrain. The timber business took its place—wood remains the county's leading crop—and poultry farming came along after the Second World War, but the big timber mills were (like the chicken-processing plants) all built elsewhere. There are poorer counties in East Texas, but San Augustine is today a backwater even in a backward, isolated area.

Most Texans simply disown the whole region. "Behind the Pine Curtain," they call East Texas. Why, the people there aren't really even Texans, I was once told in Houston; they're the ones who were afraid to come out of the woods during the great westward movement.

And much about San Augustine does feel preserved from another era. Not only the plantation houses—slave-built from virgin longleaf pine—but many of the older houses in town (1990 population: 2,430) have the wide porches and twelve-light windows, the fluted Doric columns and classical pediments of the antebellum South. On the courthouse square, farmers sell watermelons, okra, potatoes, and yellow squash from pickups parked next to the jail. Bags of seed are piled on a canopied sidewalk in front of an old brick hardware store. The only stoplight in town—and San Augustine is the only real town in the county—blinks sleepily at one corner of the square.

Across the railroad tracks, in a black neighborhood still known as the Quarters, unpainted shotgun shacks lean under tall pines and great, spreading maples. The Jerusalem CME, the oldest black church in Texas, organized in 1845, stands on a modest plot, its bowed walls still shaken by gospel hymns on

Sunday mornings. On the porches in the Quarters, old folks nod in weathered armchairs; in the backyards, roosters crow from woodpiles. The atmosphere of deep, premodern slumber is broken only by the passing of a glistening violet Nissan miniature pickup, its side windows smoked, its chassis lowered almost to the ground, with a gold-flaked stiff chain around the license plate, a young black man at the wheel, and percussive hip-hop pounding from the cab.

Though a big stone courthouse sits at the center of the square in downtown San Augustine, the old two-story brick jailhouse next door takes up far more symbolic space in the county's collective consciousness. Eight dim, battered cells and all their unhappy memories fill the second floor; downstairs is the sheriff's office. Official authority in the rural South has always tended to be concentrated in the sheriff's office, where the monopoly on violence enjoyed by a county's chief law enforcement officer often invests him with a psychological power that can be incomprehensible to outsiders.

The South became a one-party state after Reconstruction, and in the system of power and patronage that emerged in virtually all rural areas, violence was always close to the surface. In the 1890s, the Populists, in a movement born of the economic desperation of workers and small farmers, briefly challenged the ruling Democrats, and in San Augustine they managed to capture the sheriff's office. The first Populist sheriff was gunned down in the street in 1900 by a political rival. A few weeks later, his successor, who also happened to be his nephew, was shot, and *his* brother and uncle were killed, in a downtown shoot-out with leading Democrats. This particular political feud, which was also a clan feud, led to a number of other deaths. The murderer of the first Populist sheriff later became sheriff himself, and when he was removed from office for malfeasance he confronted *his* successor, who shot him dead in the courthouse square. By that time, though, the Democrats were back in control of the county—and they have not been seriously challenged since.

The saloons where much of this frontier-style violence found its spark were closed by Prohibition, which came to Texas in 1918. But the illegal liquor business thrived in perennially depressed, lightly policed San Augustine, and this trade, too, gave rise to frequent violent disputes. Like most Bible Belt communities, the county stayed dry after the repeal of national Prohibition, thus insuring that moonshining and bootlegging would continue. The families who controlled the liquor trade became increasingly powerful and brazen. They began to terrorize their neighbors, going on a legendary binge of robbery, rape, assault, and murder until finally, in 1935, the Texas Rangers were sent in. The state officers took control of local law enforcement, forcing out the sheriff and bringing the outlaw clans to justice. Four thousand people gathered on the courthouse square to thank the Rangers.

This famous Depression-era scene was, from the descriptions I heard and

read, strangely similar to the one that occurred on the night Operation White
Tornado came down, fifty-four years later, when a crowd again gathered on
the square and cheered as handcuffed suspects were led into the squat old jail.
There were plenty of people still around who remembered both events—
including Hulon and Ruby Kelly. But these scenes were, in the eyes of many
San Augustinians, less the stuff of history or heroics than what Roger Hale
called "politics." And politics mostly meant the permanent, raw swirl of power
around the sheriff's office.

In San Augustine people talk about "the sheriff"—or "the high sheriff"—as
though he were an intimate, fundamental, inescapable fact of life, like oxygen
or aging or family. They dream about him, turn to him in every sort of ex-
tremity, blame him for every sort of distress. More than once, I overheard residents in their cups declaring that their lives would be utterly different if only
so-and-so were sheriff. Presidents are marginal figures by comparison.

"The sheriff ain't just the *law* around here," Cecil Clark explained. "He's also
responsible for the *economy*." No one around Cecil's house seemed to disagree
with this idea—nor with Cecil's assessment of the county's foremost personality over the last half-century. "Nathan Tindall," Cecil said, tapping a cigarette
ash carefully into his shirt pocket. "Now that was a sheriff had something to
offer the *public*."

Nathan Tindall grew up in Depression-era San Augustine. His parents were poor tenant farmers on the Attoyac River, in the western part of the county; as a boy he rarely even saw the town of San Augustine. His family belonged to Pentecostal and Baptist country churches; they and their neighbors moved in a separate social universe from the Episcopalians and the Methodists who worshipped in the big white churches in town. As a teenager, Tindall became a mule skinner—an independent logger with a mule team—and earned a name as a hard worker blessed with extraordinary strength. "For a white man, Nathan was almighty stout," a veterinarian named Tom Blount told me. "He could pick up a 128-pound sack of oats with his teeth and throw it up on the back of a truck."

In 1943, at the age of eighteen, Tindall joined the Navy. He served in the Pacific, as a military policeman, and was wounded near Kwajalein. When he came home to San Augustine after the war, one of the first things he did was run for sheriff. It was an unusual move for a twenty-one-year-old, but Tindall was unusual. "Hell, I was just as settled at twenty-one as I am now," the sixty-nine-year-old Tindall told me. "I grew up young, for some reason, and never did change."

"Nathan was strangely even-tempered," Dr. Blount recalled. "Almost unnaturally so. Also, there wasn't a scared bone in him."

Aided by the general popularity of returning soldiers, he was elected. A photograph of the young sheriff, taken in 1950, shows a smooth-cheeked, round-faced, blue-eyed country boy in a tall white Stetson. He looks kindly and calm, almost shy. Studying the photograph, Tindall—now portly, gray-haired, nearsighted, and nothing like shy—remarked to me wonderingly, "I don't believe I'd vote for a kid that young."

The job paid $4,500 a year, and with it came a late-model, cream-colored Ford with a red light mounted in the center of the grille. Tindall found that sheriffing suited him. He knew the woods, where most of the county's moonshining and bootlegging went on, and he was willing to go to considerable lengths to do his job. He didn't attempt the impossible—shutting down the illegal liquor trade. He simply kept enough pressure on the bootleggers and moonshiners to insure that their power didn't get out of hand. The bootleggers' lawyers, notably Smith Ramsey and his brother Ben, were formidable opponents. The Ramseys were members of the old, landed elite of San Augustine—Ben served as lieutenant governor of Texas in the 1950s, and Smith was routinely described as the most powerful man in town. Tindall, who never did win the support of most of the San Augustine Old Guard, had to work around them. "One time, I waited till Smith was on vacation and Ben was busy in Austin," he recalled. "And then I rounded up twenty-eight bootleggers, and I persuaded that judge, who usually did whatever Smith told him to do, to hit those boys with the maximum fine, a thousand dollars each. I could run the sheriff's office for three years in them days on twenty-eight thousand dollars."

Tindall's approach to serious crimes was also, according to himself and others, tenacious and inventive. "I'd do about anything to catch a thug," he told me. "I remember, once, this old boy had murdered his mother-in-law, and I knew how these boys always like to talk about what they done, so I saw them all in there one night, and I crawled up under the house, where I could hear them clear as could be. And here was this old boy tellin' them others, 'Don't tell the sheriff this, and don't tell the sheriff that.' After a few minutes, I heard pretty much everything I needed to know."

Charles Mitchell, the San Augustine district attorney (and Smith Ramsey's nephew), grew up in San Augustine in the 1960s. "You couldn't do a thing here without the sheriff knowing about it," Mitchell told me. "He just pretty well *handled* it. One thing you have to say for Nathan: He is good at solving crimes."

Tindall's wits were his main weapons, literally. In a county where virtually everyone seems to carry a gun—where grandmothers pat their aprons significantly when the subject is small pistols and self-defense, where people still hunt deer and squirrel and possum for meat irrespective of the season, and where I was regarded with disbelief and disdain by local young women (Lanee Mitchell among them) after admitting that I traveled unarmed—Tindall never carried a gun.

"He's a six-gun sheriff without the six-gun," said Sam Malone, a local printer and longtime East Texas newspaperman.

"He was always such a disappointment to me and the kids," Willie Earl Tindall, Nathan's wife, told me. "He didn't wear a gun, and you know how he made an arrest? He'd call them on the telephone and tell them to meet him at the jailhouse."

Tindall even made murder arrests over the telephone—perhaps fifty of them, he reckons, through the years. His peculiar authority was difficult to account for, according to Sam Malone. "He tells you to do something, you just better do it. Not because he'll hurt you physically, or even throw you in jail. He's just a queer nut. There ain't no explaining him."

Tindall, being a politician, loved to get his picture in the paper. "Nathan was always showing off," Gary Borders, who edited a newspaper in San Augustine for five years in the 1980s, recalled. "He once called me up to go out with him. He had solved the Case of the Stolen High School Band Instruments. We went out there, and the band instruments were right where he said they would be. He went on and on about his own brilliance, as if he had just solved the crime of the century. Finally, I managed to ask how he had come to suspect the boy who did it. The boy's mother had called him up, Nathan said, and told him that her son stole the stuff."

In truth, solving crimes and making arrests are not the major part of a rural sheriff's job. "Mainly, the sheriff in a county like San Augustine has to know the people, and how to get their problems solved," a state police sergeant told me. "If two guys got a beef, he might just throw them both in a cell and let 'em fight it out. Or maybe run one guy out of the county." Character judgments, in other words, count for at least as much as crime judgments.

In the end, the rural sheriff, for all his autonomy and local power, is in a service profession, and the parameters of his job description have a tendency to expand indefinitely. "In San Augustine, if you're out of water, the sheriff's supposed to bring you water," Willie Earl Tindall said. "If your car breaks down, the sheriff's supposed to carry you home. If your lights go out, and you can't get the electric company, it's the sheriff's job to bring you a flashlight. It's pathetic, but that's the way people think here."

Tindall took this "political" side of his job so seriously that he essentially put himself on twenty-four-hour call for forty years. His nights off were so short that he often slept in his office. He and Willie Earl were married in the jailhouse with two deputies as witnesses and Nathan wearing his uniform. Their honeymoon—to the nearby and not even slightly scenic town of Hemphill—lasted two hours.

They were, in some ways, an unlikely couple. Married to a man not known to have read a non–comic book since the Second World War, Willie Earl was most at home in the depths of a research library. She was for many years the social sciences librarian at Stephen F. Austin University in Nacogdoches, thirty-five miles west of San Augustine, before becoming the superintendent of schools in San Augustine. She had two master's degrees, and was working on her doctorate in Texas history at the University of Texas in Austin. She was president of the local chapters of both the Texas Historical Society and the Daughters of the Republic of Texas, and spearheaded the founding of a local Black Historical Society. She had a big, tobacco-cured voice, a broad face, little pierrot eyes with brows raised high in an expression of permanent surprise, and a great raucous laugh. When I asked her if "Willie Earl" was an, uh, common name in San Augustine, she said, "Sure it is. There's three others running around here wearing it right now. 'Course, they're all black males."

Nathan Tindall had one major interest besides sheriffing, and that was making money. He started out by providing logging equipment to other men and soon became a pulpwood contractor. He bought and sold stands of timber, and acquired a fleet of logging trucks, a truck dealership, and, finally, a small sawmill. He also became a land trader. By the 1970s, Tindall's businesses were grossing more than two million dollars a year. Many of his employees were ex-residents of his jailhouse. Tindall's standard response to a jobless man who asked for work included providing him with a chain saw, a bobtail truck, and directions to some obscure patch of woods.

His record keeping was loose at best, and his lending policies were liberal, with the result that half of San Augustine eventually owed him money. The areas of overlap between his businesses and his work as sheriff, and the potential for conflicts of interest, were endless, and local muttering about corruption and the exploitation of public office grew louder with the years. Still, Tindall was reelected again and again.

His generosity helped. Tindall himself reckoned that he "gave away" a million dollars while he was sheriff. "Hell, I paid for over fifty babies to be born," he told me. "Everybody, black or white, knew that if a baby was coming and there was no money, you just had to call the high sheriff."

"The sheriff's office used to look like a bank," Gary Borders recalled. "People actually stood in line to borrow money from Nathan. Some paid him back, but my impression was that most never did."

Cecil Clark, who did his share of truck driving and pulpwood hauling for Tindall, said that he would have lost his family's house on Farm-to-Market Road 1277 if Tindall had not stepped in and made the mortgage payments during a bad patch in the seventies. An old black man named Willie Harp, who lived in a shack off a dirt road in the northwestern part of the county, told me that the only reason one of his daughters was able to attend college and climb out of poverty was that Mr. Nathan had paid for her education.

Tindall's warm relations with his black constituents irritated some whites, who took to calling him "the nigger sheriff." Particularly offensive in the eyes of such whites was his habit of shaking hands with black friends in public. "Tindall was *for* the nigras," one old white man told me. "Used to be, white folks would get together when a black bothered them, and take him out and trim him up a bit—talk to him or whip him, whatever was needed. But Tindall wouldn't even cooperate with a nice local lynch mob."

Tindall didn't remember any lynch mobs. "I was just treatin' the blacks the way they *make* you treat 'em now," he told me.

He was not above enforcing the segregation of Jim Crow days. There was an infamous incident at a local café in the 1950s between a Tindall deputy, Cecil Clark's brother Thelious (who had joined the Army and was home visiting), Thelious's new wife from Germany, and a dose of tear gas. "That hurt me bad with the black community," Tindall recalled. Hard feelings over the episode lingered even after he and the Clarks had made up their differences.

On the whole, though, Tindall's support in black San Augustine was deep and wide. He was seen as the rare powerful white man who treated the races more or less equally, and as the rare sheriff who tempered law enforcement with leniency. "He wasn't no big crusadin', whip-snappin' sheriff," Sam Malone recalled. "He was a practical man livin' with poor, practical people." If a prisoner in Tindall's jail had a job and a family, the sheriff usually let him out in the mornings, so that he could go to work, and locked him up again in the evenings. His employment agency cum pulpwood business only enhanced his popularity with blacks, who needed the work. This was what Cecil Clark meant when he said that Tindall was a sheriff who had something to offer the public.

Tindall cultivated his support in the black community by holding free barbecues and, at election time, by "hauling votes"—providing free transportation to the polls, courtesy of operatives like Roger Hale. The black vote, which routinely went more than 80 percent for Tindall, became the key to his electoral lock, particularly after the civil rights period and the increase it generated in black voter registration.

The civil rights movement actually had relatively little impact on San Augustine. White resistance was deep: public schools were segregated until 1970, and even then integration occurred only under federal court order—and the all-white school board resigned in protest. The movement inspired some local struggles—over segregation in the town's cafés and the bus station's waiting room, over the redrawing of district boundaries to create a black-majority county precinct—but a generation later few people remembered those victories, and the signs of black progress when I visited were, in truth, scant. "Even for the South, this town is not what you would call advanced," Leroy Hughes, the principal of San Augustine High School, told me. Hughes, who is black, grew up in Jackson, Mississippi. "San Augustine is about where Jackson was twenty years ago," he said. Most towns in East Texas have at least a Martin Luther King, Jr., Boulevard to mark the passage of the civil rights movement; San Augustine had no such memorial. The town was more than 50 percent black—the schools were nearly 60 percent black—yet the leading local service organizations, the Lions and the Rotary Club, were still exclusively white.

And yet many whites were, I found, still bitter about the "forced integration" of the schools. One amateur historian even compared the civil rights period with Reconstruction, when the "*first* federal army of occupation" had come to San Augustine, he said, to promote black supremacy. In truth, local history has been written almost exclusively from a white point of view—and nearly everything I learned about the county's past from black sources, which are chiefly oral, gave an opposite version of the same events. Certainly, Reconstruction, which lasted eight years in Texas, was a time of profound upheaval and included a spasm of black political mobilization that was far more traumatic for San Augustine's whites than anything since. Freed slaves walked away from their masters, often to reunite with their families. Local planters were driven off their plantations; one, Jesse Burnett, was killed. Schools for black children were started, some with help from the state's Freedmen's Bureau, and black literacy began to spread.

The local center of black resistance was a district known as the Pre-Emption, in the northern part of the county. No part of San Augustine today swarms with more ghosts. After Emancipation, ex-slaves flocked to the area. It had been lightly settled by whites, for it was hilly and heavily wooded, roads were poor or nonexistent, and the soil was sandy. Unclaimed land could be "pre-empted" (homesteaded) for as little as fifty cents an acre. In the free-for-all of Reconstruction, the Pre-Emption became a black stronghold. An ex-slave named Harry Garrett even organized a military company there. "He would assemble them at night to the sound of a horn which could be heard for a long distance, and the company would spend several hours in drilling," wrote G. L. Crocket, a local historian. "One house in the neighborhood was fortified by large logs, laid along the yard fence with notches cut in the top for gun rests." Alarmed whites organized, according to Crocket, a "Klan of the Invisible Empire of the Ku Klux" to intimidate "obnoxious negroes," captured the fortified house, and drove Harry Garrett out of San Augustine.

The Pre-Emption remained a neighborhood known for its proud black inhabitants—not sharecroppers, like the black farmers in the more fertile redlands, but landowners. (San Augustine had few, if any, free black inhabitants before Emancipation, and therefore lacked the early African American bourgeoisie that developed elsewhere—the educated elite meant to provide what W.E.B. Du Bois famously dubbed the "Talented Tenth" and saw as instrumental to race upliftment. The county did not, however, lack for social distinctions among blacks, partly based on the antebellum labor division between house slaves and field slaves, but increasingly based on landowning, church and financial standing, and the economically slight but socially crucial difference between families seen as "proud poor" and those considered "sorry poor.") The black settlers of the Pre-Emption logged and cleared their pastures and fields by hand. They grew corn, peas, cotton, watermelons, peanuts. They raised hogs and cattle and farmed with mules. Cash was scarce—crop prices were chronically depressed, and black wages in the logging industry stayed under a dollar a day well into this century—but food was usually plentiful. Aside from sugar and baking soda, people raised nearly everything they ate. Barter was the main system of exchange. Conversations with those who grew up in the Pre-Emption evoke, even after allowing for nostalgia, an agrarian community with a powerful spirit. People worshipped at little clapboard Baptist churches in the woods and in summer gathered for baseball tournaments with black teams from all over East Texas and western Louisiana.

Still, the leitmotif of local black history is racial harassment and oppression. The traditional indignities of going to town included having to step off the sidewalk for whites, having to bow and scrape and, if you had a car, having to park it out in the old wagonyard. There was peril in simply passing through certain white communities in the southern part of the county, where wrathful backwoodsmen liked to whip black train passengers from the platform. There were storekeepers who whipped black debtors in the alley or took title to their land as payment, sheriffs who arbitrarily arrested and fined—"whipped you with the billfold"—and lawyers who took land as payment. The Burlesons and McClanahans, white bootlegger clans, terrorized black farm families for years, robbing and raping and burning, hijacking crops bound for market. Some cotton farmers whipped their workers; rednecks ran you off the road if your car had whitewalls and forced you to turn the tires around right there. And always, of course, there were lynchings. Laverne Clark's grandmother told her about a lynching just across the road from Laverne's house, and Laverne herself tells the story of the man who was lynched and lived. "He had put something down his mouth so his neck wouldn't break, and they wouldn't cut off his wind," she said. "So they took him down and shipped him out of here, thinking he was dead. And he got away. But he could never come back here."

Texas ranked third in the nation in lynchings in the first decade of this century—seventy-three counties in East Texas recorded lynchings during those ten years. And the hangman was not a figure out of the ancient past. Near the western end of the Pre-Emption, I was told, lived two brothers whose father was publicly hanged on the courthouse square.

Greertown, where Cecil Clark was raised, is in the eastern end of the Pre-Emption, near the old Greer plantation. (There was actually more than one black Greer clan, for even in a community as small as San Augustine some blacks with the same name may not be related. The black Garretts, for instance, descend from workers on a plantation that, in the 1860 census, had 132 slaves. Most of the slaves were unrelated, of course, but many took the Garrett name. The white Garretts, for their part, had "pretty well played out in San Augustine," I was told. So, apparently, had the white Greers.) Cecil, born in 1940, grew up as the countryside was starting to empty. The war pulled large numbers of people into the military and to jobs in shipyards and factories in Houston and Beaumont, and to defense plants out in California. After the war, many chose not to return to life behind a plow or on the end of a crosscut saw. Small-scale Southern farming was becoming, in any case, less viable—Cecil's father had to drive trucks long-distance to supplement his farm's meager profits from cotton—and black farmers, unable to finance new equipment and expansion, were disappearing fastest. Between 1940 and 1960, the rural black population in Texas fell 30 percent; the number of black farmers fell 70 percent.

In Greertown, in the early 1960s, the farmers tried to survive by forming the Greertown Community Club, pooling their resources to buy an old tractor and raising corn, peas, and watermelons cooperatively. The result was an epic watermelon harvest. Cecil Clark, whose father was one of the cooperative's founders, remembers huge watermelons hoisted into the branches of trees to keep them from spoiling on the ground before trucks took them to market. But the trucks never came. The Greertown farmers had dreamed of gleaming eighteen-wheelers hauling their produce to supermarkets in the North, the way they took the produce of nearby white farms. But the supermarkets refused to buy from them, their agents claiming, according to Willie Harp, another of the cooperative's founders, that the one old Greertown tractor couldn't get the melons out of the fields fast enough. The Greertown farmers suspected collusion between the supermarkets and their white competitors. Nathan Tindall sent some of his trucks to help, but he had no contacts with Northern supermarkets. In the end, most of the watermelons rotted in the fields, and the cooperative collapsed.

There is no black commercial farming left in Greertown, or anywhere else in the Pre-Emption. Those black-owned fields still under cultivation are leased to white farmers, who use Mexican itinerant labor and sell their crops each year to the supermarkets before they're even planted. Most of the old fields are now forest again, thickly overgrown with slash pine. Driving the rutted dirt road down through the Pre-Emption, it's actually hard to spot all the spectral farmhouses standing off in the trees. And it's haunting to learn, standing at a desolate fork four or five miles southwest of Greertown, that the old Pre-Emption ballfield once filled a great clearing there with crowds for baseball tournaments, and for the all-night barbecues and outdoor dances that accompanied them. (I once stopped to ask directions at one of the few occupied houses along the Pre-Emption road, and a tall, slim, very old black man—probably a fastball pitcher, I thought, in his prime—peered at my cap and asked shyly, "You with the Yankees?")

Perhaps half the land in the Pre-Emption still belongs to blacks, and title to much of that is hopelessly mired among absentee heirs. The few octogenarians still living on their farms are the survivors of more than a century of threats and inducements—from white merchants and local authorities, from the timber companies (International Paper is the largest landowner in the Pre-

Emption today), and, most recently, from land speculators who, spurred by visions of Houston orthodontists seeking second-home sites (or, at the least, deer-hunting leases), turn up at Greertown churches and family reunions with checkbooks. Among the Clark clan, Cecil had hung on to a few acres near Clarktown. Hulon Kelly had inherited fifteen acres out in East Liberty—though title was so tangled that nothing more complex than timber leasing could be done with the property. Ruby Kelly's father owned 122 acres in Brushy—and yet it too had become ensnared in the courts. A few years ago, one of Ruby's sons was arrested for cutting down trees on land the family still insists it owns. He ultimately got two years in jail for his trouble.

Laverne Clark was interested in my reporting and liked to hear about what I'd learned, though she was sometimes amazed by my naïveté, my willingness to chase down stories that were to her (and she always turned out to be right) clearly fabricated. She was also sometimes exasperated by what she saw as my arrogance. Once, when I tried to tell her about the fruits of my research into early land titles in the Pre-Emption, and how some of the more colorful stories about black dispossession were apparently unfounded, she erupted, "Bill, you will never understand what black people been through around here. The *abusements*, how it make you *feel*. What happened here is we go into a place that ain't got nothin', clean the land, cut the trees, build a house, grow some crops—I mean, *clean* the land—and they just let us go on workin' it till they decide they want it, and then they come in and tell us we don't got the right papers, and they take it away, don't pay us nothin'. *That's* what happened here. It don't matter what you find out in books."

Laverne, like a lot of black people in San Augustine, considered the broadcast of the TV miniseries *Roots* a watershed event in local historical awareness. She cried and cried while watching the program, and her sister Mary Barnes told me that she didn't think it should ever have been broadcast, but Laverne said, "I'm glad they went and showed it, even if it did upset a lot of people, upset the white children to see how their people done treated our people. It started some fights, I know, but people got to know what happened here, how we got to this." Ruby Kelly told me that she had found watching *Roots* unbearable: "It was just like the stories my mama told me." And while Laverne and her mother plainly shared a powerful sense of what their ancestors had suffered at the hands of whites, Laverne worried that the younger generation was losing that history. She was concerned about the neglect of June Teenth, the day the slaves were freed in Texas. "It's our Fourth of July," Laverne said, and in her youth it had been celebrated with big community barbecues and even parades. Nowadays, only old folks even seemed to remember it.

Young Lanee, for her part, disdained everything she considered "politics."

Her own sense of local history and its racial abyss was, nonetheless, acute. Once, as we were driving past the Ezekiel Cullen House, an antebellum tourist attraction in the center of town (and the headquarters of the local chapter of the Daughters of the Republic of Texas), I pointed out the house and Lanee sniffed, implausibly, "I never seen that place before." She grimaced, then explained, "They don't tell the black kids here too much about that stuff." (Cecil, while passing a pillared plantation house, complete with historical plaque, on a country road, put it more bluntly: "To me that plaque mean slavery, that's all.") Lanee refused to see a local doctor widely known as a segregationist. She was also certain that the chronic shortage of jobs in San Augustine was exacerbated by racism. "Just look at the stores around here, the banks, the offices, who's working in them," she told me. "Whites hire whites." According even to some local businesspeople, she was not wrong. Sam Malone, the newspaperman, was unusual in that he hired black workers for his printing shop, but he was convinced that doing so hurt his profits. "Some of these redneck businessmen would sooner cut off their arm than hire a black," he said. "And because I do they won't let me have their printing."

Whether Malone was right or not, such suspicions have a way of becoming self-fulfilling. Certainly, I never had to search in San Augustine to find pungent examples of white racial animosity. One of the town's leading businessmen told me that his name for the public housing project down the street from his establishment was "the nigger hatchery." A revolt was in progress at the main white Methodist church because a racially mixed couple had tried to join. The Methodist minister, the Reverend Clayton Gilpin, a newcomer from Houston, supported the couple, but said the furor had helped sour him on San Augustine. It was related, he said, to another furor that erupted when he let the high school's homecoming dance be held in the church gym. The high school itself had stopped holding dances years before, apparently because of objections, raised primarily by white parents, to black and white students dancing together.

Many blacks and a few whites, including Rev. Gilpin, saw the lack of recreation and entertainment for young people in San Augustine—the county had no bowling alley, no skating rink, no public swimming pool, no movie house—as yet more evidence of the white community's fear of teenage racial mixing. That fear definitely ran deep. One of the more worldly, liberal people I met in San Augustine, a woman whose social values were formed, she told me, during the sixties while she was away at college—and who was appalled, she said, by her teenage daughter's materialism and snobbery—also told me that she would go to any length to keep her daughter from dating black boys. (Local interracial romance had, of course, a long and mostly secret history, linking more black and white families than some cared to admit. Cecil Clark's white grandfather had belatedly, and quietly, acknowledged Cecil's father as his son. "But my white cousin don't know me on the street," Cecil said. "I never been inside his house.")

Amid the general poverty, there were always a few black people who managed to make a decent living in San Augustine, even after black farming became obsolete. This local elite consisted primarily of schoolteachers, insurance agents, funeral home owners—largely because white undertakers refused to handle black corpses—and, above all, those enterprising souls who supplemented legal incomes with moonshining and, in later years, bootlegging. Smith and Ben Ramsey, the old-money lawyers, had many black bootlegger clients. One of them was Bud Watts, a World War II veteran, who told me that, despite the many arrests he suffered and fines he paid, he still managed to buy a new Ford coupe each year. He used the cars on his supply runs up to Shreveport or down to Apple Springs, where he would fill his "turtle hull"—his car's trunk—with Red Bird, Old Forester, Southern Comfort, and cases of Falstaff. Sometimes he even took out the backseat. "Get a thousand dollars of liquor in there."

The bootlegging business in San Augustine ended abruptly in 1972. Its demise was an unintended consequence of a rare local civil rights triumph: the redrawing of electoral district boundaries to create a black-majority precinct. This redistricting effectively insured the election of a black county commissioner—the first since Reconstruction. But it also led to the repeal of Prohibition in the newly drawn precinct, where residents promptly voted to "wet up"—to legalize liquor sales. And thus was shut down one of the few local avenues of black economic opportunity. Nathan Tindall's job got easier overnight, but old Bud Watts, who opened a small bar on the west side of town, sighed when I asked him about it. "I wish it was still bootlegging times," he said. "Now most your money just goes to the government."

THREE

There were also white bootleggers in San Augustine, among whom Dave Husband, who later took the hard fall in Operation White Tornado, was easily the best known. His father and his grandfather had been bootleggers before him, operating from their homestead on the Attoyac River, so Husband had been in the business since he was a boy. By all accounts, he was a savvy trader. With legalization, he quickly opened a liquor store at the intersection of U.S. 96 and State Highway 21, just west of town, where the new black-majority precinct started.

Husband's liquor store prospered, and by the early 1980s he was a major regional wholesaler and a wealthy man. He became something of a community burgher, known for his generous disbursements to youth groups such as the 4-H Club. But he never lost his outlaw predilections. A compulsive gambler, he took to wearing expensive jewelry and Rolex watches, and liked to brag about the time Louisiana Governor Edwin Edwards sent a helicopter to fetch him for a gambling date. He dabbled in low-level rackets. "Dave was always selling a box of nails at half price," John Mitchell, then the county attorney, recalled. Husband sold legitimate goods from a general store next to his liquor store—fresh fish, eggs, metal culverts. He also had the local U-Haul dealership, and became a busy land trader. With the money he didn't lose gambling, he built onto his house and, by the mid-eighties, the old Husband homestead on the Attoyac, where Dave now lived with his wife and two teenage children, looked like the suburban spread of a partner in a Dallas law firm.

Although Nathan Tindall had arrested Husband for bootlegging many times, the two men were friends. Tindall later disputed stories that they were extremely close, but after Husband's father died, in 1961, when Dave was sixteen, Tindall, in his role as all-purpose protector of the county, did look out for the family in ways that the Husbands never forgot. Certainly Dave, once he got established as a legitimate businessman, became a prominent backer of Tindall's, sponsoring campaign barbecues for him on the courthouse square. And the two men were firmly paired, in the eyes of the Old Guard, as upstart poor boys from Pentecostal families down on the Attoyac.

Husband was on unusually friendly terms with law enforcement in general. He supplied free liquor to the parties and reunions of various agencies, and took Texas Rangers, highway patrolmen, sheriff's deputies, park rangers, San Augustine's town policemen, and just about anybody else in uniform off on hunting weekends. (Tindall, a lifelong teetotaler and a nonhunter, may have been the only lawman in Deep East Texas who missed out on these stag weekends.)

Campaign barbecues notwithstanding, Tindall's friendship with Husband probably hurt him politically. Tindall's association in the public mind with a motley crowd of jailhouse hangers-on—some of them ex-inmates, all of them the sort of men who hope that a cop's power will rub off on them—definitely hurt him politically. But Tindall, who was never particular about appearances, shrugged it off. "I never had a preacher come to me with no information," he told me. "It's the thieves that come to you with something, after they done got themselves into something. That's the ones that tell you what you need to know."

And for many years he could absorb the damage. The list of people with grudges against him grew—it eventually included not only most of those he had sent away to the penitentiary, and their families, but also most of those he had defeated in elections, a category that ultimately contained, according to Tindall, fifty-seven men, and *their* families. He did lose one election in the 1950s, and he once resigned as sheriff for a term in the seventies. Demographics began to work against him, too, after the state dammed the Angelina River, which forms the county's southern border, in 1964. The dam created Sam Rayburn Reservoir, a two-hundred-square-mile fisherman's paradise whose wooded shores soon sprouted second homes, trailer parks, retirement communities, and other attractions for white strangers with scant interest in the affairs of the sleepy little town of San Augustine, twenty-five miles north, and with no electoral loyalty to the backwoods boss whom local whites called "the nigger sheriff." Still, Tindall's popularity as a dispute settler and old-time paterfamilias was so great that he was all but invincible politically, his everyday power in the county—especially after the Ramseys passed from the scene—seemingly absolute.

"It was just lucky for San Augustine that Nathan is a good man," Willie Earl Tindall said. "Because he pretty much made up the law himself, whatever he thought was fair. Fortunately, most of what he thought was fair *was* fair." While Mrs. Tindall could be expected to judge her husband's performance charitably, it was true that he enjoyed a rare freedom—very rare for a sheriff in East Texas—from charges that he abused those who tried his patience.

But Tindall wasn't the only San Augustine official making up the law as he went along. According to Mark McDaniel, an itinerant lawman who joined the town police force in 1986, nobody in San Augustine followed the rules. "I had worked all over Texas and Louisiana, and I'd never seen anything like it," McDaniel told me. "We'd arrest somebody, and sometimes there'd be no paperwork at all. It was *strange*. They had never even run a search warrant. When I wanted to go to a J.P. with a probable cause, they said, 'We don't do that here.' It wasn't just Tindall. It was everybody. And I got to be the same way, six months after I started."

McDaniel heard the rumors about Tindall being corrupt. "People would say that Tindall could make sure that a DWI never went on your record," he said. "That's ridiculous. The sheriff of San Augustine, Texas, has no say about what does or doesn't go on your record in Austin. But people here don't understand that. They're just so used to thinking that the high sheriff is all-powerful."

A lesser but similar awe surrounded other peace officers in San Augustine. "People here are obsessed with law enforcement," McDaniel said. "Most places, nobody really notices who the cops are. Here, I hadn't been on the job a month and I had an invitation to dinner at someone's house every night of the week. You're a little celebrity." In such a climate, petty corruption was rampant, according to McDaniel. "We never bought beer or whiskey," he said. "We never paid for the food at our cookouts. You know, when you're making eleven hundred dollars a month you're always ready for a free six-pack. And our biggest buddy—nobody likes to admit this now—was Dave Husband. Every night we'd meet over at his store—the highway patrol and everybody— drink Cokes, eat chips, whole-head cheese, whatever we wanted."

Long after Nathan Tindall left the sheriff's office, some people were, I found, still muttering that he had been corrupt, and not merely on a petty, complimentary-six-pack scale. But in virtually every case these people refused to be specific in their allegations. Charles Mitchell sighed and said, "There's always going to be somebody to say that whoever is in the sheriff's office is crooked." I also heard, over time, plenty of defamatory (and unfounded) rumors about Tindall's successor, an ex-butcher named Charles Bryan.

But much of what I heard also reflected, I thought, a communal paranoia, a radical distrust of all institutions, that is widespread in East Texas. (This paranoia seems to coexist, in some cantankerous way peculiar to the place, with the habit of depending on the sheriff for every little domestic thing.) "All they ever do in the sheriff's office is change bootleggers," declared Y. W. (Bo) Ruth, a black electrician in his eighties, unwilling to retire a good motto just because bootlegging happened to have disappeared. A white scrap dealer named Blue Perry gave me his formula for business success in San Augustine: "If you can just stay harnessed up with the thieves, you'll be all right." Heading out of town on State 21, I often passed an imposing, pillared, hilltop mansion. The house had been built during Prohibition by a merchant known as Baby Jack Matthews, and San Augustinians were fond of saying that it had been built with bootlegging money. It was more likely that Matthews had simply made some money trading with bootleggers, and perhaps selling supplies to moonshiners, and yet the myth about the big house, the idea that all gains are ill gotten, clearly spoke more resonantly to local historical tastes, while confirming the most popular piney-woods theory of capital accumulation.

Nathan Tindall, who harbored few illusions about the world's virtue supply ("Fifty percent of the people is doing things that ain't right, and not too many of them goes to the penitentiary," he told me, shrugging), naturally denied the charges that he grew light-fingered in office. And an informal survey of some of those who worked with him when he was sheriff—two county judges, the county treasurer, the district attorney, the county attorney, the town attorney, the town police chief, various deputies, the only two real newspapermen in town—yielded no one who credited the charges that he was corrupt.

Willie Earl Tindall claimed that, although she knew of her husband's legendary generosity, she never realized how much money his businesses were making until she started reading about it in the press. "If I'd known that—are you kidding? I would've had my butt in a Cadillac the next minute." But Nathan, the work-focused child of the Depression, never changed his ways to reflect his wealth—he never went on vacation or wore anything but his sheriff's uniform—and by the time Willie Earl realized they were millionaires, they weren't.

Tindall's business fortunes—along with the Texas economy as a whole—turned down sharply in the 1980s, particularly after he bought the San Augustine Sawmill in an effort to keep it from being closed. "He saw himself as the savior of the county," Gary Borders recalled. "And it just about wiped him out." Tindall lost the mill, and then a deep recession in the wood business and a disastrous investment in a floundering local bank plunged him close to bankruptcy.

The strange thing about Tindall's fall from financial grace, according to those who were there, was that it hardly seemed to affect him. He just kept sheriffing night and day, and claimed not to miss the money. His self-confidence, they said, seemed entirely undiminished.

Such unflappability was actually not hard to picture, for by the time I met him, Tindall was selling used cars on U.S. 96, having been turned out of office by the voters, drubbed fearfully in the press, and hounded for years on end by various federal investigators; yet "humbled" was still about the last word that would have come to mind to describe him. He bustled around the car lot, popping hoods and turning ignitions for a succession of solemn young shoppers, shouting instructions to a stream of "hey-boys," black and white, who wheeled up in battered pickups or crawled out from under jacked, delaminating Buicks. He took me into his office, a grubby box at one end of a sagging mobile home, where, between telephone calls full of business dickering, he bragged for two hours about all the timber he had cut and all the crooks he had caught, and shook his head sadly over the performance of his successor. "He knows about as much about sheriffin' as he does about jet airplanes," Tindall said.

The peculiar authority that Sam Malone noted in Tindall does not arise from his physical presentation. Tindall's boots that day were muddy, his shirt rumpled. He wore ill-fitting brown jeans with an oil rag hanging from a front pocket and a pair of rubber-handled pliers protruding from a back pocket. One lens of his thick, steel-rimmed glasses was severely smudged from, he said, a recent encounter with battery acid. His speech was by turns fumbling, gusty, intense, distracted, and enthusiastic. It was frequently punctuated with laughter. When Tindall saw that some of his humor went right past me, he looked at me quizzically, and then seemed to decide that it would all take too long to explain to a Yankee. And when a heavy-browed young black man in coveralls came in, saw that I was taking notes, and started questioning me, Tindall just grinned and let him interrupt.

"People call me Frog," the young man said eagerly.

"I put him in jail for dope," Tindall said.

Frog's eagerness to talk to a journalist vanished. He said it was true, and went about his business.

Frog, I noticed, had addressed Tindall as "Cap'n," and the title somehow sat comfortably between them.

Over the weeks that followed, I often saw Tindall driving somewhere in the company of Frog and some of his equivalents—four or five of them crammed into the cab of a truck, off to cut some timber or pull another truck out of the mud. And the more time I spent in San Augustine—a place where black residents maintain that there are white shop assistants who still won't hand them change directly—the more I came to see how unusual Tindall's common touch truly was. I once watched him and Frog having lunch together at the Hill Top Barbecue. They teased each other cursorily while they waited for their food; then both plunged into plates of barbecued ribs, eating silently, side by side, and hardly looking up except to nod to friends and neighbors as they came through the door. I mentioned to my own lunch companion—Ilester Porter, a furniture restorer, who owns the Hill Top—that Tindall certainly seemed to be a democratic sort. "Thank you," Porter said. "He's *too* democratic."

I later asked Porter what he meant. Porter, a middle-aged black man who was decidedly not a Tindall supporter, tried to explain. "The sheriff in a place like San Augustine has one real job," he said. "That's to keep the poor man, black or white, poor, and let the rich man get richer. If a poor man gets into something that lets him stack up a few thousand dollars, the sheriff's got to find some reason to bust him, take away that money by a fine. And he's gotta leave the rich man alone, let him do what he wants. Nathan Tindall didn't do part of his job. He didn't care *who* got rich, long as he was making money himself. He let white trash like Dave Husband get rich. That's why the rich folk decided to get rid of him, finally. And once them people over on the other side of the tracks decide you're out, you're *out*."

There was a crucial change in the mixture of law enforcement in San Augustine after bootlegging was rendered obsolete. Marijuana farmers, whose crop thrived in the fertile forests of East Texas, effectively replaced moonshiners in the local underground economy, and marijuana traffickers replaced bootleggers. And, while Nathan Tindall had little trouble keeping track of local people who got involved in marijuana—some were farmers who had fallen on hard times, and others were ex-bootleggers looking for a new trade, or underemployed loggers looking to turn a remote clear-cut into a gold mine—he sometimes found that he needed help when the scale of growing or dealing was larger, was regional rather than local. Though it was a point of pride with him to call for outside help as rarely as possible, he did occasionally call on the state police, with whom he had always been on good terms. Marvin McLeroy, a senior detective in the state narcotics office in Lufkin, recalled taking some of his men to stake out a large field of marijuana that Tindall, who didn't have the manpower to watch it, had found deep in the woods in San Augustine County. The growers got spooked and escaped, but the state police tore out sixty thousand plants.

"Of course, working in San Augustine was always a unique experience," McLeroy told me. "Because if it wasn't cleared with Nathan it didn't happen. He knew absolutely everything that happened there. I could drive through the county, not even stop for a cup of coffee, and when I got back to my office the phone would ring and it would be Tindall wanting to know what I was doing. The man had *resources*."

Rickey Allen, another state narcotics officer, said, "I went over there to San Augustine once to bust a dealer named Bo Barnes. Nathan asked me, 'What's he got?' I told him something like five pounds of pot. Nathan wanted to just phone the old boy and tell him to get on down to the jailhouse with the dope. I told him I didn't want to do that. I wanted to go out there with a search warrant. Nathan said, 'A *search* warrant?' Finally, we just drove out to Bo's trailer, and Nathan hollered for him to come on out, and he did. Then Nathan told him to go back in and get all his dope and cash. And Bo did it. He brung out four or five pounds of pot and twenty-three hundred dollars. We arrested him, but Bo kept saying it was all a mistake. See, he had been dealing coke, and

Nathan had told him to stop, so Bo figured that meant it was okay to go back to selling pot, because the Captain didn't tell him he couldn't."

Federal agencies were not among Tindall's resources. He had worked with the FBI when it was chasing draft evaders during the Vietnam era, and he claimed to have always had cordial dealings with the feds. But his deep reluctance to invite them into San Augustine was well known, both locally and in the federal offices in Beaumont and elsewhere. Charles Ruth, a former federal magistrate in Beaumont, said, "Tindall didn't think he needed the FBI, and the FBI is trained to be egomaniacs, so there was a problem." Marvin McLeroy said, "Nathan and San Augustine have been a thorn in the side of the feds for a *long* time." Thus, when the federal government—not just the FBI but the Drug Enforcement Administration, various task forces, and every ambitious federal prosecutor in America—got more interested in the drug trade during the ever-escalating war on drugs of the mid-eighties, Tindall was not necessarily aware of the fact.

Around the same time, cocaine began to replace marijuana as the main commodity in the East Texas drug trade. Cocaine moved much faster than pot, in every sense. It cost more, yielded a higher profit, involved much higher levels of the criminal world, was far harder to interdict, and, in the form of crack, which soon caught on locally, wreaked a social and medical havoc on its users unlike anything associated with marijuana. "Cocaine is just another level," Mark McDaniel, the itinerant lawman, said. "It's *hard* to bust. And Tindall didn't have the training, the people, the knowledge, the technology."

Tindall did have a notion, though, about who was bringing cocaine into San Augustine, and he mentioned it to McLeroy, of the state police, in 1987. The suspect was Lenard Jackson, a local black man who had lived for many years in Houston but still had family in San Augustine. Jackson's brother Herbert was the county's first black commissioner, and he was still in office. "But we didn't go after Lenard Jackson, because he lived in Houston," McLeroy told me. "And Nathan, you know, probably didn't contact anybody else who could've done something. Nathan only talked to people he liked."

Lenard Jackson, who was born in 1948, grew up in Greertown. Like Cecil Clark, he was descended from the ex-slave Claiborne Greer; in fact, he and Cecil were second cousins. Frank Jackson, Lenard's father, was a farmer and logger; he and his wife had fifteen children. Lenard, the eighth, was in the tenth grade at the segregated high school in San Augustine when Frank died, in 1966. Lenard left school and went to work hauling pulpwood. Like his older siblings, all of whom had already left for California or Houston, Lenard saw plainly that his chances of making a decent living in San Augustine were bleak. He went to work pouring steel in a refinery in Lufkin, a hundred-mile round trip from Greertown, for two dollars an hour, saving fifty dollars a week through the plant credit union. After two years, he quit and went to California to visit his relations—"California was a big word then in East Texas," Lenard recalled—but he ended up moving to Houston in 1969.

There was plenty of work; Houston boomed throughout the 1970s. Jackson joined the construction workers' union and started as a laborer. He rose to labor foreman, concrete foreman, general foreman. He was, from all accounts, a ferociously hard worker. He took a second job at night, and with his savings he bought a garbage truck. He landed a contract to haul garbage from Burger Kings, and found a dump that stayed open until midnight. As a labor foreman, Jackson became a kind of one-man hiring hall for other young men from San Augustine. Thus, when he went out on his own as a construction contractor, in the mid-seventies, he had a pool of loyal, experienced workers to draw on. By that time, he had married Girtha Mae Polley, from East Liberty—his mother's home place, a few miles northeast of Greertown—and had bought his first house, a bungalow out among the gas works and bayous east of Houston. His company started pouring foundations for Sambo's, a chain of twenty-four-hour restaurants. "There were a lot of jokes," Jackson recalled. "You know, 'Got a bunch of Sambos out here doing the Sambo's.' But that didn't bother me too much. The work was good."

The work was very good, especially once Jackson had begun winning contracts to build the little L-shaped shopping centers, known as "strip centers," that surround Houston in their multitudes. By the early eighties, his company, LJ Construction, employed eighty people, including most of Lenard's eleven brothers, and had jobs going all over the metropolitan area. "If we was in Houston, and we was ridin', I could show you some of the buildings we made to come up out of the ground," Herbert Jackson, who occasionally worked for Lenard, told me. "All the parking lots we paved. You wouldn't believe it. Seems like we must have poured half the concrete in Houston." Only Herbert and one disabled sister stayed for extended periods in Greertown with their widowed mother, but all the children, led by Lenard, contributed to the maintenance of the old place, and to the regular replacement of their mother's Ford with a new one. To many people in black San Augustine, the Jacksons were an exemplary family: hardworking and dutiful toward their elders. Laverne Clark regularly held them up to her own sprawling, impoverished clan as a model of industry and solidarity.

Herbert worked as a policeman in Nacogdoches, a seventy-mile commute from Greertown, before he was elected county commissioner. Much of a county commissioner's job in San Augustine is indistinguishable from that of a road crew foreman. The county commission has real budgetary power, though, and for that reason certain entrenched white elements were, according to Herbert, determined to oust him. "They tried a lynching-without-a-tree," Herbert told me. "They even indicted me to the grand jury." I asked what he had been indicted for. Herbert shrugged, and pulled on a longneck Coors. "In this county, a group of white people could get together and say, 'A Negro ate our car,' and they would be believed," he said. The effort to oust him failed.

We were sitting on the front porch of the Jackson family's house, looking southeast across a small yard where collard greens grew, across the pale pastures and dark forests of Greertown, to distant hills. It was a beautiful October afternoon; the only sound was a huge oak tree rattling dryly in the wind. Herbert, a thin, dark, mutton-chopped man, forty-five years old, was wearing flashy black cowboy boots. He was wary with me, but hospitable. He had won a second term as county commissioner, but—after Operation White Tornado sent Lenard and another brother, Roy, to prison—had failed to win a third. But Herbert kept steering our conversation away from his political career, and from his brothers' legal difficulties. He clearly preferred reminiscing about the Greertown of his youth, when the fields were busy with people, and Indians still lived in the sassafras thicket down yonder, and the family smokehouse seemed to be always full of curing beef, ham, bacon, sausage, and chitlins.

Lenard, having become a prosperous contractor, bought a lot in Pearland, a flat, windy exurb south of Houston, and built a sprawling, one-story Spanish-style brick house with six arches across the front and tinted windows. This house acquired mythic proportions back in San Augustine; Roger Hale told me that it was worth $750,000, though its real value was perhaps $150,000. It was a powerful symbol, in any case, of a local boy's success in the city. Jackson bought another such symbol: a secondhand Rolls-Royce—not, he later said, because he particularly liked the car but because his wife liked it and because it would hold its resale value. (He continued to drive a pickup truck.) He raised rabbits in his backyard, and on weekends he held barbecues for the many young San Augustinians who worked for him. Success had its burdens, however. The fact that Jackson was widely admired and considered a fair employer sometimes put him in a difficult position. "If you said you were from San Augustine, and needed money, I'd find something for you, because I knew how it was, trying to get started," he recalled. "But that meant I worked a lot of San Augustine guys I didn't need. And that hurt me down the line."

When the Texas economy crashed and burned in the 1980s, Houston construction went with it. Jackson's business began to suffer from competition with what he called "Spanish guys"—undocumented Mexican laborers working for Anglo contractors for four dollars an hour. Some of Jackson's workers had been making more than a hundred dollars a day. He lowered that to eighty, and then, when things got desperate, to sixty.

At some point—exactly when is a matter of dispute—Jackson went into the illegal drug trade. First marijuana, according to the state narcotics police, and then cocaine. "When my construction business started going down, I had a lot of things to keep up, people to take care of," he told me. He didn't want to say more. (He had an appeal pending.) But then he added quietly, "I liked the con-struction business, even working sixteen hours a day, a whole lot better. The drug business is *dangerous.*" He paused. "And look what it does to people." We were sitting in a visiting room in a federal prison near Dallas, but it was clear that Jackson was not referring to his own situation—serving fifteen years, with no chance of parole—but to the ill effects drugs have on their users. He is a round-faced, soft-spoken man with a steady gaze. It wasn't difficult to pic-ture how younger men, particularly young men from the same background, would look up to and follow such a calm, avuncular character. And, as it hap-pened, there was a surplus of underemployed young men hanging around Jackson's world in Houston by the latter half of the eighties—guys from San Augustine looking for work, hoping to make some money.

Although Lanee was only twenty-three, I found her deeply—almost weirdly—nostalgic. She loved to reminisce about what she called her "good old-fashioned country upbringing." The far better time she remembered had ended perhaps five years before. "When I was little, we lived in a big old white house up the hill from where we're at now," she said. "We had a big old garden. Used to tote water up from the stream, water our tomatoes. Used to plant seeds and fertilizer, and my grandpa be comin' up behind us with his mule, coverin' over the seeds. We had a white cow, called her Ol' Lily. Churned our own butter—best you ever had. We drank a lot of water. Had a big old iron dipper, good old cold water. Seemed like the dipper *made* the water taste good."

Lanee even remembered fieldwork fondly. "Summertime, we hit that pea field," she said. "Everybody be ready at five A.M. when the pea truck come through, jump on. Pickin' peas was *work*, but we got used to it, and we used to have fun. Even after I had Johnathan, I used to get out there, just tuck him up in the shade. Sometimes we pick with Mexicans. They pick *everything:* green peas, you name it. You're supposed to pick just the purple ones. You pick the green peas, you won't have nothin' to pick in two weeks. The Mexicans killed a snake once, killed it and ate the meat. Asked us if we wanted some. Uh-*uh*. And then bees come when the peas bloom, those little yellowjackets, millions of 'em. They sting you sometimes, but I rather be stung than get a bull nettle on me. Them really hurt, and the only way to stop it hurtin' is to pee on the knots it give you. One time my sisters were wrestlin', and one of them fell into a bull nettle, got knots all over her back. It was bad, and we called the boys over. Who want to pee on her back? They *all* wanted to pee on her back. But she got to pick the one, you know, and he did it, so it was better till we got home. We made good money out there. One kid could make up to eight hundred dollars in one summer.

"One time, some white people drivin' by saw us in the field pickin' and they stopped and wanted to take our picture. Guess they liked seein' black people out there pickin' peas. So me and my cousin Kay let 'em take our picture, standin' by the scale with a big old bag of peas. We was sandy and nappy and barefooted, and wearin' these old caps. Hey, we used to get so sweaty out there. By time we quit, we was *funky.* We finally get home, we all go in that one small room we could afford to keep cold, just fall asleep dirty. It felt *good.* Wake up, take our baths. Lukewarm water." Lanee shook her head. "Those were the best days of my life, and I didn't even know it. I'd give anything to go back to those days, even though I was out in the field. I'd rather be out pickin' peas in *winter* than up there at Tyson's."

Lanee frowned, then raised her eyebrows high and burst into a big, incongruous horse laugh. It was her customary way of clearing the air after delivering some complaint or bad news. She even guffawed once after telling me how, when Johnathan was a baby and she was again pregnant, her ex-husband (they divorced when Johnathan was three) pushed her down, causing her to miscarry—"and broke the rocking chair, too!" She often made some bittersweet, aw-shucks remark, complete with horse laugh, as she left her parents' house in the morning, pulling on her showercap and climbing into a car with four other women, all of them in showercaps, for the long ride to the Tyson plant.

Lanee's fond memories notwithstanding, the Clarks' place on Farm-to-Market Road 1277 was not the stuff of rural agricultural idyll. The house was part of a small, closely knit black settlement, known as Kellyville, after its eldest residents, Hulon and Ruby, but Kellyville was not a traditional farming community like Greertown or Brushy. Its scatter of a dozen small brick houses and trailers only appeared in the 1960s and 1970s, and nearly all the land around it was white-owned and wooded. People still raised vegetable gardens, and kept a few cows and chickens, and were in and out of each other's houses, borrowing food and tools and videotapes, but no one did any serious farming, and the logging trucks that roared down 1277 kept it from ever feeling too restful. Most tellingly, there was no church in Kellyville—on Sundays, people made their way to their "home places," or to their parents' or their grandparents' home places, in other parts of the county.

Lanee dreamed, in fact, of moving back to Greertown, and toward that end had been renovating an old house on her paternal grandfather's property there. She and a former boyfriend (a Greer) had put up new windows and wallpaper and were about to install new plumbing when they broke up. On a tour of her family's land in Greertown, she gleefully pointed out a massive pecan tree, half a dozen plum trees, and a potato bin built by her grandfather, insisting I admire the dryness of the bin on a wet winter day. "It's so peaceful here," she said. "You can really think good out here."

Lanee was more susceptible than most to this sort of rustic daydream—few others who've done fieldwork (and none of her sisters, several of whom, lacking full-time jobs, still picked peas in summer) rhapsodize about it. Many country people were quite pleased to move to town—even if, as in San Augustine, it often meant moving into a federal housing project. Nola Oliphant and her family, for instance, moved into Sunset Hills, the older of the two San Augustine projects, after their house near Greertown burned in 1974. Nola's daughter, Sarah, who was eighteen then, remembered the joy of moving to town, and of having electricity for the first time. "I used to hate Saturday mornings," she told me. "I wanted to be watching Bugs Bunny, Popeye, Tom and Jerry, and here I'm off in the woods totin' water back to a Number Three tub, for washin' clothes. Life's more *convenient* in town."

Sunset Hills, which consists of eight or nine two-story brick apartment blocks at the north edge of town, between the Quarters and U.S. 96, originally represented a major improvement in local housing for the poor. But the buildings were now dilapidated, and the atmosphere seemed to me deeply depressed. A sign in the manager's office listed fines: PLAYING ON GRASS, five dollars; SITTING ON AIR CONDITIONS UNITS, five dollars; NO BRIGHT COLORS ALLOWS, fifty dollars per brightly painted room. Most of the residents were unemployed; most were on public assistance; all were black; two-parent families were nearly unknown. And yet all fifty-two apartments were rented and, in a county with no homelessness, Sunset Hills had a waiting list. Cedar Hills, the other project, on the south side of town, was better maintained and even more in demand. Still, it was one of Lanee's dearest wishes that she and Johnathan not end up in the projects. After her divorce, she had been unemployed and collected food stamps for a year, and the experience had left her with a powerful aversion to public assistance. Being insulted by welfare bureaucrats—that was for people who were sorry poor.

But the bucolic imagery that enthralled Lanee was in fact broadly popular in her community, especially in the churches. Pastoral scenes hung on the walls; they illustrated the prayer books and calendars; they even adorned the paper fans passed out in summer—Christ as shepherd, a lamb in his arms, a staff in his hand, standing on the flowered bank of a stream, surrounded by trees and mountains. The appeal of such scenes may have been primarily to older people. Certainly, very few young people—and almost no young men— were at the Sunday services I attended at various black churches in and around San Augustine, where elderly women and young children seemed to be the main constituencies. The smaller country churches nearly all struggled just to keep their doors open. Lanee was a member of her mother's church, Maryland Baptist, down in the Brushy community where Laverne grew up. Like other black rural communities, Brushy had lost much of its population, and Maryland Baptist only survived because enough of its members were still willing to make the trip from wherever they lived now to the clearing where the church sat off a red-dirt road.

To an outsider exhilarated by the beauty of its sylvan setting, Maryland Baptist actually sat strangely in the countryside, for even on a flawless autumn morning all the church's shutters were drawn tight during Sunday service. It could just as easily have been a stormy night in Detroit outside. And when the preacher, a heavyset man known as Deacon Barnes, started searching during his sermon for an example of God's underappreciated magnificence, he ended up pointing to an unshaded lightbulb burning in the ceiling—never mind the glorious sunlight dancing everywhere outdoors. But then, as it happened, there was no dearth of glory inside the church once Deacon Barnes got up to preaching speed, exhorting believers to trust in the Lord—his constant, grinning refrain, "Isn't that *something?*" and Laverne's shouted response, "Sho' 'nuf!"—and, especially, once the choir started singing. Laverne and her family—her daughters, sister Mary, and mother—formed the heart of the Maryland Baptist choir, and their renditions of "Lord, I Know You Been So Good" and "Leaning on the Everlasting Arms" absolutely soared that morning, with Laverne's piano and towering, bluesy solos taking the music into the high country of exaltation.

After the service, while the tiny congregation lingered to chat in the clearing, I casually asked someone the name of a nearby hardwood tree and found myself being led through the underbrush by half a dozen women in high heels and Sunday dresses, intent on introducing me to the medicinal secrets of the forest. This here is sassafrass; use the root to make tea to keep your blood in line. This here is holly; its tea will make a mother's milk flow. Cowslip is good for colds, pine sap for worms, fever weed for fever. Briarberry vine is for when your stomach is running off; snake root tea is good for the liver. And this, *this,* is bone-set. You boil up this root, drink the tea, and all your aches and pains will go away. Botanical disagreements broke out and were settled by great-grandmothers peering through microscope-thick bifocals. Clay dirt, all agreed, is good for sprains, and pregnant women often eat it. Lanee, though she was not pregnant, ate some by way of demonstration, and laughed at my expression. "Mmm-*mmm,*" she said. You can stop babies from eating dirt, I learned, by letting them eat a little graveyard dirt. A gaggle of excited children were plucking weeds for identification and pretending not to hear the shouts about keeping their Sunday outfits clean.

In the days of Lanee's good old-fashioned country upbringing, children were better behaved. "We wasn't allowed in the house in the daytime," she recalled. "Just played outside all day, makin' mud pies and such. Decorate 'em with flowers. Nowadays, you couldn't *pay* these kids to go outside and make mud pies. They just want to sit up in the house and watch TV. We wasn't allowed to watch TV except kids' shows: Mickey Mouse, Donald Duck. Then, back outside! Used to be, kids wasn't allowed to sit in the room with adults, look up in their faces while they talkin'. You try that, you get whupped. That was good, because it meant kids didn't know about sex till they was teenagers. I didn't know nothin' about it till ninth or tenth grade. Nowadays, with TV and hearin' the adults talk, they *know*."

Children's diets were healthier, too, according to Lanee. "Most of our food came out of the garden. Corn and tomatoes and greens. Only thing we didn't raise was sugar. We didn't have no choice about what we ate. Sometimes just greens and bread, no meat. Whatever we had, we ate, and if you didn't want it, you went to bed hungry. Nowadays, a kid has a choice—if he don't want what you got, you can go to the store, get him chips and candy.

"We had a table in the kitchen, and we ate there, like other families do." She sighed. "But then a lot of things got broke and wore out, lamps and tables, and we couldn't afford to replace 'em all. Then me and my sisters started gettin' all these babies, and now there ain't enough room for everybody around a table. The little kids don't care. They like just eatin' chips or a sandwich in front of the TV. But I think it hurts my parents, especially my mama. She likes nice things."

At one time, Laverne was in fact known for her housekeeping. "We called her 'the white lady,' " her sister Mary remembered, laughing. "That was because she always kept her house so nice." Laverne and Cecil's house was now sparsely furnished. The living room, which had no table or rug, was dominated by a big velveteen couch facing a big TV, and the few decorations on the walls—a framed copy of the Ten Commandments; a quotation from Corinthians: "And now abideth faith, hope, love, these three; but the greatest of these is love"—were all hung safely above a child's reach. Meals were catch-as-catch-can affairs. In the months I was around, the only old-fashioned Southern meal—collard greens, cornbread, chitlins—I saw Laverne serve was, I suspected, for my benefit. Everybody wanted to see if the white Yankee would eat the chitlins. (He did.)

To hear Lanee tell it, she even missed the beatings of her youth. "I got more than my share of whippings, I think," she said. "And maybe that's why I turned out a little better—why I got a job, and been out on my own—because I got beat more." Johnathan, according to his mother, was missing out on this aspect, too, of a good old country upbringing. She tried to redress the neglect on weekends, smacking him for the slightest misstep, though he had to be a difficult child to beat. Tall and slender, loose-limbed and prancing, he was an eager, affectionate, soft-voiced boy. He was a good student—Lanee said that was because she used to read to him before he was born—and he loved to make cards and drawings for his mother. "And you give *him* something, and I mean anything, he's so happy, he'll never let it go," Lanee said. Johnathan's favorite television character was Steve Urkel, from *Family Matters*—the nerdy black kid with the horn-rimmed glasses, short pants, and white socks. He had an Urkel doll that he talked things over with. Asked what he wanted to be when he grew up, Johnathan was too shy to answer. "He wants to fix hair," his mother answered for him. But when asked what he was not supposed to do, Johnathan's answer was loud and vigorous: "Don't play with guns. Don't play with knives. DON'T DO DRUGS!"

The evils of drugs could, in Lanee's view, scarcely be exaggerated. In fact, it was the arrival of cocaine in San Augustine that really divided the good old days from the fallen present. "We didn't know about drugs yet" was her standard preface to a fond reminiscence, or, "This was before drugs." Practically all social ills could be traced to the original serpent of drugs. The difficulty of modern relationships? "You can't rely on these mens these days. They all on dope or something. You go out to work, they sell your TV for dope." Increasing crime and violence? Drugs. The terrifying creep of AIDS? Drugs.

For all their conflation, Lanee was actually not imagining these problems, not hallucinating after watching too much TV. In sleepy San Augustine no less than in the cities, they were the order of the era. AIDS, though it was rarely discussed, was already a local public health emergency, according to a county social worker. That wasn't news to Lanee. Her cousin, Dee Dee—Mary's daughter—who lived two doors away in Kellyville and worked with Lanee at Tyson, had died of AIDS, at the age of eighteen, just a couple of weeks before I met the Clarks. "Dee Dee and I were real close," Lanee said quietly. "We rode to work together every day. She slept right here." Lanee patted her shoulder. When Dee Dee got sick, Lanee nursed her. "Once I held her up in front of a mirror so she could see herself, and I made her say, 'I *want* to get better. I'm *gonna* get better.' And she said it, and for a little while she really did seem like she was gettin' better. But then she just went down and down and she died. Another one gone. She knew she was going, too." Lanee shook her head. "I picked out the dress she wore to be buried. . . . It was one of the worst funerals I been to." Lanee paused, taking deep breaths. "I'm kinda worried I mighta caught from her what she had," she said finally. "I used to handle her, kiss her forehead, never minded if I shared the same glass with her." Dee Dee, who did not use drugs, was apparently infected by a lover who remained healthy and, from all reports, sexually active. She left behind two babies, both healthy. Her mother, who also worked at Tyson, and Laverne and her daughters all cared for them.

One of Lanee's few direct experiences with drugs—she had never experimented with them—also involved nursing. Her favorite uncle, Hollis Kelly, was one of the early San Augustine cocaine addicts, and when his personal life disintegrated in the late eighties, she said, "I used to find him out on the Front"— a scruffy commercial strip on U.S. 96 that doubles as a black hangout—"and I used to take him home and make him take a bath, wash his clothes, cut his beard, shave him. And he really appreciated it, because people were kind of afraid of him in those days." Hollis was arrested in the White Tornado raid, convicted on a minor trafficking charge, and sent to prison for a year.

Drugs, like AIDS, came to San Augustine from the city. (Most of San Augustine's AIDS cases were, in the words of a social worker, "young people who come home to die.") The city, which for rural blacks had traditionally signified, above all, new social and economic opportunity, was now associated, in Lanee's mind, as in many other people's, primarily with violence and disease and social breakdown. The farthest Lanee had been from home—she had never flown on an airplane and was in no hurry to try it—was Fort Worth. She went there for a weekend once, and it frightened her. "There was a lot of *thugs* up there," she said. "And bad writin' on the buildings. I couldn't believe that. And the people we was with was laughin' at me, because I was tryin' to read this stuff, all about 'bitches' and 'hos.' But we went to a mall—it was real nice, real big—and they had these escalators. I never been on one of them before. It scared me, and I had to hang on to my friend." Lanee acted the cowering, wide-eyed country girl, then gave her big boisterous laugh. Actually, she didn't need to go to the city to learn to be afraid of it. After her divorce, she had a boyfriend named Willie Burgess, who divided his time between Dallas and San Augustine. One day, while Willie was in Dallas, Lanee got word that he had been killed in a drive-by shooting. It was, apparently, a random murder. There were no arrests. As Cecil Clark said, "'Round here, at least you have to start yourself a family feud if you want to get shot."

Lanee told me that she wanted to be what she called "a modeler," and with her long legs and pretty face it didn't seem like a particularly far-fetched ambition. "But you need a lot of free time to be a modeler—to get your hair done, your nails, shop," she said. "And free time is one thing I ain't got." You also need, of course, to move to the city, or somewhere reasonably nearby. Lanee sighed. "I'd like to get out of here," she said. "But I guess the real reason I don't move is, if I go some other place, I won't know what's going on. My people is here. Also, I'm scared what would happen if I put my kid in another school someplace. Someplace else, he might get *shot*."

And so she stayed, making the long commute to the "chicken poultry," as people called the Tyson plant, and dreaming of the good old days before drugs. Black people in big cities often carry around with them a fond image of the rural place that they or their ancestors came from. Memories of sharecropping, hunger, and the real world of Jim Crow may compete with that pastoral, but its enchantment increases with the difficulties and discouragements of life in the inner cities. Meanwhile, in the bucolic backwoods of San Augustine, a young woman was similarly enchanted—by an image of her community as it was before.

F I V E

Was there an arc of decline in black San Augustine similar to the arc that seemed so relentless in New Haven? Lanee certainly thought so, and while listening to her it was hard not to recall Anjelica Morgan's saying, "Every generation gets worse." Anjelica, too, had blamed the decline of everything on drugs. The economic straits of the two communities were different—the abrupt obsolescence of black farming in the South was a more ambiguous development than the disappearance of manufacturing jobs in the North, which was an unqualified calamity—but the symptoms of social disintegration were disturbingly similar. The two-parent family had clearly become an endangered species in both communities, and teen pregnancy—so often identified as the starting point in the cycle of contemporary poverty—was just as common in black San Augustine as it was in black New Haven. Lanee herself had been pregnant at her high school graduation—"I couldn't even see my shoes," she said. Indeed, at the time I arrived in San Augustine, five of Laverne Clark's seven daughters had reached high school, and not one had graduated before becoming pregnant. And those who had married had, like Lanee, subsequently divorced. The era of sturdy, property-owning, fifty-year unions like Hulon and Ruby Kelly's—and of all the social stability and coherent child-rearing such marriages provided—was apparently gone for good.

But there were more ways to see these questions than mine—or Lanee's. Once, Laverne and I were discussing the difficulties that her daughters had each had finishing their educations—she still had two preadolescent girls at home, and the subtext of our conversation, at least on my side, was concern that those girls should, if possible, not follow in their older sisters' teen-pregnant footsteps—and I started quoting recent figures about the poverty rate among unwed mothers. Laverne wasn't buying. "Marriage got nothing to do with it," she said. "*I'm* married, and *I'm* still poor. Lots of times, a husband's more trouble than he's worth." I persisted, citing percentages and statistics, trying to tie them to her daughters' chances of happiness, and Laverne began to look disgusted. "You just talking about *money,*" she said. "That ain't what life is about." We happened to be sitting in a school bus parked in Laverne's driveway, and for some reason I decided that it was time for a lecture on the true face of American poverty. When I got to the part about there being more whites than blacks living in poverty in the U.S. today, Laverne exploded. "I don't know where you heard *that,*" she said. "Not around *here.* Who you think owns everything in this country? Break it *down,* Bill." Laverne's lips, normally full and expressive, were compressed in an angry line. She shook her head. "Now get offa my bus," she said. "I gotta go fetch them chirrun home."

It later occurred to me that I knew a few figures to back up Laverne's point about who "owns everything in this country"—such as the fact that the median white household owns nearly ten times as much as the median black household (a far more profound figure than mere disparities of income). There was also, however, a world of assumptions behind our respective ideas about poverty and marriage. I came to the subject girded with the conventional certainty that two-parent households are both more prosperous and better for the children in them than "female-headed households." Laverne came to it from another, more empirical angle. My extrapolation from the high poverty rate among unwed mothers—that Laverne's daughters ought, if possible, to get married before having kids—was in fact questionable. While married couples in general were less likely to be poor than single mothers, it did not follow that young women confronted, as the young black women of San Augustine surely were, by a shortage of "marriageable" (reliable, securely employed) young men, would escape poverty by getting married.

Indeed, Laverne had seen it work the other way more often than not. Young women got married and, especially if they had children, found themselves scrambling to survive with husbands who were often unemployed, underemployed, irresponsible, unfaithful, alcoholic, jealous, or violent, and were in any case usually poor themselves. Government regulations often reduced or eliminated the public assistance benefits of women who married, and the everyday anxiety and deprivations of poverty housekeeping tended to corrode the bonds of love. A young woman, particularly one with a child, was frequently better off remaining in the bosom of her extended family, where systems of mutual kin support were well established.

My notion that teen pregnancy was a dire mistake also came from another world—one where most kids went to college and abortion was largely unstigmatized. In Laverne's world, abortion was, in the Christian fundamentalist spirit, an abomination, and college was only for the academically gifted, the exceptionally determined, and the wellborn. The protracted adolescence that I, as a deracinated college graduate from a big city, took to be a sensible norm— the delay of parenthood deep into one's twenties and thirties—is, of course, an anomaly, little known in most of the world. It was very little known in Laverne's world. Laverne had borne her first child at sixteen. For her daughters, only vehement proscription of sex or vigilant contraception—neither exactly common features of American teenage life—was going to break the natural progress from sexual maturity to sexual activity to pregnancy. In the end, the reasons not to get pregnant weren't especially compelling. Babies were work, yes, but they were also joy, and a source of pride, and they marked a welcome passage for the young mothers into adulthood. The family was supportive—there seemed to be no disgrace attached to unwed motherhood—and it was not as if promising professional careers were being stunted. At San Augustine High, fewer than one fourth of the students who managed to graduate went on to college, and most of those went to junior colleges. None went out of state. Social classes everywhere tend to reproduce themselves, and few if any of the young black women I met in San Augustine had any sense that a world of greater options awaited them elsewhere.

Pondering these questions in San Augustine, where the long shadow of centuries of African American experience seemed to fall more heavily across modern life than in any Northern city, I found it useful to recall that black America, particularly its rural Southern precincts—where a large majority of black Americans lived until the Great Migration of 1910–1970—has always been a world apart, kept by force outside the American mainstream, developing its own folkways, family structures, language, music, politics, and religious traditions in complex interplay with (and resistance to) their counterparts in the dominant culture. Thus, early childbearing, for example, has been not only common but powerfully endorsed among black people for as long as they have been in the American South. During slavery, young black women faced less risk of being sold away from their families and lovers if they had babies. Slave-owners, barred from importing more unpaid labor by the abolition of the international slave trade from American shores, encouraged their slaves to reproduce prolifically. Later, when most black Americans lived as sharecroppers or subsistence farmers, having many children was prudent for the same reasons it has always been prudent for the world's peasantry—high rates of infant mortality, the need for helping hands, old-age insurance. The Protestant churches that most rural blacks joined in the nineteenth century did try to stigmatize births out of wedlock, but such preachments were so at odds with the parishioners' reality that they were never taken too seriously. There is evidence that even slavery provided an environment more congenial to the institution of lifelong marriage than sharecropping, with its radical economic insecurities.

Turn-of-the-century social reformers, including W.E.B. Du Bois, concerned about the scarcity of stable two-parent households in black urban ghettos in the North, used to blame the disordered habits of poor migrants from the rural South. More recently, the South has become, for many people, the symbolic home of black family values, a bastion of order and tradition, uncorrupted by urban license. In New Haven, it may be recalled, Terry Jackson's year in Mount Olive, North Carolina, was always said to have done him a world of good. The symptoms of social disintegration, particularly the disappearance of the black two-parent family, might be equally extensive down South, but the sense of crisis and chaos that had come to permeate the Northern urban ghetto was more intense. Part of that difference was just the greater threat of violent crime in the city, but much of it stemmed, I thought, from the free-fall that so many urban families felt themselves to be in. The North had once offered a promise: jobs in industry and government, upward mobility. And many families *had* made it, not only into the unionized working class but, in the second or third generation, into higher education and the American middle class. For most purposes, these families, or at least their more fortunate members, had escaped their centuries-long captivity at the bottom of the American color caste system, and had gained the status and outlook of an American-style "ethnic group." But the millions of less fortunate were understandably desperate as they saw the golden doors of opportunity closing.

In the rural South, meanwhile, most blacks were still firmly barred by caste from the possibility of middle-class prosperity. It wasn't an exotic "culture of poverty" that kept them from this possibility; it was poverty itself, and the social isolation that accompanies it. The young black women of San Augustine weren't short of "family values"—indeed, their attachments to their families were as deep and durable as any I've run across. What they were short of was decent jobs, and men with decent jobs. They settled for unwed teenage motherhood because there was nothing better in sight.

In truth, the breakdown of the black two-parent family in the postwar era has only paralleled the breakdown of the American two-parent family. Between 1960 and 1990, the number of children born out of wedlock to black women tripled; the number born to white women rose by eight and a half times. This breakdown has been more thoroughgoing at the bottom of the economic pile, particularly where the two-parent structure was never strong. And, even after all the downward mobility suffered in recent years by urban working-class families, the poverty rate among rural blacks remains much higher than the rate among urban blacks. So the economic base for stable nuclear families among poor rural blacks has remained painfully thin.

Laverne and Cecil Clark were each, in fact, on their second marriage. His first had produced four children and ended in divorce. Her first had produced three children, and ended after a couple of unhappy years in San Francisco, where her first husband worked in a shipyard and Laverne was lonely and, at the age of twenty-one, finally took a bus back home. She and Cecil met a short time later, while he was home for the weekend from Houston, where he had a job driving a truck for a frozen food company. When the two of them married, a few months later, he moved back to San Augustine. Cecil and Laverne recalled their courting days fondly—the café where they met, the car he drove then—but it was clear that Lanee's memories of better housekeeping days were not unfounded. The inexorable destruction of her household finery by the rising waves of young children and grandchildren still pained Laverne, who no longer had the energy for child-rearing that had once led her to throw legendary kids' birthday parties, featuring Cecil in a rabbit suit. The growing tyranny of the television precisely marked that loss of energy. Meanwhile, a fancy black-skinned Barbie in an immense blue-and-pink homemade dress—this doll lived inside a plastic bag on top of the VCR on top of the TV, high above a child's reach—expressed what remained of Laverne's determination to have a few flashy, delicate *objets* around her.

But Laverne had too much sense of history to bathe the past in the nostalgic light favored by Lanee. The bad old days in black San Augustine had simply been too bad. Some black San Augustinians were better off materially now—particularly old people, whose Social Security benefits let them live in greater comfort and security than they had ever known. Even the welfare families in the projects, though pitied by their neighbors, often counted themselves lucky to have escaped the centuries of agricultural peonage. At least they now had a few dollars in their pockets once a month. Laverne was right, of course—money ain't what life is about—but it was easy to look around San Augustine and see vast progress from the not-so-long-ago days when blacks were expected to drink only grape soda and risked a public beating if they were seen drinking Coca-Cola.

It was also easy, however, to see, simply by watching TV, the gulf that still separated black life in San Augustine from life in the American mainstream. At the Clarks' house, where the big-screen in the front room played nearly twenty-four hours a day, the cognitive dissonance was constant. Most of the TV shows seemed to emanate from some distant galaxy, some infinitely wealthier and more orderly nation than the one that contained Kellyville and the Pre-Emption. Indeed, the only shows that seemed to consistently engage much sustained attention were the afternoon freak shows, with their motley adulterers and worst-case families airing their wounds and treacheries: now here were some *truly* pitiful people. Otherwise, the basic frame of reference, the shared American experience presumed by the makers of a sitcom set in yuppie Manhattan, seemed to me largely absent from the Clarks' front room. That may have been changing among the kids. Cecil would be poring over his Bible in the evening, prospecting for inspiration for the next day's sermon or funeral service, while all around him his children and grandchildren haphazardly soaked up *Seinfeld* and *Beverly Hills 90210*. They probably didn't catch every inside joke and postmodern nuance, but they were all pop-culture fluent, and the older kids, with their hip-hop jargon and in-vogue warmup jackets and reverence for brand names, seemed ripe for conversion, despite their poverty, to the American religion of liberal consumerism.

Laverne and Cecil, while always making me feel overwhelmingly welcome, also saw me as an emissary from the outside world. Cecil would say, "Finnegan, what we're talking down here ain't really even English, is it? It's just a kind of slang." Laverne, in the wake of one of our arguments about the origins of poverty, teased me after I finished making a call home to New York, saying, "So you tell them about the poor little black lady you're trying to straighten out down here?" Her expression was hard to read for a moment, and then her face split open with a great, gold-toothed peal of laughter. Laverne was interested in Africa, and she ruefully appreciated the irony that I, a white man, had lived there, while she, an African American, would almost certainly never even visit. She wanted to know "what it is about you and black people, Bill," and she found it odd that I was clearly more comfortable hanging around her house in Kellyville than I was anywhere in white San Augustine.

Some of her older children also looked at me askance. Her first-born, Lavender, known as Punkin, once asked me sarcastically, "So you guess you got everything you need to know about how we're livin' down here in the *country?*" LaCecil, known as Pelo, who was born next after Lanee, was the one who accused me of being a federal narcotics agent. She was wrong, of course, when she claimed that she and I had danced together at a nightclub on the Front shortly before the big drug raid, and my protestations and "proofs" of my identity seemed to slowly persuade her to accept the possibility that I really was who I said I was. But the other possibility—that I was a fed—remained in the air, it seemed to me, not only for her but for everyone who had heard her accusation. And, I decided, there was a sense in which she was right—to the extent that I brought a "national" perspective to bear on the affairs of poor black people in San Augustine, I *was* a fed.

Pelo was full of questions about places I might have seen and she had not (though Laverne hushed her, gesturing toward her then-pregnant belly, when she once tried to ask me about urban homosexual subcultures—it seemed that local superstition had it that a pregnant woman who discussed homosexuality would make her baby homosexual). Pelo also liked to pull my leg. She insisted that since I was in Texas I should be out meeting what she called Real Texans. By way of demonstration, she tucked in her chin and started barking and drawling about cowboys and cattle, pronouncing "Lufkin" with so much down-home force I thought my ears would pop. It was a strikingly good caricature, not unrelated to Roger Hale's famous impersonation at the cattle auction. On the morning I went to visit Hale, Pelo shook her head balefully. "Louisiana," she said. "Uh-*uh.* That's the hoodoo country over there. They take your picture when you cross the bridge. And when you come back they give you a doll looks just like you—with pins stuck in it! Be careful over there!"

(Actually, the only other thing I heard about "hoodoo" was over in Louisiana. A young white deputy in De Soto Parish, who had participated in Operation White Tornado, told me that some of the black drug dealers he pursued believed in witchcraft—though, just to confuse things, the local witches they patronized lived back across the Sabine River, in Texas. The deputy showed me some charms he had taken off a suspect that morning, including a bag of saffron—for warding off spells—and a doll dressed in prison stripes, with a pearl-handled pin stuck in it. The prisoner doll was meant to insure that its owner stayed out of jail. "Didn't do the trick," the deputy said, chuckling, and he threw the doll on a photocopy machine, producing a spooky image for me to take away. He also showed me another doll, which he said he used in interrogations. By threatening to stick a pin in it, the deputy said, he could make black suspects quake with fear and tell him what he wanted to know.)

Pelo and I once watched a TV program about the isolation of poor rural mothers. Afterward, her aghast comment was, "They don't have to live in that *poverty;* they should get the government to *help* them." Pelo at the time was twenty-two, unemployed, overweight, the mother of two-year-old twins, unmarried, and pregnant—and yet she had not, it seemed, identified at all with the women on the TV. Later she asked me, "America is the richest country in the world, right, Bill?" And she seemed disturbed when I said, "By some measures, no." It was as if the mere fact of being American—and perhaps the miscellany of late-model cars and trucks that filled their yard—reassured Pelo that her family was not actually poor, never mind the monthly scramble to make loan payments and avoid repossessions. (One of her favorite expressions was, "Woofin' to buy"—which it took me some weeks to understand as "We're fixin' to buy.")

Pelo's grandmother, Ruby, seemed to have a more realistic fix on the family's situation. She remembered the days of far greater hardship—when her mother had sewed her slips to wear to school out of flour sacks dyed with tree moss, when she had worked in white-owned cotton fields and done laundry for white people. ("Some of them was just mean. Mama and me washed for a white lady, and maybe she be givin' us a can of sour milk. Lot of the time we'd have to put soda in that milk to drink it. Boil it. We *had* to drink it. They wasn't goin' to give you nothin'. Work you to death. I know none of them ain't livin' now, and I never did rejoice at the death of any. But they was *mean.* And they didn't have to be that way. We didn't make ourselves. God made us all.") Ruby recognized, however, that her children and grandchildren were still facing long odds. She worried that some white teachers at San Augustine's schools had been lowering standards for black students, and while she was proud of a granddaughter who was in college in Houston she refused to accept that any of her offspring were not taking advantage of all available opportunities. "They all work hard," she said. "For us, it's a tight fight with a short stick."

For any black person who stayed in San Augustine, even modest success required a medley of occupations, beyond the staples of pulpwooding and the chicken poultry. People raised a few head of cattle, leased out land if they had any, drove unlicensed taxis, ran unlicensed hair salons, did white people's laundry, gardening, housecleaning. Cecil preached and repaired trucks. Laverne drove a paper route. She and her kids picked peas in summer. Above all, people started small businesses—everyone seemingly agreeing with young Terry Jackson's statement that "in this economy, you got to own your own." Hulon Kelly had for years run a small store in Kellyville. Cecil and Laverne then ran a small recreation center in the village, with a pool table and a jukebox. It never made much money, and they had had to shut it down after local drug dealers started using the joint to make connections. Lanee talked about opening what she called a "country club" in Kellyville—a reincarnation, I gathered, of her parents' failed recreation center. Meanwhile, her half-brother Timmy Price, Laverne's boy from her first marriage, who had spent some years working in his father's office-cleaning business in California, talked, somewhat more concretely, about setting up Lanee in a small liquor store on the Front.

Just as in New Haven, though, the most concrete opportunities for young black entrepreneurs clearly lay in the illegal drug business, which was exactly where a large fraction of what Roger Hale insisted on calling San Augustine's "black business talent" had been going since at least the mid-1980s.

SIX

Cocaine made its way into Deep East Texas by various routes. Some came from Los Angeles, through family contacts with the Crips and the Bloods, the vast L.A. street gangs. A gang member in trouble with the law in L.A. would come to hide out with his country grandparents, find that the local cocaine market was ill protected or nonexistent, and move to establish a franchise, bringing in drugs overland from the West Coast. Most of the East Texas cocaine trade remained, however, in the hands of local entrepreneurs. Being near Houston was convenient. The Cali and the Medellín cartels had both established large-scale cocaine import-and-distribution operations there.

American dealers bought from the Colombians at whatever level they could afford. The domestic dealerships were ethnically segmented—white and Latino traffickers sold powdered cocaine, mostly to white and Latino users; African Americans sold crack, mostly to black users—but were otherwise diffuse and loosely structured. The sophistication and corporate-style discipline of the Colombian suppliers were regarded with awe by many of their retailers. "They won't even do business with nobody that starts using drugs," a black former crack dealer in Houston told me. "They find out you're using, they just kill you." This rule, if it was ever applied, was definitely not followed in San Augustine in the mid-eighties, when Arthur Watts and Willie Ray (Blue Tick) Edwards, two part-time pulpwood haulers and full-time ne'er-do-wells, hooked up with a couple of low-level Colombian dealers, brothers named Aldon and Ivan Aguirre, in Houston, and began to run small quantities of cocaine up into the woods to support their own habits.

The demand for cocaine exploded with the invention of crack. In East Texas, makeshift legions of small-time dealers began shuttling between Houston and their hometowns. The Arthur Wattses and Blue Tick Edwardses were unlikely to be left alone in a business with such volume and cash flow, and in San Augustine they were soon joined by an older, far cannier, and more sober businessman: Lenard Jackson. According to the FBI, Jackson started buying cocaine in kilogram quantities from a Colombian named Celestino Morales, who was linked to the Cali cartel, and some of the young men who worked in Jackson's construction firm started carrying it with them on their frequent trips home to San Augustine.

One of Jackson's couriers was Harlon Kelly—Laverne's brother Hollis's son. Harlon had been working for Jackson for several years, since his graduation from San Augustine High. Neat, serious, and soft-spoken, he had been voted the handsomest boy in his graduating class. He was best known, though, for his ability to work. At the age of five, according to his family, he had started hauling pulpwood with his grandfather, Hulon, and he had rarely been without a job since. He hauled hay, did plumbing, painting, and landscaping at the Cedar Hills housing project, sacked groceries at the supermarket. Even after he moved to Houston and started working construction for Jackson, where the pay was by far the best he'd seen, Harlon continued to take second jobs—as a gas station attendant, as a United Parcel Service driver during the Christmas rush. Harlon and Jackson understood one another, because they were cut from the same mold: quiet, clever, ferocious workers, intent on escaping the poverty into which they had been born.

But when Jackson's construction business began to falter, Harlon's pay fell, and by 1987 there were periods of unemployment. Harlon, who could not abide being out of work, had heard that Jackson had started dealing drugs. Jackson, according to Harlon, tried to discourage him from going into the business, but Harlon was keen. "All I cared about in them days was making money," he told me.

Kelly started buying "eight-balls" (one eighth of an ounce) of powdered cocaine from Jackson, carrying them up to San Augustine, and selling them off in small quantities. Within a few months, he had saved ten thousand dollars. This was fantastic money, yet Harlon found he didn't care for the drug business. Addicts were unreliable, often unpleasant associates. He had never used drugs himself. "I got a personal grudge against drugs," he told me. "Because of my daddy." And so Harlon quit dealing and returned to Houston, where he got a job driving a container truck, and then went back to work for Jackson on a big road-construction project. The road project took him all over East Texas, and as far north as Longview. Then, in late 1988, the general contractor on the road project declared bankruptcy, throwing Jackson's crew out of work.

Jackson and Harlon, on their way back to Houston, stopped in San Augustine for Christmas. Harlon, seeing that the drug business was better than ever, decided to stay. He thought he would try to deal in larger quantities—ounces and half-ounces—and thus have less contact with addicts. Jackson agreed to put him on salary—five hundred dollars a week—and let him stay in a modern ranch house he now owned up behind the old Jackson family farm in Greertown. Harlon was joined at the ranch house by his younger half-brother,

Steven Kelly, who is an "outside" son of Jackson's, and who had also been thrown out of work by the downturn in his father's construction business. The Kelly brothers were soon doing a roaring business from the ranch house, building a network of sub-dealers, many of them former high school classmates who had either stayed in San Augustine or, like them, returned unemployed from Houston. These sub-dealers, who included Roger Hale's son Daryl, were usually not drug users—though some, like Harlon, had parents who were addicts.

Crack caught on in San Augustine mainly in poor black neighborhoods—in the Quarters and, especially, in the Sunset Hills housing project. "It was a good high," Shirley Bell, a Sunset Hills resident, told me, simply. "Something to do. And everybody else was doing it." Bell's son, Michael, who was a former classmate of the Kellys', objected to his mother's smoking crack, though his authority on the subject was limited by the fact that he was selling it himself. In fact, Michael Bell became one of the more successful local dealers. He had not had a job since high school—and had never left San Augustine—but he started driving a new car, bought a number of quarter horses (including one that was reported to have cost nine thousand dollars), and, in early 1989, vacationed in Acapulco with Daryl Hale and another friend. "Easy money," his mother said flatly. "Everybody saw it, everybody wanted it."

Sarah Oliphant, she who had pined for Saturday morning cartoons before her family moved to town, got hooked on crack in November 1988. She soon lost her job, and eventually her health. "These whole projects, we was really lookin' rough and ugly," she recalled. "Everybody skinny and sickly. I wore a sweater cap 'cause I wouldn't comb my hair. I got down to ninety-eight pounds." That was perhaps half of what Oliphant weighed when I met her. "She was po' as a snake," her mother put in.

A few whites got into crack, though the illegal drugs of choice among whites remained marijuana and methamphetamine, or speed, both of which are produced locally, the East Texas woods being almost as convenient for meth labs, which produce a powerful telltale odor, as for pot growing. Among the few white crack addicts who gained the trust of the black dealers in San Augustine was Dave Husband's daughter, Sheila Fussell.

The radius of the San Augustine cocaine market grew well beyond the county's boundaries during the first half of 1989. Customers and small-time dealers from the surrounding counties started making their way to San Augustine—to Jackson's ranch house, or to Sunset Hills, or to Blue Tick Edwards's trailer out on a country road known as Spur 85—to score. Some San Augustine dealers went on the road, renting a motel room in, say, Center, Texas, the next town north, for a weekend and selling off a load of rocks or powder to local users. For San Augustine's young entrepreneurs, who were accustomed to being patronized by their traditional rivals in Center (proud home of the Tyson plant where Lanee worked) as the natives of a backward county without industry or initiative, it was sweet turnabout.

Another kind of socioeconomic turnabout was occurring within San Augustine, as a growing number of young black men began to display unprecedented buying power at local car dealerships and at clothing and jewelry and furniture stores. In some cases, these were the same establishments that had once punished the ancestors of these prosperous new customers for nonpayment of their bills with whippings or forced land title transfers. The drug dealers paid cash. Steven Kelly insisted that he and Harlon were always low-key—"Our dress code and lifestyle were normal; I even wore jeans and my Redwing boots." But some of their sub-dealers, such as Michael Bell, who favored thick gold chains and mirrored sunglasses, were less discreet. The most startling image of new black prosperity, though, and surely the most difficult for many whites to accept, was Lenard Jackson, up from Houston, tooling around in his blue Rolls-Royce.

Dave Husband, people often said, went into the drug trade simply because he couldn't bear the thought of Jackson's being a more successful entrepreneur than he was. More likely, Husband, who owned a tavern where a lot of small-scale drug dealing went on, just saw a business opportunity too tempting to pass up. "Daddy was raised to bootleg, and somewhere back in his head he probably never saw no difference between bootlegging and the drug business," Sheila Fussell told me. "He told me later that he'd started losing most of his liquor business to the drug business. And he just 'wanted to see what the drug business was like.' Those were his words."

Jackson apparently welcomed Husband's entry into the trade, perhaps on the theory that Husband might divert some of the unwelcome law enforcement attention he himself had begun to attract. According to the FBI, Jackson introduced Husband to Celestino Morales in Houston, and Morales began to supply Husband with cocaine directly. In San Augustine, Husband dealt mainly in wholesale quantities, though Blue Tick Edwards recalled Husband coming around to his trailer, ostensibly to help him break down a package and cook it up into crack, but really, Edwards believed, to watch his retail sales operation, to collect his payment before Edwards could spend it, and, if possible, to steal a few of Edwards's customers.

How extensive did the San Augustine drug trade become? The FBI later said that seventy-five pounds of cocaine, with a street value of more than $3 million, was passing through the county each week by mid-1989. These figures, if accurate, would have made San Augustine a major regional drug-distribution center. But other law enforcement officials, such as Kenneth Kidwell, of the Drug Enforcement Agency in Tyler, questioned whether the drug problem in San Augustine was really any different from or bigger than in other East Texas communities. Certainly, young dealers like Harlon and Steven Kelly, who saw their involvement as short-term and relatively shallow, and both claimed they had decided to quit dealing altogether shortly before they were indicted, were stunned to find themselves described by prosecutors and the press as "drug lords."

Be that as it may, Nathan Tindall's main challenger in the 1988 election for sheriff—Charles Bryan, a local butcher—made "drugs" virtually the entire basis of his campaign, and it was soon clear that he was reaching voters with his message. People frightened by the rapid growth of the drug trade, or by the ravages of crack, began moving toward Bryan. This group included both whites, some of whom simply didn't like the idea of blacks' getting uppity—a prejudice that "drugs" covered nicely—and blacks, who had traditionally voted for Tindall but were now worried that he wasn't doing enough to stop drugs.

It wasn't true that Tindall was doing little or nothing about the problem. He had suspected Lenard Jackson a year earlier, after all, and had reported him to the state narcotics police then. He ran regular stings on dealers and users, and harassed the more hapless mid-level dealers, like Blue Tick Edwards, mercilessly. "Mr. Nathan arrested me so many times," Edwards recalled. "He picked me up every two or three months. Caught me once in the projects with some cocaine, and got me and my wife thrown out of Sunset Hills. That's how we ended up in my trailer."

Charles Bryan was in some ways an unlikely challenger. He had grown up in the southern part of the county, come to town as a teenager, gone to work for his father, and spent many years in the family grocery business and then in the meat business. He was not known as an especially sharp businessman, and he was unsubtly snubbed by self-made peers like Nathan Tindall and Dave Husband. "He was raised with a little bit of a silver spoon in his mouth," Tindall sniffed. Bryan's hobby was raising and selling show horses. He and his wife belonged to the highly respectable First Baptist Church, whose members included some of the oldest families in San Augustine. Thus, when the town's Old Guard, long dissatisfied with Nathan Tindall's performance as sheriff, considered alternatives, Bryan was ready to hand. He was photogenic enough— he was tall, heavy, firm-jawed, and white-haired, and wore a huge white cowboy hat—but he had none of the natural politician's bonhomie. He had, moreover, no experience in law enforcement.

Still, a consensus clearly formed among voters that it was time for a change in the sheriff's office—that, for whatever reasons, cocaine was getting away from Tindall. The high sheriff lost the Democratic primary to Bryan in the spring, and then, when Tindall managed to get his name on the ballot for the general election, he lost again in November.

Cecil Clark and I left for the woods at dawn. We drove south in his pickup, a clapped-out 1980 Ford Explorer with a Bible on the dashboard. We were both sipping coffee against a chill that seemed to have settled in for the winter. "Another wet year, I don't know, Finnegan," Cecil was saying. "Get too muddy to log, man can't work, man can't feed his family." He coughed, long and hard. Man can also catch pneumonia, I thought. Cecil had been treating himself for flu with a bitter tea he called merlin-and-pinestraw, its elements gathered from the woods. "You know, I can't get a job in a big manufactory because the insurance say I'm a risk," he said. "Because I'm fifty-one years old. That's why I'm still out here pulpwooding."

We were headed down Ayish Bayou, where the woods are scattered with ancient clan settlements with names like Hebron and Pisgah and Little Flock. The county roads were damp and deserted. Finally, behind a little Baptist church in a clearing, we found Cecil's battered bobtail truck and skidder. The truck was loaded with maybe thirty pine logs, each roughly fourteen inches thick and nine feet long. Cecil had cut them down, limbed them, and dragged them out of the woods the day before. We set off for the sawmill in the bobtail, which roared and jounced like an untuned tractor.

"She's a sorry old thing," Cecil said, meaning the truck. "Nowadays, you don't got a tree-length rig, you in the *sufferin'* line. And I mean an eighteen-wheeler, and a lot of big machinery." Cecil's one-ton had just a simple stiff-boom loader. I had heard many black people say that local banks would loan only a white man enough to buy a tree-length truck. And there clearly was a racial division of labor among independent loggers in the piney woods. "That's right," Cecil said. "We the shortwooders, because that's where there ain't no money, and the work's more dangerous."

Daylight was general now. We made our way slowly toward the mill, which was near a place called Grapevine. "If I was more interested in money, I'd have gone into the drug business," Cecil said. "Because that's where the money is."

I couldn't tell if he was serious. Cecil wasn't above testing my credulity for laughs. "That's right," he said. "But I just woulda stayed one year. Because that's all it takes in that business. One year, and then you can retire."

"That's what they all say."

"That's true. And look where they at now. All in the pen." We entered the devastation of a timber company clear-cut. "Now this is a real bad idea," Cecil said. "It gonna wipe out the wood industry. Plus, these trees help purify the air some kind of way. That's why the air is so clean around here. The water—everything is cleaner up here."

"You sound like Lanee."

Cecil laughed. "Or maybe she sound like me." He pointed at my notebook. "All that paper you all use up in New York? That paper come from somewhere. Possibly it come from right *here.* Lotta sweat went into getting that wood out of here. Lotta blood. Men died to make that paper. Some of them big-shot preachers in New York? I don't think they know about this." He jerked his thumb back toward the logs we carried.

At the sawmill, which turned out to be a family operation, Cecil drove up onto a scale. A white woman weighed the truck, graded the logs, and directed Cecil to an area of the yard where similar logs were stacked and where one of her sons was operating a crane. After he unloaded Cecil's logs, she told me, she would weigh his truck empty to determine Cecil's payment. Another son was working on a huge screaming saw nearby, and another was working on an even noisier debarker. Above the din, the woman told me, "We do our own millwright work. We got a big order from the Mexican national railroad for industrial-grade crossties. That's really keeping us going. We use everything off a log. Boards off the sides, ties out of the center, bark and edges for the chipper—that's to make paper—even board ends for firewood."

As Cecil and I, his business at the mill done, headed up the road, he mentioned that he had once lost three fingers in a sawmill accident. "Lost 'em in a chain sprocket," he said. "Carried 'em to the doctor in a napkin. He sewed 'em all back on." Cecil waved a work-gnarled hand. "God been good to me. Showed me the way, let me do His work. You know, I got licensed as a preacher back in 1964, but then I drifted away from it. My ministry only stabilized about nine years ago, when I started pastoring at St. Matthew's, up in Greertown. Then I got a couple more churches."

We wandered down a maze of red-dirt roads into an area known as the Steep Creek community. "Somebody want to clear some land for an orchard," Cecil said. We came over a rise. "Oh, my. Every truck in Texas already here." From beneath one of the trucks parked in the brush, two legs in overalls were sticking out stiffly. Seeing my alarm, Cecil laughed. "That's just old Hulon, mechanickin'," he said. Down a hillside, chain saws whining, we found Cecil's brother-in-law Hollis Kelly, his stepson Timmy Price, and a teenage nephew named J. C. Barnes. We arrived just as they dropped a sixty-foot pine, which hit the ground with an impressive whump.

The trees being cleared were mostly hardwood: pin oak, red oak, sweetgum. The men moved with amazing ease over the thick brush and unstable, fallen trees, wielding their saws—even Hollis, who had some kind of cancer, now apparently in remission, and was still rail-thin. To keep me occupied, I was given the only safe task available, one that even I could not screw up: measuring fallen trees with a ten-foot-six-inch stick, making marks for the cutters. The diciest part of the day's work turned out to be hoisting the logs up onto the bobtail truck: getting chains from the stiff-boom loader around them, then swinging them through the air into place. Cecil was in charge of figuring the many angles and movements and quick, scary weight transfers before they occurred. I was especially nervous watching young J.C. help with the loading, for I knew that his father, who was also known as J. C. Barnes, had been killed in a pulpwood-loading accident.

Later that day, a complicated truck reshuffle put Cecil and me on a long drive through the county in his pickup. At my instigation, we started talking politics. Cecil was president of the local chapter of the NAACP—a chapter that had become, he admitted, rather moribund. In fact, the NAACP had never been much of a factor in San Augustine until, in 1988, it had suddenly made a name for itself by helping organize a protest in Hemphill, in neighboring Sabine County. One of Cecil's three church congregations was in Hemphill, and it seemed that a young black man named Loyal Garner had been beaten to death in the Hemphill jail. Three white officers had been acquitted of violating Garner's civil rights by a local jury composed of eleven whites and one black (and the black juror worked as a housemaid for one of the white jurors). Cecil had held a protest meeting, which got a great deal of local attention, especially after the Ku Klux Klan threatened to attack the church where it was held. The Klan never did attack, but, Cecil said, "I was followed, told they were going to run me out of town. Somebody came in and tore up my pastor's chair and left a drawing of a lynched man on my desk. But, you know, they had been misusing white peoples in that jail, too. A white woman came to me and said they beat her daughter to a peppermint stick up in there."

A coalition of activists from Hemphill and elsewhere came together and demanded justice for Loyal Garner. The officers were eventually tried again, on murder charges, in Tyler, Texas—where Garner had been transferred to a hospital and actually died—and convicted. Cecil still didn't feel entirely safe in Hemphill, he said. The officers were now in prison, but their families were still around, and some relative could, he figured, decide to come after him at any time. But the standing of the NAACP had shot up throughout the Deep East Texas black community as a result of the Garner case.

"But that's how I made my big mistake," Cecil said. "Got too big for my britches. Because that was about when Charles Bryan got elected sheriff, and so I went and told this white man"—a reporter, he meant—"that if Charles Bryan screwed up the NAACP would be on his ass, too, like a fly on shit. That's what I said. Next thing, a lady we know who was working in Charles Bryan's house heard his wife say at the dinner table that they needed to get me and the NAACP. And the next thing I knew I was bein' arrested for child molesting."

That was in April 1989. The crime, according to the indictment, had occurred nearly a year and a half before. The victim was a niece of Cecil's who lived in Kellyville; she had been eleven years old at the time. Cecil vehemently denied the charges, and Charles Mitchell, the district attorney, told me that, though he had planned to try the case, he was not optimistic about winning a conviction. But then Cecil had saved him the trouble, surprising everyone by entering a plea of No Contest. He did so, he told me, because his lawyer had told him that to win an acquittal they would have to demolish publicly the credibility of his niece, as well as that of her mother, whom the Clarks believed had put her daughter up to making the accusation in the first place. Cecil didn't want to do that to his niece, he said. In return for his plea, he received a suspended sentence, a fine, and ten years' probation.

Far worse than the legal penalties, however, was the damage to his reputation. The elders at one of his churches decided to replace him (his congregations in Hemphill and in Greertown chose to retain him). In a vote of confidence, he was reelected president of the Baptist Ministers' Conference of the Sabine Valley Association. He also kept his position as NAACP president. But his effectiveness as a civil rights advocate was drastically diminished, just as he believed the sheriff's office intended it to be.

Then there was the impact on him and his family. (Of the impact on the victim and her family, I knew little. I never got to know them, though I often saw them around Kellyville, where the incident was all forgiven and forgotten, I was too frequently told.) Laverne had stood next to her husband during his court appearance, and still stoutly asserted his innocence, though the pain in her eyes and her voice when she talked about it were unmistakable. Their children had also suffered, needless to say.

As for Cecil himself, he told me, with a heavy sigh, "I swallowed a *hunk.* Thought it about choke me. But God stood with me. Because He knew I never did no such act. I'm payin' here, but I ain't gonna pay on the other side."

We drove in silence, between walls of forest and through clearings bisected by the long tin roofs of chicken houses.

"I'm all right with God, and that's all that matters," Cecil said suddenly. "It don't matter what people think. What matters is the truth. I lied to play the system, to make a deal, but God done forgive me that lie. I suffered. Many times I just had to stop and cry. I even considered suicide. But then one night I had a dream. And the Lord told me to go to the Scripture, and I did. And it told me to carry on with my ministry. And so I did. After what happened to me, a man is never supposed to speak again, rest of his life. Just hang his head down. And I hung my head down for a while. But not no more. Now I go everywheres they ask me to preach. And I feel the Lord inside me. My preaching is getting better and better, too."

Cecil was, in fact, in heavy demand as a preacher again by the time I met him. But his days as a political activist seemed over. He had been a prominent supporter of Nathan Tindall, and had even signed, with fourteen other black preachers, a petition of support for him in the last sheriff's election. But he would be staying clear of all future sheriff's races, he said, no matter who ran. "Uh-uh," he said. "Uh-*uh*. They tried to shut me up." He paused, and nodded. "And they did shut me up."

Lanee was as vehement as her mother in defense of Cecil. Her version of events emphasized the crack addiction of the victim's mother, and charged a boyfriend of the mother with molesting the girl. Like others I had spoken to around San Augustine, she seemed to think her father had made a mistake by not defending himself in court and thus reclaiming his good name. "People always like to think the worst thing," she said. "They believe that make life more interesting."

We were sitting outside a Dairy Queen, slightly west of town, in my rental car, eating hamburgers after church. We had been speaking in careful generalities because Johnathan and one of his young cousins were in the backseat, murmuring happily over milkshakes. Lanee finished eating, meticulously cleaned her hands, and ordered me to drive to a car wash a short distance up U.S. 96. "This car been gettin' embarrassing," she said, indicating with distaste the dried red mud covering everything up to the windows.

At the car wash, which was self-serve, Lanee waved away my efforts to help. I rolled up the windows and, with Johnathan and little Lavetta, sat inside while Lanee hosed us down with soapy water, blasting the hubcaps and the thickest mud deposits with a high-pressure stream, striding back and forth in her high heels and swank, navy blue church dress. She completely ignored both our mugging at the windows and the occasional hoots and car honks that her performance attracted from passersby. Admiring her absorption in her work, it struck me that this was one of Lanee's chosen roles in life: cleaning up. When her favorite uncle, Hollis, seemed to be killing himself with crack and nobody knew what to do, she dragged him home and bathed him and shaved him. When her favorite cousin, Dee Dee, was dying of AIDS, Lanee mopped her brow and laved her with kisses.

Not that nursing was Lanee's vocation. She had actually worked for a while at a nursing home in San Augustine, and she had not liked it. "Certain time of year, it seemed like the patients all started dying," she told me. "And we had to clean them up. It was too sad. And the pay was sorry: $4.52 an hour. Also, some of the old men, their things still be gettin' hard. Then they want you to wash it! 'I ain't washin' that thing! He can wash it his*self.*' Even Tyson's is better'n that."

I had been up to the Tyson plant in Center, where Lanee worked, and had taken the tour. It was a vast place, employing more than a thousand people and processing more than a million birds a week. Starting pay was $5.15 an hour, although some of the grislier jobs, in places like the hanging pen (very dark, very smelly, birds still alive) and the kill room, paid more. On the whole, it was a hectic, noisy, reeking, gory assault of an environment, with temperatures ranging cruelly from one hundred degrees (eviscerating room) to sub-freezing (pre-loading), and I wasn't surprised to learn that one third of all employees quit each year. Lanee was in the labeling department, a chilly but clean area—no blood or fat on the floor—where she and about thirty other workers weighed birds, labeled them, and tossed them into cardboard boxes. As I passed through labeling, accompanied by the plant manager, Lanee caught my eye and winked.

We were released from my car to admire Lanee's work. A few stalls down, a bearded young white guy was polishing a gleaming new tree-length truck and trying not to stare at us. I waved. He shyly waved back. His rig was of the type that cost $65,000 and required a well-disposed bank. A honk and a shout came from the highway, "Nay Nay!" That was Lanee's nickname. The shout came from a purple miniature pickup with smoked side windows, cruising slowly past. Lanee turned and shouted back. "That's just a cousin of mine," she said. She shook her head. "He older'n me, but he got a kid's mind on him."

We climbed back in the car. As we pulled onto the road, the purple pickup passed again, going the other way. Lanee sighed. "He went to the city for a while, ran the streets up there," she said, speaking again of her cousin. "It don't make no difference. Here and there, they both dead ends."

Lanee wanted to show me a house in town she was planning to rent with a roommate. "My parents' house gettin' too crowded," she said. Her new place turned out to be a tumbledown tin-roofed place with a dirt yard and no foundation, near the old Jerusalem CME church, on the edge of the Quarters. I asked Johnathan if he looked forward to living there. "Don't gotta ride the school bus," he said quietly. Their roommate, Lanee said, would be a young woman known as Juicy. "She nice, but she kind of wild. Me and her went out to a club in Pineland the other night, had a lot of fun. But she brung this white girl from her work with us, and the white girl got kind of drunk and started talkin' 'nigger' this and 'nigger' that, just because she heard Juicy doin' it. I didn't like that. It ain't the same when white people say it."

We drove back to U.S. 96, where Lanee pointed out a low-roofed plywood hut near the southern end of the Front. "That's where our liquor store gonna be," she said. The building could scarcely have been more modest, but the location was prime. It was right next door to the Watts Café, a shabby but popular pool hall and tavern. There were three liquor stores already nearby, but also within shouting distance were two convenience stores, four gas stations, a Laundromat, a take-out chicken shack, and the car lot where Nathan Tindall worked. By local standards, this was a bustling retail district. Even Dave Husband had seen fit to do business here. Just south of Lanee's place-to-be was Husband's old tavern, the Bull Club, where a fancy neon sign was still disintegrating in the window. And next door to that had been Husband's liquor store, which was, according to many San Augustinians, a gold mine before it was shut down and confiscated by the federal government.

EIGHT

Along with their radical distrust of institutions, rural East Texans tend to a conventional suspicion of outsiders. In San Augustine, Operation White Tornado only deepened the local paranoia. People I interviewed constantly insisted on anonymity for the most innocuous observations, and more than once I had interview subjects suddenly grab at my jacket pockets to see if I wasn't, you know, hiding a tape recorder in there, heh heh. Local people habitually mistrust each other as well. Once, in the Hill Top Barbecue, I heard an old black man call to a group talking in the kitchen, "Y'all ain't framin' up on me in there, are you?" His tone was jocular but his concern, I came to understand, was chronic. And the discovery that professional undercover officers, even federal agents, had moved among them undetected for months, seemed to have made a special impression on people.

Having a writer in town was apparently, to some San Augustinians, no less appalling. At the San Augustine Inn, the motel west of town where I stayed, a night clerk wanted to know what I was doing there. When I told her, her eyes narrowed under painted brows and her tobacco-ruined voice sharpened. "You ain't gonna write nothin' bad about us, are you?" She reminded me that a writer from *Texas Monthly* had come through town in the 1970s, "and after what he wrote he never could show his face here again. If he did, some folks here would peel the skin right off him, in one-inch strips." She demonstrated the skinning process she had in mind, her mouth twisted in sadistic concentration. She pressed me about who I had interviewed and, deducing that I was interested in the politics of the sheriff's office, she glowered. "Don't you say a thing about that 'round here, if you know what's good for you," she said. Nathan Tindall was a crook, she informed me, and Dave Husband "was a bad, bad man." On the night that Tindall lost the election, she said, Husband had showed his opinion of the results by selling cocaine from his liquor store all night, right over the counter! She imitated a fiend at work, a sort of American peasant folktale Satan, doing evil in the night.

Whether Dave Husband was even selling cocaine in 1988, from his liquor store or anywhere else, was a matter of dispute. The U.S. Attorney's office believed that he got into the cocaine business in 1987. Nathan Tindall believed that, if Husband ever got into the drug business, it was only in 1989, after he, Tindall, had left the sheriff's office. Certainly, the FBI's efforts to get Husband to sell cocaine to various informants who approached him in his store in 1989 were rebuffed. Marvin McLeroy, of the state narcotics office in Lufkin, who played a major role in Operation White Tornado, told me that, after Charles Bryan took over the San Augustine sheriff's office, Bryan and his men began to make life more difficult for Husband—who had been, after all, a prominent Tindall supporter—and that their petty harassment of Husband and his liquor customers made Husband more wary in his illegal dealings than he might otherwise have been. In fact, McLeroy said that if Tindall had won the election and remained as sheriff, White Tornado might have been an easier operation all around.

It began as two separate investigations—one local, the other external. The local effort was the initiative of Larry Saurage, the chief deputy sheriff hired by Charles Bryan when he took office. Bryan, though he looked the part of a Texas sheriff, had wisely grasped the fact that his career as a butcher and grocer had not prepared him for a leadership role in law enforcement, and had gone looking for an experienced chief deputy. Saurage, a well-traveled lawman who was then working narcotics down in Chambers County, between Houston and Beaumont, fit the bill. He came to San Augustine in January 1989, and within a few weeks he had brought in Betty Donatto, a black undercover narcotics agent from the Liberty County sheriff's office (Liberty is next door to Chambers) to help him put together drug cases in San Augustine. Donatto, passing herself off as Bennie Lee Thibodeaux, a good-time girl originally from Louisiana, was paired up by Saurage with a local informant, who helped her infiltrate the county's drug scene, starting in the Sunset Hills housing project.

Meanwhile, Marvin McLeroy had begun his own investigation in San Augustine the previous September, prompted by persistent reports that Lenard Jackson, Dave Husband, Blue Tick Edwards, Arthur Watts, and Daryl Hale were dealing drugs, and by rumors of corruption in the sheriff's office. McLeroy, without informing any local agency of his activities, used informants to buy cocaine from Arthur Watts and Daryl Hale, and eventually invited federal authorities into the investigation. (Charles Bryan, while still a candidate for sheriff, had also contacted the U.S. Attorney's office in Beaumont about the drug problem in San Augustine.) Stuart Platt, an assistant federal prosecutor, now took charge of the investigation, with field command going to FBI Special Agent Zechariah (Zack) Shelton. Platt and Shelton's chief quarry in San Augustine was, from the outset, Nathan Tindall—whom Shelton later described to me as "a true boss-hog sheriff." The state and federal investigators continued to shun local law enforcement in San Augustine. For local assistance, they turned to the Shelby County district attorney's office, in Center, and to Robert Cartwright, a young policeman in Port Arthur, whose father, John Matthew Cartwright, was a patrolman in the San Augustine town police.

But then, in March, Platt and Shelton's men began to run across Betty Donatto's trail in San Augustine. Concerned that her investigation might inadvertently abort theirs, they went to the Liberty County sheriff's office, learned of Saurage's operation, and contacted Saurage. According to Shelton, Saurage was angry to discover that outside agencies were working on his new turf. He agreed to cooperate, however, with the FBI and the state narcotics office, though his boss, Charles Bryan, whose ability to keep professional secrets was untested, was to be left in the dark. John Matthew Cartwright's superior, the town chief of police, was also left in the dark—even though the command center for Platt and Shelton's operation was set up in a trailer in a pecan orchard behind Cartwright's mother's house. (That spring, a tornado rocked the trailer and gave rise to the operation's catchy title.) For Chief Deputy Saurage, actively running undercover agents and informants right under the nose of even an inexperienced sheriff soon proved to be more trouble than it was worth, and in April, he and his colleagues let Charles Bryan in on the operation. According to the FBI's Shelton, "We just told Bryan, 'Stay out of our way, and we'll make you a hero.' "

Betty Donatto, a sleepy-eyed, soft-voiced, russet-haired woman in her early forties, remained the key agent of the combined operation. She had been doing police work for only a few years, having previously worked as a computer operator in California and as a journalist in Liberty County, but, once she started in law enforcement, she had risen quickly, becoming a small-town police chief and then discovering she had a talent for undercover work. The informant she worked with in San Augustine, a local crack addict named Bo Garrett, had been dubious about her at first. Her skin was too light for her to pass unaccosted in the black drug world, he thought. But the Louisiana cover story, Donatto figured, would help ease suspicion, since Louisiana was known for its mixed-race population, and her real upbringing in a black family in East Texas gave her the ability to blend in socially.

"It worked good," she told me later, in a restaurant in Houston. "We just told people I was Bo's girlfriend, living in Houston. I started out buying twenty-dollar rocks, and moved on up to one-fifties. If people wondered why I never smoked, I told 'em I worked for the airlines—'Hey, I gotta take a pee test tomorrow.' I'd say I was just up there to see Bo, and I was buying for somebody in Houston. I was driving a white Corvette—a seized vehicle from Liberty County. That got their attention." Donatto laughed lightly. "I mean, San Augustine was *sad*. A lot of the people there didn't even have cars. It was like they had no connection to the outside world. After a while, I started feeling like Santa Claus. I used to buy a box of chicken, maybe a case of beer, and drive up into the projects, and they'd all come crowd around the car, ask me for chicken and beer, and tell me everything that was going on. 'Hey, Jackson's in town!'

"Nobody was afraid of the town police. The crooks were afraid of Tindall, and they told me to watch out for him, because he still ran the show, even if he was in the background. But San Augustine was pretty unusual—at least, when I was there. It was so open and free. And you could kind of understand it, because you're really away from everything up there. If you had the right amount of money, it was like you could set up your own little world, and nobody could touch you. I could see how Dave Husband and Lenard Jackson thought they'd never get caught. There were all these weak-minded people around who they could just control. In the projects, the Ranch"—Lenard Jackson's house in Greertown—"was considered Heaven."

Donatto befriended some of the local crackheads and dealers, including Sarah Oliphant and Michael Bell. She bought cocaine from Blue Tick Edwards, out in his trailer on Spur 85, sometimes encountering Roger Hale there (these encounters helped put Hale away), and ultimately managed to overcome the suspicions of Willie Earl Dade, Tindall's ex-deputy, and buy half an ounce from him in a tavern on the Front, for six hundred dollars—the largest purchase she made in San Augustine. She had no luck buying dope from Dave Husband, however. "The word was, Husband didn't deal anything small. It was half a kilo on up, and you needed an introduction. We tried to make buys with a couple of different informants, but they both failed. I was there for the second one. It was a white girl from Jasper, who said she'd bought from him before. But Husband just said he didn't know what she was talking about."

Donatto knew that a major target of the federal investigation was Nathan Tindall. "They told me to find out anything I could about Tindall being crooked," she said. "But all I ever got was hearsay."

Eventually, Donatto made her way out to the paradise of Lenard Jackson's ranch house, in the company of a young woman, "a hyper crack smoker" whom she watched make a buy from "Jackson's sons," as she knew Harlon and Steven Kelly. Donatto later began going out there on her own, and succeeded in buying half an ounce of crack from Roy Jackson, one of Lenard's brothers. Roy subsequently invited her "to go partying to Louisiana with him." Donatto wanted to go, but Shelton and Saurage thought it sounded too risky. "Zack was a nervous wreck about me," Donatto recalled. "I appreciated that, because working in San Augustine was lonely. Working undercover for a long time gets weird. They say you should never do it for more than three months. You forget who you are. You can't think about anything else. I'd go home to Liberty County to see my daughter, but all I could think about was how I wasn't really getting what the feds wanted. I actually couldn't wait to get back in my dirty jeans and my Corvette, and this straw hat I always wore up there."

One of the investigation's local informants was a small-time dealer named Ricky Davis. Fitted out with a tape recorder, Davis allegedly managed to buy half an ounce of powdered cocaine in April from Dave Husband's brother Buck—though the tape ran out before the deal was consummated. Davis claimed that in the past he had bought cocaine from Dave himself, as well as from Husband's son, Neil. Davis had a credibility problem, though. When his controllers heard that he was still selling drugs, even while he was informing, they took him to a secluded park in San Augustine to discuss the matter with him. Davis denied the reports heatedly. Then Betty Donatto stepped out from behind a tree. "He had been selling to me," Donatto said, laughing. "He didn't know I was a narc. Ricky about fainted. We worked together after that. But he was always a nervous wreck."

In May the FBI began tapping the telephones of more than a dozen "subject individuals" in and around San Augustine. In Agent Shelton's application to a federal district judge for permission to do more wiretapping, including of Nathan Tindall's phone, he concluded, "Normal investigative procedures have been tried and failed." Some of these failures were evident in the application itself; it described Michael Bell as being married to his mother, assured the judge that Dave Husband owned the San Augustine Inn (this would have been news to Husband), and twice described Husband as Nathan Tindall's nephew. "Affiant believes," wrote Shelton, referring to himself, "that Nathan Tindall was integrally involved in providing protection to various cocaine dealers." He added that he suspected Tindall might be laundering money for Husband and Arthur Watts through a local bank where he was then working. Shelton even managed to interpret Marvin McLeroy's report that Tindall had approached him about Lenard Jackson's activities in 1987 as evidence that Jackson must have started paying off Tindall then.

The additional wiretaps were authorized, and the investigators, listening in from their trailer in the pecan orchard, continued to gather information on the San Augustine drug trade. Some of the dealers, although they were usually infuriatingly vague and wary on the phone, made some reasonably incriminating remarks, but Tindall never said anything of interest. "I'm just lucky that Dave Husband and them others never had accounts at my bank," Tindall told me. "Because if they did the feds would have put that on me, called it laundering."

In late May the commanders of Operation White Tornado decided it was time to pounce. Betty Donatto was astonished. "I couldn't believe they wanted to pull the cord *then*," she says. "I had just worked my way up from the projects to the Ranch, and I only needed a couple more months. We could have got more on the Houston connection, Louisiana, the Colombians. Zack Shelton knew I thought it was too soon. But he said Ricky Davis said the crooks were getting suspicious of me and were going to bump me off. Except everybody knew that Ricky was a nervous wreck. He just wanted the whole thing to end."

And so, late on the rainy afternoon of June 2, 1989, a vast paramilitary convoy, complete with newspaper reporters and TV camera crews, streamed into San Augustine, carrying more than two hundred heavily armed agents from the FBI, the Drug Enforcement Administration, the U.S. Customs Service, the U.S. Marshals, the Bureau of Alcohol, Tobacco, and Firearms, the Army's Criminal Investigation Division, the state highway patrol, the state police, the Texas Rangers, and sheriff's offices in half a dozen nearby counties and parishes, with a helicopter thundering overhead. Houses, taverns, trailers, and liquor stores were raided on the strength of seventeen federal search warrants. Property was seized and suspects arrested on the basis of three sealed federal indictments and sixteen criminal complaints. In the TV footage, burly agents swarm up the Front, ordering frightened black people down on their faces in the mud. Lenard Jackson and his wife, who had attended the high school graduation of a niece and a nephew up in Shelby County that afternoon, were stopped on the highway by a patrol car backed up by a helicopter. Lenard was made to stand spread-eagled, his hands on the hot hood of his Rolls-Royce, a gun at his head. Dave Husband was arrested at his store. Willie Earl Dade was found in his girlfriend's trailer, about to cook up a batch of cocaine—the only drugs actually found in the raid. Little or no resistance was offered. The only injury occurred when Blue Tick Edwards, surprised in his trailer, tried to flee, and dislocated his shoulder in the ensuing struggle. "Me and my wife just been laying up in the bed all day, using drugs and making love, and I didn't know what was going on," he said later. By nightfall, thirty-one suspects had been taken into custody. Tindall, who had not been named in either the indictments or the complaints, was not arrested.

Betty Donatto was there for the raid, but did little. "I was in a vehicle with some FBI guys," she recalled. "And they had every type of gun you can name. Machine guns, AK-47s. Of course, they didn't need all them guns and dogs and a helicopter in little San Augustine. But I kept quiet. I just figured, This is really gonna make Larry and his sheriff look good. That's what this is about." And on the courthouse square that evening, watching the crowd applaud and the TV cameras jostle for position as Lenard Jackson was hustled handcuffed into the jail, Donatto marveled at Charles Bryan's performance. "Larry's sheriff," who had been so firmly excluded from Operation White Tornado, was reaping the reward that Zack Shelton had promised him. "There he was, shaking hands and grinning and accepting all the credit," Donatto recalled. "And I told my captain, Tom, who came up from Liberty County for the raid, 'I can't *believe* this.' At the end of the whole situation, I just had to give that man an Academy Award."

NINE

Naturally, Nathan Tindall said that, if it had been up to him, he'd have conducted Operation White Tornado by telephone, just calling up the suspects and telling them to come on down to the jailhouse and bring their dope. He'd probably have got more dope that way than the pittance the feds found, too, he reckoned. (Actually, some suspects who weren't in the county at the time of the raid, such as Harlon and Steven Kelly, who were in Houston, only heard about it secondhand. The Kellys, having seen the news reports on television, turned themselves in to the police the next morning.) Why did the feds stage the raid when they did? According to Tindall, it was because they were nervous because he had just started work as an investigator for Charles Mitchell, the district attorney (who knew nothing about Operation White Tornado), and they were afraid that he might break up the drug trade himself, stealing all their glory. As it happened, Mitchell let Tindall go immediately, reasoning that the former sheriff would not make an effective investigator while under a cloud of federal suspicion.

That cloud only darkened in the days after the raid, as veiled and not so veiled charges began to rain down on Tindall. Stuart Platt explained to reporters that Operation White Tornado had been necessary because local law enforcement in San Augustine had been "compromised." Larry Saurage said that he had found in San Augustine a sheriff's office that was "a hundred years behind the times." Meanwhile, the FBI, during detention hearings in Beaumont, testified, according to the Beaumont *Enterprise*, that "Tindall was difficult to work with and offered little cooperation on drug investigations." The press got in its licks: UPI tarred Tindall's entire career with the drug brush when it reported: "Federal investigators said the drug trade ran rampant in San Augustine County during Nathan Tindall's almost 40 years as sheriff." Or, as the *Houston Chronicle*, apparently buying the notion that the county had been a piney-woods gangland until June 2, put it: "Many San Augustine residents blame the years of blatant criminal activity on former Sheriff Tindall."

It seemed only a matter of time before he would be indicted, his disgrace complete. On the day after the drug raid, Tindall was served with a federal court order to turn over the bank records of seven of the White Tornado suspects, and a few weeks later he was subpoenaed to appear before a federal grand jury in Beaumont to answer allegations by one of the suspects that he had taken payoffs. In early July, Tindall's house was searched twice in one week by Zack Shelton and Larry Saurage. On the second visit, they were accompanied by IRS agents. Tindall's tax records were seized, along with dozens of old guns he had taken from the evidence room at the sheriff's office when he left, and a small bag of marijuana. The marijuana was a prop that Tindall had been using for years in antidrug lectures at schools, and the guns still had evidence tags on them—Tindall had left instructions that anybody who wanted to reclaim a weapon should contact him—but the episode did little to improve his press. SEARCH OF EX-SHERIFF'S HOUSE NETS GUNS, DRUGS was how the Beaumont *Enterprise* played it, illustrating its story with a photograph of Charles Bryan with the confiscated arsenal. The San Augustine *Tribune,* a timid weekly in normal times, actually ran verbatim several paragraphs of the search warrant that Larry Saurage had sworn out in order to enter the home of the county's former boss hog.

Bryan, Saurage, Shelton, Platt, and Platt's superior, U.S. Attorney Bob Wortham, were the local (and not so local) heroes of the hour. Zack Shelton was shown on ABC News making a speech on the San Augustine courthouse square, where, according to Peter Jennings, residents were "cheering the police who liberated their town." As a news story, Operation White Tornado worked. It had good guys, bad guys (Lenard Jackson's seized Rolls-Royce made countless TV appearances, as the lurid emblem of a black man's ill-gotten gains), and a great little official-corruption angle. It also revealed a vivid new front in the war on drugs—a picturesque, one-stoplight Southern town—and even some San Augustinians seemed pleased to see the raid in that quasi-national context. Dr. Curtis Haley, a conservative local landowner and physician, circulated a public resolution, signed by some six hundred of his neighbors, thanking Bob Wortham and his colleagues and urging them, "Please continue with your crusade of providing a Drug Free America not only in this community and county but all others in the great state of Texas."

Virtually nothing was said publicly about the disparity between the amount of cocaine alleged to have been moving through San Augustine—the often repeated seventy-five pounds a week, worth more than $3 million—and the amount actually found during the raid. Two hundred agents making a lightning strike had turned up only five ounces of drugs. Bob Wortham, the U.S. Attorney, repeatedly pointed out that some $2 million of property had also been seized in the raid, but this seizure was less of a law enforcement coup than it sounded, for most of the property involved consisted of very public assets like

Dave Husband's liquor store and house, his brother Buck's house, the Watts Café, Lenard Jackson's houses in Greertown and Pearland, Blue Tick Edwards's trailer, Willie Earl Dade's trailer, and the various vehicles of the numerous suspects. (And some of this lucre, including the Watts Café and Dave Husband's house, was ultimately returned by court order to its owners.)

The White Tornado defendants, for their part, could not seem to win for losing. Barely a week after the raid, it emerged that Dave Husband was now suspected of having buried the bodies of an undetermined number of undocumented Mexican workers on his land. Government bulldozers began turning acres of rolling pastureland into a vast open-pit mine while the press corps camped out under the trees. Husband had employed illegal Mexican labor for years, and five undocumented workers had, in fact, been found in a trailer behind his liquor store during the drug raid. But the workers found in the trailer later signed a joint statement asserting that, contrary to press reports, they had not been beaten by Husband. And no bodies were ever found.

The number of defendants rose eventually to fifty-seven, and the guilty pleas began to flow in early August. Daryl Hale, Roger's son, was the first White Tornado defendant to agree to cooperate with prosecutors in exchange for reduced charges—a single count of conspiracy to distribute cocaine. By the end of September, Blue Tick Edwards, Willie Earl Dade, Roger Hale, Edgar Price, Michael Bell, Ivan Aguirre (Aldon Aguirre was still at large), and more than a dozen others had pleaded out. Each time someone pleaded, the remaining defendants grew more nervous, for it meant another finger quite likely being pointed at them. Thus did the stampede build, to twenty and thirty and forty guilty pleas. By early 1990, Dave Husband and Lenard Jackson and their immediate families and associates were the only significant defendants left.

But the federal prosecutors still did not have the man they wanted: Nathan Tindall. Lenard Jackson and company probably knew nothing incriminating about Tindall, the prosecutors thought, and so the issue did not figure in the negotiations with them. In March those negotiations finally resulted in guilty pleas that brought down sentences of fifteen years on Lenard and ten years each on his brother Roy, his son Steven Kelly, and Harlon Kelly. (Because these were federal sentences, they contained no possibility of parole.)

Dave Husband was another matter. The prosecutors' first offer to Husband was five years, and the return of his liquor store. Husband, convinced that the evidence against him was weak, turned it down. As his fellow defendants began to cooperate, agreeing to testify against him, the offers from the prosecutors got less generous. Finally, in September, Husband agreed to plead guilty and to cooperate with the government in exchange for a sentence of twelve years, the forfeiture of his store, and a dismissal of the charges against his son. Cooperating with the government meant telling investigators what he knew about Nathan Tindall.

And then Husband's lawyer, Joseph C. Hawthorn, of Beaumont, made a colossal mistake. After coming to a verbal plea agreement with the prosecutors and with the federal judge, but before formalizing the agreement in court that afternoon, he let his client be debriefed by Stuart Platt, Zack Shelton, and Malcolm Bales, one of Platt's colleagues. In barely half an hour, Husband told the government the sum total of what he had on Tindall: nothing. "And Tindall was it," Hawthorn said later. "He was our only bargaining chip." That afternoon, the judge decided he didn't like the sentence, and after a private conversation with Platt and Bales he rejected the plea agreement. Hawthorn's appeal to have the judge recused from the case was denied. And the government was no longer interested in any plea agreement with Husband.

Six months later, on the day that his son was to enter a guilty plea, Husband, now frantic about his son, whom he had drafted into the drug business to begin with, made the government an extraordinary offer. He would plead guilty to every charge against him—eight felony counts—if they would just assure him that his son wouldn't go to jail. The prosecutors agreed immediately. And Dave Husband, who was then forty-four years old, was subsequently sentenced, under the mandatory minimums that attach to all federal drug violations, to life in prison without the possibility of parole.

Except for its incongruity among the punishments received by the other White Tornado defendants, Charles Mitchell had no problem with the sentence Dave Husband got. He had no problem, for that matter, with asking for the death sentence when a capital murder case came his way. He did, however, have reservations about the way business was now being conducted in federal courts. "The new evidentiary rules in these drug cases, allowing what would ordinarily be hearsay, and so forth, are pretty outrageous," he told me. "I mean, it's not much of a challenge to try a case when you're allowed to use evidence that would be inadmissible in a state court." It's also not much of a challenge, under such rules, to win guilty pleas from defendants once fellow defendants start testifying against them. Mitchell believed that in the Texas courts, where he did his prosecuting, most of the cases against the White Tornado defendants would have been much more difficult to win. The evidence simply wasn't there. And Dave Husband would have walked free after a state court sentenced his son Neil to ten years for possession with intent to deliver cocaine, in what even Mitchell, who prosecuted Neil, agreed was a subversion of Dave Husband's plea agreement with federal prosecutors. But when Husband's lawyer argued in the Fifth Circuit Court of Appeals that the plea agreement had been broken, the federal prosecutors contended that they had no control over state prosecutors; the judge agreed, and let Husband's life sentence stand.

Mitchell also had questions about the perennial federal investigation of

Nathan Tindall. "If they really believed that he was putting fines in his pocket, they just needed to send an agent up here driving drunk," he said. "That's what I'd do. Buy him three or four quarts of beer, send him up here throwing bottles out the window. That would be pretty easy to clear up." With Tindall out of office, the feds were reduced to chasing shadows. "I could get on that phone right now and say, 'Tindall's got a cow out here,' " Mitchell told me. "And they would figure out a federal crime he's committing and be *on* his butt."

Why are the federal authorities so intent on Tindall?

"Well, they want to do what's right," Mitchell said. "If there's a dirty sheriff, they want to prosecute him. But, of course, sheriffs' offices are also a fountainhead—or a cesspool, depending on how you look at it—of publicity."

The wave of publicity that accompanied Operation White Tornado left Mitchell unmoved, at best. "It was all just media hype," he said. "Lawyers in the square, holding a pep rally—that borders on unethical behavior. Am I supposed to call a pep rally every time I go to try a murder case? Tell the world, 'I'm going to cut out killing'? It would be popular, but it wouldn't mean very much." The raid itself had been a pointless display, in Mitchell's view, since of all the suspects only Dave Husband and Lenard Jackson could conceivably have fled prosecution. Routine arrests would have sufficed for everyone else.

Within the law enforcement coalition that mounted Operation White Tornado, there were inevitable strains. Larry Saurage disappeared on weekends during the investigation, annoying Zack Shelton. Shelton himself got on people's nerves—by the time it was over, some of the state officers had taken to calling him, with acid insincerity, "the great Zack Shelton." Shelton did seem fond of his own press clippings—when we met, he suggested I check out a *Penthouse* article about his role in the investigation of Sheriff James Wade, of Orange County, near Beaumont, which resulted in Wade's conviction on federal drug and corruption charges. (That investigation was called Operation Falling Snow.) Like the federal prosecutors he worked with, Shelton seemed keenly aware of all the good things that came to those lawmen who helped nail a crooked sheriff.

But serious strains developed between the feds and the San Augustine sheriff's office in the aftermath of the drug raid. The main point of contention was the division of spoils—who got what among the assets seized and ultimately forfeited. While Charles Bryan had been allowed to claim a major share of credit for the raid, his office was allotted just 5 percent of the proceeds—the same amount that went to the San Augustine town police, and only a third of what the Liberty County sheriff's office received. According to federal officials, these allotments were determined by the actual contribution of each agency to the operation. Sheriff Bryan, who had evidently come to believe his own claims, was furious, and let the world know it, even vowing publicly not to let the FBI back into San Augustine County. This was an empty threat, and federal officials responded by publicly announcing that the San Augustine sheriff's office had played no substantial role in Operation White Tornado, and by privately voicing scorn for Bryan's abilities, even suggesting that his incompetence had helped scuttle a post-raid investigation that might have netted major drug dealers in Houston. Eventually, the importance of the San Augustine drug trade was subtly downgraded by federal authorities. "I *like* local law enforcement to think that the biggest problems in the world are in their own backyard," Bob Wortham, the U.S. Attorney in Beaumont, told me. "That way, they take things seriously." Stuart Platt, Wortham's assistant, said, "You could do these types of cases in every town in East Texas."

Post-raid squabbling also broke out in San Augustine itself. Curt Goetz, the mayor, designed a stone marker for the courthouse lawn to commemorate White Tornado, but Charles Bryan and Larry Saurage were outraged when they discovered that Goetz's own name would be chiseled near the top of the list of the heroes of the raid, just above the names of Charles Mitchell and Jack Nichols, the county judge—this despite the fact that Goetz, Mitchell, and Nichols had, by their own admission, not even known about the investigation until the raid occurred. And Larry Saurage's name was relegated to the bottom of Goetz's marker. Sheriff Bryan made his objections known to Goetz. "I told him just what I'd do if he put that thing up," Bryan told me. "I said I'd wrap a chain around it, pull it out of the ground with my truck, drag it over to his house, and dump it in his front yard." The marker proposal was tabled.

Somehow, nearly all of White Tornado's principal characters managed to get together at a one-year anniversary celebration, dubbed Drug Independence Day, on the San Augustine courthouse square in June 1990. Curt Goetz, Bob Wortham, Stuart Platt, and Zack Shelton all spoke, along with U.S. Representative Jim Chapman and Kenny Houston of the National Football League's Hall of Fame. (Larry Saurage boycotted the celebration, though his name was on the program as a host.) Blackhawk helicopters from the U.S. Customs Service flew in for the day, and President Bush sent a telegram. Final success in the war on drugs was the consensus prediction: "Our commitment to eliminating narcotics cannot be diluted," Representative Chapman proclaimed. Media coverage was enthusiastic.

But for those who read to the end of the list of nearly two hundred official invitees in the program for Drug Independence Day, there was a small surprise waiting: N. L. TINDALL. The disgraced ex-sheriff evidently still had some influential local supporters. The federal authorities were still pursuing him—they were about to subpoena the records of his myriad land trades—but he had still not been charged. After all the bad press he had received, and all the federal investigative attention, the fact that he was alive at all as a public figure seemed remarkable.

It even seemed to amaze the state police. More than a year after the anniversary celebration, I was talking to a group of state narcotics officers in Lufkin. I mentioned that I had heard that Tindall was thinking about running for sheriff of San Augustine County again. There was a long, stunned silence. Finally, Rickey Allen, a huge, bearded undercover agent, spat tobacco juice into a can and said, "Seems like Nathan survived a pretty hard little old punch over there." I had the impression that the other old narcs in the room were struggling not to smile.

T E N

Everyone in San Augustine knew someone who was "in the pen," and it seemed it had always been that way. But Operation White Tornado had torn through the community like nothing else in memory. Dozens of families were devastated by the raid, and by the wrenchingly heavy prison sentences insisted on by federal prosecutors. A new generation of ghosts was created, sowing a new crop of sorrow.

Ruby Kelly lost a son, Hollis, and two grandsons, Steven and Harlon. Although Hollis was locked up for only a year, Harlon and Steven were serving ten years each. Ruby especially missed Harlon, whom she and her family called Mack. "He was such a lovin' child," she said. "He wasn't a sassy child. And he worked hard, hard, *hard.* I seen him workin' in the woods with Hulon until his eyes, from lookin' up pullin' that loader with the sun shining directly into 'em, be full of red. But he never fussed or nothin'. They just *hauled* wood."

We were standing outside a rude, uninsulated shack in Kellyville. Ruby and Hulon had been living there since their house burned down a few years back. It was evening, and Ruby wore an old striped dress and a blue bandanna from which a few white curls peeked. Despite an autumn chill, she was barefoot. She turned away from me for a moment, and silently watched her son, Lon L., unload firewood from a pickup truck onto a huge pile next to her house. She and Hulon had been talking about moving into a neighbor's empty house trailer, which would be warmer than the shack. But the monthly rent for the trailer would be two hundred dollars—a prohibitive sum. Ruby wasn't thinking about rents or keeping warm, though; she was thinking about Harlon. "He was a *smart* child," she said, almost to herself.

When Harlon first went to prison, he and his grandmother talked on the phone almost every day. But neither of them could afford the bills. "Now we just write letters," she said. "He always been a churchgoing person, but he real religious now. He send me Bible lessons. I send him Bible lessons. We study the Bible together. The Lord is with him now." She paused, peering off into the distance again. She'd been playing with an old kitchen fork while we talked. Now she raised it to her brow, the tines pointed away from her, and waved it in the general direction of Fort Worth, where Harlon sat in prison. It was a strange, almost shamanistic gesture, rich in the forest twilight with suggestions of supernatural sympathy. "Mack told me if he don't make it back, he'll be okay," Ruby said softly. "'If the Lord calls me, my soul will be saved'—that's what he said. But it make me feel good to know he's trusting in God, because now I feel he won't do no wrong." What she meant, I realized, was that Harlon was not at risk for suicide. "I feel like he gonna come home."

Bud Watts, who graduated from high school in the same class with Ruby Kelly, lost a son—Arthur, Jr.—and two grandsons in White Tornado. "Mr. Bud" was the genial ex-bootlegger who, when Prohibition was lifted in the county, became a saloon keeper, turning a barbecue shack he had owned since the 1940s into the Watts Café. Now seventy, a widower, he was alone in his little white clapboard house on the Front when I visited him. His son phoned, he said, from prison every day. He sighed. "Yes, that drug raid really hurt us. It about killed us dead. It was good from catchin' with those drugs, but I say, 'Fine 'em, maybe give 'em some time, but then give 'em probation, and don't take everything they got.' They gonna make some bad people out of these boys."

(Ruby Kelly agreed with her old classmate about the need for antidrug campaigns—she had, after all, watched her son Hollis struggle for years with cocaine addiction. "Drugs is kinda rough," she said. "Colored peoples been thinkin' they could make a little livin' sellin' that stuff, that's all. It's a shame." Ruby also believed, however, that White Tornado was too harsh. "Nathan Tindall would've handled it better," she said simply. "Charles Bryan, he ain't no sheriff.")

Since the raid, Mr. Bud, who once belonged to the San Augustine Chamber of Commerce and seemed likely to become, after Herbert Jackson, the commissioner from the county's black-majority precinct, had renounced politics. "I used to get involved in elections, but now I just cast my vote," he said. "Getting involved is a dangerous business, if you're on the losing side." Nathan Tindall's troubles began, in Mr. Bud's view, when he found himself on the losing side.

Few people had lost more, of course, than Dave Husband and his family. Like Ruby, Husband's wife and daughter were, I found, trusting in the Lord. Shortly before the White Tornado raid, Sheila, who had been abusing cocaine for years, had stopped taking drugs, and by the time I met her she was a clear-eyed, gracious, evangelical Christian and mother of two sturdy blond boys. She and her husband were living in a trailer on some relatives' land out in the western reaches of the county.

Sheila pulled out a family photograph album. There was her brother, Neil's wedding day; Dave shaking his son's hand; her mother, Gail, adjusting Neil's white tuxedo. They were a big, handsome, prosperous-looking family. Sheila shook her head, and turned the page. There was an old black-and-white of Dave Husband, Sr. A tough-looking man, he was sitting backward in a metal folding chair under a tree, shirtless and staring unsmilingly into the camera. "Grandaddy was somewhere between a steelworker and a bootlegger," Sheila said thoughtfully. He looked like both. *His* father, I recalled, was also a bootlegger, until he got religion and founded a Pentecostal church down near the Attoyac.

Gail Husband had gone back to another Pentecostal church, the one she attended as a girl. "We rarely went to church while we had the store," she told me over the telephone. "Church people kind of frown on somebody selling whiskey all week and then coming to church on Sunday. But since all this happened I've accepted Jesus Christ as my Lord. And He has been my savior." Mrs. Husband was working six days a week as a secretary in a hospital in Lufkin, going to community college at night, and rarely ventured into San Augustine. "A lot of people in San Augustine who I thought were my friends have shunned me since the bust," she said. "Nathan and Willie Earl Tindall haven't shunned me. I feel like they're still my friends. But that's about it."

Mrs. Husband blamed her husband for getting into the drug business, but she also blamed Charles Bryan for recruiting witnesses to testify against Dave at his detention hearing, so that he was never granted bond. Bryan's son Michael, whose convenience store on U.S. 96 stood next to the Husbands' old liquor store, profited directly from Dave's absence, she said. "It's called eliminating the competition." Even Sheila, who radiated forgiveness—and insisted Charles Bryan had been nothing but kind to her—said cryptically, when the subject was justice, "San Augustine is not a judicial system, it's a politics."

Mrs. Husband, who had only been able to afford to visit her husband once since he was sent to Leavenworth to begin his life sentence, spoke about him through gritted teeth. "Sometimes I hate Dave," she said. "And sometimes I still love him. I got a lot of mixed emotions. I'm afraid he's got his head in the sand, though. He's not facing his own situation."

I visited Dave Husband in prison, and he did seem freshly stunned by his sentence, though it had been handed down nearly a year before. He said that his lawyer hadn't told him it would be life without parole, that he had only said "it would be a considerable amount of time." Husband was a big man with a receding hairline and a crafty manner, but the gambler's confidence for which he had once been famous in Deep East Texas seemed to have vanished. Now he reminded me of Buck Barrow, the Gene Hackman character in *Bonnie and Clyde*, in the scenes after he's been wounded and reduced to desperation. Leavenworth Federal Penitentiary is an overpowering place even for a visitor. "Taking everything you've worked for all your life, that's pretty hard," Husband murmured. "Getting a life sentence, that's extra hard." Of Nathan Tindall, he said, "I could probably have told a lie on him and walked home. But I'm not going to tell a lie on no one." Husband was working as an orderly at Leaven-worth, sweeping and mopping floors for eleven cents an hour. His dreams had seemingly narrowed to one: "I'd like to be closer to home so my people can come see me."

Lenard Jackson's wife, Girtha Mae Polley Jackson, who was driving with her husband when he was arrested, didn't wait for the last act of Operation White Tornado. In December, while Lenard was still plea-bargaining with the U.S. At-torney's office, she committed suicide in Houston.

The possibility that Nathan Tindall might rise from his political grave—and the likelihood of his resurrection seemed to grow with each passing week that win-ter—posed an interesting question: Were San Augustinians in general, despite all the official hoopla, unhappy with the results of Operation White Tornado?

Certainly the local economy had been flattened by the drug raid. The late Edward Clark, the county's leading banker, said, "Money totally disappeared from this town after the drug bust. Stores that had been selling hundred-dollar hats, fifty-dollar shoes, their customers were just gone." Even more, perhaps, than businesses, poor families felt the raid's impact. Susan Ramsey, a social worker, said, "Some of my clients did better after the raid. They stopped doing crack, and started getting their hair done. Later on, though, the financial repercussions began to be felt." Mary Warren, the county's welfare director, said, "That bust just ruined the economy here. It's as simple as that. It in-creased our caseload directly."

The economic blow delivered by the drug raid wasn't simply a matter of re-moving a few dozen free-spending cocaine dealers from the county. There was a more general chilling effect, according to many black residents. "Like we used to have street jams out by my house," J. C. Barnes, the teenage pulpwood hauler, who lived in Kellyville, told me. "Street jams," he explained, were big parties, with music and dancing (but no drugs that he ever saw). "Then, after the drug raid happened, we never had another one. People used to come over from Lufkin and Nacogdoches. Now, ain't nobody interested in coming here."

And it wasn't only black people who were put off San Augustine by the raid. At a restaurant called Raymond's, north of town, a barmaid told me, "This place used to be a gold mine. It was open seven nights a week." Raymond's was open two nights a week by the time I visited, and on the night I ate there I was the only patron. What happened? "A drug bust happened," the barmaid said, making a sour face. She was a young, tousled-looking white woman and Ray-mond's, I learned, was and always had been a segregated establishment: whites only. Had the former patrons all been drug dealers? "Some of them was. But none of them got arrested. Mostly, there was just a lot of money in circu-lation. Now San Augustine's like a ghost town. There's nothing for young people to do here. The old families that own this place don't want nothing to change. They won't let nothing come in here. And this new sheriff, he don't care about helping people, the way Nathan Tindall did."

"They won't let nothing come in here."

It was the complaint that young people in San Augustine—especially young black people—made constantly. According to Bud Watts, business opportunities for young blacks were actually worse now than when he was young. "I don't know what these banks expect these young folks to do," he said. "They won't even let me cosign a loan for 'em, and my record is good—I don't owe them a penny up there." Ruby Kelly said, "Seems like the men don't want the coloreds to have nothin' to do. And you know it takes a job to buy."

Curt Goetz, the mayor (he later became the county judge), conceded that there had once been some truth to the allegation. The county's old Bourbon elite, he said, had traditionally resisted any development by outside capital, fearing competition. But the old family holdings had broken down until there was now really none large enough to be threatened by development. Goetz, who had also served as president of the local chamber of commerce, had tried to lure industry to San Augustine. "And these big companies say, 'Yes, we'd like to establish ourselves in small towns in the Sunbelt, in a cheerful atmosphere,'" Goetz said. "But they mean much bigger towns. They mean Nacogdoches, which has twenty-five thousand people. We have twenty-three hundred. They want infrastructure—rail, hotels, airports. They want to be on a major thoroughfare." Goetz even went to Benton, Arkansas, headquarters of the Wal-Mart Corporation, to try to get a Wal-Mart for San Augustine. "Apparently, we're right in the middle of a dead geographic area for Wal-Mart."

Goetz got the same kind of answer from McDonald's and Kentucky Fried Chicken. K mart also turned him down. He tried to get a prison: many other counties in East Texas have one, and prisons are a dependable source of jobs. But the state turned down the county. Ultimately, Goetz decided that San Augustine's best economic hope was its very sleepiness. "Our real raw material is our basic tourism quality," he said. Efforts to put the town on the tourist map had been halting, however. There was a new visitor information center, but it rarely saw any business. After I had trouble finding a postcard of San Augustine, the director of the visitor center told me that postcards were indeed a good thing to have in a tourist town. But the cost of producing them, she said, could run into the hundreds of dollars.

There was little official unemployment in San Augustine, but most of the county's employers were small, family-operated businesses that didn't pay Social Security taxes or workmen's compensation, insuring that laid-off workers weren't eligible for unemployment compensation and were thus never counted by the state. And many people were self-employed. "Pulpwood hauling is still the main thing," Mary Warren, the welfare director, said. "But a lot of our clients do that and don't tell us about it, so they can collect food stamps. We have to ask our clients how they manage on their income. If they get busted for drug dealing, and we see their name in the paper, well, then we know." The limits of local opportunity directly affected the school-dropout rate, according to Warren. "Kids say, 'Why should I finish school? I can go gut chickens now, or I can wait two years, and get a diploma, and *then* go gut chickens. I'd rather make those two years of wages.'" These limits also fueled the drug trade, she said. "No wonder so many of these kids are ready to go out there and sell a rock of crack, when they can make more money in a few minutes doing that than they can from a week in the chicken plant."

Though Operation White Tornado was a setback to the local drug trade, it was far from a death blow. Two years after White Tornado, Larry Saurage ran another drug sweep that netted eighteen arrests. Seven months after that, a town patrolman told me, "I wish we could get the feds back in here." But most people said that the biggest local cocaine dealers—and all the real drug profits—were now up in Shelby County. The San Augustine dealers were being forced to run to Center for supplies. And these new local wholesalers were apparently not under the control of a discreet, nonviolent businessman like Lenard Jackson. A couple of the older Shelby County dealers had been arrested in White Tornado, and some tough young guys from Houston, whose grandmother lived in Shelby County, had come in to take over the market. Known as the Uzi Brothers, their leader was arrested for murder shortly after I arrived in San Augustine. He was eighteen, and the crime had been strictly big-city: a drive-by shooting on the main drag of the black section of Center. The victim was a twenty-two-year-old woman. The killer was convicted and sentenced to twenty-five years to life.

The most incisive critic of Operation White Tornado was, surprisingly, Betty Donatto. As Bennie Lee Thibodeaux, she had ended up personally making most of the cases in White Tornado. But the longer she had spent in San Augustine, the more mystified she had become about what, exactly, state and federal law enforcement were doing there.

"At first it made sense," Donatto told me, when we talked in Houston. "The feds said, 'People here in San Augustine are fed up—they want something done about the drugs now.' But after I got to know the scene, and saw how *small* it was, things stopped making sense. The problem was, the feds were trying to make it seem like more than it was. The quantities were all wrong. In fact, when they yanked the string I was upset, because I only needed a couple more months to really figure out what was going on. But then I decided that maybe they didn't *want* me to see that there *weren't* seventy-five pounds coming up from Houston every week."

Donatto was silent for a minute or more. I knew that she had been working lately on international smuggling cases for the Houston narcotics squad. She knew the difference between large and small drug shipments.

"It's all politics," she went on. "Sticks and stats, that's what we say—arrests and big numbers. There's so much money available for drug programs now, and every region wants that money, so they put you out there, telling you to get those sticks and stats. Liberty County loaned me out, and we made big bucks on my seizures. We got $175,000 just for my work. But what did we really *do*? I went back to San Augustine for that one-year celebration they had. I was kind of scared to go back. I mean, they'd built it up so much, and built up my part in it, and people's families could have been really mad at me. So I just stood in the crowd with a hat on, and sunglasses, and Malcolm"—Malcolm Bales, the assistant federal prosecutor from Beaumont—"accepted an award for me. Then I just snuck off, and on the drive home I just cried. It just seemed so, so . . . I mean, all these people got promotions and raises, and what had we *done*? Here they were celebrating, with all the politicians, and a barbecue at the sheriff's house, and everything else, and unless I really missed something, *there just wasn't that much dope there.* Thinking about those heavy sentences, and all those families we'd hurt . . . I tell you, the more you get into narcotics on the law side, the more you see the politics."

I had heard that Donatto, after her performance in White Tornado, had been offered a job by the FBI. When I asked her about it, she said that she had decided not to pursue it. As a matter of fact, she had pretty much decided to get out of law enforcement altogether. She was taking night courses, hoping to start a new career, as a drug rehabilitation counselor. "It just seems like a better way to help people," she said.

ELEVEN

"This Larry Saurage's town now."

Thus Sarah Oliphant, who once let Saurage's agent Betty Donatto befriend her, and spent a year in prison as a result. Oliphant was now back in San Augustine, living with her mother and her two sons in the Sunset Hills projects, and she had the local power situation dead right. Chief Deputy Sheriff Saurage received a higher salary than Sheriff Bryan, he had the power to hire and fire, and he made all the law enforcement decisions that counted.

He was in his late forties and came from Beaumont, but he had worked all over Texas and Louisiana as a lawman, a prison guard, a telephone lineman. He was sandy-haired, six feet tall, with a wide, weather-lined face and an unusual, imposing build: barrel-chested and bullnecked but surprisingly light on his feet. His voice and his manner were rich with natural authority. When his deputies brought in a roaring drunk driver, Saurage said firmly, "Bennis, you're going to spend a few hours with me now," and all belligerence vanished and the prisoner was booked. His language was a mixture of police jargon and down-home vernacular. "He ain't nothin' but an old snake head," Saurage might say of a disliked lawyer, "but we'll still dispose the case." Most of the sheriff's department business seemed to find its way to Saurage's office, and the chief deputy, his cowboy boots propped comfortably on his desk, made no pretense of consulting with anyone as he delivered his instructions; he simply ordered the town judge to sentence a vandal to ten days, or the chief of police to pick up a suspected burglar. On one wall of his office was a framed plaque from the Police Officers' Hall of Fame, which Saurage had won in 1985 for his role in a homicide investigation down in Orange County. Taped to another wall was a bumper sticker reading, MY ASSAULT RIFLE: 0, TEDDY KENNEDY'S CAR: 1.

Saurage had brought an aura of big-city police work to San Augustine. He might hang out in the jailhouse on a balmy evening with the other deputies, park rangers, and highway patrolmen, chewing tobacco and talking coon dogs and squirrel dogs and where the bass were biting on Sam Rayburn Reservoir, and I once saw him catch a stray horse on a highway at dusk, fashion a bridle from a jumper cable, and walk the animal half a mile back to the house where it belonged, tethering it there and going on about his business without leaving a note—classic rural sheriff work. But Saurage had been a cop in Houston and Orange and Chambers County and he did not let people forget it.

He had a big-city cop's respect for paperwork, in drastic contrast to Nathan Tindall's style of office management. He also brought to San Augustine his wide experience as a narcotics officer. After all, the war on drugs had been Charles Bryan's campaign platform, and hiring Saurage had been his one big strategic deployment. Saurage brought in undercover agents, turned suspects and prisoners into informers ("snitches," he called them, with a fierce, musical pronunciation that was half affectionate, half contemptuous), and generally made life difficult for the local dopers and dealers.

Bryan, meanwhile, in the day-to-day role of sheriff, seemed a little uneasy, as if he weren't quite sure what to do next. When I dropped by his office in the jailhouse, he always seemed to have time to talk, and his mind was often on unofficial matters. One morning, I found him studying a jar of epoxy at his desk. "Horse bit my car," he explained.

I accompanied Saurage and some of his fellow officers on an antidrug operation. They brought a young black man down from an upstairs cell in the jailhouse, taped a remote microphone to his belly, and drove him to a spot behind the junior high school. The young man lay down on the seat of the cruiser to avoid being seen and explained from there that he had just returned from six months in the state penitentiary, which was why he had agreed to snitch today. He darted into the woods behind the school, then made his way into the Sunset Hills housing project. We drove around to a vantage on U.S. 96, and watched him wander through the scatter of buildings, his microphone picking up garbled snatches of conversation, which we strained to hear on a walkie-talkie. "It helps if you speak a little Swahili," a white patrolman told me. Saurage grimaced. "It's a way of life," he said. "Welfare, laying around smoking cocaine, having babies. I'll never understand it."

The informer gained entrance to an apartment and apparently found a group of people smoking crack there. He tried to buy a rock but was told that the dealers, who were outside in a car, wouldn't sell to him, because they believed he was a snitch. He persisted, and eventually the woman whose apartment it was went out, scored a rock, shaved off a piece for herself, and sold the remainder to the informer for twenty dollars. We drove back around to the school, and soon the informer emerged from the woods, looking scared but triumphant. "Got 'em," he said, handing over a small, yellowish rock.

Half an hour later, armed with a search warrant, a patrolman kicked in the door of the apartment. Inside, four startled women, including Sarah Oliphant, silently raised their hands. They were sitting on a couch watching cartoons on

TV: Woody Woodpecker, Daffy Duck. There was no dope in sight. John Matthew Cartwright, now the chief of police, went to search the bedrooms. One of the women on the couch—heavyset, middle-aged—curled her lip. "Can't go visitin' no more," she said. "Law gonna kick the door down." The apartment's resident, a sallow, middle-aged woman named Beulah, found her voice. "What's this all about?" she said.

"Larry be here in a minute," Cartwright said. "He'll tell you."

Saurage, who had been detained by jailhouse business, showed up. "Hoo-wee," he said, pointing at Oliphant and shaking his head. "What we got here?"

"Hi, Larry," Oliphant said.

The apartment search turned up no drugs, though a crack pipe was found in Beulah's pocket and confiscated. The four women were let off with a stern warning from Saurage and, in Beulah's case, a broken door, a charge of delivering cocaine, and an agreement to give a statement against the dealers who had sold her the crack. The dealers—four young black men—were found hanging out at the car wash up on U.S. 96. There were no drugs on them, either, but one of them, Rodriguez Hill, had thirty-four dollar bills in his pocket, along with a scribbled list of names and dollar amounts. Hill was arrested and booked for driving without a license and without a seat belt.

"You seen *New Jack City?*" Saurage asked me later. "Good. Because that's exactly what we got here. It's the American Dream, except it's a nightmare."

San Augustine didn't really resemble the apocalyptic Harlem of *New Jack City*, I thought—though Rodriguez Hill might have relished the idea that it did. He was twenty-one, beefy, and mad as a snake. He wore a little denim fishing cap. At the jailhouse, he glared at me with narrowed eyes. After I told him I was a journalist, his attitude changed abruptly. He was actually from Louisiana, he said, but had been raised in San Augustine. "You say you from New York? Hey, up there they don't fuck around. Law gets in their face, they shoot 'em dead. They play for *real.*" Hill had evidently seen *New Jack City* and mistaken it for a documentary. I wondered if he watched it repeatedly, as Terry in New Haven did. "We fixin' to start doin' the same thing 'round here," he added. "People sick and tired of the law jumpin' on 'em all the time."

Hill was allowed a phone call, which he used to try to raise his bond, set at $265. I went back to Saurage's office, and found him listening in on an extension. He put his finger to his lips; he was taking notes. It seemed that Hill was calling someone in Center whom Saurage believed to be his drug connection.

After the call, Hill was put in a ground-floor holding cell. He immediately started shouting up the stairs to the prisoners in the long-term cells on the second floor, accusing a man he assumed had led the police to him. The prisoners called back that he was mistaken. "We *know* the motherfucker done did it," one yelled. "We seen him go off from here!" The real informer's name was bellowed, repeatedly. Larry Saurage eventually went back and interrupted this colloquy. He reminded Hill that he was out on bond on another charge, glared at him until he dropped his gaze to the floor, then returned to his office, shaking his head.

Maybe it wasn't New Jack City, but drug-related violent crime was finding its way into the piney woods. At an Exxon station on U.S. 96, I was surprised to find the attendant sitting behind inch-thick, bulletproof glass and making change through a steel trough. Such security struck me as needlessly serious and urban until one Sunday afternoon when a local crackhead persuaded the attendant to open the booth's door to hand him an oilcan. He hit her on the head with a brick and robbed her. (She was hospitalized, he was caught by two local men, and three days later, after pleading guilty to aggravated robbery, he was sentenced in state district court to fifty years.) A few weeks later, at the San Augustine Inn, another local addict attacked and nearly killed the desk clerk, an elderly woman, in the course of an early-morning robbery.

The only violence I actually saw in San Augustine came during a high school basketball game. Center was the visiting team, and passions were running high. During the first half, Richard Carl Davis, a black patrolman, went into the bleachers on the Center side and arrested a young black man. It seemed the suspect had tried to scare some local students by flashing a gun. The weapon, tucked in his waistband, turned out to be a Glock 10-millimeter automatic pistol, with fourteen bullets in the clip. "Them Center guys *all* got guns," said the young man sitting next to me. "They don't leave they *house* without they guns." Hearing that, I thought the small, noisy gym seemed suddenly very small indeed, and I found myself studying the crowd, especially the young black men in it, with new interest. There weren't many white kids at the game, and none on the San Augustine team, and though the cheerleaders were mostly white girls—performing endless, earnest versions of hip-hop-based routines ("Too, Too, Too Legit to Quit")—white people seemed distinctly irrelevant to whatever was really happening that night, both on and off the court.

Then, during the third period, a fight broke out in the stands. There were screams, shouts, and a swirl of furious punching that seemed to twist through the crowd. It lasted a minute or two, appeared to involve four or five young men—while dozens of bystanders, including an old woman mashed against a railing, were involuntarily involved—and it ended when a swarm of cops, coaches, and administrators managed to hustle the fighters out the door and into squad cars. While the fight lasted, people dove for cover throughout the gym, fearing that gunfire might break out—the young men arrested were, in fact, the buddies of the gunman arrested earlier. But the most frightening moment came when Richard Carl Davis reentered the gym carrying an AR-15 assault rifle, strode to the center of the floor—the game had stopped when the teams had fled to the locker rooms—and began to wave the rifle around, shouting at people to take their seats. The crowd crouched as one. "He gonna *start* a shoot-out that way," the young man next to me said. "He trigger happy!"

That was the end of the excitement—the game resumed, and Center won at the buzzer—but the incident left me with a raft of questions. Had this fight been just an old-fashioned high school sports brawl, a traditional dust-up? Or did the automatic pistol change everything, the way such weapons had changed life in the cities? Gun-toting was certainly nothing new in East Texas, but was this not a strange new generation, peculiarly indifferent, like the drug posses in the cities, to the safety of bystanders, as its dominant males settled their quarrels? Center had already had one drive-by shooting. And the sheriff's office in San Augustine had immediately labeled the gymnasium mêlée "drug-related," because the men arrested were allegedly involved in the drug trade in Center. The first young San Augustinians I talked to about the fight emphasized, too, that the Center guys were "gangsters"—you could tell by their long denim coats and cut-up jeans—and members, as such, of a species that had not yet emerged in San Augustine.

But the more I asked around about the fight, the less novel it seemed. At the Clarks' house later that evening, two of Laverne's teenage daughters, one of whom had been sitting where the brawl broke out, described it for their mother in personal, almost homey terms. Whether "Little Gary" had first slapped "Little Eric," or whether "Big Mark" had thrown the first punch, were disputed points, but nobody who knew the principals believed drugs had anything to do with it. "This happens every time Center come down here," Laverne's daughter Lyndorie, who was a high school senior, said. What was more, Laverne approved of Little Gary's behavior. "That's *good*," she said. "Gary got to show some aggression. He need that. He usually don't stand up for hisself."

I was appalled, but everyone just laughed when I said so. Hadn't I seen Coach Ford run up there and get into it, helping out his old student Gary? (I hadn't.) Didn't I see that white boy from Center try to jump in? Gary's girlfriend had kicked him in the head a few times and he quit. (I missed that, too.) I had obviously missed most of what occurred, and though I would never have the jolly attitude toward homeboy's performance that my companions did, the whole incident had begun to sound much like the turf-and-testosterone dramas from my school days.

Richard Carl Davis's performance was another matter. It was part of an ominous escalation in aggressive behavior by local lawmen that had, only a few months before, produced a tragedy. It happened on a Saturday night when a number of "homecomings"—family gatherings, usually held in the fall, when far-flung relatives return to their rural homesteads and churches—had filled black San Augustine with people in a festive mood. After the Watts Café closed, people lingered outside, continuing the party. Richard Carl Davis arrived, and found himself in a confrontation with Varron (Bo) Lane, twenty-five and drunk and armed with a .22 rifle. Davis pointed his shotgun at Lane's chest and ordered him to lay down the .22. Lane did so. Then, unarmed, he advanced on Davis. Davis pulled the trigger, killing him with a single blast.

A local grand jury declined to indict Davis. On the evening after the grand jury handed up that decision, I happened to run into one of its members at Sheriff Bryan's house. White and in late middle age, she was a member of the town's Old Guard ("We been here since 1853," she informed me). The grand juror made it clear that she wouldn't have dreamed of indicting Davis. She owned a police scanner radio and loved to listen to it at home, and Richard Carl Davis, she said, "is just so cute on there sometimes." I probably didn't understand, she said, what the police had to deal with in San Augustine. "People who don't associate with that one particular segment that's always causing trouble, or don't have a scanner, just aren't aware of what's going on. It takes constant effort and time to keep this element down."

Sheriff Bryan and his wife agreed that it was so.

Some time later, I happened to visit the grand juror shortly after seeing Richard Carl Davis brandish the assault rifle at the basketball game. I mentioned the incident. "Well, have you ever been around blacks before?" she asked. "They like authority. They like somebody to have more power. You have to do that with them. Richard Carl was the one killed that Lane nigger."

TWELVE

The rumors that Nathan Tindall might run for sheriff again turned out to be true. While the federal authorities were still making noises about indicting him, Tindall was making campaign sounds. "I miss it, sheriffin'," he confessed to me. "I miss helpin' the underdog. The man on top don't need help." We were sitting in his dilapidated office at the car lot. Flies buzzed around a couple of aging loaves of white bread on his desk. "I was just about finished with sheriffin'," he said. "But now I have a lot of people coming in here—hundreds—saying they're gonna put me back in. So I'm thinking about it." By early 1992, he was doing more than thinking about it. His candidacy became official in January. The Democratic primary—the only election that mattered in San Augustine—was in March.

Charles Bryan and Larry Saurage seemed stiff with disbelief that Bryan had to face Tindall again. When Sam Malone wrote a syndicated column about great East Texas sheriffs he had known, and put Tindall on the list, Bryan and Saurage were apoplectic. Didn't *anybody* realize that this man had been disgraced, had been permanently discredited? The fact that Malone did not include Charles Bryan, the hero of Operation White Tornado, on his list of great sheriffs only increased the insult.

As the campaign began to heat up, law enforcement in San Augustine became even more political than usual. Waiting in the sheriff's office, I overheard Bryan, discussing an aggravated assault charge arising from a clan feud in Black Ankle—a no-win case, politically—tell someone over the phone, "Well, I thought I'd let Larry handle this, it bein' comin' up on election time." Bryan winked at me, though we both knew he wasn't kidding.

Saurage pleaded political inexperience. "I never been through anything like this before," he said. "I always just worked as a cop. I let the sheriff, whoever he was, worry about politics. But that won't work here."

He was right, it wouldn't. Tindall made Saurage an issue in his campaign ads in the *Tribune*—not Saurage's job performance but that he lived too far from town to be of use in an emergency, and that he had an unlisted phone, and that he held a part-time job outside the county (as a highway flagman), and, most important, that he had been hired to cover for Sheriff Bryan's inadequacies. As I heard Tindall put it in an impressively brief speech at a campaign pie supper in a crowded schoolhouse, "You all probably got your minds made up already. I got experience. You all know how it was here for forty years. And it's $35,800"—the combined salaries, according to Tindall, of Saurage and his wife, Shetresa, who also worked in the sheriff's office—"that you're paying this year for experience. I think Mr. Saurage done a pretty good job. But Mr. Bryan ain't really done nothing."

Saurage, sitting in the audience, looked restless and angry. Shetresa, a suntanned, well-built woman in her thirties, rubbed her husband's broad back steadily, clearly trying to keep him calm.

The Saurages lived down near Sam Rayburn Reservoir, in a modern, pale brick house surrounded by horse pastures. They liked being away from things—they were nearly twenty miles from the town of San Augustine—because, as Shetresa said, "This is the strangest place. You get the nicest people in the world living right next door to the most terrible people in the world." Barbecuing on their deck, riding horses, watching TV, the Saurages could escape the inbred, premodern weirdness of San Augustine. And when it all got to be too much, and they thought about moving elsewhere, all they had to remember, Larry said, "was how much the good, decent people of this county need us."

Black San Augustinians, in particular, were easily identified, according to the Saurages, as either good and decent or not. "The good blacks," as Shetresa put it, had no significant criminal records, liked and cooperated with the police, and, above all, supported Charles Bryan for sheriff. The other kind (the majority) supported Nathan Tindall. The Reverend Clois Rodgers, for instance, a successful insurance agent and one of the leading black campaigners for Tindall, was "a piece of shit," according to Larry, and "straight NAACP," according to Shetresa. (Rev. Rodgers actually had nothing to do with the NAACP.) Cecil Clark was, of course, "nothing but a piece of shit," in Larry's view. Not only did Clark's NAACP presidency count against him, and his former public support for Tindall, but the old snake head was a convicted child molester.

Shetresa and Larry had arrived in San Augustine at around the same time, though not with each other. Shetresa, who was born in Abilene, had lived in various faraway places, including Libya and Nigeria—her father was in the oil business. In Houston she met and married a man from San Augustine. They moved to town and bought a hardware store. Larry had arrived with his third wife, Jane, who went to work in the jailhouse as a clerk and dispatcher. When Shetresa left her hardware store husband for Larry, Jane was dismissed (and divorced) and Shetresa got her job.

Shetresa quickly discovered that she simply loved law enforcement. "Now I just can't imagine ever doing anything else," she told me. Though she had missed Operation White Tornado, she soon started talking about it as if she had been there. Some of the White Tornado agents she grew to dislike—"that little queer bastard" was her epithet for one of the more prominent officers—and others, such as Betty Donatto, she came to admire passionately. "You'll find nothing but respect for Betty Donatto in this jailhouse," she told me. Clearly, Donatto had not shared her second thoughts about her role in White Tornado with the Saurages—nor with anyone else in San Augustine, as far as I could tell.

Shetresa seemed to enjoy especially the information-gathering aspects of her job. The sheriff's office kept files on people—not only official arrest records, but informal jottings on index cards—and Shetresa spent a great deal of time browsing among, and updating, these cards. In a county of eight thousand souls, they had files, she estimated, on five thousand people. It was a great way to get to know San Augustine.

The county's traditional election campaign pie suppers were for white voters only. Black San Augustinians were wooed by other means—phone banks, barbecues, free rides to the polls—only around Election Day. In the meantime, they were mostly ignored by the politicians. Black people got together for homecomings and funerals and Baptist Church synods and music-saturated revival meetings, though, and I made my way to some of those. One Saturday night in February, there was a Senior Choir Musical held out at Mt. Dena Baptist Church, in the eastern part of the county. The big building was packed to the rafters for a program of church choirs, gospel groups, and soloists from all over Deep East Texas and the nearby parishes of Louisiana. The Maryland Baptist choir performed, with Laverne Clark singing lead, deep and flat and soulful, on "Lord I Know You Been So Good." Later, I sat with Laverne and Ruby and Mary and listened to the True Vine Baptist choir, the Greertown Gospel Singers—an all-male a cappella group, not one of whose members looked to be under seventy—and the incredible Gospel Messagers from Mansfield, Louisiana.

Laverne's enthusiasm for the performers was vast and catching. She had the Spirit. Like much of the audience, she clapped and sang or hummed along, or punctuated performances, with perfect musician's timing, with calls of "Amen" or "Sho' 'nuf" or just "Mm-*hmm.*" If a singer of obvious talent started out hesitantly, Laverne might shout "Come *on* with it!" ("Calm own widdit!") and gesture urgently toward herself. And the tempo and temperature of the performance seemed to me to lift instantly.

But at some point that evening it occurred to me that Laverne was, in the official scheme of things in San Augustine County, a bad person. That is, she was a bad black person. She was proud, and known for her pluck, and she did not trust white justice. She was not enthusiastic about Charles Bryan, and she was enthusiastic about the NAACP, and in any conflict between white authorities and black people, everyone knew her first sympathies would always lie with the latter. She had never been in trouble with the law, but she had plenty of friends and relatives who had, and she saw no reason to denounce them or distance herself from them. I knew Laverne as the beloved Sister, who, when she wasn't at church or at choir practice or driving her school bus, spent nearly all her time looking after her grandchildren, counseling the love-troubled, or running some mission of mercy—on the afternoon of the Mt. Dena musical, she'd been taking care of a retarded girl from town whose parents desperately needed a break. And yet the sheriff's office, where local power was so fearfully concentrated, knew Laverne as something quite different. It saw black people like her as being on the wrong side in San Augustine—as part of the problem. It was an incongruous notion, to say the least, as we sat there clapping and swaying along with all the singers, shouters, mystics, and testifiers who took the stage at Mt. Dena.

Laverne and Cecil Clark's house was a kind of refuge for stray characters who found themselves in San Augustine. There was almost always someone around to talk to. Children usually outnumbered adults, and toys, tricycles, and long-suffering puppies and kittens littered the house and yard. Unless it was raining or dark, somebody always seemed to be working on a car or pickup or bobtail truck. ("We got some *good* mechanics round here," Lanee assured me. "Shade tree—the best kind.") In Cecil and Laverne's front room, somebody always seemed to be asleep on the big velveteen couch, oblivious to the din of TV, babies, and conversation swirling around them.

That conversation, to my surprise, rarely concerned the sheriff's race, even at the height of the election campaign. People were apparently exercising, at least around me, the discretion that went with the view that local politics was, as Bud Watts put it, "a dangerous business." (Cecil, who could testify to that, seemed to be sticking to his vow to stay clear of this race.) The communal obsession with the sheriff found other ways to express itself, however. "Charles Bryan's my grandfather, you know," a young woman told me one night, perfectly deadpan, and then refused to retract the claim, though everyone else on hand howled with laughter. "Oh, yeah?" her sister asked. "With *that* hair?" But then the same sister turned to me and said, quite seriously, "You should go ask Charles Bryan about some of his little nigger babies running around out here."

I got lots of bad advice of this sort. It represented, more than reporting leads, I thought, a kind of immersion course in local legend and fantasy. Cecil even once offered himself as a cover subject, saying, "Why don't you put a picture of me on the back of your book, with a rope around my neck, and a big old tree, and Charles Bryan pulling on the other end?"

The TV lent an antic, absurdist touch to the proceedings at the Clarks'. For the most part, it was watched only fitfully, when conversation lapsed. Even pro football broadcasts were of interest only because of a gambling "board" administered by Punkin that, for a dime a chance, gave the neighborhood bettors an opportunity to win ten dollars. The gambling bore a merely arithmetical relation to the game—it had nothing to do with which team won—and when I once showed an interest in the game itself I was asked, in a room that suddenly went quiet, if I were by any chance a, ah, *football fan?* It was clear that a football fan was regarded as a certain kind of white man—not necessarily anyone's favorite kind.

Occasionally, a local news story would really capture viewer attention. One that did so while I was around concerned an eighty-four-year-old black woman in Kilgore, Texas, who had been shot to death in her bed by police officers during a drug raid (they found no drugs). This tragedy was the talk of black San Augustine for days. I overheard an older couple discussing it over breakfast at the San Augustine Inn. "They wanna come in your place, they just come in. All they gotta think is somebody using that stuff. You can't control it if somebody might be using that stuff, but they gonna come right into your house. Old lady like that, she can't walk, but she hear something she gonna rise up, want to see what it is. My mama was just like that. Ain't no reason to *shoot* her."

Much of the talk in the Clarks' front room was casually apocalyptic. The Bible said that the end of the world was coming soon, and people seemed to be in a mood to believe it. Cecil said that since last time it was a flood, next time it would be fire. Pelo wanted to know if we would know each other in Heaven, or would these earthly friendships be forgotten? Laverne thought that they would be forgotten, that we would all be new beings over there—a prospect that didn't seem to displease her. Lanee didn't say much in these discussions. It wasn't that she wasn't apocalyptically minded, or that she wasn't a churchgoer—she was both—but that she wasn't, as far as I could tell, really a Christian fundamentalist. She lacked the literalist faith, the old-time religion, of her parents. Ultimately, I thought, that probably left her even more alarmed about the future.

Some of the household's fatidic mood flowed from Cecil's absorption in the Bible, which on the evenings before he was scheduled to preach could be intense. But much of it also arose, I slowly understood, from the fresh trauma of Mary's daughter Dee Dee's death. Dee Dee's two small children were always underfoot, and while they seemed cheerful and vigorous, many of their cousins and aunts and uncles, not to mention their grandmother, were still grief-stricken. Dee Dee's twelve-year-old brother hadn't had a good night's sleep in months, and now refused to go to church—God had let him down. He had started running around with a wild older cousin, and he and his younger sister had become terrified of dying, and their grades at school had plummeted.

The atmosphere at the Clarks' was further darkened by financial desperation. The rainy winter meant that Cecil's income from hauling pulpwood barely paid his expenses. Laverne's job driving the school bus covered insurance and utilities and little else. Lanee's paychecks and Pelo's welfare checks and Cecil's fees for preaching helped defray food and car and house payments, but it was all being done on the impossible, procrustean bed of poverty economics, with nothing left for the unanticipated, such as illness or injury, let alone the inessential, like a family vacation or the police scanner radio that Laverne wanted. ("I'm nosy," she explained.) "Cecil got to get something sturdy," Laverne told me repeatedly, meaning something more reliable than pulpwood hauling. Laverne's second daughter, Lyndra, having finished a course in cosmetology in Center, was starting work as a hairdresser. And Lanee and her half-brother, Timmy, were still planning to open their liquor store, which Lanee hoped would be her ticket out of the chicken poultry by summertime and, if it did great business, might even help keep her parents' leaky financial boat afloat.

Like most families, the Clarks had a deep fund of stories they enjoyed retelling: the time Laverne caught some "car hoppers" (repo men) from Nacogdoches trying to make off with a neighbor's car in Kellyville and, using a shotgun for emphasis, persuaded them that they needed to get their operation approved by Nathan Tindall first; the time Lanee found Lynn Karen, then a toddler, trying to get a cute but quite dead raccoon, which Cecil had shot and left in a box in the kitchen, to drink from her bottle; the time Hulon's saw jumped and cut his jugular and he nearly died. Laverne's personal reminiscences, particularly late at night when people started falling asleep around us, were often more philosophical. Once, she told me about how she finally came to appreciate the blues, after an upbringing that was strictly gospel music. "I never knew what the blues *meant* till after I got married and started really caring for people I was involved with," she said. "Now I done lived some of what the blues is about, and I love that music. Bobby Bland, B. B. King."

She interrupted her reverie and pointed at the TV. "This is something you need to see, Bill." It was a newsmagazine piece about a sociological experiment: two young men, one black and one white, with identical qualifications, applying for jobs, trying to rent rooms, trying to buy cars. The white man consistently got hired while the black man got turned down. The black man was also charged more for identical purchases. "You got any questions, Bill? I hope you do."

Hanging out at the Clarks', arguing about race and poverty and local history with Laverne, sometimes put me in mind of what the American "native anthropologist" John Langston Gwaltney, in his book *Drylongso*, calls "core black culture." "Core black culture is more than ad hoc synchronic adaptive survival," Gwaltney writes. "Its values, systems of logic and world view are rooted in a lengthy peasant tradition and clandestine theology . . . It is a classical, restricted notion of the possible." Gwaltney extols "the prudent masses of black people," and neatly predicts the clash of my pop social science with Laverne's "classical" empiricism: "Black Americans are, of course, capable of the same kind of abstract thinking that is practiced by all human cultures, but sane people in a conquest environment are necessarily preoccupied with the realities of social existence." (The philosophical distance between this fierce, hard-earned realism and the expansive, infantile imperatives of consumerism was what made the rural black South at least a partial exception to the rule of mass culture among the places I studied for this book.)

In Gwaltney's model, the margins of core black culture, while they exclude those who become either unusually assimilated to the majority culture or criminally antisocial, are generously wide, and embrace the great majority of black Americans. Even the scapegrace Roger Hale, it occurred to me, fell clearly within those margins—and thus merited the solidarity of prudent, upstanding folk like Laverne. Most of Hale's misadventures and "devilment," such as the cattle-auction caper, were harmless, and took place, after all, in the context of the detested "conquest environment." More to the existential point, according to Laverne, he kept his sense of humor.

He wasn't the only one. I watched part of the Clarence Thomas confirmation hearings on TV at the Clarks'. The hearings sparked heated discussions as some viewers, including me, found Anita Hill's accusations of sexual harassment believable and others, including Laverne, insisted that she was a spurned lover, lying to have her revenge on Thomas. "You don't understand how much these black women hate it when a black man chooses a white woman over them," Laverne insisted. She got abundant support from the other women present, including her own daughters, and I naturally found it difficult to argue that I *did* understand. But then I thought Laverne overreached badly one evening when she pointed at Clarence Thomas's wife, sitting grimly by his side, and announced that she knew exactly what that white woman was thinking. Everyone in the room turned to hear what that might be. I got ready to assail whatever Laverne came up with. "She's thinking, 'I *knew* I never should've married this nigger.'"

Surrounded by gales of complex, abandoned laughter, I decided I was out of my league.

THIRTEEN

Nathan Tindall had a campaign strategy. He had always done fine in the northern half of the county. That was where he grew up, where the town of San Augustine was, and where nearly all of the county's black people lived. But the southern half of the county was white, heavily wooded, and crowded with strangers, particularly along the shores of Sam Rayburn Reservoir, and that was where he had effectively lost the 1988 election. And so, one sunny afternoon in February, he headed south on Farm-to-Market Road 1751 in a big, brown, diesel-powered Buick with a stack of cardboard campaign signs in the backseat, a box of nails, and a hatchet. I went with him. We passed a fuel truck, and Tindall indicated the driver. "There's old thing," he said. "He ran against me oncet. Fifty-seven people done tried that."

We drove for a while behind a pickup displaying a bumper sticker, ONLY SICK PEOPLE NEED DRUGS. These stickers were ubiquitous in San Augustine: the town police had distributed them. "You know, there was just as much hell being raised about drinking when I came in as there is about drugs now," Tindall said. "And the same people who used to raise hell about drinking, now they're all drinking and condemning drugs. But I seen ten times as much trouble caused by alcohol as I seen caused by drugs."

We passed the Chinquapin community, and crossed State Highway 103, an east-west artery that divided the county into northern and southern halves. I'd once visited an abysmally poor white family living in a trailer off 103, east of Chinquapin. The head of that household was a single mother in her early forties with nine sons; she looked closer to sixty. She told me that she'd grown up nearby, with an alcoholic father who "got shellshocked over in Vietnam, in World War Two. I guess that's why he mostly drinked all the time." Interviewing her had felt like taking a quick trip to some very harsh and distant land.

"Used to be some good farming country down through here," Tindall said. "Cotton, far as you could see, both sides of the road." The old cotton fields were now scruffy stands of slash pine. Tindall's father-in-law, Earl Woods, had come from this part of the county. We passed the cemetery where he was buried, in a tiny community known as Little Flock. "I used to know every person in this county," Tindall said. "Every little old pig trail. I knew how many dogs they had, how many kids, what they did for a living, legal and illegal."

Tindall pointed out a shack back in the woods. "I found a man hanged hisself in that camp house down there," he said. "He shot a friend of his out hunting, thought he was a deer. Never did get over it. Hanged hisself from the door."

We came upon an old man, opening a mailbox next to the road. Tindall stopped. "Hear of anybody up here that's not for me?" He gestured east, to where an old farmhouse stood on a hill.

"No, I ain't heard nothing agin' you."

"But those are the people I gotta talk to," Tindall muttered.

We pushed on. "You know, the country's a lot thinner populated now," Tindall said. "They all moved down onto the lake." Tindall pointed to a shack in a muddy lot. "I arrested this old boy for stealing a skidder tire," he said. "I tried to get him to do right, but he wouldn't."

We were passing through endless stands of slash pine. At a crossroads, Tindall got out and nailed one of his signs to a tree. With the hatchet, he hacked off twigs that obscured the sign. Red on white and exceedingly plain, the sign said simply ELECT N. L. TINDALL SHERIFF, and underneath, in smaller print SAN AUGUSTINE COUNTY. From what I had seen of local traffic, I estimated the sign would be passed by maybe one vehicle every two or three days.

We crossed back into small holdings, and eventually ran across another old white man, walking with a dog.

"That's a good-lookin' dog," Tindall said, bringing the Buick to a halt.

"That's a *good* squirrel dog," the man said fiercely, and then, without missing a beat, asked, "How you think you gonna do?"

"I think I'm gonna do better."

"I think you're gonna *win*."

As we pulled away, Tindall said happily, "Now he wasn't for me before, I think. And he's the leader of a little community back in there. Whatever he does, they'll do."

Finally, in late afternoon, we reached the lakeshore district, leaving behind the ancient, half-deserted clan communities—Hebron, Pisgah, Little Flock, Veach—for a world of modern settlements named Edgewater, Paradise Hills, and El Piñon Estates. Suddenly there were mobile homes, vacation homes, and hulking recreational vehicles everywhere. In the distance, glimpsed through the trees, was the shining expanse of the reservoir. This was the country Tindall needed to conquer.

But he didn't seem to know where to start. "I'm telling you, them people come and go down here, and ain't nobody knows 'em," he said. "I don't even know how many of them *votes*. That's the heck of it."

We found our way into a trashy little development, with trailers and gim-crack shacks crammed between the trees. "There's a *lot* of people back in here," Tindall marveled. "But you gotta know somebody that can tell you who stays here, and who just comes in for the weekend. I used to *own* this land, but I don't know nobody here."

Tindall stopped and nailed a sign to a tree, just under another sign that said FISH with an arrow pointing to a trailer.

On a road along the lakefront, we stopped at a market. It was the liveliest place we'd seen since leaving San Augustine. There were motorists getting gas, shoppers in the aisles, and a motley group of fishermen hanging around the counter. Tindall hopped out of the car and approached the fishermen, who regarded him blankly. "Tindall," said Tindall. It was the first time I had seen anyone in San Augustine County not recognize him. They didn't even seem to know his name. He started handing out cards that said ELECT N. L. TINDALL. The fishermen took them silently. Tindall left a stack next to the cash register. The woman behind the register looked at them dubiously.

We drove down to an inlet on the lake. Tindall parked and sat quietly, studying the water. "Used to pull a lot of bodies out of here, when they first dammed it up," he finally said. "Folks here, they wasn't used to big water, high waves. They'd drown in wintertime, and it'd take the bodies fifteen to forty days to come up."

Sam Rayburn Reservoir had passed its prime, I had heard, as a bass-fishing destination. Artificial lakes were great for the first few years, but the bass population then went into a long decline. And yet some people still saw Sam Rayburn as the salvation of San Augustine. Stuart Platt, the assistant federal prosecutor who directed Operation White Tornado, saw it that way. All the outsiders, the retired people who had come to live along the lake, had changed the county for the better, he told me. "It will never be the same Old Guard place again," he said. Of course, he added, "It was Operation White Tornado that really broke the spell of Old San Augustine."

Tindall and I headed back north on Farm-to-Market Road 705. Tindall spotted a familiar house and stopped. It was a truly terrible little tin shack, possibly the most disreputable place we'd seen all day. Two rusted-out school buses lay on their sides in the weeds beside the shack. "An old alcoholic lives here," Tindall said. He got out of the car, and nailed one of his signs to the alcoholic's front gate. As he climbed back into the car, Tindall was chuckling. "Now that may hurt me," he said. "But it'll tickle him. He's a good old boy."

FOURTEEN

Laverne Clark, who does not drink alcohol, let her children know that she was not delighted about them going into the liquor business. But when she saw that they were determined, she let the matter drop. For Lanee, a successful store would mean not only being able to quit the hated chicken poultry but, perhaps, finally, to finish fixing up her house in Greertown. And so, in early 1992, she and Timmy and Bud Watts's grandson, Arthur III—a heavyset, easygoing twenty-year-old known as Buddy—finally opened for business, in the little plywood hut at the southern end of the Front.

The real initiative behind launching the store had been Timmy's. Though he was only twenty-six, Timmy was, by local lights, an experienced businessman. He had studied general business for a year at East Texas Baptist College, in Marshall, on a basketball scholarship (he was six feet five inches, quick and strong). When his father, who had the office-cleaning business in San Francisco, fell ill, Timmy went out to help him. He ended up running the company, which cleaned banks and offices and employed fifteen people, many of them from Deep East Texas. After his father died, Timmy moved to Houston, where he started another janitorial business. Now he was back in San Augustine, living at his mother-in-law's place out in Black Ankle with his wife (who had recently left the Air Force) and their young son, hauling pulpwood for his grandfather. He still had plenty of irons in the entrepreneurial fire, including a vintage Ford pickup he was restoring and planning to drive to California to sell, a new house near Lufkin that needed a water line, and the liquor store. Getting a liquor license had taken nine long months, but now that they were open he and Lanee and Buddy were working hard.

"One problem here is that our competition is trying to close us down," Timmy said. He meant that the two white-owned liquor stores on the Front had, along with the town police and the sheriff's office, persuaded the San Augustine city council to try to close the Watts Café—which was next door to the store and provided much of its business—as a public nuisance. The police harassed the tavern's customers, according to Timmy and others, in ways they would never harass the patrons of the white taverns in town. "When Tindall gets back in, that stuff will stop," Timmy said. "I already talked to him about it."

Another problem with doing business in one's hometown was its near-familial closeness. Timmy preferred California. "Out there, you meet some-body, you might never see them again. Here, you meet somebody, you probably gonna see him every day from then on. Pretty soon, he be wantin' to borrow money. It become a bad friendship. At the liquor store, people already expect us to give them everything. In California, you'd just have regular customers."

Deep as the legacy of racial disadvantage runs in a place like East Texas, Timmy was wary of invoking it. "Sure, this town is prejudiced, but I'm sick of people talking about how the white man ain't doing nothing for black people," he said. "It don't matter what color people are. Whoever you are, you gotta *work* in this world. You gotta start your own businesses, not sit around waiting for the white man to be nice to you. You don't get nowhere by talking about black this, white that all the time." He indicated a poster on the wall of the liquor store—COLT .45 MALT LIQUOR SALUTES BLACK ACHIEVERS, the poster declared, next to pictures of Martin Luther King, Jr., General Colin Powell, and Shirley Chisholm. "I'm not off into any of that stuff," Timmy said. "I don't even know who Malcolm X is. All I know is the name." He was referring, I guessed, to the reigning passion among local black youth for Malcolm X T-shirts and X base-ball caps. (Another favorite T-shirt had the legend AFRICA—KENYA UNIVERSITY under zebras, spears, and an African shield.)

Timmy's contempt for black nationalism did not necessarily pit him against his more race-minded peers. The most politically sophisticated young black I met in San Augustine, a union steward at the Tyson plant named Quincy Bratchett, who had attended Prairie View A & M University in Houston, and had served as a medical technician in the Air Force—and wore a T-shirt, when we talked, that said THE BLACKER THE COLLEGE, THE SWEETER THE KNOWLEDGE—could come up with only one name when I asked him about young black business talent in San Augustine: Timmy Price.

So many of Timmy's peers in San Augustine, including his first cousin and close friend Harlon Kelly, had, when *they* got serious about making money, gone into the drug trade. Why had Timmy not? Those who stayed clear of drugs were sometimes said to be "scary" of arrest. Timmy didn't strike me as the scary type. He was really, I thought, just hardheaded. Where others were romantic capitalists, hoping to take big risks and make big money, he was cool and realistic. Although his mother had been lonely and homesick as a young woman in San Francisco, returning to East Texas when Timmy was a baby, Timmy actually liked the anonymity of the city, where nobody tried to borrow his money.

Timmy's bootstrap politics seemed connected to his awareness that his generation was facing a brutal economic future—a broad pattern of downward mobility, not unlike black New Haven's. His and Lanee's grandparents, Hulon and Ruby, were poor but owned land and logging trucks. Timmy's paternal grandfather owned a small construction company in California, and made a good working-class living. His parents' generation was in general no better off than his grandparents', and often less secure. Laverne and Cecil owned a house, but scrambled to pay every bill. Meanwhile, Timmy's many sisters and half-sisters were all unmarried with children, owned no property, still lived mainly with their parents, and had, on the whole, extremely poor economic prospects. As old Bud Watts had said, the banks had been better to him than they would ever be to these young people.

Timmy, perhaps heeding his mother's exhortations to follow the example set by the hardworking, family-minded Jacksons—Laverne didn't see the Jacksons' recent setbacks as any reason to retire their model—was intent on building solid, family-based assets. "What I'm trying to do is set my family up in businesses," he told me. "The money in the liquor store is mine, but Lanee is the owner. I'm setting her up. I'll be like a father to her. Buddy will train her. All she has to know is the prices of things." The fact that Lanee was a good-looking young woman helped the store's prospects. In fact, Timmy had specifically instructed her to flirt with their male customers. Young or old, city or country, they appreciated that.

I stopped by the liquor store one Saturday night in February. Lanee was behind the counter, wearing tight jeans, a flowered shirt, and gold chains featuring a Mercedes symbol and an L. She was doing a steady business, and obviously enjoyed catching customers as they came in the door with a hearty "May I help you?" (Some of the men had the presence of mind to reply, leering, "Oh, yes!") Many of those who came in were just in town for the weekend, from Dallas or Houston or Shreveport, most for family reunions or church homecomings or funerals. "Only reason I ever seem to get back to San Augustine is for funerals," a young factory worker from Dallas told me. These prodigal sons and daughters often stayed at the San Augustine Inn—big family groups rolling up in vast Buicks with California plates or in sleek rental cars from Houston.

Though Lanee hadn't yet mastered the cash register or all the prices, she seemed to be moving plenty of beer and liquor, wine coolers and cigarettes and snacks. A set of bright posters, provided by Bud Light, featuring white and black women in snug bathing suits and short, snug dresses, contributed to the little store's air of cheerful seduction. On the counter were stacks of Nathan Tindall's campaign cards and notepads—ELECT N. L. TINDALL SHERIFF IN 1992. Customers picking up the Tindall items nodded to each other and said, "Cap'n comin' back."

Some customers did double-takes when they saw me in the store. White people rarely paused on this part of the Front, let alone hung around. But the hostility I sometimes felt on the Front wasn't racial, I was told. "People just think white men are narcs unless they're with the absolutely right people," Timmy said. "And a lot of people got family members sitting in the pen behind narcs." Young Buddy Watts qualified, I knew, as an absolutely right person, and he was sitting beside me that night, huge and absorbed in a Joseph Hansen paperback thriller. Nobody in black San Augustine would want to mess with Buddy, I had heard, nor with Timmy Price. In fact, the store's proprietors said they had no fear of robbery. They kept a gun, which Timmy called a "machine," under the counter, but it was just for dealing with rowdy drunks. Even with all the weekend visitors, the tone in the store was densely familiar. Ancestral jokes flew back and forth, and after people left, Lanee would sometimes translate for me. "That guy, he was kiddin' the other guy because his brother shot the other guy's brother in the behind one time. That's why they call each other cousin now."

Some fairly heavy-looking characters came in. When a big man with no neck and a shaved head, dressed in a full-length black leather coat and a black leather hat with a wide, stiff brim entered, swiveling to survey the street with cold yellow eyes before shutting the door, I found other things to stare at until after he had left. When I asked Timmy who the hell *that* was, he laughed. "That's my cousin, Marcus Davis," he said. "He was in the military. He disabled now. Gettin' ready to go to school, be a hairdresser." I said I didn't think Marcus looked like the hairdresser type, and Timmy roared with laughter. "He ain't no gangbanger," he said. "It's just this town make him be lookin' like that. He look like that in the big city, he know he be dead in a week."

Across the highway, between a rundown Laundromat and old Mr. Bud's house, an indelible emblem of Saturday night on the Front appeared: a young guy wearing a black-and-silver L.A. Raiders jacket and a baseball cap turned backward began walking back and forth, a blaring boom box on his shoulder, arms akimbo, hip-hop–style, in front of a long-distance log truck that had been parked for the night. The truck was piled high with big, shaggy, sap-dripping, fresh-cut pine logs. Louie the Lumberjack meets the Notorious B.I.G.

Lanee detested rap music. "It's *nasty*," she said. That night, she had an example ready to hand in a tape that Buddy was playing. The album was by a duo calling themselves the Convicts—their jacket photograph showed two young black men behind bars—and it featured raps with titles like "Woop Her Ass" and "Wash Your Ass" and "I Love Boning." Lanee, the youthful nostalgist, preferred soul singers like Al Green and Luther Vandross. While working in the liquor store gave her a chance to flirt and joke with old schoolmates, it also brought out her grandmotherly side. A big guy about her age came in, and she said, "See this guy? He can draw anything. He got *talent*." But when the young man turned away, she whispered, "He just got in with the wrong crowd."

Pretty much everyone who frequented the nightclub next door was in with the wrong crowd, according to Lanee. To my surprise, she said she thought the Watts Café should be shut down. "The only people that goes in there is the people what don't count to nothing," she said. "No jobs, no willingness to work, just drinkin' all the time, don't know how to act." It would be different, she said, if the club's habitués were better dressed. Lanee didn't seem worried about the effect that shutting the club might have on her store, nor about how her views differed from Timmy's, Mr. Bud's, and, for that matter, those of every other black person I'd heard discuss the subject. What was more, Lanee said she hoped Nathan Tindall lost the sheriff's election. He was a nice man, she said, "but he never did enough to stop the drugs that's hurtin' our people."

Lanee and Johnathan had moved into town. Now it was a Saturday morning, and Lanee's least favorite music was booming from her new roommate Juicy's stereo: the gangsta rapper Ice Cube railing against "house nigger scum" on an album called *Death Certificate*. Lanee's new house wasn't any more prepossessing up close than it had been at first glance; the windows were taped over with plastic, the porch listed perilously, and the front door was fastened by a cheap padlock. But rent was only forty-five dollars a month, and after Kellyville the place seemed spacious. There was even a formal dining room with a fully set table, including folded cloth napkins in the wineglasses—a room that would be used twice a year, Lanee said, on Christmas and Thanksgiving.

I had come to fetch her and Juicy and Johnathan. We planned to go to a matinee at a moviehouse in Nacogdoches, but I was early and I had the flu, so I tried to nap while they did laundry and ran errands. Lanee had bought a new bedroom set, all black lacquer and mirrors. On the walls of her room were a painting on velvet of an improbable sea wave with a lavender maw and lacy froth, and a framed photo of herself looking like a romance novel's idea of a law student—all neatness and seriousness in a dark blouse, posed in front of shelves of leatherbound books. The only book in the house seemed to be Lanee's Bible—a big, inexpensive, white-covered version in which she kept important papers: a credit-union statement, Dee Dee's funeral program, a Mother's Day card from Johnathan. There were also a few black-themed magazines: *Jet, Jive, Black Romance, Bronze Thrills*. Seeing me thumbing through these, Lanee laughed. "Them's some good old books," she said. A remake of *Stagecoach*, starring Bing Crosby and Ann-Margret, was playing unwatched on the TV, its sound track annihilated by Ice Cube's threats.

Lanee brought me tea and TheraFlu. "You lucky you don't work at Tyson's," she said. "They don't give you no time off for nothin' now, no matter what's wrong with you. They even say you can only go to the funeral of an *immediate* relative, not a cousin or a friend. And then you gotta bring the obituary with you, *signed.* You ever hear of anything like that?"

Not since the Middle Ages, I said.

Lanee had in fact been working hurt, I knew, since an ex-boyfriend had paid her a visit a couple of weeks before. "He had a gun on him, and he'd been drinking," she said. "He slammed me against the wall here on the porch—left a knot on my head, kinda messed up my back. He kept trying to pick a fight with my new boyfriend, Scottie. Kept asking if we loved one another. Wouldn't leave. I finally got the law on him, and they made him leave." Lanee had spent five years with the ex in question. They had fixed up the old house in Greertown together, planning to get married and live there. "But he ran around with too many other womens. Plus he was jealous, wanted to control me too much." She frowned. "I won't get married again unless it's an equal partnership. I'm through with this the-man-is-king-of-the-house stuff."

Her ex-husband had also been unfaithful and violent. "Sometimes I think I oughta just stop *doing* it," she said. Then she laughed. But it wasn't just black guys who were useless, she said. She'd had white boyfriends, too. "And you know how they always say black men are better in bed?" She seemed to be considering the matter. I tried not to look too interested. "It ain't really true," she concluded. "It just depends on the man."

Johnathan was in high spirits, capering through the house in long johns. Lanee regarded him loweringly. "I don't got a good hold on him," she said. "I'm not really raising him. I only see him to kiss in the morning, and kiss good night. Other people raisin' him. Whoever he's around all day."

Juicy, too, seemed to be in high spirits. A big-hipped, sharp-eyed young woman, she was standing in the front doorway, drinking coffee and exchanging loud greetings with passersby. Ogling a young man going by on foot, she called back to Lanee, "Who dat? He a pretty li'l ol' fella!"

Lanee said she didn't know him.

I fell asleep.

I awoke to a great commotion. It seemed that Johnathan had been standing behind a door that struck him when Lanee opened it. For this microscopic sin, she dragged him into the laundry room and smacked him half a dozen times, shouting while he screamed. After his beating, Johnathan skulked and whimpered around the house while Lanee continued to storm and threaten. When she finally left to buy groceries, I tried to talk to Johnathan—and found he had completely lost his voice. He opened his mouth, but no sound came out. I knew that Lanee believed the rearing of obedient children required a regular course of beatings. But was this mute cowering really the result she wanted?

Lanee and Juicy decided they wanted to see *Juice,* yet another violent film about gangsta rappers in New York. I said I didn't think Johnathan should see such a film. The women seemed surprised, but we agreed to leave Johnathan at Laverne and Cecil's in Kellyville. He was still too subdued from his beating to protest.

After the movie, it was Lanee who seemed subdued. On the ride back to San Augustine, she said, "If the Lord bless me to see my son hit nineteen years old, I'll be thankful. That's nineteen long years." A minute later, she announced, "We had it *easy* growing up. We never had to worry about no dope dealers, or gettin' shot, or AIDS. It's much worse now."

I felt like pointing out that the good old-fashioned country upbringing that Lanee idealized was meant to protect children from just the kind of destructive sex, glorified violence, cynicism, and nonstop profanity featured in movies like *Juice*, to which she had seemed pleased to take her son. But that, of course, was not my job.

That evening, however, at the Clarks' house in Kellyville, I got in my digs. Lanee started bragging to the crowd on hand that she had given Johnathan— who, scampering with his cousins, seemed fully recovered—a real good whipping that morning. She called me as not exactly an eyewitness, but as an earwitness certainly. I realized that she was just trying to show her family and friends that she was a good mother, capable of doing what had to be done. But I said I hadn't heard a thing. Lanee glared at me, and said that was impossible. I insisted I hadn't heard a thing.

FIFTEEN

The sheriff's race became, inevitably, a referendum on Operation White Tornado. Charles Bryan helped make it so by again designating drugs as the main theme of his campaign and by constantly bringing up his own participation in the famous raid. Nathan Tindall took the bait, going into gleeful detail in his newspaper ads about the falling-out between the sheriff's department and the federal authorities. Bryan responded angrily, citing earlier, more generous federal assessments of his role, and repeatedly suggested that it had been Tindall's laxness in office, if not his outright corruption, that had necessitated the operation to begin with. Although the names of Dave Husband, Willie Earl Dade, and other former Tindall cronies now sitting in federal prisons never appeared on Bryan campaign flyers, they loomed behind his darker suggestions about his opponent. And their weight in the electoral balance was unknown.

Tindall, for his part, refused to denounce Husband or his former chief deputy; he insisted that Dade had gone into the drug trade only after he left the sheriff's office and found himself ill, broke, and unemployed, and he publicly doubted the strength of the evidence against Husband. "They came up here for *me,* not Dave Husband," he said. "And I don't know what he did or didn't do." Tindall rejected, however, the popular notion that he had been Husband's closest friend. "Everybody wants to talk like I was sleeping neat with him, but I only saw him about once a month! *I* didn't go with him to Las Vegas. *I* didn't go with him to the Houston Livestock Show. Hell, all these others was doin' the goin'. I was doin' the *workin'.*"

Tindall didn't say who had gone with Husband to the Houston Livestock Show, to which San Augustine sent a barbecue team comprised of the county's leading (white male) citizens, but I had already heard that the team of the mid-eighties had included not only Husband but the Mitchell brothers, the president of the local bank, and Charles Bryan.

Bryan had had various dealings with Husband, it seemed. He had sold Husband the land where his liquor store stood. He had traded with other White

Tornado defendants, too. Michael Bell—the young king of the Sunset Hills projects, who had never held a job since high school—had bought his brace of expensive show horses from Bryan. Even before the drug raid, some of these transactions had raised eyebrows; people wondered where Bryan imagined that Bell had come by all his discretionary thousands. And after Bryan took office, Bell apparently started claiming he enjoyed the sheriff's protection, pointing to the horses as evidence. While there was almost surely nothing to this claim, and nothing untoward about Bryan's dealings with Husband, either, such convergences showed how closely interwoven most lives were in a place as small and isolated as San Augustine. Outsiders—journalists, say, from Houston or Beaumont (or New York)—often made more of these relationships than they merited. Presumably, local people knew better.

But this was another level of the race: local experience, the county's self-understanding, contending with powerful but remote judgments—with a federally endorsed array of heavily coded drug war imagery. Except for the new people down on the lake, most San Augustinians knew Bryan and Tindall personally. Tindall's campaign ad promises to "come when called, immediately as I always have," appealed to that knowledge—to residents' memories of his decades as sheriff.

The drug problem in San Augustine was real—even if, taking the long view, Tindall reckoned alcohol had caused more trouble—and the pressure that Larry Saurage put on local dealers and their customers gave concrete expression to Sheriff Bryan's overriding concern. But there was more to running the sheriff's office than conducting drug stings, and the drugs theme had as much symbolic as real significance. In the lexicon of many whites, it was, of course, code for lawless blacks, and evoked a great range of criminal stereotypes, from the hapless and desperate addict to the fiendish, nouveau riche pusher. It also represented everything that threatened people's children and—for some, like Lanee—everything that had gone wrong with the modern world.

I kept having to remind myself that most of the voters in San Augustine County—at least two thirds of them—were white. Since I spent most of my time in the town of San Augustine, which was more than half black, and in rural areas like Greertown and Kellyville, which were entirely black, my sense of the county's electorate was skewed. I had to seek out white voters to interview, and when I did so I found that the main issue for whites in the sheriff's race was not drugs but, put simply, black people and how to control them—the same issue that has warped white Southern politics since antebellum days. "A lot of white people supported Nathan Tindall down the years just because they believed he kept the blacks in line," an elderly white woman—a vociferous supporter of Charles Bryan—told me. Her sister, also a Bryan supporter, said,

"Truth is, the blacks pretty much had the run of the county when Nathan was in office. They behave better under Charles."

Actually, everybody knew that it wasn't up to Charles Bryan to make black people "behave"; it was up to Larry Saurage. And there was much debate about whether local black people "respected" Saurage or only feared him. Tindall supporters—who turned out, as the campaign neared its end, to include virtually everyone who held elected office around the courthouse, including the county judge, the county attorney, the city attorney, the district attorney, and the district clerk—generally believed that Saurage had done nothing but alienate black San Augustinians. "The black community is really disgruntled about the way they've been treated," Joanna Johnson, the district clerk, told me. "Just because they're black doesn't mean they're automatically criminals. Every person that's arrested, he's got a family out there."

There was a deep, irrational fear among whites in San Augustine—just as there is among whites in American cities—of a violent rebellion by blacks. "If you just keep pushing 'em, putting pressure on their little clubs and what have you, trying to shut 'em down, there's gonna be—well, I don't want to call it a riot, but let's just say a lot of hard feelings," Joanna Johnson said. "People who go out to these joints at night, they respect Nathan Tindall. They'll mind him. They don't feel like they're having something put *on* them all the time. They don't respect this sheriff." She meant Charles Bryan.

Whatever people's view of Bryan, the man they had to deal with was Larry Saurage. I watched Saurage wade into the middle of a quarrel in the Watts Café one night, and while it was impossible to know what anybody there thought of him, his intervention was effective. A tall, heavily muscled man in his twenties—who had been a top local athlete as a teenager, before his body and soul were wrecked by alcohol, drugs, and prison—had attacked a young woman, and was threatening worse. Saurage, arriving on the scene, stopped him cold with a finger in his face and a few sharp words, then took him by the arm and led him down the Front. A few minutes later, Saurage returned alone, lightly scolded the remaining gawkers, and left in his cruiser. "That boy works for me," he told me. "He's one of my snitches is all."

The imagined black insurrection would start, it was widely assumed, on the Front, probably at the Watts Café. And so the Front was, in a curious way, a focal point of the sheriff's race. Roughly half a mile long, it actually went by many names. The newspaper called it "the 96 strip." Some old-timers called it "Skid." Larry Saurage called it "the Cut," hitting the word with almost as much underjawed force as Pelo Clark, playing a Real Texan, did "Lufkin." Old Bud Watts, who had been doing business in the neighborhood since before U.S. 96 was built, claimed that people once called it "Happy." It ran from the J & J Car Wash, on a hill at the northern end, to the Hill Top Barbecue and Fat

Daddy's Video and Tires, on the next hill south. In between were four gas stations, four liquor stores, two convenience stores, a Laundromat, a gun shop, a locker plant, the Henry Harp American Legion Post, the car lot where Nathan Tindall worked, the Watts Café, a white bar and restaurant called Doodle's, a take-out chicken shack, a few private homes, and half a dozen shuttered businesses. It was a scruffy, forgettable strip, and long-distance traffic on 96, while it was forced to slow for a traffic circle at the intersection with State Highway 21—downtown San Augustine was half a mile east—rarely paused except for gas. What made the Front so symbolically important, which is to say politically important, was that it was a place where black people gathered and white people had to pass them.

Blacks gathered on the Front partly because it ran past the Quarters and the Sunset Hills projects, but also because it was not the courthouse square, where the jailhouse presided and all the shops and businesses were white-owned and white-run and the sour spirit of Jim Crow still hung over the town. Even the white-owned establishments on the Front were more egalitarian somehow. At dawn, a dozen older black men in blue jeans, checked shirts, and baseball caps might assemble in the all-night convenience store (the one owned by Charles Bryan's son) at the traffic circle, sipping coffee sleepily, ruing the night's hard freeze—"That frost come down *early* last night"—and gruffly organizing the complicated rendezvous of men and equipment for the coming day's work in the woods, while outside younger guys waited glumly, sleeping in the dark cars and pickups scattered around the lot: the muscle for the day's pulpwooding.

Late that afternoon, the same group of older men might reconvene in front of the shuttered Bull Club, their pickups parked at crazy angles, cold cans of Old Milwaukee raised, voices rich and tired, laughing, everybody in a much better mood. Or, if rain had shortened the day, a pair of young loggers might make their way to the Watts Café before noon, their jeans muddy, each with a quart of beer in hand, one wearing an old HUSBAND'S LIQUOR STORE cap and grousing, "We got about a cord out of there this morning, and then we bogged down. I told him, but that boss got a head like a goat!" At that hour, the jukebox would be silent, the pool table unused. A couple of older men might be sitting quietly smoking in the window, watching the traffic pass on 96. At night, the scene at the club was younger and rowdier, but the point is that, for all its raffishness, the Front was a place where ordinary black folk felt comfortable.

And whites did not. On my first night in San Augustine, I asked a young white woman in town where I might find a restaurant. The only place still open, she said, was Doodle's. Getting there would be a problem, though, because I was on foot. She got out a map of the town. "See, all this here"—she indicated the Front—"is blacks."

John Mitchell, the county attorney (later a district judge), said there were plenty of precedents for the campaign to shut down the Watts Café. "There's always been, periodically, these little uprisings, mainly in the churches, about how we've got to 'clean up the cafés.' " But the Watts Café was, in some ways, a special case. "In the old days," Mitchell said, "the cafés weren't right on the highway, where whites had to drive by them. They were back in the black neighborhoods, or out in the country." Those early cafés were, I imagined, the famous juke joints, back when East Texas was a cradle of country blues. What a long fall it had been to the Watts Café, where live music was unknown, and where the next generation's Leadbelly was truly unlikely to surface. "Now that they're in town," Mitchell went on, "the young blacks want to claim more public space. And they consider the city council's move against them to be racist. And they're right. It is."

The public space being contested between blacks and whites extended beyond the Front. When backwoods whites complained that they didn't like to go into town "because the niggers don't know their place no more," they were objecting to a host of things, including the burly black boys who dominated the high school football team, towering unapologetically over the white cheerleaders, and to the wildly colored, extravagantly accessorized, miniature Japanese pickups that young black men drove up and down the Front, hip-hop blasting from the cabs, 2 BAD 2 BE 4 GOTTEN scrawled in super-fancy lettering on the tailgates. Sometimes the pickups ventured uptown (though I never saw one pass the jailhouse). The trucks themselves seemed unnatural—with bumpers and hubcaps of brightly colored plastic, they looked like rolling pieces of hard candy. And lowering the chassis to within inches of the pavement made, in context, a ringing statement: "I don't go down rutted-up old dirt roads, bouncing through the sand pits to some old home place. I don't travel hog trails. I don't work in the fields."

In some places, the contest for space grew literal and even violent. At the Cedar Hills housing project, the white nonresident manager, George Ramsey, had built a high iron fence around the place and put an armed guard at the front gate, where a sign said ALL VISITORS MUST SHOW PROOF OF IDENTITY AND LEAVE BY 10 P.M. Some of the more cosmopolitan whites in town were embarrassed by Ramsey's fence, noting sheepishly that it looked pretty bad from a civil rights point of view, but I heard no public objections. Cedar Hills residents and their friends raised their objections privately, but vehemently. At a city council meeting five months after the fence's completion, Ramsey reported that it had just been damaged for the fourteenth time. Everything from crowbars to dynamite was being used against it. But Ramsey and his repair crews had no intention of abandoning the fight. Symbolically, the power of the fence was intensified by the presence of a large white mansion on the hill overlooking the projects. The mansion's owners had, in fact, sold the land for the projects to the government.

But the Watts Café had become the central local metaphor for black disorder and white control, and its importance to the sheriff's race was not lost on the candidates. Nathan Tindall said, "I told that big Watts boy I don't want those old drunks that hang around there saying they're for me. White people hear them talking about me, that's bad for me. But what can you do? There's only about ten or fifteen drunks hang around down there, don't work, see 'em there all hours of the day. But they can cause a lot of trouble."

They did cause trouble for Tindall, in the closing weeks of the campaign, when a town patrolman began playing a videotape he had assembled for civic groups, such as the Rotary Club. The tape showed late-night police visits to various black nightclubs, including the Watts Café. The purpose of showing the tape, which was ill lit and impossible to follow without narration, was, the patrolman told me, "to let these people know what's going on in their town after they go to bed and roll up the sidewalks at nine." It was also to boost support for the effort to shut down the Watts Café. The all-white audiences for the tape were riveted by it—especially by the part where the police stormed into the Watts Café on Christmas Eve while the evening's disc jockey shouted, "Vote for Tindall in '92!"

The big white churches in town—Baptist, Methodist, Church of Christ— were all backing Bryan. Everyone, including Bryan, said so. What that would mean in the election, however, nobody knew. There were no official endorsements from the pulpit, no rock-solid white voting blocs, no tracking polls— and most people, black and white, were wary of saying publicly who they supported. Sam Malone said, "There's an old-family, white-supremacist element here, but it's damn hard to put your finger on it." There were also what Malone called "redneck do-gooders" among the town's Old Guard—these were the more conservative members of the big white churches and were all Bryan supporters.

But it was here that the race issue began to blur into the class issue. "There's an older group that sees Nathan and Dave Husband in the same category—as low-class farm kids who can deal with other low-class folks, like blacks," John Mitchell said. "Because Nathan employed a lot of the same guys he arrested, he came to be seen as pro-black, pro–lower class." Tindall was, in other words, still the "nigger sheriff" to many whites.

SIXTEEN

Looking for a break from politics, I drove up to Greertown. Beyond the house where Herbert Jackson lived with his disabled sister and his eighty-year-old mother, the road had been ruined by winter rains. I parked and continued on foot. It was a brilliant afternoon. I was walking northeast, through stands of pine and chinquapin. Perhaps half a mile along, on a knoll at the end of the road, I came to Lenard Jackson's fabled ranch house, once regarded as Heaven by the ragged denizens of Sunset Hills. It was a modern brick place, nothing special, painted white, with blue-gray shutters and trim. Birds were nesting in the mailbox. In the windows, NO TRESPASSING signs, now fading, had been plastered by the U.S. Marshal. The house had been seized by the federal government, along with Lenard's one-third share of a hundred-acre tract of Jackson family land just south of here, behind St. Matthew's Baptist Church. There was a fine view to the south and east, across rolling woods and watermelon fields. Two older houses, both long abandoned, also stood on the site; an ancient, unpainted settler's shack and a small frame house on blocks. A dead Bonneville Safari station wagon was parked in the weeds; on its front seat lay a waterlogged pamphlet, THE CHEMICALLY DEPENDENT ADOLESCENT: GUIDEBOOK FOR THE CONCERNED PERSON. In the windows of the ranch house, hundreds of big red wasps were trapped behind the glass.

It was already possible to imagine the story of Lenard Jackson and Operation White Tornado—and, perhaps, the suicide of Girtha Mae Polley Jackson—being subsumed into the rich oral history of the Pre-Emption. Part of it would be about how the government came and took some more black people's land. Part of it would be about how a local man went off to the city and came back with some of its wealth and some of its corruptions. Visiting with the few old black people who still lived in the Pre-Emption, I had heard many land-loss sagas, and had glimpsed different facets of people's notions about the city. Willie Harp, a widower who was born in the Pre-Emption in 1913 and still hunted squirrels and deer, and sang, memorably, with the Greertown Gospel

Singers, had told me about a "little grandgirl" of his, a teenager in Dallas, who was addicted to crack. Harp had gone up to Dallas to talk to her, and to comfort her mother, but he was still worried sick. "These cities are just no good for these kids," he said. Harp's neighbor, T. G. Clark, who was born in the Pre-Emption in 1915 and had nineteen children with four different women, had told me about how some of his grandchildren liked to come up from Houston in the summer to visit. Those city people got a peculiar kick, he said, out of his hogs and cows and mules. Clark showed me around his place, pointing out butter churns and crosscut saws and a blacksmith's anvil and a spinning wheel, all while regaling me with tales about how his great-aunt's husband had been killed by the Burlesons over some bootleg whiskey, and how he had fended off the advances of a white lady who was trying to get his land.

But while hiking back down from the ranch house to my car, it struck me that there soon wasn't going to be any oral history of the Pre-Emption for the story of Lenard Jackson and White Tornado to *join,* that it was all coming to an end. The people of the Pre-Emption were dying off, and there was no one to replace them. All of San Augustine was a backwater, but oblivion was truly preparing to close over this ancient black community's head.

Dr. Tom Blount, the veterinarian, was also a local historian. He lived with his mother in a grand old farmhouse west of town and he owned a vivid sense of just how far outside the American mainstream San Augustine stood. "We're an oppressed people," he told me. "We're living in a wealthy, high-tech country, but all we have to offer is raw materials: cotton, timber, chickens. You can see the oppression in people's eyes. You can see it in their faces. It's here, and it's been here. Some of us have had the good fortune to get an education, but even that's not a real relief. It just helps you understand it better. I have a cousin who moved to Houston a long time ago and married a psychiatrist; they take vacations in Europe. That's just another world; people here only see it on TV. I've been to other countries myself. But most people here have never been anywhere, and the truth is that Deep East Texas just keeps falling farther and farther back. In the 1920s, this house had three telephones, hooked into three different exchanges. By the time I came along, in 1940, phones were a thing of the *past.* We didn't have one, even though my granddaddy was a doctor. And we didn't have indoor plumbing either. It wasn't until the fifties that those things started coming back. The Depression carried us backwards here. It was a real lick to this county, and in some ways we never recovered."

Dr. Blount was from one of San Augustine's oldest families—his great-great-grandfather, Stephen Blount, signed the Texas Declaration of Independence—but he seemed to have little to do with the town's Old Guard. Like many scions of distinguished local families, he was land rich and cash poor. The house he shared with his mother was in bad shape, and its dilapidated grandeur, its sagging ceilings and peeling wallpaper, its faded portraits and squirrels in the rafters, were as Old World as they were Old South—they put me in mind of some ancient family manse in a permanently depressed part of rural France. Blount said he had never thought of leaving San Augustine. "But my kids probably would have come out better if I had. Very few that come out of San Augustine High School now can pass a university entrance exam."

While I couldn't say that I saw in anyone's eyes the "oppression" Dr. Blount described, and while I had certainly seen poorer, more degraded places in America—both urban and rural—it was nonetheless true; the deep, systemic poverty of San Augustine was fundamental to any understanding of its relationship to the rest of the country. The county's poverty rate was 50 percent higher than that of New Haven, and no child raised there, black or white, was going to Yale, or to anywhere comparable. San Augustine was a place where new cars and trucks and house trailers began to appear in late spring, at what people called "income time"—when income tax refunds were received—and where those things then started disappearing through the summer and fall, as they were repossessed.

It was also a place where many people believed that, as Cecil Clark put it, "The sheriff ain't just the *law* around here. He's also responsible for the *economy.*" This wasn't true, any more than was the idea, especially popular among outsiders, that a rural sheriff (or anyone else) could really "run" a county. Even in a lightly populated place like San Augustine, there are far too many people doing far too many different things for any one person to be on top of much of it. But it all had its figurative truth, particularly for the weaker and more provincial residents. This social psychology was, broadly speaking, feudal, and Nathan Tindall, with his sawmill and truck fleets and pulpwood contracts, with his thousand and one personal loans and customized fine-payment schemes—with, in short, his profound understanding of the grim economic facts of life in his county—had reigned for decades as San Augustine's democratically elected liege lord.

And when Tindall's grip on the forces of disorder, concisely represented by the cocaine trade, had seemed to grow uncertain, Charles Bryan had come along and defeated him at the polls.

Now, however, in the 1992 race, the choice between the two men was no longer between a known and an unknown. After a term with Bryan as sheriff, voters knew what they were getting if they chose him. They were getting Larry Saurage, a professional lawman whose duties did not include powering the local economy, and who seemed, at least to some, to have a firm grip on the forces of disorder. They were getting the war on drugs, and a man who could call for outside help. It was as though an action hero had walked out of one of the endless cop shows on TV.

Of course, Bryan's campaign turned on the allegation, expressed with varying degrees of subtlety, that Tindall had been corrupt, and that his own signal achievement had been to clean up a dirty county. This was another aspect of the drugs theme, and an indispensable one. It was a risky strategy, though, for it asked people to accept that San Augustine had been a den of pushers and thieves, that the county had needed cleaning up so badly that the feds had to be called in and the community's problems exposed to the world. This was the story the outside world got, the story of White Tornado. But it was a tricky thing to sell locally, and it got trickier over time, as the drug problem persisted and the local retail economy failed to recover. (Larry Saurage never mentioned, I noticed, that he had called in the feds before, when he was working in Orange County. In that case, Saurage had charged that, among other things, the sheriff and his friends were "queers.") There were many people ready to believe, in the best East Texas paranoid tradition, that Tindall had been crooked, but there were many others who, if they were to reach that conclusion, had to revise their own long experience of the man who had been sheriff since before they were born.

Tindall's supporters liked to say that it was statistically impossible that he could be corrupt. "I think he's probably the cleanest person in America," Judge Jack Nichols told me. "He's been investigated by everybody but the CIA." Plenty of mobsters, I imagined, could make the same argument. Unlike a gangster, though, Tindall had lived the least secretive of lives. He had hardly been out of the public eye for forty years. Indeed, what he reminded me of was neither a crime boss nor a crime buster, but a veteran baseball manager, some crusty old field general like Earl Weaver or Sparky Anderson, surveying the opposition and his tender charges, making calculations too complex—and informed by too much experience—to explain to the casual observer (a reporter, say). He was tireless, paternal, eccentric, vain, endlessly competitive and yet stoically philosophical. Casey Stengel meets Marcus Aurelius.

His opponents' philosophy, meanwhile, was a piney-woods Manichaeanism. The world of Bryan and Saurage was divided into the blessed and the damned, in the Christian fundamentalist style, with drugs helping draw the bright line between the two. It was a highly abstract version of the county, and a throwback in some ways to the boss man days of segregation, and yet, paradoxically, it served to connect San Augustine to the modern world and the rest of the country, through the war on drugs and a new, bureaucratic, urban style of policing.

But perhaps the more relevant philosopher was Emerson, who wrote that in any political contest there were really only two parties, "the party of the Past and the party of the Future." Call them memory and hope. Tindall was memory, the muddled genius of a particular American place; Saurage was hope, a generic American dream.

SEVENTEEN

Election Day was cold and sunny, with a sharp breeze shaking the new leaves on the pin oaks. It was Super Tuesday across the South, but Bill Clinton signs were rare sights around San Augustine, where it was BRYAN FOR SHERIFF hand-painted on the windows of the gun shop on the Front and ELECT N. L. TINDALL nailed to the tree trunks along the farm-to-market roads.

I stopped by the courthouse, which was a polling station, and was surprised to find that the poll judge there was a close relative of Charles Bryan's. I was even more surprised to find, upstairs in the courtroom, one of Bryan's more passionate supporters presiding over the counting of ballots. Nobody else seemed to find anything strange about these arrangements.

I didn't see either of the candidates until late that afternoon, when I ran into Tindall in the bar at Doodle's. He didn't belong in there—he was the man who had never had a drink in his life—and yet he seemed at ease. The joint was crowded, full of animated white people I hadn't seen before, and Tindall moved through the throng, shaking hands. Where had all these people come from? Were they just in town for the election? When Tindall saw me, he laughed. He pointed me out to two badly dressed, sunburned men and said, "When this fella come here, he thought I was Al Capone. I don't know what he thinks now." After Tindall left the bar, I had a drink with the badly dressed men. They were oil workers, from an offshore rig in the Gulf. They were also friends of Dave Husband's. They said Husband had phoned the bar earlier, and he was due to call again later, to hear how the election came out.

Downtown, on the courthouse square, a huge chalkboard had been set up. The names of all the candidates, from the Democratic presidential hopefuls to the would-be constables of the county precincts, had been carefully written in. As the only countywide race being contested, the sheriff's column, with spaces for returns from each of the county's eleven precincts, took up most of the chalkboard. After sundown, a shivering crowd began to gather in the square, collecting ten deep before the brightly lit chalkboard.

I went inside the county clerk's office, where the returns would be reported first. Several dozen people, all white except for one young clerk, were milling around. The first ballot boxes began to arrive, hushing the crowd. The county clerk intoned the tally from each box as it came in. It was soon apparent that Tindall's southern-county strategy had not worked. By the time the box from Hebron arrived—carried by a huge young man with an Old Testament beard flowing down his chest and the big metal box clasped in his arms like unwieldy news from God—Tindall was nearly five hundred votes behind.

I wandered outside and joined the crowd in front of the chalkboard on the square. About half of the results in the sheriff's race had been posted, not enough to predict a winner yet, though the trend of things was becoming obvious. The crowd, which was predominantly white, was, just as in the bar at Doodle's, full of faces I hadn't seen before. Country music blared from the pickup trucks slowly circling the square—the county's silent white majority seemed to be putting in a rare appearance. I spotted Laverne Clark, and went and stood with her and a small group of other middle-aged black women. One of the women, heavyset and merry-faced—and the mother, I realized, when we were introduced, of the hapless young man who had carried a hidden microphone into the Sunset Hills projects on the day I accompanied Larry Saurage and his men on a drug raid—was amusing her companions with a raucous running commentary on the election. When a young white man behind us asked about a result he couldn't see on the chalkboard, and Laverne turned to help him, our foul-mouthed raconteuse growled, just a little too softly for him to hear, "I ain't telling him shit." The other women giggled fiercely, shaking their heads.

There was a potent racial element to this election, clearly, and the people around us were being, I thought, conspicuously quiet about the sheriff's race. They talked instead about the presidential primary, where Bill Clinton was cleaning up his competition. Our fearless commentator snorted. "I don't care about *that*," she said. She pointed to the right-hand side of the chalkboard, where votes for sheriff were being tabulated. "I care about *this*." Appreciative chuckles rose around us from both blacks and whites.

As a Bryan victory began to look certain, our merry interpreter's commentary darkened. "Uh-*uh*," she said. "He gonna *really* whup us now. Gonna send *every* black boy to the pen who ain't already there." She turned to me. "You lucky you live in New York. He gonna *whup* us. Four more years!" The other women in our little group were laughing helplessly now. Laverne, who was hiding her face inside a silvery flowered shawl, was laughing so hard she sounded half delirious. "You laugh, girl," her friend scolded her. "I ain't goin' outta my *house* for the next four years!" But Laverne just kept laughing, her voice trilling down in beautiful, church-choir descants, her eyes flashing above her shawl at me, as if to ask whether I understood yet just what it was that was so funny.

Voter turnout had been, for San Augustine, unusually low—only 60 percent. It had been especially low, people said, among black voters—a fact that presumably contributed to Tindall's crushing defeat. He had received only 41 percent of the vote.

Many of Tindall's supporters were grasping for explanations, shocked by the magnitude of his loss. His black supporters, in particular, had been quite unprepared for it, since virtually no one in the black community had had a good word to say about Charles Bryan. But the Captain was not coming back.

I stopped by Charles Mitchell's office, and found the district attorney in a subdued, reflective mood. "Nathan's losing is part of something bigger that's happening," he said. "East Texas is moving away from the old-timey sheriff. It's happening in other counties, too—Shelby, Jasper, Nacogdoches. Used to be you had a skunk under your house, a fight with your wife—hell, if your house was on *fire*—you called the sheriff. And that's the kind of sheriff Nathan Tindall was, and what he was offering people. But it's not what most of 'em want anymore. Now various police agencies handle things. I guess it's the passing of an era. Some people still prefer the old-timey sheriff, though." Mitchell sighed. "I might be an example of such a person."

I briefly saw Tindall, late that afternoon, at the car lot on the Front. He was just pulling out of the lot, headed somewhere in his grubby Buick, and his eyes were red in the low sun. "I didn't want the job," he said, his voice as gustily confident as ever. "Other people wanted me back in there. I just wanted to help people." With that, he roared off.

Larry Saurage, surprisingly, said he was disappointed. "Why am I disappointed? Because 1,599 people voted for Tindall!" The only good part, Saurage said, was that the feds still might indict Tindall for money laundering at that bank where he'd worked. We were in Saurage's office; his boots were up on the desk. Shetresa, on the phone behind me, was saying, "A lot of the blacks are mad at us because we broke up their little crack dealing. You know." Watching Saurage stew, I understood better than I had before why people were so nervous about being on the losing side of a sheriff's election. "I stayed away from town last night for a reason," he said. "Because if we'd lost I'd have got in a fist fight for sure." He shook his head angrily. *"After all the work Betty Donatto came in here and did."*

On the morning after the election, Lanee seemed unconcerned. She said she hadn't even bothered to vote. I asked why.

"Because they just gonna put in who they want," she said sulkily.

Did she mean that the election was fixed?

"Sure they cheat on the count!"

Lanee's paranoia and cynicism were almost exquisite. Truly, though, politics didn't interest her. They weren't going to put the world back together the way she thought it should be. (They could help take it apart, though. Three months later, the local authorities, led by Larry Saurage, shut down the Watts Café, and three months after that Lanee and Timmy's liquor store was out of business.)

What did concern Lanee that morning was me—specifically, what I would wear when she and Juicy took me to a nightclub they liked in Pineland. It was kind of a glamorous place and Lanee was not sure my wardrobe was up to it. I noticed her studying my feet unhappily. "Ain't you got some other *shoes?*" she asked.

Was there something wrong with burgundy Rockports?

"Look like . . ." she began. "Look like . . ." Her face screwed up in a losing battle with amusement. Finally, she hit me with a huge, sweet horse laugh.

BOOK THREE

La Vida Loca

Now the clash is different, no longer between opposing sets of values, but between values and the violent vacuum. The substitute for culture presented to newcomers was invented at the conjunction of entertainment and advertising; it may still be called culture, but neither Rambo nor Madonna has the character required to get a troubled child through the night.

—Earl Shorris,
Latinos: A Biography of the People

Rosa and Rafael Guerrero first found their way to the Yakima Valley, in central Washington State, in 1977. They were a young married couple from Tacoaleche, a farm town in Zacatecas, in central Mexico, more than two thousand miles away. Poor and barely educated, the Guerreros had packed up their two small children and left everything they knew, hoping to find, in their words, *una vida mejor*—a better life. Traveling by bus, they crossed the international border at Tijuana on tourist visas. They worked, illegally, for a few months in a factory in California, then pushed on to the Yakima Valley, where Rafael had a nephew. They found jobs on a grape farm near Sunnyside, a town of about ten thousand people in the lower valley. The work paid $2.90 an hour. Less than two hundred miles from the Canadian border, the Guerreros settled down, sent their children to school, and produced two more sons. Once, after five years in Sunnyside, Rafael was seized by the immigration authorities and deported to Mexico. But he quickly recrossed the border on foot, made his way back to his family, and did not lose his job. In 1986 Rafael and Rosa took advantage of a national amnesty and got green cards. In 1994 they became United States citizens. They were still working on the grape farm.

The Yakima Valley, one of America's richest farming regions, has been starkly dependent on Mexican labor for more than fifty years. Irrigation canals built during the New Deal carry immense amounts of water from the Cascade Mountains down into the valley, which gets mild winters and three hundred days of sunshine a year. Apples, peaches, pears, grapes, cherries, hops, mint, asparagus, and a dozen other food crops are grown in elysian abundance on large, highly profitable farms. During the Second World War, when farmworkers left en masse for better-paying defense jobs around Seattle, the federal government shipped thousands of Mexican *braceros* to the valley to help with the harvests, and after that the area became a regular stop on the great migrant farmworker trail, which surges annually from deep in Mexico, and today fans out across most of the agricultural United States. The last Anglo and American Indian farmworkers in the Yakima Valley (the Yakima Indian Reservation covers the west side of the valley and the adjacent foothills of the Cascades) were displaced in the 1970s by a wave of undocumented Mexicans whose willingness to work for low wages made them irresistible to growers. Twenty thousand Mexicans in the Yakima Valley got green cards under the 1986 amnesty, and an equally large number of migrants decided to "settle out" there. (Three million people, including one million migrant farmworkers, took advantage of the amnesty nationwide.)

Sporadic attempts to unionize Washington's farmworkers were, until the mid-eighties, crushed by the growers. After the 1986 amnesty, however, many newly legal workers became determined to improve their lot, and the United Farm Workers of Washington State, the most ambitious organizing effort yet, was launched in 1987. The UFW-WS had won a series of state legislative victories, extending standard labor protections to farmworkers and their children, but in 1994, when I started visiting the Yakima Valley, the union had yet to win a single contract with a grower. Its best chance of winning a breakthrough contract was at a group of farms owned by the Château Ste. Michelle winery, where its organizing had been highly effective. Rosa and Rafael Guerrero worked at one of those farms. They were union members, and vigorously supported a consumer boycott, called by the union, of the wine sold under various labels by Château Ste. Michelle.

I first met the Guerreros through their union. When I arrived at their house—a small, stuccoed three-bedroom on a wide, sun-bleached street in Sunnyside—they were just getting home from work. Their oldest son, Juan, who was then eighteen and also working at Château Ste. Michelle, trudged silently from the car into the back of the house. Rafael and Rosa, in boots and dusty jeans, gave me shy smiles and three-part solidarity handshakes, complete with light knuckle punches. We sat drinking Cokes in their living room, surrounded by family photographs and artificial flowers in hanging baskets.

The Guerreros were both copper-colored, sun-weathered, broad-faced, compactly built. That evening, they looked slightly glassy-eyed from exhaustion, but they politely answered my questions with long, carefully phrased narratives. Their most pressing problem at work, they said, was a new type of shears that *la compañía* had given them for pruning. These shears were damaging their hands, they said, and they were afraid they might eventually be crippled. The union provided a channel for resolving such problems. But what they really wanted was a contract, reached through collective bargaining.

"We only want what the whites have," Rafael said quietly, referring to the Anglos who worked inside the Château Ste. Michelle buildings, and who belonged to the Teamsters. "Normal benefits, job security, an end to discrimination, dignity."

According to the Guerreros, Château Ste. Michelle, which was owned by

UST Inc.—a holding company whose most profitable subsidiary was the United States Tobacco Company—had been bringing ever more sophisticated tactics, including "consultants" from California, to bear on the union and its members. Here, I thought, were workers locked in a struggle as old as serfdom—it was their bad luck that it happened to be taking place in the capital-triumphant 1990s.

Juan emerged, freshly showered, in a clean T-shirt and baggy pants. His parents excused themselves and went to wash up. I asked Juan how he liked working at Château Ste. Michelle.

He looked at me as if I were crazy. "It sucks," he said. Throwing himself onto a kitchen chair, he looked past me at the television, where his two younger brothers were watching Snoop Doggy Dogg strut and threaten on MTV. Juan was several inches taller than his parents, and had a radically different affect. Where they were plainly from campesino backgrounds, with forthright, stolid manners, he had a lean, liquid grace and a distinctly ironic presence. They spoke only Spanish; his English had no Spanish accent. He had an open, intelligent, handsome face, a chipped front tooth, and five earrings. He wore his hair, which was bleached faintly henna-colored on top, in the sort of chopped-off bowl cut that I associated with undergraduates devoted to the Pre-Raphaelites.

I asked him about the farmworkers' union.

"I don't know anything about it," he said. "When I get to work, I just—" He mimed pulling a pair of tiny headphones delicately over his ears. "I put on the Walkman, and that's it. I don't talk to anybody, and people don't talk to me. They're like, 'Why don't you talk?' But it's just not my scene. They're all like old people. It's just not me."

I was shocked. John Steinbeck had prepared me for Rafael and Rosa, but not for Juan. I asked what he listened to on his Walkman.

"Nirvana. Smashing Pumpkins. Pearl Jam. Alternative, techno, some rap."

A beeper went off, and Juan pulled it from his pocket and checked the number displayed. Then he turned and studied me, cocking his head, seeming to take me in for the first time. "You really from New York?" he said.

When I was Juan's age, I thought Mexico was cool. It was the wild place, where we camped on the beach, bought beer without hassles, and howled at a foreign moon. Juan, who had visited Mexico only once since his parents brought him north, did not think Mexico was cool. "Their roads are ugly," he said. "Their houses are made out of mud or chalk or something, and a lot of them are falling down. Their food is weird. They don't have corn dogs, they don't have pizza. In fact, there are no real stores or restaurants. The stores and restaurants are just, like, *in the houses.*" When Juan and his friends wanted to get wild, wanted to escape adult supervision, wanted to drink, they went out in the country around Sunnyside, gathering in old barns and abandoned home-steads, just as rural and small-town American kids have done forever. That was their Mexico, you might say.

So Juan was, to me, both enigmatic and strangely familiar.

Rafael and Rosa were very worried about him. They were no more enthusiastic about his working in the fields than he was; it was not the future they had foreseen for him. But Juan had started getting into trouble, mainly for fighting, in his early teens, and after a spell in juvenile detention he had finally been kicked out of school. The job in the fields was a stopgap, it was hoped, until he resumed his studies. In the meantime, the Guerreros seemed a bit stunned by the variety of perils that raising kids in *El Norte* had turned out to include. As I got to know more about Juan's life, I was a little stunned myself. Juan, for his part, usually managed to seem spectacularly casual about almost anything that happened. To him, of course, his life was normal.

Hanging out with Juan meant, I found, hanging out with Mary Ann Ramirez. The two were inseparable.

"Juan and I have the same thoughts," Mary Ann told me. "We think *exactly alike*, and everybody else thinks we're weird, but we're not. They'll all be like tired or drunk or whatever, and we'll just be talking, talking, talking. Last night, we talked almost all night."

"Almost," Juan confirmed.

The three of us were driving around Sunnyside in my rental car. Hanging out with Juan and friends also meant a lot of aimless cruising. "Did you hear that guy at that party last night say he was from L.A.?" Juan asked Mary Ann. "Everybody who comes up here says they're from L.A."

"And you're supposed to be impressed!" Mary Ann shouted. "Did you hear what Cuco said?"

"About us being little rockers? Little snowboarders?"

"Yeah!"

I was keeping a list, which was swiftly growing, of local youth insults. Now I added "rockers" and "snowboarders." I had met Cuco Zesati. He was a burly junior at a local "alternative" high school—the place where students with discipline problems at the regular school were sent—and was a close friend of Juan's.

"He just doesn't like our hair," Juan said.

"Almost all Juan's friends have the same hair," Mary Ann informed me. I had met enough of Juan's buddies by then to know what she meant. "But Juan has the best!"

Mary Ann's speaking voice, at least when she was feeling pleased with life, was an ebullient shout. She was fair-skinned, fine-boned, and extremely pretty, with a full head of long brown hair and a ton of nervous energy. Although she was born in Sunnyside, she had lived in many places—in Seattle, Texas, Germany (a stepfather in the military)—so that her speech was full of tramontane expressions like "y'all" and "fixin' to git." She talked fast and, like Juan, had no Spanish accent.

"Did Juan tell you we're going to Alaska this summer?"

"No."

"We are! Ten of us are going. We're going to work in a fish cannery. Make mass cash. It's gonna be fun, dude!" She punched Juan in the shoulder.

"Yeah," he drawled. "It is."

I asked Mary Ann, who was the same age as Juan, what she wanted to be when she grew up.

"Prison guard," she said. "The pay is good, it's secure, it's clean." She paused. "But I'd rather be a psychiatrist. I'd be really good, I think. It takes a lot of years of college, but I could do it. I'd like to specialize in sexual problems. People don't like to talk about it, but sexual problems cause a lot of other problems. Don't you think?"

I didn't disagree. But I had trouble picturing Mary Ann as a prison guard.

"Yeah, I'm probably not big enough," she said. "And if I ever *go* to prison I'm so small they'll probably toss me around ten times."

Juan laughed. "She always has to add on something," he said. "She doesn't just get tossed around. She gets tossed around *ten times*."

"You like the way I talk!"

"I do."

Juan and Mary Ann made, I thought, a striking couple. Mary Ann insisted, however, that they were not one. As she put it to me, "Everybody thinks we're boning each other, but we're not."

I didn't say so, but I could see how everybody might get that idea.

"We're just friends," Mary Ann protested.

"Yeah," Juan said, unconvincingly. "She's just like one of the guys."

"These other girls just can't stand it that I like to kick it with Juan and his friends. Hey, did you see that?"

Mary Ann indicated the occupants of a vintage Chevy. She and Juan were constantly spotting friends, enemies, and telltale combinations of other teenagers as we cruised. Downtown Sunnyside consisted of a dozen low-rise blocks of modest shops and offices. Most of the commercial (and teenage social) action was out along the Yakima Valley Highway, on the north side of town, where a strip with a couple of shopping malls, a K mart, a new Wal-Mart, and a complete collection of fast food outlets straggled along for several miles. To my eye, it was a generic American setting, but to Juan and Mary Ann it was home: dense and full of drama. About the group in the Chevy, Juan pronounced, "Those guys are all potheads, that's why they're together."

Mary Ann concurred with this analysis, then howled dolefully, "My mother is going to be so pissed! I haven't been home since yesterday, and she's got Victoria!"

Victoria was Mary Ann's baby daughter. She had been born in Texas when Mary Ann was living there with an older sister. The baby's father had stayed in Texas. "He was no help," Mary Ann said simply, when I asked. "All he wanted to do was party out."

"Maybe you should go home," Juan said.

"I should, but they're in Toppenish at the flea market."

I pointed the car toward Toppenish, a town fourteen miles up the valley from Sunnyside. Mary Ann's mother sold wedding accessories at a flea market there. Mary Ann said, "You know, someday Victoria is gonna walk all over me, just like I did to my mom. That's how it works." We got on Interstate 82 and were soon sailing through broad muddy fields. "My problem is I'm too young to be a mother," Mary Ann said. "I still just want to kick it with my friends. I'm a teenager! I want to party out!"

We left the interstate at Granger—the poorest town, it was said, in Washington. Parts of the three-block main street looked like rural Latin America. Most of the people in Granger were Mexican. We passed a general store called the Mercado Michoacáno—many of the recent immigrants to the valley came from the southern state of Michoacán. We passed an old brick building that housed a radio station called KDNA. Radio Cadena ("Radio Link") was, for my money, one of the best things about the Yakima Valley. "The Voice of the Farm-worker," and one of the few Spanish-language public radio stations in the United States, it provided public service broadcasting *and* a propulsive, highly romantic sound track of Mexican music to drive to. Unfortunately, Juan and Mary Ann loathed KDNA, and rather than have them suffering grimly through mariachi, I ceded control of the radio while I was with them and thus heard a lot of gangsta rap and alternative rock.

On the old highway to Toppenish, Mary Ann suddenly yelled, "Juan! Look at the asparagus rows!" There were strips of water, each catching a pale strip of sky, lying between the crop rows, and the effect of staring perpendicularly into the fields at sixty miles per hour was apparently fantastic. Off in the west, I could see Mt. Adams, a twelve-thousand-foot glacier-covered peak in the Cascades, shining in the late-winter sun.

As we came into Toppenish, Mary Ann said, "I just hope Victoria doesn't look like a little wab." Wab—short for wetback—was, I had already discovered, the single most popular local youth insult. "Whenever my mom has Victoria for more than a couple of hours, she's totally wabbed out—ribbons everywhere, little sandals, frilly socks. Not the frilly socks!"

Victoria turned out to be dressed more or less as Mary Ann feared. And her mother was even angrier than anticipated. The flea market was inside a tent at a crossroads on the edge of town. We had barely entered the tent before Juan and I found ourselves backing between the booths of cheap housewares under a hail of Spanish insults, among which I caught *callejeros*—street dudes. We retreated to the parking lot, where, after a few minutes, Mary Ann appeared, empty-handed and on the verge of tears. We headed back to Sunnyside. Mary Ann fumed, her voice low and desolate. "She can't do this. She's not her daughter!"

"She'll cool down," Juan said.

"I wish I still had my Firebird," Mary Ann moaned. "I used to go out and sit in it when I felt bad, listen to the Cranberries, or Skinny Puppy. I really, *really* miss that car."

We dropped Mary Ann at her mother's house in Sunnyside. It was a few blocks from the Guerreros' and looked much like it: modest, ranch-style, a tiny yard. She gave Juan a distracted kiss and said, "Don't call me if y'all are doing anything fun."

As we drove off, Juan said, "Her mom was *pissed.* Could you understand what she was saying?" He laughed. "My mom gets mad, but she never talks like that."

We drove west on Lincoln Avenue. Juan turned to study a police car parked outside a convenience store. Then he sank back into his seat and sighed. "This must look like a normal town to you," he said. "But it's not. It's really totally weird."

Sunnyside was, in fact, fairly weird. A sign on the highway described it as the HOME OF THE ASTRONAUT BONNIE DUNBAR. Its best-known annual event was the Country Christmas Lighted Farm Implement Parade, and its city council had almost the same pale, middle-American cast that it had at the turn of the century. And yet most of the people in Sunnyside were, according to every recent census, Latinos. Before the 1986 immigration reform, this majority had apparently been even less visible than it was when I started visiting, but to the casual eye there was still little sign that the town was jammed with new immigrants from Mexico, that every spare trailer and garage was rented by farmworkers and other poor tenants. On hot summer weekends the city park filled with Mexicans, most of them single men in cowboy hats and tooled leather belts out looking for some shade and a cool breeze. But these gatherings, which mightily disturbed some Anglo old-timers, were the exception.

Much of the Yakima Valley had the same quality—of separate worlds interacting as little as possible. The newest immigrants retained, naturally, the closest ties to Mexico. A Spanish-language soccer league, with teams named after the players' home villages in Michoacán or Jalisco or Oaxaca, played year-round. When the leftist politician Cuauhtémoc Cárdenas, who nearly won the Presidency of Mexico in 1988 (and did become mayor of Mexico City in 1997), visited the United States in 1990, he came to the valley to see his constituents. Valley residents had asked the Mexican government to open a consulate in the city of Yakima so that they wouldn't have to keep crossing the mountains to Seattle for visas. When they couldn't afford (or didn't trust) doctors or pharmacies, many patronized *curanderos* (traditional healers) and bought prescription drugs (illegally) at the *botánica*, the same way they did (legally) in Mexico.

Though the great majority of Mexicans and Mexican Americans in the valley were poor and uneducated, a few had made the long trek from the fields into the middle class. Myrna Contreras-Trejo, for instance, a lawyer and a judge pro tem—the first Latina to hold that job in the Yakima Valley—spent her early years on the road with her family, who were migrant farmworkers until they settled out in the village of Mabton, a few miles south of Sunnyside, in the 1960s. Contreras-Trejo's high school counselor had advised her to become a secretary, and she was still in the fields picking grapes two days before she left for the University of Washington.

Many Anglos and American Indians openly resented the new arrivals. Mexican men frequently married Yakima Indian women, displeasing the tribe's elders. While white poverty in the valley was comparatively rare, many whites believed that the Mexicans either were taking jobs that were rightfully theirs or were bankrupting local government by going on public assistance, or both. I often heard whites, when they thought there was no one around but us Anglos, dis both Mexicans ("spics") and Indians ("prairie niggers"). Contreras-Trejo told me, "The prevailing attitude still is 'You should pick the apples, cut the asparagus, and get out of here—go back where you came from.'"

Some of the local racism was strangely unconscious. A Latina who worked at KDNA told me about a white Methodist minister who told her that he was a racial liberal but that he was having trouble persuading his more conservative parishioners to be tolerant. "They say they think Mexicans are just one level above animals," the minister told the KDNA woman, who was a college graduate. "So if you could just give me some proof that they're wrong, I'd be obliged." The KDNA woman took a deep breath after she told me this story. "*Proof*," she said. "That was the part that really got me, him using that word."

In the late 1980s, the Yakima Valley had gained a reputation as a regional drug-trafficking center. Many Anglos blamed their Mexican neighbors for this, too; and the trade routes for cocaine (from South America) and black-tar heroin (from Mexico) that passed through the valley did follow the migration routes of Mexican farmworkers. The 1986 immigration reform apparently stimulated this trade, as some of the traditional importers of illegal labor, known as coyotes, fearing that the market for their product was about to disappear, turned to a more compact, less perishable, more profitable product—cocaine—to pack into their old camper-pickups for the long run from Mexico to the Pacific Northwest. Family-based Mexican smuggling organizations controlled the bulk trade, according to the Drug Enforcement Administration, which opened a regional office in Yakima in the late eighties, and the valley served as a distribution center for a vast area that included Seattle, Spokane, western Canada, Idaho, and Montana. (The local market for cocaine was largely Anglo. Skilled technicians at the huge nuclear facility in Hanford, thirty miles east of Sunnyside, were said to be especially fond of blow.) Though most of the river of drug cash seemed to flow back to Mexico, a fraction stayed in the valley—mainly in the pockets of local lawyers, such as George Trejo, Contreras-Trejo's husband, a successful criminal defense attorney who specialized in drug cases.

The drug trade in the valley was, considering its volume, relatively peaceful—more so, anyway, than in most American cities. There was, however, a startling amount of urban-style violent crime unrelated to drugs: murder, robbery, drive-by shootings. Many Anglos, once again, blamed immigration from Mexico for the violence. As it happened, many Latinos did the same; that is, a shockingly high percentage of the region's violent crime was being committed by youths—in 1993, Yakima County might have been the only place in the country where more juveniles than adults were indicted for murder—and most of those youths were Latinos. And Latino adults, who tended to be at least as unhappy as their Anglo neighbors about youth crime, said that little or none of it would have happened back in Mexico.

The worst crime in recent memory had been the slaughter, in 1993, of an Anglo family of four in their rural home near Granger. Two boys, Miguel Gaitan and Joel Ramos, each fourteen years old, had been convicted of those murders. The boys told authorities that they had intended only to rob the house, and had been surprised to find the owners home. But those close to the case all had something to say, I found, about the boys' desire to impress the leaders of a Latino youth gang in Sunnyside known as the Bell Gardens Locos.

The Yakima Valley was home to dozens of youth gangs. Still a new phenomenon, the gangs were overwhelmingly Latino, and police blamed them for most of the valley's youth crime. Though gang crimes rarely happen in schools, public concern became so great that in 1991 the Sunnyside School District decided to hire a "gang awareness coordinator" from California named Donavon Vlieger. (This decision sounded much like Charles Bryan's hiring Larry Saurage to come to San Augustine County to fight the local war on drugs—and the more I learned about Vlieger's work, the greater the similarities seemed.) A former deputy sheriff from Los Angeles, Vlieger persuaded the school authorities that the only way to stop the growth of gangs was by dramatically confronting anyone who appeared to be involved. From all accounts, Vlieger took Sunnyside's junior high and high schools by storm. He stunned those students who were, in his opinion, "gang-involved" with extravagant verbal abuse. He advocated suspension and expulsion for suspected gang members, and such punishments quickly became the norm.

One of the boys Vlieger suspected—and ultimately succeeded in having banned from Sunnyside High—was Juan Guerrero.

I attended one of Don Vlieger's "gang awareness seminars" for teachers and school administrators. It was held at the East Valley Middle School, forty miles up the valley from Sunnyside and a few miles east of the city of Yakima.

Classes were dismissed early so that the entire faculty could attend. The atmosphere was strangely boisterous, as if the thirty-odd teachers were looking forward to being entertained. Vlieger did not disappoint. Trim, blond, in his mid-thirties, with a thick brown mustache in a vulpine face, he had a showman's élan: snappy but relaxed, folksy but vaguely glamorous, in the Southern California law enforcement style. This was clearly a presentation he had made many, many times. A brochure he distributed noted that he had been on radio and TV and had received "nationwide attention" in major metropolitan newspapers.

After some jokey opening remarks, Vlieger showed a video about gangs in Los Angeles. It seemed to have been made for use by local police. According to the video, there were five types of gangs in L.A. The "Latin" gangs were the biggest, and had three distinguishing features: they were "turf-oriented," "superstitious Catholics," and "big on machismo." Black gangs, by contrast, were primarily about money. Asian gangs existed, even though "the Asian people are law-abiding." Then there were white gangs, whose specialties were drugs and gay-bashing. Finally, there were "stoner" gangs, who smoked marijuana, took LSD, and practiced Satanism. The video ended with a lesson on how to read graffiti, "the newspaper of the streets." Vlieger continued the lesson with some of his own slides of graffiti, pointing out the upside-down cross (a common Satanist symbol), the goat's head (more Satanism), and the ubiquitous FTW (for "Fuck The World").

The gang problem in the Yakima Valley had its roots in Southern California, Vlieger said. The connection was clear throughout the Pacific Northwest, where the names of certain tough Los Angeles neighborhoods—Pomona, Hawaiian Gardens, Bell Gardens—were incongruously popular as gang names. The great dividing line among Latino gangs in California, between *Sureños* (southerners, traditionally from south of Bakersfield, with heraldic attachments to the number thirteen, the color blue, and the letter M) and *Norteños* (northerners, from north of Bakersfield, claiming the number fourteen, the letter N, and the color red), also divided the Yakima Valley gangs into opposed camps. Vlieger drew three concentric circles on a chalkboard to show the membership structure of a typical gang. In the center was the hardcore leadership, in the first ring the "associates," and in the outer ring the "affiliates/wannabes." "If some pooh-butt from California comes up here, he pops straight into the hardcore leadership."

Vlieger had some logical-sounding things to say about the appeal of gangs. "Gangs are how kids gain power over their environment, which is a basic need we all have," he told the teachers. "They're also fun, they're exciting. And, contrary to popular belief, gangsters don't have low self-esteem. They are into a *powerful* behavior. They feel *great* about themselves. How else can a twelve-year-old walk down the street and make adults scatter?"

His condemnation of gangs was, however, unequivocal. "Gangs are the worst thing a kid can get into, worse than drugs. Gangsters don't graduate, druggies sometimes do. A gang is a negative social group. It destroys members and communities, it produces sorrow and pain. It's antisocial behavior with a support group. Football teams are *not* a gang, even if their players do something antisocial. If you're a gang member, going to jail gives you prestige. It means you went down for the set, it's career enhancement. Jail means exactly the opposite of what it would mean for me and you. Gangs have a humiliating, medieval approach to women. Girls who want to get jumped into a gang are required to pull a train. I don't need to tell you what that means."

The East Valley Middle School staff seemed rapt. Mostly women, nearly all Anglo, they listened carefully, and tittered grimly at the occasional sarcasm.

"Here in the valley, you're never going to have a metropolitan gang issue," Vlieger told them. "You'll have a rural gang issue. It will be different. More crimes will be solved. But it's going to be just as violent, because your gangsters are going to be looking to their cousins in L.A. for leadership."

There was much they could do, Vlieger assured the teachers. He had had great success in a troubled school district in Los Angeles County, reducing gang activity there by 25 percent. "The first thing is to watch the attitude," he said. "It's a way of life, it's a way of thinking. It's also a way of dressing—so you need to know what gang clothing is. It's khakis, it's Dickies, it's web belts, it's bandannas, it's colors, it's people dressed all in black. We take photos of clothing, of notebooks covered with gang graffiti, and we show the photos to parents. We say, 'Take a little time because your child is at risk for losing their school experience.' Some parents get the message and take action before it's too late. But we can't save the troublemakers. We need to take care of the compliant kids first."

A chorus of agreement rose from the teachers, including a cry of "Hear! Hear!"

Vlieger went on, "We can deal with the noncompliant with whatever time and resources we have left. You can't put healthy people with sick people and expect the sick to get better. You have to isolate the problem. That's why we enforce the letter of the law for gang members. We get them for jaywalking, spitting, almost anything they do."

Vlieger showed examples of items that could be confiscated as evidence of gang affiliation. There was a school notebook with writing in "Gothic script" on the cover, and a T-shirt, promoting a magazine called *Teen Angels*, covered with a lush tropical drawing of soulful *cholos* (Chicano tough guys) and worshipful women. It seemed clear, watching the teachers paw disapprovingly through the goods, that what we had here was one culture (Anglo, adult) trying to forbid the imagery of another (Latino, young). A grandmotherly teacher sitting beside me made this explicit when she turned to me and whispered, "He dislikes the culture. It's as simple as that." For a moment I thought she was talking about Vlieger. Then I realized that she was picking up a whispered narrative, begun earlier, about her son. "Even though he's a grown man, six foot six, he's afraid to walk in the mall," she said. "Says he just doesn't like Mexicans, and he's going to move his family out of here." None of her other children felt similarly, the teacher said. "He just had a bad experience with some Mexican kids when he was small, and he never got over it." Something comparable was happening in local education, she said. "The city of Yakima is growing to the west, and the school administrators out there, in the middle and high schools, are very determined to keep the Mexicans out of their schools," she said.

East Valley Middle School was, incidentally, 85 percent Anglo. According to its principal, with whom I talked after the Vlieger show, the school had no gang problem. Some of its students were "stoners," she said, who smoked marijuana and took LSD and speed. And every now and then she saw a bit of graffiti.

I later caught up with Vlieger in his office at Harrison Middle School. He described his work in Sunnyside as a success. "We've quit the 'poor kids' syndrome," he told me. "We now tell them what we expect from them, and we remove those kids who give us trouble. It's an anxiety shift, from administrators to kids."

Chico Rodriguez, Jr., a Sunnyside High alumnus in his mid-twenties, who was Vlieger's assistant, vigorously endorsed everything his boss said.

"I used to carry around a big pill to my presentations," Vlieger went on. "And I used to tell people, 'It's big. It's going to hurt going down. But take it or you're going to die. It's as simple as that.' Next to a war, this is probably the most threatening thing to our society. It's anarchy. And what's next?"

A teacher, a middle-aged white woman, came in with a tiny tin-and-cardboard spinner—the sort of thing you might find in a box of Cracker Jack. Was it gang-related? Vlieger turned the toy over a couple of times and showed it to Rodriguez. Both shook their heads. Nah. The teacher left.

A bell rang, and the halls outside filled with children, most of them Latino. Barely one third of the students in Sunnyside's public schools were Anglo; in recent years, many of the town's white children had been transferred to private schools. The Sunnyside Christian School, for example, had increased its enrollment by 44 percent since 1985. It had few—very few—Latino students, and sent at least 80 percent of its students on to four-year colleges. Meanwhile, Sunnyside High School sent perhaps 20 percent of its students on to four-year colleges.

I asked Vlieger how he had landed up in Sunnyside.

"I used to drive a truck, turned Seattle every week. I didn't like it because of the rain, but whenever I came over here to pick up potatoes I loved it. Then I became a deputy and got into real estate pretty heavily, and did well. When I decided to move here, I transferred my real estate from Southern California, and that's worked out very profitably. Property values have gone up thirty to forty percent since we arrived." Vlieger did not live in Sunnyside—"I never police the town I live in"—but he did have extensive business interests there. Thus, the fact that youth gangs continued to thrive in the town, if not in the schools, concerned him financially as well as professionally. "If Sunnyside doesn't beat the gang issue, the economy will deteriorate. People don't want to live where they don't feel safe, and that hurts property values. Sunnyside is small enough that it *can* beat the gang issue. But the police have no dedicated anti-gang resources—not yet. We're working on that."

I asked Vlieger about Juan Guerrero.

He snorted. "Juan's crazy," he said. "The look in his eyes. He's violent. He's intelligent. A bad prognosis."

Some time later, I talked to Chico Rodriguez, Jr.—whose father, Chico Sr., was a Sunnyside police officer—without Don Vlieger present, and I found he was careful to distinguish his own approach to the students from Vlieger's. "I try to be more subtle," he said. "I don't disrespect them. I don't get in their faces and tell them they're trash and puke."

"He was crazy," Juan said when I asked him about Vlieger. "He called me into his office and said he saw me downtown. He said I was throwing gang signs at him, threatening his life. I didn't even remember seeing Vlieger downtown. But he didn't want to hear that. He just kept calling me all these names. It was almost like he wanted to fight."

Juan's brother Rafael Jr.,who is five years younger than Juan, had a terse analysis of his older brother's history of problems with authority. "He smirks." Ralph, as Juan called him—and as he preferred to be called—was a calm, shy, heavyset boy. His parents described him as *más leyista*—more legal-minded, or maybe they meant law-abiding—than Juan. (Rosa and Rafael were trying to explain to me Juan's failure to understand the importance of the farmworkers' union. Rafael Jr., they said, understood better.) Ralph went on, "Juan's problem is he giggles, and people don't like it."

Others said the same thing. Cuco, of the alternative high school, said, "Juan laughs at people. He don't give them no respect. That's why they all go crazy and want to fight him and expel him from school."

Juan did not look like a fighter. He wasn't stocky or heavily muscled or scarred. In baseball terms, he was a lithe, strong-armed left fielder, not a fireplug catcher. In high school, he ran cross-country, a sport that would seem to suit his build. And yet he also studied Tae Kwon Do from an early age, earning his black belt at fourteen, and he had a formidable local reputation, not just in Sunnyside but among teenagers throughout the valley, as a street fighter. "For some reason, he really knows how to throw his things," a friend of his named Saul Zaragoza told me.

I asked Mary Ann Ramirez about it and she said, "You know, it's unbelievable. Everywhere we go, Juan has beaten somebody up—at least one person in every group, at every party. I hate it! I mean, it doesn't impress me none that he can fight good. What it means is that we can't go anywhere without somebody calling him on. It sucks!"

Juan shrugged when I asked about it. "Yeah, I been in a lot of fights, and I usually win," he said. "But I say, let's forget about fighting, let's go out and do some other fun activities."

Saul Zaragoza said, "When big guys get beat up by little Juan, they can't handle it. Some people are just born fighters, but the guys Juan beats up can't accept that."

Mary Ann said, "Juan's not big, but he's strong, and he's really, really fast. Plus he knows all the karate high kicks. I saw him fight a guy named Roy at Safeway two weeks ago. Roy was beating up a friend of Juan's and it made Juan mad. So he ran right at them, and he jumped up so fast and so high and he hit Roy, who's really tall, right in the chest with both feet. It was awesome! The fight was over, just like that. The cops came, and Juan got a ticket. Nobody else got one. But that's how it is. Everybody's like, 'Yeah, yeah, Juan, beat him up!' But when he's going to jail nobody's like, 'Hey, take me with you!'"

Juan had been charged with more misdemeanors related to fighting than he could count. When he was seventeen, he pleaded guilty to second-degree assault, a felony, and was sent to a youth camp in western Washington for five months. He subsequently spent five months in a group home in Richland, thirty-five miles east of Sunnyside.

His incarceration was a great blow to his parents. Their shame, sadness, and frantic concern did not stop them from questioning the treatment Juan received, however. "Juan is no angel," Rosa told me. "But he didn't do all the things the police said he did."

Rafael said, "Even though I can't convince him about what he should do and shouldn't do, I understand Juan. Why? Because I was like him when I was his age. My friends and I were wild. I got in a lot of fights. The difference was that the police didn't watch us so closely. They weren't afraid of us, and they didn't arrest us for every little thing. There is a lot of discrimination here in Sunnyside. Even in Mexico, where the rich *hate* the poor, we didn't have discrimination like this."

Juan did not carry the marks of his time in detention any more visibly than he did the traces of his brawling. "Being locked up was weird," he told me. "It's like the whole world has stopped. There's a little world in there, but you just wish you were outside. You wonder what everybody's doing. There's a lot of fighting in there, especially on weekends. Most of it's racial. Like this black guy called me a spic in the forest. I said, 'Call me that again and I'll kick your ass.' And he did, so I kicked his ass. Another Mexican guy helped me. Later on, though, that black guy and I got to be friends. But some of the whites in there were KKK. There weren't enough of them to do what they wanted to do. They'd just say, 'White power,' just to rub your face in it." Juan looked at me wryly.

When he got home from Richland, in late 1993, he was barred from returning to Sunnyside High. Although he had been attending public high school without incident while he was living in the group home in Richland, the fact that he was now eighteen gave the Sunnyside High authorities broad powers to bar his enrollment. Teana Robbins, Juan's parole officer, argued for his reinstatement. Don Vlieger, she recalled, led the charge against it. Bob Thomas, who was then the school's vice principal (he later became the principal), was also against it. "He was considered dangerous," Thomas told me. "His presence on campus. You could feel it in the air."

Later, Thomas added, "He's a good-looking kid, and he seemed better educated than most that are involved. And his parents were pretty active in trying to get him back in. But the Guerreros were the type of parents who scream discrimination. It's a type of parent, and kids who are raised in that environment tend to have problems."

Within weeks of the decision to keep him out of school, Juan was in the grape fields, under his Walkman, working alongside his parents. His plan, once he got a general-equivalency diploma, was to start community college in Yakima. A bunch of his friends, including Mary Ann, had the same plan. They were going to get a house in Yakima, and part-time jobs, and be roommates. "After Alaska, when we'll have a bunch of money saved up," Mary Ann told me. "It'll be great! Right, dude?"

"Right," Juan said. "No doubt about it."

THREE

Juan, pace Don Vlieger, scorned gangs. When he was in junior high, he briefly thought they were cool and he joined a schoolboy gang called the Little Valley Locos. But the kitschy ritualism, the romanticism, the heavily Chicano atmosphere of *cholo* gang style were a poor fit for the ironic individualist whose favorite musician by the time he got to high school was Kurt Cobain. Juan left the LVLs, as they were known, after only a short association.

Curious about the Sunnyside gang world, I spent a little time with what passed for the LVL high command—a pack of attitudinous teenage brothers named Flores. Their father, Victor, a squat Chicano from Fireball, California, was a *veterano*—a gangbanger of an earlier generation. He drove a small, heavily modified truck—lowered to the ground, with the roof sawed away. He and his wife worked in the fields, spoke English together, and had a tidy little house in Sunnyside. Their boys slept in the basement, which had its own entrance and felt like a clubhouse.

The first time I stopped by the Flores basement, I spent an hour talking to Victor Jr., who was then eighteen. Stocky, like his father, he pointedly avoided meeting my eye. Instead, he sat at a tiny, well-lit desk in a corner of the basement, hunched intently over my business card with a pen, covering it with elaborate script. The walls above the desk were papered with gang-style art.

"New York?" Victor Jr. said, finally. He drew down his mouth. "I like to move to the city."

"Why's that?"

"Easier to do crimes there." He drew his mouth down farther. He did not look up. Victor Jr. had a peculiar, extremely powerful-looking jaw—it looked as if it belonged on somebody twice his age and twice his size—and an expressive mouth, which he drew down to droll effect. Furiously "tagging" my card, he looked, at the same time, about eight years old. "They got a lot of killers there," he went on. "And stripping bars. You ever been to a stripping bar?"

He gave me a mischievous glance, then returned to his work. Victor Jr.'s nickname, I recalled, was Camel, conferred for his strong resemblance to the cigarette-ad character Joe Camel. People called him Victor Camel—to distinguish him from the various other Victor Floreses in his family. One of the other Victor Floreses, Camel's cousin, was known as Mister Whisper because he was deaf. Yet another one, an uncle, was El Spooky—I wasn't sure why.

Camel's younger brother Lee, who looked about fifteen, emerged from the shadows of the basement, yawning. He stared at me as he stumbled past. It was nearly midday, so I asked him why he wasn't in school. He muttered something unapologetic and went upstairs.

Camel snickered. "He ain't been to school for two years."

"What's he doing?"

"Chillin'. Kickin' back. Doin' tattoos."

Camel indicated a butterfly on his forearm. He had, for a teenager, an amazing number of tattoos. He was shirtless that day, and I could see at least half a dozen, including a rose on the back of a hand, LVL here and there, a huge SUR, for *Sureño*, across his hairy belly, and a blue teardrop falling from his left eye.

There was doo-wop playing on a tape deck, so we talked a bit about music. I asked what kind he liked.

"Oldies," he said, gesturing toward the tape deck. "East L.A. stuff. Motown. Rap. *Corridos*—especially Chalino Sánchez." (*Corridos* are popular Mexican ballads, typically celebrating the exploits of cowboy drug runners in western and northern Mexico. Chalino Sánchez, who called himself El Bandido Generoso, wrote and sang great *corridos* until he was killed in Mexico, in 1992.)

I asked Camel about a feud that the LVLs had been having with the Bell Gardens Locos.

He sneered. "Them BGLs been prank-calling my house," he said. "They're just a bunch of punks."

The feud was getting violent, I had heard. Knifings, drive-bys.

Camel shrugged. "It don't make no sense because we're all *Sureños*," he said. He looked at me with a theatrical impassivity. "*Sureños hasta la muerte*," he said.

I asked about various people I had met around Sunnyside. Don Vlieger?

"Punk." Camel spat the word.

The principal of the high school?

"Punk."

The chief of police?

"Punk."

Juan Guerrero?

Camel paused, the plosive already on his lips. I was thinking about Juan's towering rep as a street fighter, and figured Camel was thinking the same thing. Finally, he said, "*Prep.*"

That was it, I thought, exactly. Juan might not look preppy to the Sunnyside school system, or the police, or Don Vlieger, but from Camel's end of the telescope he was strictly from J. Press. Juan scorned the subcultural refuge of gang life; he was bored by its florid, dead-end ethnicity. He cared little for La Raza, and was not prepared to turn his back on the wider world. "He ain't down," Camel said gruffly. Indeed, no one who knew Juan well seemed able to picture him "claiming a *klika*," being "down for the set." When Rosa and Rafael worried aloud about him, they never mentioned, as the parents of so many other young Latinos did, the lethal allure of the gangs. Mary Ann laughed at the idea. "Juan's his own gang," she told me. "He and his friends are just into something totally different."

The reasons had to do partly with class. Most of Juan's close buddies—Saul Zaragoza, Richard Negrete, Junior Salazar, Aaron De La Cruz, Joaquín Rodriguez—came, as he did, from solid homes, had parents with jobs, spoke English well. None of them had uncles doing hard time in state prison. (Camel had two.) They could all walk the mainstream American walk to an extent that few Latino gangbangers could. "Juan and his buddies know how to behave appropriately," Teana Robbins, the parole officer, told me. "They handle stressful situations pretty well. Besides that, they're awesome athletes. They fight, just like the gangs, except they always win because they're in shape. These other guys are heavy drinkers, heavy dopers, fools—kids who will almost surely be career criminals."

But even as Juan steered clear of formal affiliations, either with a gang or with organized (as in school) sports, his misadventures forced a collective identity on him. In jail, for example, he became a nationalist. "That's when you need some other Mexicans," he said. "So in there I'm like, 'Yeah, I'm *Mexican*,' but out here it's like, 'Who cares?' In there, some guy paints a Mexican flag and I'm like, 'All *right*.' But out here I don't have any real strong feelings about it."

The street-fighting life also creates strong group identifications. Thus, Juan knew his friends primarily as those who would back him up in a beef. He and Cuco, for instance, had been fighting side by side since they were little kids. "Juan is the only person I know that will never leave me stranded," Cuco told me. "We been in so much stuff together, and he's *always* got my back." Cuco's scorn for snowboarders—and his preference for a sort of rockabilly haircut—did not seem to affect this bond.

Juan, when asked how he defined himself, shrugged and said that he was indeed a snowboarder. Snowboarding, like its close cousin downhill skiing, is not cheap to pursue, so Juan and his friends actually spent a limited amount of time at the various ski areas north and west of Sunnyside. But snowboarding, which is like skateboarding on snow and infinitely cooler, by teenage lights, than traditional skiing, is not simply a sport. It is an attitude, an argot, a look. The look is grunge, basically, with some gymnastic, speed-demon undertones. And while skateboarders and snowboarders bear a vague resemblance to traditional Chicano *cholos*—with their baggy plaid shirts and baggy khaki pants, their sawed-off figures and baseball caps worn backward—the two sensibilities are cultural worlds apart. Snowboarders are descended from surfers and skiiers, from Austrian outdoorsmen and Okie hedonists, while *cholos* come from Pancho Villa, from Latin notions of honor and manhood, from *el barrio* and *la familia* and jail.

As Juan and I sit discussing these matters in his parents' living room, his youngest brother, Eddie, who is six, periodically interrupts by smashing Juan in the face. Eddie is wearing a pair of huge boxing gloves, garishly painted with the Stars and Stripes, and his blows, which are delivered with all his might, look painful. Juan ignores them, pushes Eddie away, keeps talking. Indeed, he seems to notice the pummeling only after Eddie knocks off his hat. It's a green corduroy baseball cap bearing the name of a surfwear company, Quiksilver. Juan carefully resettles it on his head, bill to the back. Ralph appears and takes Eddie outside, where he puts on a pair of gloves and proceeds to whale the tar out of Eddie, who laughs uncontrollably.

Rafael stops in. It's a Saturday evening, and he is dressed to the nines—long black leather rain slicker, white cowboy hat, fancy boots. He and Rosa are going to a dance tonight. After he departs, Juan says, "My mom and dad used to win dance contests at the Branding Iron, in Toppenish."

I ask Juan if he owns any Western clothes.

"Not even," he says, and laughs. "You mean like my dad? No way! It's not even me. I'm not saying it's never going to be me, but at the present time it's not. I can't even dance Spanish."

Mary Ann can't dance Spanish, either. "It's too *hard,*" she says. "Too many different steps and styles. My mom tried to teach me, but I couldn't do it." Mary Ann's mother, who comes from Monterrey, in northeast Mexico, has also tried, without success, to teach Mary Ann how to cook proper Mexican food. Mary Ann is not, however, a total washout on the Mexican-heritage front. "I speak Spanish really good," she says. "Better than my sisters. People say, 'You sound like a wetback!' " She also had a hell of a *quinceañera*—the traditional fifteenth-birthday bash for Mexican girls. "We rented a white limousine and kept it for thirteen hours," she says dreamily. "A whole bunch of us went riding around Sunnyside in it. My dress cost twelve hundred dollars. The whole *quinceañera* cost fifteen thousand."

Mary Ann shows me a photograph album of her *quinceañera*. "I felt like a queen," she says. But that party was a last gasp of affluence for her and her family. Reynaldo Hinojosa, the stepfather who footed the bills in those days, got busted for drug trafficking. Mary Ann's mother now visits him in a federal prison camp in Oregon.

Mary Ann lays down the album to attend to Victoria, who is fussing. We are in the tiny front room of Mary Ann's mother's house. Victoria is a bright-eyed baby, with coloring and hair from her father, who is half Korean, half black. Mary Ann, who is uncharacteristically subdued, settles Victoria facedown across her lap. It was a previous stepfather, she says, who took the family to Germany—which she remembers as fantastically clean and calm, with amazing parks. Her best friend spoke no English, so Mary Ann learned German. After her mother divorced that husband, she took her daughters back to Seattle. There she worked as a nursing assistant and they lived in not-so-genteel poverty. Then, when Mary Ann was in the sixth grade, her mother met Hinojosa, who had a landscaping business in Seattle and a ranch near Brownsville, Texas. Hinojosa began to make big money in the drug trade, and he bought Mary Ann's mother a house in West Seattle. "His kids from his first marriage didn't like us calling him 'Dad,' " Mary Ann recalls. "But he was like a real dad to us. And it was so *nice* having all that money. We lived in a rich neighborhood, all doctors and lawyers. I went to a real nice school. My mom knew what my dad was doing. But she just told us, 'Look, I'm happy, and we're not living in the projects anymore.' "

After Hinojosa's arrest, Mary Ann and her mother moved back to Sunnyside. They still had the means to rent a good-size house in a predominantly Anglo part of town. "I hung around with preps then," Mary Ann says. "White kids. We partied hard. I was only in the eighth grade, but I was already into drugs—coke, weed, alcohol." After a falling-out with her mother, Mary Ann went to Texas, where she lived with her oldest sister, who was then a social worker. By the time she came back to Sunnyside, she had Victoria, and her mother had moved to a poorer, more Mexican part of town and was selling at the flea market in Toppenish. "My old friends, the preppies, are all walking now," Mary Ann says. She means that they're graduating from high school. Mary Ann, who is studying for her GED, sighs. "I wish I was walking, mostly because of my mom."

Victoria is now asleep. On my way out, Mary Ann's mother, who seems to have decided that I am not a street dude, after all, stops me for a chat. She is an intense, attractive woman of about fifty. Our idle conversation about the craziness of kids these days turns suddenly emotional. Her eyes fill with tears and her voice with anguish. "How can we teach them to work? How can we teach them to stay off welfare?"

Mary Ann's mother's concern was well founded. Her two older daughters had both escaped the fields (where she worked as a girl) and were decently employed in Seattle—one as a paralegal, the other as a store manager—but the dark spiral of downward mobility, of children growing up to find themselves worse off than their parents, haunts Mexican immigrants as badly as it haunts any group in America. In fact, the Latino school dropout rate, which is roughly 30 percent, is higher—far higher—than that of any other major ethnic group. Latinos will soon be this country's largest ethnic minority, outnumbering African Americans. They are already more than 10 percent of the population, and, if present trends continue, fifty years from now, according to the journalist Earl Shorris's study *Latinos*, there will be a "Latino underclass of enormous size"—perhaps twenty-five or thirty million souls.

Why Latinos are, on the whole, faring so poorly is a question with many answers. The category itself is too broad; Cuban exiles in south Florida, who are prospering, have little in common with illiterate Guatemalans in rural California. This diversity works against the accumulation of national political power, as does the fact that Mexican Americans, who are the largest national bloc among Latinos, have a relatively poor record of voter registration and turnout. Latinos thus do much worse than, say, African Americans at securing their share of civil service jobs. Like African Americans, they suffer extensively from the practice of redlining by banks, which stunts economic development in barrios across the country. While millions of Latinos have entered the American middle class since the Second World War, their collective experience has in many ways remained fundamentally different from that of earlier immigrants from Europe. Most have retained close connections to their homelands—often, in the case of Mexicans, settling only a short distance from the border. Most have faced much more intense discrimination than the most despised white immigrants endured—discrimination that until the civil rights revolution included de facto racial segregation. Above all, the great recent wave of poor Latino immigrants has poured into a postindustrial economy that has a limited demand for unskilled labor.

The age-old American immigrant's dream is, in short, not working out for millions of Latinos. Even in little Sunnyside, far from the vast, bleak barrios of East Los Angeles, the pattern was stark. "The kids whose families have just come from Mexico are the best off," Deirdre Gamboa, a first-grade teacher in Sunnyside, told me. "Their families are stable. They're studious and well behaved. It's after they've been here awhile that the families start to fall apart. Not all of them, of course, but it really is consistent. The kids who have the most trouble have been here awhile. In so many cases, whether from drugs or alcohol or whatever, child care just seems to break down."

Even the children of migrant workers, whose schooling was constantly interrupted and haplessly restarted, seemed to thrive in comparison with the children of the not so recently arrived. There was another pattern, too: an earlier arc of upward mobility that had carried bright Latinos of the baby-boom generation into the professions. Myrna Contreras-Trejo, the lawyer and judge, and Deirdre Gamboa's husband, Guadalupe, a labor lawyer, were two shining members of this cohort in the Yakima Valley. But it was a very small group, really. Of sixteen first-grade teachers at Deirdre Gamboa's school, she was the only one who spoke Spanish—and she was an Anglo from Canada. The school, meanwhile, was 70 percent Latino. Gamboa offered a succinct explanation for the consistent failure of the immigrant dream among her students. "I think the racism here begins to take a toll," she said. "People realize they're second-class citizens, and things start to fall apart."

Or, I thought, if they're teenagers they start to fall into gangs. Here Don Vlieger's gang typology seemed apt: Latino gangs do tend to be less about making money than they are about identity. Thus, while in many American communities impoverished teenagers, as we have seen, go into the drug trade—where gangs are, as in New Haven, often an integral part of the drug business—in the Yakima Valley the two scenes were separate and distinct. There were teenagers who sold drugs on a small scale, of course, mostly to their peers, but the serious drug trade—"the business," as Juan and his friends called it—was effectively closed to nervy kids of the sort who staffed it elsewhere. "It's all wabs," according to Mary Ann. She meant Mexicans, like her stepfather Hinojosa. She meant the badly dressed, mostly undocumented migrants who inhabited the shadows and margins of life everywhere in the valley, generally beneath the notice of Americanized kids like her. Mary Ann was actually sympathetic to the migrants' plight. "A lot of them come up here expecting to get a job, and all they can get is in the fields," she said. "It's *sad*." At the same time, she respected and feared their economic desperation. When it came to the drug trade, she said, "If you tried to pick up some of their business, even if you were in the biggest gang around here, they'd just kill you."

The county's criminal courts handled a steady traffic of low-level smugglers and dealers, many of them from Oaxaca and Michoacán. Typically, the defendants were tiny, dark-skinned young men, often illiterate, who spoke no English. Most, hoping to pass through the relatively lenient juvenile justice system, claimed to be under eighteen—even some graying desperados who were clearly closer to forty. While these men were by no means representative of Mexican immigrants in the valley, they were the real-life denizens of the *corridos*—the hustling campesinos hoping to hit the jackpot and build themselves a narco palace back in the hills of Oaxaca. And in the minds of alarmed Anglos, they got lumped together with Juan and Mary Ann and Juan's parents and Guadalupe Gamboa and every other Latino in sight under the heading of the valley's "Mexican problem."

But Juan and his friends confronted a quintessentially American problem, which was how to become Americans. The assimilation they faced was a sloppy, complicated business in which parents were not much help. While Juan's family had avoided, thanks in large measure to his parents' commitment to the farmworkers' struggle, the pattern of postimmigration implosion described by Deirdre Gamboa, Juan's awe of authority had not been enhanced in the process. Mary Ann might have survived her mother's serial marriages and her beloved stepfather's brief prosperity and long imprisonment with her dreams of becoming a psychiatrist (or a prison guard) intact, but her life had already involved far more exposure to failure and havoc than to discipline and success. Assimilation is inevitable; the question was which of the many layers of America each of these kids would assimilate *to*. The possibilities had to be both confusing and terrifying. And in the meantime Juan and his friends enjoyed a highly American aimlessness. They cruised, ate junk food, worked dead-end jobs, watched rock videos, called each other on their beepers, raised a little hell.

On the whole, they seemed unimpressed with me. Indeed, they seemed to see me as something of a loser. I had, for example, no beeper. *Why not?* The most hapless kid in Sunnyside could afford to rent a beeper, to keep in touch with his buddies. What if my office wanted to talk to me? My cars were also alarmingly bland. And a mortifying fault: I had no opinions, no *standards*, when it came to food. A group of us would pull up to the drive-through window at McDonald's, say, and I would simply take whatever I was handed and eat it, not even bothering to check if they had put the right amount of sauce on my Big Mac. Meanwhile, the discriminating adolescents riding with me would be unpacking their custom-ordered burgers and fries, checking for cheese consistency and pickle arrangements, sternly sending back anything that wasn't up to scratch. The customer was, after all, always right. That's what *their* bosses were forever telling *them*.

In their own cars, I learned, seating arrangements were crucial. The car owner (or owner's offspring) drove, of course, and the other front window ("shotgun") was the most desirable passenger spot. The least desirable was the "bitch seat"—the middle position in the back. It was very difficult for a boy to look cool riding there, squeezed between two other boys, with no window of his own. Girls didn't usually mind the bitch seat. Some of them even seemed to like it. Mary Ann was an exception. But then she acted more like a boy than like a girl. She took whatever seat she could grab, and she defended it. She drank as hard as the boys, and she did the same drugs, too.

When I first met Mary Ann and Juan, they had been doing "wall hits"—sucking gasoline fumes out of a plastic bag until they fainted. "It was my idea to try it," Mary Ann said. "I thought it would be fun. But it's scary. I blacked out once and saw the world coming to an end. People said I kept going, 'The world's coming to an end, the world's coming to an end.' I'm never gonna do gas again."

"Me, neither," Juan said. "Too weird."

On a Saturday morning in early spring, Juan and Mary Ann and Ralph and I took off for the mountains in my rental car. "Boarding!" Mary Ann crowed. She started slam-dancing against Juan in the backseat. "I've wanted to try it forever!"

Mary Ann had resigned herself to not coming snowboarding with us after her mother had said that she couldn't watch Victoria. But then Rosa had volunteered to help, and we had left the two women chatting amiably. "So now our moms can be friends, dude," Mary Ann said, chortling.

"That would be weird," Juan mused.

The fruit trees had a blush of red in their branches. Otherwise, the valley was a muted canvas: gray on gray, brown on brown. Orchard heaters, deployed to fight a cold snap, stood among the trees like short, rusty, abstract sentries.

Juan and Mary Ann passed the miles discussing their friends. "Nick's started talking all black," I overheard Juan say. "He's, like, 'Yo, homeboy, wussup?' So people are, like, 'Yo, nigger, nothin'.'"

"Just so he doesn't get all into gold chains and shit," Mary Ann said. "The blacks in Texas, especially the drug dealers, are really into flashing their money. Gold teeth, gold rings. I'm glad people aren't into that here. It starts too many fights."

Later, as we rode past the city of Yakima, I heard them talking about a group they called the Trogs. I asked who they were. Juan laughed. "The little monsters," he said. "That's what everybody calls the Flores kids. You said you talked to Camel."

We headed west into the Cascades. At a truck stop in the foothills, Juan and I watched a big dirty cat sunning itself in a gas station window. "He just like lives here," Juan said wonderingly. "Just laying there in the sun watching people like us go by. Probably thinks we're strange."

Back on the road, conversation turned to the MTV program *The Real World,* which Juan and Mary Ann and Ralph never missed. A self-described "reality-based soap opera," it followed a troupe of young roommates whose everyday lives were taped and turned into weekly shows. Juan and Mary Ann discussed the characters as if they lived with them. One guy had been kicked out of the house for hitting on his female roommates—Juan and Mary Ann weighed the evidence against him. Ralph jumped in occasionally with factual corrections, and Juan and Mary Ann deferred to him. "Ralph always puts in the *right* last word," Juan told me.

"I don't think you and me and Aaron and everybody will have any of these problems in Alaska, or when we get our place in Yakima, do you?" Mary Ann asked.

"I wouldn't say so," Juan said.

"Yes, you will," Ralph whispered, looking slyly at me.

It occurred to me that house-sharing, having roommates, while not unknown in Mexico, was another assimilation rite. It was the way American kids left the family nest. That was, of course, just one reason the subject interested Juan and his friends. In class terms, their Alaska summer work plan had a migrant labor aspect, while their Yakima community-college dream was solidly middle-class-aspirant. Snowboarding was also, in its own grunge way, a piece of class aspiration—that was why it was mildly controversial when Juan and his friends claimed it. I wondered what Juan's peers who were leaning the other way and "talking all black" thought of his taste for the alpine-resort scene—whether they ever called him a coconut, meaning brown on the outside, white on the inside.

It was wall-to-wall Anglos when we arrived at the White Pass Ski Area. We rented snowboards—my treat—and fooled around for a while on a beginner slope, with Juan showing the rest of us the basics. Then we straggled onto a chairlift and were borne up into the mists. Coming down the mountain, Ralph and Mary Ann and I seemed to crash every few feet. Ralph, particularly, struggled. Juan concentrated on instructing his brother while Mary Ann and I pooled our ignorance and counseled each other down the hill. She had excellent balance and, though she tended to scream when she picked up speed, took the frequent hard falls without complaint. I was fascinated by what I could see and hear of Juan's pedagogical method. He simply stood at a certain distance from Ralph and yelled at him, addressing him as "fucker." His yelling was not angry or impatient, and his pronunciation of "fucker" was odd—it put greater emphasis on the second syllable, and drew out the "r." I was worried that some passing skier or area official might take offense, hearing Juan yell, "Get up, fucker," over and over, to the prostrate, gasping Ralph. But the hill was uncrowded, the fog was thick, and nobody seemed to notice. And Ralph seemed unfazed.

After lunch, Ralph, who was exhausted, took a long break. Mary Ann, who fell even more often than I did, urged Juan and me to go on without her, which we ungallantly did, taking run after run in deep snow east of the chairlift.

But we learned just how ungallant we had been only at the end of the day when we reconvened and found Mary Ann propped on a bench at the rental-return counter with her leg in a splint. It seemed she had gone snowboarding alone, had wrenched her knee, and had lain in the snow for an hour before she was found and carried on a sled to a clinic. The doctor had told her to get an X ray when she got home; she had a possible hairline fracture. "But it don't hurt," she claimed cheerfully, "now I got this thing on it." We carried her to the car, and tried to make her comfortable in the backseat.

There was no slam-dancing in the backseat on the long ride home. There was, however, much cuddling, rustling, cooing, and giggling. The splinted leg did not seem to be an issue. Ralph, riding shotgun, slept nearly the whole way to Sunnyside. At one point, Mary Ann announced, "You got chick lips, you know that? Juan's got lips like a chick!"

"You got 'em, too," Juan said softly.

"First we think the same," Mary Ann murmured. "Now we got the same mouths."

The police kindly showed me their version of Sunnyside. A big blond detective tossed me a huge sheaf of computer printout, listing all the local arrests for the last few years. "Just check out those names," he said. Alvarado, Alvarez, Asuncio—virtually all the names were Hispanic. The detective took me into the evidence room, where he tossed me a kilo brick of cocaine. On the shelves were shotguns, assault rifles, big Dirty Harry six-shooters, 9-millimeter pistols, a lethal-looking crossbow. The detective opened a file drawer and pulled out a filthy bundle of cash. "Twenty-four thousand bucks," he said. "Found it in a trailer. The wetbacks we took it from never even asked for it back." He handed me a set of cockfighting spurs, and said I could keep them. Then he pointed at my hands, which were white with cocaine dust. "Better not take a drug test real soon," he said.

We went for a drive. The detective was good company—cynical and funny. He had been a Sunnyside policeman for sixteen years, and claimed to love the work. "Never a dull moment. It's cop heaven." He introduced me to one of his confidential informants, a Chicano chicken-farm foreman who had, in a previous life, smuggled farmworkers and then cocaine. I listened to them plot the capture of a local thug, a drug dealer who had taken to pistol-whipping his enemies. Later, we cruised around Sunnyside. The town looked peaceful, but on a rowdy night, the detective said, there were probably two hundred shots fired inside the city limits. "Luckily, we don't have a lot of good marksmen." He pointed at a bar on the highway called the Dark Horse Inn and said, "You go in there, a white guy, there won't be a sound except the clicking of automatics."

A nearby Mexican restaurant, he said, was "the biggest drug front in town." Its chief rival for that distinction, he said, was a Mexican clothes and music shop downtown.

As it happened, I was a customer of each of these shady establishments. I bought cassettes of the Mexican music I heard on KDNA at the downtown shop. I also stopped in there sometimes to ogle the fringed turquoise cowboy shirts and bright purple jeans—the wabbed-out gear that so horrified the likes of Mary Ann and Juan. The shop was usually packed with wholesome-looking farmworker families; its staff was natty and helpful. The Dark Horse Inn, it was true, was less wholesome—though its patrons could not very well have been armed, since everyone was frisked for weapons at the door. I went to the Dark Horse to hear the ranchera bands, and to watch the stylish dancers circling clockwise around the floor. Some of the older couples seemed to have been dancing together for decades.

As for the Mexican restaurant down the road—La Fogata, "The Lighthouse"—it was about my favorite place in the Yakima Valley. The food was cheap and good, the atmosphere calm and civilized. I was first taken there by the director of KDNA, and later by a Latina social worker, both of whom described the hardworking family that owned and ran the place as model immigrants. In the back, separate from the restaurant, was a bar. It was clean and comfortable, with a couple of pool tables. The bar's clientele seemed to be exclusively male, Mexican, working-class—farmworkers, cowboys, carpenters, plumbers. Some of the men brought in guitars, including tiny, fat-bodied instruments with a high, sweet, sad, mandolin-like sound. When the jukebox was silent, they played and sang old Mexican ballads.

An Anglo sales clerk in Sunnyside, overhearing me say I liked La Fogata, once sternly advised me that it was an infamous drug den. I asked if he had ever been inside the place. He hadn't. Don Vlieger also warned me against La Fogata. "They hate white people in there," he said. "They won't even wait on you."

Juan's objections to La Fogata, on the other hand, were strictly culinary. I never succeeded in getting him to eat at any of the Mexican food wagons, known as *taquerías,* parked along the Yakima Valley Highway, although some of them were excellent. But one day I dragged him to La Fogata. He, too, had never been inside the place. He ordered his meal elaborately, in Spanish, trying to ensure that he didn't get any salsa picante, or too much cheese, or any of the other things he disliked about Mexican cuisine. Still, when our food came, he looked ill. He picked at his rice and beans, looked inside a taco, blanched, and pushed away the plate. The fearless champion of the streets seemed undone by the sight of a jalapeño pepper. And he looked less than inspired by the smiling *michoacános* who bustled between the tables. He waited politely, miserably, while I ate, and afterward asked meekly if we could stop at Pizza Hut. We picked up Mary Ann on the way.

FIVE

Wanting to see how things with Juan and his family and his friends would play out over time, I withdrew for a few months. I kept the cockfighting spurs on my desk in New York, and phoned Sunnyside every now and then, but essentially I was out of touch until the fall. Then I made my way back to the valley.

Rosa and Rafael, I found, had been giving *la compañía* hell. Rafael had gone to a UST Inc. shareholders' meeting in Greenwich, Connecticut, where, surrounded by hundreds of nonplussed men in suits, he had stood up, wearing his best cowboy hat, and, though shaking with nerves, had given a fiery speech about how one of their companies was exploiting farmworkers in Washington State. He spoke in Spanish, with a union official providing simultaneous translation. The speech was coolly received in Greenwich, but a big hit back in Sunnyside.

Rosa, meanwhile, had just returned from a demonstration near Seattle. It seemed that *la compañía*—a relatively modern, liberal employer as agribusiness firms go, and very conscious of its public image—had sponsored a series of outdoor concerts, and that the union had succeeded in persuading some of the entertainers, such as Willie Nelson and Jackson Browne, to cancel their engagements. Other performers had refused to cancel, and the union had set up picket lines outside the shows. Traffic had been tied up, and press attention had been generous. Rosa showed me photographs of Ralph marching in the demonstration, and of herself standing next to a huge cutout picture of Tony Bennett.

Juan, too, had finally got some politics. It seemed that the company had transferred him to another farm, some fifty miles from Sunnyside, where a group of antiunion workers imported from California was strong. The intrusive, pro-company diatribes of his new coworkers got on Juan's nerves. They offended his rebel's sensibilities, not to mention his sense of family loyalty. He took to wearing a UFW button on the job, and to countering the antiunion speeches he heard each day on the bus from Sunnyside with a raised fist and a firm cry of *"La unión!"* Rafael and Rosa were, of course, delighted. But then Juan was laid off.

"They knew I would talk to the people," Juan said. "So I'm jobless."

His unexplained absences from work, which had apparently become frequent, might also have had something to do with it, I heard.

I asked about the expedition to Alaska to make mass cash in a fish cannery. Juan looked uncomfortable and mumbled something. Apparently, no one had gone. Neither, I gathered, was the Yakima house-sharing idea coming together as planned. When I asked about Mary Ann, Juan looked extremely uncomfortable. It seemed they had broken up.

I asked Juan why.

"The guys decided," he said tightly. We were in his parents' living room. He kept his eyes on the TV.

I waited.

"It was just too weird," he finally said. "Having a chick hang out with us, getting drunk, doing everything."

Not sitting in the bitch seat, I thought.

"I kept saying, 'Hey, let's go pick up Mary Ann.' But we never did. It wasn't my car, so I couldn't really do anything about it. They just stopped picking her up."

Juan clearly didn't want to talk about it.

What he did want to talk about was a recent series of fights. First, it seemed, he and Cuco Zesati had brawled on a country road with two brothers from a gang called the Ghetto Boys. Then, just a few nights before my return, one of the brothers, David Muñoz, had attacked Juan and three friends with a baseball bat as they drove past a local hospital. No one had been hurt, but Muñoz had succeeded in smashing all four side windows of Richard Negrete's car before they could get away. "That guy is really, really crazy," Juan said. Finally, while Juan and his friends were at the police station reporting the baseball bat attack, a major fight broke out around the corner from the Guerreros' house. Three people ended up in the hospital, including Cuco, who had been stabbed in the back with a *sword.*

"This town is getting so messed up," Juan said. "I'm not going out at all now."

I found Mary Ann at her mother's house, sitting on the floor in the front room, sorting through baby clothes. She looked tired. Her hair was different, though I couldn't decide exactly how. She and Victoria were moving to Seattle, she said. They were going to live with her sister. She already had a job lined up. I asked what had happened with Juan.

She sighed. "He just didn't feel the same, I guess," she said.

She folded a whole stack of clothes before she went on. "His mother was really upset. She wanted us to get married. But, you know, Juan always had this other little girlfriend on the side," she said wearily. "Rachel. She's young. She's not his equal. She'll just see him when he wants to see her. His friends all have girls like her, beeping them all the time, waiting for them to call. I'm not like that. I guess I was too much for Juan. Too much like him."

I asked if it had come down to a choice, for Juan, between her and his friends.

Mary Ann stared at me, long and hard, her eyes full. She nodded. After a while, she said, "So I wasn't going to just hang around. I just got into something completely different."

I reached out and took her left wrist and turned it over. On the inside of her forearm, pricked into the pale flesh below the elbow, was a big, new-looking tattoo. SURENA'S 3CE, it said, in spidery black Gothic script.

"I told you," Mary Ann said. "I got into something totally different."

What Mary Ann had gotten into was the Little Valley Locos—Camel's gang. "People don't understand about gangs," she told me. "Gangs are like a family. My mom and I couldn't get along, you know. She would always just push me out the door. So where could I go? I've always hung around guys. And I was, like, looking for myself. So Camel got me into the LVLs. I got corded in by nine guys."

Corded in?

"They corded me in," she said impatiently. "They beat me up. I got a black eye, but I fought hard. I never cried. Some *guys* cry. I got mad because they ripped my T-shirt. It wasn't the shirt—I got mad because my back was bare. But somebody gave me another shirt. And after that they knew I could handle mine."

I asked if she had been romantically involved with Camel.

Mary Ann looked incredulous. "*No*," she said. "You don't understand. I was never disrespected in the LVLs. They never touched me. They never tried to rape me. They might make a joke—'You have a nice butt,' or something—but they'd immediately get really embarrassed after they did it. Being the only girl, I got a lot of attention. A *lot*. And that made me want to stay. Some of those guys, they worshipped the ground I walked on. My tag name was La Genius. They called me that because they said I knew everything. It's up on the wall in the alley behind the Flores house: La Genius."

I went by the Flores house and found Camel and his brother Lee hanging out in the basement with a scrawny, talkative LVL *vato* named Frankie Mendoza, also known as Spider. I asked them about Mary Ann.

"Mary Ann used to be like high society," Frankie said. "She lived over by the Hill"—an expensive part of town—"and she hung out with the preppies. That was till her dad got locked up. Then she fell. First, she hung out with Juan Guerrero and those guys. Then us."

"She was crazy," Camel said. He laughed lightly. "She used to act like a guy. Saying stuff to other guys, *fighting* with guys. Jumping in whenever we were fighting."

"She was a freak," Frankie said. "An addict. Weed, coke. We called her La Genius at first, but later we called her La Marijuana."

"I did her tattoo," Lee said. "You seen it?"

I said I had.

"Nice, eh? *Sureña por vida.*"

They all laughed.

I asked if they had seen Mary Ann lately. There was an awkward silence.

"Naw," Camel said, finally. "She went to jail and they scared her in there. So she ain't really down right now."

The LVL basement crew suddenly felt like a backup band without their torch singer.

"You been talking to them BGLs?" Camel demanded to know, changing the subject. "What are them punks saying about us?"

A couple of days later, I asked Mary Ann if she had indeed gone to jail.

"Sho' 'nuf," she said. "What happened was, in July I got in a fight in the parking lot at Price Chopper. I was shopping with Victoria, and this chick started cussing me out, calling me bitch and pussy. It was because I was going out with this guy she used to go out with. But I didn't want to fight her, because of Victoria. But then she started kicking my car, and she punched me in the face twice. So I felt like I had no choice. After a while the cops came, and they said I had some outstanding warrants. So they locked me up. At first I didn't really care, but then they started saying that they might take away my daughter, and I got scared. I really, really didn't want that to happen.

"After four days, I made trustee. The cops liked me, so I got to smoke and walk around and even hold Victoria one time, for ten minutes. Then the jail got too crowded, and they moved me to Grandview. That jail was crowded, too, but that was where I met Brandon. He's twenty-one, he's white. He was just in jail for a few days on some old MIPs"—convictions for having been a minor in possession of alcohol. "Since I was a trustee, I got to talk to the men, and Brandon and I found out we were like the only ones in the whole jail who liked 107.3, the alternative rock station. So that was kind of how we got together. And then I ended up answering the phones when all the cops had to go out because of a bank robbery. So I got early release, after only eleven days—for substantial assistance during a serious situation or some shit. And since I've been out I've just been really careful. I've been like totally avoiding the gang life. Me and Brandon have a good relationship. He treats me like a woman, the way I want to be treated. We're going to Seattle together."

"You been talking to Mary Ann?"

Juan was sprawled, as usual, on his parents' couch. Outside, the street was hot and bright; inside, the room was dim and cool and loud with the music of Smashing Pumpkins.

"She tell you about her little gang?"

A bit, I said.

"You know, when she stopped hanging out with our crowd, she like suddenly disappeared," Juan said. "And when she reappeared she was like a freak. She was all dressed down, with a tattoo on her arm. Getting in all kinds of trouble, fighting with other gang girls. I was like really depressed about it. She just took us all by storm."

An operatic song came on, full of booming rock violin. I picked up the Smashing Pumpkins compact disc box and read the song titles on it: "Disarm," "Spaceboy," "Silverfuck," "Mayonnaise."

"She tell you about getting corded in?" Juan asked.

"She did. She said she got a black eye and a ripped shirt." I waited a beat. "I don't think there was any sex."

Juan looked at me steadily. "Really?"

I said I would bet on it.

Juan turned away. "That's not what I heard," he said. His relief was audible. "That's what freaked me out." He sat up and peeked briefly through the curtains at the street outside. "But I would never ask her about something like that, you know. Not unless I was really drunk."

It was peculiar but distinct, this sense of delicacy that Juan and Mary Ann still seemed to have about each other. Drugs and alcohol were their truth serums, letting them discover if they really did think alike. They still struck me as a dream pair: two halves of a whole proposition. And yet Juan had blown it. Conditions were never auspicious for love on an equal basis, and now Mary Ann was off to the Emerald City without him.

Juan seemed to be serious about not leaving his parents' house. Whenever I pressed him about his indolence, he said that he would soon start studying for his GED. There was an adult education center in Sunnyside, he said. After hearing him say this four or five times, I told him that, if such a place existed, I doubted he even knew where it was. He laughed and said I was wrong. I challenged him to show me. He said, "Any time." Now, at my insistence, we were going to look for the center.

"But first can we go by McDonald's and pick up Sammy?" Juan asked. "He gets off work now."

We drove out to the fast food ghetto on the highway. Sammy turned out to be a chunky kid with an unfinished, forlorn face and a self-deprecating smile. He didn't quite have The Hair. He jumped in the backseat.

"So what have you been doing?" Sammy asked Juan. "Just kicking back at home?"

"No, dude," Juan said. "I've been cutting asparagus in the backyard, picking apples. Hard stuff. Not little sissy stuff like flipping patties."

Sammy said nothing. I had heard Juan's friends discuss the notion, widespread among their parents, that all of them were spoiled because they had not worked in the fields as children. Surprisingly, most of them agreed with this analysis—even Richard Negrete, whose parents owned a small farm and gave him a car and an allowance. So Juan was goofing on, among other things, the idea that fieldwork built character. His parents' backyard wasn't big enough to grow two stalks of asparagus in, let alone apple trees.

Juan directed me easily to the adult education center, a low white building near the railroad tracks. Inside, we found a pleasant young Latina behind a desk. The center had just closed for the afternoon, she said. She worked for a state farmworker-assistance program that used the same offices. As we were leaving, Juan suddenly pulled up. "Hey," he said. "*I'm* a farmworker."

"So you are."

Juan went back to the desk and collected a sheaf of handouts. When we got to the car, I noticed that we were alone.

"Where's Sammy?"

Juan peered back toward the education center, shielding his eyes from the sun. "He's still in there," he said. "Talking to that girl. Looking at the stuff they got." Juan laughed. "Sammy's just trying, you know, to *fit in.*"

Juan's self-awareness was becoming unnerving. His deadpan put-ons about apple picking versus patty flipping, his parking-lot mordancy about *fitting in.* He was starting to remind me of Bartleby—perennially preferring not to. Juan seemed, that is, to balk at every road put in front of him: school, sports, gangs, the fields, the union (he lost interest as soon as he was fired), even the life road represented by Mary Ann. (I, like his mother, thought he was crazy to pass her up.) Although his peers seemed not to have adopted the term yet, what he was acting like was a slacker: lying low, listening to music, smoking dope, laughing at people. Basically waiting for something more interesting to turn up.

He knew he was blowing it. Teana Robbins, his juvenile parole officer, had invited Juan to speak to a group of gang kids she convened each week from the Sunnyside junior high school. "He amazed us," she told me. "He gave a really good lecture about staying in school. He said, 'Don't waste your high school years like I did.' Even though he had been banned from school, not dropped out, he took responsibility for his own problems. He should do more guest speaking. It would probably help him as much as anybody else."

His parents were now more worried than ever. Rosa said, "We could throw Juan out of the house because he's eighteen and he's not contributing. Lots of families do that. But he would just do worse in the streets." She talked often about sending him to stay with relatives in Mexico, where it was safer—an idea that plainly held zero appeal for Juan. Rafael, for his part, spoke eloquently and sympathetically about Juan's difficulties with authority, and about how he needed to decide what he wanted, not let his life be dictated by unsought confrontations. But he rarely spoke about these things to Juan. "My dad won't give me any advice directly," Juan told me. "He just tells me things through other people, like you."

Rafael was also eloquent on the subject of my work. "Guillermo," he would say, his eyes glowing. "Your words will outlive all of us. What you hear and see, what you write in your books, will be kept in the libraries of the world forever."

Rafael's vision, so optimistic (unduly so, in my case) and bibliocentric, stood in stark, depressing contrast to Juan's ahistorical, rock-video weltanschauung. His clear, uncorrupted Spanish was also a far cry from Juan's minimal, slang-heavy English. It wasn't that Juan spoke Caló, the truly impoverished Spanish-English mix of the American-born Latino lower class. (This is the patois of the gangs and prisons, used by the functionally illiterate who effectively speak neither Spanish nor English; it has a maximum vocabulary of perhaps fifteen hundred words.) It was that he had never been successfully led into the world of books, where the standard English he spoke might be strengthened. And it wasn't that he was incurious about the world beyond Sunnyside. On the contrary, Juan was constantly asking me questions. When Malcolm X appeared in a hip-hop video, he asked me about him, and seemed enthralled while I told him the story of Malcolm's life and death.

The conundrum that had first struck me about Juan—how he could not share his parents' unionism—had come to seem less of a mystery. To me, Rosa and Rafael were exemplary immigrants. Lacking the capital to start a business like La Fogata, they had thrown themselves into the labor struggle with heartbreaking dedication. Contrary to the school principal's view that they were "the type who scream discrimination," I saw them as the type who actually believe in the ideals of equality and opportunity. I sometimes wondered if Juan found his parents' decency and dedication oppressive, or if his indifference to their ideals was just part of a standard-issue adolescent rebellion. But Juan, from everything I could tell, admired his parents. The unhappy truth was that the pop culture that formed so much of his world view simply provided no referents for their kind of heroism. The nobility of labor was no longer even a minor value in the devouring consumerism of the America where he was growing up.

In fact, Juan had been raised with a dense admixture of values, Mexican and American. The ancient code of *machismo* clearly informed his fighting life, and his failure to thrive in school or at work might well be attributed to the sort of cultural liability that conservative poverty theorists, such as Lawrence M. Mead, believe afflicts many African Americans and Latino immigrants. Juan's parents, however, could hardly be described as fatalistic, resigned to their low status, or unwilling to work hard—the standard cultural slurs laid on poor Latinos. No, Juan's anomie was not Third World but thoroughly American.

And the ironic attitudes he so often struck probably had as much to do with the need to be always negotiating between Latino and Anglo cultures as they did with any postmodern sophistication. Such dexterity breeds distance, if only to mask insecurity. For all I knew, Juan's reluctance to visit Mexico might really derive from a fear that he would be too *pocho*, too *agringado*—too gringoized—for the tastes of his Old Country relatives and peers.

But Juan's experience beyond the Yakima Valley was really pathetically slight. And some of it—such as the racialized violence in juvenile detention, where the white kids were "KKK"—constituted an introduction to an America almost too bleak and shameful to contemplate. In part, though, his isolation and inexperience were simply a function of poverty. He had, for instance, never been on an airplane. (Neither had Lanee Mitchell, in San Augustine, nor Terry Jackson, in New Haven—and all three had mentioned this fact about themselves unasked, each quite aware that it marked them as poor folk in frequent-flier America.) I once asked Juan if he had ever seen the ocean. He said he had seen the Atlantic a couple of times while he was at the youth camp in western Washington. I must have looked surprised. He blushed and quickly corrected himself. "I mean the Pacific. See? I'm already forgetting my oceans. I really gotta get my GED." After he was fired from Château Ste. Michelle, he made a foray over the mountains to Seattle, looking for work with Richard Negrete in Richard's car. The ceiling tiles in the Kingdome, Seattle's main sports arena, had apparently started falling off, forcing the arena to close, and Juan and Richard were hoping to get on an emergency repair crew. "But we never got there," Juan said. "I mean, we got close. I could see the Kingdome and everything. But Richard changed his mind and said he just wanted to go to a mall and hang out. So that's what we did. It was stupid. We could have made some money. I really wanted to check out Seattle."

But Mary Ann would be checking it out first, it seemed. "That's good," Juan said weakly. "That's good for her."

One morning, Juan and Cuco and I were driving past Mary Ann's mother's house. On impulse, I pulled in. Mary Ann came out the front door grinning manically. "Hey, you guys, y'all come to say good-bye?"

Juan and Cuco were grinning, too, but shyly, looking down at their shoes. We stood around in the front yard, shooting the breeze. Mary Ann was wearing a tank top and a pair of very short shorts. As usual, she looked smashing. "Y'all want to meet Brandon?" she asked. "He's great! He's white, he's rich. He's got real long hair."

Juan and Cuco seemed amenable to meeting Brandon, though in no rush to do so. Suddenly, both of them turned and stared intently at a pickup truck passing on a cross street.

Mary Ann made a face at me. "When are these guys going to grow up?" she stage-whispered. "They're nineteen years old!"

I was confused.

Juan explained, "Those are the guys that stabbed Cuco."

Cuco was still staring after the pickup truck. Earlier, he had shown me the sword wound in his back. It was huge, deep and curving and still raw. He would never have been stabbed, he said, if Juan had been with him that night. But the guys he was with all fled, leaving him alone with a gang of angry enemies. "I was lucky they didn't kill me," he mumbled.

Now Cuco turned back to us, his face flushed and set.

"So, Cuco," Mary Ann said, trying to lighten the mood. "You're letting your hair grow. I like it. Pretty soon it's gonna look like Juan's!"

I only realized how serious were the tensions swirling around Cuco and Juan when I attended a closed-door meeting of the Sunnyside police and school officials. The meeting was a regular weekly affair with a set topic: youth violence. After a brief discussion of recent stabbings and drive-by shootings in the feud between the Little Valley Locos and the Bell Gardens Locos, talk turned to the mélée that had landed Cuco and two others in the hospital, and to its likely ramifications. Juan's name came up repeatedly, and it was suggested that his recent brawl in the countryside with Cuco and the Muñoz boys had somehow led to the big fight in town. The principal of the high school asked if Juan could possibly be tied to the town fight, but a police officer, who knew that Juan had been in the station at the time, said he could not. "But this thing ain't over yet," Wallace Anderson, the police chief, said. "You people in the schools, stay in touch with us, and stay spun up on this thing. Because if these people show up on your doorstep in the right combination, you got big problems right away."

Oliver Hernandez, a handsome, heavily muscled young officer, announced, with obvious pride, that he had recently arrested Juan at a party. "I took him in for trespass," he said. "He tried to resist me."

The consensus view at the meeting was that the young warrior they most needed to watch was David Muñoz. "He is very dangerous," a detective said. "He'll probably kill somebody before the end of the year." Muñoz, the detective said, had been especially irascible ever since Juan Guerrero "butt-stroked him between the eyes during the little disagreement they had out in the country."

David Muñoz called him, I discovered, Juan Guerro. It was as if he could not bring himself to pronounce the hated surname (which means, as a matter of fact, "warrior"). Muñoz and I were sitting at a picnic table in a park in Sunnyside. It was a bright Saturday morning and he was wolfing down an Egg McMuffin. An awful stench from the stockyards filled the air, as it often does in Sunnyside, but Muñoz was in no danger of smelling it, for his nose was still swollen and discolored. He snorted uncomfortably and blew his nose frequently. The clout he had received between the eyes had not been from the butt of a shotgun, as the police believed, but, he said, from the end of a baseball bat—his own bat, which Juan had taken from him in the course of their brawl, and then used to jab him in the face. "Faggot hit me with my own bat," he snarled. "He's gonna pay for that." It was, presumably, the same bat Muñoz had used in his spectacular one-man attack against Richard Negrete's car outside the hospital. This bat, I had heard, was metal—much better against windshields, Muñoz explained, than wood. I asked if he had been at the hospital because of his nose.

"*Chále*," he said. *Chále* is gangspeak for *no*. "This don't need no hospital. I was there for my sister. She was having a baby."

I had turned up unannounced at Muñoz's family's house that morning. It was an old farmhouse a few miles east of town, with a yard full of trash and chickens. Inside, it was dim, roomy, and impressively squalid. I recalled a story Teana Robbins had told me about visiting there. Just as she arrived, two of David's brothers had started fighting. Then their mother had gone after the younger one with a pitchfork. The younger boy managed to call 911, bringing the sheriff to the house. After peace was restored, the older boy expressed his feelings by grabbing a rooster and quietly wringing its neck. My arrival occasioned nothing so vivid. Somebody went to rouse David, who came out and stared at me grumpily, then suggested I take him to McDonald's.

He was slim and dark, not tall, with a scraggly goatee and a forward-thrusting, bantam's body. He was sixteen and good-looking, but he had a strange, furious light in his eye—and a remarkable number of scars on his face and hands. As we drove into town, he informed me that his tag name was El Diablo Azul, the Blue Devil. "I got an all-blue suit," he said. "Blue flannels, a blue rag, blue jeans, blue T-shirt. Because the gang I'm in is blue." I elected not to mention that the tag name I had heard Camel Flores and the LVLs use for him was not the Blue Devil but Caveman. Muñoz's gang, the Ghetto Boys, was allied with the Bell Gardens Locos and was therefore also at war with the LVLs.

I knew Muñoz had recently been released from jail. I asked about his troubles with the law.

"They were trying to get me for some rape charges," he said. "Some fuckin' LVL bitch. They didn't have no evidence, just her word. I fucked her but I didn't rape her. So they dropped that charge. But then they got me for auto theft. I fuckin' jacked it smooth, even put the truck back, just like it was, just a few more scratches, but that bitch told on me. I should kill her."

Muñoz had three uncles currently in jail, he told me. A fourth had died in state prison a few years before. "They called it suicide, the fuckin' bastards," he said. "The cops hanged him. He was a professional thief."

In the park, while he ate his breakfast, Muñoz extolled the courage and loyalty of the Ghetto Boys and their allies, sometimes leaping to his feet to emphasize a point. He issued elaborate threats against their enemies, especially a *leva* (turncoat) who had left the Ghetto Boys to join the LVLs. "Stupid faggot," Muñoz growled. "Thinks he's better than us. I'll kick the fuck out of him. He's too slow now. But, you know, us TGBs got a lot of good fighters. The biggest boy we got right now is Ramón. That fucker can throw blows! We sent one guy to the Marines, Izzie. He was a wrestler in high school. Every gang has their fighters, their crazy guy (that's me), their artist. Hector's our artist. He's the one that tags it up. TGB, all over town. You seen it?"

I said I had.

"For reals, man." Muñoz seemed pleased. "Whatever's clever, homes," he said.

Muñoz was quiet for a minute. Then he grew agitated. "See, I come up with some crazy shit," he said. "I start things, and if one of my friends won't go along with it, well, he goes *down* right there."

Sounds like fun, I said.

Muñoz stared at me. Then he snickered. Then he asked if I knew Junior Salazar.

I said I did. (Salazar was one of Juan's friends.)

Muñoz asked if I knew where Salazar lived.

I did, but I asked Muñoz why he wanted to know.

"A BGL bet me a hundred dollars to a machine gun that I can beat up Junior Salazar," he said. "Why don't you show me where he lives?"

Another time, I said.

Muñoz wanted to know who else I knew in Sunnyside. I didn't want to mention Juan or Cuco or the LVLs, so I mentioned Mary Ann, who had by then left for Seattle.

"I wish I could fuck her," he said immediately. "Just to make the LVLs mad." He laughed. "But it's good if she really went away, because she was causing a lot of problems, making the LVLs think they're big shit, making them confident."

It was now late morning, but the park was still deserted. Muñoz and I watched three Mexicans—two women and a young man—pass on foot. They were brightly, unfashionably dressed, and carried plastic shopping bags. "Check it out," Muñoz said. "They're in another world, you can tell. Peaceful. *Mexican.* Even that young guy won't fight. He doesn't have time for that. He doesn't even know about nice T-shirts like this." Muñoz fingered his own, not particularly nice T-shirt. "They're more poor. They just have to work. But Mexico, you know, is *bad.* It's the best place to be. It's all the same as here, only it's better, because there are more things to do. Ride horses, whatever. My grandmother down there is rich. She owns a lot of land. I got cousins in East L.A., too." We watched the Mexicans disappear around a corner. Muñoz spat. "Everything's turning crazy in this world," he said. "*La vida loca.* Everything *is* crazy in this world."

I didn't disagree.

"I'm going to declare a truce," Muñoz announced. "But just with myself. I won't tell nobody, because that would be showing weakness. I can't show weakness because I got a lot of respect here, and I would lose respect. They love me, my homeboys, so I have to live up to myself. That's what everybody's doing here, living up to their reputations. And I got one of the biggest ones here, so I got to work hard." He laughed. Self-mockingly, I thought. "For reals, man. That's a trip."

But first, Muñoz planned to kill Cuco and Juan. "I'm ready to retire them," he said. "And I'm gonna have plenty of chances. Just the other day I had a gauge"—he meant a twenty-gauge shotgun—"and my stupid little brother wanted me to kill Cuco. It was right here." He indicated the edge of the park. "But it was broad daylight. Everybody's gonna see me. That's stupid. I know where them guys live, Cuco and Juan Guerro. I know where they hang out. But I better not say where, because I just be making myself stupid. Can't trust nobody."

Muñoz gave me a sly look. He was getting agitated again. "Those guys are *levas*," he said. "Two-faced bastards. Sometimes they claim a gang, sometimes they don't, just so they can have an alibi. I don't care if Juan Guerro is a black belt. I been needing to throw a squabble with that boy for a long time. Now he went and fucked up my nose with my own bat. So I'm gonna fuck his nose up. Cut it off and make him eat it. Hurt him like he hurt me."

With that, Muñoz gave me a look of such pure vengeful rage that I shivered in the noonday sun.

The next morning, I took Juan to breakfast at a diner on the highway. He looked hungover and preoccupied. He pushed the menu away. "I don't think I can deal with a hamburger yet," he said.

I asked what was on his mind.

"Last night, at a party, this guy, Dan Perez, started firing guns in the dark," he said. "And there was like a little flame coming out of the barrel each time he shot. It was *bad*. I can't stop thinking about it. It was"—Juan peered into the middle distance, looking for words—"*very interesting*."

"Was anybody hurt?"

"Nah," Juan said. "It was at a country spot we call the Barn. There were like thirty cars there. It was stacked. It was crazy. These guys, the Aztecs, from Mabton, started calling on Perez, who's old, like in his twenties, and used to be in the PBGs—the Playboy Gangsters, from Yakima. They were like, 'What's up, buster? You're a bitch. Why you be narkin'?' They were red-dogging him, beating on him. He didn't say nothing. He just got away, went to his car, and came back with this big old rifle, I don't know what kind, and a nine-millimeter. And he starts going, 'Wussup? Wussup? Who wants a piece of this?' Boom! Boom! Boom! 'What you got? What bitches are ready now?' Boom! Boom! Boom! There were a lot of shots. It was crazy."

Juan was now gazing out the diner window, still with a faraway look. I asked if he knew that David Muñoz was after him. A caul of boredom fell across his face.

"Different people have been saying they're going to shoot me for four or five years," he said. "Guys from Grandview, Prosser, Mabton. The PBGs. City Life. This Chinese gang from Seattle, the Tiny Boys, came and broke out our front windows last year. Lots of other people. There's nothing special about this one. They all pass. Where do they go off to? I can't even remember some of their names. Awhile from now, it'll be like, 'David Muñoz? Oh, I remember him. I *think*.'"

Beyond the diner window was the vast expanse of the Price Chopper parking lot, harsh and empty on a Sunday morning. Juan's eyes were flat as he studied the acres of asphalt.

"If we were still juveniles, it would be a lot more serious," he said, finally. "People would really get hurt. When we were juveniles, we could destroy people with bats and crowbars and just get community hours. Now it's different. You don't hit somebody with a crowbar now unless you want to go to jail."

David Muñoz, I thought, was still a juvenile. And the boys who murdered the family of four near Granger, hoping to impress the BGLs, had been fourteen years old. Life seemed to be getting increasingly dangerous for Juan, with the likes of Muñoz so eager to "retire" him.

"I'm just tired of the whole thing," Juan said. "My close friends aren't even gang members. I just think the gangs suck, to tell you the truth. I didn't always think so, but I grew up, got older. I'd rather go to concerts, go boarding, go water-skiing. It's these other guys that want to keep on battling."

At that moment, we were unexpectedly joined by Rosita Castillo, an exuberant social worker who had helped me get my bearings when I arrived in Sunnyside. I introduced her to Juan.

"I've heard a lot about you," she said. *"¿Cómo estás?"*

"Okay," Juan said, without enthusiasm.

"Except for the guys who want to kill him," I added.

"That's the street life," Rosita said. She turned to Juan. "You should go down to Mexico for a year. Go out and risk your life with the bulls in the plaza, just to get one kiss from the Queen of the May, or to dance the first dance of the *baile* with her."

Juan struggled to look interested, but his expression said, *"As if."*

Rosita chuckled. She had been raised in the U.S., and then, as a young mother, had returned to Mexico for a number of years. Those years, she had once told me, were among the happiest of her life. Now she said to me, "You can't tell them till they're ready to listen."

We took Juan home.

Then we drove around Sunnyside for a while in Rosita's car. "There's just no *place* for *los Mejicanos* here," she said. "No place for the youth especially. Look at it."

"It" was a dispiriting sprawl of roads, highways, fields, trailer parks, labor camps, parking lots, convenience stores, shopping malls, waste ground—the public space in semi-rural America. It was indeed bleak, and most Latino immigrants surely couldn't afford much private space as a refuge from it.

"What's needed here in *la valle* is something like *la plaza* in Mexico," Rosita declared. "A place where everybody goes to hear music, and say hello, and the men circle around in one direction, and the women walk together in the other direction. That would be so much better than this endless cruising in cars!"

. . .

I went to talk to Cuco about David Muñoz. I found him at the alternative high school, which was in a small, corrugated-tin building right on the highway. The school looked like the office shack at a car lot. We stood outside and talked in the traffic roar.

Cuco said he was aware of Muñoz's threats. "I hate that kid," he said. "I want to teach him a lesson. He and his buddies chased me into Payless the other day. I had to borrow some of their bats. Even with this thing"—he indicated his sword wound—"I was ready for them."

"How is your back?"

"Itchy," Cuco said. "And I'm depressed, because I still can't rebound, and basketball practice is already starting." He watched the traffic pass. "But I wish I was in real high school," he said. "Seeing everybody with their faces painted for Spirit Week . . . High school is so much fun. I'm gonna tell my kids, 'Don't do like I did. I went to high school *in one room.*'" He threw his chin disdainfully toward the tin building behind us.

At least he was *in* school, I said.

"And I don't want to mess that up," he said emphatically.

Another good reason to stay away from David Muñoz, I suggested.

"People like to fight," Cuco said. "You can't stop that. But I just keep telling them, 'Let's take it into the country, and don't take no weapons, and settle things that way.' That's what Juan and me did with those Muñozes. But these young kids won't go along with that. With them it's all guns and knives and drive-bys, and big mobs of people bum-rushing you. They want to make a name for themselves. So it's hard for guys like Juan and me to avoid them."

Juan, I said, seemed stuck. Drifting, disengaged.

"Yeah," Cuco said. "He just won't take any help. I tried to get him in here, but they didn't want him. And I've been trying to hook him up with, you know, the helpfulness people. But he acts like he just don't care."

The "helpfulness people" were, essentially, Rosita Castillo. She ran a small group for young ex-offenders, trying to structure their time after school with art and community service projects and some minimum-wage clerical work. She had shown me a couple of colorful *piñatas* that her group had made, and said she was very interested in getting Juan involved. But when I asked Juan about it, he looked at me with disbelief. He had in fact checked out the program, he said, but had found it "corny." And I had to admit that, even to my mind, it just wasn't him at the present time.

"I've seen the future, and it is murder." This Leonard Cohen line, from the Oliver Stone film *Natural Born Killers,* kept running through my mind over dinner with Juan and his girlfriend Rachel. We had driven up to Yakima because Juan was still reluctant to go out in public in Sunnyside. And we had seen *Natural Born Killers* because it was his all-time favorite movie. On the drive up, I had asked Rachel if she knew David Muñoz. She said she did. In fact, Muñoz had once stabbed her cousin Arthur three times through the back. Her cousin had survived, she said, but still had trouble with his lungs. "He's not strong no more," she said matter-of-factly. Rachel, who was in the eleventh grade, struck me as strangely placid. She was American-born, dark-haired, and very attractive. She spoke with no Spanish accent. In all the months I had known Juan, this was the first time I had met her.

I asked Juan what he liked about the film.

"Everything," he said passionately. "The way they like divide the screen into two or three parts, and show you different things at the same time, so when Mickey is like doing something you can see exactly what he's thinking while he's doing it. It's like an acid trip. And just the violence—all the shooting, bam bam bam, all like in slow motion. It's beautiful. It's exciting to watch. And the way the whole world is just crazy—the way it really is, but even crazier. The only thing I don't like is when they get famous, when it's Mickey and Mallory this and that, and they're in all the magazines and on TV, like celebrities. That's just so much what you already expect. That's *too much* like the real world."

I asked Rachel how she liked the film.

She shrugged, obviously surprised to be asked. "It was okay," she said.

I thought about how Juan and Mary Ann would have dissected the movie in one of their frenetic all-night talks.

After we got back to Sunnyside and had dropped off Rachel at her parents' house, Juan told me that he had some news for me. Rachel, he said, was pregnant. "Pretty weird, huh?"

I didn't need to ask if she would carry the baby to term, or if she would keep it. She would, of course.

Oliver Hernandez, the muscle-bound policeman, was a local boy. He had wrestled for Sunnyside High, then joined the Marines and seen the world: California, Asia, Saudi Arabia. After Operation Desert Storm, he came home. He first went to work in the school system as a security officer, and was shocked, he told me, by the level of crime and violence he found there. The social atmosphere in Sunnyside had badly deteriorated, he thought, in the last few years. He admired Don Vlieger's efforts to restore order in the schools. Vlieger was not inhibited, Hernandez said, by the kind of dense familiarity that, for example, he and Chico Rodriguez, Jr., usually had with the families of the kids who were messing up. "They might be our second cousins or whatever." But Vlieger was not coming back to the Sunnyside schools this year, I discovered—his contract had expired. And Hernandez was now a policeman, concerned with bigger troublemakers.

Such as Juan Guerrero, I suggested.

Hernandez grimaced. "A typical smart-ass," he said. "After I arrested him the other night, and I got him down here to the station, he got in my face and tried to call me on. I was unarmed, and I threw him across the room, and that was the end of it. I don't care what he's saying now, he *didn't* have handcuffs on. You know, that guy's probably not going to last very much longer. A lot of people I've talked to want to beat him up royally. He's also in danger of us taking him out for doing something stupid. We see his attitude toward cops. He'll probably either get killed by somebody, possibly by the police, or else he'll kill somebody."

My understanding of Juan's situation was changing. His resemblance to Bartleby now seemed slight. He was not simply balking at a set of unsatisfactory options. He was in fact badly trapped and in real danger. I couldn't tell how seriously to take David Muñoz's threats, or Oliver Hernandez's extremely ominous words. If Juan did get killed by the Sunnyside police, it would be cold comfort to have evidence of premeditation. I also didn't know whether to tell Rosa and Rafael about the things I had heard around town.

Rosa already seemed beside herself with alarm. She was more intent than ever on the idea of sending Juan to Mexico. "But first, he must get citizenship," she told me. "In case something happens. I keep telling him he must go get the papers, but he never goes." I wasn't sure if Rosa understood Juan's reluctance to leave the house during the day. Was there anywhere else, I asked, besides Mexico, where he might be sent? His older sister was in Arizona, Rosa said, but Juan didn't want to go there, either. He sometimes talked about Wenatchee, Washington, ninety miles north of Sunnyside, where his friend Aaron had relatives and a job, but Rosa and Rafael were against that. They liked Aaron, but he and Juan had a tendency to kick up their heels when they got together.

My understanding of how Juan had gotten himself into this fix had also changed. Gangbanging, for a start, now made much more sense to me. Latino gangs had degenerated since their founding days, when they functioned as community self-defense units against the depredations of Anglo rednecks in Texas and California—such, at least, was the myth—but even in these self-lacerating times it seemed perfectly understandable that a Camel Flores or a David Muñoz would choose to be in a gang. Those two actually struck me as bright kids—I had also spent a little time with the BGLs, whose denizens made Camel and Muñoz look like Nobel laureates—but their shared hunch that the future held little more for them than poverty and futility was irrefutable. So why *not* live as large as they could while they could—claim some space, some teenage glory? This *was* their dance with the bulls.

Juan, admittedly, was a different matter. He, too, might suffer from what one Latino anthropologist has called "multiple marginality" in America, and yet he still seemed hopeful that he might have other chances in life, a trajectory that might be all his own. But what did I know about Juan, really? The principal of the junior high school in Sunnyside recalled him by saying, "He had a real charming side to his personality, which we only rarely saw." How many sides of Juan's personality had I seen? I had never even seen him fight. Other kids were in awe of how much "heart" he had, but that didn't mean just physical courage, coolness under fire, the ability to fight and to tolerate pain. It also meant the capacity for violence, for hurting other people. Oliver Hernandez was right; Juan did say he was handcuffed when he tussled with Hernandez at the police station. And I would never know which one of them was telling the truth.

Brooding over these matters in my motel room in Sunnyside, I had a curious flash of memory: I was once in a gang myself. I had completely forgotten about it. It was in junior high school, in Honolulu. It was a racial gang—whites only—at a school where whites were a small minority. We called ourselves the In Crowd. Our ostensible raison d'être was self-defense; before I joined, I was regularly attacked simply for being white and because I had no gang to back me up. But the truth was that we were an offensive force, fighting constantly and joyfully. Some of the fights were fair, but many were not. I still cringe when I remember some of the attacks I took part in. More to the point, I can half recall what a life of adolescent fighting felt like: rich, dramatic, absolutely vital. For me, it all faded abruptly when my family moved back to a middle-class suburb of Los Angeles. I paid nothing for my thrill ride in the street-fighting world; even the school officials whom I had alienated were out of my life. And in high school, too, my friends and I paid little or nothing for our adventures on the far side of the law, our "experiments" with drugs and petty crime. We were white, we were college-bound, so they were juvenile hijinks. Does it even need saying that for Juan and his friends the rules were fundamentally different?

■ drove over to the Guerreros' one afternoon. Ralph was just getting home from school. Juan was asleep in his room. I had brought some forms for Ralph: an application for a program meant to help underprivileged eighth graders get on an academic track toward the University of Washington. Ralph seemed pleased when I told him that his grades were good enough to qualify. As we were filling out the forms, Juan shuffled into the living room, wearing only a pair of sweatpants. There were two fresh scars on his right arm.

Ralph left for wrestling practice. I asked Juan about the scars. He stared at them for a minute, as if he hadn't seen them before. "This one's from that fight with the Muñozes," he said finally, indicating a long, healing slice above his elbow. "And this other one was just stupid." He fingered what looked like a big, nasty burn on his bicep. "A bunch of us were drunk, and decided to burn ourselves with cigarettes. Some of them came out better than this. This was supposed to be a face, but you can't really see it now."

Juan picked up the forms that Ralph and I had been working on. He studied them. "Cool," he said. "The little professor."

I asked if he knew anyone who had gone to the University of Washington. "Maybe some people a few years ago," he said. "Some really smart kids. Maybe some white kids more recently. But nobody I could call a friend."

I had once, in desperation, asked Rosita Castillo to introduce me to a college-bound Latino, and she had brought me a teenager from Michoacán. He had been in the U.S. less than five years. When he got to this country, he said, he couldn't even read Spanish. Now he had a 3.3 grade point average. He still worked in the fields with his family. His favorite subjects were biology and mathematics. He wanted to go into hotel management. He reminded me of Asian kids I had known in school in California. He had less in common with Juan, I decided, than I did.

I was starting to feel a bit undone. I was leaving for Seattle the next day.

I thought I would try to see Mary Ann. I asked Juan if he had any message for her.

"Just stay in touch," he said softly.

I asked if his parents knew yet about Rachel's pregnancy.

"I told 'em. They were pretty upset at first. But now my mom's starting to get into it. She's looking forward to having a baby around. She wants us to get married."

And?

"I seem not to really want to right now."

"You should be a diplomat," I said.

Juan laughed. He turned on the TV and went to the kitchen in search of food. Finding myself unable to watch another minute of Snoop Doggy Dogg, I wandered around the living room, noting some old Santa Claus stickers on a window—an assimilated touch; Mexicans welcome the three wise men at Christmas, not St. Nick—and a small plaster shrine on the wall. The shrine held a figure of a young boy and, except for a small crucifix, was the only religious touch in a room full of family photographs, china geese, and martial arts trophies.

"That's Santo Niño de Atocha," said Juan, wolfing down a slice of cold pizza. "He's from Mexico, from Zacatecas. He's like my mom's favorite saint. He's bad. He helps you. I want to go see him."

"Really? To Mexico? You?"

"Yeah," Juan said. "I think he's cool. In a way."

I was starting to feel undone again. Juan looked at me sympathetically, as if I were the one trapped in a nightmare. He shrugged. "It's all cool, in a way, I would say," he said.

In Seattle, Mary Ann and I went to a plush waterfront restaurant for dinner. She seemed different—as if her native enthusiasm were now under firmer control. She wore pearls, heels, light makeup, an expensive-looking dress. She looked like a prosperous college student—maybe an MBA candidate—and she seemed delighted when I said so. She said she was thinking about moving to the university district, on the north side of the city. My hotel was in that neighborhood, and I could suddenly picture her there, waitressing in a coffee bar, taking some classes, inhaling college-town culture in great eager draughts.

In the meantime, she and Victoria were living on the south side with her sister, her sister's boyfriend, and their baby daughter. I had found my way to their apartment by looking for a drug rehab center, which was across the street. "It's still the ghetto," Mary Ann had said, sighing, as she gave me directions. "Mainly Hispanics. It's even got gangs." Her place of work, the Sky View Casino, which I had asked to see, was also less glamorous than I had imagined it from Sunnyside. I had pictured a revolving baccarat club on the roof of a skyscraper overlooking Puget Sound, but the Sky View Casino had turned out to be a bingo parlor in a rundown shopping center in the woods on the edge of the city. Mary Ann said she liked working there; she had just received a raise and would soon have enough money saved to get her own apartment and a car. "Brandon and I really want our own place," she said. "He's in Grandview right now helping his dad, but he's got a job lined up over here."

Mary Ann was still keen on Brandon, evidently, but when the conversation turned to Juan she surprised me. She asked me what I thought would become of him. I told her that I had recently asked him where he hoped to be in ten years' time, and that he had replied, "Seattle."

Her eyes burned into mine. "If it was up to me, he'd come up here right now," she said. "Things could still work out. We could both get jobs . . ."

A vein of self-contradiction ran through much of our conversation. On the one hand, Mary Ann was still passionate about the LVLs. "I still won't talk to *Norteños*," she said vehemently. "They got 'em here, too. More than in Sunnyside. But I'm not going to be a *leva* just because I'm over here. I may not be kicking it with my homeys, but I'm still *Sur.*" She went on to denounce various enemies in Sunnyside, including David Muñoz, whom she called Caveman.

But Muñoz was also a *Sureño,* I said. In fact, there seemed to be few *Norteños* in Sunnyside. All the feuding was among *Sureños.* I said something facetious about the narcissism of small differences.

"I don't know about that," she said. "But I know where I'm from. I know what I claim. It's the people I've known the longest. If I had grown up around different people, I might have gone *Norte.* I admit that."

It was a strange, sideways argument we were having, over our salmon and chocolate mousse—about identity and fate and free will.

At the same time, Mary Ann kept returning to her fantasy of a future for herself in Seattle that would have nothing to do with her gang-girl past. "I want to drive a Lexus," she said. "I want to wear a nice suit and come in to work on one of these ferries, like from Bainbridge Island. I want to carry a briefcase, a really nice leather one, and have a big office, and a big desk, and a bunch of people working for me. And I want to have my daughter in a private school. That's all."

I said I thought these things might be within her reach if she finished college. I was uneasy, though, with the peculiar shallowness of these set-designed ambitions. I wondered if Mary Ann felt it as well. What had become of her dream of being a psychiatrist? Was the city to her really just a place where one got to carry an expensive briefcase? When she talked about gangs or about Juan, vexed though the subjects might be, there was a wholeness to her, a force and solidity that were missing when she stargazed about Bainbridge Island.

After dinner, we went for a drive around Seattle. Mary Ann navigated. As we passed through a posh shoreline district, she exclaimed, "This neighborhood is perfect! It's all white people. A lot of Jewish people. Have you ever seen the way Jewish people dress? The women? It's like unbelievably nice! They have *no* problems in this neighborhood."

"Do you mean they have no *Sureños?*" I asked.

"I mean they have no *Norteños.*"

Things in Sunnyside continued to close in on Juan. In November 1994, a sixteen-year-old named Pedro Cárdenas, a member of the Ghetto Boys, was stabbed to death in the Park-N-Pak parking lot. The police rounded up the usual suspects, including Juan and Cuco. They gave Cuco a polygraph test, which he passed. They had no evidence against Juan, and released him. (Two members of the LVLs were eventually charged with second-degree murder; one pleaded guilty to first-degree manslaughter, the other to second-degree assault with a deadly weapon.)

But David Muñoz was not interested in evidence. He had a long list of people whom he blamed for his homeboy's death, a list topped by Cuco and Juan. "If the cops can't get them, *we'll* take them out," Muñoz told me. "No more fighting, just what-it-takes." He meant murder, of course.

Juan continued to lie low. "It wouldn't be smart to go out," he said, a few days after the Cárdenas killing. "I don't want to be the next guy in the paper that died. I'd rather just read about it."

While the death of Cárdenas had fired up some of his enemies, the threats to Juan still did not begin or end with David Muñoz. "Rachel and I tried to go shopping at Wal-Mart the other day," he told me. "And this big-assed Nee-gro guy in there wanted to fight me. He had a big-assed *pan* in his bag and he chased me around the store with it. I guess he thought I was with some guys who beat him up once. He never caught me, luckily, and they arrested him— even though he used to be a supervisor in that same Wal-Mart."

Juan mentioned that he was looking for a job, but said there were restrictions on where and when he could work. "It has to be an evening job, so I don't have to go out when it's light," he said. "And it has to be out of town. If I'm sitting there in some warehouse or convenience store in Sunnyside, my enemies can just find me. That would be dangerous for everybody."

A few weeks later, there was another ominous development. "Ralph got harassed by some BGLs yesterday," Juan said when I phoned. (I had gone back to New York.) His voice was tight. "He was in a store, wearing a maroon sweater he made in school, so these guys said he was a Blood, a *Norteño*. They called him a faggot and a punk, and stuff, and the store owner called the cops. Ralph thinks they just saw his sweater. He doesn't think they got a good look at him. At least that's what we're hoping."

I asked Juan if he felt responsible.

"Yeah," he said. "I might have to get involved. Pound a few heads, just to show them to kick back and leave him alone. They're just young guys, Ralph's age, but there are ten or fifteen of them. Some are Ghetto Boys. One is David Muñoz's cousin. But I don't know yet if they know Ralph's my brother. That's what I need to find out."

Were Rosa and Rafael aware of the threats their sons were facing? When I spoke to Rosa on the phone, she seemed preoccupied with Juan and Rachel's baby. She was still lobbying for a wedding. "It is my tradition that they should get married," she told me.

"That's right," Juan said after she gave him the phone. "It's her tradition, not mine." His mother, he said, was actually thrilled about the approaching birth. She was already negotiating with Rachel's mother over child care—hoping to maximize her own time with the baby. Rachel did not plan to take time off from school.

As things turned out, Juan and Rachel became unwed parents at the end of March 1995. They named their daughter Jasmine Jay Tasha Guerrero. I asked Juan how they had come up with Tasha. He said, "I heard it off a rap group. It's some chick who raps, and it just stuck in my head as a bad name."

Within a few weeks, Rosa and Rafael had another reason to celebrate; *la compañía* and *la unión* had come to a historic agreement. After eight years of boycott and bitter struggle, management had caved in. Château Ste. Michelle's farmworkers would be allowed to decide, by secret ballot, whether they wanted the UFW to represent them. The election was held in June, and the union won easily. Collective bargaining began, and a contract was signed in November 1995.

Juan, however, missed all the fiestas held in honor of the union's victory. He missed them because he was in jail. Nothing particularly dramatic had occurred. He had had some outstanding charges from 1994, for being a minor in possession of alcohol. Then the police had given him a ticket outside Taco Bell after they found a joint in the ashtray of a car he was driving. Then, a week later, there was a fight at the AM/PM Mini-Market. The police picked up Juan in connection with the fight. When he appeared before the municipal judge, charged with fourth-degree assault, he took the opportunity to plead guilty to the earlier ticket for marijuana possession. This was a major mistake. He had no lawyer. He didn't think he needed one. All the charges he faced were misdemeanors. But the judge, knowing his juvenile record, immediately handed Juan the maximum sentence for misdemeanor pot possession: one year in county jail.

Rosa and Rafael frantically filed papers and found a lawyer. But it is difficult to appeal a guilty plea successfully, and they made no headway. Rosa, according to Ralph, could not stop crying.

Juan phoned me from jail. "I tell her it's cool," he said. "It's not like I'm hurt." He sounded as plaintive as I had ever heard him. But when I asked him how he was holding up, his voice steadied. "They think it's going to crush me," he said. "But it's not going to crush me. I'm just going to kick back and do my time. I'll take it from here. You know what I mean?"

When we said good-bye, Juan gave me the street farewell: "Laters."

The next time he called, a week or two afterward, Cuco was with him in jail. It seemed that the police had ultimately charged Cuco with assault for the mélée that had gained him his sword wound. Cuco sounded stunned. He kept saying, "It's not fair. It's not fair. I ain't been in no trouble for nine months."

I spoke to Juan separately, and he explained, "Cuco's supposed to graduate next week. He already rented his cap and gown, and everything. He was gonna be the first one in his family to graduate. Everybody thinks the cops did this to him on purpose, because they hate him. He's calling anybody he thinks might be able to help him."

But nobody could help Cuco, though Rosita Castillo tried mightily. In the end, he missed his graduation and, like Juan, was sentenced to one year in county jail.

Mary Ann, to my disappointment, moved back to Sunnyside. Things in Seattle had not worked out, she said. She would not elaborate. She got a job at K mart, doing inventory and pricing. "It's on the management training track," she said proudly. She was still seeing Brandon, who was also back with his parents, in Grandview. But she was trying to find a way, she said, with a naughty little laugh, to visit Juan in jail without Brandon finding out, "because he'll flip his lid." In the meantime, she had taken to visiting Jasmine, Juan's daughter. "Rachel doesn't like it," Mary Ann said. "But I took her a little baby outfit and a little bear, wrapped up like a present, with a card from Victoria, so that was okay. Mainly, I just visit the baby when she's with Juan's mom. I saw her yesterday. She's *so beautiful!*"

NINE

Juan's year in county jail did not crush him. His release, in April 1996, was pretty harrowing, though. Mary Ann had by then left Brandon, but she had not waited for Juan—she and Victoria had returned to Texas. Juan moved back in with his parents in Sunnyside. A few days later, the Guerreros' house was attacked, late at night, by what Juan described as a mob of twenty BGLs. Most of them seemed to be young guys simply looking to make a name for themselves by taking out Juan. Some of them might also have been looking to avenge, however misguidedly, the death of Pedro Cárdenas. Juan and a friend who happened to be visiting fought them off at the front door with shovels, but the windows of his parents' cars were all smashed out. Rosa and Rafael were in shock. The entire family was obviously in grave peril (and their daughter, Ana, had come home from Arizona with her husband and baby, increasing the household's vulnerability), and the police seemed unable (or unwilling) to help. No one dared even to sit in the living room, for fear of drive-by fire. It was clear that Juan couldn't stay there. The question was where he should go. As always, Rosa favored Mexico, and Juan rejected the idea. Rosa phoned me, and asked me to talk to him.

Because I thought Juan sounded genuinely ready to leave the Yakima Valley, and because the situation seemed urgent enough to justify my crossing the journalistic lines, I made a desperate suggestion. If he could think of nowhere to go, I said, I would come up with some places for him to check out, and would cover his travel expenses. If he was too damn American to go to Mexico, I said, let him claim his rightful share of the American open road. First stop, San Francisco, where I had some friends who could show him around. Juan, unafflicted by my ambivalence about muddying the reportorial waters between us, liked the plan. Within a day or two, his parents had bought him an old car, his friend Sammy had agreed to go with him, and the two of them had set off.

Eight hours later, somewhere in Oregon, driving drunk in the rain at night, Juan lost control of the car, rolled it, and totaled it. Both he and Sammy escaped serious injury as well as arrest. Even more impressive to me, they didn't turn around and go home, but pushed on to San Francisco by bus.

My view of Juan and Sammy's adventures in the Bay Area came filtered through a skein of missed appointments and botched rendezvous. I had never quite grasped what a hick Juan was until he started phoning me for advice on the smallest matters urban (and some matters not so urban—his first question was always, "Hey, what time is it?"). Numerous misunderstandings could have been avoided if he (or Sammy) had only known that a hotel desk takes messages for its guests. One friend of mine who managed to find them bought them both watches. He also saw that they were carrying an absurd amount of luggage (one carful), made them edit it down to two bags each, and helped them ship the rest home. The main connection I wanted Juan to make was with a magazine called *YO!* (Youth Outlook), which is published by Pacific News Service but written and edited by young people, some of them former street kids from the barrio. Sandy Close, the PNS executive editor, had suggested that the scene might interest Juan—it had captured the interest, even altered the life-course, of some kids with backgrounds similar to his, she said. Juan and Sammy eventually made it to PNS, and they seemed to like what they saw there, particularly one or two young women. I found that, when they weren't where I expected them to be, I could usually reach them at *YO!*

Juan liked San Francisco, but he said he was ready to check out some other towns, too. I was also ready for him to move on—he and Sammy seemed to be spending money at a furious rate, some of it, I suspected, on overpriced marijuana. I had managed to find Mary Ann, who was living near Houston, and she was eager to see Juan. En route, I suggested, he might like to visit El Paso, where a friend of a friend had offered him and Sammy the use of her basement guest room. So they caught a bus to El Paso. I gathered that they had a good time there as well, give or take a street fight or two. Certainly, after they got bumped from their basement digs by a new set of guests, they were again spending freely—staying, according to my sources, in one of the better hotels in town. I decided it was time for them to resume touring—on what I announced would be their last tranche from me. (There turned out to be one more.)

But Mary Ann now seemed to be getting cold feet. As she explained it to me, she had just acquired a new boyfriend. His name was Frank. He was an ex-gangbanger who still, Mary Ann said, "claimed thirteen." But he was twenty-two years old, had a job as an X-ray technician, and, to hear her tell it, was the soul of maturity. He owned, moreover, a nice pink 1994 pickup truck "with a really good system." Juan and Sammy, meanwhile, were planning to arrive by *bus?* Mary Ann didn't exactly forbid them to come, but her enthusiasm had clearly dimmed. She mentioned that she was living in Pearland—the same Houston exurb, I realized, where Lenard Jackson of San Augustine had bought his fabled house. Mary Ann hated it. It was too white, too snobby, she said. She planned to move soon to Alvin, Texas, ten miles away, where there were more Mexicans.

After Juan and Sammy got the word from Mary Ann that it might not be a cool time to visit, they caught a bus to Fort Worth instead. Juan, it seemed, had family there—including a nineteen-year-old female cousin who was married, he said, to a seventeen-year-old boy who had "faked her out about his age." Juan moved in with them. (Sammy pushed on to Houston, where *he* had family.) Juan found a job doing maintenance in a clothing warehouse for $5.50 an hour. His parents, happy to hear that he was settled and employed, sent him money to buy a car. He got a green 1979 Monte Carlo.

And yet Juan was restless in Fort Worth. "Yeah, they're my blood," he said, when I asked about his Fort Worth relations. "But they're not my type of people. They're too Mexican. For me, Mexico is just a place to visit."

One day, without saying anything to anyone, Juan got up and drove to Houston. He found his way to Alvin. He had not called Mary Ann in advance. Still, she seemed thrilled when he turned up. Frank stormed off in his pink truck. Mary Ann had just secured a job managing a small apartment complex; the job came with an apartment. Juan moved in with her and Victoria. Mary Ann also had a job at a pharmacy. Juan was impressed. "You should see her," he told me. "She's got it *together.* She dresses up like a business lady. When she goes out of here in the morning, she looks *good.*" Juan baby-sat Victoria while Mary Ann worked. Frank did not return. He did, however, disappoint those of us who had previously been impressed with his maturity by sending a young woman over to Mary Ann's apartment to beat her up. "I thought she was my friend, too," Mary Ann explained. "She said she wanted to use the bathroom. So I let her in. Suddenly she started punching me. She got me once in the lip, once in the forehead. But that was all. Nothing too bad."

Each time we talked that summer, Mary Ann proclaimed her delight at being reunited with Juan. It was fate, she declared, destiny, like something you might read in a book. My story about them now had a happy ending, she frequently pointed out. Texas, of course, was not perfect. "It's too racist, too hard," she said. "Washington is more alternative, more laid back." But Juan could not return to the Yakima Valley anytime soon, she knew. The town of Alvin, she now said, was "pretty strange. It's the Home of Nolan Ryan. So everything is Nolan Ryan. He's got a museum here, and a McDonald's, and a bank." Mary Ann liked to drive down to the beach at Galveston, where there were waves and she could eat fresh seafood. Both she and Juan planned to start taking classes at a local community college in the fall.

But Juan had a strange new ambition. Once he got his general-equivalency diploma, he told me, "I wanna be a cop. I hate cops, but I'll be different. I'll be a cool cop, not a fuckup. If somebody's cool with me, I'll respect them. But if they get rough with me, I'll get rough with them. Handcuff 'em, then chain 'em up like a dog, and throw 'em in the back, so we can laugh about it later." Juan laughed softly. "And if I can't get into the police academy, I'll go for prison guard. That would be cool, too."

In the meantime, Juan seemed preoccupied with his parents' disapproval, repeatedly expressed over the phone, he said, of his impulsive flight from Fort Worth. "My mom, especially, thinks I should've stayed," he said. "But I just don't think I have to stay someplace where I'm miserable, just because I got some family there and a job. If I'm not happy, I say, 'Fuck it, move on to a new place.'"

This was something new, I thought. Juan, the American individualist, had long battled with his parents' Mexican-village sense of family ties and obligations, not to mention class solidarity. Now here was Juan the American nomad, nervously claiming his God-given right to hit the highway whenever the mood took him.

The mood, I feared, would probably take him often. He had found Sunnyside, his own hometown, "totally weird," and for good reason. But would any other place ultimately strike him as not weird? Coming to the Yakima Valley, as I had, from the intimate rural universe of San Augustine, the lack of any coherent polis in Sunnyside—let alone of a benevolent despot, a caudillo like Nathan Tindall—had been conspicuous. MTV-raised farmworkers' kids like Juan ended up gazing out into a society that, beyond the most immediate circle of family and friends, looked deeply atomized and alien. Even Terry Jackson, in New Haven, who had enjoyed none of the profound parental support that Juan did, and who was never more than a young-black-male case file to the local authorities—there was certainly no Tindall in the Elm City—had seemed more at home in his world. Terry, too, had finally had to leave home, and he would always face harsh odds as an uneducated black man in the great American economic casino and social wilderness, but he would surely never flee his family for being "too black," or think to reinvent himself as a snowboarder.

Juan did miss Sunnyside. "I think about my friends a lot," he said. "But if I go back I'll just go to jail for fucking somebody up. And I am *not* going back to jail. I called Cuco and told him to come down here. If he likes it, he can stay, get an apartment, bring his girlfriend. I told him, 'We can just live like normal people. Go to bars after work, have a beer, not be always chasing people, or getting chased by the fucking BGLs.' But he says no, he likes Sunnyside. That's because he doesn't know anything *but* little Sunnyside. What a dork."

This, too, was new: Juan the cosmopolitan.

I was surprised, at first, that Rosa and Rafael were not more enthusiastic about Juan's having landed safely in the arms of the bright, ambitious Mary Ann. Then I learned that Mary Ann's happily-ever-after vision of their life together was hers alone. I phoned one day while she was at work and Juan was home baby-sitting. "I don't see myself staying with Mary Ann," Juan said matter-of-factly. "I want to live the guy life for a while. Get a place with Sammy. Make it like long-distance, like thirty-five minutes' drive away. Just come over here when I want. Me and Sammy, we'll be roommates, just make our money. On weekends, fuck it, we do what we want."

BOOK FOUR

The Unwanted

The followers of the established religion intrenched themselves behind a . . . fortification of prodigies; invented new modes of sacrifice, of expiation, and of initiation; attempted to revive the credit of their expiring oracles; and listened with eager credulity to every imposter who flattered their prejudices by a tale of wonders.

—Edward Gibbon,
The Decline and Fall of the Roman Empire

Film companies used to come to the Antelope Valley, in northern Los Angeles County, to shoot high-desert scenes. It was empty country, a good backdrop for Westerns. Now they came when they needed to burn down or blow up a housing tract. For the fiery climax of *Lethal Weapon 3*, Warner Bros. used a development called the Legends, at Avenue J and Thirtieth Street West, in Lancaster. The Legends had become available after its financing failed, leaving forty-eight large, Spanish-style homes (each named after a legendary American—Babe Ruth, Marilyn Monroe) unfinished. Mel Gibson and Danny Glover went on a memorable rampage through the place, which was now a wasteland (tumbleweeds, shopping carts, graffiti-covered sofas) surrounded by a high brown wall. Ten blocks away, at Avenue J and Fortieth Street West, another abandoned tract sat weathering in the desert sun.

The transformation of the Antelope Valley from rural desert to modern suburbia—with neighborhoods, literally, to spare—was very sudden, a historical jump cut. In 1980, the combined population of Lancaster and Palmdale, the valley's two main cities, was 60,000. By 1994, their combined population was 222,000, an increase of 270 percent. Estimates of the valley's total population by 1996 ranged as high as 400,000. This hyperexpansion was first sparked by housing prices in Los Angeles and its nearer suburbs, which soared during the 1980s, and by white flight from an increasingly Latino and Asian city. The Antelope Valley had been considered too remote for commuters, but the completion of the Antelope Valley Freeway, snaking over the San Gabriel Mountains, helped change that. (There were also major building booms to the east, in Riverside and San Bernardino counties, and to the south, in Orange County.) In the Antelope Valley, one could buy for $200,000 a new house that might cost $400,000 in the San Fernando Valley (forty miles south, population: 1 million plus). What was more, the air was cleaner and the streets were safer. The commute to jobs in the city was at least an hour longer each way, but that was the trade-off. And so the desert brought forth swimming pools and convenience stores beyond number, and wide empty streets as far as the eye could see.

Then, in 1990, the Southern California economy, staggered by cutbacks in the aerospace and defense industries, fell into a deep recession. Los Angeles County alone lost more than half a million jobs, and property values throughout the region collapsed. Few places were hit harder than the Antelope Valley. Housing prices fell by as much as 50 percent, land prices by as much as 90 percent. Abandoned housing tracts began to dot the subdivided desert. Boarded-up shopping centers and bankrupt school districts followed, along with a wave of personal financial disasters so severe that *USA Today* dubbed Palmdale "the foreclosure capital of California."

The special ferocity of the local recession was fueled in part by the valley's unusually direct dependence on aerospace and the military. Even when the area was lightly populated, in the fifties and sixties, its major employers were Edwards Air Force Base, NASA, and a few large defense contractors. The new-minted bedroom communities of Lancaster and Palmdale thus remained in some measure military-industrial company towns—at a time when both parts of this dual identity were coming under crushing economic pressure.

And yet the Antelope Valley's population continued to grow. Between 1990 and 1994, Palmdale was the second-fastest-growing city in the United States, Lancaster the sixth-fastest. As a rule, the valley's newest residents were poorer and darker than their predecessors, lived in more crowded lodgings—new home construction having essentially stopped—and were more likely to rent. Still, the valley remained, in a county where whites were a minority, overwhelmingly white (68 percent), home-owning, and dominated politically by conservative Republicans of the pro-growth, anti-tax stripe. (Latinos, who will soon be the county majority, accounted for just 21 percent of the valley's population, African Americans for 7 percent.) And the reasons most people gave for moving out from the city—less crime, less congestion, less smog, cheaper housing—had not changed. The valley remained particularly attractive to families with children. Indeed, the *Sacramento Bee* called it "the last great breeding ground of Southern California."

This was not a cheerful thought, for the valley's supersonic growth had led to overcrowded, often chaotic schools, which were prone, especially at the secondary level, to lose track of students. According to the high school district's superintendent, nearly 45 percent of the entering students did not finish with their class. The valley's teen pregnancy rate was also startlingly high. As in New Haven and the Yakima Valley, and many other American communities, rising juvenile crime was a major problem, and its root was usually identified in the Antelope Valley as "unsupervised children"—that is, the huge number of kids whose parents could not afford after-school care and often didn't return from their epic commutes until long after dark. A sheriff's department spokesman in Lancaster estimated that fully half of the valley's children were unsupervised after school.

He also said that there were, not coincidentally, more than two hundred youth gangs represented in the valley—though what the police considered a gang, and how they managed to count them (there was, after all, no licensing bureau), were pertinent questions. Local politicians, while they acknowledged that latchkey children were a community problem, tended to say that government had no place providing baby-sitting services, and in any case they couldn't imagine where money might be found, in these tight-budget times, for public after-school programs. With many neighborhoods devoid of adults from early morning to night, it was no mystery why the most popular youth crime in the valley was burglary.

The imploded local economy had changed everything for many of the valley's kids. Less than a generation before, a Palmdale High graduate was virtually assured of a local job "bucking rivets" at Lockheed or Rockwell for $11 an hour, with wages typically rising to $16 an hour within a couple of years. (For skilled aerospace workers, including those without college degrees, salaries were commonly $60,000 to $80,000 a year.) The same graduate now, if he or she could find a job in the valley at all, would most likely be making minimum wage at Taco Bell or in telemarketing. And the job market outside the valley was not much better. Moreover, according to Dr. Martha Wengert, a sociologist at Antelope Valley College, the valley's young people knew that this economic downturn was not cyclical, that the Cold War was over and the aerospace and defense jobs were not coming back. "They are very aware that they're not going to make it the way their folks did."

In truth, this sort of awareness was mostly confined to white kids, since black and Latino kids tended to have a different family history. As it happened, the racial dynamic in the valley, particularly among kids, was strangely dense and explosive. Some of the friction arose, unsurprisingly, when middle-class white families found their ever more affordable neighborhoods filling up with rowdy, impoverished refugees from the inner city. But many of the nonwhite newcomers were middle-class professionals themselves. The Antelope Valley was thus a place where widespread white insecurity and downward mobility intersected with significant black and Latino upward mobility—an intersection that made for an altogether different kind of social friction.

The toxins released by this situation found especially vivid expression among the valley's teenagers—in the widespread desertion of school, in prodigious drinking and drug abuse, in a general mood even more apocalyptic than the American adolescent norm, and, most startling to a visitor, in the popularity of white-supremacist and neo-Nazi skinhead gangs.

The leading illegal drug in the valley, among adults as well as teenagers, was crystal methamphetamine, a dangerous and addictive stimulant whose longtime consumers tend to suffer from violent rages. The drug is often linked to child abuse, and the Antelope Valley in fact had one of the highest child abuse rates in California. A particularly horrific series of violent infant deaths in 1991 and 1992—seven in twelve months—had helped focus public attention, after methamphetamine was tied to six of the seven killings, on drug abuse by parents and guardians. But the popularity of methamphetamine had not waned, nor had the abuse rate declined, and social workers who dealt with troubled families tended to see a spiral of decline that frequently started with unemployment. "This economic downturn is a major stressor on families, a domino-effect stressor that often leads directly to child abuse," said Esther Gillies, the director of the Children's Center, a treatment center for abuse victims in Lancaster. Gary Lippmann, a senior probation officer for the Antelope Valley, told me, "People get downsized and within a year or two they're into the system, doing things they wouldn't normally do. They've walked away from the house and mortgage, they're on food stamps, they start taking it out on the kids."

Of course, most jobless parents do not take out their frustrations on their children, and the classrooms at Antelope Valley College were packed with former aerospace and defense workers gamely pursuing retraining for jobs in new fields. But even those who had managed to keep their jobs through the cutbacks were "upside-down"—that is, they owned houses that were no longer worth as much as their mortgages—if they had bought during the boom, as most homeowners in the valley had. This circumstance left people both acutely vulnerable to a layoff and blocked from leaving the area without suffering financial ruin, creating an air of desperation, I found, even in comfortably middle-class households.

The desperation in poorer neighborhoods, in the trailer parks and low-rent apartment complexes where single-parent families were the norm, public assistance was the main source of income, and youth gangs seemed to multiply daily, was of another order. Indeed, the grim panorama of suburban teen pregnancy, school dropouts, juvenile delinquency, and downward mobility on view in the Antelope Valley was sometimes enough to suggest the formation-in-progress of a new class. Jerry Cohen, a gang prevention officer with the county probation department, worked for many years "down below," as valley residents called the rest of Los Angeles County. He had recently started working in Lancaster. "And out here is really my first experience with a lot of white dysfunction," Cohen told me. The similarities to the country's failing inner cities were unmistakable.

I grew up, a generation ago, in a then–outer suburb of L.A., and when I started spending time with teenagers in the Antelope Valley I figured I had a head start on understanding their world. As it turned out, my youth might as well have been spent in Katmandu for all the clues it gave me in this new realm. There was a street war raging in Lancaster, between a white-supremacist skinhead gang known as the Nazi Low Riders and a rival gang of antiracist skinheads who called themselves Sharps. Although this arcane, semi-doctrinal conflict fascinated me long before it escalated to homicide, no adult could shed any real light on it. I needed guides, native bearers, informants. That was where Mindy Turner came in. Mindy, who was seventeen, knew all the principals in both the Sharps and the Nazi Low Riders. In fact, she was caught in the middle of their strange and deadly struggle herself.

Mindy was having the kind of casually harrowing life that I was starting to regard as common. She was living with her mother, Debbie, her younger brother, Matthew, and an older half-brother, Chris, in a four-bedroom white stucco ranch-style house in Lancaster, the valley's largest town. Debbie, who worked behind the counter at Thrifty Drugs, had bought the house with the settlement she got after her husband, a crane operator, was electrocuted on the job in 1989. Mindy recalled, "They came to get me at school and said, 'Your dad's gone to be with your dog and your grandpa in Heaven.' I've never gotten over it. Whenever I get sad, I start thinking about it and just cry."

Debbie remembered Mindy being deeply troubled by the idea that her dad had never been baptized, and thought that was probably why Mindy later became a Mormon—because she wanted to be baptized herself. Actually, before Mindy became a Mormon, she had wanted to become Jewish. But that had turned out to be too much work. Becoming a Mormon was relatively easy. All this was before Mindy got addicted to crystal methamphetamine and became a Nazi, in the ninth grade.

Mindy and her mother shared blond good looks but otherwise presented sharply different faces to the world. Debbie was hearty, outgoing, an ardent water-skiier with a big, charming laugh. Mindy was pale, fashionably thin, moody, intense. Her manner oscillated with unnerving speed—from jaded worldliness to girlish enthusiasm, from precocious grace to gawkiness, from thuggish cynicism to naked vulnerability. She spoke in fluid bursts, as if she had to express each thought before she changed her mind. Her accent was middle class—standard California white suburban—with a few oddments, such as "Dang!" (to express wonderment), thrown in.

In her mother's day, Mindy's looks might have made her a homecoming queen. But Mindy had stopped going to school in the tenth grade. "I'm not a people person," she told me. "I didn't like all the little gossip circles that went on there."

Mindy was actually chased out of her first high school by another student. "There was this big fat girl who said she was going to kick my butt. I was afraid she was going to squish me, so I transferred." Her grades had been falling, in any event. She had always been a good student, earning B's, but had slipped academically in junior high (as a disturbingly high number of American girls do). In the seventh and eighth grades, she became first a "hesher"—into heavy-metal music and smoking marijuana—and then a "hippie," into reggae and smoking marijuana. She also became sexually active, though without any long-term involvements. "I went through boyfriends really fast." Her lovers were mostly older, some were much older. "I was kind of looking for a father," she told me.

About Mindy's Nazi period, she and Debbie and I seemed to agree, at least at first, on a narrative that put it firmly in the past, casting the whole episode as a nightmare from which they had thankfully awoken.

Spike Lee had helped get her into it, Mindy said. She and a friend, she explained, had gone to see *Malcolm X*. They found they were the only whites in the audience, and a black guy had asked them sarcastically if they were in the right theater. "That's why I hate Spike Lee. Because he's a racist. And that's when I started thinking, if the black kids can wear X caps, and Malcolm is calling us all 'white devils,' what's wrong with being down with white power?"

Her real political inspiration, though, was methamphetamine, also known as crank, crystal, ice, or simply speed. The Nazi Low Riders were one of her speed connections. "They're all tweakers," Mindy told me. Tweakers were speed addicts. "Speed is just so cheap here. And it makes you feel so powerful, so alert. It also makes you really paranoid."

The NLRs' hangout was the Malone household, in a run-down neighborhood in downtown Lancaster. Andrea Malone, a single parent, had three teenage sons, all white-supremacist skinheads, and she worked long hours, giving the kids the run of the house. Mindy, who had grown bored with Mormonism, became a regular there, snorting speed, smoking dope, and becoming fast friends with the NLRs. They called her a "skin bitch," though she refused to shave her head. "My dad always said he loved my long blond hair, so I wouldn't cut it off." She and the other NLR girls—"they called us Property of the NLRs, not members, it's this weird thing"—fought with girls from rival gangs, including Sharps. But Mindy insisted she never took part in random attacks on black people—something the NLRs specialized in. "I just used to sit in the car and watch, while they'd get out and be, like, 'Go back to Africa, nigger,' and beat people up."

At first Debbie had no idea what was going on. "I talked to Mrs. Malone on the phone a few times," she told me. "She seemed really nice. I used to drive Mindy over there, and walk her to the door, even though she'd get all mad. The Malone kids and some of the others used to come over here. I knew they were prejudiced, but as long as they acted civilized they were welcome. When they started talking about how black people were no good, I'd point out the door and they'd apologize. I even took them roller skating. I never thought they'd really influence Mindy. She's so strong-minded. I think it was the drugs."

The NLRs were into tattoos: swastikas, skulls, Iron Crosses, lightning bolts —though lightning bolts were permitted to be worn only by those who had killed a black person. Mindy got a big swastika on one hip. "I wanted to get my dad's initials, but then I decided I wanted that done professionally," she said. "My mom got really mad when she saw it."

Mindy's skinhead friends were also into guns. In early 1995, one of her boyfriends, Jaxon Stines, went with a group of NLRs to the house of another boy whom Mindy had been seeing, and fired several shots through a bedroom window, aiming for the other boy's bed. No one was hurt, but Mindy was picked up by the police for questioning, and Jaxon pleaded guilty to attempted murder.

Debbie was by then deeply alarmed about the company her daughter was keeping.

Soon after that, three NLRs fired six shots into a car carrying four black people, including a baby, outside Antelope Valley High School. Again, no one was seriously injured, but the incident got plenty of local press. Mindy clipped the stories. These were her homeboys, on page one.

Mindy was by that stage a full-tilt tweaker with a daily habit. She had lost a great deal of weight. She rarely slept. Finally, she became so dehydrated that she had to be hospitalized.

While she detoxed, with her mother keeping away her skinhead friends, Mindy seemed to snap out of her gang-girl trance. "I just realized I didn't hate black people," she told me. "Some of the nicest people are black. Also, I'm totally infatuated with Alicia Silverstone, and she's Jewish. I've seen *Clueless* like eleven times. So how could I be a Nazi?"

But the NLRs did not take apostasy lightly. "They started calling my house, saying they were going to kick my ass. They started driving by here, throwing bottles at the house." Two NLR girls, Heather Michaels and Angela Jackson, were particularly incensed. "Angela said she was coming over here to kill me. I was scared, but I told her, 'Fine, come over, whatever.' But she never came. Heather, especially, is really, really mad at me. They all say I'm a race traitor."

As it happened, I had met Heather, who had in fact denounced Mindy, with great vehemence, as "a fuckin' race traitor bitch." This comment had come out of nowhere. I hadn't mentioned Mindy, and did not react when Heather suddenly brought her up and clearly knew somehow that I knew her. Her rage twisted her mouth with frightening force.

Debbie Turner took measures. She had an electronic security system installed around the house. "It got really bad after Jaxon went to jail," she told me. "They started coming by here. I was afraid they were going to shoot at the house. It was very scary. I started calling the cops."

Mindy showed me a letter she had received. It was from Willie Fisher, the leader of the NLRs in Lancaster. He was in prison, but he was scheduled to be paroled soon, and the NLRs were eagerly awaiting his return. He was the oldest, toughest, and smartest of them, Mindy said. His letter, which had been written before Mindy left the gang, was decorated with big, crudely lettered, messianic (and often misspelled) slogans: LIFE and DEATH and RESORRECTION and THE PERFICT HATE . . . N.L.R. SKINHEAD. There was a big swastika drawn across the bottom of the page, and two lightning bolts. "Willie has bolt tattoos," Mindy said quietly. She folded up the paper. "I wrote him a letter telling him I didn't believe in the same stuff anymore, and I liked black people and everything, and if he could accept that we could still be friends. He still hasn't written me back."

Debbie had been paying for a series of painful, expensive laser procedures to remove Mindy's swastika tattoo. The final cost would come to several thousand dollars. And that was essentially how we talked about Mindy's tour with the NLRs during my first visits, in early 1996, to the Turners' house—as a nasty accident whose scars were now being, not without cost, erased. Mindy was even back in school, through an independent-study program.

At the same time, we all knew that things were really more complicated. For one thing, Jaxon had been released, after just six months in jail, and he and Mindy were seeing each other again. "Me and Jaxon have been through so much together," she told me. For example, she said, a few weeks after her seventeenth birthday, she had had an abortion. "I wanted to keep it," Mindy said. "Because I knew that if Jaxon and I ever broke up I would still have some communication with him because we would have a kid together. But then we decided we just weren't mentally ready for it. We fight all the time. Plus I was afraid that if we had a kid and Jaxon stayed friends with those people the kid would be brought up around all that hate."

Jaxon's gang status was actually ambiguous. He still hung out with the NLRs, and they still considered him one of them, but he didn't publicly "claim" NLR. In any event, his association with the NLRs extended no automatic protection to Mindy, who had therefore turned to the antiracist Sharps, her erstwhile enemies, for protection. The Sharps, however, were in no particular hurry to help her—leaving her in an even more vulnerable position. As for my own role in this drama—it may be that Mindy and I each had unspoken (and unfounded) hopes that my company might serve to give some of her ex-comrades pause in their campaign to punish her.

But the idea that the Nazi Low Riders represented the sole, or even the main, threat to Mindy's welfare was really just a dramatic convenience. They were bad news, certainly, but there was very little good news around, and plenty of other, less cartoonish threats to be parried—not just by Mindy but by all her peers and counterparts.

T W O

The future was always a hot commodity in the Antelope Valley. When I was a boy, the area was mostly talked about as the future home of the Palmdale International Airport—a vast facility that would eventually replace dinky little LAX. I pictured supersonic aircraft zipping from Japan to California in a couple of hours, requiring miles and miles of runway to land. By then, greater L.A. would be so big, the Antelope Valley would be somewhere near the middle of town. High-speed monorails would connect every corner of the megalopolis to this Tomorrowland-type hub. It never happened, of course, but road maps of the valley still show, with dotted lines, the outlines of the proposed mega-airport, and plenty of money changed hands over the years as land speculators and the local alfalfa farmers tried to cash in on rumors that the thing might get built after all.

The top-secret military aircraft being developed at Edwards Air Force Base (the test-pilot heaven in *The Right Stuff*) also helped give the valley its futuristic sheen. Michael Singer, a valley native and now a Lancaster city councilman, remembers looking up from a classroom daydream in the early 1960s and seeing an XB-70 Valkyrie, a huge, delta-winged bomber, executing a low, slow fly-by. Another time, from the school yard, he and his classmates saw a B-52 drop an X-15. Kids prided themselves on knowing the names of the planes and the pilots, he said. There were still, in the 1990s, in the words of one valley resident, "lots of spooky planes flying around at night," and the Space Shuttle, which was built in the valley, was still landing at Edwards. And a kind of reflex enthusiasm for the future still seemed to infuse most of the public rhetoric one heard, even in the crashed new-housing market—billboards standing in acres of empty scrub announcing the approach of ANOTHER FINE BEAZER COMMUNITY!

But a sense of backlash against all the development boosterism also pervaded the valley. Much of it was economic—the bitterness of the thousands of financially trapped homeowners. Some of it was environmental—the area had become prone to epic dust storms. But I also got a sense of generational backlash. I never met a teenager, for instance, who seemed to have any real interest or pride in the valley's rich aerospace history, or in the B-2 bombers that Northrop was still building at Plant 42—a facility with more floor space than the Astrodome. Dave Kennedy, an English teacher at Quartz Hill High School, near Lancaster, told me that he had been taking an annual poll of his senior students. For three years running, when asked about their post-graduation goals, more than 90 percent of Kennedy's seniors had proclaimed their first ambition to be getting out of the Antelope Valley.

The constant complaint I heard from kids was actually not about the lack of future opportunity, but about the lack of things to do in the meantime. On weekend nights, those teenagers who had not fled down below all seemed to rattle from parking lot to parking lot, endlessly cruising the same shopping centers and ghost malls—getting stoned, getting drunk, looking for parties, fighting, anything to kill the boredom. One Friday night, I was returning from a ska show in Hollywood with a car full of Sharps. It was late, and most of my passengers were asleep, but as we crossed the mountains, and the vast grid of amber streetlights that covered the floor of the Antelope Valley hove into view, one of the skinheads sighed and said, "Oh, I was hoping they maybe dropped an atom bomb on it while we were away."

Mindy Turner's favorite escape from the valley was going to raves in the city. I asked her about a small poster on the wall in her bedroom, advertising something called THE INSOMNIAC RAVE.

"Oh," she said. "*Oh.* That was so great. It was the first real rave I went to. *Dang.* It was in Hollywood. Raves are like big parties, with all different races dancing. They're not really known to the cops. And there's never any fights. The people like rent a warehouse and they have deejays and everything. You have to phone for directions just before it happens. The Insomniac Rave had an *Alice in Wonderland* theme. A lot of people were in costume. There were big rabbits walking around, queens, guys in tall hats. I took Ecstasy, and I just danced all night. Usually I'm self-conscious when I dance, but not that night. A guy started squirting me with cold water from a squirt gun and"—Mindy threw her head back, giving a convincing demonstration of rapture—"*it felt so good.*"

She sighed. "Jaxon can't stand it that I go to raves," she said. "He says I don't act white. But what is acting white? Me and him have been getting drunk almost every night lately, and I ask him, 'What do you think black people do that's so different from whites? They just sit around getting drunk and listening to music. Drive around in cars. Just like us.'"

I looked forward to hearing Jaxon's counterargument. In the meantime, he and Mindy seemed to fight nonstop. "I don't see why we can't be together and just have different beliefs," she said.

"Beliefs" made up a strikingly large part of Mindy's world. The word some-times referred to racial attitudes, but it just as often encompassed questions of religion, sex, politics, music, history, or personal heroes. Kicking around teenage Lancaster, I sometimes felt like I had fallen in with a thousand little cultural commissars, young suburban ideologues whose darkest pronounce-ment on another kid—a kid deviating from, say, the hardcore punk anarchist line on some band or arcane point of dress—was, inevitably, "He's *confused.*"

Mindy's own beliefs were nothing if not eclectic. Her brave and principled rejection of racism, even her devotion to Alicia Silverstone, did not mean she had embraced enlightened liberalism in all matters. She still had a soft spot, for instance, for Adolf Hitler—she claimed she was the only NLR who had actu-ally read *Mein Kampf*—and her all-time favorite "leader" was still Charles Manson. "My mom thinks I'm sick, but I think he's cute," she told me. "In a weird, gross way, I think he's attractive. He has the real fuck-you blood. He's been in jail for so long but he doesn't let it bother him. He acts as his own lawyer. He talks for himself. I've read some of *Helter Skelter.* I wouldn't, like, buy a poster of him and put it up. My mom wouldn't let me do it if I tried. But I don't think it would fit my room, anyway, with all my nice John Lennon and Beatles stuff."

We were talking in Mindy's room, where the walls were indeed adorned with Beatles posters. Her father, she said, had been a big John Lennon fan. Her own favorite musician at that moment was Tori Amos—a frail-voiced, folk-rock poetess whose music was popular with sensitive, alienated teenage girls. But Mindy also loved Trent Reznor, of Nine Inch Nails, whose best-known lyric was "I wanna fuck you like an animal!" I asked about a framed photograph, set next to her bed, of a shirtless, tattooed young man. The picture had obviously been taken in prison.

"That's Tory," she said. "He's my brother." She meant close friend, not blood relative. "He's twenty-three. He says he's in love with me, but he knows I can't get over Jaxon. He's in for armed robbery. I didn't know him too well before he went to jail, but then we started writing letters. We're going to Florida together after he gets out. He's SFV Peckerwood."

The Peckerwoods were a white gang, known mainly for mindless violence and methamphetamine dealing. (They should also be known for having the worst gang name in America.) They were big in the Antelope Valley but bigger, reportedly, in the San Fernando Valley, or SFV. They were biggest of all in prison. "Tory has his beliefs," Mindy said. "He believes whites are better than blacks, and he'll never eat or smoke after a black person, whatever that means. But he knows I don't think like that, so we don't talk about it. He's got WHITE PRIDE tattooed on the backs of his arms in Olde English."

Now she pointed at another rave poster and said, "This one is happening this Sunday. Probably in Hollywood. You should come. Me and my friend

Stephanie and her boyfriend Mike are going." I said I would be glad to go along, my heart sinking at the thought of an entire night in a warehouse with a bunch of kids on Ecstasy. This rave was to be called, inscrutably, the Return of Fuck—No Screw on Monday.

"Maybe Darius can come," Mindy said.

I must have given her a strange look, because she added, hastily, "I just want to see him dance."

Darius was Darius Houston, one of the Sharps to whom Mindy had turned for protection. Darius was half black, half white, and was probably the NLRs' least favorite skinhead. "I don't think Darius really likes me," Mindy said. "Because when I hung out with the boneheads"—this was the generic term for racist skinheads—"I used to call him a nigger. All the Sharps have good reason to hate me. I was stupid."

I knew Darius pretty well by then, so I agreed to ask him to come along to the rave on Sunday. I asked Mindy if she might be hoping to become a Sharp herself.

She said no. "Most people here say, 'Mindy Turner? Oh, you mean Nazi Mindy.' So I don't want to start being Sharp Mindy. I want to be just *Mindy*. If somebody asks me what I am now, I just tell them I'm Free Unity. That's not a gang. It's just what I believe."

"Sharp" stands for Skinheads Against Racial Prejudice. It is not, as I first thought, a local Antelope Valley sect. Skinheads claim Sharp throughout the United States, in Europe, even, reportedly, in Japan. There is no formal organization—just an antiracist ideology, a street-fighting tradition, and a few widely recognized logos, usually worn on jacket patches. Sharp's raison d'être is its evil twin, the better-known white-supremacist and neo-Nazi skinhead movement. Many, if not most, skinheads in this country are actually nonpolitical (and nonracist) and simply resent the disastrous public image that the boneheads give them. Sharps do more than resent it.

"It's all about working-class"—this was the surprising reply I kept getting from the Antelope Valley Sharps when I first asked why they were skinheads. All of them, I found, were amateur social historians, determined to rescue the skinhead movement—or simply skinhead, as they call it—from the international disrepute into which it had fallen. In their version, which seems broadly accurate, the original skinheads emerged in England in the mid-sixties out of other youth cultures, notably the "hard mods" and the Rude Boys, stylish Jamaicans who wore porkpie hats and listened to reggae and ska. Skinheads were clean-cut, working class, nonracist ("two-tone"), and tough. They loathed hippies for reasons of both class and hygiene, loved soccer and beer, fighting and ska, scooters and Fred Perry tennis shirts. They wore extra-shiny boots, extra-wide Levis, and narrow braces. The meticulous, distinctive look they developed has been described as a "caricature of the model worker." For a detailed history of skinhead, the Antelope Valley Sharps all urged on me a book, published in Scotland, called *Spirit of '69: A Skinhead Bible.*

By the seventies, the movement had been hijacked, according to the Sharps, by the anti-immigrant National Front in England. Skinheads had already become notorious for "Paki-bashing," but that was at first less racial, the Sharps insisted, than territorial. In any case, it was the second wave of British skinhead that crossed over to the United States, in the late seventies, as part of the great punk-rock cultural exchange, and by then neo-Nazism and white supremacism were definitely in the mix. Traditional American racist and neo-Nazi groups began to see the political potential in skinhead in the mid-eighties, and a host of unholy alliances were formed between racist skinheads and old-line extremist organizations such as the Aryan Nations, White Aryan Resistance, the Church of the Creator, and the Ku Klux Klan. The Anti-Defamation League, which monitors neo-Nazi skinheads in more than thirty countries, estimated in 1995 that there were only thirty-five hundred active neo-Nazi skinheads in the United States—a figure apparently derived from a narrow definition of its subjects, since there were, from everything I could tell, more white-supremacist gang members than that in California alone. But after a decade of hate crimes and racist violence, white-power skinheads were becoming increasingly familiar figures in the American social landscape, particularly among teenagers, who tended to know much more about them and their rabid views than adults did.

"The boneheads are looking *forward* to a race war."

"They like Bic their heads, and grow out a little goatee so they look like the devil, just to scare other kids."

"They're all on some harsh drug."

"*Somebody's* got to stand up to these guys," Darius Houston said.

Six or seven Sharps were sitting around Jacob Kroeger's mother's house in Lancaster. They were a picturesque lot in their boots and braces, their extra-short ("flooded") jeans, their Andy Capp–type "snap caps." Some sported "suedeheads," others had skulls that gleamed. Most were white kids and, though girls came and went, it was clear that all the main players were boys. They were voluble with me, and easy with each other, even though the mood that evening was rather grim and besieged. This was late 1995, and Darius's girlfriend, Christina Fava, had just been involved in a nasty incident with the Nazi Low Riders. It seemed that a girl from the NLRs had called her a "nigger lover" in a hallway at Antelope Valley High School, where Christina was a junior. A black student named Todd Jordan, who knew and cared nothing about skinheads, had become involved on Christina's side, and the next day half a dozen NLRs had jumped Todd on a deserted athletic field, stabbing him five times with a screwdriver. Todd was now in the hospital. The doctors were saying he would not play basketball—he was on the school team—again. Christina, for her part, was transferring to a new school.

And this wasn't the only violent attack of the preceding weeks. Less than a month before, some two dozen NLRs and their allies had stormed Jacob's house during a party, knocking down the front door, chasing everyone out, breaking windows, smashing holes in the walls. The house was still being repaired, as I could see, and there was some question about whether or not it had been insured against Bonehead Attack.

Somehow, I said, being a Sharp seemed to mean, more than anything else, a lot of fighting with white-power skinheads.

I was wrong, I was assured.

"It's the music, the fashions, the friendships, the whole lifestyle."

"It's like a big fuckin' family."

"Everybody's got everybody else's back."

"It's all about working-class."

This curious, almost un-American class consciousness among the Antelope Valley Sharps turned out, upon examination, to be a very American miscellany. The kids themselves came from a wide range of backgrounds, everything from two-parent middle-class families to drug-addled welfare mothers who dumped them on the streets as adolescents. For some, "working-class" meant, I learned, simply having a job, any job, as opposed to being a "bum." For others, it was synonymous with "blue-collar," and it distinguished them from richer kids who might decide to be skinheads and buy all the gear but who weren't really streetwise and so might just have to be relieved of their new twelve-hole Doc Martens.

Sharp membership was itself in constant flux. Earlier that year, there had been scores of kids in the valley claiming Sharp, but the antics of some of the "fresh cuts" had started causing problems for the inner circle, who were tougher and more deeply committed to skinhead and had to tell the new guys to cool it. There were still dozens of kids "backing it up" when I started visiting—young antiracists who said they were punk rockers or traditional skinheads or unity skins—but only a handful actually claiming Sharp. Hanging out with the Sharps and their allies, I came to see that there was, in fact, much more to their little brotherhood than rumbling with the boneheads. They were a haven, a structure, a style, a sensibility, set against the bleakness, uncertainty, and suffocating racial tension of teenage life in the valley.

For Darius, in particular, Sharp was a godsend. An orphan since his mother died when he was thirteen, he had been a skater and a punk rocker before discovering skinhead. As a half-black kid in a largely white town, being raised by various white relatives—it was his white mother's family that had settled in the Antelope Valley—he had always been something of an outsider. Skinhead, as he understood it, was a complete, ready-made aesthetic and way of life. It was exotic yet comfortable, it fit. He identified with its "blue-collar pride," its underground energy, and its music, and he was soon playing bass in a multiracial ska band called the Leisures. Darius was a stickler for the dress code. Indeed, one of his main complaints about the boneheads seemed to be that they were always doing "cheesy" things like writing slogans in felt pen on their jeans and T-shirts and bomber jackets, instead of getting proper patches. He was planning, he told me, to get a huge tattoo on his back of a crucified skinhead with the caption THE LAST RESORT, which was, among other things, the name of a legendary skinhead music shop in London. Unfortunately, the mere idea of a black skinhead drove neo-Nazi skinheads into a fury, so Darius had been fighting on a regular basis for years. He was a skilled fighter—he once showed me a kick-boxing trophy he had won—but the backup that the other Sharps provided was still, for Darius, a lifesaver. Going to school had become too dangerous, so he was on independent study. After graduating, he said, he planned to join the Navy and become a medical technician. He was eighteen, beefy, soft-spoken, watchful, with skin the color of light mahogany. When we met, he was homeless and had been sleeping on a couch in Jacob's mother's house.

Billy Anderson, another Sharp, was sleeping on the other couch. He was seventeen, pink-skinned, big-boned, round-faced. He came from a chaotic family, plagued by alcoholism and drug abuse. According to both Billy and his older sister, a punk rocker who lived down below, their mother, who had been on public assistance most of her life, was a methamphetamine addict, given to tearing up carpets and tearing out phone wires in search of secret microphones; her current husband was an alcoholic; her previous husband was a tweaker; their favorite aunt died of a heroin overdose; and their father, who lived in a trailer park in Compton, was a pothead. "It's so wack to see your parents all tweaked on drugs," Billy said. "That's why I've never tried any drugs." Drinking and fighting were all right, though, he thought, particularly if you were fighting boneheads, whose crudity and racism gave the name of his beloved skinhead a white-trash taint. Like Darius, Billy was on independent study when we met and was planning to join the Navy. He had been into skinhead since he was fifteen, and he always seemed to be "dressed down"—in immaculate, classic skinhead gear—which was a feat, since he was usually homeless and broke.

Jacob Kroeger still had his hair when we first met, though he was getting ready to become a full-fledged Sharp. Eighteen, sardonic, fair-haired, he was a rare, second-generation Lancaster native. Jacob struck me as a street-fighting liberal (an even rarer breed), so affronted by the boneheads' racism that he was ready to defend his town's good name with his fists. After a clash with the NLRs that left one of them with a gash in his scalp, Jacob told me, "I just hope it knocks some *sense* into his head." His mother was often away with a boyfriend, leaving her house—a modest ranch-style bungalow in a seedy older tract—to become, at least for a while, the Sharps' main hangout.

Christina Fava claimed to be horrified by what Jacob and his younger brother had been allowed to do to the room they shared—they had totally covered the walls with graffiti, much of it obscene, including some vivid pornographic tableaux—but she didn't let it stop her from coming around daily in her parents' late-model, black-and-silver, 4 × 4 sport-utility vehicle. Her romance with Darius was unpopular at home, she said, so much of her hanging out was semi-clandestine. Christina was slim but not fragile, and when I met her she had just trimmed her blond hair into a "fringe," which is the standard skin girl haircut and made her look reasonably tough. She was the only non-racist in her family, she said. In fact, she had an uncle who had been in prison and joined the Aryan Brotherhood, a widely feared white prison gang. Christina doubted that Darius would really join the Navy. "He just says it so that all his friends will say, 'No, don't go!'" she said, not unkindly. "He always does that. 'I'm ugly.' 'No!' 'I'm moving.' 'No!' He can't leave his friends."

Justin Molnar was another regular at Jacob's. He played keyboards for the Leisures, and claimed traditional skinhead, though he had gone through many phases, including grunge, punk, glam, and Gothic rock, before finding what he called "my niche." Justin, who was twenty, lived with his parents in a swank tract west of Lancaster, and was close to his family—he even bowled in a league with his parents and sister. Short and almost comically intense, he was studying engineering at Antelope Valley College. Though he told me he backed up Sharp, he was clearly less enthusiastic about fighting than some of the others, causing them to question privately just how down for the cause he was.

Johnny Suttle was also taking classes at the college, but nobody questioned how down he was. He was twenty, half Mexican, half Anglo, diminutive but super-aggressive. He worked graveyard shifts at a Taco Bell, and had a great deal to say about skinhead. On the patriotism question, for instance, he was one of those who said the Paki-bashing by the founding skinheads had been justified, because the victims were buying neighborhood pubs and kicking out the local boys. Skinhead was about loyalty—to your class, hometown, soccer team, *and* nationality, according to Johnny. Thus, if a Japanese or a Chinese skinhead decided to beat up a foreigner, it was okay, "because they're just defending their country, and that's good," he said. "The thing is, America is not a white man's country, never mind what the boneheads say. It's a melting pot. And we're about defending that."

Johnny always seemed ready to weigh the moral dimensions of violence. His girlfriend, Karen, had immigrated from Khomeini's Iran with her parents, and she had told him about the revolutionary regime's practice of hanging thieves from the lampposts. Johnny couldn't argue with it. "I'm sure people started thinking twice before they boosted anybody else's shit!" (Karen's parents were cool, he said. "They're racist about blacks, but that's just because they can't understand why some of them are kind of loud and obnoxious. And they totally hate Armenians, but that's just an Iran thing.") I once heard him deliberate one of the timeless questions: Was it ethically permissible to drop bonehead chicks before taking on the boneheads? The answer, ultimately, was yes. While it was not right to hit females, bonehead chicks were simply too dangerous to leave standing while you fought their boyfriends. They would probably stick a knife in your back. Ergo, they had to be dropped at the outset. Q.E.D.

Jacob's mother, Sheryl, an attractive, weary-looking woman in her thirties, was dubious about the Sharps. At one time, she had admired them for standing up to the racist bullies in the community, she said. "But then I got my house smashed up. I've got three kids, including a ten-year-old daughter, and I don't want anything worse to happen. I just wish the whole stupid thing would go away."

"**W**e believe in Hitler's ways," Tim Malone, of the Nazi Low Riders, explained. "But that don't mean we worship him. He was smart, but he was a homosexual. I think what he did with the Jews was right, mainly. They was coming into Germany, buying up the businesses, treating the Germans like slaves. I think he killed *more* than six million. That was just all they could find."

Chris Runge, another NLR, told me that Hitler had actually been working for the Vatican. "That's why the Jews were put in the concentration camps. The Pope went to Hitler and said, 'These people aren't giving in. We'll give you weapons, we'll give you ammunition.'"

It took me some time to get past the NLRs' mistrust of strangers bearing notebooks, but once I did I found them garrulous, even fascinating, expounders of misinformation and sulfurous opinion. Chris Runge seemed to be the theorist of the Lancaster clique. He was nineteen, hairless, blue-eyed, pale-skinned, with an athlete's physique and an odd manner that, at least with me, alternated between an exaggerated serenity and a worried seriousness—an alternation occasionally interrupted by big, goofy smiles. "I'm basically what you call a political Nazi," he said. "A lot of these Nazis out here are unorganized. They're mostly street skins, like Storm Troopers, doing the dirty work. I want to start getting them organized. I'm not down for the government, but I'm interested in military service, because that's really getting inside the political system. I want to know how to use weapons, and get inside the government, so I can help bring it down and start my own. You saw what happened in North Carolina? We're already in there."

Chris was referring to the discovery, in late 1995, of a group of violent white-supremacist paratroopers at Fort Bragg.

"People don't really understand what Nazism is about," he went on. "They think it's all just Adolf Hitler. But Nazism is about a society with no upper class, no lower class. We'd have equality. We wouldn't have homelessness—because we keep the factories going and everybody has a place. It's like a machine, a robot. Democracy doesn't work. As you can see right now, it's falling apart. With a Nazi government, we'd just take out all the unwanted and start over again—even whites, if they're doing the same thing as the niggers are. . . . I'm here for the future. I'm for a lot of restrictions. You can't let too much freedom in." Chris gave me one of his big, blue-eyed smiles.

He grew serious again. "White supremacism just comes from growing up and seeing what's happening in society," he said. "We're going down. I mean, what's up with all this United Negro College Fund? Why is there no United White College Fund? We're just all sitting out here on the corner while they're getting all the scholarships." He frowned. "I haven't seen any of them yet show me they really deserve to be in this society. They deserve to be taken out—any way possible."

Chris was trying to change his own ways, he said. "Before, I was just like a street thug. 'Fuck you, nigger!' I see 'em in an alley, say, 'Hey, you're in the wrong neighborhood,' and beat 'em down. But our superiority is a superiority of the *mind.* You can't kill 'em all. You gotta be smarter. Whites are more civilized, so you should act more civilized—present yourself in a good manner, so people respect you."

Chris credited a recent eight-month stint in jail for his new insight. He had been convicted for participating in the same drive-by shooting that sent Jaxon Stines, who was his best friend, to jail. And he had "found the Lord" in his cell, he said, an experience that seemed to be the source of his beatific grins. It may have also softened some of his judgments. Of Mindy, for instance, Chris merely said, "She's confused. She's young." This was notably gentler than the pronouncements of other NLRs on the subject. Chris even showed some self-awareness when he talked about his life. He told me that his mother's ex-husband used to beat her so badly when he was drunk that she would come lie in bed with Chris in the hope that it would make him stop. It didn't. "And that's a lot of the hate I got inside me now," Chris said quietly.

Chris's mother was, by all accounts, a serious tweaker. (His grandfather was an executive with the Xerox Corporation, Chris said—a point of reference, perhaps, for his bitter assessment, "We're going down.") She and he had moved to the Antelope Valley when he was thirteen. He had dropped out of school in the ninth grade, and had largely been on his own since. For a while, he was a Deadhead, following the band around California, and he had lived for a patch in Oakland. When we met, he was working at a Burger King and living with the Malones.

The Malones' house was still the NLR hangout. Though I stopped by many times, day and night, I never saw Mrs. Malone there. She worked in a plastics factory in Pasadena, more than an hour's drive away, and, according to Tim, she left the house at dawn and got home only late in the evening. When I first met Tim, who was seventeen, he had just spent two months in jail; he had been locked up as a suspect in the Todd Jordan stabbing, but had been released for lack of evidence. He was wiry and well built, with close-cropped dark hair and, tattooed on the back of his neck, an Iron Cross. He described himself as "more of the Gestapo Storm Trooper type than a political Nazi—the type that's ready to go to war over things. There's gonna be a race war around the year 2000."

I asked Tim how he had become a Nazi. He said that his father had been a Hell's Angel, "so it was kind of inherited." His dad drank, did speed, and abused his mother—that was why his parents broke up. The family had lived in a black neighborhood in Montclair, east of Los Angeles, where Tim, at the age of ten, joined a local Crips set for self-protection. He was the middle brother of three, and his joining a black gang did not please his brothers. "Both my brothers was punk rockers, into speed metal, and they used to beat me up, trying to teach me a lesson," he said. "I thank them for it now. I was on the wrong road. You gotta stick with your own race. Now ain't nothing I hate more than a wigger." (This charming term means "white nigger.") The news that Tim was an ex-Crip helped explain why he often sounded like a white thug doing a flawless imitation of a black thug. He even had a set of elaborate hand and arm gestures that I had never before seen a white kid use—the same moves gangsta rappers use in performance.

Tim and his brothers, Jeff and Steve, became skinheads after moving to the Antelope Valley, in 1992, and meeting the local neo-Nazis. They were, however, no longer calling themselves Nazi Low Riders, he said. I was surprised; that was what everyone, including the police and the press, called them. But it seemed that Willie Fisher, the leader of the Lancaster NLRs, had been beaten up when he arrived in prison claiming NLR. "It's a prison gang," Tim explained to me. This had obviously been news to the Lancaster set. "You gotta be in prison to be a member. That's why they jumped Willie, because he never been in prison before. See, NLRs are a clique off of Aryan Brotherhood, and Aryan Brotherhood ain't recruiting no more. Now it's just everybody white in prison. But Willie's been talking to the older homeboys, so now it's cool. But we're under his wing, so if we mess up, the older homeboys will take it out on him. So we gotta jump up and take the blame for any brothers in trouble, jump up if anybody disses NLR, back it up a hundred percent. See, you can be down for NLR but not claim it yet, because you're not eligible."

Stints in juvenile detention—Tim had twice done time for methamphetamine possession—evidently didn't count toward NLR eligibility. "But the real NLRs can always just call on us if they need something taken care of," Tim said. "They just say, 'Hey, brother,' and we take care of it." The once and future NLRs of Lancaster were, in any case, eagerly awaiting, as Mindy said, the release of their leader, Willie. "When he gets out, he might take us all to Idaho," Tim said wistfully. "That's a white-power state."

In the meantime, they were a warm little nest of vipers. "We're all family," Tim said. "Even the little kids. Trouble's son, who's only, like, nine months old, already knows how to Sieg Heil." Tim imitated an infant giving a Nazi salute, and laughed. (Trouble was the street name of Robert Jones, one of the three NLRs, as I shall continue to call them, charged with firing into a parked car full of black people, including a baby, in Lancaster in 1995. Jones was convicted and sentenced to twelve years. One of his companions, Chris Parker, fondly known around the Malones' house as Evil, was the shooter; he got twenty-two years.)

There were certain limits that even Tim acknowledged, though. "Like my little sister, we don't want to get her into it too bad yet," he said. His sister, who was always parked in front of a TV playing video games when I came by the house, was, Tim estimated, approximately ten. (He really had no idea.) "She knows how to salute, and throw up a W"—that's a white-power gang sign, done with crossed fingers—"but one day she got down to it with some black kid at school, called him a nigger, and the school called my mom, and she got mad at us, because she knew where my sister picked it up."

The ranks of the boneheads were swelling, Tim said. Everywhere he went in the Antelope Valley, guys were throwing Nazi salutes at him. "Some of them I don't even know," he said. "We get hooked up that way." Standing in the Malones' front yard, talking with Tim and his friends, I did notice a startling number of passing cars honking in greeting, with white arms often jutting out the windows. The NLRs would respond with quick, stiff-armed salutes and the occasional deep shout, "White power!" Then they would grin. This, I thought, was why the local Sharps called their hometown Klancaster.

"When we first come up here, there was hardly any blacks," Tim told me. "So there wasn't much trouble. But then they started hearing about this place, wanting to come up here, starting stuff, thinking they're hard. So we're just trying to push 'em back."

The NLRs' main enemies, however, were the Sharps. "Most all Sharps are straight pussies," Tim said vehemently. "They're just a bunch of preppy white boys who want to run with the blacks because they're afraid to fight them."

The one Sharp who most infuriated Tim and his friends was, of course, Darius Houston. "There's no such thing as a black skinhead," Tim fumed. "Skinheads are *white*. Everybody knows that. Darius is bullshit."

I asked Tim if he knew where skinhead originated.

"Germany," he said. He wasn't sure when.

I asked if he had ever read anything about skinheads.

"There really ain't no book about skinheads," he said. (There are many.) He had heard about a magazine, though, a neo-Nazi "skinzine" called *Blood and Honor*, published in Long Beach, California. He asked if I could help him find some copies. "They'll hold some concerts out here for us, we heard."

On the whole, the neo-Nazi skinheads I met in the Antelope Valley seemed to have only vague, subpolitical connections to the white-supremacist world beyond their turf—through the methamphetamine trade, through prison gangs and outlaw motorcycle gangs, through racist music (white-power punk bands like Skrewdriver and Rahowa—for "Racial Holy War"—and country-and-western lynch-mob nostalgists like the Coon Hunters). They knew and admired groups like the Ku Klux Klan and White Aryan Resistance but, as far as I could tell, had little or no contact with such organizations.

I did meet one young man at the Malones' who was clearly not from the valley. He said his name was Scott Larson (I doubted that), that he was nineteen (he seemed older), and that he came from Ventura, a town on the coast north of Los Angeles, where he belonged to a gang called the Ventura Avenue Skinhead Dogs. Scott was wound extremely tight; he could not sit still while we talked. He was barechested and prison-yard fit, with a swastika tattooed on his chest and swp (for Supreme White Power) on one shoulder. He told me that all his older male relatives were Klansmen, and that he had just served eight months in jail, "for stabbing a nigger." Before that, he said, "My girlfriend got killed by four niggers. They knew my truck—it had a big swazi on the back—and we were coming home from a movie, just sitting at a light, and they just started capping. They were aiming at me, but they got her, twice. Now all them niggers is six feet under. But I'll be with her soon!"

Scott didn't think too much of the Antelope Valley. "This is all petty here," he said. "But I'm trying to get these guys organized. That's why I'm here."

Scott reckoned the American race war would be with us "in about ten years. And after that it'll be all segregated. Each city will be, like—Lancaster will be white, L.A. will be Mexican, New York and San Francisco will be niggers." In the meantime, he said, "We're against everything about blacks. We're against black gangs, black kids, everything. Fuck niggers!"

There were always kids at the Malones' house, and I noticed a number of them gathered around now, listening to Scott. "We're just like the Nazis," he went on, grinning intently. "We're the Storm Troopers, trying to get everybody *out.*"

Trying to get who out of where? I asked.

"Trying to get all the niggers and Mexicans out of *existence.*"

Among the kids who were usually around the Malones' were some who could not have been more than ten. I wondered if their parents had any notion what kinds of things their children were seeing and hearing there. Not all the older kids were skinheads—one regular, Tom Forney, who was perhaps seventeen, and who always seemed to be fiddling with an electric guitar, had a long red ponytail—and not all the NLR skinheads were willing to talk to me. Tim's older half-brother, Jeff, whose gang name was Demon, was polite to me but kept his distance. Angela Jackson, one of Mindy's tormentors, was often around but elusive. I sometimes heard her mention Mindy—loudly refusing to use a stick of lip balm, say, that she thought Mindy might have touched. She once sat in the kitchen and told me a few things about herself—that she lived with her grandmother, that her father had died of a heroin overdose, that the Antelope Valley had used to be all white people but was now full of "toads"— but mostly she stayed in front of the TV with the Malones' little sister.

Angela, who was seventeen, struck me as intelligent but eerily immature. She was chunky, wore boys' clothes, and, whenever I was around, seemed to be wearing a strange, sweet, dissociated smile. The NLRs called her La La, and Tim Malone told me that even he had to defer to her passion for taking revenge on the defector Mindy. "I'd really just like to work with Mindy, and get her back this way," he said. "But my brothers and sisters think she should be punished, so I keep quiet."

The attractions of the Malones' house as a hangout were not mysterious. The illicit atmosphere was exciting—all the in-your-face racism, the edge of violence, the skinhead outrageousness, the sex-and-drugs-and-rock-and-roll. The house was like a child's idea of a pirate's den: scruffy and run by tattooed brigands. I even got the feeling sometimes that a rough, retrograde, neo-communal sort of social experiment was being conducted. A boy would be opening a can of beans to heat up on the stove. Someone would bellow, "Only bitches cook in this house!" The boy would drop the can, while onlookers guffawed. Angela would tear herself away from the TV and finish opening the can, declaring herself "a skin bitch, a Featherwood." Someone at the window would shout, "Check out this Fender!" And the others would rush to the window to study two young Latinos walking past the house carrying a guitar. The questions in the air were charged and clear: Can they be robbed? Right here and now? In front of this reporter guy from New York? What can we *not* get away with?

Antelope Valley officials tended to say that white-supremacist skinheads were less of a problem than they seemed. Deputy Chris Haymond, head of the sheriff's gang detail in the Antelope Valley, told me that, while there were perhaps a hundred neo-Nazi skinheads in the valley, they were dwarfed in number by the thousands of black and Latino gang members who had moved up from Los Angeles in recent years. Whites accounted for less than 10 percent of the valley's gang membership, Haymond said, and white-power gangs for far less than 10 percent of the gang-related felony crimes. A local anticrime panel, ordered by the county's Commission on Human Relations to report on racist skinhead activity after a series of violent incidents, agreed that the problem was insignificant, and blamed the press for "over-reporting certain events."

Latino and African American activists disputed this view. George Salas, a retired civil engineer and president of a coalition called Latinos for Social Justice, told me story after story of racist harassment and assaults in the valley that had led to arrests not of the perpetrators but of the Latino complainants. "The white racist problem has been growing tremendously here," Salas said. "The police are simply in denial about it." Linda Thompson Taylor, president of the local chapter of the NAACP and a nine-year valley resident, told me, "This has become a frightening community." Pete MacEachern, a juvenile probation officer for the county, said, "I see lots of white-power kids, and the problem has been steadily growing for the last five to seven years." When he first got to the valley, MacEachern said, "I thought the Palmdale Peckerwoods were ornithologists, kids with monocles looking at birds." He knew better now.

The Sharps thought they knew why the police played down the racist skinhead problem—"because the cops are haters themselves." And the NLRs, while quick to complain of police harassment, also loved to tell stories about sympathetic officers. Tim Malone told me, "One deputy who arrested me for speed possession apologized to me later on. He said, 'I'm white-power, too, but there's a time to be racist and a time not to be racist. I need a job to support my family, and if I'm all racial I'll lose my job.'" Chris Runge said, "I've had police officers tell me they believe whites are superior. They say, 'I share your views, so stop running around out here on the street like these other people. I'm white and I'm doing my job: getting the unwanted off the streets.'" These tales may have been fantasies, of course, but the record of both active and passive sympathy for white supremacism in American law enforcement is long, and Southern California has contributed more than its share to this tradition.

Certainly some of the descriptions I heard of local white-power gangs from Antelope Valley officers were odd. One gang expert told me that the Peckerwoods were "kind of hippies revisited: free love and dope." Another sergeant at the sheriff's office told me that Sharps had been responsible for the stabbing of Todd Jordan, and when I asked about the NLRs—six of whom his office was then holding as suspects in the Jordan stabbing—he said, "I would say they have very strong beliefs as far as race is concerned." They also had strong screwdrivers. This sergeant, for what it was worth, more than doubled Deputy Haymond's estimate and said there were two hundred active Peckerwoods in the valley.

Billy Pricer, a former deputy and a preacher at a valley fundamentalist church, ran the only local gang prevention center. His clients were sent to him by the juvenile courts, and roughly half of them, he said, were white. "Our white-power counselees often have involvement with the occult," he told me. "They're the most frightening group we see. Virtually all were abused, sexually and otherwise, as kids, and they hate the world. They talk about 'the power.' They like the ability to intimidate, to control."

Beverley Louw, then the principal of Lancaster High School, reported similar experiences. "The most serious problems I ever have with kids are with white supremacists. I'd take any black gang or Hispanic gang or Asian gang over white supremacists. They appear to have absolutely no conscience. Our strategies for working with gang kids just don't work with white-supremacist kids. They won't be part of a discussion group or counseling. It's almost like a religion. They're reading Nazi stuff. They have more material with which to *pattern* their hostility, their opinions, more references. They're into power. Some are very socialistic. They're not into possessions; they just want to control people's minds."

Whatever the felony crime figures for gangs of different hue, the white-supremacist aroma filled the valley with a special pungency, I found, and not only among kids. Christian Identity—an apocalyptic, racist, and virulently anti-Semitic doctrine that enjoys great sway among far-right militias today—was extensively promulgated in the Antelope Valley by a Klansman named Wesley Swift, who founded a still-influential sect called the Church of Jesus Christ Christian in Lancaster in the late 1940s. Crackpot populism and paranoia were still flourishing locally. At the time I started visiting, a group associated with the Freemen—the racist cult that came under FBI siege in Montana in 1996—was holding bimonthly seminars at the best hotel in Lancaster. The object of the seminars was, essentially, to teach people how to secede financially from the United States, and they were reportedly hugely popular, despite being quite expensive. Larry Grooms, the editor of the *Antelope Valley Press,* told me he thought the same desperation that drove adults to such seminars drove their children into white-power gangs.

The police might have been right—the Bloods and Crips might have been feuding, quietly, somewhere in the valley—but the gang tension you could not miss was between the Sharps and the boneheads. If you went to Brunswick Sands Bowl, a bowling alley on the Sierra Highway in Lancaster, the jacket that caught your eye, worn by a spike-haired teenage punk, was the one with a huge patch on the back snarling NAZI PUNKS FUCK OFF. Watching the boy in the jacket bowl with his friends, your major concern would be whether the boneheads might dare to attack him right there on Family Night. If you went to the only real teen hangout in Lancaster, a coffee shop called Hang 'n Java, which had a pool table, music, and an Internet connection, the tense conference taking place at the counter would be between the owner and a group of Sharps. When I went, I found her throwing them out. She supported them, she maintained, but she could not risk their business, because if the boneheads saw them in there, they'd come back at night and shoot out her windows. "And I can't pay the insurance," she said tightly.

Larry Grooms told me about a white boy who, in 1993, as a sophomore at Antelope Valley High, began hearing from racist skinheads that he had to break off his friendships with black and Latino kids. When he refused, they threatened him. Finally, a death threat was followed by a drive-by shooting that missed. The boy's terrified parents went to the police about the shooting. The police did nothing. The parents reluctantly sent the boy to Texas to stay with an uncle. The boy finished the last two years of high school there, while his parents back in California cried themselves to sleep at night.

I seemed to run across variations of this grim tale wherever I went. Some of them made even less sense. After interviewing one school administrator, I asked in passing about his plans. He said that he was thinking of moving his family out of the Antelope Valley, that he was no longer comfortable there. I asked why, and he told me about a fearsome beating that one of his sons, a high school senior, had recently received as he was leaving a party. The attack had been totally unprovoked, he said. Then the administrator mentioned that his son had been a successful child actor on television, and that his assailants had been white supremacists. The attack suddenly didn't seem so inexplicable. The victim, I thought, had simply been too bright and shiny for the boneheads to let pass. But the part that had most disturbed his father was the police response. His son could identify several of his assailants, but the police were not interested. They didn't even want the names for future reference. I asked for the names. The administrator declined to give them to me. They had decided just to let the incident go. His son was graduating in a few weeks and would then go off to college. I mentioned the names of some of the white-power kids I knew. When I got to Jaxon Stines, the man's face colored. "That's one of them," he said quietly.

Darius said he would gladly go to the Return of Fuck rave with us, and Mindy seemed pleased. I didn't tell her about the angry glare that Christina gave me when she heard me tell Darius that Mindy would be there. Neither did I tell Mindy what Johnny Suttle had said when I asked him about Mindy's plea for protection. He had grimaced unsympathetically and said, "She's an instigator." That was what boys called girls who changed gangs, or went from a boyfriend in one gang to a boyfriend in another, or acted in any way to set boys against one another.

There was some question about whether Mindy herself would be able to go to the rave because her mother had grounded her after finding her passed out, stark naked, on her bed with her head next to a bowl filled with vomit. Too much vodka with Jaxon, Mindy told me. It was now two days later, and still several days before the rave. We were waiting for Jaxon to come over, so that he and I could talk, and Mindy still seemed to be feeling tender.

"I hate light," she said. Her voice was flat and small. "My mom thinks I'm a vampire because I sit in my room with the music on and no lights. I won't even take acid if the sun's out."

Mindy was fond of LSD. "The last time I took it was on my birthday. That was fun. I do it as often as I can. I don't know how many brain cells I have left. I've never taken acid with Jaxon, but I want to."

She also liked cocaine. "Because it makes your mouth numb. I like to be numb. Speed lasts longer, but it makes you paranoid, so you end up doing stupid things."

The stupid things she'd done on speed seemed to be legion.

"Like, once Heather and Angela and I were tweaking, and we saw two girls holding hands, and we were really grossed out. We just said, 'We're going to show them that's not allowed.' We didn't have any weapons, but we really stomped them. One girl had to go to the hospital. I don't even remember her name. I felt bad afterward, but I couldn't undo what had already been done."

Usually, Mindy said, she didn't like fighting. "But one time I walked up to this cheerleader I hated, when I was tweaking with the boneheads, and just hit her in the face. Just because she was so conceited. She tried to grab my hair, so I hit her in the stomach really hard. Then I kneed her in the face while she was falling down. Then I called her 'a trendy cheerleader' and spit on her and walked away. Jaxon saw it. We were both tweaking and drunk. I heard she quit being a cheerleader the next weekend, just because of the fight." Again Mindy said, "I feel bad about it now. But I don't plan to apologize."

Debbie had shown me a photograph of Mindy, age five, in a tiny cheerleader's outfit, adorably imitating the big-girl cheerleaders. Mindy at five already knew all the cheers and routines, Debbie said. The photo had been taken at an afternoon football game somewhere in Canyon Country, the next set of suburbs to the south. That was where the Turners lived, in a tract called Sky Blue, before they moved to the Antelope Valley.

"Hitler did a lot of speed," Mindy said, incongruously. (She was right. Hitler was an extraordinarily heavy tweaker, especially during the last years of his life.)

I mentioned that I had recently read (in *The New York Times*, no less) that "young men use methamphetamine for sexual stimulation." Mindy scoffed. "When Jaxon's tweaking, I could dance naked in front of him with a porno on the TV, and he still wouldn't be interested."

She went outside for a cigarette. Her mother didn't allow smoking in the house. I joined her in the backyard, which had a small swimming pool and a basketball hoop. I asked Mindy when she started smoking.

"Fifth grade. We went to the roller-skating rink, and I saw my friend Mary Helen smoking with some boys. I ran and told her mom and got her in trouble. But I thought she looked *so pretty* smoking that cigarette. Later I went and stole one from my mom's purse. That's how I started."

We could see Matthew, Mindy's thirteen-year-old brother, in the kitchen, plundering the refrigerator. "You know, Matthew's one of the reasons I quit the Nazis," Mindy said, her voice suddenly full of feeling. "He really looks up to me. He's a good athlete, and he's going to be playing basketball and football in high school, and he's going to have to be able to get along with black people. And it won't work if he gets into something disgusting like I did: 'nigger' this and 'nigger' that."

I noticed, not for the first time, a clacking coming from inside Mindy's mouth. I asked about it. She stuck out her tongue. It was pierced with a heavy silver stud. "I've had this for a long time," she said.

She also had a ring through her navel, above which she had her name tattooed in longhand. Her mother absolutely couldn't understand that tattoo. "I mean, your own name? Why?" Debbie asked me. "Is it so that some guy can look down there while you're doing it in case he forgets your name?"

I once asked Mindy what she wanted to be when she grew up.

"Exotic dancer," she said immediately.

I asked what that meant.

Dancing on a runway, slithering around a pole. She wasn't sure what else. She had seen exotic dancing in movies. She had also seen it advertised on a sign near the Los Angeles International Airport. Her mom had told her that her dad used to visit the place by the airport.

Debbie, I felt certain, was unaware of this ambition. She and I had talked about Mindy's future, and she had seemed distressed, even without the prospect of her daughter's becoming a stripper. "She used to want to be a lawyer," Debbie said. "Then she wanted to be a psychologist. Now she wants to be a fashion photographer. That's a long way down."

Debbie also didn't know that Mindy was not going to school. Her independent-study program required her presence only one hour a week (to hand in completed assignments and receive new ones), but she had quietly abandoned it. Mindy's cynicism about school was fierce. "The only reason they care if you ditch is because they get money for each kid that shows up, and if you don't show up they don't get it." Her aversion to school was equally intense. "I'd rather sweep the streets than go to school," she declared.

She had recently quit a part-time job doing telemarketing. "I did it for three months," she said. " 'Hi, my name is Mindy, and I'm calling on behalf of blah blah school, and we're putting together a two-foot-by-four-foot full-color school sports calendar for our spring season. About a thousand calendars are printed.' Et cetera. Unfortunately, the boneheads got the number there, and Heather and Angela started calling me all the time, saying they were going to kick my ass. Also, my supervisor, who was old enough to be my grandfather, started sexually harassing me. Then Jaxon got out of jail, and I quit so I could spend more time with him. They still owe me a hundred bucks. Where is he?"

It looked like Jaxon might not show. I asked what had become of the boy Jaxon had tried to kill in the drive-by.

"James Walters," Mindy said. "He's around. He was on Jerry Springer, because he's white-power, he claims Palmdale Peckerwood, but his sister, Jennifer, was with a black guy named Kevin who got killed by a cop—shot six times, right here in Lancaster. Kevin was really nice. One time I was on acid and having a bad time, and he, like, calmed me down. Jennifer was pregnant by him when he died. The baby's so cute. The show was called 'Stay with Your Own Race.' James yelled at his sister, and at the end of the show they brought out the baby. It was pretty cool."

Jaxon whipped into the driveway in a small, dark car. Mindy jumped up, sat down, jumped up again. Jaxon came into the yard through the chain-link gate, a lean, wary-looking figure in a white T-shirt. He nodded at me, glanced at Mindy.

"We're going camping," he said.

"Can I go?" Mindy asked.

Jaxon didn't reply. He and I went inside and sat at the dining-room table. Mindy followed us in. "Where are you going?" she asked.

"Cottonwood."

"Can I go?"

Again, Jaxon didn't reply. He was a pale, good-looking kid with deep-set eyes and a large, unfortunate, silver ring through his nose. ("I hate it. It makes him look like a bull," Mindy said.) His head was shaved except for a small, wispy patch on top. Mindy watched him miserably while we talked.

He had recently turned eighteen, he said. He and his mother and his older brother had moved to the Antelope Valley in 1990 from the San Fernando Valley. He had been kicked out of school in the ninth grade for fighting and truancy, and since then he had bounced around, living here and there, including a stint with his father, an unsuccessful rock musician who drove a school bus in Northern California. "I've hitchhiked all up and down California," Jaxon told me. "Every place is just as boring as this is." He had a studied jadedness, a cool anger in his eyes that undoubtedly served him well, I thought, in dealing with other boys—and probably brought many girls, not just Mindy, to his feet. With adults, his manner was less likely to charm. He was plainly intelligent. He got his high school diploma by passing an equivalency exam at the age of fifteen. Since getting out of jail, he had been living with his mother and stepfather in Palmdale and working as a repair-line operator for the phone company, where his mother was a computer technician. He planned to go to college at some point, he said, with a slight sneer.

Mindy interrupted, pleading and petulant. "Can I go camping with you?"

Jaxon ignored her. I couldn't. "Have you got sleeping bags?" I asked Jaxon.

"I've only got a mummy bag."

Mindy scurried down the hall in search of camping equipment.

Jaxon's parents divorced when he was three, he said. "My brother was the good little preppy. He never got caught for anything. I was the bad one. They were sending me to shrinks from the fourth grade." He and his family had been living in Reseda, a lower-middle-class section of the San Fernando Valley, when Jaxon, under the influence of an older neighbor, got into skinhead. "I shaved my head when I was, like, nine," he said. "This guy used to take me to hardcore punk shows. He was a Reseda Hood. The Reseda Hoods were racist but not all Nazi and aggressive about it. Some of the bands at those old hardcore, straight-edge shows were, like, Slap Shot, Uniform Choice, No For An Answer. They're hard to find these days. But most of the bands I like have sold out, gone unity. Even the Venice Suicidals, who used to be like a skater, punk-rock-music gang, just whites and Mexicans mainly, now it's all mutts—Cambodians, Samoans." Jaxon sneered.

His version of skinhead was a mix. "It's a music scene, plus being down for who you are, not giving a fuck what other people think. Traditional skinhead is being down for the government, fighting for your country. I'm not into that. This is a good country, but I would never fight for the government. Why should I, when this government has been dicking me around all my life?" Surprisingly, considering that he had been warring with the Sharps for several years as part of the NLR cohort, Jaxon said he esteemed Darius's beliefs. "Darius has the right idea," he told me. "We've talked. In fact, he used to be vegetarian straight-edge. That's no drugs, no drinking, no sex—nothing. Not too many people can follow that." Jaxon was even critical of certain younger NLRs. "Some of those guys don't know what skinhead is about. They're just a bunch of dumb little kids doing dumb shit, and they're going to end up spending their whole lives in prison."

But Jaxon's sympathies were decidedly with the racist side of the skinhead schism. He was familiar with *The Skinhead Bible* but said, "That's more nonracial than where I'm at. I'm not, like, Mr. Nazi—I'm not saying that all non-whites should be executed. And I know some black and Mexican people who are cool. But the majority of them are just welfare-mooching scumballs. I don't want to hear your sob story about how my great-great-grandfather owned your great-great-grandfather." Jaxon's anger became less cool when he began addressing the imaginary object of affirmative action uplift, the fictive mendicant asking him for a handout. And his sneer deepened until it severely distorted his face. "I'm not going to baby you because of your ancestors!"

He shrugged. "Whether I like it or not, I'm racist," he said, more calmly. "My mom doesn't agree with me. She's not prejudiced. But I like to consider myself less ignorant than most racists. They're all preparing for race war, race war. But it's never going to happen. Or, you could say, it's already here." He shrugged. "I'm just proud of what I am. But being proud of being white doesn't mean I'm proud of every piece of white trash out there snorting speed."

I asked him about drugs.

One of the conditions of his parole, Jaxon said, was random drug testing. He gave a small, bitter bark. "The funny thing is, speed probably used to keep me out of trouble. It made me so paranoid. That's why I didn't like doing it with my friends. They'd get spun and they'd be all, like, 'Let's go out with guns and rob people,' and shit, and I'd be all paranoid so I wouldn't want to go." He pursed his lips. "My friends will always be my friends, but I don't have to go along with everything they do."

Mindy reappeared, lugging an armful of gear, including an old, square-bottomed sleeping bag that she displayed proudly. "Where's Cottonwood?" she asked.

Jaxon didn't reply.

. . .

Jaxon was right: his mother didn't agree with him. A political liberal with a degree in anthropology, she lived with her second husband and her two sons in a big, cathedral-ceilinged house in a gated community. "I don't know why Jaxon holds those racial views," she told me. "I keep hoping it's just a teenage rebellion, and he'll grow out of it—that it's not how he *is*." Other parents I visited in the Antelope Valley seemed equally mystified by their kids' passionate "beliefs." Debbie Turner described herself as a "George Carlin for President" liberal, totally unable to comprehend Mindy's enthusiasm for the likes of Manson and Hitler. A local college professor who, dissatisfied with the valley's public schools, had sent his children to one of the few alternatives—a Baptist school with higher academic standards—told me that one of his sons, who didn't like the Baptist school, plunged headlong into Satanism, where he had terrifying visions of killing his own brother. Billy Anderson's stepfather, a hippie carpenter and Vietnam veteran, said that, while he was glad Billy was not a racist, he could not begin to understand what skinhead was about, even in the Sharp version. He had read the lyrics of a song Billy wrote and found them "really scary—profane, sexual, violent. I tell you, this headbanging thing he's into makes rock-and-roll look like a walk in the park."

Schools clearly failed to provide most parents and children with any common cultural ground. Sheldon Epstein, a high school principal in Lancaster, who had a cheerleader daughter, told me, "My wife and I are big-time supporters of our daughter's school. But most of the kids are just not bonded with their schools, so for them that school-spirit piece is missing. It's the parents who have school spirit now, not the kids."

In fact, only some parents had what Epstein meant by school spirit. Among the tens of thousands who worked over the mountains, relatively few had the time or energy to involve themselves in their children's schools (or any other community activity) after their brutal commutes. And then there were all those too consumed by their own troubles even to raise their children. I found, that is, a startling number of kids in the valley being raised not by their parents but by their grandparents, and the prevalence of this arrangement was confirmed by everyone I asked, from social workers to the high school district superintendent. Many explanations were offered, including the exceedingly high child abuse rate. "Mom often has to make a choice, whether to keep the boyfriend who is the molester or keep the child who is the victim," said Caroline Pettway, a county probation officer in Lancaster who worked on child abuse cases. "You'd be surprised how often she chooses the boyfriend, and the child goes to the grandparents."

But the most common explanation by far for this mass displacement of children was methamphetamine addiction among parents, particularly mothers.

Indeed, the quiet devastation revealed by a few weeks of visiting struggling families in the Antelope Valley, where so many peoples' stories were haunted by absent, addicted relatives—ghostly legions, as I came to see them, of tormented white women, either strung out on speed, or sitting in prison, or already dead from an overdose—was starkly reminiscent of the better-known syndrome that had left so many African American grandmothers rearing the children of their crack-addled daughters in the inner cities.

Experts tend to say that methamphetamine is even more destructive than crack. Cocaine is made from a natural substance that human enzymes can break down; methamphetamine is entirely synthetic. It provides, therefore, a much longer high per dose—at the same low unit price as crack. The euphoria that the two drugs produce is similar, and abusers of each suffer from paranoia, depression, hallucinations, and violent rages. But methamphetamine brings on these symptoms faster than crack does. Americans, particularly college students, truck drivers, and assembly line workers, have been taking speed, of course, for generations, usually in pill form, but the methamphetamine of the 1990s is a souped-up new model that can be smoked, injected, or snorted, and it is far more addictive and wasting than its predecessors. It is also, unlike cocaine, domestically produced—it can even be manufactured, dangerously, in stove top labs at home—although, by the mid-1990s, the wholesale trade was becoming dominated by Mexican organizations that either set up their own labs or simply smuggled finished methamphetamine into the country. The Mexicans were slowly replacing the outlaw motorcycle gangs in the West and Southwest who traditionally ran speed labs in rural areas (including remote parts of the Antelope Valley) and controlled distribution.

Meth's popularity, meanwhile, was soaring. Between 1992 and 1994, meth-related deaths rose nationally by 145 percent. In Los Angeles they rose 220 percent. Meth-related hospital admissions rose nearly 2,000 percent between 1986 and 1996, according to the Drug Enforcement Administration. "It's absolutely epidemic," a DEA spokesman said in 1996. Four hundred and nineteen speed labs were busted in California alone in 1994. The drug hadn't yet reached the East Coast in significant volume—even though I heard kids in New Haven dreaming eagerly about "ice" as early as 1990—but it was spreading swiftly across the Midwest. In Polk County, Iowa, which includes Des Moines, 90 percent of those being committed to mental institutions in 1996 reported methamphetamine use. The drug's long-term effects could be, according to some doctors, indistinguishable from paranoid schizophrenia. Horror stories about methamphetamine "rage reaction" abounded. In New Mexico, a tweaker who had also been drinking decapitated his fourteen-year-old son with a hunting knife and hurled the boy's head from a speeding van.

Methamphetamine was popular mainly with white people. In the Antelope Valley, where white families falling into poverty were being hit hardest by speed, those same families also tended to suffer from a range of problems not necessarily related to drug abuse, such as underage pregnancy. Some of these problems were multigenerational. Sheldon Epstein's school offered the valley's only program for pregnant minors. "And I find that the happiest members of the program are the prospective grandmothers, who are usually very young themselves," he told me. Most of these proud young grandmothers were white, he said, as were the many mothers who came in for interviews with their hands and arms covered with tattoos. "It kind of makes it tough to argue against gang affiliation and tattoos."

Again, the violence of gang life and the bizarre economics of the retail drug trade struck me, in the suburban variations I found in the Antelope Valley, as little different from their more publicized counterparts in the inner city—from what I had seen and heard in the ghetto in New Haven. An immature white eighteen-year-old named Christopher, whom I met in a juvenile detention facility in Lancaster, told me that, to become a member of the San Gabriel Valley Peckerwoods, he had been required to "kill a fool." So he had shot a transient under a bridge. "I was high. I didn't feel nothing. The other bros saw it, so I was in the gang." Another boy I met in the same facility—a pale, pimpled seventeen-year-old named Joseph—told me that, at the age of fifteen, he had been "running a trailer park, selling all the dope," at Avenue I and Twenty-Seventh Street East, in Lancaster. "We had, like, three apartments all to our owns," he said. "I'm the head of the Little Antelope Valley Peckerwoods." His mini-empire came crashing down, he said, when his underage girlfriend's parents turned him in to the police for having sex with her. He also got busted for strong-arm robbery of a Sears in Palmdale—a caper he attempted while high on methamphetamine.

I later met Joseph's mother, Glenda, when she happened to come to juvenile court—where I was observing the proceedings—with her fourteen-year-old son, John, who was there to plead guilty to stealing a motorcycle. Glenda was a methamphetamine addict, then on probation and required to take a weekly urine test. Her sons had lived more often with her parents, she said, than with her. She was pregnant when we met, and planning to marry her boyfriend, a laconic Chicano named Richard. Joseph and John were not happy about the marriage. John was in fact so unenthusiastic about having a half-Mexican sibling that he had been threatening to kick his mother in the stomach in the hope of causing a miscarriage. Though he was barely five feet tall, John's arms and hands were already covered with tattoos—the words LOVE and HATE were spelled across his knuckles. Richard, when I visited him at the mobile home he shared with Glenda and John north of Lancaster, took a gentle view of his troubled stepson-to-be. "There's a kid in there," he said. "When his little six-year-old cousin comes over here, and he's playing with his G.I. Joe on the floor,

John gets down there with him and he's right into it. But then, if he sees us watching, he jumps up and he's gotta be all tough."

About the threats to his unborn child, Richard, who was an old gangbanger from the San Fernando Valley, sighed. "He's just real, real jealous of this baby brother that's coming. He keeps saying, 'Every time you buy him something you gotta buy me something—and he ain't just gonna have his own way around here!' I tell him, 'John, this is a *baby.*'"

About the racial tension with his stepsons, Richard was also low-key. "John don't know what he is," he said. "Sometimes he thinks he's white, sometimes brown, sometimes black. I tell him to be proud of what he is, not just try to be the same as whoever he's hanging out with. Last week it was this Mexican heroin addict named Eddie, an older guy, been in the pen. They were slammin' heroin together all week. Glenda said it mellowed John out, but I said there are better ways to mellow him out than heroin. Now he's running around with this black guy named Damien, who's a Crip, so suddenly John's coming in here throwing all these Crip signs at me. I just tell him to cool it."

When I talked to John, he told me that he claimed Pacoima Flats—Richard's old gang. He also told me about jumping a group of Sharps in Lancaster, and about fighting with the NLRs, and about a long-running feud with a gang I hadn't heard of before called the AFKs, which John thought stood for Ass Fucking Kings—either that, or Ass Famous Kings. He hadn't been to school in several years, he said. I noticed that he had a tattoo, on his left arm, of a wizard throwing lightning bolts. "But I didn't kill no niggers to get these," he said sheepishly.

I met another fourteen-year-old in the detention facility, a tiny, fine-boned boy named Dustin, who had a stronger—indeed, an almost exquisite—sense of himself. Dustin's mother had died of a cocaine overdose when he was eight, and his father and his brothers, who lived in Lancaster, were hard-shell white supremacists. "I come from a really racial family," he said. "But I refuse to be like that. I'm not a gangbanger, I'm just a plain person. I describe myself as unique." One of his older brothers was a Nazi skinhead who, along with one of their stepbrothers, was, he said, "so wacked-out on acid. And the acid dealers around here are *really* racial." Dustin had been in foster care—"on placement," as it's said—and was now doing time for burglary. He was scheduled to go back to his father's house soon. "But I told them, my father and my brothers, I'm not going to stick around for a lot of race talk, and if they start it up I'll just go on placement again. There's a nice lady that wants me." Dustin pulled his jail-issue sweatshirt sleeves down over his hands as we talked.

I later met his father. He was a short, sunburned, bulbous man with gray hair down to his shoulders, thick arms covered with tattoos, and a long gray beard that fell halfway to his stomach. His beard was liberally decorated with food when we talked. He was glassy-eyed drunk. He confirmed that he had a skinhead son who was fighting with the Sharps. "They want to be black, and he just don't believe in that," he said, with flammable breath. But he would not let me speak to his son.

I did meet less beleaguered kids in the Antelope Valley, including some who were clearly college-bound. Natalie Blacker, for instance, was the editor of the school newspaper at Quartz Hill High. Natalie was one of Mindy's idols—"I'm totally in love with her" was how Mindy put it—and she was friendly with the Sharps. Natalie was a feminist and had started a consciousness-raising group for girls at her school. (*Her* idol was Naomi Wolf.) She nagged her friends not to let their boyfriends treat them badly—Jaxon's cavalier treatment of Mindy was, she told me, a great example of what girls should not put up with—but she cheerfully acknowledged the depth and staying power of the sexism and racism she opposed. She was totally shocked, she told me, when Mindy fell in with the boneheads, and delighted when she renounced them. "But you really have to be strong to do that, to stay neutral here. This is a place where every-body feels the need to be in a clique."

In truth, I met few teenagers in the valley who seemed able to see much be-yond the immediate world of their peers. Martha Wengert, the sociologist at Antelope Valley College, told me, "Kids here have very little to identify with. Their families have moved around a lot. This area has grown so fast that neighborhoods are not yet communities. Kids are left with this intense longing for identification."

An ambitious effort to get teenagers to channel that longing into school was under way at Lancaster High, a fiber-optic-laden facility that opened in the fall of 1995 and accepted only ninth graders, intending to build school spirit from the bottom, year by year. Lancaster High students wore uniforms. Teachers were encouraged to wear red, white, and blue. The curriculum was demanding and old-fashioned—"fifties-style," according to Beverley Louw, the school's dy-namic first principal. "Our hope is that *we* can create the culture, and that way not lose our students to the kinds of fragmented subcultures—the heshers, the skinheads, and so on—that you find kids joining elsewhere."

Ms. Louw, a popular, empathetic educator, had been in Antelope Valley schools, at various posts, for ten years, but after six months at the helm of Lan-caster High, she already sounded pessimistic. She had too many students she couldn't help, she said, kids who arrived at school with too many deficits. Be-sides that, the Sharps and the neo-Nazis were already fighting at her school, and outright racial clashes were also starting to occur. I heard kids complain that the uniforms they wore were dangerous because they concealed the alle-giances of potentially dangerous schoolmates. I heard others talk about the thrill of "day parties," when a hundred or more kids cut school together to get drunk at the house of somebody whose parents were away. How could the classroom compete with such excitements? "Parties are the core of existence," one valley teacher told me. "School is a sideshow."

Ms. Louw, who grew up in South Africa, said, "Everything is in such flux here, which unsettles kids. The *homelessness* among kids is just enormous. I've never seen anything like it. It's invisible to outsiders because they don't live on the streets, but they move from place to place, living with friends or relatives or whatever. And lack of supervision is the key, I think, to most of their problems. It doesn't help that we're on the edge of Los Angeles, because this is a place without a core and *it* is a place without a core. I see L.A. as just this group of people waiting for a producer to walk by and discover them, or waiting to see somebody famous, and here in the Antelope Valley we're on the edge of *that*. No wonder kids don't know what to do with themselves. No wonder so many of them worship Charles Manson. They idolize him because he had a commune out here somewhere, and they think of him as being from the Antelope Valley. He makes more sense to them, I suppose, than a lot of other things. I had a straight-A student commit suicide when I was principal of the continuation school. The kids said she did it on a dare. Her father came to the funeral in a yellow leather suit. I couldn't believe it. A *yellow leather suit.*"

FIVE

The group that was supposed to go to the Return of Fuck rave grew and shrank and then grew again. Then Darius dropped out. He told me that Christina didn't want him to go, that she didn't trust Mindy. Mindy was disappointed. "I just wanted to show him that there are places where people don't fight," she said. I wondered if Darius knew that one of the ways that rave promoters reportedly kept fights to a minimum was by not letting in anyone who looked even remotely capable of violence—a door policy that just might have excluded a big, tough-looking black kid in traditional skinhead regalia. Mindy was got up for the evening in a tartan miniskirt, knee-high white boots, and white tights. Her friends Mike and Stephanie were more casually dressed.

As it happened, we never got out of Lancaster. Jaxon intercepted our little convoy as we were leaving town and shouted something from his car that persuaded Mindy that we should return to her house. There, she and Jaxon got into a long screaming match on the patio. The neighbors were treated to many versions of his belief that she was on her way to Hollywood to "fuck niggers," to a host of other baroque grievances, and to her pleas, shouts, and, eventually, convulsive sobbing. Stephanie, Mike, Mindy's older half-brother, Chris, and I each tried to intervene, without success. Mindy became inconsolable and renounced her desire to go to the rave. Jaxon, in a nice turnabout, urged her to go, complaining that she was too dependent on him. This went on for hours. Once I saw that the outing was shot, I made an appointment with Stephanie and left, annoyed but also relieved to have avoided the goddamn rave.

"Mindy's a needy person," Stephanie said, when we met. "She's sensitive, but she doesn't really think about her future. She's just looking for someone to take care of her. Not that you'd know it by the boyfriends she chooses!" Stephanie laughed. "She's really generous—she comes over and helps me with my homework. I don't know why she can't do her own. She was a good student before she started hanging out with the boneheads. But I was so happy when she finally blew them off. She was too stressed out from that scene. She got so sick. I saw her in the hospital. She just, like, blended into the bed!"

Stephanie had had her own bouts with methamphetamine, but she also seemed to have cleaned up. She was seventeen, half Jewish, half Guamanian, and lived with her father, an electrician, in a small apartment in Quartz Hill. She and Mindy had been friends since junior high. Somehow their friendship had survived Mindy's time with the NLRs. (Mindy said she refused to join in the gang's ritual denunciations of Jews out of loyalty to Stephanie.) Stephanie planned to go to college, she told me, and become a lawyer like her uncle, who lived in Orange County. In the meantime, she was a jovial, rather worldly girl with a sleepy smile and a doughty, adenoidal laugh.

As consolation for having missed the rave, I told Stephanie and Mindy we could go to dinner wherever they liked. The fanciest place they knew in the Antelope Valley turned out to be a Red Lobster franchise. By the time we got there, some weeks later, Mindy's home situation had changed totally, and then changed again. First, Debbie's boyfriend, Tom, and his teenage son had moved in with the Turners, over Mindy's objections. Tom had been a friend of Mindy's father's, which she said made her mother's romance with him "creepy." Tom was also "trying to act like he's my dad," Mindy said, "and he's not." Tom's son, furthermore, was sexually harassing her, she said, but everybody, even her mother, took his side when she complained. (I once heard the boy sniggeringly order Mindy to "lick my balls" and when she bellowed, "Fuck you!" the parental wrath did indeed fall on her.) And then, suddenly, only a week after moving in, Tom and his son had moved out. "I woke up this morning, and all Tom's furniture was gone!" Mindy actually sounded disappointed.

"*That* was quick!" Stephanie chortled.

We ordered our Maine lobster and Louisiana catfish (in the California desert) while Mindy and Stephanie went over the latest threats against Mindy from the NLRs. They sounded dire, as always. Stephanie sighed. "See, that's how gangs are," she said to me. "Dangerous, hard to get away from. Just tonight, before you came, these gang guys I used to hang out with called. They're MTC—that's Mexicans Taking Charge—and they wanted to take us out tonight. I told them no, and they started talking real rough."

"I told them I only go out with white guys," Mindy said. "Just so they would leave us alone. And this one guy goes, 'That's because white guys have small dicks.' *I'm sure.*"

Mindy and Stephanie looked at each other, then erupted in laughter.

Mindy told us about a dream she had had the night before. "I dreamed me and Alicia Silverstone got married. I don't remember that much about it, but we had a big house in Beverly Hills, and I was really, really happy. Apparently we adopted a kid, because there was a boy playing in the backyard."

"In dreams, marriage means death," Stephanie said. "If you dream about marrying someone, that means they're going to die."

Mindy gave Stephanie a long, alarmed look. Stephanie shrugged, as if to say, "I didn't make up the rules of the world."

The two of them began reminiscing about rock concerts.

"Tell him about Metallica!" Stephanie said.

"The first time I pitted was at a Metallica concert," Mindy told me. "I was tweaking so bad. I'd done like three or four lines on the way there—it was at Cal State Dominguez—and I was really, really dehydrated. So Stephanie and I got down in the pit and we just started *flying* around. Then this *huge* Mexican guy who's all drunk falls over right on top of me, and I'm, like, 'Please, please get off me. I'm dehydrated and I'm going to puke on you.' And he's all, 'Okay, okay.' Then somebody picks me up and throws me in the air, and I just start floating, up above the crowd. They carry me up toward the stage, and this is just as Metallica is coming onstage, and this is when I was totally in love with James Hetfield, their lead singer, so I was just *tripping.* Then they threw me toward the stage, and I landed on these security guys. We all fell down, and they were, like, 'Are you okay?' Then I just fainted. Totally. I was too excited."

Stephanie and I were eating heartily. Mindy was picking. The girls started talking about Stephanie's fiancé, Vince. It was the first I had heard of him.

What about Mike, I asked. He seemed like a nice kid.

"Vince is in jail," Stephanie explained. "And he'll be in for a long time. First he was in for armed robbery, then he tried to escape and a guard got killed."

Stephanie had not known Vince, it seemed, before he was in jail. She had met him through a friend.

"And this is your fiancé?" I said. "You guys are weird."

Mindy and Stephanie looked at each other, smirked, and burst into giggles. I could see how they were such good friends. They shared a dark, useful sense of the absurd.

"I just hope my mom doesn't blame me for Tom leaving," Mindy said suddenly.

"Yeah," Stephanie said. "What's she doing tonight?"

"Probably out getting drunk," Mindy said. "Shit-kicking at some cowboy bar. I love it when she gets drunk. She's so funny. But I hate everything cowboy—especially cowboy boots!"

Stephanie murmured sympathetically. Cowboy stuff sucked.

"I would never, ever, ever wear cowboy boots," Mindy went on fiercely. She paused. "Except maybe if we were all getting together for like a family photo in Western outfits. Then I would."

Stephanie made a small, assenting sound. She understood.

.   .   .

I didn't really think Mindy was weird. No more so, anyway, than anyone else where she found herself growing up. One day we went to the Antelope Valley Mall to get the latest Tori Amos release. We stopped in at a shop called Hot Topic, where Mindy wanted to look for a poster. All the posters on sale seemed to be of dead rock stars: Kurt Cobain, Jim Morrison, Jimi Hendrix, Janis Joplin. I started talking to a young salesman with a pierced eyebrow, many tattoos, and an elaborate haircut. He said the shop was part of a chain specializing in "alternative, music-related fashion." There were rock-band T-shirts, skirts, socks, a line of "Satanic jewelry," a rack of pastel snap caps—"Old men come in and buy those sometimes," the young man laughed—and a book section devoted mainly to palmistry, "magick," and dream interpretation. This was probably where Stephanie came to learn about death and marriage in dreams, I thought. Mindy joined us, and it turned out she and the salesman were buddies. "Show him your Lizard King," she told him. "He's a Jim Morrison freak," she told me. The salesman looked around, saw no reason not to, and pulled up his shirt to reveal a spectacular, multicolored, unfinished tattoo of a kelly green, phantasmagorical lizard on his thin chest. He pulled down his shirt. On his scalp, under a patch of short hair, I could see what looked like a block of writing in Japanese.

"Get any boneheads in here lately?" Mindy asked.

"Always," said the kid. To me he said, "We try not to stock anything the boneheads would buy. So we don't sell, like, red shoelaces. But there's always something they'll come in for, something everybody else wants, too, like bomber jackets, or these narrow red suspenders."

I asked about a rack of Army surplus gas masks.

"Those are good for doing nitrous oxide," the boy said. "Or you can convert them into bongs. Or just use them for rioting!"

He and Mindy laughed.

"They're good for raves, too," Mindy said. "You cover your face with Vick's Vapo-Rub, and your face goes numb, and *dang,* you get really high."

We stopped for lunch at one of the period burger joints in the mall. Mindy mentioned that she had driven to San Diego the night before with Jaxon. "We went by this big Mormon temple down there," she said wonderingly. "I just saw it from the freeway, but it was all lit up, and I felt the Spirit move inside me." She took a tentative bite of her lunch. "So I think I might start going to church again."

She pushed her food away. I urged her to eat.

"I'm too fat," she said. "I did the Cindy Crawford tape this morning for an hour, but I'm never going to get this flab off my thighs if I keep eating."

There was no detectable flab on her thighs. Indeed, I thought she looked too thin, and I said so.

"Oh, you don't know how I can get. I used to be really chunky, and I don't want to end up with a big butt like my mom."

Mindy asked if I had heard about Trent Reznor, of Nine Inch Nails, living in Tex Watson's old house. Tex Watson, I recalled, was a member of Charles Manson's merry tribe. I said it sounded unlikely. Mindy said she believed it, though. "I'd love to go there," she said. "I'd even go so far as to see the murder pictures. I don't know why. I like blood. I like the taste of blood."

Maybe, I said, there was something to her mother's vampire theory after all.

"I've cut Jaxon," Mindy went on. "He didn't mind. I've cut myself. Steve Malone"—Tim Malone's younger brother, known among the NLRs as Li'l Trouble—"cut me with a knife right here." Mindy indicated her upper arm. "And he drank from there. I've tasted Steve's blood. He's got good-tasting blood. And Jaxon's blood is really, really sweet."

Mindy wanted to know what the NLRs were saying about her. Had I met Heather at the Malones' house?

I had met her, I said, though not at the Malones'. I didn't relay any of Heather's curses.

"She could probably kick my ass," Mindy said pensively. "But maybe I could hold my own for a while." She considered the matter, then sniffed, "She just thinks she's the big Aryan Mother. Was she wearing her Slayer T-shirt?"

She was, I said.

Who else had I met?

I mentioned the guy who called himself Scott Larson.

"I know him," Mindy said. "He likes me."

"No, he doesn't," I said. I had seen Scott, out in the Malones' front yard, grabbing his crotch and making lewd suggestions to every female who passed. "He's a sociopath. He may want to sleep with you, but that's different from liking you."

"I know." Mindy sighed. "I'm totally caught in the middle. Darius and those guys don't like me, either. Darius just tolerates me, that's all."

I asked her what it was about guys in jail that she and Stephanie liked so much. (And they were not the only girls I had met in the valley who had prisoner boyfriends or fiancés.)

"I don't know," Mindy said. "It's sick, I guess, but I just find it really attractive. I guess it means they're capable of doing something really spontaneous, without regard for the consequences."

"Like shoot somebody."

"Yeah. They're adventurous. And they're tough, usually. There's nothing else to do in there but work out."

And dream about the girls who write to them, I thought. And, prison segregation being what it is in California, be "down for their race" or risk getting killed. Mindy started telling me about visiting her "brother," Tory, in Tehachapi. Debbie, who wanted to meet this convict who was phoning her daughter, had driven her up there, and Mindy had worn a skirt that she realized only later, she said, became transparent when the light was behind her. She laughed gaily as she described it, and I felt a little sorry for Tory. This was another aspect of the attraction, of course—the incredible power that a Stephanie or a Mindy suddenly had in a relationship when the other party was locked up. It was a romantic omnipotence that they were unlikely to find, certainly, with many guys on the outside.

What about when these inmates were released, I asked.

"Good question," Mindy said. She sounded worried. "Tory gets out in May, and my mom is afraid he only wants me for the money I get when I turn eighteen in December. The money's from the settlement from my dad. I wasn't supposed to tell Tory about it, but I did." She chewed her lip. "Then there's Jaxon." She sighed. "I don't know. Tory got really mad when I told him I wasn't a racist. Plus I told him I was going to paint my car black and white—you know, paint a checkerboard pattern around the bottom, for two-tone. The car's in our garage. It's this little '74 VW bug my dad gave me. I've never driven it because I don't know how to drive a stick. I want to get it pin-striped, too, and inscribed IN MEMORY OF DAD. But Tory said if I get it painted black and white, he won't even ride in it. He hates anything two-tone."

The passions inspired by two-tone—by, that is, the idea of difference, of racial-cultural integration—often have a fundamentalist quality, as if psychic survival itself were at stake. Not everyone gets to choose, however, which side of this philosophical frontier to occupy. Darius Houston had had two-tone thrust upon him, as it were. After the death of his mother, he had gone to live for a while with her husband before last, Richard, who had come to this country from Germany. Some of Richard's relatives had fought for the Nazis, Darius said—the *real* Nazis—"but they were forced into it." Though Darius didn't stay in touch with the black side of his family, he told me that he believed his father "was Mandingo. He had paintings from there and everything. I think his people came over here from Africa on their own." (The other Sharps, having heard this theory, nicknamed Darius "Mandingo.") Darius also believed that his musical ability came from his father, who had been a talented saxophone player. His mission as a skinhead, he once told me over dinner, was "trying to oppose the delusion of racism."

We were sitting in a funky, family-run Salvadoran restaurant in Lancaster. I asked Darius what it felt like to be the target of so much bonehead ire.

He looked embarrassed. "Even white-powers are people, so you have to respect them," he said. He sipped his lemonade, then added, "Unless they don't respect me. Which they don't." He shrugged. "Most skinheads fight. It comes with the book. It comes to you."

I suggested that it came to him more than to most.

He agreed. "But it's cool." Then he admitted, "I can control myself with a lot of people, but some people—white-powers—I can't always control myself with."

Somehow Darius had avoided any serious trouble with the law. I hated to think what would happen to him in prison, though. I once asked a Palmdale skinhead and ex-con named Juan about Sharps in jail. Juan, who was not a Sharp but who, as a traditional skinhead, vigorously backed up Sharp in the valley, snorted. "Ain't no such thing," he said. "There was this Sharp dude in the joint, a big white dude, real buff. He had BAY AREA SKINHEADS tattooed across his back in big red letters, and he had a black girlfriend who wrote to him and sent him a picture of herself. He also had a crucified skinhead on his right arm—that means two-tone, you know. So I thought he was cool, and the other Chicanos thought so, too. But the other white guys didn't know. And then one day he was in the weight room, pressing, and some guy got pissed off at him and started saying he was a nigger lover, and he had a nigger girlfriend. And these Aryan Brothers heard the whole thing, and when he didn't deny it, when he stood his ground, they went after him with a ten-pound barbell. And I mean they beat the *dogshit* out of him. Half killed him. When he finally came back from the infirmary, maybe three weeks later, he was just, like, not the same. He was bowed down, and he was an Aryan Brother after that. There's no such thing as a Sharp in the joint."

Even outside the joint Sharps often struck me as a fragile, if not endangered species. It was partly their hated identification with their enemies, the racists, by the public. One Christmas Eve a group of Sharps, including Darius, Johnny Suttle, Billy Anderson, and Jacob Kroeger, tried to attend a midnight mass in Lancaster. They slipped into a rear pew, perfectly silent and respectful. Then they noticed that the other worshippers were looking over their shoulders in alarm. This was a largely black and Latino congregation, and when they saw skinheads, they saw possible racist attack. The Sharps were asked to leave, and weeks later they were still bummed out about it. "We're pariahs," Jacob said.

As pariahs, the Sharps dearly loved to "clique up," as they called it, or even just to run into one another unexpectedly. Once, while I was on the highway with a bunch of Sharps, a fresh cut named Fred recalled the time he looked over and saw, in the car next to him, a bunch of Sharps. "It was so cool! Just right there on the freeway!" I asked Fred how he knew the other car wasn't boneheads. "Because it was a nice car," he said matter-of-factly. "And I've never heard of a rich bonehead, have you?"

We were traveling at the time in a two-car convoy and, when the other car broke down, we had to cram nine passengers into my rented sedan. Some of the Sharps were beside themselves with excitement. Justin Molnar kept shouting, "We are rolling *so deep!*" He made it sound like we were the Corner Pocket Crips on patrol in the 'hood. In fact, we were going to a ska show at the Whiskey A Go Go, the venerable club on Sunset Boulevard.

That was a curious evening. Only the headliners, a band called Hepcat, met with the complete approval of the Antelope Valley Sharps. The other acts had all "sold out," it seemed, in various ways—they played their ska too fast, or mixed in some Satanism, or some punk. (I liked all the bands, particularly an aggro punk group from Michigan called Mustard Plug, who wore sneakers and black-and-mustard bellhop uniforms with the trousers cut off at the knees. Their lead singer kept barking existential refrains like, "You live in a box, you die in a box," and, "When I grow up, I wanna be . . . *white trash.*") Hepcat's two black front men, only one of whom appeared to be West Indian, were old pros who mugged for each other and could just as easily have been doing James Brown. (Indeed, when they got bored, they did expert little James Brown and even Sinatra riffs.) They openly disdained the crowd, which consisted mostly of young white skinheads, and they sternly ordered them "not to be throwing no gang signs at *us.*" Johnny Suttle was also disgusted by all the action down in the mosh pit. "You're not *supposed* to pit to this music," he told me angrily. "All these hippies and punks think they can just shave their heads and throw themselves around at a ska show like they own the place, like they're real skins. They're not. They can't."

After the show, in the parking lot behind the club, Johnny stunned me by suddenly throwing open the door of my car and scrabbling frantically under the front seat, shouting, "Where's my blade?" Before I could ask what he thought he was doing, he came up with an evil-looking throwing knife and was gone. It seemed that someone had spotted a group of boneheads, and dozens of skins from the ska show crowd were now off in hot pursuit. As things turned out, they didn't catch them, but Johnny and the others returned grimly exhilarated from the chase. I was unhappy about the knife, and said so. Nobody seemed overly impressed. I was also appalled that the Sharps were so quick to decide that perfect strangers were mortal enemies. How did they even know their prey were boneheads? Boneheads, after all, hate ska, and rarely come to Hollywood. They just knew, they said. You could tell.

You really could tell, I found, at another show I attended with the Sharps. It was an oi show in San Bernardino. Oi music, which gets its name from a Cockney greeting, is a hard form of punk rock, and it appeals to the whole range of skinheads. The headliners at the San Bernardino show were a cult band from Britain called the Business, who had been around so long that they even appeared in *The Skinhead Bible.* The Antelope Valley Sharps were deeply thrilled to be seeing them, and before the show I took snapshots with Johnny's camera of each of them standing next to bored-looking members of the band. Darius,

Jacob, Juan, Johnny, and four or five others had made the long trip over the mountains in a heavy rain. San Bernardino is an old, hard-used city east of Los Angeles. On a recent listing of 207 American cities ranked as places for bringing up children, San Bernardino came in number 207. The oi show was held in an old wrestling arena near the railroad tracks.

There were several hundred skinheads inside, most of them white but many of them Latino or Asian. Cliques milled around, exchanging elaborate tribal greetings with other cliques and taking snapshots together. All was mellow, all was unity, I was assured. No boneheads had come. A couple of punk bands played, and there was some moderate thrashing in the pit, which was a big, brightly lit, cement-floored space in front of the stage. I retreated to one of the wooden bleachers that rose on three sides of the arena. And that's where I was, looking down on the crowd, when the Orange County Skins arrived. They were in uniform and in formation. Their uniform consisted of black combat boots, white trousers, and the white tank tops known as "wife beaters." Their formation was a sort of flying wedge, which knocked people aside with swift, efficient violence as they swept toward the middle of the pit. There were no more than thirty of them, but they were all big, muscular white guys and their paramilitary coordination overwhelmed each bit of startled resistance. They easily seized the center of the arena, under the lights, turned to the stunned crowd, and raised their arms in Nazi salutes, bellowing, "White power! White power!"

There was a lengthy pause, during which everyone seemed to consider the boots of the invaders. Whoever approached them first was certain to get his teeth kicked in. Then the crowd rushed the boneheads, and a bloody mélée began. It seemed to be all boots and fists. Security at the door had been very tight—a guard had even taken away my pens, tartly demonstrating how someone could jab out my eyes with one of them—so the possibilities for injury presumably had some limits. I caught glimpses of Sharps I knew, flailing away—particularly Darius, who is tall and, as a black skin, seemed to be the focus of a great deal of Nazi fury. But Darius stayed on his feet, blessedly, and seemed to have plenty of help as he spun and kicked and punched. There were a couple of distinct rounds of fighting, as the arena's security force struggled to push the combatants apart. The Nazis were badly outnumbered but preternaturally fierce, and each time they seemed to be contained and moving toward the exit they regrouped and attacked in another direction.

Then I saw Darius running toward the rear bleachers, where I was perched. He was holding one eye—pawing at it frantically—and zigzagging blindly through the crowd. I had a horrible premonition that he had been stabbed in the eye. I ran down the bleachers to meet him, and tripped and twisted my ankle. A security guard had to help us both stagger out through a back door into the rain. Darius, still pawing at his eye, threw himself face first into a puddle. He splashed water into his eye. "Somebody Maced me!" he shouted. I felt a rush of relief. Darius rose up, blinking, gasping. "It's okay," he said. "It's okay. I can see." The door behind us flew open, and another casualty came reeling out. Darius sprang to the door, caught it, and, without another word, was gone—back into the roaring fray.

SIX

"**W**hat the Orange County Skins did at that oi show?" Mindy said. Her tone was petulant, scornful. We were sitting in her room. "These boneheads out here could never think of that. They're just into speed. The original Nazis did no drugs, didn't smoke pot, drink beer, anything. They just trained for war, twenty-four/seven. These guys out here have no right to call themselves Nazis. That's why I don't like them."

This, I thought, was different. Mindy had previously disliked the NLRs for a lot of reasons, but not because they failed to emulate Hitler's men properly. And, for the record, many of Hitler's elite troops were in fact tweakers (though not in the führer's league when it came to dosage). But Mindy was upset, so I didn't argue. It seemed she had been jilted by Jaxon for a younger girl named Casey.

"Okay, I'm not fifteen and six feet tall with two pierced nipples!" she wailed. Casey was apparently all these things. "Okay, I'm immature and selfish! He's right. I am. I was spoiled when I was young. But he is so selfish, so conceited, so immature, so arrogant!"

I still didn't argue.

"Plus, he won't give me my baby blanket back. My dad gave it to me. It's my security blanket. I'm all 'Give me my blanket.' He's all 'Give me my CD.'"

Mindy's pager beeped. She pulled it off her belt and read the number it displayed. Calling her pager's number yielded a message with her voice talking very rapidly over a hard-driving punk tune: "Leave me a message and tell me why you want me and if it's good enough I'll call you back."

"I would have gone to jail for Jaxon," she went on bitterly. "For that drive-by. They didn't have anything on me. I had an alibi. But I would have gone. But Jaxon didn't want me to go. That's why he confessed."

Mindy fell silent, studying a pair of boots sitting in a corner. "Look at those things," she said. Someone had scrawled "23" on one heel and "16" on the

other. "Twenty-three is for W, sixteen is for P," Mindy said. "White Pride. I ruined a good pair of boots. Everybody knows what that means. I can't wear
them out."

The phone rang. Mindy answered it. She listened for a while, grunted. After
she hung up, she said, "That was Zack. He's in Alabama. He's my best friend. I
have a lot of best friends. He's a speed freak. He *loves* speed. He's in college."

The phone rang again. Mindy listened for a minute, then hung up, smiling.
"That was Rocky. He's been up all night, slamming speed, probably."

I had met Rocky. He and Jaxon played together in a two-man punk band
they called Wallpaper. These monologic calls from tweakers seemed to be
cheering up Mindy.

We drifted out to the living room and found Debbie just coming in from
work. "You tell him about how you're going back to school or I'm going to
send you to live with Grandma?" Debbie asked.

Debbie had discovered that Mindy was skipping her independent-study appointments, and had grounded her. Mindy carried off the groceries that Debbie had brought home. "My mother still lives in Canyon Country," Debbie told
me. "It's better for kids, I think. Mindy would probably never have got into all
this bad stuff there."

"The Antelope Valley sucks!" Mindy called from the kitchen.

Debbie seemed to have recovered from the Tom fiasco. She had played for me,
a few days before, an angry, funny country tune, by the Forester Sisters, called
"Men!" It was from a collection called *Great Divorce Songs for Her.* She had made
some lousy romantic choices since her husband died, she said. Her first
boyfriend had turned out to be a cocaine freebaser who resented her kids and
was after her settlement money. At least she got rid of him. Actually, she said,
she and Tom were talking again. It sounded to me like they might reconcile.

Debbie noticed me admiring an upright piano with hand-carved panels. "I
think it's from Nebraska," she said. "I think my mother's family brought it
when they first came West, way back when."

I asked if she or Mindy played.

Debbie guffawed. " 'Heart and Soul,' " she said.

I asked for a recital.

"Mindy!"

Mindy trudged in from the kitchen. Mother and daughter sat down at the
carved piano. They began to play "Heart and Soul," which I have always loved.
But Mindy kept playing her part too fast for Debbie to keep up. She seemed to
be doing it just to annoy us both.

Mindy and I drove down to Canyon Country one night. The area is a large,
shapeless carpet of suburbs and shopping centers thrown onto rough, dry

mountains. The billboards greeting commuters driving through from the Antelope Valley urged them to consider relocating: SLEEP AN EXTRA HOUR! Mindy's grandparents, Pearl and Jerry Chandler, lived in an upscale mobile-home park near the freeway. Only Pearl was home when we showed up.

The carved piano was not, she said, from Nebraska. But she was. Pearl and I sat in her spotless living room—her trailer was a triple-wide and felt as big as any middle-class house—while Mindy darted in and out, alternately listening to us and playing on a computer in Jerry's office. When Pearl said that she and her parents were living in Compton in the early forties, Mindy's eyes went wide. Compton? The famous ghetto 'hood of Ice-T and Niggaz Wit' Attitude? "At the end of the street was a dairy," Pearl said.

"It's probably a KFC now," Mindy said.

"No, I believe it's a minority neighborhood," Pearl said.

Pearl was decorous, candid, very grandmotherly. She had been a bookkeeper. Now she did fancy cake decorating. She had four children, many grandchildren and step-grandchildren, and she had been married to Jerry, who was her third husband, for twenty-one years. Jerry was a senior orthopedic technician at a hospital in the San Fernando Valley. Every Christmas, Pearl said, she and Jerry put on a big Christmas party, with a Santa Claus and presents for their grandchildren and the neighborhood kids. Sometimes a hundred people attended.

"And every year I tell myself I'm not going to sit on this guy's lap," Mindy said, referring to Santa. "And every year I end up sitting on his lap."

Mindy bounded back to the computer. She seemed, in her grandmother's house, suddenly about ten years younger, as if she had magically regressed to a calmer, more constrained, less sexualized, less bored self.

"Debbie was a good kid," Pearl said. "She was athletic. Insisted on competing with the boys, and this was before women's lib. She wasn't really college material, but after she graduated she always worked hard. And she was always so outgoing. Mindy is just the opposite. She's shy, and never wants to do anything on her own. I've always kind of hoped she would be a writer. She has written some of the prettiest poems. She has the ability to go to college, if she only puts her mind to it. But now I'll be happy if she just goes back to school and graduates."

Mindy brought us a printout to admire—a banner she had made reading THE BEATLES.

"We've wanted her to come live with us," Pearl said. Mindy gave me a look of melodramatic horror and sprinted from the room. "I've talked to her when she's been crying because these white supremacists were threatening her," Pearl went on. "She needs to get out of there. But we've been clear: 'You will live by our rules.' My husband is very strict. We've had lengthy talks with

Mindy about her beliefs. She got associated with those people because she was looking for something. She got mixed up with the Mormon church for a while, too. But it was really shocking to hear her say those things when she was with the white supremacists. It's just so different from our beliefs. I *hope* she's really left them."

Mindy reappeared with a new banner: JAXON STINES. She made a wry face, as if she didn't know how that name had got there, and fled.

"Jaxon has been over here," Pearl said wearily. "She never brought these other kids—these skinheads—around. Even after Jaxon got out of jail I let him come over once, because Mindy was trying so hard to convince us he had changed. I'm willing to give anybody another chance. But he hadn't changed. When he came over for Christmas, Jerry told Mindy, 'You tell him there will be black people here and we don't want any problems.' "

At that moment, Jerry came home. Tall, overweight, with a piercing gaze, he eased himself into a chair and confirmed Pearl's recollection. "I told Mindy that if Jaxon said one word to a black or Hispanic guest of ours I would take him around the corner and beat the living shit out of him." Jerry did not want me to think he was a liberal. (He need not have worried.) "My heritage is from the South, and I would be a hypocrite if I didn't tell you that I don't want my son to marry a black woman. But when Pearl and I got married our best man was a black man."

Mindy came out and kissed Jerry, whose gaze softened as he studied her face. The computer she was playing on was hers to take home, he said. He was getting a new one, and she and Chris and Matthew could share this one. All kids needed a computer at home nowadays, he said. Mindy kissed him again and skipped back to her new toy.

Looking after her, Jerry said, "Mindy is probably the biggest frustration I have in my life now. I feel bad that I haven't been more of an influence on her."

Talking with the Chandlers about Mindy's travails, I could see how Jerry might, in fact, be a very strict guardian. His ideas could not have contrasted more sharply, anyway, with Debbie's. She believed that simply forbidding children something usually backfired. "I know it always just made me more determined to do it, whatever it was," she once told me. "You have to be flexible, try to understand kids but also outsmart them. Not that anything I've done has worked particularly well with Mindy." I tried to picture Mindy living with her grandparents, but could only picture a great clash and meltdown.

"The problem is, society requires both parents to work," Pearl said. "Single parents also have to work. So kids are left to raise themselves. That's why they have no respect, no discipline. There's no one to teach them how to care, how to love, how to *live*. So they form these groups and, right or wrong, those are their families."

Various Sharps and NLRs had told me the same thing, of course. But it was sadder, somehow, to hear it from a consummate grandmother in her big, clean, cozy mobile home.

But absent parents are only the proximate cause of youth waywardness. A far more general abandonment is in progress. If most parents must work outside the home, the obvious institution to take up the caretaking slack is the school. There are American communities that have begun to reckon with this imperative, but they are a small minority, and the Antelope Valley was not among them. In California as a whole, school funding had been *falling* for a generation. When I was in junior high, in the mid-sixties, the state's public schools enjoyed the seventh-highest per-pupil spending in the country; by 1995, California's per-pupil spending ranked forty-seventh nationally. School bond issues that passed in all fifty-eight California counties in the 1950s now failed more often than not. A property-tax revolt in the 1970s began a process that between 1973 and 1992 reduced state and local taxes by 25 percent. This long-wave contraction forced a general defunding and dereliction of public services—the state had to close 1,100 of its 2,150 library branches—but its deepest import was surely the growing refusal of adults to pay for the education of children.

Alongside this refusal came a historic shift of public welfare monies from children to the elderly. Between 1970 and 1996, the poverty rate for children and adolescents in California more than doubled—to 27 percent. During the same period, poverty among the state's elderly was nearly wiped out. Sky-high child poverty rates are not, of course, a disgrace exclusive to California. Neither is California alone in defunding public schools, as parents and children in poor and working-class neighborhoods all across the country know well.

But just as crime rates tend to track closely with poverty rates, vast amounts of public spending have been diverted to law enforcement and the penal system. The California prison budget in 1975 was $200 million. By the year 2000, it will be $5 billion. Between 1981 and 1996, the number of prisons in California nearly tripled. Between 1980 and 1995, the state's incarceration rate quadrupled; by 1995, it had the highest youth incarceration rate in the country.

The money for all these jails and prisons came, in effect, directly out of the state's higher-education budget. Between 1986 and 1996, California built nineteen prisons and one state university. When I graduated from high school in 1970, the state had what was often described as the finest public university system in the world. Tuition was negligible—$219 a year in 1965—and scholarships were plentiful. By the 1990s, scholarships were scarce, and fees at the University of California in 1997 were $3,799—nearly five times, in constant dollars, what they had been thirty-two years before. Between 1991 and 1994, the state's university and college system lost two thousand professors and two hundred thousand students to budget cuts. State spending on prisons came to exceed spending on higher education for the first time in memory, and the disparity is expected to grow for the foreseeable future. Again, these were not just regional trends. As Mike A. Males pointed out in his chilling 1996 book *The Scapegoat Generation: America's War on Adolescents* (from which some of the figures above are taken), "California is an egregious example, more advanced in its splits over generational wealth and politics than other states. But it is not the only example."

Nancy Kelso, a middle-aged lawyer in Palmdale who had many juvenile clients, rejected the view, which she said was common among her peers and colleagues, that they had grown up in a Golden Age when children obeyed their parents and ordinary people felt safe and God was in his Heaven. "I remember the Red Scare," she told me. "I remember suffocating pressure to conform. I remember a lot of bad things." She also remembered, however, a radically different opportunity structure. "When I graduated from high school, in 1962, it was like a *deal*, a contract, between the adults and me," she said. "All I had to do was get a B average and halfway behave myself and I was guaranteed a free education at a top public university, like Berkeley. And that was my *backup*. If I could get into a private school, I could get a California State Scholarship—for Stanford, Pomona, USC, anywhere. This wasn't a loan, this was *free*. My four siblings and I all took advantage of it. Our dad was a five-dollar-an-hour nonunion machinist in Glendale. We all became productive, responsible citizens. And the kids who didn't learn anything at school—and there were plenty of them in those days, too—usually seemed to do okay. The wild boys went into the Army, got some discipline, chilled out, grew up, came back, got their job at Lockheed or driving a big lawn mower for the city. They could support a family on that. I tell you, I would have a *lot* more anxiety about what was going to become of me if I were growing up now."

In 1996, out of a graduating class of about four hundred, Palmdale High School sent exactly six students into the University of California system. Less than 10 percent of the class went on to any four-year college at all.

Listening to Nancy Kelso, I kept thinking of Chris Runge grumbling about "the unwanted." He and his friends looked forward to a "Nazi government" whisking this surplus population from sight. Of course, he and his friends undoubtedly felt that they themselves were the real unwanted. And they were not wrong. But one of the ironies of their predicament was that the withdrawal of resources from education and other social services by wealthy older generations was fundamentally racist—it was primarily, that is, a withdrawal by older whites from the support of those aspects of public welfare, including public education, that seemed to benefit a large number of nonwhites. And yet the collapse of educational opportunity caused by this withdrawal was being suffered by all nonaffluent children and families. "Affirmative action" was merely the name that many whites gave to their sense of disfranchisement. Martha Wengert, of Antelope Valley College, said of her students, "College kids as a whole want to be thought of as tolerant and accepting, but affirmative action is a red-button discussion topic with them. White kids are absolutely convinced that they can't get into UCLA because those other people are taking their spots."

Issues of race and opportunity were especially loaded in the Antelope Valley, of course, because of the extent of white downward mobility. Esther Gillies, of the Children's Center in Lancaster, put it bluntly: "Black families who move to the valley are often moving up. White families who move to the valley couldn't make it down below." While I heard many whites complain about lower-class blacks and Latinos settling in the valley, I often sensed that they were really more concerned about the middle-class minority families in their midst. Todd Jordan's family lived, I noticed, in a grander house than those of any of the white-power kids who stabbed him, and Todd's father was definitely on the premises. Some black and Latino refugees from the city still went back to their old neighborhoods for church on Sundays, but many were starting new churches in the valley, livening up the endless, rectilinear, numbered and lettered streets (Salt Lake City redux) with gospel singing and Spanish-language masses. I talked with black parents who pronounced themselves delighted with their new, racially integrated neighborhoods (the valley had developed so fast that the insidious patterns of residential segregation had not taken root) but even they expressed wariness about staying on once their children reached high school age. In the words of one well-educated black mother of three, "That's when the white-supremacist thing seems to kick in."

After a long series of violent attacks by racist skinheads, the Los Angeles County Board of Supervisors in 1995 ordered its Human Relations Commission to study skinhead activity in the Antelope Valley. The commission's report declared, "It is a frightening time that we live in. The Commission warns all communities in Los Angeles County that skinheads and hate groups are not isolated pockets of alienated individuals, [that] they have a potential to grow and recruit young people in the current climate of deep social discontent." The report described an "emerging white underclass"—elsewhere, an "embittered white underclass"—whose members "find good jobs hard to come by and . . . are no longer guaranteed access to the good life simply by being white males." Given this "climate," the commission's mandate "to develop a strategy . . . to eliminate the skinhead problem in the Antelope Valley" sounded unrealistic at best.

White females are not "guaranteed access to the good life," either. And they too can, of course, become white supremacists, in some cases exceptionally fierce ones. Young Heather, the "Aryan Mother" of the NLRs, actually denounced Chris Runge to me as "confused" for his alleged deviations from the hard racist and homophobic line. And a willowy, ice-blond sixteen-year-old girl named Ronda Hardin, who was loosely associated with the NLRs, once unnerved me by talking, in a breathy, high, almost reverential voice, about "my hatred." She smiled faintly when she said it, as if the thought of this burning racial animus itself evoked a kind of tender awe. I didn't get the impression that Ronda was thinking about the decline of the University of California as we spoke, nor probably about the emergence of an embittered white underclass—though she did tell me proudly that all of her older brothers were skinheads, and that two of them were in prison for murder. And yet the frame around everything she said was nonetheless, I thought, a sense of loss—loss of a marginal color-caste privilege that, in her mind, was supposed to keep black people beneath her socially, and in that way somehow prevent the worst from happening to her. Because she lacked that reassurance, her beloved hatred seemed to be a main prop of her self-respect.

It was difficult, but not impossible, to picture Mindy in such a state. Her friend Stephanie talked about her recovering "her true self" when she left the boneheads. But I saw Mindy still groping in search of a self, an identity whose "truth" would inevitably be relational. And the sad fact was that she had found no consistent, organizing structure for her days since leaving the NLRs—not school, not a job, not a new gang, and not, despite her efforts, a steady, loyal boyfriend. She found comfort in youth culture, in rock music and drug-powered pleasure, but the message she received from the larger culture was cold; she should be thin, beautiful, and passive so that males would want her. She would do almost anything, it sometimes seemed—even become an unwed teenage mother—to try to fasten a male to her side. At one level she was, as she said, forever in search of a father. But the male attention she attracted was double-edged at best. She once told me about how the father of one of the NLRs came on to her. He was a methamphetamine "cook"— a speed-lab supervisor—who lived with his parents. "He said we should get a motel room, and he would be a *total gentleman* with me," Mindy said, her expression a perfect combination of horror, amusement, and query—as if I might be able to tell her what a "gentleman" was. "I said no as nicely as I could."

One didn't need to be a shrink to see that Mindy was depressed. She was apathetic, morbid, and self-destructive. Her self-esteem was clearly hostage to whatever Jaxon did or had to say about her. In the end, it wasn't really so unimaginable that, if she were to turn her anger outward, maybe with the help of methamphetamine, Mindy, too, could again start blaming the Other— black people, lesbians, cheerleaders—for making her feel so bad.

But I only knew her as a sardonic, self-interrogating girl. Other kids might fetishize their "whiteness," pointing to their pale forearms during interviews with me and insisting, apropos of nothing in particular, "I'm *proud* of my race." The Mindy I knew considered such displays ridiculous, even pathetic. (One white-power kid I talked to said, "*I'm* down for my race, are *you?*" And when I said I wasn't, he sneered with unfeigned contempt and disgust, as if to say, "Well, what earthly use *are* you then?" He, in other words, considered *me* pathetic.) Still, Mindy was prey to the same forces that drove her peers to think of themselves in such embattled, illiberal, essentialist terms. Those forces, it should be emphasized, were in the world they found, the world they were entering. The spectacle of rabidly racist teenagers horrifying reasonable parents and grandparents was thus, in a sense, misleading. Kids might express the issues in their lives more vividly, more baldly—and more physically—than adults, but they didn't invent an issue like race; they inherited it. And they constructed their terrifying "beliefs" out of the terror they felt.

The Sharps, for all their antiracism, were, I decided, really no use to Mindy. The only way they would ever take her in and protect her from bonehead wrath was if she were to become romantically attached to one of them. Indeed, the Sharps' view of women sometimes seemed as backward as the boneheads'. I once heard Jacob Kroeger teasing a girlfriend who belonged to Natalie Blacker's consciousness-raising group by using a Rush Limbaughism to describe Natalie—calling her a "feminazi," of all things. But the true state of gender affairs among the Sharps was for me made clear when I heard another Sharp casually denounce *Natalie* as "an instigator." I asked what that meant, and got a muddled reply. What it meant, I knew, was that she was a female who was friendly with the gang but who was not "property of." As Mindy mused, "It seems like you just can't be out on your own." For girls, this truism of tribalized teenage life had an extra oppressive dimension.

There are many versions of what happened in the little brown tract house on East Avenue J-4 in Lancaster on the night of March 9, 1996. I heard at least two dozen. A few facts are undisputed. The Sharps were having a party. There were roughly fifty kids there, most of them white, not all of them antiracists. A keg of beer was flowing. Darius, who was drunk, got into a dispute in the kitchen with Ronda Hardin, who was wearing a bomber jacket with a Confederate flag patch on one sleeve. The dispute may have been over the patch. Darius may have choked Ronda. In any case, Ronda fled. Tom Forney, the ponytailed guitarist who hung out at the Malones', remonstrated with Darius for attacking Ronda. A number of Sharps beat up Tom. Not seriously hurt, he also fled. A boy named Sebastian McCrohan drove Ronda to the Malones' house. When the NLRs heard what had happened, three of them—Tim Malone, Jeff Malone, and somebody named Javier—went back to the party with Sebastian and Ronda in Sebastian's car.

The boys went inside. Ronda remained in the car. A confrontation took place almost immediately, not far from the front door. Jeff Malone, the quiet nineteen-year-old whose gang name was Demon, waved a knife at a girl who approached him. He was wearing sneakers and wraparound sunglasses. She later said she had been trying to warn him to leave. Darius, standing in a knot of his friends, threw a cup of beer at Tim Malone. One of the Malones challenged Darius. The NLRs were standing in close formation, their backs against a living-room wall. Darius ran toward them, a knife in his right hand. With his first thrust, he stabbed Jeff Malone through the heart. Jeff fell. His friends dragged him out the door.

Ronda ran to a neighbor's to phone the police. Sebastian drove Jeff to the hospital. On the way, Jeff's friends tried to stop the bleeding. Tim was slapping his brother hard in the face, shouting, "Breathe! Breathe!" To Sebastian, he yelled, "Run this light! Go! Go!" It was only a few minutes' drive to Antelope

Valley Hospital. By the time they got there, Sebastian said, Jeff's body was cold. They carried him inside. He was pronounced dead an hour later.

"Homeboy deserved it," Johnny Suttle said. "He shouldn't have come to that party. He wasn't invited."

Johnny himself wasn't at the party. He was at Taco Bell, working. But he heard about the stabbing soon after it happened, and he helped direct the Sharps' flurry of subsequent moves. The party had broken up immediately, and Juan, Fred, Billy, and Jacob had bundled Darius away. They drove first to a cemetery behind Antelope Valley High, and there, at Juan's suggestion, they all spat on the bloody knife and buried it under a bush. Next, they went to a park and cleaned up Darius, whose clothes and arms were covered with blood. Then, unaware that Jeff was dead, they dispersed for the night.

But the news was soon flying around town. Jacob was lying in bed a couple of hours later when he got a phone call. He jumped up and woke his mother, brother, and sister. Within minutes, they had packed their bags and moved to his grandmother's house. Some of Darius's relatives were also on the move before daybreak. NLR death threats were already in the air.

Johnny called the police in the morning, and he liked what he heard. The police had interviewed a number of witnesses, and to them the killing sounded like self-defense. Johnny, who knew where Darius was hiding, agreed to bring him in for questioning. He did so, and Darius was questioned but not arrested. Darius then went deeper into hiding, with some relatives in Orange County.

The police wanted the knife used in the killing. They also wanted to know why, if the stabbing *had* been self-defense, the knife had been thrown away. The Sharps, frightened by police mutterings about possible charges, asked me to accompany them to the cemetery to look for the knife. This was now three days after the killing. I declined to go with them. They eventually retrieved the weapon and turned it in.

The killing became a crossroads of sorts for the Sharps. Johnny, who was nothing if not down, took a hard line. "We gotta get *more* aggressive now," he told me. "You always gotta show the boneheads you're crazier than they are. That's the only way they won't fuck with you. If you punk it and run, you're finished."

Jacob, on the other hand, decided to let his hair grow out—"to hang up my boots and braces," as he put it. When I asked him why, he looked nonplussed. "Why? Death, that's why," he said. "This is just not a win-win situation." His friends understood, he said. He would still back them up. He just wouldn't claim skinhead. Like many Sharps (and ex-Sharps), Jacob was angry at Darius. "Why did he do it? He had no right to play God, to take another man's life. And now we all have to lie low. We can't go out and get drunk like we used to. We just have to stay in our houses and watch for boneheads."

Jacob's house was actually empty. As the Sharps' old hangout, it was now too dangerous to live in. In fact, less than a week after the killing, Jacob's entire family moved to Utah, where his mother's boyfriend had relatives. Jacob refused to go with them. He'd spent his whole life in Lancaster and he didn't want to leave. But a few weeks later he, too, moved to Utah.

Billy Anderson wanted to leave the valley, but he had no plans to grow any hair. "I'm a skinhead for life," he said. "I just hate this place. I totally despise it. The boneheads are multiplying like cockroaches, and we're just getting smaller and smaller. Everywhere else, the skinheads outnumber the boneheads, but we're stuck in this dead-end desert town where people are raised on hate. I just want to go up north, where it's more secluded and nobody knows me and I can just start over. Go to college, live with my friends."

The Sharps as a group seemed intent on putting Jeff Malone's death behind them as fast as possible. They joked about "that killer party," and soon began referring glibly to "the time Darius shanked that fool." But they each had their own odd angle on the tragedy.

Justin Molnar said his first thought after seeing Darius stab Jeff Malone was for the Leisures, their ska band. "Right away, I knew we were going to need another bass player," he said. "And probably a new name, too, because without Darius it's really not the same band." Justin was also angry at Darius. "Because it affects all of us. We all have to change our routines. I can't take my girl to the movies dressed like a skin." He was now less inclined than ever, he said, to claim Sharp. "I'm not that political. I hate boneheads because they make people think that our pure little movement, just kids listening to ska, that we're all like them: racists. That's it." He shrugged. "I'm not a violent person. I don't mind a boxing match, but to throw your life away, your whole career, just in twenty seconds, just by pulling a trigger or shanking somebody, that's such a waste. There's too much I want to accomplish."

Natalie Blacker thought that the death of Jeff Malone would be the end of the local Sharps. Darius, she said, would be unable to return to the valley soon, if ever. "And without Darius I just think the Sharps here will dwindle," she said. "It's so terrible. Darius has so much potential. And just before he got into that fight in the kitchen he was so happy. I was talking to him and he was saying, 'This is such a mellow party. It's going to be so much fun.'"

Natalie had mixed feelings about her friend Christina Fava's reaction to the tragedy. Christina, who as Darius's girlfriend was now in real peril, had chosen not to lie low. She still went to school, still worked in a shop on Lancaster's main drag. She talked to Darius on the phone regularly, and drove down to see him every chance she got. "I mean, it's great that she's so loyal," Natalie said. "But girls around here can be too loyal. Sometimes it's like Christina doesn't realize that he *killed* someone."

. . .

Mindy realized, and she was devastated. We were sitting in the Hang 'n Java coffeehouse, in Lancaster, a week after the killing, and she could not seem to take her eyes off the floor. "I keep thinking about this one time with Jeff," she said. Her voice was low and dull. "It wasn't that long ago. We were at a party, and he was on a trampoline, just jumping up and down, and he was *so happy*. We went back to my house, and he was hungry, and all I could find was a can of pork and beans. He wouldn't even let me heat it up for him. He just ate it cold. I can't get that out of my mind."

The Malones were about to bury Jeff, and Mindy was not invited to the funeral. "They should think about what Jeff would want," she said. "Jeff would want me there. But I'm not a Nazi, so I'm not welcome." Her breath was ragged. "I think I'll go buy this Danzig CD Jeff liked and listen to it while they're having the funeral. One of his favorite songs is on there. He sang it to me one time when we were lying on his bed. I had such a crush on him. He always had a crush on me, too. I remember one night lying on the roof of his house, just rubbing Jeff's head until we both passed out."

Tears were trickling down Mindy's cheeks. We sat and sipped coffee in silence for a couple of minutes.

"The NLRs will never forgive me for saying Darius was fine," Mindy said suddenly. "It was true, though, he really was good-looking. But I've lost all respect for him now. If I saw him, I wouldn't even talk to him. I would just give him a dirty look."

Mindy seemed unaware that Darius had left town to avoid mishaps worse than her dirty look.

"I don't want to go back to being a bonehead," she said. "But the way things are happening out here . . . I don't want to have a label on me, but Tim says I already have one. He says I'm a 'gang hopper.' "

It was news to me that Mindy was talking to Tim Malone. As it happened, Tim had just told me that the NLRs were on strict orders from Willie Fisher, who was still in prison, to do nothing. The police were watching them, he said, expecting them to retaliate against the Sharps. This ceasefire might mean that Mindy herself was safe, at least temporarily, I thought—a hopeful possibility that I mentioned to her. She thought about it but seemed uncomforted.

"Willie is an evil person," she said quietly. "Evil, and wicked, and sweet, all at the same time."

Two burly young men had come into the coffeehouse and were standing behind Mindy. Both wore baseball caps, and both had goatees. I wondered if they were boneheads. As they began to walk past us, one of them turned and gave me a startling, sparkly-eyed look right in the face. It was a practiced, frightening, prison-yard challenge. I had never seen the guy before, but I now had no doubt whatsoever that he was a neo-Nazi. He kept walking. The skin on the back of my neck was crawling. Mindy hadn't noticed a thing.

"Once, I was drinking beer at Jacob's," she said. "And I asked Darius what he wanted to be when he grew up. And he said, 'An elephant.' Is that the sweetest thing you ever heard? An *elephant*." Mindy shook her head. "People keep asking me, 'What's wrong?' And I say, 'Oh, my friend killed my friend.' That's the way it's been coming out. It doesn't matter if they disagreed in their beliefs."

The spooky guys in the baseball caps were now chalking pool cues. I didn't know what to make of them, except that with one glance I had felt jolted out of my journalist's protective pocket for the first time, really, in months of visiting the Antelope Valley. I was so distracted that I suggested we leave, and we did. We drove to Stephanie's. Mindy told Stephanie that she couldn't hang out that night, though. She wanted to go home and finish a poem she had been working on for Mrs. Malone.

When I asked Tim Malone how his mother was taking Jeff's death, he said, "Like she should. Hard and dry."

That wasn't true, I found, when I talked to her. Mrs. Malone was tearful and despondent, and was wishing aloud that she had never moved her family to the Antelope Valley. "I wanted to get Tim away from the gangs in Montclair," she said. "But there are bad influences here, too, and my boys have gotten under their wing, and I'm hardly ever home to protect them." She knew almost no one in the valley, she said, and added, "But I've met more people in the last few days, people just calling up to offer condolences, than I'd met in the three years before this happened."

Even Heather Michaels, the NLRs' fierce "Aryan Mother," wasn't "hard and dry" when we spoke. "They didn't want no trouble," she said, meaning, improbably, the NLRs who had rushed to the party that night. "If they wanted trouble, they would've taken guns. They thought there was just five or ten Sharps there. Then they get there, turns out it's like fifty or a hundred Sharps." Heather's eyes welled at the thought. "If one of us had killed this nigger, or even stabbed him, we'd all be locked up," she snapped.

Tim Malone said the same thing, calling the police treatment of Darius "reverse discrimination." He and Chris Runge and I were standing in the Malones' front yard, watching traffic pass and talking desultorily. It was a sunny afternoon. Both of them were barechested and wore boots and jeans. Tim had on a pair of red suspenders, which he occasionally pulled up over his shoulders but mostly left to dangle. Chris, I noticed, was not flashing his goofy smile.

"Vengeance is mine, saith the Lord, and tenfold," Chris intoned. "Darius will get a lot worse than what Jeff got."

Tim nodded, his face both somber and livid. "That's right, brother," he said. To me, he said, "You know, we didn't expect Darius to be there. Because he usually runs if he thinks we might be coming."

I asked what had happened.

"We saw him in there, standing with his friends, and when he saw us he started bouncing up and down." Tim demonstrated. I had seen Darius do that fighter's bounce during the mêlée at the oi show in San Bernardino. "We saw him pull something out and hide it behind his leg. We figured it was Mace. Then somebody offered me a beer, and when I went to take it Darius threw a cup of beer at me. I caught it, threw it down, and called him on." Tim demonstrated his quick reactions, his forceful challenge. " 'Come on, nigger, let's go! Right now! Mace me!' Then I spit in his face."

Nobody else had remembered the scene quite this way.

"Then four guys rushed me, and Darius came in behind them, low, and reached around me and stuck Jeff. I saw it go in. It was a pocket knife, with a black handle. Jeff didn't even know he'd been stuck. Then he looked down at his shirt and saw it. He went, 'Fuck you, nigger!' " Tim imitated Jeff crouching, both middle fingers raised before him like guns. Again, nobody else remembered anything like this. "Then we all started backing up toward the door. Jeff didn't go down till we got outside. We dragged him to the car, and we beat the shit out of him on the way to the hospital. 'Wake the fuck up!' But he died before we got there."

We stood and watched the traffic pass. I asked if Jeff had said anything in the car. "No," Tim said. "But I know what he would have said: 'Get that nigger!' "

Tim and Chris looked at each other, their shaved heads slowly nodding.

I found Darius somewhere in the suburban wilderness of Orange County. We met at a Taco Bell. Juan and Christina were also there. Darius looked much the same—a little warier, less abashed, slightly exhilarated. We had talked on the phone a few days before, and I had asked how he felt. "I'm going to be more mellow," he had said. "I was sick the first couple of days. I haven't felt that feeling since my parents died. Some people probably get off on it, and some people don't like it. I don't like it. It's weird. You've taken somebody's life, and they're never coming back on this earth. At the same time, you feel happy because he was, like, your enemy."

To my amazement, Darius didn't know the name of the person he had killed. At first I thought he was just confused by the fact that the newspapers were calling Jeff by his real father's last name, Crowther. But Darius said he hadn't seen any newspapers. He just didn't know the guy's name. If he hadn't seen the papers, I thought, then he also probably didn't know that the *Antelope Valley Press* was describing him as a "mulatto."

I ran Tim Malone's version of the killing past Darius and Juan. When I got to the part about Jeff's noticing he had been stabbed, throwing up his middle fingers in defiance, and bellowing, "Fuck you, nigger!" Juan and Darius gaped.

"He did what?" Juan said.

I told them again.

Juan and Darius looked at each other. Darius laughed. Juan shrugged. "Okay," Juan said. "They want to go out in a blaze of glory. That's cool. They can have their story."

In Darius's version, the boneheads had arrived with two knives. Darius had kicked one of them loose—he wasn't sure who was holding it—and then picked it up. That was the knife he had used to stab Jeff. None of the other witnesses I interviewed had seen this kick, or anything like it. Darius, I thought, didn't look abashed enough as he told this story.

I watched Christina from the corner of my eye. She fidgeted, checked her watch, said nothing. I noticed her studying Darius, her expression both cool and oddly contented. This fugitive skinhead was her main project now, even the center of her life. Other kids in the Antelope Valley were starting to talk about her with awe. Her black boyfriend—*Mandingo*—killed a bonehead. He was in hiding. She stuck by him, defying her parents. It was a romantic role, far larger than ordinary valley teenage life. I wondered if Christina still had the shrewd perspective on Darius she had shown when she told me that he didn't really want to join the Navy, that he just wanted to hear his friends say, "No!"

Christina and Juan set off on the long drive back to the valley.

Darius took me to meet some new friends he had made. "It's a good thing I cliqued up with some other heads," he said. "Because Huntington Beach is just a few miles from here, and that's where the O.C. Skins are from. Remember those guys from the oi show? I heard they're looking for me. So I need people to watch my back."

Darius's friends lived in a vast low-rise apartment complex. We passed through an empty white-brick foyer and were buzzed into a courtyard that seemed to ramble on for blocks—through plots of grass and stands of tattered bamboo, past a lighted swimming pool, around a thousand plastic tricycles and abandoned toys. All the ground-floor apartments had sliding glass doors without curtains. Behind them, virtually in public, people watched TV, ate sushi, and scratched their bellies, oblivious of path traffic like us. There were Asians, Latinos, blacks, whites, bikers, yuppies, buppies, old Samoans, young Cambodians. It was a Free Unity world, I thought. It felt like a vision of the next American century: ramshackle, multiracial, cut-rate. White supremacists, it struck me, fear the future for a reason: It's going to be strange and very complicated.

We came finally to the apartment of Darius's friends. But they were not there. Some other guys were, and they let us in. They looked like skaters. Two were white, one was Asian. They were smoking a bong, listening to music. Darius and I sat on a couch to one side and talked. He was staying with one of his many half-brothers, he said, not far away. He was thinking about moving to Germany. He had a lot of relatives in Germany. First, though, he was going to enroll in the local community college to learn German. Then he thought he might join the Navy. In the meantime, he thought Christina should move down here. It was too dangerous for her in the Antelope Valley now.

I wasn't sure why Darius wanted me to meet his new friends. But I figured I had seen enough of his new world. It was just a more historically mature Antelope Valley, I thought. I wished him luck. We shook hands, finishing off with a clean, only slightly self-conscious solidarity knuckle punch. And then I made my way back out through the long, complex, low-rise courtyard of the future.

The first time I talked to the Lancaster prosecutor in charge of investigating Jeff Malone's death, he shared with me his feeling about gang killings in general. "I say lock 'em all up in a room and prosecute the survivor," he said. I took this to mean that Darius did not have to fear prosecution.

Later, when a decision was officially made not to prosecute, the same assistant district attorney explained his reasoning to me. The victim and his friends had gone to a house where a hostile or opposing gang was having a party. The victim had a knife. He attacked Mr. Houston. Mr. Houston's claim that the knife he used belonged to the victim or to the victim's friends was not credible. But it was not illegal for him to possess that knife inside that house. There were conflicting eyewitness versions of the attack. It was certainly not a particularly vicious attack. The fact that a single knife thrust had killed the victim was simply bad luck. The crucial question for the prosecution was whether a jury could be persuaded that the killing had *not* been self-defense. That seemed unlikely; the victim was a Nazi skinhead, who would not be viewed sympathetically. Mr. Houston was on his own turf, minding his own business. "I'm not saying Mr. Houston is a great guy," the prosecutor concluded. "He's not. He's a jerk. You need to call me in about six months to see if he is still alive. I do not believe he will be."

To the Malone family's bitter contention that it was really because Jeff was a skinhead from a poor family that no one would be prosecuted for his death, I could think of no rejoinder. It was true.

Tim Malone and his friends wanted to move to a "white-power state"—and several of them eventually did—and in this respect they were alarmingly ordinary. White Americans of all economic classes have started moving in significant numbers out of cities, not just to the suburbs but to faraway, white-majority regions like the Rocky Mountains and the Intermountain West. White flight of the traditional variety appears to be turning into interstate flight. The implications of voluntary regional racial segregation are unnerving, to say the least.

But the months I had spent in the Antelope Valley were, for me, unnerving less for what I had glimpsed there about likely American futures than for what I had begun to see about the past, including my own. As I saw it now, I had grown up in what amounted to a white-power enclave. My family had moved to Woodland Hills, at the western end of the San Fernando Valley, when I was six. This was before school busing, and the schools I attended, all of them public, were virtually, if not literally, 100 percent white. My parents supported a civil-rights-era fair-housing campaign, and they battled, unsuccessfully, with some of the local racists over efforts to integrate our neighborhood. Black people remained a distant clan—athletes, entertainers, and the muscle-bound guys on the sanitation trucks that ground through the streets at dawn. I spent the week of the 1965 Watts riot in Newport Beach, down in Orange County, bodysurfing. When not in the water, I lay in the hot sand listening to a couple of local urchins, whose parents came from Alabama, talk in a way I had never heard before, about "killing niggers."

When I was thirteen, we moved to Honolulu, where I suddenly found myself in a racialized world. The little gang I eventually joined to protect my back at school, the hopefully named In Crowd, was whites-only. My best friends were not in the gang, though. They were three Hawaiian brothers, the Kalakukuis, and a Japanese kid named Ford Takara. Ford and the Kalakukuis were, like me, avid surfers; that was how we'd met. Glenn Kalakukui, the eldest brother—a gifted surfer and a thoroughly cool guy—was my hero. In the course of time, my two worlds merged; Ford and the two older Kalakukuis joined my gang at school, integrating it without a fuss, and I joined their surf club. I was devastated when my family moved back to L.A., where the waves were boring and gangs were, at least in our part of town, unknown. There was nobody as cool on the mainland, I thought, as the Kalakukuis.

Laverne Clark had asked me what it was about me and black people. It was many things, I told her, but in the beginning it was simply escape—flight from the arid 'burbs of my sheltered youth, out into the great world where Hawaiians, Mexicans, Africans (and African Americans) lived. My interests changed with age, from ad hoc personal anthropology and low-budget travel to politics, power, and war, which in turn led me to journalism. I had seen some hideous things as a reporter. But I'd never lost my interest in people from other . . . backgrounds, as Laverne would say.

So the Antelope Valley had been an odd destination. Having stalked the unfamiliar, the far-from-home, for much of my adult life, I had come there looking for the kind of place where I grew up, the ineffable tract homes and saplings of the Southern California suburban frontier. (In Woodland Hills, those saplings were now beefy redwoods.) And I had found the valley more disturbing, in many ways, than the other communities featured in this book. It was the wealthiest of them, certainly, but it was also the least coherent. Its young people seemed the most seriously lost, its public spaces the most forbidding. Now and then, wandering across its stupendous parking lots, I would think of Terry Jackson, and wonder how he might fare if he were dropped onto the turf of the Palmdale Peckerwoods and the Nazi Low Riders. The image nauseated me—less the thought of any physical violence Terry might suffer than the fear, the psychic violence I imagined him enduring, alone in white-supremacist America. Juan Guerrero's stories about the "KKK" white boys in juvenile detention had made me feel similarly ill. And this nausea was different from anything I had felt even on bad days in Mozambique or El Salvador. It contained, I realized, more shame.

My unease tended to intensify around Jaxon Stines. The problem was, I identified with him. He grew up in Reseda, in the middle of the San Fernando Valley, which happened to be where my family had lived until I was six. Most of my earliest memories were set in sweet, starter-home Reseda, when the tracts there were still surrounded by walnut farms. Thus, Jaxon's stories about becoming a racist skinhead at the age of nine—listening to loud, angry bands with names like No For An Answer—in *Reseda* flabbergasted me. I could understand, easily enough, that times had changed, that I had grown up during the long postwar boom, when the American social and economic pie was sharply expanding, especially for middle-class whites, and that Jaxon had been born on the post-1973 downslope. His parents were, in fact, my peers, his father a garage-band rocker who might have played at parties I attended as a teenager. And there was nothing foreordained about Jaxon's juvenile delinquency—he had a brother who had never been in trouble. But the idea that Jaxon, an intelligent kid from a comfortable household, looked out and saw nonwhites—blacks, Mexicans, Asians, whatever—as his natural enemies, and saw the world beyond the L.A. suburbs as "just as boring as this is," said everything about what, far more than economics, had changed.

I once asked Jaxon if he considered himself middle class. "I hope to be middle class," he said coolly. In his version, it seemed, his mother had made it into the middle class, with her lifetime job at the phone company (she was considering taking early retirement) and a second husband who made good money installing security cameras. Her father, now deceased, had been a car mechanic, and her mother, now remarried, had retired, financially secure, to a coastal community north of L.A. where she spent her time playing golf. And yet none of this bourgeois tranquillity would necessarily devolve upon Jaxon, who had already made some notable detours from the straight and narrow, such as the drive-by shooting that earned him a conviction for attempted murder. The ironies were thick here; if some adult had asked me, when I was eighteen, whether I hoped to be middle class when I grew up, I would have sneered as deeply as Jaxon ever did about affirmative action. Not a chance, man! And why not? Because I despised the bourgeoisie. At the same time, of course, I knew that I could probably join it if I ever changed my mind. It seemed I could have it every which way. My first job after college was as a brakeman for the Southern Pacific Railroad, where, thanks to a powerful union, I earned better pay on the day I started than the professors who had just gotten rid of me did.

Navigating the teen world of the Antelope Valley felt, at times, like wading through the sucking bogs of my own generation's crash site. Everyone close to my age seemed to have been divorced twice, had their mortgage foreclosed, maxed out their credit cards, lost custody of their kids, or been addicted to drugs or alcohol or gambling or sex or born-again religion. Even the success stories were sad. Sebastian McCrohan's father—Sebastian was the kid who drove Jeff Malone to the hospital on the night he died—had written, it was said, the Steppenwolf hit "Born to Be Wild." That was why Sebastian lived in a big, new house up in Quartz Hill. I visited that house once, to pick up Sebastian, and there, hanging around in a setting of overlit, underfurnished splendor, was a group of teenagers as surly and bad-news as anyone I ever saw hanging out at the Malones'.

Antelope Valley officialdom was not more inspiring. After the 1992 Los Angeles riots, when a campaign to rebuild the devastated sections of the city was getting under way, Howard Brooks, the executive director of the Antelope Valley Board of Trade, told the *Los Angeles Times* that help would not be forthcoming from the valley. "With budget crunches all over, I can't get real enthusiastic about sending money to L.A.," he said. "The people in that community burned down their community. I'm sorry about that. Why'd you do that?"

I once asked Mindy if she had any interest in politics. She looked at me as if I were mad. Juan, Lanee, Terry—it had been the same, I realized, everywhere I had gone. Everything official was either "corny" or corrupt. What mattered were only the most immediate dramas: friends, family, love, money, drugs, liquor, music, movies, parties, fights, the cops. Even the Sharps, whose antiracism was, in my view, profoundly political, scornfully denied any interest in "politics." There were less alienated kids around, of course—I usually met them on college campuses—but beyond this well-lighted circle of the well-adjusted, among the millions of American young people "out here on the corner," as Chris Runge put it, the disconnect with civil society, with democratic institutions, was all but complete. This dislocation was not their fault. Speaking generationally, it truly was "a measure of our failure, not theirs."

As the second Clinton administration got under way, Mindy remained caught between the Sharps and the NLRs. Christina Fava, having heard that Mindy spoke ill of Darius because he killed Jeff Malone, announced her intention to kick Mindy's ass. "But I can kick Christina's ass, I think," Mindy said. When Mindy heard that Johnny Suttle had been threatening to "piss on Jeff's grave," she was outraged, and she told Johnny so, over the phone. He laughed, then told her that the next time they met in the mall she had better watch out.

Mindy and Jaxon continued to break up and reconcile on a weekly basis. During one of their reconciliations, Mindy actually befriended his other girlfriend, Casey, and got to inspect her amazing body, including her pierced nipples. "She keeps saying *I* have the perfect body," Mindy said happily. "But my mom's put me on these stupid birth control pills now, so I'm totally fat. I'm up to one-fifteen."

Jaxon continued to hang out with the Malones, and he was at their house when it was hit by a drive-by shooting, allegedly committed by a black gang. No one was hurt. Then three NLRs, shouting racial epithets and wielding a machete, attacked two black teenagers—a boy and a girl—on the street in Lancaster. The boy was slashed four times. The victims' families contacted the Nation of Islam and its officers held a press conference in Lancaster. A spate of retaliatory attacks on whites by blacks followed. It seemed that a version of the long-awaited race war was finally coming to the Antelope Valley.

Tory's release from prison began to impend, and it threw Mindy into a panic. She had stopped opening his letters, wanting to prove her loyalty to Jaxon. She vowed to avoid his visits. "I'm being kind of a bitch," she said. "But I don't know what to do. It's a seesaw, a teeter-totter." After Tory was released, he moved in with his mother in Canyon Country, and the next time Mindy and Jaxon broke up, Mindy and Tory got together. A week or so later, she told me, "Now I'm with Tory and everything's fine. We're not even fighting about our beliefs, because I've sort of changed kind of a lot. I'm saying 'nigger' and everything. But I feel bad, because I told myself I wasn't going to do that anymore."

Debbie Turner reconciled with her boyfriend, Tom, and each time I called they seemed to have a new plan to leave the Antelope Valley. First it was Fresno. Then it was Arizona. Mindy said she would not go with them.

Then Mindy and Tory started fighting—over Dennis Rodman. "I said I liked his hair," she said. "And he said I was sticking up for a black guy." This sounded very much like the old life with Jaxon, who was always after Mindy to stop watching basketball and football because they were "black" sports. (He approved only of ice hockey.) But, Mindy said, she was trying to show her loyalty to Tory, so she was getting a new tattoo on her lower back. It was going to be Tory's initials, one on either side of her spine.

Then she and Tory broke up. Luckily, Mindy told me, she had had only one of his initials tattooed on her back before they split. And she got that covered up with a new tattoo: a black rose with a spider web attached to it.

Debbie, meanwhile, had abruptly rented out the Turners' house and moved with Tom to Arizona, and Mindy, to my surprise, had moved in with her grandparents in Canyon Country. At their insistence, she got a job, as a ride operator at an amusement park called Magic Mountain. There she met a young mechanic from Canada named Dave. When things got difficult with her grandparents, as they inevitably did, Mindy moved into an apartment in Lancaster with Dave.

Debbie, when she met Dave during a visit to the valley, found him strangely "normal." He wasn't a white supremacist. In fact, he had no criminal record at all. Was Mindy finally going for a new type? Dave's great passion, Mindy said, was for lowered, heavily customized pickup trucks. The Antelope Valley was apparently a center for the lowered-truck world. That was why Dave had moved there. Unfortunately, Mindy found lowered trucks (and their devotees) tedious beyond words.

Mindy lost her job at Magic Mountain in the spring, when a trial on Court TV began to fascinate her so much that she skipped work for ten days. Three neo-Nazi skinheads, all paratroopers at Fort Bragg, North Carolina—these were the same soldiers whose exploits had shown Chris Runge the extent of Nazi infiltration of the U.S. government—were accused of murdering two black civilians. The victims had been chosen at random. Mindy's special interest was in James Burmeister, a twenty-one-year-old who was found guilty on two counts each of first-degree murder and conspiracy, and received two consecutive life sentences. "He's really good-looking," she reported. She began to write to Burmeister. He wrote back. Mindy sent him a picture of herself. "He's really nice," she told me. "He likes Jagermeister. I like Jagermeister." She laughed. "But that doesn't mean I'm going to go out and kill black people."

Burmeister and his buddies—an investigation revealed that there were twenty-one neo-Nazi soldiers at Fort Bragg—sounded, both in Mindy's descriptions and in the press, very much like the Lancaster NLRs. Burmeister even had an older brother who had graduated, he said, from Quartz Hill High. One difference, I noted, was that in Burmeister's crew the tattoo one got after killing a black person was not a lightning bolt but, according to *The New York Times*, a spider web—Burmeister had been trying to "earn his spider web," the police said, with the murders. Another difference, Mindy said, was that Burmeister, though he listened to a lot of racist skinhead music, also liked Tori Amos. "I couldn't believe that," she said. "Not that many guys like Tori Amos." For her, this passionate correspondence consumed much of the summer of 1997.

Dave looked askance, naturally, at Mindy's blossoming relationship with Burmeister, particularly because she had not yet found the nerve to inform the jailed skinhead that she had a live-in boyfriend. "We fight about it all the time," Mindy told me. "I'm just afraid James will stop writing me if he finds out I have a boyfriend. I guess I'm pretty flirtatious. That's probably my problem. But those guys in prison feel bad enough already." She was making plans, she said, to visit Burmeister in North Carolina as soon as she received an insurance payment from her father's death.

Midnight at the Casino

We have now entered a new phase, in which adults all over the world have to recognize that all children's experience is different from their own.

—Margaret Mead,
Culture and Commitment

Why is this such a strange and difficult time to grow up in America? The baroque array of perils faced by the young people in these stories suggests that there may be no comprehensive explanation. (Single-factor explanations are always suspect, anyway.) And the uniqueness and the seriousness of this generation's struggles can, of course, be overstated. Wild, lost, misunderstood youths have been a main feature of the American social landscape since the invention of adolescence (which occurred, according to historians, in the mid-nineteenth century). Adults, for that matter, have been wringing their hands over the uselessness of the next generation at least since Hesiod deplored "the frivolous youth of today" in the eighth century B.C. No decimating war or famine has torn through the United States lately, nor anything as traumatic as the Great Depression. Still, the past quarter of a century has produced the first generation-long decline in the average worker's wages in American history, and the stresses on kids and families have been ferocious. This turmoil, moreover, is our turmoil and thus, by definition, momentous.

How representative are the kids in these stories? I did not, as I have said, go looking for types, and I've concentrated on communities caught in social and economic downdrafts—places where relatively few young people are, for example, going on to college at a time when most young Americans go to college. So this is not a representative cross-section of contemporary youth. And yet I believe that nearly everyone, young and otherwise, feels these downdrafts, feels their fetid, chill breath on the streets and in the culture if not closer to home.

And the malaise that afflicted so many of the kids I met—the oppressive sense of reduced opportunity—is more general, I think, than some indices of social progress might suggest. College enrollment, for instance, is not what it appears. Two thirds of American high school graduates now go on to some form of higher education, but, according to a recent survey of students in degree programs, "fewer than one in six of all undergraduates fits the traditional stereotype of the American college student attending full time, being eighteen to twenty-two years of age, and living on campus." The large majority of college students today are, it seems, "nontraditional"—older, working, living off campus, attending part-time, or going to corporate-sponsored profit-making schools. Some of this devolution is useful—some of it even represents an expansion of opportunity—but the sheer popularity of higher education tends to obscure a critical fact: Three quarters of the American work force do not have four-year college degrees. And, again, the real wages of those without college degrees have been falling—for men, women, blacks, whites, Latinos, and, especially, young people—since 1973.

As with the hopeful notion of "college," so with "middle class." Reporting these stories, I often found myself fantasizing wearily about just what combination of talent, effort, luck, and transformation it might take to lead Terry Jackson—or Juan Guerrero or Mindy Turner—through the storms of their youthful troubles and into the broad haven of middle-class life. This comforting image—the vast, placid waters of the American mainstream as a site of redemption—not only keeps open the possibility of a happy ending to these kids' fraught journeys; it also subtly assumes that I (and you, my readers) live in the peaceable kingdom where they may yet arrive. This idyll has some basis in fact; I really was a visitor from another class in most of the settings described here, and middle-class prosperity and respectability really are—among the poor, the downwardly mobile, and the hard-pressed—life outcomes to be keenly desired. What needs revision, it seems to me, is the image of the middle class as a vast, welcoming place—the default home of nearly all Americans.

There are many ways to define "middle class," all more or less arbitrary. The term itself is a wildly popular self-description—polls show large numbers of rich and poor Americans claiming, with equal improbability, to be middle class—and this national passion for middle classness is not new. A century ago Matthew Arnold wrote, "That which in England we call the middle class is in America virtually the nation." What is new is that the middle class, defined by almost any measure, has been shrinking conspicuously for some time. Defining it simply as a relative income range—between half the median family income and twice the median family income—sheds light on the nature of that shrinkage. Among college graduates, people have been leaving the middle class in both directions: the percentage of college graduates making less than half the median income has grown slightly since 1969, while the percentage making more than twice the median has grown significantly. Among adults of prime working age at all other levels of educational attainment, however, both the middle class and the upper tier shrank notably between 1969 and 1995, while the percentage filling the lower tier more than doubled. In other words, during the last thirty years or so, the ranks of the upper middle class and the rich have grown overall, the middle class has shriveled for every category of educational attainment, and the ranks of the working poor have grown enormously.

Of course, we usually understand middle-classness as more than just an income range. A college degree, for instance, is now generally considered a class-entrance requirement, and the fact that more Americans than ever are receiving degrees suggests that the middle-and-above category must be growing. But the percentage of Americans with degrees is still far smaller than the percentage generally reckoned to be middle class. The truth is, for the postwar generation now nearing retirement, a middle-class standard of living was widely achieved by the unionized working class—by families whose workers lacked college degrees. And it is this once-broad avenue of opportunity that has been inexorably narrowing, with far-reaching social consequences.

I think the kids I've written about all understood, one way and another, this ill-starred trend—and understood it, on the whole, better than I did. Middle-classness, as Jaxon Stines recognized, is a tenuous, contingent, unstable condition. My sunny assumption, largely unexamined before I began this book, that membership in the American middle class was more or less automatic for those born into it—and was at least attainable by most of those willing to work for it—was, I now think, unfounded. Social mobility in America runs in every direction, and these days it does not necessarily run upward. Not everyone, after all, can go to college; even the postindustrial economy requires unskilled workers to fill the tens of millions of menial jobs that cannot be shipped overseas. Some of the income advantage conferred by a college degree has recently eroded, moreover, as multinational companies have found ways to export even highly skilled jobs to low-wage countries.

Globalization, as it is grandly called, is one of the major reasons—and they are all interlinked—for the stagnation, or worse, of most Americans' incomes and economic prospects. The decline of labor unions (hastened by labor-market deregulation) is another. The rapid growth of low-wage service-sector jobs is a third. Automation and the large-scale immigration of unskilled workers, combined with a relentless drop in the value of the minimum wage—a drop slowed but not reversed by recent legislation raising it to $5.15 an hour—have also put long-term downward pressure on the pay of all nonsupervisory workers. Finally, growth in corporate profits, unrelated to growth in productivity—and thus at the expense of wages—has weakened the bargaining position of workers, blue- and white-collar alike.

Described this way, in terms of large, impersonal economic forces, the deteriorating position of American workers sounds unfortunate but inevitable, almost a tidal flow, ordained by the laws of nature. But it is governments that decide to deregulate, to accommodate capital rather than labor, to tax one constituency and not another. Political agency, while not always evident, and not always accountable, drives much of what passes for necessary pain under capitalism. Poverty in the United States, which is easily the wealthiest nation the world has ever seen, is no longer a matter of scarcity. It is a matter of political economy, of deciding how wealth will be distributed.

The recent rise in inequality should not, however, be construed as an aberration, a departure from the American norm. Wealth and income have always been unequally distributed in this country. The wholesale movement toward greater equality—indeed, toward mass prosperity—that began after World War II was the historical exception, made possible by a constellation of circumstances that will not soon be reproduced.

While young people may have no other era with which to compare their times, they nonetheless sense the rot in the structure of opportunity more acutely than the rest of us simply because they are its main victims. For students whose families are not rich, it might be the spiraling rise in college costs. For those slightly older, it might be the steep decline in home-ownership among younger families since 1973. Or it might be the even steeper (and directly related) decline in entry-level wages. For those in trouble, it might be the blood-chilling enthusiasm of officials, starting with politicians, for prosecuting, sentencing, and imprisoning juveniles as adults. During the 1996 election season, candidates from Bob Dole on down seized on the scare term "superpredator," meaning violent, very young criminals from whom only the most draconian measures could protect us—never mind that the juvenile crime rate, like the crime rate generally, was falling.

Lisa Sullivan, the community activist in New Haven, said, "These kids know that the whole society hates who they are. And they can't *help* who they are." She was talking about inner-city black kids, but recent surveys indicate that the fear and loathing extend to young people generally. A study released in 1997 found that more than 60 percent of American adults believed that young people's failure to learn fundamental moral values such as "honesty, respect, and responsibility" was " a very serious problem." For young people, the negative views of them held by their parents' generation—expressed in public policy as well as in opinion polls—must constitute a harsh lesson in the moral limitations of adults. As Walter Kirn, a young writer, recently put it, "First the members of the 60's generation hated their parents. Now they hate their kids."

But the picture that stays with me as an image of my generation's performance as parents is of Terry Jackson's mother, Anjelica, having heard that Terry was in trouble, perhaps even involved in a shoot-out, missing the last bus into New Haven and running after it, mile after mile, but never quite catching it—and then always telling the story of her failure with an air of self-congratulation. I think of Chris Runge, the neo-Nazi skinhead, saying, "I'm for a lot of restrictions. You can't let too much freedom in." In those stark, unsettling words, I hear a generation in bleak reaction to parents and caretakers who placed too few restrictions on their own needs and appetites.

Blaming individual parents for their children's alienation and failure to thrive is too easy, though. Families struggle to survive against a powerful tide of social and economic forces today, and all the parents depicted in these stories suffer that tide's destructive effects to some (usually large) degree. Even those parents who do virtually nothing but work and sacrifice—think of the Clarks in San Augustine, or Rosa and Rafael Guerrero in the Yakima Valley—see their kids get into trouble, give up on school, or simply get trapped in poverty. Everyone looks for a magic formula. Remember Roger Vann, in New Haven, extolling Kwanzaa as a family holiday, telling parents, "If you educate your children correctly in the seven principles, they won't turn on you when they become teenagers, the way they do today." Lacking the formula, people look for someone to blame. I think of Terry's various caretakers all pointing fingers, recalling one another's derelictions—and then of Terry himself, sadly serene, seeming to understand himself as more than the product of his family's failings.

For what it's worth, I blame the government. There has been a disastrous lag in policy response both to deindustrialization and to changes in the American family—particularly, in the latter case, to the fact that more and more mothers have entered the paid work force. These changes in the family have actually been occurring over generations—the breadwinner/housewife system, as it is called, the first form of the modern family, has been in decline since 1890—but public assistance has always been problematic because, as the family historian Arlene Skolnick points out, "support for children and families in America has been generally based on the assumption that families are inadequate if they are not self-sufficient." The failure to publicly subsidize child care in the face of the overwhelming need for it has been unusually short-sighted, however, even by laissez-faire standards. Now that welfare "reform" is forcing additional millions of poor mothers into the paid work force, the Clinton administration has introduced a modest package of tax credits and grants to expand child care for working families. But this plan, if it passes Congress, will barely begin to address the problem, and it will do nothing, of course, for the millions of American children already injured by being left poorly supervised or unsupervised.

"Big government" is unpopular at the moment, although it's sometimes difficult to tell if that is because of what it does, what it fails to do, what it stopped doing, what it started doing, what it's rumored to do, or for whom it does whatever it does. The correct answer is, I suppose, some combination of all these. But for those of us who grew up during the long postwar boom, it is easy to forget just how large a role government programs played in the spread of mass prosperity—starting with the New Deal and including, crucially, Social Security, the Federal Housing Administration's home loan programs, the G.I. Bill, the antipoverty programs of the 1960s (particularly Medicare and Medicaid), the industrial subsidies and jobs programs (though they were not called that) of the immense Cold War military buildup (including construction of the interstate highway system), and, above all, wave after massive wave of investment in public education. It is easy to forget because, having reaped the benefits of all this public investment, my generation (and our parents') decided at some point that paying taxes on our hard-earned incomes had become an undue burden, was almost un-American, and a Reagan-style amnesia became convenient to all the tax-cutting and privatization that followed. Thus, over the past generation, government has withdrawn support for education, poor children, public works. It has also largely stopped regulating business and trade—allowing deindustrialization to proceed unhindered in the name of "competitiveness."

It isn't that government has receded from our lives. Indeed, in the suburbs of the Antelope Valley, I was stunned by how much kids talked about "the government"—and by how fierce and personal that talk was. "I'm down for the government," one would declare. "What has this government done for *me?*" another would demand. As in the inner city, everyone seemed to feel the state, particularly the police and courts, crouching hungrily at the edge of their lives. There are 1.7 million Americans in prison and jail today—more than three times the number who were locked up in 1980. We have the world's second highest incarceration rate—six times higher than Britain's, seventeen times higher than Japan's. This grotesque orgy of imprisonment is driven primarily by the politically irresistible, utterly ineffective "war on drugs." Even for an old-school fan of the public sector, it's become difficult to feel any enthusiasm for a government whose activism seems to consist mainly of harassing and jailing citizens. Those who hoped that a Clinton administration might slow or reverse this trend have been bitterly disappointed.

While most of the young people I've written about here consider politics irrelevant to their lives, their alienation does not preclude a growing measure of class consciousness. Kids sense that class lines in America are hardening. Many still seek to cross those lines through education, and some succeed. Those not bound for college know that their best hope for upward mobility lies in owning a business: a fish restaurant, in Terry's case; a liquor store, in Lanee Mitchell's. Worthy as they are, these ambitions are not the stuff of collectivist political culture. Timmy Price, Lanee's cousin, preferred, it may be recalled, to run a liquor store in the anonymity of big-city California rather than in his hometown because out West nobody asked to borrow money. Timmy's commitment to family-based enterprise and accumulation was so thoroughgoing that he rejected even the mildest appeals to black solidarity—"I'm not off into any of that stuff." But most people, including most young people, are suscepti- ble to group identifications larger than their immediate families. Indeed, most of the kids I met for this book seemed to be shopping, more or less actively, for something to belong to, something to believe in.

In my introduction, I nominated liberal consumerism as the reigning ideol- ogy of contemporary American mass culture. By no means an original notion, it seemed worth keeping in mind nonetheless while reading stories about poor and downwardly mobile kids and families. I opposed consumerism, broadly, to fundamentalism. There are many fissures in this scheme, however, and innu- merable nonfundamentalist admixtures and subcultures, particularly youth subcultures, seeking to fill the intellectual vacuum left by the bland hegemony of liberal consumerism. Thus, on any sustained wander through the world of American youth, one meets, as I did, an endless array of ardent skaters, skins, rockers, ravers, rebels, heshers, punks, Goths, jocks, Rude Boys, hippies, preps, nerds, snowboarders, Sharps, Bloods, Crips, *Sureños, Norteños,* gangstas, Unity rappers, neo-Nazis, cheerleaders, Satanists, and straight-edge anarchists. This is just an arbitrary, incomplete catalogue of a few high-profile formations— the kind that tend to have their own magazines, Web sites, fashion lines, and music playlists, not to mention "beliefs." There are thousands of smaller sects and splinters and tendencies, gangs and subgangs and cliques, rising and falling all the time, each with a party line on a range of cultural issues, large and small.

To my mind, such groups offer more than just companionship and struc- ture—they also offer what was called in my student days an analysis. Even the most mercenary drug posse can be said to do this. Kids form and join groups in part because these groups help explain to them their place in the larger scheme of things. That place often includes class and ethnicity, often very pre- cisely defined. Nearly all of these niche-subcultures are "pre-political," at most, and very few place much emphasis on a critical reading of history. Still, they represent the means, the framework, through which a great many young Americans encounter the world. They connect private and public life. To the extent that young Americans have ever been interested in society as a whole, these groups' diverse, overdetermined interpretations of events have largely replaced traditional political understanding.

And here lies a large historical irony. American workers have never been po- litically organized by class, not on a large scale over the long term, in social- democratic parties, as their counterparts in every other industrial democracy have. The standard explanation for this anomaly has been the extraordinary amount of upward mobility in the United States—both the chance for individ- ual families to cross class lines and, more important, the nearly constant rise in the national standard of living since the beginning of the industrial revolution.

Now, in the postindustrial world, this two-hundred-year rise appears to have slowed greatly, if not stopped altogether. Most workers are losing ground. Their kids, moreover, seem acutely, if inchoately, aware of that fact. The time might seem ripe, then, for wide recognition of a shared plight, particularly considering the speed and power of modern communications.

And yet the net impact of the much-vaunted information revolution seems to have been so far, if anything, depoliticizing. The swelling national (and international) entertainment state implacably homogenizes culture through mass marketing, while the less centralized new media, including cable TV and the Internet, quietly atomize through niche marketing and their inevitable detraction from the life of real (nonvirtual) communities. Popular cynicism about politics deepens, and consumerism reigns triumphant, effectively unchallenged, at a moment when most Americans could really use some new ideology.

It is not necesary to romanticize any earlier, more "organic" era—of heavy industry, or heavy public investment, or a long-lost agrarian republic—to recognize the peculiar stresses of these times. After all, Americans have been suffering from some sort of future shock since the Pilgrims landed. Marx lamented the "everlasting uncertainty and agitation" of life under capitalism 150 years ago, memorably crying, "All that is solid melts into air, all that is holy is profaned." This is a sentiment that the protagonists of each of my stories here would understand, I think. All of them sometimes felt like hiding, certainly. Think of Terry in New Haven, dreaming of locking the door and just pulling the blankets up over his head all day; of Juan, lying low in his parents' house, murmuring, "It's all cool, in a way, I would say"; of Mindy, preferring darkness to light; of Lanee on the old family farm in Greertown, showing me, on a wet winter day, the potato bin built by her grandfather. "See how dry it stay," she said. As for my own analysis—my middle-aged outside-agitator's take on their various situations—none of these kids could much relate to it. In the end, I basically shared Juan's parents' unionist views, and you saw how nonplussed Juan was by those (except when he wasn't, briefly). Fortunately for all concerned, my job was to listen.

It may be worth noting, still, that in 1996 the AFL-CIO dispatched more than a thousand "Union Summer" students to twenty cities across the country to learn labor organizing—a wavelet of activism that could actually presage more significant action if the U.S. labor movement continues to revitalize, and if more Americans are persuaded that their economic prospects stand a better chance of brightening through collective bargaining than through a lucky lottery number. As it is, though, the general mood of kids strikes me as more Gothic than Gompers: millennialist, depressed, widely disposed to see the world as corrupt—as a casino where the games are rigged. Cliques and gangs may serve as relief from the atomized, latchkey life so many

American adolescents lead—you never see skinheads bowling alone. But from what I have seen, the ideological void left by consumerism tends to get filled among kids not by considered, historically informed activism but by apathy, frustration, hedonism, nihilism, or an excess of the emotional detachment known as cool (or, alternatively, by the fiercest, most vivid doctrines available, from militant turf defense—being down for your set—to full-blown race nationalism). Without significant adult involvement in their projects, many kids tend to enact, I fear, hometown versions of *Lord of the Flies.*

Few of these afflictions of the age are exclusively American. Labor union membership has been falling globally. Welfare states have been scaled back or dismantled throughout the industrialized world. Poverty and inequality are growing in much of Western Europe, as are all the modern social ills. Young people in Europe face a wall of generational economic disadvantage and future downward mobility at least as high as that faced by their American counterparts, along with chronically high unemployment. And their political response has been, on the whole, no more coherent. Racist skinheads and other far-right youth movements flourish in dozens of countries. I recently happened to be in Guernica, the Spanish town where more than 1,600 people died in a bombing raid by Hitler's air force called down by General Franco. On a railway station wall there, I saw a spray-painted slogan: LOSS SKINS. No hot-eyed American bigot could have a darker, more bent sense of history than that.

It is often said that in this age of the global corporation, there can be no coherent political response, at the national level, to the eroding position of workers everywhere. The old Keynesian policy remedies for the excesses of capitalism lose their effectiveness when capital becomes too fluidly international. Perhaps that is why socialist parties, pale and centrist as most of them have become, now govern most of Western Europe. European voters seem to have decided, at least for now, that in the trade-off between "economic efficiency" and the possibility of social peace, there is much to recommend the latter.

What price are Americans willing to pay for social peace? This seems to me a central question. We jail the poor in their multitudes, abandon the dream of equality, cede more and more of public life to private interests, let lobbyists run government. Those who can afford to do so lock themselves inside gated communities and send their children to private schools. And then we wonder why the world at large has become harsher and more cynical, why our kids have become strange to us. What young people show us is simply the world we have made for them.

INTRODUCTION

page xiii "the economic prospects of most Americans have been dimming": Since 1973, there has been a steady decline in the average earnings of American production and nonsupervisory workers—a category that includes teachers, clerks, factory workers, and a wide variety of service-sector workers and accounts for more than 80 percent of all wage and salary employment. Average hourly earnings for workers in this vast category fell from $12.72 in 1973 to $11.46 in 1995; average weekly earnings fell from $469 to $395 over the same period. (All figures in 1995 dollars.) Among males, hourly wages for white-collar *and* blue-collar and service occupations fell over this twenty-three-year period. Indeed, wages fell for workers at all education levels except those holding advanced degrees—a group that comprised only 8 percent of the work force in 1995.

Younger workers, and younger families, have been hit particularly hard by these declines. Entry-level wages for male high school graduates fell 28.1 percent between 1973 and 1995; for female high school graduates, 19 percent. For male college graduates, they fell 10.9 percent; for female college graduates, 6.1 percent. The median income for families headed by someone under the age of twenty-five fell from $25,876 in 1973 to $18,756 in 1995; families headed by someone between the ages of twenty-five and thirty-four saw their median income fall from $39,411 in 1973 to $36,020 in 1995. (All figures in 1995 dollars.) One important result of these declines: Home-ownership among those between the ages of twenty-five and thirty-eight fell sharply between 1973 and 1993.

Only a large increase in the number of wives working for wages prevented the family income picture from being considerably darker. The median income of all married couples with a wife not in the paid labor force fell more than 12 percent between 1973 and 1995. For husbands in families with children, hourly wages fell between 1979 and 1994 for all income brackets except the top 5 percent.

Upper-income workers and families have been the exception to the general stagnation and decline in national income. While the average income of families in the bottom 80 percent (ranked by income) fell slightly between 1979 and 1994, the average income of families in the top 1 percent rose by a stunning 87.5 percent between 1979 and 1989, the last year for which figures are available. Top executives have done especially well. In 1973 the chief executive officers of major American companies made 44.8 times the pay of the average worker. By 1995 they were making 172.5 times the pay of the average worker—a ratio more than twice the average in other advanced economies.

Lawrence Mishel, Jared Bernstein, John Schmitt, *The State of Working America, 1996–97* (Economic Policy Institute, 1997), pp. 140, 143, 169, 174, 176, 48, 83, 88, 51, 84, 60, 227–8.

Home-ownership: Jeffrey Madrick, *The End of Affluence: The Causes and Consequences of America's Economic Dilemma* (Random House, 1995), p. 211.

page xiii   "unemployment rate": The official unemployment rate for November 1997 was 4.6 percent, the lowest since October 1973 ("Job Growth in U.S. Posts Huge Jump; Wages Also Climb," *The New York Times*, December 6, 1997). Not surprisingly, median hourly wages ticked up 1.4 percent between mid-1996 and mid-1997 (EPI Data Card: Wages, Economic Policy Institute, August 15, 1997). Still, a Federal Reserve report issued in December 1997 found that, while labor shortages were widespread, "the bulk of the American work force is still not winning sizable wage increases" ("Fed Survey Finds Wages Still Contained," *The New York Times*, December 4, 1997).

page xiii   "median household income has fallen": Median household income in 1996 was $35,492—2.7 percent below its 1989 level. Even during the "Clinton recovery," as the current expansion has been called, the median earnings of full-time male workers continued to fall. In 1996, families in the bottom 80 percent of the income scale remained below their 1989 income level. (Daniel H. Weinberg, U.S. Census Bureau, Press Briefing on 1996 Income, Poverty, and Health Insurance Estimates, September 29, 1997; Jared Bernstein and Lawrence Mishel, "Family Income Up Over Past Year, but Still Fails to Regain Pre-Recession Level," briefing paper, Economic Policy Institute, September 29, 1997; "The Tide Is Not Lifting Everyone," *The New York Times*, October 2, 1997.)

Median household income would have fallen much farther if Americans had worked the same number of hours each year. But the average number of hours worked rose steadily between 1982 and 1997, while the average number of hours worked by husbands and wives rose dramatically. ("More Work, Less Play Make Jack Look Better Off," *The New York Times*, October 5, 1997; Barry Bluestone and Stephen Rose, "Overworked *and* Underemployed," *The American Prospect*, March/April 1997, pp. 63, 66.)

page xiii   "national poverty rate has risen": In 1989, when I began this book, the national poverty rate was 13.1 percent—32.4 million people were officially poor. In 1996 it was 13.7 percent—36.5 million people. (U.S. Census Bureau, March Supplement to the Current Population Survey, 1997.)

The failure of recent economic growth to bring down the poverty rate was, according to the economist Rebecca M. Blank, "historically unprecedented." In 1993, "when the rate of aggregate economic growth (after inflation) was 3 percent—a very healthy growth rate indeed—the proportion of Americans who were poor in that year actually *rose*" (emphasis hers). (Rebecca M.Blank, *It Takes a Nation: A New Agenda for Fighting Poverty* [Russell Sage Foundation/Princeton University Press, 1997], p. 54.)

Even in the "Clinton recovery," the ranks of the very poor—those subsisting on incomes less than half of the poverty threshold—grew. In 1995, there were 13.9 million very poor; in 1996, there were 14.4 million. The number of people lacking health insurance coverage also grew—to 41.7 million in 1996, up 1.1 million from 1995. (Weinberg, U.S. Census Bureau, September 29, 1997.)

It should be noted that the official poverty rate is an arbitrary figure, devised in the 1960s by taking the cost of a minimum subsistence diet and multiplying it by three, on the assumption that food should consume no more than a third of a family's income. This standard has often been attacked as inadequate (see Patricia Ruggles, "The Poverty Line—Too Low for the 1990s," *The New York Times*, April 26, 1990).

page xiii   "growth in the number of low-wage jobs": Between 1973 and 1995, the percentage of American workers earning less than a poverty-level hourly wage rose from 23.5 to 29.7. During this period, the percentage of workers earning less than 75 percent of a poverty-level hourly wage nearly doubled. A "poverty-level wage" is what a full-time, year-round worker must earn to sustain a family of four at the federally established poverty threshold—in 1995, that was $7.28 an hour (in 1994 dollars). Workers earning less than a poverty-level wage don't necessarily live in poverty—they may belong to a family with fewer than four members, or, as is often the case, other members may contribute to family income. Still, the number of full-time, year-round workers living in poverty is also growing—in 1994, 1.5 million Americans of prime working age (twenty-five to fifty-four) worked full-time, year-round, and yet remained in poverty. (Mishel, Bernstein, Schmitt, pp. 150, 341; interview with Jared Bernstein, Economic Policy Institute, September 26, 1997.)

Among new jobs created, the great preponderance of jobs with below-average pay finally began to abate during the "Clinton recovery"—78 percent of all new jobs paid below the average in 1992; by 1995, the figure was down to 55 percent. ("The New Jobs: A Growing Number Are Good Ones," *The New York Times*, July 21, 1996.) The stagnation of middle-class wages in the face of new-job improvement was sometimes explained by the phenomenon of "trading down" within a job category—or, as the *Los Angeles Times* put it, "when someone loses a $75,000 job and accepts a new $50,000-a-year position, it is counted as one 'good job' lost and one 'good job' gained—no net change." ("Quality of Most New Jobs Better Than Expected," *Los Angeles Times*, March 13, 1996.) Indeed, two thirds of those who lose jobs end up making less at their next jobs, according to the U.S. Labor Department. ("Confusion as an Economic Indicator," *The New York Times*, November 2, 1997.)

John E. Schwarz, in a comprehensive calculation of opportunity versus need, found that an average American household of four, dependent upon employment for a living, needed, in 1994, $25,000 a year "to be able to reach the minimum level of a mainstream standard of living," and that the shortfall of adequate jobs now available stands at 16 million and growing. (John E. Schwarz, *Illusions of Opportunity: The American Dream in Question* [W. W. Norton, 1997], quotation from p. 64.)

page xiv   "most poverty in America is . . . neither Northern nor urban nor black": In 1993, for example, of families living in poverty, 27.1 percent were black, 48.1 percent were white, and 20.7 percent were Latino. Among the poor that year, 42.8 percent lived in central cities; the rest lived in small towns, suburbs, or rural areas. (Blank, pp. 16, 29.) Poverty rates, meanwhile, were higher in the South and in the West—and in the nation as a whole—than in the Northeast. (Mishel, Bernstein, Schmitt, p. 374.)

page xiv   " 'postmodern poverty' ": Jacqueline Jones, *The Dispossessed: America's Underclasses from the Civil War to the Present* (Basic Books, 1992), "Postmodern Poverty in America," pp. 267–92; quotation from p. 271.

page xv   " 'double truth' ": Benjamin DeMott, *The Trouble with Friendship: Why Americans Can't Think Straight About Race* (Atlantic Monthly Press, 1995), p. 59.

page xv   "the illegal drug trade offers more economic opportunity": While the terrifying violence of the inner-city street drug trade of the late 1980s and early 1990s declined in the mid-1990s, this decline reflected increased discretion and sophistication on the part of dealers rather than a decline in the trade itself. The situation in poor Brooklyn neighborhoods in 1997 was typical. As *The New York Times* reported, "the disappearance of drug-related violence hasn't meant the disappearance of drugs. Dealers quietly sell cocaine from inside a store. . . . Teen-age dealers receive coded messages by beeper and discreetly meet customers in neutral locations or deliver drugs to their homes. . . . There are few indications that fewer young men and women are eager to enter the drug trade. The teen-agers convicted of drug dealing said in interviews that they have seen no increase or decrease in the number of their peers turning to drug sales. Narcotics investigators, state officials, Brooklyn residents and agency officials . . . said they have seen no decrease either." ("Where Has Your Neighborhood Drug Dealer Gone?" *The New York Times*, August 17, 1997.)

Some observers have argued that the epidemic of crack cocaine abuse began to run its course as the generation that saw its parents succumb to addiction learned to stay away from the drug, but this has actually been true since the epidemic's early days. As I found in New Haven, and other reporters and researchers have found elsewhere, crack's popularity has always been concentrated among adults. Even teenage dealers have rarely been users, and the rate of detected crack use among young arrestees fell off steeply in most cities from the late 1980s onward. ("Drop in Homicide Rate Linked to Crack's Decline," *The New York Times*, October 27, 1997.) The latest national survey reports that "the market for cocaine is generally stable," and that crack smokers "are likely to be older, poly-drug users." (*Pulse Check: National Trends in Drug Abuse*, Office of National Drug Control Policy, Summer 1997, pp. 7, ii.)

page xvii   "bright kids from the 'burbs almost always abhor": One notable exception to this rule is the sociologist Donna Gaines. See her *Teenage Wasteland: Suburbia's Dead-End Kids* (Pantheon, 1990).

page xvii   " 'If young people feel no connection' ": Christopher Lasch, "The I's Have It for Another Decade," *The New York Times*, December 27, 1989.

page xvii   "poverty among Americans over the age of sixty-five": In 1970, 24.6 percent of Americans over sixty-five lived below the federal poverty line; this figure had dropped to 10.5 percent by 1995. In 1970, 15.1 percent of Americans under eighteen lived below the poverty line; by 1995 this figure had risen to 20.8 percent. (Andrew Hacker, *Money: Who Has How Much and Why* [Scribner's, 1997], p. 63.)

page xvii   "national child-poverty rate is by far the highest": The Luxembourg Income Study, in a 1995 report funded by the National Science Foundation, found that, after welfare payments had been figured in, the United States had the highest child-poverty rate—20.8 percent—among the eighteen countries it surveyed. Australia had the second-highest rate—14 percent—and Ireland, at 12 percent, was the only nation in Western Europe among those studied with a rate above 10 percent. ("Low Ranking for Poor American Children," *The New York Times*, August 14, 1995; Mike A. Males, *The Scapegoat Generation: America's War on Adolescents* [Common Courage Press, 1996], pp. 7–9.)

page xvii   "1996 welfare 'reform' ": In the first year after the president signed the Personal Responsibility and Work Opportunity Reconciliation Act of 1996, the grim predictions of the bill's opponents had not come to pass. State-administered welfare-to-work programs were largely succeeding in the low-unemployment economy, and some of the bill's most onerous provisions had been reversed by the administration in its 1997 budget negotiations with Congress. It remained likely, however, that the new welfare system's long-term effect on the well-being of children would be harmful. (See Mary Jo Bane, "Welfare As We Might Know It," *The American Prospect*, January/February 1997, and Peter Edelman, "The Worst Thing Bill Clinton Has Done," *The Atlantic*, March 1997, for analyses of the new welfare law by officials who resigned from the Clinton administration in protest over it.)

page xviii   "the 1996 budget of the Children's Defense Fund": Children's Defense Fund, "The State of America's Children—Yearbook 1997," p. 10.

page xviii   "the American Association of Retired Persons": Executive Director's Report, *AARP Bulletin*, June 1997, p. 15.

page xviii   "a brutal squeeze on public school funding": In 1995 the General Accounting Office "cited $112 billion in pressing construction needs in the nation's 80,000 existing schools at a time when school districts are spending $5 billion a year to repair and expand buildings." This colossal backlog was the product of a generation of neglect. Meanwhile, national public school enrollment reached 51.7 million students in the 1996–97 school year, a record high, and is expected to rise to 54.6 million within ten years. ("Enrollments Soar, Leaving Dilapidated School Buildings Bursting at the Frayed Seams," *The New York Times*, August 25, 1996.)

Per-pupil spending actually rose 61 percent between 1967 and 1991, but little of that increase found its way into the ordinary classroom, going instead to areas like special education, school lunches, and dropout prevention. (Richard Rothstein, with Karen Hawley Miles, *Where's the Money Gone? Changes in the Level and Composition of Education Spending* [Economic Policy Institute, 1995], p. 1.)

In California, per-pupil spending fell from seventh-highest in the nation in 1965 to forty-seventh in 1995, a decline begun by a property-tax revolt in the 1970s and deepened by repeated budget cutbacks and failed school-bond issues. (Males, *The Scapegoat Generation*, pp. 2–3, 12; "Public Elementary and Secondary Education Statistics: School Year 1995–96," U.S. Department of Education, National Center for Education Statistics, May 1996, adjusted for regional costs in "Quality Counts: A Report Card on the Condition of Public Education in the 50 States," *Education Week on the Web*, January 1997.) For a detailed look at California's abandonment of public services, see Book Four, "The Antelope Valley," Chapter 6.

page xviii   " 'There are no books at home' ": Dr. Martha Wengert, Antelope Valley College, interview, February 21, 1996.

page xix   "away from the movement toward racial equality": Affirmative action programs, which have been responsible for much of the occupational and economic progress made in the post–civil rights period among blacks, in particular, but also among other minorities and women, have come under increasing attack and, in many areas, are being rolled back or abolished. Recent court decisions have greatly restricted the minority set-asides that have given opportunities to businesses traditionally excluded from public contracts. While these sorts of remedies for group injustice have obvious problems, and are susceptible to obvious abuses, they are not being replaced by other remedies, let alone more effective ones. For recent arguments in support of affirmative action, see K. Anthony Appiah and Amy Gutmann, *Color Conscious: The Political Morality of Race* (Princeton University Press, 1996), and Barbara R. Bergmann, *In Defense of Affirmative Action* (Basic Books, 1996).

Stephan Thernstrom and Abigail Thernstrom, who oppose affirmative action, make the novel suggestion that black economic progress achieved before the development of affirmative action and set-asides—and black economic suffering in the era since—show the ineffectuality of such programs. (Thernstrom and Thernstrom, *America in Black and White: One Nation, Indivisible* [Simon and Schuster, 1997], pp. 234–35, 449–51.)

page xix   "upward transfer of wealth": See Sheldon Danziger and Peter Gottschalk, *America Unequal* (Russell Sage Foundation/Harvard University Press, 1995), and Edward N. Wolff, *Top Heavy: The Increasing Inequality of Wealth in America and What Can Be Done About It* (New Press, 1996).

page xix   "Harvard Project on School Desegregation": Gary Orfield, Mark Bachmeier, David R. James, and Tamela Eitle, "Deepening Segregation in American Public Schools," research paper, Harvard Project on School Desegregation, April 5, 1997, p. 4.

Even when blacks and Latinos move from the central cities to the suburbs, they tend to end up in segregated pockets. On Long Island, for instance, outside New York City, "95 percent of black residents are concentrated in 5 percent of the census tracts." ("Persistent Racial Segregation Mars Suburbs' Green Dream," *The New York Times*, March 17, 1994.)

page xix   "growth of the African American middle class": There are many ways to calculate this growth. One is to look at the percentage of African American households earning more than $35,000 (in constant 1996 dollars)—not a precise definition of "middle class," but a fair threshold measure of black upward mobility. Between 1967 and 1989, this figure grew by more than 65 percent—from 19.9 percent of all African American households to 32.9 percent. Between 1989 and 1996, it effectively stopped growing. In March 1997 the figure stood at 33.8 percent. (U.S. Department of Commerce, Bureau of the Census, Current Population Reports, P60–197, "Money Income in the United States: 1996," Appendix B, Table B-2, September 1997.)

Figures for white households for the same periods show a more modest growth and, between 1989 and 1996, a reversal. (*Ibid.*) Indeed, fixing the "middle class" as an income range—whether an arbitrary dollar range (between $15,000 and $50,000, in 1995 dollars) or relative to the median income (between one half and twice the median)—shows that this very large "class" shrank steadily between 1967 and 1995. (Mishel, Bernstein, and Schmitt, p. 77.) For more on the shrinking of the middle class, see Epilogue.

Class position depends, of course, on wealth as much as on income—no household can be described as securely middle class unless it has the assets to sustain itself through economic setbacks—and even high-income black households remain far less wealthy than their white counterparts. (See Wolff, *Top Heavy*, pp. 15–17, 70–72.)

Educational attainment is a reliable predictor of class, but not race-neutrally—by 1995, blacks had achieved the same high school graduation rates as whites, but black men still earned far less than white men of equal education. The percentage of black twenty-five to forty-four-year-olds with college degrees more than doubled between 1970 and 1990, and black college enrollment continued to rise between 1990 and 1995. If rollbacks in affirmative action programs do not reverse this trend, and if well-educated African Americans can find well-paid jobs—two optimistic assumptions—the growth of the black middle class should resume. ("The Greening of America's Black Middle Class," *The New York Times*, June 18, 1995; "Blacks Show Gains in Getting College Degrees," *The New York Times*, June 12, 1996; "College Payoffs Lower for Blacks," Associated Press, September 10, 1991; Thernstrom and Thernstrom, *America in Black and White*, p. 191.)

page xix "'Mixed marriages' . . . are on the increase": The number of children born of interracial couples grew from five hundred thousand in 1970 to two million in 1990. ("People Can Claim One or More Races on Federal Forms," *The New York Times*, October 30, 1997.)

page xix "illegal drugs are a salient feature": A 1997 survey by the National Center on Addiction and Substance Abuse at Columbia University found that, among seventeen-year-old high school students, 52 percent said they knew someone who sold illegal drugs, 41 percent had seen drugs sold at their school, 34 percent said that half or more of their friends used marijuana, and 41 percent thought drugs were a teenager's biggest problem. ("Drugs Common in Schools, Survey Shows," *The New York Times*, September 9, 1997.) The understandable reluctance of teenagers to share with pollsters their experience with illegal drugs suggests that all of these figures (except the last) probably understate the true extent of that experience.

Least reliable of all are answers to poll questions about teenagers' own drug use. This, however, does not deter the federal government from basing antidrug policy on the results of such polls. The latest survey, conducted by the Parents' Resource Institute for Drug Education in Atlanta, showed drug use rising among younger teenagers. General Barry R. McCaffrey, the White House's drug policy director, announced these findings, observing, "It's now literally at age 10 where you can see the onslaught of drugs." ("Drug Use by Young Teen-Agers Is Found Up," *The New York Times*, October 29, 1997.)

page xix "drug trade is the heart of the nation's underground economy": Estimates of the size of the illegal drug trade often seem to be what researchers call "PFA"— pulled from the air. The White House Office of National Drug Control Policy offers an improbably precise chart of "Drug User Expenditures" (cocaine: $39.5 billion) in its annual National Drug Control Strategy, and, between 1988 and 1993 (the last year for which figures are available), its estimates ranged from $66.9 billion to $48.7 billion for total U.S. expenditures on illicit drugs. ("The National Drug Control Strategy: 1996," p. 78.) In a symposium sponsored by *The National Review*, William F. Buckley, Jr., estimated that American consumers spend $70 billion a year on illegal drugs and that the government spends another $75 billion on trying to control them, while Judge Robert W. Sweet, of New York City, using markup calculations provided by *The Economist* (December 24, 1994–January 6, 1995, p. 22), estimated the U.S. drug market at a whopping $150 billion a year. (*The National Review*, February 12, 1996, pp. 35, 44.) Finally, in December 1996, the secretary general of Interpol estimated international drug trafficking's annual turnover at $400 billion, which would make it the world's second most lucrative business, after the arms trade. ("Drug Traffic's Value Put at $400 Billion," *The New York Times*, December 16, 1996.) If these figures bear even a remote resemblance to reality, then the drug trade drives most of the cash that passes through the American underground (untaxed) economy.

page xx "'African Americans constitute 12 percent'": James A. Morone, "The Corrosive Politics of Virtue," *The American Prospect*, May/June, 1996, p. 35. (Morone's source, though uncited, appears to be Marc Mauer and Tracy Huling, "Young Black Americans and the Criminal Justice System: Five Years Later," The Sentencing Project, October 1995, p. 12.)

It should be noted that, while racially selective law enforcement can account for much of the difference between the percentage of African Americans arrested for drug possession and the percentages convicted and given prison sentences, the concentration of street drug markets in black urban ghettos and the overrepresentation of African Americans among street drug dealers undoubtedly account for some of the difference between the unremarkable percentage of African Americans using drugs and the much higher percentage arrested for possession.

page xx   "cultural 'balkanization'": Some of these critiques have been searching, others self-serving. For a fair sample, see Richard Bernstein, *Dictatorship of Virtue: How the Battle Over Multiculturalism Is Reshaping Our Schools, Our Country, and Our Lives* (Knopf, 1994); Arthur M. Schlesinger, Jr., *The Disuniting of America: Reflections on a Multicultural Society* (Norton, 1992); Dinesh D'Souza, *Illiberal Education: The Politics of Race and Sex on Campus* (Free Press, 1991); and Diane Ravitch, "Multiculturalism: E Pluribus Plures," in *The American Scholar,* Summer 1990 (reprinted in *Debating P.C.: The Controversy over Political Correctness on College Campuses,* ed. Paul Berman [Dell, 1992]).

Some conservative analysts, such as Samuel P. Huntington, have warned that multiculturalism may corrupt American foreign policy and even doom the nation to extinction. "If multiculturalism prevails and if the consensus on liberal democracy disintegrates, the United States could join the Soviet Union on the ash heap of history." (Samuel P. Huntington, "The Erosion of American National Interests," *Foreign Affairs,* September/October 1997, p. 35.)

page xx   "centripetal, homogenizing cultural forces; Afrocentrism is but a frail reed": Benjamin R. Barber, in a study of the global conflict between these forces, finds that the same imbalance obtains internationally. "Jihad" is his shorthand for indigenous ethnic and religious passions, "McWorld" the term he uses for the institutions of mass marketing. "To think that indigenization and globalization are entirely coequal forces that put Jihad and McWorld on an equal footing is to vastly underestimate the force of the new planetary markets. . . . It's no contest." (Benjamin R. Barber, *Jihad vs. McWorld: How Globalism and Tribalism Are Reshaping the World* [Ballantine, 1996], p. 12.)

page xx   " 'June Teenth' ": While June Teenth had become neglected in San Augustine, it was catching on outside Texas. The Anacostia Museum, in Washington, D.C., began sponsoring a June Teenth celebration in 1990. Seven years later, 140 communities throughout the United States and Canada were said to be celebrating it. In 1997 the U.S. House of Representatives declared June 19 "African-American Independence Day." ("June-teenth," Morning Edition, National Public Radio, June 19, 1997.)

page xx   "high-consumption, high-debt culture": Between 1973 and 1994, American household debt rose from 58.6 percent of personal income to 83.9 percent. One recent study showed household debt had reached a new all-time high: 91 percent of disposable personal income. As of December 1997, according to *The New York Times,* "American consumers are carrying about $1.2 trillion in installment credit, up about 50 percent from just four years ago, and the average credit card holder has four cards and about $4,000 in high-interest debt." (Mishel, Bernstein, Schmitt, p. 294; William Greider, "When Optimism Meets Overcapacity," Op-Ed, *The New York Times,* October 1, 1997; quotation from "Giving Credit Where Debt Is Due," *The New York Times,* December 14, 1997.)

page xxi   "liberal consumerism": I heard this term used in a panel discussion by Douglas Rae, a professor of political science at Yale, and found that it caught more social and historical nuances of the postwar phenomenon of mass consumerism than more common terms do. It is not meant to refer to contemporary political liberalism but to the classical liberalism that, with its emphasis on liberty, individualism, and tolerance, underpins all modern, nonfundamentalist social thought.

Barbara Ehrenreich makes a sly connection between "culture of poverty" theorists and critics of postwar consumerism. The latter group produced, in the late 1950s, a spate of worried books and essays on the enervating effects of "affluence" on the national character. This was shortly before American poverty was "discovered" by the mass media in the early 1960s. Commentators seeking to explain the persistence of poverty in a land of plenty seized on the anthropologist Oscar Lewis's notion of a "culture of poverty"—although Lewis had actually coined the phrase for a strictly limited purpose, and even connected it to the remedy of political mobilization—and then used it to recycle the hoary image of a heedless, self-destructive lower class. But as Ehrenreich writes, "The ideal consumer, like the denizen of the culture of poverty, is hedonistic, impulsive, self-indulgent. Nothing could better serve the consumer-goods industries than for everyone to abandon their 'capacity for deferred gratification' and become as suggestible and addicted to sensation as the poor were said to be. These were the traits that marketing men hoped to inculcate in all Americans, and especially those who had money to spend. . . . The poor—the invented poor—came to serve as a mirror for the middle class, reflecting its own dread submission to the imperatives of consumption, the tyranny of affluence." (*Fear of Falling: The Inner Life of the Middle Class* [Pantheon, 1989], pp. 52, 56.)

page xxi "more than 380,000 TV commercials": Children between the ages of two and eleven watch an average of three hours and thirty-four minutes of TV a day. Those between the ages of twelve and seventeen watch an average of three hours a day. (Nielsen Media Research, unpublished survey, December 1996.) For younger children, 82 percent of that time is spent watching channels that show commercials; for older children, the figure is 88 percent. ("Children's Viewing to All Sources [Full Day]," Nielsen Total Viewing Sources Report, Nielsen Media Research, July 1997.) Under the Children's Television Act of 1990, commercial stations are allowed to broadcast twelve minutes of commercials—that's 24 thirty-second spots—each hour during children's programming during the week. On weekends the limit is ten and a half minutes. Although the limits are higher for ordinary programming, I've used the children's-programming figures to come up with this number. The true average total of commercials viewed before age eighteen may be much higher.

page xxii "The sociologist Jennifer Hochschild": Jennifer L. Hochschild, *Facing Up to the American Dream: Race, Class, and the Soul of the Nation* (Princeton University Press, 1995), p. 5 and elsewhere.

page xxii "consumerism's mythic twin, the American Dream": There are innumerable interpretations of this overused trope, not all of them materialistic. John E. Schwarz, for instance, sees it as a source of social cohesion, reflecting "the faith that we all belong somewhere within a rational and forgiving system that in the end rewards hard work, intelligence, and sacrifice. The ethos is that everyone who steadfastly practices certain practical virtues will find a place at the table. No one need be left out, unless he or she voluntarily chooses to be." (Schwarz, *Illusions of Opportunity*, p. 16.)

page xxii "youth-gang phenomenon is so widespread": In a national survey of police gang experts, Malcolm W. Klein found that 94 percent of U.S. cities with populations of 100,000 or more—176 out of 189 cities—reported a street-gang problem.

In a random-sample survey of the 2,250 American cities with populations between 10,000 and 100,000, 38.3 percent reported a gang problem, and most said it had appeared only after 1985. Though most of these cities estimated their gang membership to be less than 500, the problem was clearly escalating. (Malcolm W. Klein, *The American Street Gang: Its Nature, Prevalence, and Control* [Oxford University Press, 1995], pp. 31–35.)

BOOK ONE: NEW HAVEN

page 3   "Newhallville, a working-class neighborhood": For histories of Newhallville, New Haven, and New Haven's black community, see Rollin G. Osterweis, *Three Centuries of New Haven, 1638–1938* (Yale University Press, 1953); Robert Austin Warner, *New Haven Negroes: A Social History* (Yale University Press, 1940); William Michael Johnston, *On the Outside Looking In: Irish, Italian and Black Ethnic Politics in an American City* (Ph.D. dissertation, Yale University, 1977), pp. 23–32, 234–89; and *Inside New Haven's Neighborhoods* (City of New Haven, 1982), pp. 97–106.

page 4   "Like every old industrial city in America, New Haven": For a valuable study of plant closings, see Barry Bluestone and Bennett Harrison, *The Deindustrialization of America: Plant Closings, Community Abandonment, and the Dismantling of Basic Industry* (Basic Books, 1982). For the invidious effects of deindustrialization and middle-class flight on the black urban poor, see William Julius Wilson, *The Truly Disadvantaged: The Inner City, the Underclass, and Public Policy* (University of Chicago Press, 1987), and *When Work Disappears: The World of the New Urban Poor* (Knopf, 1996).

In the past thirty years, according to Jeremy Rifkin, "the number of factory workers in the United States has declined from 33 percent of the work force to under 17 percent," and the number will continue to fall—to less than 12 percent by the year 2006. Automation, Rifkin contends, is replacing the assembly line worldwide. By 2020, "less than 2 percent of the entire global work force will still be engaged in factory work." In the meantime, in this country, African Americans have been disproportionately affected by deindustrialization. Rifkin cites a report by the Equal Employment Opportunity Commission showing that "black wage-earners made up nearly one-third of the 180,000 manufacturing jobs lost in 1990 and 1991." (Jeremy Rifkin, "Civil Society in the Information Age," *The Nation*, February 26, 1996, pp. 11–16; quotations from pp. 11, 16.) See also *African Americans and Post-Industrial Labor Markets* (Transaction, 1996), ed. James B. Stewart.

page 4   "overall population of the city shrank": New Haven's 1994 population was 119,604. (U.S. Bureau of the Census, 1995.) In 1990, the city's black population was 47,157. (U.S. Census, Summary Population and Housing Characteristics.)

page 4   "the seventh-poorest city in America": Special Commission on Poverty, "The Extent, Distribution and Causes of Poverty in New Haven" (City of New Haven, 1983), p. 39. This description refers to the percentage of the population in cities of 100,000 or more who were living below the federal poverty level.

page 4   "neighborhoods where the poverty rate ran as high as 40 and 50 percent": The census tracts with the highest poverty concentrations in 1990 were in a neighborhood near Yale–New Haven Hospital once known as Sodom Hill, now known as the Hill. The area, already a slum, was ravaged by extensive "urban renewal" in the 1960s. (Census-tract figures provided by the City Room at the Institution for Social and Policy Studies, Yale University.)

page 13   "The illegal drug business . . . in New Haven": For this brief history, useful interviews included: Dr. Martin Waugh, Central Medical Unit, APT Foundation, New Haven; Dr. Charles Riordan, Hospital of St. Raphael, New Haven; Dr. Richard Schottenfeld, Connecticut Mental Health Center; Dr. Charles Morgan, APT Foundation; Marie Countryman, Victor Gotay, and Jeraldine Bryant, Orchard Street Clinic, New Haven; and Major Daniel Blackmon, New Haven Police Department.

page 13 "400,000 people live in the New Haven hinterland": "Population Projections, Series 95.1," Connecticut Office of Policy and Management, September 1995.

pages 13–14 "The city's public defender for juveniles": Ray Krezinski, interview, January 26, 1990, and follow-up, August 1990.

page 16 "*New Haven Register* surveyed public opinion": *New Haven Register,* June 25, 1989.

page 16 "19,425 serious crimes": FBI Uniform Crime Reports, "Crime in the United States, 1988" (Government Printing Office, 1989), p. 78.

page 17 "most of New Haven's workers now live outside the city": Karen Gilvarg, of the New Haven City Plan Department, reported that only one out of three workers in downtown New Haven lives in the city. (Interview, March 21, 1997.)

The 1990 census found that whites comprised just under 49 percent of New Haven's population.

page 17 "a multiple shooting on the steps of the state courthouse": "3 Youths Shot as Gangs Clash at Courthouse," *The New York Times,* December 13, 1989.

Bond amounts for the suspects were reported in the *New Haven Register,* December 14, 1989.

page 17 "more than 320 shootings . . . and 34 murders": For figures on shootings and murders, see the *New Haven Register,* January 3, 1990. The murder rate per 100,000 people in 1989 was 27.4 in New Haven. In New York, the same rate was 25.0; in Los Angeles, 26.0; in Chicago, 26.9. ("No Haven," New Haven *Advocate,* January 8, 1990.)

page 17 "the New Haven police made 2,700 drug-related arrests": The figure for 1984 was 573. (*New Haven Register,* June 25, 1989.)

page 17 "The city's superintendent of schools": Dr. John Dow, interview, November 27, 1989.

page 22 "my clients' Social Register": Joan Leonard, interview, January 26, 1990.

page 26 "Soaring arrest rates were part of a conspiracy": "Warehousing black youth" has in fact become a mammoth national project. A 1995 study found that, among African American males between the ages of twenty and twenty-nine, *one in three* were "under criminal justice supervision on any given day—either in prison or jail, or on probation or parole." The war on drugs, "and not increases in crime, [was] the most critical factor leading to the rise in minority incarcerations." Between 1983 and 1993, the number of drug offenders among inmates rose 510 percent. (Marc Mauer and Tracy Huling, "Young Black Americans and the Criminal Justice System: Five Years Later," Sentencing Project, October 1995, Report Summary.)

page 26 "Kwanzaa, an 'African-based' holiday": For a sympathetic, if ambivalent, personal essay on Kwanzaa, see Gerald Early, "Dreaming of a Black Christmas," *Harper's,* January 1997, pp. 55–61.

page 27 "84 percent of families": U.S. Department of Commerce, 1990 Census of Population and Housing, Tape File 3A, General Income and Poverty Profile; also, Summary Tape File 3A, File P019.

page 29 "They expanded a previous voter registration project": Paul Bass and

Howard Altman, "Why He Won: The Soul of a New Machine," New Haven *Advocate*, September 18, 1989.

page 29   "a centuries-long story in New Haven politics": A resonant and influential version of this story can be found in Robert A. Dahl, *Who Governs? Democracy and Power in an American City* (Yale University Press, 1961).

page 30   "Blacks have always faced far more daunting obstacles": The increasingly popular idea that many blacks (and Latinos) simply missed the historical boat by arriving in American cities too late, after the heyday of heavy industry, scants the profound impact of occupational racism on the economic chances of earlier generations of black immigrants. Useful studies of different immigrant experiences in individual Northern cities include John Bodnar, Roger Simon, and Michael P. Weber, *Lives of Their Own: Blacks, Italians, and Poles in Pittsburgh, 1900–1960* (University of Illinois Press, 1982), and Theodore Hershberg, *Philadelphia: Work, Space, Family, and Group Experience in the Nineteenth Century* (Oxford University Press, 1981).

page 30   "Between 1975 and 1992, the average income": The average income of the lowest fifth of black families was, in constant 1992 dollars, $6,333 in 1975. In 1992, it was $4,255. (U.S. Bureau of the Census, "Money Income of Households, Families, and Persons in the United States: 1992," as cited in Wilson, *When Work Disappears*, p. 195.)

page 30   "Daniels's younger brother, Robert, was arrested": "Portrait of a Leading Family Enduring the Hurt of Drugs," *The New York Times*, February 26, 1990.

Robert Daniels was sentenced to four years in prison after pleading guilty to sale of cocaine and conspiracy. ("In Drug Case, Mayor's Brother Is Sent to Jail," *The New York Times*, July 21, 1990.)

page 34   "a vast urban renewal project": See Fred Powledge, *Model City: A Test of American Liberalism—One Town's Efforts to Rebuild Itself* (Simon and Schuster, 1970). The Richard Lee quote, "Our goal is a slumless city," is from a speech given to New Haven's aldermen in February 1959 and cited in Powledge, p. 42. The Willard Wirtz quote, "the greatest success story," is from "An Old Industrial City Wages Dramatic War on Poverty," Trenton (New Jersey) *Sunday Times Advertiser*, July 12, 1964, as cited in Powledge, p. 90.

page 34   "it displaced far more poor people": See Norman I. Fainstein and Susan S. Fainstein, "New Haven: The Limits of the Local State," in *Restructuring the City: The Political Economy of Urban Redevelopment*, eds. Susan S. Fainstein, Norman I. Fainstein, Richard Child Hill, Dennis Judd, and Michael Peter Smith (Longman, 1986), pp. 47, 49.

page 42   "when the town's founding Puritan elite was displaced": See Dahl, *Who Governs?*, pp. 11–31.

page 42   "superintendent of New Haven's schools": Dr. John Dow, interview, November 27, 1989.

page 43   "Jesse Jackson's 1988 campaign": For a searing analysis of the 1984 Jackson campaign as ritualized media event and occasion for opportunism on the part of black elites, see Adolph L. Reed, Jr., *The Jesse Jackson Phenomenon: The Crisis of Purpose in Afro-American Politics* (Yale University Press, 1986).

page 44   "Dr. James Comer": Dr. Comer is a prolific author and educational reformer. Some of his recent ideas about child development, schools, and black families can be found in *Waiting for a Miracle: Why Schools Can't Solve Our Problems—And How We Can* (Dutton Signet, 1997) and *Rallying the Whole Village: The Comer Process for Reforming Education*, eds. James P. Comer, Norris M. Haynes, Edward Joyner, and Michael Ben-Avie (Teachers College Press, 1996).

page 45   "the reasons not to deal drugs must seem weak": For a lively comparative study of the careers, legal and illegal, of poor urban youths in black, white, and Latino neighborhoods, see Mercer L. Sullivan, *"Getting Paid": Youth Crime and Work in the Inner City* (Cornell University Press, 1989).

page 50   "Dopebusters, who . . . chased the drug dealers out": After this success in Washington in 1989, the Nation of Islam began winning government contracts to provide security in public housing projects around the country—in Pittsburgh, Philadelphia, Los Angeles, Chicago, Baltimore—and also went into the private security business. Some of the government contracts were canceled or not renewed after protests by Jewish and other groups about the Nation's anti-Semitism, racism, and homophobia. ("As Farrakhan Groups Land Jobs from Government, Debate Grows," *The New York Times*, March 4, 1994; "Baltimore Must Drop a Contract, HUD Says," *The New York Times*, November 11, 1995.)

page 65   "the AIDS virus, which has cut a terrifying swath": Dr. Alicia Roach, epidemiologist, Connecticut Department of Health, and Dr. Jerry Friedland, AIDS Program, Yale School of Medicine, interviews, March 1997.

page 66   "Connecticut contains some of the nation's worst ghettos": The poverty rate in Hartford, according to the 1990 census, was over 26 percent. For Newark, it was 25.7 percent; for East Los Angeles, 23 percent. ("Maptitude Census Data Disk," produced by the Caliper Corporation.)

    Connecticut's 1996 per-capita income, according to the U.S. Commerce Department, was $33,189, the highest in the nation. ("Region Lags in Gain in Personal Income," *The New York Times*, April 29, 1997.)

page 67   "A New Haven drug treatment administrator": Dr. Charles Riordan, Hospital of St. Raphael, interview, December 7, 1989.

page 67   "The commander of CAPACT operations": Commander Leonard Gallo, New Haven Police Department, interview, January 29, 1990.

page 68   "Science Park": Carole Bass, "Science Park Grows Up," New Haven *Independent*, March 30, 1989.

page 78   " 'streetcorner men' ": The best examination of this inner-city subculture is Elliot Liebow, *Tally's Corner: A Study of Negro Streetcorner Men* (Little, Brown, 1967).

page 79   "the lead story in the *Register*": "Cops Nab 15 in Drug Sweep," *New Haven Register*, April 29, 1990; "Saying Drug Gang Is Broken, New Haven Police Arrest 15," *The New York Times*, April 30, 1990.

page 86   "40 percent of Job Corps participants drop out": "Remnant of the War on Poverty, Job Corps Is Still a Quiet Success," *The New York Times*, February 17, 1992.

page 88   "The state had lost an estimated 200,000 jobs": "Winning the Cold War and Losing a Job," *The New York Times*, February 9, 1993.

page 89   "it fell by more than 10,000 people": In 1990, the population had been 130,474. In 1994, it was 119,604.

page 89   "a new kind of urban redevelopment": See Paul Bass, "The Bulldozer's Back," New Haven *Advocate*, July 25–31, 1996.

page 89   "an iconoclastic new police chief, Nicholas Pastore": See "Chief With High Profile Uses Streets to Test New Theories," *The New York Times*, November 1, 1991; also, Paul Bass, "Saint Nick," New Haven *Advocate*, December 22–28, 1994.

page 89   "a student was shot on campus in 1994": "Student Is Shot at a High School in New Haven," *The New York Times*, November 10, 1994.

page 89   "several of the big drug posses were . . . broken up": Bass, "Saint Nick."

page 89   "the first known Colombian connection in New Haven": "The Battle of the

Drug Trade in Fair Haven," *The New York Times,* Connecticut edition, February 4, 1996.

page 90 "in West Haven, starkly inferior maintenance and services": See Paul Bass, "The Two 'Two Cities' Tours," New Haven *Advocate,* June 27–July 3, 1996.

page 90 "The best hope for many deteriorating American cities": David Rusk, the former mayor of Albuquerque, advocates the creation of "metro governments" of various types. "For many small and medium-size metro areas, the surest way to avoid or reverse patterns of racial and economic segregation is to create metro governments. This can be achieved by expanding the central government through aggressive annexation policies, by consolidating the city and county, or by fully empowering county government and abolishing or reducing the role of municipalities." (*Cities Without Suburbs* [Woodrow Wilson Center Press, 1993], p. 123.)

Jane Jacobs, the great urbanist, has long ridiculed the idea of expanding urban jurisdictions, arguing for smaller, more manageable polities. In *The Death and Life of Great American Cities* (Random House, 1961), she quotes an unnamed wit saying, "A Region is an area safely larger than the last one to whose problems we found no solution." Jacobs goes on to describe New Haven, in some detail, as a city of manageable scale. And yet she was writing in 1960, when New Haven had—according at least to the 1950 census figures she used—nearly 165,000 residents. The city has since lost more than a quarter of that population and has become so much poorer that its problems no longer respond to merely local treatment (pp. 411–12; quotation from p. 410).

BOOK TWO: DEEP EAST TEXAS

page 96 "'what you would expect to find in a large metropolitan area'": "Federal, State, Local Lawmen Sweep East Texas Counties," Nacogdoches *Daily Sentinel,* June 4, 1989.

page 96 "The county . . . has only eight thousand inhabitants": The exact figure, according to the 1990 census, was 7,999. (U.S. Department of Commerce, 1990 Census of Population and Housing.) The poverty rate was 29.7 percent. (*Ibid.,* Selected Characteristics by Poverty Status.) The black poverty rate was 48.8 percent. (*Ibid.*)

page 96 "of fifty-four people ultimately convicted on various charges, fifty were black": John M. Bales, United States Attorney's Office, Beaumont, Texas, interviewed by Pete Wells, researcher, August 1994.

page 96 "San Augustine County is 28 percent black": 1990 Census, Selected Characteristics of the Population.

page 99 "San Augustine County has fewer people living in it today than it did in 1900": The county's population peaked in 1920 at 13,737. (Texas Agricultural Extension Service, "Long-Range Extension Program," 1981, p. 23.)

page 100 "The town of San Augustine, laid out in 1833": G. L. Crocket, *Two Centuries in East Texas: A History of San Augustine County and Surrounding Territory, from 1685* (1932; facsimile edition, Hart Graphics, 1982), pp. 103–4.

page 101 "the county's 1870 census": "1870 Edited Census of San Augustine County," ed. Mrs. McXie Whitton Martin, 1983 (privately published).

page 101 "1990 population: 2,430": *Texas Almanac and State Industrial Guide 1994–1995* (Belo, 1995), p. 266.

page 102 "The South became a one-party state after Reconstruction": V. O. Key, Jr., *Southern Politics in State and Nation* (Knopf, 1949).

page 102   "In the 1890s, the Populists . . . briefly challenged the ruling Democrats":
For the Populist movement, see Edward L. Ayers, *The Promise of the New South: Life
After Reconstruction* (Oxford University Press, 1992), pp. 249–82; Lawrence Good-
wyn, *Democratic Promise: The Populist Movement in America* (Oxford University
Press, 1976), pp. 213–43; Robert C. McMath, Jr., *Populist Vanguard: A History of the
Southern Farmers' Alliance* (University of North Carolina Press, 1975), pp. 90–109;
and C. Vann Woodward, *Tom Watson, Agrarian Rebel* (Macmillan, 1938). For events
in San Augustine County, see Joe F. Combs, *Gunsmoke in the Redlands* (The Naylor
Company, 1968), pp. 22–88.

page 102   "a legendary binge of robbery, rape, assault, and murder": Ben Procter, *Just
One Riot: Episodes of Texas Rangers in the 20th Century* (Eakin Press, 1992), "Leo
Bishop and the San Augustine Crime Wave," pp. 59–73.

page 105   "The Ramseys were members of the old, landed elite of San Augustine":
For a fine sketch of Smith Ramsey, see Richard West, "The Petrified Forest," *Texas
Monthly*, April 1978, pp. 107–15, 163–79.

page 107   "By the 1970s, Tindall's businesses were grossing": *Ibid.*, p. 163.

page 108   "public schools were segregated until 1970": *Ibid.*, p. 176.

page 108   "signs of black progress . . . were . . . scant": A notable sign of black political progress came in 1995, when Gertrude Lane, who is black, was elected mayor
of the town of San Augustine. Lane was not, however, a particularly forceful advocate of black interests. The town's business went on exactly as before and, when
charges of mismanagement and racism in the police department were aired in
1997, Lane's view was that, in the words of the Beaumont *Enterprise*, "racial slurs
are OK in private conversation." ("San Augustine Needs Stability," editorial, Beaumont *Enterprise*, November 16, 1997.)

page 108   "The town was more than 50 percent black": The town of San Augustine's
black population was 1,318, according to the 1990 census.

page 109   "Reconstruction . . . was a time of profound upheaval": Crocket, *Two Cen-
turies in East Texas*, pp. 346–49.
    For less myopic studies of Reconstruction, see Eric Foner, *Reconstruction: Amer-
ica's Unfinished Revolution, 1863–1877* (Harper & Row, 1988); Leon F. Litwack,
Been in the Storm So Long: The Aftermath of Slavery (Knopf, 1979); Kenneth M.
Stampp, *The Era of Reconstruction, 1865–1877* (Knopf, 1965); and John Hope
Franklin, *Reconstruction After the Civil War* (University of Chicago Press, 1961.)

page 109   " 'He would assemble them at night' ": Crocket, pp. 347–48; quotations
from p. 347.

page 110   "Texas ranked third in the nation in lynchings": Alwyn Barr, *Black Texans:
A History of Negroes in Texas, 1528–1971* (Jenkins, 1973), p. 135.

page 110   "a plantation that, in the 1860 census, had 132 slaves": William Garrett
also owned 36,751 acres. His large white-pillared house, complete with preserved
slave bell, is owned today by nondescendants.

page 111   "Between 1940 and 1960, the rural black population": Barr, *Black Texans*,
p. 196.
    The same decline occurred throughout the South. In 1920, one of every seven
American farmers was black; by 1982, only one farmer in sixty-seven was black.
(Osha Gray Davidson, *Broken Heartland: The Rise of America's Rural Ghetto* [Free
Press, 1990], p. 37.)

page 111   "Perhaps half the land in the Pre-Emption still belongs to blacks": A. E.
Whitton, land surveyor, San Augustine County, interview, February 9, 1992.

pages 111–12   "International Paper is the largest landowner": *Ibid.*

page 112 "Nowadays, only old folks even seemed to remember it": To Laverne Clark's surprised satisfaction, a local movement to resume observation of June Teenth started up in 1996 with a baseball tournament, a dance contest, a barbecue, and a parade.

page 132 "not one had graduated before becoming pregnant": This pattern continued with the next daughter, Laverne's sixth, who got pregnant during her senior year. She later set up housekeeping in the Cedar Hills housing project with the father of her baby, and at the end of 1997, although still not married, the couple were expecting their second child. Laverne's older daughters, meanwhile, despite the seemingly long odds against marital happiness, continued to try their luck. Lyndorie briefly married a young man who ended up in state prison for drug dealing. Lyndra married, more lastingly, a longtime boyfriend with a steady job in a sanitation department in the next county north, and they bought a house together. Then Lanee, in 1995, while singing at a regional church musical with Laverne, met James Derrick Jones of Shreveport, Louisiana. They were married in 1996. Lanee and Johnathan moved to Shreveport, where Jones worked in a paper mill, earning more than twice the wage that Lanee had earned at the Tyson plant—it seemed that not all of the economic opportunity once represented by the cities had disappeared. They lived in a safe neighborhood, Lanee reported, where most of their neighbors were white. She and Johnathan sorely missed San Augustine, though, and frequently met with Laverne and other family members at a roadside spot midway between Shreveport and San Augustine. "It's like Dorothy says in *The Wizard of Oz*," Lanee told me wistfully at the end of 1997. " 'There's no place like home.' "

page 133 "the median white household owns": U.S. Bureau of the Census, "Household Wealth and Asset Ownership: 1991" (1994), cited in Jennifer L. Hochschild, *Facing Up to the American Dream: Race, Class, and the Soul of the Nation* (Princeton University Press, 1995), p. 43.

  Another fact that might have interested Laverne was a long, slow decline in the poverty rate among black, female-headed families. The rate remained atrociously high, but, between 1973 and 1995, while the poverty rate among white, female-headed families rose from 24.6 percent to 26.6 percent, it fell among black, female-headed families—from 52.8 percent to 45.1 percent, a nontrivial decline, as economists say. (Lawrence Mishel, Jared Bernstein, John Schmitt, *The State of Working America, 1996–97* [Economic Policy Institute, 1997], p. 322.)

page 133 "a shortage of 'marriageable' . . . young men": The term comes from William Julius Wilson, who, in *The Truly Disadvantaged: The Inner City, the Underclass, and Public Policy* (University of Chicago Press, 1987), actually came up with a Male Marriageable Pool Index (pp. 95–106).

page 133 "where systems of mutual kin support": The definitive ethnographic work on this subject was Carol Stack's *All Our Kin: Strategies for Survival in a Black Community* (Harper & Row, 1974), in which she examined kin networks in a poor black community in a Midwestern city. Anne R. Roschelle argues, in *No More Kin: Exploring Race, Class, and Gender in Family Networks* (Sage, 1997), that such support systems among poor black and Latino families have been eroded over the past twenty years.

page 134 "no disgrace attached to unwed motherhood": There is abundant testimony that this lack of stigma has become more widespread in recent years. In black communities, the stigma was probably always stronger in the urban North than in the rural South. Elaine Bell Kaplan, studying teenage mothers in East Oakland and Richmond, California, found *their* mothers and grandmothers angry with them for getting pregnant. (Kaplan, *Not Our Kind of Girl: Unraveling the Myths of Black Teenage Motherhood* [University of California Press, 1997].)

page 134 "fewer than one fourth of the students who managed to graduate": Leroy Hughes, principal, San Augustine High School, interview, September 25, 1991.

Among adults over twenty-five in San Augustine County, fewer than 10 percent had college degrees. Among black adults over twenty-five, fewer than 3 percent had college degrees. (U.S. Department of Commerce, 1990 Census of Population and Housing, Summary Tape File 3, Selected Characteristics by Educational Attainment.)

page 134 "During slavery, young black women faced less risk": "Demonstrated early (and then high) fertility greatly increased a married or unmarried [slave] woman's value to her owner and therefore diminished the likelihood of her sale. . . . [The birth of a child] not only diminished the probability of the physical separation of its mother from her family of origin but also made a marriage, and the future of a new slave family, much more secure." (Herbert G. Gutman, *The Black Family in Slavery and Freedom, 1750–1925* [Vintage, 1976], pp. 75–76.)

page 134 "Slaveowners . . . encouraged their slaves to reproduce": "An early end to the slave trade, followed by a boom in cotton and plantation slavery, dictated a policy of encouraging slave births." (Eugene D. Genovese, *In Red and Black: Marxian Explorations in Southern and Afro-American History* [Vintage, 1971], p. 87.)

"Enslavement required more than that human chattel produce commodities: it also required—especially after the abolition of the overseas slave trade—that the slave labor force reproduce itself. Few realized this better than the slaveowners themselves. . . . The system put a high premium on females who began early to bear children, inside or outside of marriage." (Gutman, p. 75.)

page 134 "Protestant churches . . . did try to stigmatize": See E. Franklin Frazier, *The Negro Family in the United States* (University of Chicago Press, 1966), pp. 89–101.

page 134 "even slavery provided an environment more congenial": Herbert Gutman's *The Black Family in Slavery and Freedom* documents, at length and with eloquence, the remarkable adaptive strength of the black family in slavery. Nicholas Lemann, in *The Promised Land: The Great Black Migration and How It Changed America* (Knopf, 1991), convincingly renders the hardships of sharecropping in the Mississippi Delta and the regular year-end disappointments that led to "the great annual reshuffling of black families between plantations in the Delta" (p. 20). As Gerald Jaynes has pointed out, the sharecropping system virtually required a male-headed family as a labor unit. Its rigors and frequent displacements nonetheless placed severe strains on settled family life. (Even slave families tended at least to stay put from year to year.) For contemporary accounts of black sharecropping life by academics, see Charles S. Johnson, *Shadow of the Plantation* (University of Chicago Press, 1934; Transaction, 1996); John Dollard, *Caste and Class in a Southern Town* (Yale University Press, 1937); Hortense Powdermaker, *After Freedom: A Cultural Study of the Deep South* (Russell & Russell, 1968); and Gunnar Myrdal, *An American Dilemma: The Negro Problem and Modern Democracy* (Harper & Row, 1944; Transaction, 1996). All cited in Lemann.

page 134 "social reformers, including W.E.B. Du Bois": "Among the lowest class of recent immigrants and other unfortunates there is much sexual promiscuity and the absence of a real home life. . . . Cohabitation of a more or less permanent character is a direct offshoot of the plantation life and is practiced considerably." (W.E.B. Du Bois, *The Philadelphia Negro: A Social Study* [University of Pennsylvania Press,

1996], pp. 192–93; also quoted in Lemann.) DuBois believed, however, that at the time—*The Philadelphia Negro* was published in 1899—loose-living slumdwellers were a small minority. "Of the great mass of Negroes this class forms a very small percentage and is absolutely without social standing. They are the dregs which indicate the former history and the dangerous tendencies of the masses." (p. 193.) (It should be noted that these passages were written near the beginning of a long and extremely distinguished career, and that this sort of Victorian, not to say Calvinist, moralism was not characteristic of Du Bois's mature work.)

E. Franklin Frazier was another African American academic from the North who held a dim view of the habits of migrants from the South—see his *The Negro Family in Chicago* (University of Chicago Press, 1932). Lemann advanced an updated version of the migrating-family-disorder theory in 1986 in *The Atlantic*, contending, "Every aspect of the underclass culture in the ghettos is directly traceable to roots in the South—and not the South of slavery but the South of a generation ago. In fact, there seems to be a strong correlation between underclass status in the North and a family background in the nascent underclass of the sharecropper South." ("The Origins of the Underclass," June 1986, p. 35; a second installment of this article appeared in July 1986.) Lemann's argument was disputed by William Julius Wilson in *The Truly Disadvantaged*, who pointed out that "the systematic research on urban poverty and recent migration (that is, migration in the second half of the twentieth century) consistently shows that southern-born blacks who have migrated to the urban North experience greater economic success in terms of employment rates, earnings, and welfare dependency than do those urban blacks who were born in the North." (p. 55.) Lemann replied, indirectly, in *The Promised Land* by asking if a sharecropper background did not emerge nontheless as a disadvantage *among* black Southern migrants to Northern cities. (Lemann, *The Promised Land* [Vintage paperback edition, 1992], p. 287.)

page 135   "Between 1960 and 1990, the number of children": Rebecca M. Blank, *It Takes a Nation: A New Agenda for Fighting Poverty* (Russell Sage Foundation/Princeton University Press, 1997), p. 35.

Among American teenagers, who tend to be unwed, the birth rate has actually been falling throughout the 1990s—most dramatically, as it happens, among black teenagers, where it fell 21 percent between 1991 and 1996. Despite these declines, the black teenage birth rate was still nearly twice the white rate, and the United States still had the highest rates of teenage pregnancy, teenage birth, and teenage abortion in the developed world. ("U.S. Life Expectancy Hits New High," *The New York Times*, September 12, 1997.)

page 135   "the poverty rate among rural blacks remains much higher": In 1992 the poverty rate for rural blacks was 40.8 percent; for urban blacks, 31.9 percent. (*Blacks in Rural America*, eds. James B. Stewart and Joyce E. Allen-Smith [Transaction, 1995], p. 5, Table 1, "Median Income and Poverty Rates by Residence and Race, 1992," citing U.S. Bureau of Labor Statistics.)

page 140   "Cocaine made its way into Deep East Texas by various routes": For this account, useful interviews included: Zechariah Shelton, Federal Bureau of Investigation; Ken Magidson, U.S. Attorney's Office, Houston; Stuart Platt, U.S. Attorney's Office, Beaumont; Wayne Padgett, Marvin McLeroy, and Rickey Allen, Texas Department of Public Safety, Lufkin; and Tom Lantini, Drug Enforcement Administration, Houston.

page 140   "Arthur Watts and Willie Ray (Blue Tick) Edwards . . . hooked up with a couple of low-level Colombian dealers": Willie Ray (Blue Tick) Edwards, interview,

Seagoville Federal Correctional Institute, Dallas, January 23, 1992; Harlon Kelly, interview, Fort Worth Federal Correctional Institute, January 22, 1992.

pages 140–41 "According to the FBI, Jackson started buying": Zechariah Shelton, FBI, interview, September 27, 1991.

page 142 "The radius of the San Augustine cocaine market grew": Padgett, McLeroy, and Allen, Texas Department of Public Safety, interview, October 15, 1991; Robert Davidson, De Soto Parish Sheriff's Office, Mansfield, Louisiana, interview, September 19, 1991; Karren Price, Shelby County District Attorney's Office, Center, Texas, interview, September 20, 1991.

page 147 "Loyal Garner had been beaten to death in the Hemphill jail": "Ex-Policemen Are Convicted in Texas Killing," *The New York Times*, May 4, 1990; "Death as a Ripple in Deep Racial Current," *The New York Times*, May 11, 1990.

page 150 "the Tyson plant in Center": Jack Gardner, general manager of Tyson's Center plant, interview, February 4, 1992.

page 152 "a writer from *Texas Monthly* had come through town": Presumably Richard West, author of the article "The Petrified Forest," cited above.

page 153 "The U.S. Attorney's Office believed that he got into the cocaine business in 1987": Platt, U.S. Attorney's Office, Beaumont, interview, September 27, 1991.

page 153 "It began as two separate investigations": For this account of Operation White Tornado, useful interviews included: Larry Saurage and Charles Bryan, San Augustine County Sheriff's Office; Bob Wortham and Stuart Platt, U.S. Attorney's Office, Beaumont; Zechariah Shelton, FBI; Padgett, McLeroy, and Allen, Texas Department of Public Safety; Betty Donatto, Houston Police Department; Karren Price, Shelby County District Attorney's Office; Robert Davidson, De Soto Parish Sheriff's Office; Lenard Jackson; Harlon Kelly; Steven Kelly; Willie Ray (Blue Tick) Edwards; and Dave Husband.

page 156 "Agent Shelton's application": "Affidavit in the Matter of the Application of the United States of America for an Order Authorizing the Interception of Wire Communications," filed in the U.S. District Court for the Eastern District of Texas, Beaumont Division, May 24, 1989, pp. 21, 25, 45, 51, 55; quotations on pp. 4, 54.

page 158 "Stuart Platt explained to reporters": "Officers Say They Arrested 31 Suspects," Beaumont *Enterprise*, June 4, 1989.

page 158 "'Tindall was difficult to work with'": "Raids Expose Well-Rooted Piney Woods Drug World," Beaumont *Enterprise*, September 24, 1989.

page 158 "'Federal investigators said the drug trade ran rampant'": United Press International, "Former Deputy Pleads Not Guilty to Drug Charge," July 12, 1989.

page 158 "'Many San Augustine residents blame'": "Celebration Tinged by Trepidation," *Houston Chronicle*, June 10, 1989.

page 159 "Tindall was served with a federal court order": "Former Sheriff Leaves Job in DA's Office," Beaumont *Enterprise*, June 4, 1989; "Ex-Sheriff to Testify in Drug Probe," *Houston Chronicle*, July 6, 1989; "Tindall's House Is Searched for 2nd Time," Beaumont *Enterprise*, July 8, 1989.

page 159 "SEARCH OF EX-SHERIFF'S HOUSE NETS GUNS, DRUGS": Beaumont *Enterprise*, July 6, 1989.

page 159 "The San Augustine *Tribune*, a timid weekly": "Sheriff Recovers Evidence Room Property from Tindall Home," San Augustine *Tribune*, July 6, 1989.

page 159 "Dr. Curtis Haley . . . circulated a public resolution": "Referendum of the People," reprinted in the San Augustine *Tribune*, June 29, 1989.

page 159 "only five ounces of drugs": John M. Bales, U.S. Attorney's Office, Beaumont, interviewed by Pete Wells, researcher, August 1994.

page 160   "the bodies of an undetermined number of undocumented Mexican work-ers": "Rumors Spark Hunt for Bodies," *Houston Chronicle*, June 24, 1989; "San Augustine Man Again Denied Bond," Tyler *Morning Telegraph*, August 18, 1989.

page 160   "Daryl Hale, Roger's son, was the first": "Defendant Enters First Guilty Plea in San Augustine Cocaine Case," Beaumont *Enterprise*, August 4, 1989.

page 163   " 'Our commitment to eliminating narcotics' ": Drug Independence Day Celebration program, June 2, 1990.

page 175   "he was sentenced in state district court to fifty years": "50 Years for Two Involved in Local Beatings," San Augustine *Tribune*, January 23, 1992.

page 177   "Richard Carl Davis . . . in a confrontation with Varron (Bo) Lane": "San Augustine Shooting Investigated by Rangers," Shelby *Light and Champion*, September 6, 1991.

page 184   "John Langston Gwaltney, in his book *Drylongso*": John Langston Gwaltney, *Drylongso: A Self-Portrait of Black America* (New Press, 1993), quotations from pp. xxvi, xxix.

page 203   "The county's poverty rate was 50 percent higher": The poverty rate in New Haven, according to the 1990 census, was 19.5 percent. ("Maptitude Census Data Disk," by the Caliper Corporation.) The poverty rate in San Augustine County was 29.7 percent. (1990 Census, Selected Characteristics by Poverty Status.)

page 204   " 'the party of the Past and the party of the Future' ": Ralph Waldo Emerson, "Life and Letters in New England," in *The Complete Works of Ralph Waldo Emerson*, vol. 10 (Houghton Mifflin, 1903), p. 323.

page 207   "Voter turnout had been . . . unusually low": "Bryan Returned to Sheriff's Office in Tuesday Election," San Augustine *Tribune*, March 12, 1992.

BOOK THREE: THE YAKIMA VALLEY

page 211   "1986 . . . national amnesty": The Immigration Reform and Control Act of 1986 granted amnesty to illegal immigrants. Intended to slow the pace of illegal immigration, the law imposed sanctions on employers who hired illegal immigrants. It proved largely unenforceable, however, and illegal immigration continued unimpeded. ("Tide of Migrant Labor Tells of a Law's Failure," *The New York Times*, November 4, 1992.)

page 211   "The Yakima Valley . . . dependent on Mexican labor": Erasmo Gamboa, *Mexican Labor and World War II: Braceros in the Pacific Northwest, 1942–1947* (University of Texas Press, 1990), pp. 2–5, 128–31; "A Northwest Region's Family Ties to Mexico," *Christian Science Monitor*, August 14, 1992; Erasmo Gamboa, professor of ethnic studies, University of Washington, interview, September 29, 1994; Roger Finch, educator, Wapato, Washington, interview, February 14, 1994.

page 212   "Twenty thousand Mexicans in the Yakima Valley got green cards": Nicholas K. Geranios, Associated Press, August 5, 1991.

page 212   "Three million people": "Tide of Migrant Labor," *The New York Times*, November 4, 1992.

In 1997 the Binational Study on Migration produced the first authoritative estimate of the annual flow of Mexican workers into the United States. The Mexican-born population living in the U.S., it found, was between 7 million and 7.3 million, of whom 4.7 million to 4.9 million were legal residents and 2.3 million to 2.4 million were illegal. ("U.S.-Mexico Study Sees Exaggeration of Migration Data," *The New York Times*, August 31, 1997.)

page 212   "the United Farm Workers of Washington State": This union was allied—and, after 1994, formally affiliated—with the better-known United Farm Workers of America, the California-based union founded by César Chávez in the 1960s, which, in the early 1970s, had a membership of eighty thousand. (See Dick Meister and Anne Loftis, *A Long Time Coming: The Struggle to Unionize America's Farm Workers* [Macmillan, 1977], pp. 119–234.) The California union's power faded after growers refused to renew contracts and Chávez turned away from public life. It recently began serious organizing again, winning victories for rose, grape, mushroom, and strawberry workers under the leadership of Arturo Rodriguez, Chávez's son-in-law. ("Chavez's Son-in-Law Tries to Rebuild Legacy," *The New York Times*, June 30, 1997.)

page 213   "'consultants' from California": These consultants included, according to the union, Adam Ortega and Tony Mendez. Ortega headed the Grape Growers and Workers Coalition, an anti-UFW organization in California, and was associated with the Dolphin Group, a right-wing political consulting firm in California. Château Ste. Michelle admitted that Ortega had been hired to fight the UFW organizing effort in Washington State. Mendez, who was himself an organizer for the UFW in the 1960s, subsequently became a successful union buster, working for a succession of large California farms. ("Fact Sheet #2," United Farm Workers of Washington State, AFL-CIO [Sunnyside, WA], 1994.)

page 218   "most of the people in Sunnyside were . . . Latinos": Sunnyside's population was 57 percent Latino—6,423 out of 11,238—in 1990, according to the U.S. Census, Summary Population and Housing Characteristics.

page 218   "the leftist politician Cuauhtémoc Cárdenas": Geranios, Associated Press, August 5, 1991.

page 218   "Valley residents had asked the Mexican government": *Christian Science Monitor*, August 14, 1992.

page 218   "many patronized *curanderos* (traditional healers) and bought prescription drugs (illegally)": "Illegal Trade in Imported Medicines Grows," *The Washington Post*, April 14, 1992.

page 219   "white poverty in the valley was comparatively rare": The (non-Hispanic) white poverty rate in Yakima County was 11.8 percent, while the rate for Latinos was 40.4 percent and the rate for American Indians, the third-largest ethnic group in the county, was 42.4 percent. (U.S. Department of Commerce, 1990 Census, "Poverty Status in 1989 of Families and Persons by Race and Hispanic Origin.")

page 219   "'The prevailing attitude still is'": The *Yakima Herald-Republic*, after many years of avoiding the subject, published, in early 1995, an ambitious, weeklong series of articles about Michoacán, the state where many local Mexicans had roots. The paper sent four reporters to Michoacán and produced a wide-ranging, sympathetic portrait of the region, its people, and those who had left for *El Norte*, particularly the Yakima Valley. But Anglo readers of the series were, on the whole, less *simpático*. An avalanche of complaints hit the paper. A sample of published comments: "The way I feel on this Mexico thing is that . . . this is America and we don't want to learn about Mexico"; "Instead of sending your reporters down to Mexico, you could just send them to Top Food—there's plenty of Mexicans there"; "I just wish to object to your encouraging any more Mexicans to come up here and take advantage of the poor beleaguered taxpayer." (*Yakima Herald-Republic*, March 4 and March 5, 1995.)

page 219   "a regional drug-trafficking center": Susan Beck, Pamela Brown, D. M. Osborne, "The Cocaine War in America's Fruitbowl," *The American Lawyer,* March 1990, pp. 82–89; "Drugs Find Home in Heartland," *Chicago Tribune,* September 10, 1989; "Rural Washington City Becomes a Cocaine Hot Spot," *USA Today,* November 7, 1989; "The Yakima Connection," *The Missoulian* (Montana), March 15, 1995.

page 219 "coyotes . . . turned to a . . . more profitable product": Chief Wallace Anderson, Sunnyside Police Department, interview, March 17, 1994.

Another version I sometimes heard was that coyotes who stayed in the business were requiring desperate clients to smuggle small amounts of cocaine in order to pay for their passage.

page 219 "Family-based Mexican smuggling organizations": Robert Dreisbach, Drug Enforcement Administration, Yakima, interview, March 22, 1994.

page 220 "high percentage of the region's violent crime": Yakima County had the second-worst violent-crime arrest rate for juveniles in Washington State—behind only King County (Seattle)—in 1993. Eight juveniles were indicted for murder in the county that year, compared with seven adults. (*Yakima Herald-Republic,* editorial, September 9, 1994.)

Michael E. Schwab, Yakima County Juvenile Court Commissioner, interview, September 23, 1994.

page 220 "little or none of it would have happened back in Mexico": Mexico and other countries in Central America and the Caribbean have been deluged in recent years with criminals and gangbangers "made in the U.S.A."—deportees returned to their homelands after felony convictions under a program mandated by Congress in the late 1980s. El Salvador, for example, was the unwilling recipient of four thousand felons, mostly teenagers and young adults, between 1993 and 1997, and the country suffered a major crime wave. According to a local police subcommissioner, "Many of the most violent offenses, like murder, kidnapping, and robbery, are committed by people who have been in the United States and are sent back here without any prior notice, with all the bad habits they developed there." ("In U.S. Deportation Policy, a Pandora's Box," *The New York Times,* August 10, 1997.)

page 220 "The worst crime in recent memory": Press reports; interviews with police and gang members.

page 220 "Yakima Valley was home to dozens of youth gangs": Street gangs are fluid structures, especially when they are new—as most of the gangs in the valley were at the time I started visiting—but their local proliferation and tenacity were beyond question, to judge from interviews with school officials, students, parents, police, parole officers, jail prisoners, social workers, self-described gang members and ex-members, and local news reporters. For some of the problems in defining what constitutes a gang, see Malcolm W. Klein, *The American Street Gang: Its Nature, Prevalence, and Control* (Oxford University Press, 1995), pp. 20–30.

page 220 "Don Vlieger's 'gang awareness seminars'": There is a cottage industry in what Malcolm Klein, director of the Social Science Research Institute at the University of Southern California and an experienced gang researcher, calls "the suppression slide show," in which big-city cops and ex-cops visit smaller towns, often for a fee, where local leaders are worried about the growth of a gang problem. They lecture their audiences about what to expect and how to combat gangs and, in some cases, such as Vlieger's, stay to design anti-gang programs and serve as long-term consultants (quotation from Klein, *The American Street Gang,* p. 165). "Gang experts" with law enforcement backgrounds tend to favor hard-nosed suppression programs, which have a poor rate of success—though no poorer, perhaps, than other approaches to gang prevention. Street gangs thrive where poverty is rife and young people feel little connection to larger social networks. The proliferation of gangs over the past ten or fifteen years in the United States has been phenomenal. (See Klein, pp. 31–35.) For a range of views on the subject, see *Gangs: The Origins and Impact of Contemporary Youth Gangs in the United States,* eds. Scott Cummings and Daniel J. Monti (State University of New York Press, Albany, NY, 1993).

page 222   "reducing gang activity there by 25 percent": Vlieger's promotional brochure included a testimonial from the superintendent of a school district, possibly the same one cited in his lecture, saying that he helped effect "a 21 percent decrease in the number of referrals to the school discipline committee."

page 223   "Barely one third of the students in Sunnyside's public schools": Bob Thomas, principal, Sunnyside High School, interview, September 21, 1994; Dennis Birr, principal, Harrison Junior High School, interview, September 26, 1994; school secretary, Sunnyside Christian School, interview, September 27, 1994.

page 224   "youth gangs . . . concerned him financially as well": In 1997, his employment by the school district having come to an end, Vlieger ran for the Sunnyside city council on a pro-business, anti-gang platform. He and a bloc of three followers all won seats, giving them a majority on the seven-member council that took office in January 1998.

page 225   " 'Even in Mexico . . . we didn't have discrimination like this' ": Anti-Latino racism shows up vividly even in opinion polls. The National Opinion Research Center at the University of Chicago, which has been surveying racial attitudes for many years, found in 1990 that 74 percent of non-Latinos believed that Latinos were more likely than whites to "prefer to live off welfare"; 56 percent believed they were lazier than whites; 50 percent believed they were more violence-prone; 55 percent believed they were less intelligent; and 61 percent believed they were less patriotic. For beliefs about African Americans, most of these astonishing numbers were even worse. ("Whites' Racial Stereotypes Persist," *The Washington Post,* January 9, 1991.)

    Equally distressing police attitudes toward minority youths and gang involvement came to light in 1993 in Denver, where the police department compiled a list of 6,500 suspected gang members that included the names of 3,691 African Americans—a truly startling figure when one considers that it was, according to *The New York Times,* "equivalent to two-thirds of the male blacks in the city between the ages of 12 and 24." ("2 of 3 Young Black Men in Denver Listed by Police as Suspected Gangsters," *The New York Times,* December 11, 1993.)

page 232   "the Latino school dropout rate": While the Latino dropout rate in 1995 was 30 percent, the white rate was 8.6 percent, and the black rate was 12.1 percent. ("Hispanic Education Fact-Sheet," National Council of La Raza [Washington, D.C.], July 1997, citing U.S. Department of Education statistics.) For Latinos, moreover, educational attainment was not necessarily the road to economic equality it appeared to be. Just as black men earned far less than white men of equal education, "the mean 1990 income for white males who completed four years of college was $40,636, and for Hispanics it was $25,911. The sad truth is that for Latinos more education means more inequality." (Carola and Marcelo Suárez-Orozco, *Transformations: Immigration, Family Life, and Achievement Motivation Among Latino Adolescents* [Stanford University Press, 1995], p. 60.)

page 232   "Latinos will soon be this country's largest ethnic minority": Latinos were 10.7 percent of the population in 1996; African Americans were 12 percent. By the year 2005, Latinos are expected to outnumber blacks. By the year 2050, Latinos are expected to comprise 25 percent of the population; blacks, 13.6 percent. ("The New U.S.: Grayer and More Hispanic," *The New York Times,* March 27, 1997, citing a 1997 U.S. Census Bureau report, "Demographic State of the Nation.")

Latinos already outnumber blacks in four of the ten largest cities in the United States—Los Angeles, Houston, Phoenix, and San Antonio—and may outnumber them in New York City. In Miami and El Paso, Latinos comprise an absolute majority. ("Hispanic Population Outnumbers Blacks in Four Major Cities as Demographics Shift," *The New York Times,* October 9, 1994.)

page 232 "'Latino underclass of enormous size'": Earl Shorris, *Latinos: A Biography of the People* (Norton, 1992), p. 228.

page 232 "a relatively poor record of voter registration": Among Latino adults who are U.S. citizens, 58.7 percent were registered to vote in the 1992 elections. By contrast, 74 percent of eligible whites and 67.2 percent of eligible blacks were registered. In the election, 90.7 percent of registered whites voted, as did 84.6 percent of registered blacks. Among Latinos, the turnout was 82.5. The result: 484 of every 1,000 eligible Latino adults voted, compared to 671 whites and 569 blacks. (Louis De Sipio, *Counting On the Latino Vote: Latinos as a New Electorate* [University of Virginia Press, 1996], pp. 89–90.)

The soaring Latino population nonetheless ensures growing electoral power. In the 1996 elections, the number of Latino voters in California rose by 28.6 percent, while the number in Texas rose by 48 percent—to 15.1 percent of the total votes cast. ("Southwest Voter Research Notes," William C. Velásquez Institute, San Antonio, TX, Spring 1997.) In the near term, the Democratic Party stands to gain in both states—two out of three new Latino voters in Texas registers Democratic, and the Republican governor of California, Pete Wilson, saw his Latino support fall from 44 percent in 1990 to 25 percent in 1994 after he campaigned for a ballot initiative to cut off public services to illegal immigrants. Republican Party officials have recently been indicating, however, that they realize the future importance of Latino votes. ("California G.O.P. Faces a Crisis as Hispanic Voters Turn Away," *The New York Times,* December 9, 1997; "G.O.P. Tries to Win Hispanic Support Reagan Once Had," *The New York Times,* November 21, 1997.)

For an optimistic assessment of growing urban Latino political power and participation, see Peter Beinart, "New Bedfellows: The New Latino-Jewish Alliance," *The New Republic,* August 11–18, 1997, pp. 22–26.

page 232 "their share of civil service jobs": According to Shorris, writing in 1992, African Americans, while making up 12.1 percent of the population, held 17.8 percent of civilian federal jobs. Latinos, who were then more than 9 percent of the population, held only 5.1 percent of civilian federal jobs. (*Latinos,* p. 427.)

page 232 "redlining by banks": Racial discrimination in lending and mortgages became known as redlining in the 1930s after the federal Home Owners' Loan Corporation developed a ratings system for the risks involved in making loans to specific urban neighborhoods, and the least desirable neighborhoods were coded red. African American and Latino neighborhoods were invariably coded red, and loan applications from their residents were rejected as a matter of course. Private lending institutions had long practiced the same sort of discrimination, and although redlining has since been outlawed, enforcement of anti-redlining laws has often been lax. (Douglas S. Massey and Nancy A. Denton, *American Apartheid: Segregation and the Making of the Underclass* [Harvard University Press, 1993], pp. 51–52, 199, 206–12.)

page 232 "much more intense discrimination": Mexican Americans, in particular, suffered through many decades of second-class citizenship, facing discrimination in schools, jobs, housing, hotels, restaurants, and movie houses. While not formally barred from voting, their participation in elections was effectively restricted by poll taxes, which were required in Texas until the 1960s. Some counties in Texas prohibited them from voting in the "white primaries" of the Democratic Party. (Mario T. Garcia, *Mexican Americans: Leadership, Ideology, and Identity, 1930–1960* [Yale University Press, 1989], p. 41.)

page 232   "The age-old American immigrant's dream": Median income fell sharply for Latinos between 1972 and 1996, whether measured by households, families, or individuals—and this was true for U.S.-born Latinos as well as immigrants. While Latino median family income remains slightly higher than that of blacks, the poverty rate among Latinos is now higher. (U.S. Department of Commerce, Bureau of the Census, Current Population Reports, P60-197, "Money Income in the United States: 1996," Appendix B, Tables B-2, B-4, and B-5, September 1997; "Hispanic Households Struggle Amid Broad Decline in Income," *The New York Times*, January 30, 1997; "New Reports Say Minorities Benefit in Fiscal Recovery," *The New York Times*, September 30, 1997.)

The disturbing pattern I found in Sunnyside—the children of newly arrived immigrants doing better in school than Mexican American children or immigrant children who had been in the U.S. longer—has been noted, I have since learned, by various researchers. Carola and Marcelo Suárez-Orozco compared the attitudes toward school and schoolwork among Mexican youth in Mexico, immigrant youth, second-generation Mexican American youth, and white American youth, and found a disastrous decline in enthusiasm and motivation from the Mexicans and the immigrants, who shared a high level of optimism, to the Mexican Americans, who seemed to become engulfed by anger, alienation, boredom, and an expectation of failure. While the white kids professed to dislike school and their teachers at least as much as the Mexican Americans, they were less haunted by the prospect of failure. (Carola and Marcelo Suárez-Orozco, *Transformations*, Chapters 2 and 5.)

Rubén Rumbaut found, in a study of five thousand schoolchildren in California and Florida (all "either foreign born or U.S. born with at least one foreign-born parent"), that while immigrant children did better in school than their U.S.-born classmates—foreign-born children who had lived in the U.S. for five to ten years had a substantially higher grade point average than the U.S.-born children of immigrants—their performance declined as they became more Americanized. The worst-performing children in Rumbaut's study were those who described themselves as Chicanos—neither Mexican nor American. (Rubén G. Rumbaut, "The Crucible Within: Ethnic Identity, Self-Esteem, and Segmented Assimilation Among Children of Immigrants," in *The New Second Generation*, ed. Alejandro Portes [Russell Sage Foundation, 1996], pp. 119–70; quotation from p. 128.)

For a sunnier view of the situation of Latinos, see Gregory Rodriguez, "The Emerging Latino Middle Class" (Pepperdine University Institute for Public Policy, October 1996), which shows earlier Latino immigrants enjoying a higher income and lower poverty rate than more recent arrivals, and U.S.-born Latinos doing better economically than foreign-born, in a five-county area in Southern California. There is, however, no doubt that new immigrants are poor, or that they work hard. The employment rates for foreign-born Mexican men in Los Angeles—among those who did not finish high school (who are the majority)—are more than double the rates for African American men of the same educational level. (Roger Waldinger, Lewis Center for Regional Policy Studies, UCLA, unpublished data.) But

immigrants who entered the U.S. labor market in the 1960s did so at a far more op-
portune time than those who have arrived since 1980, and they progressed economically much more rapidly. The newcomers "find themselves not only at the
bottom but at a bottom that is increasingly removed from the top and from which
exit is hard to find." (Roger Waldinger, "Ethnicity and Opportunity in the Plural
City," in *Ethnic Los Angeles,* eds. Roger Waldinger and Mehdi Bozorgmehr [Russell
Sage Foundation, 1996], p. 458.)

page 233 " 'People realize they're second-class citizens' ": Shorris makes the same
point while distinguishing between anti-Latino racism and intra-Latino *racismo,*
which works against the poorer, the darker, the less educated, and the more recently arrived. "*Racismo* prevents entry into the society by demoralizing the newcomers so that they do not dare to seek a new social contract. Racism prevents
newcomers from making a new social contract no matter what concessions they
are willing to make; it is the dominant society's refusal to negotiate, a lockout.
Racism and *racismo* are the great counterrevolutionary forces arrayed against
every Latino who seeks to establish a new social contract in the United States."
(*Latinos,* p. 171.)

page 233 "in the Yakima Valley the two scenes were separate and distinct": Scholars
debate the overlap between street gangs and drug gangs generally. Malcolm Klein
believes that it was heavily overdrawn in the 1980s, particularly by the Drug Enforcement Administration, which saw a vast street-gang distribution network for
crack cocaine. (*The American Street Gang,* pp. 40–43, 112–35.) Martín Sánchez
Jankowski, however, in *Islands in the Street: Gangs and American Urban Society* (University of California Press, 1991), convincingly describes the operations of "entrepreneurial" gangs in three cities.

page 233 "county's criminal courts handled a steady traffic": Latinos, who comprised 23.9 percent of the population in Yakima County, received two thirds of the
convictions for drug dealing in 1991. (1990 U.S. Census, Summary Population
and Housing Characteristics; "Who's Getting Busted for Hard Drugs?" *Yakima Herald-Republic,* July 26, 1992.)

page 246 "Caló, the truly impoverished Spanish-English mix": Shorris, *Latinos,* p.
176.

page 246 "conservative poverty theorists, such as Lawrence M. Mead": In *The New
Politics of Poverty: The Nonworking Poor in America* (Basic Books, 1992), Mead contends that "the work attitudes of many of today's seriously poor were shaped, in
part, by their origin in the Third World." (p. 151.) American poverty near the end
of the twentieth century differs from earlier versions, he writes, in that it is "much
more passive and enduring. The origin of this resignation lies in the formative
experiences of the heavily poor groups. History has not confirmed for them the
Western faith in the possibility of individual achievement. Hispanic immigrants remember their roots in Latin America, where governments have often been preda-
tory, the culture resists material progress, and upward mobility for the masses has
been lacking." (p. 152.)

Mead also compares the energy level of Latino immigrants unfavorably with
that of other immigrants, providing an explanation for his impressions that de-
serves points for originality. "If entry is easy due to geography or lax government
controls, immigrants will more often display a passive, Third World temperament.
Thus, Asians or Arabs who have to cross oceans to get to the United States are more
likely to be more upwardly mobile than Hispanics, for whom access is easier." (pp.

153–54.) This flight-time yardstick would seem to commend the industry of African immigrants. Somehow, in Mead's scheme, it doesn't.

The explicitly conservative culture-of-poverty analysis has its roots in the work of the political scientist Edward C. Banfield, best known for his books *The Moral Basis of a Backward Society* (Free Press, 1958) and *The Unheavenly City* (Little, Brown, 1970). (The best-known application of this approach remains the "Moynihan Report," a 1965 memorandum by Daniel Patrick Moynihan, then an assistant secretary in the Labor Department. Without mentioning a "culture of poverty," Moynihan aligned himself with the concept—and provoked an endless series of attacks from the left—by citing a "tangle of pathology" in African American families as a prime cause of black poverty. See Moynihan, "The Negro Family: The Case for National Action," reprinted in Lee Rainwater and William L. Yancey, *The Moynihan Report and the Politics of Controversy* [M.I.T. Press, 1967], pp. 39–125.) Banfield scorned liberal social reform, and he helped lay the groundwork for Charles Murray's counterfactual but highly influential Social Darwinist assault on the welfare state, *Losing Ground: American Social Policy, 1950–1980* (Basic Books, 1984). For an authoritative and critical account of the conservative interpretation of poverty, see Michael B. Katz, *The Undeserving Poor: From the War on Poverty to the War on Welfare* (Pantheon, 1989), pp. 9–35, 137–65.

page 256 " 'multiple marginality' ": "The lives of the street youths who comprise the barrio gang reflect multiple stresses and pressures, which result in a multiple marginality." (James Diego Vigil, *Barrio Gangs: Street Life and Identity in Southern California* [University of Texas Press, 1988], p. 1.)

page 262 "*la compañía* and *la unión* had come to a historic agreement": "Union, Winery Settle Dispute," *Seattle Post-Intelligencer,* May 4, 1995.

BOOK FOUR: THE ANTELOPE VALLEY

page 271 "the combined population of Lancaster and Palmdale": In 1980, Lancaster's population was 47,882; Palmdale's was 12,277. (U.S. Bureau of the Census.) In 1994, Lancaster's population was 119,186; Palmdale's was 103,423. (U.S. Bureau of the Census, 1995.)

For the Antelope Valley, which includes a number of unincorporated communities, population estimates ranged from 291,000 (Los Angeles County Children's Planning Council, 1996) to 332,000 (*Los Angeles Times,* March 27, 1995) to 344,000 (California State Department of Finance, 1995) to 411,000 ("Demographic Information," City of Lancaster Department of Community Development, May 1995, p. 14; this figure includes areas of the valley that are not in Los Angeles County).

Some economists thought the valley's population could reach 600,000. ("Escape from L.A.: Antelope Valley Towns Surge," *The Washington Post,* January 29, 1991.)

page 272 "Los Angeles County alone lost more than half a million jobs": The county lost 510,000 jobs between 1990 and 1995. ("Burbank: A Cinderella City Where Fantasy Pays the Bills," *The New York Times,* March 12, 1996.)

According to a Rutgers University study, "Employment in Los Angeles County's aerospace, electronics and instruments industries fell by 47% between 1988 and 1994." In the missiles and spacecraft industry, it fell 67.2 percent. (Michael Oden, Ann Markusen, Dan Flaming, Mark Drayse, "Post Cold War Frontiers: Defense

Downsizing and Conversion in Los Angeles," Working Paper No. 105, Center for Urban Policy Research, Rutgers University, 1996, pp. 14, 27.)

For the failure of a recently improving local economy to replace many lost jobs, see "A Jobless Recovery," *Los Angeles Times*, March 17, 1996, and Peter Schrag, "Regressive Recovery: California's Curious Comeback," *The American Prospect*, July/August, 1997, pp. 60–64.

page 272　"property values throughout the region collapsed": Residential building permits in Southern California fell by 85 percent—from more than 140,000 to barely 20,000—between 1989 and 1993. ("Nation's Land of Promise Enters an Era of Limits," *The New York Times*, August 24, 1993.)

The value of the average single-family home in Los Angeles fell 27 percent between 1990 and 1995. ("Maybe a House Is Just a Home," *The New York Times*, March 22, 1996.)

page 272　"Housing prices fell by as much as 50 percent": "The median home price for the Antelope Valley dropped from more than $160,000 [in 1990] to $116,995 in the third quarter of 1995." ("Rebound After Hitting Bottom," *Los Angeles Daily News*, December 10, 1995.) "Some homes now are worth two-thirds, even half, of what buyers paid in the 1980s." ("Driven to Extremes: Hard Days and Nights in the Antelope Valley's New Suburbs," *Los Angeles Times*, June 24, 1996.) By July 1997, the median home price had fallen to $86,900. ("A.V. Market Report," Antelope Valley Board of Realtors, August 17, 1997.)

Ronald B. Halcrow, licensed realtor and economics professor, Antelope Valley College, interview, February 20, 1996.

page 272　" 'the foreclosure capital of California' ": "The City of Broken Dreams," *USA Today*, November 21, 1995.

page 272　"its major employers were": The three largest local employers as of June 1994 were still Edwards Air Force Base, Lockheed Aircraft Company, and Northrop Aircraft Corporation. ("Demographic Information," City of Lancaster, May 1995, p. 13.)

page 272　"Palmdale was the second-fastest-growing city": Palmdale's population grew by 47.2 percent between 1990 and 1994; Lancaster's grew by 22.5 percent during the same period. (U.S. Bureau of the Census, 1995.)

page 272　"the valley's newest residents were poorer and darker": "Class Struggle Unfolds in Antelope Valley Tracts," *Los Angeles Times*, June 24, 1996.

page 272　"the valley remained . . . overwhelmingly white": Los Angeles County Children's Planning Council, "Antelope Valley Service Planning Area Resources for Children, Youth, and Families," May 1996, pp. 5, 18, citing 1994 census data.

In the 1990 census, the ethnic breakdown of Los Angeles County was 40.8 percent white, 37.8 percent Latino, 10.6 percent black, and 10.2 percent Asian. (Cited in "In California, the Numbers Add Up to Anxiety," *The New York Times*, October 30, 1994.) Many analysts believe that Latinos have since passed whites as the largest ethnic group, and will soon comprise an absolute majority.

page 272　" 'the last great breeding ground of Southern California' ": Donald Rawley, "They Kill Their Young in Los Angeles' Last Suburb," *Sacramento Bee*, May 22, 1994. The quoted phrase is an indirect quotation of an unnamed San Fernando Valley realtor.

page 272　"nearly 45 percent of the entering students": Superintendent Robert Girolamo, Antelope Valley Union High School District, interview, February 21, 1996.

At Antelope Valley High School, more than 50 percent of the freshmen who enrolled in 1994 had left by the end of what would have been their junior year. ("Transferees at a Disadvantage, *Antelope Valley Press*, December 21, 1997.)

For the teen-pregnancy rate, I relied on an unpublished study by the United Way, Lancaster.

pages 272–73　"A sheriff's department spokesman . . . estimated": Sergeant Bob Denham, L.A. County Sheriff's Department, Antelope Valley Station, interview, December 20, 1995.

page 273　"Local politicians . . . tended to say": Interviews.

page 273　"the most popular youth crime": Sgt. Denham, interview, December 20, 1995.

page 273　"a Palmdale High graduate was virtually assured": Chuck Slay, Palmdale High School teacher and guidance counselor, interview, March 19, 1996.

page 273　"middle-class white families found their . . . neighborhoods": "Class Struggle Unfolds," *Los Angeles Times*, June 24, 1996.

page 273　"nonwhite newcomers were middle-class professionals": "Staking Their Claim on the Suburbs," *Los Angeles Times*, March 18, 1991.

pages 273–74　"The leading illegal drug in the valley": Rawley, *Sacramento Bee*, May 22, 1994.

page 274　"the Antelope Valley . . . had one of the highest child abuse rates in California": "Child Deaths Rise in Antelope Valley; Neglect: Geographic Isolation, a Lack of Services and Drug Use Are Blamed for the Alarming Increase in Fatal Abuse Cases," *Los Angeles Times*, September 6, 1992; "Child Abuse Death Toll Continues to Rise in High Desert," *Los Angeles Times*, October 29, 1992; "Cases of Alleged Child Abuse Rise 13% to 774 in the Antelope Valley," *Los Angeles Times*, April 3, 1993; and Esther H. Gillies, executive director, Children's Center of the Antelope Valley, interview, March 19, 1996.

page 274　"the formation-in-progress of a new class": Some students of American poverty periodically decry the emergence of a "white underclass"—e.g., Charles Murray, "The Coming White Underclass," *The Wall Street Journal*, October 29, 1993. The poverty rate among whites has in fact risen over the long term—from 9 percent in 1979 to 11.2 percent in 1995—even as the black poverty rate has fallen. The percentage of whites earning less than a poverty-level wage has also risen—from 21 percent in 1973 to 26 percent in 1995—substantially more than the same percentage for blacks. Some analysts attribute the growth in white poverty to social trends—Murray focuses almost exclusively on the rise in "illegitimate" white births—while others point to structural changes in the economy that have harmed the white working class. (Mishel, Bernstein, and Schmitt, *The State of Working America, 1996–97*, pp. 152–53, 303.)

Using an arbitrary definition of "underclass"—adults aged nineteen to sixty-four who did not finish high school, are on public assistance, and are either never-married mothers or long-term unemployed males—William P. O'Hare and Brenda Curry-White found in 1992 that non-Hispanic whites made up 36 percent of this group, while African Americans were 38 percent. In rural areas, non-Hispanic whites comprised a majority—55 percent—of the group. (William P. O'Hare and Brenda Curry-White, University of Louisville, "The Rural Underclass: Examination of Multiple-Problem Populations in Urban and Rural Settings," Population Reference Bureau, January 1992, as cited in Isaac Shapiro, "White Poverty in America," Center on Budget and Policy Priorities [Washington, D.C., 1992], p. 15.)

Unlike poor blacks, who tend to be concentrated in central cities, poor whites tend to live in more economically diverse communities. There are, however, "white underclass neighborhoods"—using varying criteria from the 1990 census, researchers at the Ford Foundation and the Urban Institute found between 378,000 and 1.6 million people living in such neighborhoods—and nearly all of them are in cities and towns hit hard by economic downturns driven by deindustrialization. ("The White Underclass," *U.S. News & World Report,* October 17, 1994.) It was a post–Cold War version of this phenomenon that I saw in the Antelope Valley.

page 276   "a disturbingly high number of American girls": A host of books and studies have recently appeared seeking to explain the high rate of adolescent girls' failure to thrive, including the long-running best-seller by Mary Pipher, *Reviving Ophelia: Saving the Selves of Adolescent Girls* (G. P. Putnam's, 1994). On average, girls' grades don't fall in junior high, but their test scores do, and they "continue their downward slide throughout the rest of their education." (Myra and David Sadker, *Failing at Fairness: How America's Schools Cheat Girls* [Scribner's, 1994], p. 138.)

page 277   "three NLRs fired six shots": "Skinheads Open Fire on Blacks," *Antelope Valley Press,* February 22, 1995.

page 279   "plenty of money changed hands": Dave Kennedy, a teacher at Quartz Hill High School, speaking of students with deeper-than-usual family roots in the valley, said, "Their grandparents were cargo cultists, people who truly believed, 'Someday Palmdale International Airport will make us all rich.'"

page 280   "Plant 42—a facility with more floor space": Air Force Plant 42, in Palmdale, has 7.5 million square feet of floor space, along with two 12,000-foot runways (including Runway 7/25, "the strongest in the free world"), on a 5,800-acre site. ("Antelope Valley: A Business Directory and Community Guide," Lancaster Chamber of Commerce, 1994, p. 28.)

page 281   "The Peckerwoods were a white gang": Deputy Chris Haymond, Los Angeles County Sheriff's Department, Antelope Valley Station, Gang Detail, interview, February 14, 1996.

page 282   "Skinheads claim Sharp throughout the United States": George Marshall, *Spirit of '69: A Skinhead Bible* (S. T. Publishing, Dunoon, Scotland, 1994), pp. 148–50; "The Skinhead International: A Worldwide Survey of Neo-Nazi Skinheads" (Anti-Defamation League, 1995), p. 52.

page 282   "the original skinheads emerged in England": See Marshall, *Spirit of '69;* Dick Hebidge, *Subculture: The Meaning of Style* (Methuen, London, 1979); Nick Knight, *Skinhead* (Omnibus, London, 1982); and Jack B. Moore, *Skinheads Shaved for Battle: A Cultural History of American Skinheads* (Bowling Green State University Popular Press, 1993); quotation from Hebidge, p. 55, as cited in Moore, p. 34.

page 283   "a host of unholy alliances": See Moore, *Skinheads Shaved for Battle,* pp. 63–150; Jeff Coplon, "Skinhead Nation," in *Rolling Stone,* December 1, 1986; and reports by the Anti-Defamation League: "Shaved for Battle" (1987), "Young and Violent" (1988), "The Skinheads: An Update" (1988), and "Skinheads Target the Schools" (1989).

page 283   "The Anti-Defamation League . . . estimated in 1995": "The Skinhead International," pp. 1, 77.

page 283   "more white-supremacist gang members . . . in California": There are no reliable numbers. There were, however, more than forty thousand white males locked up in California state prisons (not federal prisons or county jails) in 1995. (U.S. Department of Justice, Bureau of Justice Statistics, "Correctional Populations in the United States 1995," May 1997, p. 91.) By every account, a significant percentage of California's white inmates are involved in white-power gangs. Indeed, the state's prison system exacerbates the problem by encouraging racial segregation among inmates, ostensibly to reduce security risks. Many white prisoners who are of necessity "down for their race" while incarcerated leave the white-supremacist fold after their release. Others do not, and, of course, many white-supremacist gang members never go to prison at all. ("To Keep Peace, Prisons Allow Race to Rule," *Christian Science Monitor,* September 16, 1997.)

page 288 "the discovery, in late 1995, of a group": Press reports, including "Army Report Says Racist Groups Aren't Problem at Ft. Bragg," *The New York Times,* December 23, 1995.

The Army had been prompted to investigate its ranks after three Fort Bragg paratroopers and neo-Nazi skinheads had been arrested for the murder of a black couple in Fayetteville, N.C. The report mentioned in this *Times* headline was produced barely two weeks after the killings and presaged a wider examination of extremist activity in the Army as a whole.

page 291 "Jones was convicted and sentenced": "Supremacists Get Long Prison Terms," *Antelope Valley Press,* March 30, 1996.

page 292 " 'Trying to get all the niggers and Mexicans out' ": This bizarre formulation actually reflects a significant part of American white-supremacist history. Called "whitecapping" in the South and "driving out" in the West, the practice of attacking African Americans (and, in the West, Chinese), often burning their homes, and killing or driving them out of a town or area was widespread in the late nineteenth and early twentieth centuries. Perhaps the most famous single incident was the destruction of the black town of Rosewood, Florida, by whites in 1923. (See Michael D'Orso, *Like Judgment Day: The Ruin and Redemption of a Town Called Rosewood* [Boulevard, 1996].)

page 293 "A local anticrime panel": The Antelope Valley Anti-Crime Commission, quotation from "Commission: Media Makes Skinhead Problem Seem Bigger Than It Really Is," *Antelope Valley Press,* May 20, 1995.

page 294 "Southern California has contributed more than its share": The videotaped police beating of Rodney King in 1991 was only the most notorious incident in an extremely long list. For a sophisticated examination of white supremacism's local roots, see Tomás Almaguer, *Racial Fault Lines: The Historical Origins of White Supremacy in California* (University of California Press, 1994). Michael Novick links the pattern of racist violence in the Los Angeles Police Department to white supremacism in police departments around the country—as well as elsewhere in Southern California—in *White Lies/White Power: The Fight Against White Supremacy and Reactionary Violence* (Common Courage Press, 1995), pp. 59–125, 167–202. For chilling sketches of LAPD racism, see Mike Davis, *City of Quartz: Excavating the Future in Los Angeles* (Verso, 1990), pp. 8, 271–77, 284–88, 294–96.

page 295 "Christian Identity": See Michael Barkun, *Religion and the Racist Right: The Origins of the Christian Identity Movement* (University of North Carolina Press, 1994), pp. 60–69, and James Ridgeway, *Blood in the Face: The Ku Klux Klan, Aryan Nations, Nazi Skinheads, and the Rise of a New White Culture* (Thunder's Mouth Press, 1995). For Wesley Swift's Antelope Valley period, I also consulted Robert B. Harris, "The Religion of the Contemporary Radical Right: Christian Identity, Anti-Semitism, and the Christian Coalition," an unpublished monograph.

page 295 "a group associated with the Freemen": "Militias: FBI Calls into Question Group's Teachings on Foreclosures," *Antelope Valley Press,* January 6, 1996; *Antelope Valley Press,* January 4, 1996.

page 295   "how to secede financially from the United States": While the white-separatist tax protesters of the militia movement have received extensive attention, there are also black separatists advocating tax nonpayment, notably a group called the Moorish Nation. Their arguments typically cite the Supreme Court's infamous 1857 Dred Scott decision, which denied citizenship to blacks, to prove that the U.S. Constitution applies only to whites. Adherents follow the Free Moorish Zodiac Constitution instead. ("In Tax Scheme, a Major Role for Separatists," *The New York Times*, December 8, 1997.)

page 298   "Hitler was an extraordinarily heavy tweaker": For an account of Hitler's methamphetamine addiction and "toxic paranoid psychosis" that may change your view of World War II, see Ronald K. Siegel, *Whispers: The Voices of Paranoia* (Touchstone, 1996), pp. 27–30.

page 298   "'young men use methamphetamine for sexual stimulation'": "Sharp Rise in Use of Methamphetamines Generates Concern," *The New York Times*, February 14, 1996.

page 301   "'vegetarian straight-edge'": Straight Edge, which emerged from the punk-rock club scene in the 1980s—the movement took its name from a Minor Threat lyric, "I've got a straight edge"—is even more diffuse than Sharp. Its adherents are often animal-rights activists. They're usually vegetarians. They're primarily against—sometimes violently against—alcohol, drugs, tobacco, and casual sex. Their symbol is an X, which they've been known to carve into the flesh of smokers and other sinners. (Arlene Levinson, "Over the Edge," *The Missoulian* [Montana], December 7, 1997.)

page 302   "their brutal commutes": In 1996, 30 percent of Antelope Valley residents were estimated to spend at least two hours a day on the road. ("Suburban Dreams Hit Roadblock," *Los Angeles Times*, June 23, 1996, citing the U.S. Census and the Southern California Association of Governments.)

page 302   "kids . . . being raised . . . by their grandparents": The 1990 census found 5 percent of all American children living with grandparents or other relatives not their parents—a 44 percent increase since 1980. Among these custodial grandparents, 62 percent were non-Hispanic whites; 27 percent were black. (Esme Fuller-Thomson, Meredith Minkler, and Diane Driver, "A Profile of Grandparents Raising Grandchildren in the United States," *The Gerontologist*, Vol. 37, No. 3, 1997, pp. 406, 408.)

page 303   "methamphetamine is even more destructive": "Bootlegged Chemicals for 'Poor Man's Cocaine,'" *Christian Science Monitor*, April 17, 1997; "Sinister Drug Infiltrates Rural U.S.,'" *Christian Science Monitor*, February 3, 1997; "Good People Go Bad in Iowa, and a Drug Is Being Blamed," *The New York Times*, February 22, 1996; "Sharp Rise in Use of Methamphetamine Generates Concern," *The New York Times*, February 14, 1996; Anastasia Toufexis, "There Is No Safe Speed," *Time*, January 8, 1996, p. 23; "Mexican Drug Dealer Pushes Speed, Helping Set Off an Epidemic in U.S.," *The New York Times*, December 27, 1995; "Drug Agents See Shift in Trafficking in Speed," *The New York Times*, September 4, 1994; quotation from *Time*, January 8, 1996.

The Clinton administration sought to counter the methamphetamine boom with the Comprehensive Methamphetamine Control Act of 1996, which tightened control of the sale of what are called "precursor chemicals" and increased the penalties for illegal use. President Clinton, when he signed the bill, said, "We have to stop 'meth' before it becomes the crack of the 1990s." ("Unabated Methamphetamine

Abuses," *The Washington Times,* February 9, 1997.) His "drug czar," General Barry R. McCaffrey, said, "Crack cocaine simply bowled us over in the 1980s. . . . Methamphetamine—the poor man's cocaine—may be an even worse insult to our family structure and our community life." (*Christian Science Monitor,* February 3, 1997.)

For a comprehensive study of earlier American speed epidemics, see Lester Grinspoon and Peter Hedblom, *The Speed Culture: Amphetamine Use and Abuse in America* (Harvard University Press, 1975).

page 315   "the Business . . . in *The Skinhead Bible*": pp. 116–17.

page 316   "a recent listing of 207 American cities": Zero Population Growth, the environmentalist group, offered these rankings in June 1995. ("A City Racked by Woe," *Los Angeles Times,* October 10, 1995.)

page 318   "many of Hitler's elite troops were . . . tweakers": Siegel, *Whispers,* p. 28.

page 322   "There are American communities that have begun": For instance, a program designed by James P. Comer and Edward Zigler, called "The School of the 21st Century" and operating, as of mid-1996, on four hundred campuses across the country, offers year-round, all-day preschool, before- and after-school programs, and vacation programs. (Margot Hornblower, "It Takes a School," *Time,* June 3, 1996.)

page 322   "school funding had been *falling*": Between 1970 and 1995, California was the only state in the nation where real per-pupil spending did not rise. Adjusting reported per-pupil spending for regional costs, changes in poverty, and an education-relevant inflation measure, California's spending on education fell 13 percent, in constant dollars, between 1970 and 1995. (Richard Rothstein, "When States Spend More," *The American Prospect,* January/February 1998; Richard Rothstein, Economic Policy Institute, interview, November 10, 1997.)

To be fair, California's schools had to cope with a huge increase in students, many of them new immigrants, during this period. Total enrollment grew from 3.1 million in 1980 to 5.1 million in 1990 and was expected to reach 7 million by the year 2000. (Richard Walker, "California Rages Against the Dying of the Light," *New Left Review,* January/February 1995, p. 46.)

Also, the state's economic recovery, which in 1997 produced a budget surplus, is now finally allowing increases in education spending. Student fees at California's public universities will be decreased by 5 percent for the 1998–99 year. ("Our Seesaw College Fees," *San Jose Mercury News,* October 14, 1997.)

page 322   "in the mid-sixties, the state's public schools enjoyed": 1965: Mike A. Males, *The Scapegoat Generation: America's War on Adolescents* (Common Courage Press, 1996), p. 2; 1995: "Public Elementary and Secondary Education Statistics: School Year 1995–96," U.S. Department of Education, National Center for Education Statistics, May 1996, adjusted for regional costs in "Quality Counts: A Report Card on the Condition of Public Education in the 50 States," *Education Week on the Web,* January 1997.

page 322   "School bond issues that passed": M.W.M. Jones, "Voting for Local School Taxes in California: How Much Do Demographic Variables Such As Age and Race Matter?" paper presented to the Population Association of America, April 3, 1995, cited in Males, p. 12; "Schools Have Mixed Success With Bond Issues," *Sacramento Bee,* November 5, 1997.

page 322   "A property-tax revolt in the 1970s": Males, pp. 2–3.

page 322   "the state had to close 1,100 . . . library branches": "Prop. 13 Casts a Long Shadow on State Books," *Sacramento Bee,* August 4, 1996.

page 322   "Between 1970 and 1996, the poverty rate for children": Males, pp. 3, 4;
"State's Children Are Getting Poorer," *San Jose Mercury News,* June 3, 1997.

page 322   "The California prison budget": Males, pp. 2, 131; "California's Prisons:
Too Close for Comfort," *The Economist,* May 4, 1996.

In 1980, California had ninety-eight people imprisoned for sentences of one
year or longer per 100,000 population. In 1995, the rate was 416. (U.S. Department of Justice, "Historical Corrections Statistics in the United States,
1850–1984," p. 32; Darrell K. Gilliard and Allen J. Beck, statisticians, Bureau of
Justice Statistics, Department of Justice, "Prison and Jail Inmates, 1995," p. 3.)

page 322   "Between 1986 and 1996, California built": "Prisons Supplant Schools in
Budget, Critics Say," *San Jose Mercury News,* October 24, 1996.

page 322   "Tuition was negligible": 1965: Males, p. 13; 1997: "Study: Doors Closing
on Higher Education," *San Jose Mercury News,* September 26, 1997.

At U.C. Berkeley, student fees more than doubled between 1990 and 1996—rising from $1,999 to $4,354. (Berkeley Undergraduate Fact Sheet, Fall 1996.)

page 323   "the state's university and college system lost": Peter Schrag, "California's
Elected Anarchy," *Harper's,* November 1994, pp. 50–51; Males, p. 13; Anthony
Lewis, "Sunlight and Shadow," *The New York Times,* March 25, 1996.

page 323   "State spending on prisons came to exceed spending on higher education":
Between 1990 and 1997, prisons went from 4.9 percent of the state budget to 9.4
percent, while higher education fell from 12.5 percent to 8 percent. The state's universities were forced to lay off ten thousand employees while the prisons hired ten
thousand new guards. ("Crime Keeps On Falling, but Prisons Keep On Filling," *The
New York Times,* September 28, 1997.)

page 323   *"The Scapegoat Generation"*: Quotation from p. 279.

page 323   "they had grown up in a Golden Age": For a book-length rendition of this
idea—indicting not contemporary youth for the decline of American communities,
but the baby-boom generation's antiauthoritarianism, libertarianism, and worship
of the idea of "personal choice"—see Alan Ehrenhalt, *The Lost City: The Forgotten
Virtues of Community in America* (Basic Books, 1995). For a memoir of the vanished
California suburban paradise of the Space Age, and reflections on its aftermath, see
David Beers, *Blue Sky Dream: A Memoir of America's Fall from Grace* (Doubleday,
1996).

page 323   "In 1996, out of a graduating class": California Department of Education,
"High School Performance Report, 1995–96: Palmdale High," p. 181-I; Chuck
Slay, Palmdale High teacher and guidance counselor, interview, March 19, 1996;
Ray Monti, deputy superintendent for educational services, Antelope Valley Union
High School District, interview, November 10, 1997.

The career-counseling center at Palmdale High had been closed down because of
the school district's financial woes in the early 1990s. ("Valley Teens Steering Clear
of College," *Antelope Valley Press,* December 20, 1997.)

page 324   " 'Affirmative action' was merely the name": Affirmative action opponents
capitalized on this white anger with Proposition 209, a California ballot initiative,
passed in 1996, that imposed a sweeping ban on preferential treatment of minorities or women. The regents of the University of California had already decided to
halt affirmative action in admissions, and in 1997 the fruits of that decision began
to appear: UCLA's first-year law school class had ten blacks out of 381 students, the
lowest figure since the 1960s; the entering class at UC-Berkeley's law school had
precisely one black student, out of 267. At the University of Texas, meanwhile,

where the law school had lost a legal challenge to affirmative action in federal court, the number of black students in UT-Austin's law school's incoming class promptly fell from 31 to 4—out of 475. Having deduced, perhaps, that banning affirmative action was likely to bring on far worse social ills, voters in Houston, in a November 1997 referendum, rejected a proposal to end their city's affirmative action programs. ("Referendum in Houston Shows Complexity of Preferences Issue," *The New York Times*, November 6, 1997; "The Next Great Battle Over Affirmative Action," *Time*, November 10, 1997, pp. 52–54; "What Does SAT Stand For?," *Time*, November 10, 1997, pp. 54–55.)

page 324   "The commission's report": Los Angeles County Commission on Human Relations, "Skinheads in Antelope Valley: A Report to the Los Angeles County Board of Supervisors," May 31, 1995; quotations from p. 7 and Appendix A, p. 2.

page 332   "the *Antelope Valley Press* was describing him": "Dismay Felt at Killer's Freedom," *Antelope Valley Press*, March 13, 1996.

page 335   "White Americans of all economic classes": William H. Frey and Jonathan Tilove, "Immigrants In, Native Whites Out," *The New York Times Magazine*, August 20, 1995, pp. 44–45; William H. Frey, "Immigrant and Native Migrant Magnets," *American Demographics*, November 1996, pp. 1–5; William H. Frey and Kao-Lee Liaw, "Immigration Concentration and Domestic Migrant Dispersal: Is Movement to Non-Metro Areas 'White Flight'?" paper presented to the Population Association of America, March 27, 1997.

According to Frey and Tilove, citing the 1990 census, African Americans "are also leaving most of the high-immigration metropolitan areas, if not in the same numbers as whites, and their No. 1 destination is Atlanta." (p. 45.)

Economic motives, of course, drive most migration, both domestic and international. And all low-skilled workers in the U.S. have legitimate reason to be concerned about immigration. As the economists George J. Borjas, Richard B. Freeman, and Lawrence F. Katz observe, "Immigration has had a marked adverse impact on the economic status of the least-skilled U.S. workers." ("How Much Do Immigration and Trade Affect Labor Market Outcomes?" Brookings Papers on Economic Activity [Washington, D.C., 1997], p. 2.)

page 335   "civil-rights-era fair-housing campaign": This 1964 campaign's goal was actually to defeat a voter initiative that sought to prohibit the state from regulating discrimination in housing. The initiative, known as Proposition 14, passed.

For a frightening introduction to California's system of government-by-voter-intiative, see Peter Schrag, "California's Elected Anarchy," *Harper's*, November 1994, pp. 50–58.

page 337   "the post-1973 downslope": Besides being the year that the last U.S. ground troops left Vietnam, 1973 was, though few realized it at the time, an American economic watershed. Whether the cause was inflation sparked by the OPEC oil embargo, weak grain harvests, or the collapse of the dollar after Richard Nixon took it off the gold standard, the American economy slowed dramatically. Annual growth that had averaged 3.4 percent for more than one hundred years fell suddenly to 2.3 percent for the period 1973–93. Productivity, which had risen nearly 3 percent a year from 1946 to 1973, has grown by only 1 percent a year since. Median family income, which doubled between 1947 and 1973, stalled, the average wages of men and younger workers began to fall, and inequality began to rise. (Jeffrey Madrick, *The End of Affluence: The Causes and Consequences of America's Economic Dilemma* (Random House, 1995), p. 5; Sheldon Danziger and Peter

Gottschalk, *America Unequal* (Russell Sage Foundation/Harvard University Press, 1995), p. 48; "That Was Then and This Is the 90's," *The New York Times,* June 18, 1997.)

page 337   "what, far more than economics, had changed": Southern California's demographics, for one, had changed. Between 1960 and 1990, the population of greater Los Angeles had nearly doubled. In 1960, more than 80 percent of the region's population was non-Hispanic whites—and more than 90 percent was born in the U.S. By 1990, whites were less than half of the region's population, and one third of the people in L.A. County were foreign-born. (Georges Sabagh and Mehdi Bozorgmehr, "Population Change: Immigration and Ethnic Transformation," in *Ethnic Los Angeles,* eds. Roger Waldinger and Mehdi Bozorgmehr [Russell Sage Foundation, 1996], pp. 82, 87, 94.)

pages 337–38   "Howard Brooks, the executive director": *Los Angeles Times,* August 9, 1992.

page 338   "race war was finally coming to the Antelope Valley": Minister Tony Muhammad, of the Nation of Islam, stood on the steps of the Palmdale city hall and demanded that the white teenagers accused in the machete attack be tried as adults, and that local politicians stop the wave of hate crimes. "If that is not done, then I warn you, there will be a war in California, in Palmdale and in Lancaster." The hate crimes continued, however, and the youth of some of the white supremacists involved remained a factor in their favor, legally speaking. Ritch Bryant, for instance, one of the kids convicted of assaulting Todd Jordan at Antelope Valley High, was legally protected by his age when he was charged, in October 1997, with the 1995 hate-crime murder of a forty-three-year-old black man behind a McDonald's on West Avenue I. Because Bryant had been only sixteen years old at the time of the killing, he was not eligible for the death penalty. Local authorities continued to deny, ostrich-fashion, that white-supremacist violence was a serious problem, but the county officials who announced the arrests in the McDonald's case, when pressed by reporters, admitted, according to the *Antelope Valley Press,* that "there are more hate crimes in Los Angeles than any other county in the nation and that the Antelope Valley is a major contributor to the problem." ("Task Force Nets Arrest in '95 Crime," *Antelope Valley Press,* October 29, 1997.)

page 339   "Three neo-Nazi skinheads": "Ex-G.I. Draws Life Sentence for Racially Motivated Killings," *The New York Times,* March 7, 1997; "Another Soldier Convicted in Race-Based Killings," *The New York Times,* May 3, 1997; "Second Ex-Paratrooper Gets Life in North Carolina Killings," *The New York Times,* May 13, 1997.

page 340   "according to *The New York Times,* a spider web": "Army Report Says Racist Groups Aren't Problem," December 23, 1995.

EPILOGUE

page 343   "the invention of adolescence": The word has been around since the late fifteenth century, but its Latin antecedent *adolescentia* referred to a variety of age groups (some as old as thirty-five), and it was only in recent times that it assumed its modern meaning because, as Philippe Ariès explains, "prolongation of the average life-span brought into existence tracts of life to which the scholars of the Byzantine Empire and the Middle Ages had given names even though they had not existed for the generality." (*Centuries of Childhood: A Social History of Family Life* [Random House, 1962], p. 32.) The growth of the middle class, the expansion of public education, and the phasing out of child labor each contributed to the rise of what we know as adolescence. According to Arlene Skolnick, "Not until the Victorian era did adolescence emerge as a new stage of development between childhood and adulthood." (*Embattled Paradise: The American Family in the Age of Uncertainty* [Basic Books, 1991], p. 40.) Since then, the ever-increasing importance of education has led to the expanded importance—and cultural prominence—of adolescence.

page 343   " 'the frivolous youth of today' ": Quoted in M. Lee Manning, "Three Myths Concerning Adolescence," *Adolescence*, Vol. 18, No. 72, Winter 1983, pp. 823–29. Manning traces, incidentally, the emergence of modern adolescence to Rousseau's *Émile*.

page 343   "the first generation-long decline": Economic data from the eighteenth, nineteenth, and even the early twentieth century is far less complete than modern data. The predominance of agricultural work until this century also makes comparisons difficult. Still, the steady rise in the national standard of living is relatively easily traced (since the mid-nineteenth century, according to a recent calculation, "the real value of the goods and services available to an average American [has risen by] 700%"), and the few periods when the standard of living has declined or remained flat are readily identified. The Civil War, for instance, drove real wages down, as did the Great Depression. In both of these cases, however, the previous levels of prosperity were regained within a decade, and the long-term rise in the standard of living resumed. (Quotation from *Productivity and American Leadership*, eds. William Baumol, Sun Anne Batey Blackman, and Edward N. Wolff [M.I.T. Press, 1989], p. 29; other wage data from Jeffrey G. Williamson, "Watersheds and Turning Points: Conjectures on the Long-Term Impact of Civil War Financing," *Journal of Economic History* 34, 1974, pp. 537–66.) For details on wage stagnation and decline since 1973, see notes to pp. xiii and 344.

pages 343–44   " 'fewer than one in six of all undergraduates' ": Quotation from Arthur Levine and Jeanette Cureton, *When Hope and Fear Collide: A Portrait of Today's College Student* (Jossey-Bass, 1998). Many of those who pursue postsecondary education never, of course, enroll in degree programs. See also James Traub, "Drive-Thru U.," *The New Yorker*, October 20–27, 1997, pp. 113–23.

page 344   "Three quarters of the American work force do not have . . . college degrees": Lawrence Mishel, Jared Bernstein, and John C. Schmitt, *The State of Working America, 1996–97* (Economic Policy Institute, 1997), p. 174.

page 344   "the real wages of those without college degrees": For men who had not finished high school, real hourly wages fell from $12.45 an hour to $8.92 between 1973 and 1995; for male high school graduates, they fell from $14.65 to $11.87; for men with "some college," they fell from $15.43 to $13.11. For women who had not finished high school, real hourly wages fell from $7.51 an hour to $6.99 between 1973 and 1995; for female high school graduates, they fell from $9.62 to $8.95; for women with some college, they fell from $10.31 to $10.20. Entry-level wages for male high school graduates—that is, younger men—fell from $10.54 an hour to $7.58 between 1973 and 1995. Entry-level wages for female high school graduates fell from $7.93 to $6.42. For whites without college degrees, real hourly wages fell from $10.81 to $9.79 between 1979 and 1996. (All figures in 1995 dollars.) For black male high school graduates, real hourly wages fell 21 percent between 1979 and 1996. For Latino male high school graduates, they fell 22.2 percent. For black female high school graduates, they fell 8.3 percent. For Latina high school graduates, they fell 9.8 percent. (Mishel, Bernstein, Schmitt, pp.

171–72, 176; Jared Bernstein, Economic Policy Institute, interview, January 20, 1998; Ruy Teixeira, Economic Policy Institute, interview, January 20, 1998.)

page 344   "polls show large numbers of rich and poor Americans": A 1993 poll, for instance, found 91 percent of those with annual household incomes above $75,000—that is, people in the top fifth of incomes—describing themselves as middle class. The same poll found 22 percent of those with household incomes of less than $15,000—that is, below the poverty line for a family of four—describing themselves as middle class. Politicians, too, love to wrap themselves in the flag of middle-classness. "I'm a middle-class guy," insisted Newt Gingrich, the Speaker of the House, in 1996. His salary, which was not his only income source, came that year to $171,500. Another congressman, Fred Heineman of North Carolina, claimed that his annual income of $183,500 made him "lower middle-class." And George Pataki, governor of New York, addressing the issue of rent control, recently defined middle-class households as those making up to $175,000 a year, thus including 99 percent of his state's tenants in the great fold. ("Another Kind of Middle-Class Squeeze," *The New York Times*, May 18, 1997.)

page 344   " 'That which in England' ": Quotation from "A Word About America," in *Philistinism in England and America*, Vol. 10 of *The Complete Prose Works of Matthew Arnold*, ed. R. H. Super (University of Michigan Press, 1974), p. 10.

While the term "middle class" was being used in its modern sense in the United States as early as the 1820s and the American middle class grew steadily thereafter, the rise of a true middle-class majority only occurred after the Second World War. (Jeffrey Madrick, *The End of Affluence: The Causes and Consequences of America's Economic Dilemma* [Random House, 1995], pp. 124–25.)

page 344   "the middle class . . . has been shrinking conspicuously": Among college graduates, 3.9 percent earned less than half the median family income in 1969, rising to 4.8 percent in 1995; 37.2 percent earned more than twice the median in 1969, rising to 42.1 percent in 1995; meanwhile, the middle-income group fell among college graduates from 58.6 percent to 53.1 percent. Among those with "some college," 5.9 percent earned less than half the median in 1969, rising to 12.1 percent in 1995; 22.8 percent earned more than twice the median in 1969, falling to 19.4 percent in 1995; the middle-income group fell, meanwhile, from 70.9 percent to 68.5 percent. Among high school graduates, 7.6 percent earned less than half the median in 1969, rising to 17.2 percent in 1995; 14.5 percent earned more than twice the median in 1969, falling to 12.8 percent in 1995; and the middle-income group fell, meanwhile, from 77.7 percent to 70.0 percent. Among those with less than high school, 21.8 percent earned less than half the median in 1969, rising to 42.7 percent in 1995; 6.7 percent earned more than twice the median in 1969, falling to 3.5 percent in 1995; and the middle-income group fell, meanwhile, from 71.3 percent to 53.8 percent. (Mishel, Bernstein, Schmitt, p. 79.)

The overall growth between 1973 and 1996 of the group earning more than twice the median family income ("the upper middle class and the rich") can be clearly inferred from the percentage of American families earning (in 1996 dollars) more than $75,000 (actually slightly less than twice the median in each year, but the closest figure provided by the Census Bureau), which was 12.7 percent in 1973 and 20.3 percent in 1996. (U.S. Department of Commerce, Bureau of the Census, Current Population Reports, P60–197, "Money Income in the United States: 1996," Appendix B, Table B-4, September 1997.)

For a technical economic discussion of the shrinking of the middle class, see

Greg J. Duncan, Timothy M. Smeeding, and Willard Rodgers, "W(h)ither the Middle Class? A Dynamic View," in *Poverty and Prosperity in the USA in the Late Twentieth Century*, eds. Dimitri B. Papadimitriou and Edward N. Wolff (St. Martin's, 1993), pp. 240–71.

page 345   "the percentage of Americans with degrees is still far smaller": Common definitions of the middle class put between one half and two thirds of American households in that category. As noted above, only one quarter of the work force has a college degree.

page 345   "the postindustrial economy requires unskilled workers": "In the Labor Department's list of 'occupations with the largest job growth,' the top five categories are cashiers, janitors and cleaners, salespeople, waiters and waitresses, and nurses." (Paul Krugman, "What's Ahead for Working Men and Women," *The New York Times*, Op-Ed, August 31, 1997.)

page 345   "the income advantage conferred by a college degree": This erosion has occurred among men, but not among women. (Mishel, Bernstein, Schmitt, pp. 172–73.) For the export of highly skilled jobs, see William Wolman and Anne Colamosca, *The Judas Economy: The Triumph of Capital and the Betrayal of Work* (Addison-Wesley, 1997), especially pp. 87–138.

page 345   "Globalization . . . decline of labor unions . . . growth of low-wage service-sector jobs . . . immigration . . . drop in the value of the minimum wage . . . growth in corporate profits": Mishel, Bernstein, and Schmitt assign rough percentages to some of the major causes of "the recent growth of wage inequality and the deterioration of wages among non-college-educated workers," finding deunionization and the drop in the value of the minimum wage to be responsible for one third of the growth in wage inequality between 1979 and 1994; the growth of the low-wage service sector responsible for 20–30 percent; immigration and foreign trade for 15–25 percent; and "the combined effects of industry shift and globalization" for 25–40 percent. (These effects are not cumulative, they explain, but overlap, and may therefore total more than 100 percent.) (p. 20.)

The rise in the minimum wage to $5.15, which occurred in September 1997, still left it far below its average real value during the period 1962–82. (Mishel, Bernstein, Schmitt, p. 204.)

The 1995 corporate after-tax profit rate was 7.0 percent, the highest rate recorded since a comparable measure became available in 1959. (Mishel, Bernstein, Schmitt, pp. 69–71.) And yet productivity growth during the 1973–93 period fell to only one third what it was during the 1948–73 period. (Madrick, pp. 14, 207.)

page 346   "a matter of political economy": I borrow this formulation from Michael B. Katz, who wrote, in *The Undeserving Poor: From the War on Poverty to the War on Welfare* (Pantheon, 1989), "Poverty no longer is natural; it is a social product. As nations emerge from the tyranny of subsistence, gain control over the production of wealth, develop the ability to feed their citizens and generate surpluses, poverty becomes not the product of scarcity, but of political economy." (p. 7.)

page 346   "Wealth and income have always been unequally distributed": For example, 150 years ago, the richest 4 percent of New Yorkers owned 81 percent of the city's wealth. Long-range trends, moreover, have not always been progressive. The share of aggregate household income going to the poorest fifth of U.S. households fell by more than half between 1910 and 1959. (Benjamin Schwarz, "Reflections on Inequality: 'The Promise of American Life,'" *World Policy Journal*, Winter 1995/96, pp. 34–35.)

page 346   "rise in college costs": "The cost of public colleges rose 50 percent faster than inflation" between 1985 and 1995, according to Madrick, "though they were reducing the curricula and services they offered." (p. 140.) Between 1980 and 1996, state-university tuition "tripled or quadrupled" in most states, according to Nicholas Lemann. ("With College for All," *Time*, June 10, 1996, p. 67.) Between 1987 and 1996, the average cost of a year at a private four-year college rose, in constant dollars, by more than 25 percent. ("College Tuitions Climb 5 Percent, Survey Finds," *The New York Times*, September 25, 1997.)

page 346   "decline in home-ownership among younger families": "Only 34.6 percent of those aged twenty-five to twenty-nine owned a home in 1993 compared with 43.6 percent in 1973. Of those between the ages of thirty and thirty-four, only 51.0 percent owned a home in 1993 compared with 60.2 percent in 1973." (Madrick, pp. 139–40.)

page 346   "decline in entry-level wages": As noted above, entry-level wages for male high school graduates fell 28.1 percent between 1973 and 1995; for female high school graduates, they fell 19 percent. For male college graduates, they fell 10.9 percent; for female college graduates, 6.1 percent. (Mishel, Bernstein, Schmitt, p. 176.)

page 346   "imprisoning juveniles as adults": Every state except Hawaii now tries some juveniles in adult courts. Since 1987, the number of youths prosecuted as adults in state courts has risen 70 percent. Eight thousand teenage prisoners are currently being housed with adults—a disastrous policy for young inmates but one certain to be expanded if crimefighter-politicians continue to believe there are votes to be won on the issue. (Richard Lacayo, "Teen Crime," *Time*, July 21, 1997, pp. 26–29.)

page 346   " 'superpredator' ": The term was popularized by William J. Bennett, John J. DiIulio, Jr., and John P. Walters in their 1996 book *Body Count: Moral Poverty and How to Win America's War Against Crime and Drugs* (Simon and Schuster). While *Body Count* was marred by lurid absurdities ("America's beleaguered cities are about to be victimized anew by a paradigm-shattering wave of ultra-violent, morally vacuous young people some call 'the superpredators' "; "A new generation of street criminals is upon us—the youngest, biggest, and baddest generation any society has ever known"), it was widely read, if only because of the prominence of its authors. *Body Count*'s analysis of juvenile crime centered on brute demographics—more teenagers—and a tub-thumping denunciation of "moral poverty." While he was President Bush's "drug czar," Bennett contributed to the national moral tone by endorsing the idea of beheading drug dealers. (Quotations from pp. 25, 26.)

page 346   "juvenile crime rate, like the crime rate generally, was falling": Violent juvenile crime fell 25 percent between 1994 and 1995. Adult violent crime fell 18 percent. (Melissa Sickmund, Howard N. Snyder, and Eileen Poe-Yamagata, "Juvenile Offenders and Victims: 1997 Update on Violence," U.S. Department of Justice, Office of Juvenile Justice and Delinquency Prevention, June 1997, p. 16.)

page 346   "A study released in 1997": Steve Farkas and Jean Johnson, with Ann Duffett and Ali Bers, "Kids These Days: What Americans Really Think About the Next Generation" (Public Agenda, 1997), p. 8.

page 346   " 'First the members of the 60's generation' ": Walter Kirn, "Crybaby Boomers," *The New York Times*, Op-Ed, July 2, 1997.

page 347   "the breadwinner/housewife system": Skolnick, *Embattled Paradise*, pp. 11–12, citing Kingsley Davis, "Wives and Work: A Theory of the Sex-Role Revolution and its Consequences," in *Feminism, Children, and the New Families*, eds. Sanford M. Dornbusch and Myra H. Strober (Guilford, 1988), p. 74.

page 347   "'support for children and families'": Skolnick, p. 218.

page 347   "the Clinton administration has introduced": Federal legislation expanded health insurance for children in 1997, and the prospects for federally subsidizing increased child care in 1998 were generally reckoned good. ("President Plans On $21 Billion for Child Care," *The New York Times*, January 8, 1998.) A successful system of public child care requires major subsidies from all levels of government, however, as the exemplary systems in France and Sweden demonstrate. The city of Paris, for example, increased its day care budget more than fivefold between 1977 and 1997. ("Child Care Sacred as France Cuts Back the Welfare State," *The New York Times*, December 31, 1997; Steven Greenhouse, "If the French Can Do It, Why Can't We?" *The New York Times Magazine*, November 14, 1993, p. 59.)

page 348   "government has withdrawn support": Federal support for college, university, and vocational programs fell by nearly one third between 1980 and 1996. ("Why College Isn't For Everyone," *The New York Times*, August 31, 1997.) A generation of decline in support for poor children came to a grim climax—and, one hopes, an endpoint—in 1996 with the abolition of Aid to Families with Dependent Children. President Clinton's choice to head the Federal Highway Administration unwittingly revealed even a Democratic administration's reluctance to support the most basic public amenities when he suggested that repairs to the interstate highway system could be financed by private companies that would be allowed to collect tolls on them. ("Private Tolls on Interstates Discussed," *The Washington Post*, October 1, 1993.) The Clinton administration's commitment to procapital, antilabor trade policy has been no less unswerving than its Republican predecessors', even when its pursuit of free-trade agreements and "fast-track" authority has led to bruising battles with important allies like labor unions.

page 348   "There are 1.7 million Americans in prison": The most recent figures are 1,158,763 in state and federal prisons, 567,079 in local jails. (Darrell K. Gilliard and Allen J. Beck, "Prison and Jail Inmates at Mid-Year 1997," Bureau of Justice Statistics, January 1998, p. 2.) In 1980, the total number of Americans in prisons and jails was 501,886. (Jodie Brown et al, "Correctional Populations in the United States, 1994," Bureau of Justice Statistics, June 1996, p. 7.) The U.S. incarceration rate, according to the most recent calculations, is 645 per 100,000 population, second internationally behind Russia, at 690. The incarceration rate for England and Wales is 100 per 100,000; for Japan, it is 37. Drug offenders accounted for 71 percent of the increase in federal prisoners between 1985 and 1994, and 36 percent of the increase in state prisoners. (Marc Mauer, "Americans Behind Bars: U.S. and International Use of Incarceration, 1995," The Sentencing Project [Washington, D.C.], June 1997, pp. 4, 13; "'Defying Gravity,' Inmate Population Climbs," *The New York Times*, January 19, 1998.)

page 348   "'war on drugs'": For a harrowing account of drug-prohibition efforts over the past thirty years, see Dan Baum, *Smoke and Mirrors: The War on Drugs and the Politics of Failure* (Little, Brown, 1996).

page 348   "to cross [class lines] through education": Seventy-four percent of college students, asked about their goals in a recent survey, said it was "essential" or "very important" to them to be "very well-off financially." This goal outpolled all other choices. Thirty years ago, less than half of students asked the same question selected wealth as a very important personal goal. At that time, 82 percent said it was "essential" or "very important" to them to "develop a meaningful philosophy of life"—a goal that had fallen to sixth on the list by 1996, endorsed by only 42 percent. (Margot Hornblower, "Learning to Earn," *Time*, February 24, 1997.)

page 349   "diverse, overdetermined interpretations of events have largely replaced": In the wider world, among college students and adults, a similarly fierce (and related) sectarianism helps fuel identity politics, which are usually organized around ethnicity or sexual orientation. For a powerful analysis of the recent eclipse, among American progressives, of Enlightenment universalism by identity politics, both on and off university campuses, see Todd Gitlin, *The Twilight of Common Dreams: Why America Is Wracked by Culture Wars* (Henry Holt, 1995).

page 349   "The standard explanation for this anomaly": See Werner Sombart, *Why Is There No Socialism in the United States?* (MacMillan [London], 1976), an influential analysis by a German economist written in 1906 and much disputed since but never fully refuted. Michael Harrington, in a foreword to the 1976 edition of Sombart's essay, argues that there was in fact a social-democratic party representing workers that "appeared in the United States during the Great Depression. Its particularity was that it organised *within* the Democratic Party." (p. xi.) This party-within-a-party, if it existed, seems not to have survived the war.

page 350   "the net impact of the . . . information revolution": For wide-ranging critiques of the political implications of the information revolution, see Theodore Roszak, *The Cult of Information: A Neo-Luddite Treatise on High Tech, Artificial Intelligence, and the True Art of Thinking* (University of California Press, 1994, second ed.), and Bill McKibben, *The Age of Missing Information* (Random House, 1992). For an uncritical celebration of the Internet, see Don Tapscott, *Growing Up Digital: The Rise of the Net Generation* (McGraw-Hill, 1998), in which "the N-Gen" (kids born after 1977—the children, that is, of baby boomers) is sized-up for marketers and congratulated for its computer literacy and rigorous shopping. ("The availability of choice is a deeply held value in the N-Gen culture"—p. 187.) For an entertaining exploration of the social dynamics of one on-line community, see John Seabrook, *Deeper: My Two-Year Odyssey in Cyberspace* (Simon and Schuster, 1997), pp. 147–260.

page 350   "cynicism about politics deepens": In the mid-1970s, according to Madrick, "42 percent of Americans reported that they had 'a lot of confidence' in Congress. In the summer of 1994 only 18 percent had as much confidence." (p. 129.) Given the campaign finance scandals that have filled the news for much of the period since, public confidence in established political institutions is unlikely to have risen. College freshmen, meanwhile, participating in an annual nationwide poll in the fall of 1997, expressed more disdain for politics than in any year since the poll began in 1966. Only 26.7 percent thought "keeping up to date with political affairs" was essential or very important; in 1966, 57.8 percent thought so. Only 13.7 percent said they frequently discussed politics; in 1968, 29.9 percent did so. ("College Freshmen Aiming for High Marks in Income," *The New York Times*, January 12, 1998.)

page 350   "Americans have been suffering from . . . future shock": Page Smith makes this point in his great eight-volume "People's History of the United States" (McGraw-Hill, 1976–87), as cited in Skolnick, p. 10.

page 350   " 'everlasting uncertainty and agitation' ": Quotations from Karl Marx, "The Communist Manifesto," in *Capital, The Communist Manifesto, and Other Writings* (Random House, 1932), p. 324.

page 350   "in 1996 the AFL-CIO dispatched": Margot Hornblower, "Labor's Youth Brigade," *Time*, July 15, 1996, pp. 44–45; Marc Cooper, "The Boys and Girls of (Union) Summer," *The Nation*, August 12–19, 1996, pp. 18–20.

page 351   "Labor union membership has been falling globally": Between 1985 and 1995, union membership declined in 70 of 92 countries surveyed in a 1997 United Nations report. Membership declined in Britain, France, and Germany, as well as in the United States. (The biggest drops occurred in Central and Eastern Europe, reflecting the end of compulsory unionsim in the former Soviet bloc.) Membership rose sharply during the same period, however, in Spain, South Africa, Chile, South Korea, and the Philippines. ("Union Membership Drops Worldwide, U.N. Reports," *The New York Times*, November 4, 1997.)

page 351   "Welfare states have been scaled back or dismantled": "The Cries of Welfare States Under the Knife," *The New York Times*, September 19, 1997.

page 351   "Poverty and inequality are growing in much of Western Europe": The European Union is slow and parsimonious with income and poverty statistics, but the figures it released in May 1997 for 1993 showed that 17 percent of the EU population lived in poor households. Between 1988 and 1993, the poverty rate in France rose from 14 percent to 16 percent; in Germany it rose from 10.8 percent to 13 percent. Between 1993 and 1996, the number of households receiving basic welfare in France rose by 27 percent. In Germany the number of people receiving welfare rose 9.1 percent in 1995. Meanwhile, according to Mark Pearson, an international civil servant and statistician at the Organization for Economic Cooperation and Development, "there is a growing increase in income from capital, and it is very unequally distributed. . . . There has been a marked increase in household wealth in countries like France or the U.K. in the last 15 years. Perhaps you can say the extremes are increasing." (John Vinocur, "Poverty Grows Quietly Along with Wealth," *International Herald Tribune*, October 15, 1997.) Wage inequality has grown in some European countries, notably the United Kingdom, but not in others. (Rebecca M. Blank, "The Misdiagnosis of Eurosclerosis," *The American Prospect*, January/February 1997, pp. 81–85.)

page 351   "Young people in Europe face a wall": A dramatic shift by employers in many countries to hiring only part-time or temporary workers has frozen millions of young Europeans out of the high-wage, high-benefits job market that brought unprecedented prosperity to their parents' generation. At the end of 1997, there were 18 million Europeans out of work—a disproportionate number of them young—and an unemployment rate more than twice as high as the United States'. Among European workers under twenty-five, more than one third were in temporary jobs, and another one third were working without benefits. ("The Jobless Are Snared in Europe's Safety Net," *The New York Times*, November 9, 1997; "Only Employment for Many in Europe Is Part-Time Work," *The New York Times*, September 1, 1997; "It's Young vs. Old in Germany as the Welfare State Fades," *The New York Times*, June 4, 1997.)

page 351   "Racist skinheads . . . flourish": The Anti-Defamation League reported in 1995 that neo-Nazi skinheads were active in thirty-three countries. Within Europe, the greatest numbers were found in Germany, Hungary, the Czech Republic, Poland, the United Kingdom, Italy, and Sweden. ("The Skinhead International: A Worldwide Survey of Neo-Nazi Skinheads" [Anti-Defamation League, 1995], p. 1.) The neo-Nazi problem is particularly widespread in Germany, where it has recently surfaced in the armed forces. ("Pro-Nazi Incidents in German Army Raise Alarm," *The New York Times*, November 5, 1997; "First, Army Neo-Nazis, Now Racists on Internet Worry Germany," *The New York Times*, December 16, 1997.)

page 351   "socialist parties . . . now govern most of Western Europe": At the beginning of 1998, socialist parties were governing, either solely or as the leaders of coalitions, nine of the fifteen European Union countries: Austria, Denmark, Finland, France, Great Britain, Greece, the Netherlands, Portugal, and Sweden. They were also members of ruling coalitions in three other EU countries: Belgium, Italy, and Luxembourg.

ACKNOWLEDGMENTS

For a book about the daily lives of private citizens, a writer must rely on the kindness of strangers to an outrageous and humbling degree. My greatest debt is to the young people who let me hang out, observe, and rummage around in their lives. They shared their thoughts, feelings, hopes, and memories with a generosity that I will never be able to repay. I can only hope that they and their families won't feel ill served by my versions of their stories.

Many other people helped, too many to name. In New Haven, let me at least mention Paul Bass, Lisa Sullivan, Roger Vann, Deirdre Bailey, Joe Harris, Michael Jefferson, Jean Davis, William Dow, Douglas Rae, Adolph Reed, Tim Shriver, and the late Kevin Houston. In East Texas, I was blessed to hook up with the Clark and Kelly clan: Laverne Clark, Cecil Clark, Ruby Kelly, Hulon Kelly, Mary Barnes, Timmy Price, Lanee Jones, LaCecil Clark, Lavender Price, Lyndra Cartwright, Lyndorie Clark, Lynn Karen Clark, Lavetta Clark, and Johnathan Mitchell. I also want to thank Nathan Tindall, Willie Earl Tindall, Sam Malone, Charles Mitchell, Betty Donatto, Kenneth Lister, Ilester Porter, Charles Bryan, Larry Saurage, Susan Ramsey, Tom Blount, Sissy Ellimore, Richard Stewart, Jane Ayo, Herbert Jackson, Sheila Fussell, Gary Borders, and Joseph Hawthorn. In the Yakima Valley, the main debts I incurred were to Rosita Castillo, Wes Nelson, Kurt Petersen, Lupe Gamboa, Deirdre Gamboa, Teana Robbins, Ed Radder, Rosa Ramón, Jane Gargas, Refugio Zesati, Carrie Gargas, and, of course, Mary Ann Ramirez and the Guerrero family. In the Antelope Valley, besides all the kids mentioned in the text, I spent time with Robin Ray, Justin Kroeger, Chrissy Brooks, Fred Mikell, Jamie Anderson, and Jesse Alexander. I also got help from Don Ranish, Joya Frank, Chuck Slay, Fred Strasburg, Steve Gocke, Claude Smith, Larry Grooms, Holly Wolcott, Erin Zelle, Kelly Candaele, Margot Hornblower, David Jay, Lissa Levy, and Steve Ogden.

Because I was on the road so much, I cherished the hospitality of John Murphy, Daniel Ben-Horin and Jamie Stobie, Tony Peckham and Hilary Saner,

Michael Collier and Katherine Branch, Jane Creighton, Maureen and Paul Monahan, Ken Moser, Joe Gifford, Melissa and Domenic Mastrippolito, Jeannie and William Buckley, Susan and Ed Thacker, and Russell Jacoby and Naomi Glauberman. (And I hope Juan and Sammy won't forget Joe Kane, Murphy, Sandy Close, Franz Schurmann, Nell Bernstein, and Debbie Nathan.)

This book was conceived, in an earlier form, in conversations with John Sterling, a far-sighted editor whose patience and enthusiasm kept it alive for years beyond its deadline. After John changed jobs, Ann Godoff and Random House took over. Ann's sure judgments, good humor, and superb editing were the fair winds that made the homeward leg of this long journey a pleasure. My agent, Amanda Urban, never flagged in her famous ebullience. Ann's assistants, Sarah French and Enrica Gadler, helped smooth the passage to publication. Beth Pearson was a tireless and skilled production editor.

At *The New Yorker*, Bob Gottlieb gave me a rare freedom to pursue my hunches, then did his best to keep me honest with his keen nose for humbug. Tina Brown also indulged me on long, vague expeditions that often must have seemed like sure losers, and then published the results with energy and style. Her steady support has been deeply appreciated. John Bennet, my editor at the magazine for more than a decade, contributed deft fixes, sharp cuts, and insights to every passage that came his way. Deborah Garrison did wonderful work on the Antelope Valley section. Much of what ended up in these pages was fact-checked by, in order of appearance, Josselyn Simpson, Pete Wells, Aaron Retica, Bill Vourvoulias, and Blake Eskin. Their work was first-rate, and the mistakes that have undoubtedly crept back in are mine. Eleanor Gould Packard interrogated my prose with her legendary rigor, improving each sentence she touched.

Dan Kaufman came along at the eleventh hour and performed casual heroics as a deadline researcher.

Many friends read the manuscript, in whole or in part. Bryan Di Salvatore, Jim Lardner, Anne Greene, Joe Wood, Ren Weschler, George Packer, and Philip Gourevitch were especially helpful. I benefited, too, from conversations with Judith Levine, Michael Massing, Lis Harris, Jonathan Schell, Deirdre McNamer, Craig Charney, Jared Bernstein, William Spriggs, Cynthia Cotts, Caryn Davidson, Jann Sterling, and Miriam Rodriguez. Encouragement and support came in many guises, really, from the formal to the inadvertent. Some of the morale boosts I haven't forgotten came from Roger Wilkins, Michael Katz, Bill McKibben, Sue Halpern, George Trow, Mark Hertsgaard, Ray Bonner, Gerry Marzorati, Diana Wylie, Cathy Corman, the Medill School of Journalism at Northwestern University, the Drug Policy Foundation, and the echoing green foundation, which sent me, out of the blue, a generous grant. Judith Felton was a sea anchor through many storms. Residencies at Yaddo and the MacDowell Colony were useful and merry. Timely invitations to lecture, particularly one from the Yale Law School and another from the Institute of the Humanities at New York University, forced me to concentrate my ideas at key junctures of the writing.

My deepest thanks go, finally, to my parents, Bill and Pat Finnegan, who raised their kids with what I now see was a rare selflessness, and to my beloved wife, Caroline Rule, who contributed wise advice to every page of this book, tolerated my absences, and always gave me a sweet reason to come home.

WILLIAM FINNEGAN has been a staff writer at *The New Yorker* since 1987. He is the author of *A Complicated War: The Harrowing of Mozambique; Dateline Soweto: Travels with Black South African Reporters;* and *Crossing the Line: A Year in the Land of Apartheid,* which was named one of the ten best nonfiction books of 1986 by *The New York Times Book Review.* He was a National Magazine Award finalist in both 1990 and 1995, and has twice won the John Bartlow Martin Award for Public Interest Magazine Journalism. He lives in New York City with his wife.

ABOUT THE TYPE

This book was set in Photina, a typeface designed by José Mendoza in 1971. It is a very elegant design with high legibility, and its close character fit has made it a popular choice for use in quality magazines and art gallery publications.